The Challenge of Comparative Literature

———

Harvard Studies in Comparative Literature

Founded by William Henry Schofield

42

D1225518

The Challenge
of Comparative
Literature

Claudio Guillén

Translated by Cola Franzen

HARVARD UNIVERSITY PRESS
Cambridge, Massachusetts, and London, England
1993

Copyright © 1993 by the President and Fellows of Harvard College
All rights reserved
Printed in the United States of America
10 9 8 7 6 5 4 3 2 1

Originally published as *Entre lo uno et lo diverso: Introducción a la literatura comparada,*
© Editorial Crítica, Barcelona, 1985.

Translation of this volume has been assisted by a grant from the Program for Cultural
Cooperation between Spain's Ministry of Culture and United States Universities.

This book is printed on acid-free paper, and its binding materials have been chosen for
strength and durability.

Library of Congress Cataloging-in-Publication Data

Guillén, Claudio.
    [Entre lo uno y lo diverso. English]
    The challenge of comparative literature / Claudio Guillén ;
translated by Cola Franzen.
       p. cm. — (Harvard studies in comparative literature ; 42)
    Translation of: Entre lo uno y lo diverso.
    Includes bibliographical references and index.
    ISBN 0-674-10687-3 (acid-free paper) (cloth)
    ISBN 0-674-10688-1 (paper)
    1. Literature, Comparative. I. Title. II. Series.
PN865.G8513 1993   92–16810
809—dc20   CIP

For Harry Levin and René Wellek,
with all my gratitude

Contents

Contents

Preface

This presentation of perturbing problems and topics of concern to students of comparative literature began with lectures I gave at the March Foundation in Madrid in January 1980. I still remember that occasion with gratitude for the warm welcome extended to me by José Luis Yuste and Andrés Amorós. In March 1982 I expanded the material for a series of lectures given in the People's Republic of China—Beijing, Jinan, and Shanghai—before audiences of tireless listeners. I can recall today the extraordinarily close attention paid by those young Chinese students. And because of the generous encouragement of friends and colleagues in Spain as well as in other countries, I have had to continue. Finally the time has come for me to gather and express the few things I have learned or taught.

Roland Barthes, who was of course a great writer, once said that one should cite other writers the way one cites* a bull. One person who understood a great deal about both citations and bulls was José Bergamín, who spent his life, *inter alia,* modeling and remodeling strange words, idiomatic expressions, the voices of the greatest creators. I appeal here to such illustrious forebears to placate those who may be annoyed by the superabundance of citations in this volume. Since we are dealing with comparative literature, I hope that the reader will admit that these citations are functional, even useful. Criticism, which is also autobiography, comes out of a personal selection of citations. I have looked at the literatures of many countries of Europe as well as those of other continents, drawing close to them, listening to them, yielding to their best voices, reproducing when pos-

---

* *Citar* in Spanish, *citer* in French, and *cite* in English all mean to cite, *quote,* some other writer or authority, and all are also used as a bullfighting term, to signify the gesture a bullfighter makes with the cape to call the bull, when the bull has strayed too far away or his attention has wandered. In English we might say he *incites* or *excites* the bull. *Trans.*

sible their exact words. Most prose passages are given in English translation only, but poetry is printed bilingually.

Anticipating the first chapter, I would like to offer here a definition of a comparatist: a comparatist is one who dares to pester friends and colleagues, not just once but over and over. An enterprise like this one could not have been completed without consulting experts in many different fields, languages, and specialties. Fortunately, I did not lack for learned and generous colleagues both at Harvard University and in Barcelona. I remember the following with gratitude (and may those not mentioned here forgive me): Aleksandar Flaker, Tibor Klaniczay, Y. Vipper; Ralph Bogart, Gregory Nagy, Stephen Owen, Richard Sieburth, Piotr Steinkeller, Jurij Striedter, Susan Suleiman, Wiktor Weintaub; Haskell Block, Ellen Friedman, Paola Mildonian, Janice Osterhaven; Alberto Blecua, José Manuel Blecua the younger, Mario Hernández, Carmela del Moral; and my wife, Yelena Samarina. And I cannot fail to add a special greeting to my students at the Universidad Autónoma of Barcelona, who participated with such good will in the first presentation of many of these reflections during the academic year 1983–84. From the bottom of my heart, my thanks to all.

The Challenge of Comparative Literature

Part I

The Emergence of Comparative Literature

1

First Definitions

Comparative literature (a conventional and not very enlightening label)[1] is usually understood to consist of a certain tendency or branch of literary investigation that involves the systematic study of supranational assemblages.

I prefer not to say, as some others do, that comparative literature consists in an examination of literatures from an international point of view, since its identity does not depend solely on the attitude or posture of the observer. What is fundamental is the obvious contribution to the history or the concept of literature of several classes and categories that cannot be regarded as merely national in nature. Think of a multisecular genre such as comedy, an unmistakable method such as rhyme, a vast movement such as Romanticism, not just European but worldwide in scope. And I say supranational rather than international to emphasize that the point of departure is not found in national literatures, nor in the interrelationships between them.

The definition is wide, loose, and, like many others, too simple and may even represent an abuse of confidence. More than anything else it invites continued reflection on some basic dimensions of literary history. For this reason I would also like to suggest that we are faced not only by one branch—without any doubt recognized as such and established today in numerous nations and universities—but also with a trend of literary studies, or rather a form of intellectual exploration, a task spurred on by uneasy feelings and specific questions. And how may these trends be defined? How

3

may one determine a process of determination? How may one define an open itinerary, an incomplete movement, an attempt to go beyond? How may one treat an aspect of cultural history of our own time, of necessity still unfinished?

Let us approach our discipline without losing sight of this initial aspect: comparative literature as an affinity, desire, an activity chosen over other activities. I wish to go beyond cultural nationalism, beyond using literature in nationalistic ways, out of narcissistic instincts, for ideological ends. I dream, in Goethe's words, of a "world literature." (But what world? what worlds?) I shall endeavor to unravel the characteristics of literary communication, its primordial channels, the metamorphosis of genres, forms, and themes (But would the inquiry into genres not tend to merge with the history of poetics? And what is a theme?); reflection about literary history, its character, its conditionings, its temporal profile and possible meaning. I will come back to these questions later. For now let us try to elude the snare of definitions, so sinuous, so vain, and consider our field as a yearning rather than as an object, a yearning that has already been in existence for a good number of years, and will remain. The dynamic or contentious aspect—militant, Adrian Marino[2] would say—of comparativism cannot be stressed enough.

For this reason I regard the historical perspective, as I understand it, to be the right one, and that is the path I will follow in the pages to come. In order to sketch the typical features of the direction referred to, nothing could be more useful than to recall origins and ends, old debates and influential models, alliances and contradictions, the changing phases and rhythms of development.

First, however, and to begin our journey without further delay, I will sketch two outlines, one of an approach and one of a problem—both, in my view, fundamental to our inquiry.

2

The Local and the Universal

The comparatist's approach, vital for such a task, is the awareness of certain tensions existing between the local and the universal, or if you prefer, between the particular and the general. I say local, locale—place—and not nation—nationality, country, region, city—because it is worthwhile to emphasize these conceptual extremes that encompass a series of general opposites applicable to different situations: between the specific circumstance and the world (the worlds), between the present and the absent, the experience and its sense, the I and whatever is alien to it, the perceived and the longed for, what is and what should be, what exists today and what is eternal.

It seems and is in fact true that these terms and polarities belong to the field of poetry itself. Martin Heidegger, in summing up nearly two centuries of poetic exploration, called the poet the "herdsman of the Being" *(Hirt des Seins)*. Octavio Paz writes:

Art cannot be reduced to the land, the people and the moment that produce it; nevertheless, it is inseparable from them . . . A work of art is a form that is detached from the ground and occupies no place in space: it is an image. Except that the image grows because it is attached to one spot of ground and to one moment: four poplars that rise to the sky from a pond, a naked wave born of a mirror, a bit of water or light that runs through the fingers of a hand, the reconciliation of a green triangle and an orange circle. A work of art lets us glimpse, for an instant, the forever in the now.[1]

He also writes: "Real life opposes neither the quotidian nor the heroic life; it is the perception of the spark of *otherness* in each one of our acts, not excluding the most trivial ones."[2] A force comes out from an initial, concrete place and pushes us irresistibly toward other places—or perhaps beyond any place, according to the thinking of Claude Esteban in *Un lieu hors de tout lieu* (1979; A Place beyond Every Place):

> The poet has no other purpose than to undertake—and to establish—an absolute questioning within the possibilities offered him by a language. He senses that even what is rooted in the most circumstancial part of a particular destiny, a set place, an immediate time, can and should reach all the way up to the immense branches of the only tree.[3]

Tree of science as well? or of literature? I recognize the ambiguity of certain proposals that might encompass writer and reader at one and the same time. But I do not feel that such an approximation of the conditions of criticism to those of literature is out of place: a working hypothesis, nothing more, that we shall have to refine later.

The critic's situation is neither simple nor comfortable. Different and often opposing aims attract and lure him, although the options are reduced to four primary ones: first, the gap between an artistic inclination (the enjoyment of literature as art) and a social preoccupation (the work as an act, a response to the imperfections and deficiencies of the historical environs of man); second, the difference between the practical (the interpretation of particular texts) and the theoretical (the explanation, explicit or not, of certain premises and of a significant order); third, the distinction between the individual (the single work, the unmistakable writer, the originality that cultivated and written literature makes possible) and the system (the whole, the genre, the historical configuration, the generational movement, the inertia of writing); and, finally, the tension between the local and the universal that confronts comparatists in particular.

I am not overlooking the fact that these terms are intermeshed. I am not speaking of options easy to resolve, or in favor of any one stance, but of tensions, I repeat, tensions that in themselves configure a discipline, an internal structure that becomes an object for study. Thus we understand that comparatists are those who refuse to devote themselves exclusively to either one of the two extremes of the polarity that concern them—the local or the universal. It is obvious that for them specialization in one nation or one nationality is not sufficient as a task and cannot be sustained as a practical matter. And it is also true that comparatists do not operate within a sphere of extreme worldliness, of uprootedness, bloodless abstraction, a cosmopolitanism carried to the *n*th degree—in a distorted view of things that reflects neither the real itinerary of literary history nor the concrete coordinates of poetic creation.

The tasks of the writer and the critic-historian, in this case the comparatist, have certain important dimensions in common. The philologist who for professional or personal reasons limits himself to a familiarity with writings in his mother tongue has little or no resemblance to a Virgil, a Francisco de Quevedo, a Goethe, a Vjačeslav Ivanov, an A. G. Matoš, a Joyce, an Ezra Pound, a Mihály Babits, a Mandelstam, a Carles Riba, a Saint-John Perse, or a Czeslaw Milosz.

But on the other hand it would be unfortunate to overlook the fact that it is the mother tongue that offers us the most intense access—the most secure and the most intimate—to aesthetic emotion and to the comprehension of what is or what is not poetry. The coordinates of the experience of the reader, like those of the poet, are multiple, changing, successive. Sometimes when I am reading Jorge Luis Borges, for instance, I am most struck by his kinship with Vladimir Nabokov, or by his debt to English writers and German thinkers, or by his avant-garde origins that underlie an earlier less turbulent phase, true also in the case of Pound or T. S. Eliot. But at other times the linguistic roots or the cultural bonds are irresistible and take precedence over all other elements. Then I happen on one of his poems—it can be any poem, always untranslatable ("In memoriam A. R."):

> El vago azar o las precisas leyes
> que rigen este sueño, el universo,
> me permitieron compartir un terso
> trecho del curso con Alfonso Reyes . . .

> Either vague chance or the precise rules
> that govern this dream, the universe,
> permitted me to share a smooth stretch
> of the course with Alfonso Reyes . . .[4]

And also (the poet hears the notes of a melody: "Caja de música"/Music Box):

> ¿De qué templo
> de qué leve jardín en la montaña,
> de qué vigilias ante un mar que ignoro,
> de qué pudor de la melancolía,
> de qué perdida y rescatada tarde,

llegan a mí, su porvenir remoto?
No lo sabré. No importa. En esa música
yo soy. Yo quiero ser. Yo me desangro.

From which temple,
from what small garden in the mountain,
from which watch before an unknown sea,
from what bashful melancholy,
from which lost and rescued evening,
comes to me, your remote promise?
I'll never know. No matter. In this music
I am. I wish to be. I pour out my blood.[5]

How could a native speaker of Spanish of average education read a new collection of poems by Borges without feeling an elemental, almost biological delight on being submerged in his words, yielding to the pleasure of so many echoes built up over a lifetime, a prior condition to an appreciation of the magical skill that the Argentine writer exercises over the Spanish language? Here is something we must not forget: the special illusion that inspires an avid reader to rush out to get a copy of the latest book of a great poet who writes in one's own language. But that deep stratum of the psychic geology of the reader responds also—a privilege of a work of verbal art— to words that come from the past.

To take another example, remember the morning when Don Quixote and Sancho discover the sea. They are nearing Barcelona, and we the end of the book. The knight and his squire contemplate the sea with great admiration: "el mar alegre, la tierra jocunda, el aire claro . . ." (The sea was bright, the earth rejoicing, the air clear . . .).[6] But the most important thing turns out to be that it is Saint John's Eve, June twenty-fourth, Midsummer Day. And from the deepest level of his memory the native Spanish reader recalls these popular verses:

Yo me levantara, madre,
mañanica de San Juan,
vide estar una doncella,
ribericas de la mar . . .

I'll get up early, mother,
on the morning of San Juan,
I saw there was a maiden
along the shore of the sea . . .

And naturally:

Quien tuviera tal ventura
sobre las aguas del mar
como tuvo el conde Arnoldos
la mañana de San Juan . . .

Who was ever so lucky
by the waters of the sea
as was the Count Arnoldos
on the morning of San Juan . . .

As we shall see later, the reader is free to exercise the license offered so willingly by Cervantes in his prologue to the first part of Quixote. But in choosing, we simplify the text, and there is nothing to be done about it. The orientation of memory in these moments is partial and therefore incomplete in the face of the riches of literary history. I refer to history as it happened, *in illo tempore,* the history known to people who took part in it. The art of the great poet succeeds in uniting and condensing in a few words of a single language the consequences of an extremely varied succession of stimuli. However, it is rare that the horizon of a great writer is only national in scope. The author of *Don Quixote* understood and prized the impalpable irony of Ariosto, Torquato Tasso's ideas on poetics, the colloquies of Erasmus, the fantastic adventures of Amadís de Gaula and of Tirant lo Blanc, the intense eclogues of Garcilaso de la Vega, the satires of Horace, the ever-renewed metamorphoses of Ovid—all this as well as the memories of the battle of Lepanto, captivity in Algiers, the interminable struggle with Islam in the Mediterranean. And as for the "literary incompatibility of Cervantes with Lope de Vega"—as Marcel Bataillon calls it[7]—there is no room for doubt. But the author of *Quixote* took advantage of Teofilo Folengo's *Maccheronee* and of Cesare Caporali of Perugia's *Viaggio in Parnaso.* Ovid, Garcilaso, Ariosto: the literary contour of Cervantes is tripartite. The literary systems that shape him are the Latin, the Spanish, and the Italian (together with as many works translated from other languages as were available to him). Much has been written about the debt of Cervantes to *Orlando furioso;* and Francisco Márquez Villanueva dots the *i*'s in this argument very well when he points out just how far the second writer diverges from the first: "Ariosto loses himself in the legend on purpose, but Don Quixote, who holds the legend within his very soul, loses himself in a real world."[8] And that's why literary systems exist: so that writers can differ from them, or break with them, or push them aside, as the Russian Formalists insisted on so strongly, those models that had previously occupied center stage. The interweaving of the national with the international is thus evident and inescapable; more than anything else this interweaving characterized the poets' own experiences, the air they breathed in their own era, the challenges they faced. The process of literary history itself, at least in Europe and America, has always gone beyond linguistic-national or linguistic-regional borders.

In his study of the forms of versification of Hebrew poetry, Benjamin Hrushovski describes the specific nature of Hebrew literary history this way:

> A Hebrew poet, regardless of his time, was at the crossroads of three lines of development. (1) There was the historical factor common to all literatures: the tension between synchrony and diachrony, i.e., trends of the poet's generation as juxtaposed to norms of the immediate past as well as classical works. The other two factors are specific to the geographical and sociological situation of the Hebrew writer: (2) the influence of Hebrew poetry written in other countries; (3) the impact of non-Hebrew poetry of his own time and place.[9]

It is true that in the thirteenth century the Hebrew poets of Rome composed in the strophic forms of the Byzantine Erez Israel, forms based on word count and written in nonalternating rhymes, contrary to the practice of the Italian poets, who were using syllabic meters and alternating rhymes, and in contrast to the Spanish poets, who were using a quantitative versification derived from Arabic poetry. Finally those Jewish Roman poets adopted the Hispano-Hebrew meter in order to compose sonnets in the Italian manner. All of this is explained in Hrushovski's splendid study at the same time that he makes us see that the Jews and *goyim* are, from such a point of view, little less than brothers.

It would be a mistake to take as model or image of a great writer one who fits perfectly into his homogeneous cultural surroundings, restricting himself to a single language, to one literary system, to a few closed methods of versification, a suitable social circle. Perhaps this might be said of the greatest of modern poets—Shakespeare—if we are speaking only of versification, but not if we are speaking of his debt to a Plutarch or a Montaigne. And on the other hand there are countless writers of the first rank who left the cultural circle in which they were born and came into contact with strange forms and new themes; or they wandered, impelled by curiosity, or expelled or self-exiled, from place to place. I would remind you of the all-too-well-known fact that the work of Cervantes is inconceivable without his physical and literary immersion in Italy. It would be just as elementary to gloss, when citing Dante's exile, the moment when Virgil and the poet-protagonist arrive at the foot of Mount Purgatory and some souls recently landed there ask them for directions (*Purgatorio* II.61–63):

> E Virgilio rispuose: "Voi credete
> forse che siamo espertí desto loco; ma noi siam peregrin, como voi
> siete."

> And Virgil answered, "Perhaps you think we are
> acquainted with this place; but we are pilgrims like yourselves." [10]

Here I will refer only to two other brief examples of exile.

The first comes from central Europe, where a superposition or proximity of different cultures is often the norm. Ján Kollár's contributions were decisive: with his cycle of love sonnets, *Slavy dcera* (1824; The Daughter of the Slav), written in Pest, and his other writings he forged not only modern Slavic poetry but also a militant conception of pan-Slavism. [11] Kollár was the Lutheran pastor of the Slovak community of Pest; in other words, he carried out his work surrounded by other ethnic communities, primarily those speaking Hungarian and German. My second example, Rubén Darío (like Garcilaso during the Renaissance), completely and brilliantly renewed not only the forms and the language of the modern poets writing in Spanish, a change inconceivable without him, but even their way of perceiving the poetic word. "He was an osmotic writer," says Enrique Anderson Imbert. [12] What Naples was for Cervantes and Garcilaso, Paris without any doubt was for Rubén Darío, but to an even greater degree, since France—acting as *intermédiaire,* as the comparatists would say—also introduced him to Greece, to Rome, to the Mediterranean cultures. In Paris, the capital of capitals in 1893, Rubén would recount later, "I had seen the old faun Verlaine, knew of the mystery of Mallarmé, and was a friend of Moréas." [13] And one should mention many others: Théodore de Banville, Catulle Mendès, Laurent Tailhade, Rémy de Gourmont *(Le Latin mystique),* Joris Karl Huysmans *(La cathédrale),* Edgar Allan Poe, Dante Gabriel Rossetti, and Gabriele D'Annunzio. All these contacts enriched Rubén's methods of versification enormously, as shown by his return to the Latin hexameter, which he defends in his prologue to *Cantos de vida y esperanza* (1905; Songs of Life and Hope). Born in a small Central American country, Rubén never stopped traveling to other countries—Chile, Argentina, Spain, Cuba, and various others—where other poets in very different circumstances were working in the same language. As a wanderer, then, Rubén Darío fulfilled his destiny as an American writer. Created in the image and likeness of the European writer, the Latin American poet must distance himself from his historical conditioning so that, liberated, he can return to his roots—roots that include indigenous cultures, Nahuatl poetry, African rhythms. So explains Octavio Paz:

> The experience of these poets and writers proves that in order to return to our house it is first necessary for us to risk abandoning it. Only the prodigal son returns. To reproach Latin American literature for its uprootedness is to ignore the fact that only uprootedness allows us to recover our portion of reality. Distance was the necessary condition for discovery . . . Neruda had to write *Tentativa del hombre infinito,* a surrealist exercise, before arriving at his *Residencia en la tierra.* Which earth is it? It's America and at the same time it's Calcutta, Colombo, Rangoon . . . A book by the Argentinian Enrique Molina is called *Costumbres errantes o la redondez de la tierra* [Errant Customs or the Roundness of the Earth.][14]

No one insists more strongly on the peculiarity of Latin American reality than Gabriel García Márquez, but his frequent allusions to "my master William Faulkner" allow us to understand better what was needed in order for him to reinvent it. I dare to think that the comparatist—herdsman of poets—tends to resemble the writer. Throughout the centuries, according to what has been known since Aristotle's *Poetics,* it is writers who have felt most profoundly the tension between the particular and the general, or if you prefer, between the local and the universal.

3

The One and the Many

I will touch upon the problem mentioned earlier in only a preliminary and tentative way, merely in the form of a suggestion at this time. It is a question of horizon more than a premise of comparative studies—the horizon of the critic and historian this time—a condition of modern culture, a theme of final reflection. I am referring to something like a feeling of unease and a range of thought that would bring all its critical attention to bear on the polarity of the local and the universal: the debate between unity and multiplicity; or if you prefer, between monism and pluralism. To make these ideas more vivid, I offer two citations.

Borges writes in *Other Inquisitions:* "We must suspect that there is no universe in the organic, unifying sense inherent in that ambitious word." [1] Notice that Borges does not say world but universe, that is, a world not essentially disunited or diverse but considered as a unified and integrated totality. At first glance these words shock us, even irritate us, perhaps because of the negative turn of phrase used—"there is no universe"; expressed that way, the contrary idea would seem more surprising. The experience of multiplicity in the universe is common and easily observed, whereas the concept of the universe in its organic and unifying aspect does in fact appear highly ambitious to us as soon as we leave aside the laws of the natural sciences and instead begin to consider historical events, social or political institutions, cultural creations, and, among these last, literature—whose

13

unity is debatable from the point of view of the majority of those who dedicate themselves to studying it, comparatists included.

As my second example I will cite a few words of Ilya Prigogine, the eminent Belgian scientist, a Nobel Prize laureate in chemistry. During an interview in 1979 Prigogine stressed the importance of time in the natural sciences and specifically in molecular systems, whose equilibrium is affected by bifurcations of chance and the influence of other systems; thus the pertinence of the Second Law of Thermodynamics: that entropy increases as we pass from one transformation to another; that is, energy is degraded. As a consequence of this principle, the interviewer asks: Should one believe that the universe as a whole, and in spite of its diversity, its partial successes, is cooling down and tending toward a definite end? And Prigogine responds: "I cannot give you an answer. If all the things that exist are linked, if there really is a universe, then yes, certainly, the Second Law applies. But viewed from where we now stand, I am not in a position to tell you if the notion of a universe still has a meaning." [2]

The revelation of the unity of literature, going beyond historical and national differences, was a Romantic enterprise. Alexandru Cioranescu describes it very well:

> In certain Romantic spirits, those characterized by an exceptional breadth of historical vision, the idea was taking root of an underlying unity of all literatures, above boundaries of peoples and their languages. The existence of a European literary republic, whose common ideals have apparently survived all the vicissitudes of history, the presence of a more or less common ideological stream, caused those scrutinizers of the destinies of humanity to think that below the accidental forms of culture there ought to exist a fundamental, natural unity, one not conditioned by contacts, interchanges, or peculiar cases of influence or imitation. [3]

This search for essences and substrata—a centralizing ideal, example of extreme monism, little less than a neo-Platonic belief in the existence of some forms in which the individual expressions of the culture share—will cause some of the founders of comparative literature studies to feel uneasy. For example, in his inaugural lecture in Turin in 1876 Arturo Graf upheld the necessity "to search out in the various and the diverse the constant and the enduring." [4] Viewed from such an angle or with such a purpose, the historian of literature clearly comes very close either to the pure scientist—the discoverer of laws and prevailing regularities of historical time and of singular events—or to those thinkers and poets who delve into individual personal experiences in order to discover universal and even "eternal" values. Think of the young Ortega y Gasset, the author of the "Teoría del clasicismo" (1907), who postulates an immanent substance in every man at all periods of history and would like to make the classic into "a suprahistorical concept";[5] the Ortega who will later suggest that man carries within himself "all future poetry"—a store of supraindividual knowledge that the great poets would express: "every great poet plagiarizes us."[6] And think of the Unamuno of *En torno al casticismo* (1895), enemy of the distinction between the *castizo* and the international, determined to find the original human element in the most vivid reality, "what is the original, the essentially human in us, the eternal tradition" that persists in the present, the sediment of impulses and truths beneath the waves of time.[7]

The history of literature (and literary criticism: the two terms are of course indivisible)[8] has its own character and undertakes specific tasks. The student of poetry cannot and should not be confused with a scientist, nor with a philosopher, above all in questions that refer to temporal and individual dimensions of his object of study. Comparative literature has been a resolutely historical discipline; and the most responsible comparatists today regard all superhistorical or intrahistorical premises as hasty, useless, unacceptable. In addition, every idealistic posture—neo-Kantian or neo-Platonic—disdainful of individual differences, of the appearance or surface of things, is irremediably at variance with criticism of the arts—painting, architecture, music, literature, ballet, cinematography, and so forth. In these aspects of culture, it would be absurd to disregard work based on personal experience, the sensed and sensual perception, without which a work of art becomes worthless and fades away. There is no other wax, after all, except the wax that burns. One cannot follow Arturo Graf's proposal and erase the variety and the changeable character of art without also doing away with the pleasure of the spectator or reader.

I do not believe we need to dwell on such basic observations. We are not given the choice of eliminating either individual differences or a unitary perspective; neither the singular aesthetic emotion nor the integrating disquiet. The task of the comparatist is a dialectical one. For that reason, I said that this task is characterized by the constant awareness of a problem; because the investigation of dialectical relationships progressively enriches our perception of the constituent elements. On the one hand, not everything is individuality on the enchanted island that is a literary work (or we would fall into an ingenuous formalism). On the other hand, it is even more obvious that what may seem to us like a dimension or a universal component of literary history, or as arising from this always-changing and renascent morass that we call literature, is not a finished premise, easily accepted, but rather a working hypothesis, needing proof, analysis, and a body of cultural tools and knowledge much greater than we now possess. Above all else, we find ourselves facing a project, a desire, inspired by an aggregate of problems. And the witty Fernando Pessoa, with his caustic bent, wasn't far from the truth when he wrote: "since we can never know all the factors involved in an issue, we can never resolve it." [9]

Fortunately, the elements of the question become more numerous, more varied, more suggestive with each passing day. In 1971 the first International Congress of Comparative Literature to be held in Asia met in Formosa. As in other similar colloquia held in Hong Kong, North America, and Europe, the presentations included not just facts, but new proposals as well, belonging to an area that has come to be called East/West studies. The present-day leaders of comparative literature, those who have cultivated East/West studies for years, are probably the most daring scholars in the field, above all from a theoretical point of view. We will look at some examples and comment on them later. For now it is enough to note that the opening to Oriental literatures provided by East/West studies implies a truly qualitative change. The work is not aimed at simply translating or specializing in Far Eastern literatures, thus perpetuating their separation, but is meant to integrate them into a single body of learning, or rather to include them in a single interrogation. The students of East/West—horizontal axis of distant as well as distinct civilizations—on the one hand examine the literatures of Europe and America as one subject and, on the other hand, consider the specific literatures of Asia and Africa—Arabic literatures, those of India, the Chinese, and the Japanese, just to mention the principal ones. Up to now, most attention has been focused on China and Japan, the literature of China being studied with special intensity, a literature so ancient, so rich, and at the same time one that has remained so totally independent (to a much greater degree than the Arabic) from influences and contacts from abroad throughout so many centuries. This lack of genetic relations, of mutual influences, is precisely what stimulates a whole series of practical and theoretical perplexities of great interest. Let us consider a procedure such as rhyme, a form such as parallelism, a historical trajectory such as the development of the novel. Or let us suppose that we are interested in a better understanding of the nature and function of the verse epistle—one of the subgenres of European poetry dating from the time of Horace. Now we would ask: has the epistle been present in China? at what periods, in what cultural, literary, and historical contexts? What common characteristics does it share with the European? And should such common characteristics be found, how are we to evaluate and interpret them? The same questions may be asked regarding common manifestations of historical development or theoretical thought among authors of treatises on poetics in different civilizations. Here is a field where the dialogue between unity and diversity unquestionably becomes alive and tangible.

Two basic coordinates, the one spatial and the other temporal, will help to determine and define this dialogue. An extreme example of the first is the East/West difference in longitude that separates remote, independent civilizations. The supranational dimension of a theme is amply demonstrated if it spans a similar difference of longitude. But the same question arises if we examine two literatures that are close and yet quite different, such as the Catalan and the Spanish. In both cases, the critic-comparatist tests common phenomena by contrasting diverse nations or nationalities. The consideration of historical time is not necessary for differences, contrasts, and omissions to begin to be revealed. Certainly these initial revelations are insufficient. The specific character of a national literature or the existence of such a character can be found, of course, but it cannot be thoroughly understood. And the theme of a general or potentially "universal" range is even more debatable—nothing requires more careful elucidation. Thus, investigation by way of dialogue helps us to perfect our knowledge of all the components under consideration, as long as the effort doesn't become bogged down or fail. One example of a theme would be the anthology, which I will comment on later: sieve, beginning of continuity, creator of canons, instrument of self-selection of a literature. The more urgent task for the comparatist is to make sure that the theme *exists* within the framework of supranationality. And so the necessity arises for the first spatial test. We ask ourselves: What have been the principal types of anthologies, and what function have they played, not only in the West, since ancient Greece, but also in non-European cultures, such as the Arabic, the Japanese, the Chinese? And right away we discover that in these three literatures compilations have always been extremely important. It is not a matter of pure synchrony, almost always an illusion in humanistic studies, but rather a confirmation of a supranational dimension, which is of necessity a human dimension. It can turn out that a motif, a verbal procedure, an institution that we possess and know within our limited cultural and literary world, is not an ephemeral provincialism, a local usage, a chance caprice, but the property and condition of a much wider reality, perhaps occurring in almost all literatures. (It need not be present in *all* literatures for the circle of a single civilization to be broken.) An apparently modest phenomenon such as the anthology becomes more significant the moment we discover that it exists in numerous cultures. Like anthropology and similar scholarly disciplines, comparative literature definitely broadens what we wish to express, since we are required to delve into our own humanity when we say "we."

Almost simultaneously, we turn to the temporal coordinate. We have already pointed out that comparative literature has been a resolutely historical discipline. If I speak of tragedy or rhyme, I try to denote certain concrete, diverse manifestations that come to light in definite places and languages. Not so with those theorists of literature who rush pell-mell to affirm the universality of their schemes, *ex principiis,* as if one were dealing with mathematics or literature of the moon, as if they were ignorant of the disquiet of the times, unaware of social conditions, including all forms of communication. Comparatists, and other colleagues in this area, indeed live and think history. But precisely for this reason they come up against the limits of historical or historicist knowledge, and perhaps also against the limits of those themes that seemed to us potentially "universal," indivisible, ones. A new dialogue begins, no longer between locality and world, but between evolution and continuity. And as usual with all good dialogues, each speaker has to give up something. Not everything is evolution, nor is everything continuity. Since we are dealing with written literature rather than with folklore or mythology, historical knowledge carries with it a constant process of differentiation. All themes—even those of love and death—fragment and subdivide. Custom, reiteration, the cyclical return give way to change. Not only forms, words, and personalilties change, but also what men and women feel, value, and speak about. But to what extent?[10]

If the mutation of forms and emotions were total, no element, national or supranational, would resist the passage of time—neither comedy nor tragedy, rhythm nor rhyme, neither river nor flower, not even the theme of death itself—and all universality would be ephemeral and deceiving. Only change would be universal. Barren hypothesis, of course, melodramatic and destructive, since it amounts to the dissolution of the object of study, which is poetry, and of our capacity to perceive it. An extreme that we reject, either consciously or unconsciously, whenever we talk about it, while referring to a substratum of meaning with motifs of Lorca, Shakespeare, or Sappho. In my opinion, dialogue continues to be one of the most promising aspects of comparative literature: on the one hand, dialogue between certain recurrent or fundamental structures that are present in distinct literatures throughout time, and on the other hand, change, evolution, historicity—necessary and desirable—of literature and society.

The literature of exile furnishes a multisecular example. "L'exil vient de loin . . . ," wrote Saint-John Perse. The first Western writing known to us about exile was composed by Aristippus of Cyrene, a disciple of Socrates, born around 435 B.C. Diogenes Laertius gives us the title: a dialogue called Πϱὸς τοὺς ϕυγάδας (On Behalf of the Exiles). A few centuries later Plutarch wrote his treatise *On Exile*. In the modern era, from Blanco White to Pedro Salinas, from Giuseppe Mazzini to Ignazio Silone, from Karl Marx to Thomas Mann, from Adam Mickiewicz to Czeslaw Milosz, banished artists and thinkers have been legion. From one age or another, some glorious names are known to all: Ovid, Dante, Rousseau. For one thing, the exile in our time responds to special conditions (nationalisms, historical acceleration, the "out-of-joint" times, dictatorships, the expulsion of intellectuals as a class). For another thing, many characteristics of exile are repeated, seen as a certain social, political, and linguistic—or semiotic—structure; and to a certain extent, their literary consequences are also repeated. But to *what* extent? What challenges, what replies, what opportunities, what crises are reiterated? Faced with such a problem, what would have to be the comparatist's working hypothesis?

Occasionally the comparatist finds himself obliged to respond to the question: Is comparative literature a specific discipline? I believe that we can now offer a reply. Let us suppose that three things permit us to characterize a class of investigation: the themes, the methods, and the problems. The themes proper to comparative literature are easily distinguished: *the realistic European novel* is without any doubt a task for comparatists, whereas *the Spanish pastoral novel* is a subject for Hispanic scholars. But when we scrutinize the equation more closely, we find that it is flawed and cannot be regarded as valid. The theme here is the object of study, and then the difference is based solely on linguistic and quantitative grounds. The methods and approach used for analysis are identical. The conceptual tools are the same and in certain cases not even exclusively limited to the study of literature (such as comparison, according to Benedetto Croce).[11] In short, as I have tried to suggest in the previous pages, what gives life and particular character to comparative literature is a complex of problems which it alone can and wishes to confront.

Karl Vossler thought that the idea of some conjoined literatures, a "literature of the world" (*Weltliteratur*), a *bibliotheca mundi,* would be unattainable except through a rebirth of religious beliefs. Vossler fervently wished for that rebirth of faith.[12] Without being able or wishing to join him in such a longing, I do indeed share his premises. The history of comparative literature brings into sharp relief the definitive impact of the great disintegration that occurred at the end of the eighteenth century and the beginning of the

nineteenth: the one that postulated only one poetical world, only one literature—based on the paradigms presented by a single tradition, a unique or
unified culture, integrating beliefs; and the teachings of a multisecular and
almost absolute poetics. Glauco Cambon comments that with the end of
the hegemony of the classical models, there began "a process that made a
cultural universe of what had formally been a graspable universe." [13] It is
this multiverse that the critics and historians of literature confront, whether
or not they wish to or are aware of it. Regarding the early Neruda, Amado
Alonso wrote: "Our era, in the highest cultural circles, has a zeal for disintegration." [14] Zeal? Or rather ambiance, general condition, shared by critics
and creators, professors and artists alike?

"There will be no more tragedy and no more epic," Carlos Fuentes wrote
regarding Cervantes, "because there is no longer a restorable ancestral order or a universe univocal in its normality. There will be multiple levels of
reading capable of testing the multiple layers of reality." [15] Multiple layers
of reality—felicitous formulation—that, in the opinion of Italo Calvino,
literary works try to bring together or cause to congregate: "A work of
literature might be defined as an operation carried out in the written language and involving several levels of reality at the same time." [16] Plurality
of planes that perhaps corresponds to that heterogeneity of the being that
Antonio Machado saw as a replica of the problem of time and space, which
philosophy had considered to be homogeneous. When we conceive of time
without events and of space without objects—in other words, without
beings—what we do is to suppress the latter. Thus time and space "come
from the radical heterogeneity of the being. Since the being is *various* (not
one), qualitatively distinct, it requires of the subject, to be thought, a frequent displacement of attention and a sudden interruption of the work that
assumes the formation of a precept for the formation of the other." [17] Like
sparks between flint and steel, the relations of the I with the other, Machado
wrote in another place, reveal "the incurable Otherness, so to speak, underlying the life of the One . . . the Essential Heterogeneity of Being." [18]

The situation goes so far that the world can no longer be recognized or
deciphered by any symbol whatsoever, according to certain modern poets.
For example, Eugenio Montale, in "L'Eufrate":

> Non ripetermi que anche uno stuzzicadenti,
> anche una briciola o un niente puo contenere il tutto.
> E quello che pensavo quando esisteva il mondo
> ma il mio pensiero svaria, si appiccica dove puo
> per dirsi che non s'è spento.

> Don't keep telling me that even a toothpick,
> even a crumb or a nothing can contain the whole.
> That's what I thought when the world existed,
> but my thinking is changing, it clings wherever it can
> so as to tell itself it isn't dead.[19]

Can neither microcosmos nor symbol be found in a world that, Montale seems to imply, no longer exists as coherence, as cosmos? It is no longer a matter of a heterogeneity of points of view. The pluralism in question here is a pluralism of beings and not of opinions.

Having arrived now at the modern era, the uniqueness of national literature—literature that served first as substitute and refuge—is not the only fraud. Today, literature cannot be reduced to a single tradition, so tranquilly accessible to the individual talent, as T. S. Eliot supposed. Literary history, any more than can any other type of history, cannot be reduced to only one totalizing theory. Literature cannot be diminished to the perception of the reader who limits himself to the analysis or to the deconstruction of a few solitary texts. Literature does not surrender to the narrow view of the one-method and one-theory critic nor to that of the expert on a single era, a single genre. Literature cannot be curtailed to what a handful of countries of western Europe and America produce and teach. Nor can it be scaled back to whatever is regarded at a certain moment and by a certain taste as literary or not literary.

The Russian Formalists have already shown the debt owed by the great novelists of their language to the serial novel and other subliterary genres, just as Benito Pérez Galdós was indebted to stories printed in installments in newspapers, as explained by Francisco Ynduráin.[20] Andrés Amorós very rightly pointed out the stylistic traits that present-day subliterature (*Trivialliteratur*) and good literature have in common—"a very refined use of adjectives, an archaic vocabulary, use of parallelisms and oppositions, rhetorical metaphors, lapidary phrases, the structure proper for the traditional story—all this as well as the many contacts between the two." Amorós continues, "Today it seems very clear that literature and subliterature are not sealed up in separate compartments, kept incommunicado, but that there exist many channels that interrelate them."[21] Robert Escarpit suggests that the division between nations today is less significant than the differences between classes of verbal communication: the popular, commercial, oral, true romance–type, the sung, the recorded, the academic, feminist, propagandistic, pornographic, and others.[22] (Or one might think with Jan Mukařovský of distinct functions: the aesthetic, cognoscitive, informative, moral, and so on.) And the differences from genre to genre do not disappear; far from it, even though sometimes they are so distant from one another. For many people the novel is a world; for others, poetry is. And let's not even bring up the theater.

Split, shattered since the end of the eighteenth century, literature is parceled out, dispersed, broken up, but at a certain point, in spite of all misfortunes, it reconstitutes itself; and with the generations, the systems, theories, histories, anthologies, it tends to rearrange itself again and again. Like Penelope and her tapestry, it ceaselessly endeavors to put back together what was separated, whatever reading and study restore and reconstruct. Primordial to-and-fro, this double movement between decomposition and recomposition, incoherence and integrity; to-and-fro that writers know very well. I know of no thinker who has illuminated this juncture better than Octavio Paz on more than one occasion:

> Now space expands and breaks apart; time becomes discontinuous; and the world, the whole explodes into splinters. Dispersion of man, wandering in a space that is also dispersed, wandering in his own dispersion. In a universe that breaks up and separates from itself, a whole that has ceased to be thinkable except as absence or a collection of heterogenous fragments, the self also breaks apart.[23]

Among the different tensions that I have mentioned, there is none broader than the principal polarity to which I refer here: tension between the integrity of the world described by the natural sciences or encompassed by technologies, and the plurality of worlds—social, political, cultural, psychic—where we make our home, in which we do in fact live, the ones that we truly know, and that are, or configure, the horizon of humanists and creators. (Hermeneutic to-and-fro, as we shall see.)

The novelist of the Balzac type tries to construct unified worlds (the "diegesis" of the narratologs that we will examine later), but on many occasions, as Thomas Pavel points out so well, the novelist's sense of the heterogeneity of the real causes the novel to subdivide into a plurality of "narrative dominions."[24] And Bakhtin, who so vigorously stressed the plurilingualism of the novelistic genre, or "heteroglossia"—its constituent multiplicity of discourses and styles—proposes also the notion of "zones of characters" (*zony geróiev*):

> Heteroglossia is also diffused in the authorial discourse that surrounds very specific *character zones*. These zones are formed from the characters' semi-discourses, from various forms of hidden transmission for the discourse of the other, by the words and expressions scattered in the discourse, and

from the irruption of alien expressive elements into authorial discourse (ellipsis, questions, exclamation). Such a zone is the range of action of the character's voice, intermingling in one way or another with the author's voice.[25]

Let us reread one of the best novels of the past century, *La regenta* (1884), by Leopoldo Alas, "Clarín"—generally unknown outside Spain—and we become aware of the relative autonomy of Fermín de Pas, of Ana Ozores, of the Vegallanas, of the casino of Vetusta, of the workers of the city. Clarín is the first great Spanish writer who demonstrated and expressed in the form of a novel the absence of God. His testimony is representative of other modern works of fiction, narrative or poetic, where continuity and discontinuity, integrity and fragmentation are intermingled, become reconciled, or collide: open worlds, plural dominions, and zones that are superimposed and intertwined, multiplicity of languages and cultures, "plurality of systems in motion" [26] that many struggle to put together or propel—from their contradictions—toward an unforeseeable new future.

If poetry is an attempt to reunite what was splintered, the study of literatures is a second effort, a meta-attempt, to assemble, discover, or confront the creations produced in the most disparate and dispersed places and moments: the one and the many.

4

Romantic Ideals

It is well known that studies of comparative literature in the modern sense began during the second and third decades of the nineteenth century, most noticeably in France. A landmark occasion known to all was the series of lectures given in Paris with great success by Abel François Villemain (1790–1870) and published in four volumes in 1828 and 1829 under the title *Tableau de la littérature au VIIIe siècle*, followed in 1830 by the *Tableau de la littérature au Moyen Age en France, en Italie, en Espagne et en Angleterre*, in which the "amateurs de la littérature comparée" are extolled.[1] A short time later the works of Villemain's two principal successors, Philarète Chasles and Jean-Jacques Ampère, appeared. Villemain was by far the least interesting of these writers although he was a brilliant orator, ambitious, of an academic and opportunistic turn of mind.

The great period of Romantic French poetry was at hand. In 1820 Alphonse de Lamartine's *Méditations* appeared, and in 1829 Victor Hugo published his *Orientales*. Comparative studies properly speaking arose during the span of time from the end of the eighteenth century to the beginning of the nineteenth, when the first works of Romanticism emerged.[2] The idea of national literature and a modern sense of historical differentiation were necessary precursors for the study of comparative literature. There is no doubt that these specific components had to be present; it would be difficult to imagine the strong contrasts between unity and diversity without them. Certainly the concept of nationality can mean many things when applied to literature. A theoretical element is fundamental for the critic, as it is more often than not for the poet. For centuries the postulate of universality was regarded as belonging most particularly to the poet. Although different poetries and diverse poems were manifest to writers and critics, such as Renaissance poetry and Baroque poetry, the overarching poetic was and continued to be one, indivisible, normative, imperious, all-encompassing. However proud the Italians of the Cinquecento may have felt about their cultural poetical heritage going back to Petrarch and to the sonneteers of the *dolce stil novo,* the basic norms and notions of literary art, such as poetic styles and genres, were not affected by their consciousness of nationality nor by their perception of history. The unity of the poetic always triumphed over the diversity of the poetry.

One could say much the same thing about "parallels" and other traditional comparisons, common usages at that time in Rome and during the last Hellenistic epoch, terms often employed in a certain agonistic sense (*certamen Homeri et Hesiodi,* and so on).[3] In Rome the concept, dear to the Stoics, of a *humanitas* capable of embracing different peoples, idioms, and races was firmly entrenched. Comparison of Demosthenes with Cicero is common: we find it in Tacitus, in Quintilian, in the pseudo-Longinus. Greece is now regarded as the primordial comparable, or incomparable, object.[4] But this comparison with Greece does not challenge the integrity of rhetoric, its exemplary nature, the unquestionable force of its norms. The parallel between Greek and Roman writers takes up almost the whole first chapter of book X in Quintilian's *Institutio oratoria,* devoted like the rest of the treatise to the teaching of a unique and universal art.

The beginning of comparative literature involves the exploration of some national or geographic differences, as I said earlier, and of differences of a temporal or historical order. In this regard, the encounter during the Renaissance between the great Greek and Latin models was fundamental, resulting in the realization that an era might be able to distance itself from its immediate past and so be able to conceive of itself as an era in its own right. The self-consciousness of the Renaissance already foretold a historical sense of temporality. The so-called Quarrel of the Ancients and Moderns became widespread, with the comparison of periods, and the no longer incomparable but relative value assigned to the most famous poets. The Renaissance itself would nurture this dispute, as shown by the early appearance in Spain of the curious dialogue of Cristóbal de Villalón, *Ingeniosa comparación entre lo antiguo y lo presente* (1539).[5] From such a vantage point, it is unnecessary to point out that the two decisive thinkers of the eighteenth century were Giovanni Battista Vico and Johann Gottfried von Herder. A new periodization and classification of history by Vico, based on philological knowledge, went beyond the mere binary contrast between ancient and modern. More specifically, Herder did not accept the historical scheme of Johann Winckelmann, whose *Geschichte der Kunst des Altertums* (1764) asserted the hegemony of Greek art. For Herder, the norms proper for other times cease to apply to the various cultural forms of the present. As for differentiation of national character, I will mention only a few aspects of its development here.

Development, yes, or more than that: new, original, conscious invention. "In order for a frontier to be crossed," Manfred Gsteiger has said very simply, "a frontier has to exist. To put it another way, a conscious internationalism is possible only in opposition to a conscious nationalism."[6] Above all we must keep in mind the growth of a different type of nationalism, one that is all-absorbing, that supersedes and subjugates all else, devours everything, including the arts, thought, literature. François Jost distinguishes this type of nationalism from the loyalties of medieval man, attached as he was to his near, concrete environment:

> Although the Augustan concept of *patria* persisted, especially in smaller autonomous communities, medieval patriotism often consisted mainly of a feeling of attachment to a tribe, to a family and friends, to a native city or village, a valley, a countryside; in brief, the homeland, simply a homestead, was the physical and moral environment in which old habits would continue to make life easy and pleasant.[7]

Little by little the ideas of nation, state, country, national idiom, and national culture would tend to converge. This voracious modern nationalism required a considerable effort of integration, to which a patriotic conception of literature would make a significant contribution, although often a single great poet was the focus of attention: Luís Vaz de Camoëns, Adam Mickiewicz, Alexander Pushkin, Mihail Eminescu. Beginning in the seventeenth century, the greatest merit continued to be attributed to the originality of a writer (consider the censure of Pierre Corneille by Georges de Scudéry in 1636 because of the Académie Française's judgment against *Le Cid*),[8] and as a consequence borrowings and influences were also taken into account in judging a writer's work. A tenacious exploration of national peculiarities, whose principal features are all too well known, becomes evident. Béat Ludwig von Muralt in his *Lettres sur les Anglais et les Français* (1725) expresses some quite biting opinions regarding characteristic traits of the two nations ("The French despise the human race because it's not French").[9] Voltaire's brilliant preamble to his *Essai sur la poésie épique*

(1733), titled "Des différent goûts des peuples," is well known, as are the comparisons proposed by Johann Elias Schlegel (*Vergleichung Shakespears und Andreas Gryphs*, 1741),[10] neither presented in an agonistic way but in the spirit of a desire to understand and admire. The concept of "national character" or of other moral and psychological analogies was disseminated and popularized by writers such as J. J. Bodmer (1741), F. C. Moser (*Von dem Deutschen national-Geiste*, 1765), and J. K. Wezel (1781); and above all, by those like Christoph Wieland (*Das Geheimnis des Kosmopoliten-Ordens*, 1788) and principally by Herder. While avoiding jingoistic excesses, these writers endeavored to open a way for a cosmopolitanism that required a prior perception of national historical itineraries in order to be understood correctly.

The obsession with nationalism and the preoccupation with history would naturally meet in the terrain of literature, giving rise to the first national histories, which were Italian, as might be expected: from Giacinto Gimma's *Idea della storia dell'Italia letterata* (1723) to Marco Foscarini's *Storia della letteratura veneziana* (1752). In Italy a clear consciousness of a poetic patrimony appears for the first time, a patrimony uniquely and characteristically Italian, made manifest in anthologies and histories of literature. At the same time, the first multinational histories emerge, ranging from those limited to a juxtaposition of known facts and enumerations relating to various peoples—such as Francesco Saverio Quadrio's *Della storia e della ragione d'ogni poesia* (1739)—to those that propose common dimensions and genres, like the Abbot Carlo Denina's *Discorso sopra le vicende de ogni letteratura* (1760), and above all the seven volumes published in Parma by a Valencian Jesuit, Juan Andrés, *Dell'origine, progressi e stato attuale d'ogni letteratura* (1782–1799). Andrés, like the Schlegels later, makes a sharp distinction between Greek and Latin poetry. But more than anything else, his work is a vast attempt at classification, "with no sense of narrative flow," according to Wellek, "and little of continuity."[11] The most difficult task for these beginning historians was to formulate some national characterizations that would no longer be based on the "different tastes of people" or on other psychic-ethical concepts, but on true historical-literary categories.

Comparative literature becomes a plausible project when two events occur: one, when a large number of modern literatures—literatures that recognize themselves as such—come into existence; and two, when a unitary or absolute poetics ceases to be an accepted model. We then find ourselves before a fruitful historical paradox: the rise of nationalism will lay the foundation for a new internationalism. That is Joseph Texte's conclusion concerning the influence of Romantic criticism, stated at the end of the nine-teenth century, when comparative studies had attained the level of a university discipline:

> [Romantic criticism] on the one hand has given rise to a movement of each people toward their origins, an awakening of the collective consciousness, a concentration of their sparse or scattered forces on the creation of truly autochtonic works. It has provoked, on the other hand, by a contrast to be expected, a lowering of frontiers, a freer communication between neighboring peoples, a more complete knowledge of foreign works. It has been, in one sense, an agent of *concentration*, and in another, an agent of *expansion*.[12]

Romantic concentration and expansion was only beginning to offer opportune responses to the great silence left behind by the neoclassical concept of culture that had disappeared, and that was based on the normative impact and the continuity of a multisecular system of poetics and rhetoric. In earlier times literature had constituted a whole, static regulating, presided over by a cluster of masterworks, examples, and prestigious models. Thus it happened that as the eighteenth century came of age, the vast edifice disintegrated, and the old unity or universality of "humane letters" was left splintered, badly wounded. Everything that came later would be a response to this calamity unequaled in the history of poetics.

Herder, writing in his "Journal meiner Reise im Jahre 1769," laments the tendency to consider rhetoric as unique and immutable, to confuse the ancient with the modern, because he feels that "everything has changed" in the world—for example, that it would be futile to imitate today the "nature" created by the great Greek drama of the past.[13] Keep in mind that Herder detests the facile and superficial rationalism of the salons of the bourgeoisie, the deadly vulgarity of the universities. Here is a brief quote from his *Briefwechsel über Ossian und die Lieder alter Völker* (1773):

> Our pedants, who first have to cram everything together and learn it by heart so that they can stammer it out later in very methodical fashion; our schoolteachers, sextons, half-educated scholars, pharmacists, and all those who frequent the houses of the scholars, who finally acquire nothing more than an inappropriate vague language, sounding as confused as someone in death's throes, or like Shakespeare's Lancelots, policemen, and grave-diggers—these educated people, how would they compare with savages?[14]

The allusion here is clearly to the primitive fabricator of fables and poems rather than to the noble savage. Let us think of Rousseau, one of the great travelers, and one of the first anthropologists. Herder discovers and marvels at the universality of the poetic faculty:

> That would be a theory of the fable, a philosophical daydream, a genetic explanation of the marvelous and fantastic side of human nature, a logic of the poetical faculty; applied to all times, peoples, and types of fables, from the Chinese to the Jews, from Jews to the Egyptians, Greeks, Normans—how great and useful it would be! That would explain the things mocked in Don Quixote, and Cervantes would also be a great author.[15]

The opening to "primitive" cultures and to oral poetry is fundamental and decisive; they promise a new access to universality. In his *Briefwechsel über Ossian*, written with a curiosity and lack of prejudice that still surprise us today, Herder brings together a multitude of testimonies—British ballads, sagas, and other works of Scandinavian bards and skalds; Lettish roundelays; books by Cadwallader Colden (*History of the Five Indian Nations of Canada*, 1747) and Joseph Lafitau (*Moeurs des sauvages américains*) and Quechua couplets translated by "el Inca" Garcilaso.

On one side, the analytic tendency that Texte calls "concentration" will prevail: affirmation of the originality or uniqueness of each people, of its "spirit," "soul," or "genius," and of the manifestation of these qualities in popular creations and traditions, such as romances, ballads, heroic cantos. Each national literature, if it merits the term, is original. It is not a question of saying the same thing in different languages (for example, of repeating the same religious or political dogmas), but of protecting and stimulating different concepts. But this idea of culture as a mosaic of cultures harbors its dialectical antithesis, already present in Herder, that is, the attempt to understand how different voices complete one another, intertwine, and make possible the movement of history toward a broader, wider, more tolerant, self-conscious humankind. It is precisely the Herderian interest in popular poetry that leads to the Romantic discovery of a cultural archive of motifs and legends that turns out to be not local but multinational: the folklore of the brothers Grimm that initiates the study of the peregrinations of fables and themes, the beginnings of medieval romance studies (Fauriel, Raynouard, Sismondi), and the investigations of comparative mythology.

In a parallel fashion, the pre-Romantic and Romantic decades will make room for distinct impulses, very important for our theme, of a synthetic and international type. Although they are apparently very intermixed in practice, I will emphasize two principal tendencies: twin impulses, one toward unification and one toward cosmopolitanism.

The cosmopolitan or internationalist attitude reveals basic modalities of life or of cohabitation, inseparable from the social, economic, and political structures of the Europe of the beginning of the nineteenth century. Keep in mind the continuing growth of precapitalist industry during the initial stages of the Industrial Revolution, and the resulting conflicts between local interests and the interchanges brought about by commerce, technology, and the sciences. These interchanges and other socioeconomic contradictions combined with a cosmopolitan spirit that was fueled by the predominant regionalisms. Joseph Texte's first book was titled *Jean-Jacques Rousseau et les origines du cosmopolitisme littéraire* (1895). Texte (1865–1900) occupied the first chair in comparative literature, established at the University of Lyons in 1896. It is significant that Texte began by investigating the eighteenth-century origins of European cosmopolitanism, a question much debated during those years. Ferdinand Brunetière had just launched a series of contentious essays in the *Revue des deux mondes* concerning the concept of European literature. In 1884 the publication of Georg Brandes' monumental history of nineteenth-century European letters had been completed. The first volume, called *Literature of Emigrants,* included a discussion of political exiles or cosmopolites through no fault of their own (Chateaubriand, Madame de Staël, and many others). On the same subject the prestigious Danish critic wrote that one of the most characteristic aspects of European life during the first third of the century had been its internationalism: the general expansion of cultural events, the rapid propagation of literary or philosophical movements, and the wide repercussions of major political happenings. In his book Texte stressed the contribution of Rousseau—traveler, exile, and, finally, stateless person; the discovery of England by Voltaire and other great French writers of the eighteenth century—the North by the South—and the decline of direct knowledge of ancient literatures: "Romantisicm has placed in opposition to the classical influence the example of a non-Latin Europe." [16] And Texte went on to explain: "Cosmopolitan, that is to say, those identified with a too prolonged domination of the literatures of antiquity." [17]

I will point out briefly some aspects of that impulse toward unification or toward synthesis, or system, noted with notorious frequency in the thinking of the most representative critics and theorists of the time—an impulse that can often be sensed in the awareness of a contradiction, primordial among those determined to overturn the premises of all earlier classicisms, to be inexorably polemical. Think of the polarities dear to Schiller ("Über naive und sentimentalische Dichtung," 1795), or Goethe, or Adam Müller (*Die Lehre vom Gegensatze,* 1804), or Fichte and Hegel. De Sanctis sums it all up most appropriately: "study all the concepts of Romanticism and at bottom you will find an antithesis." [18] In consequence, few yearnings are more typical of Romanticism than the great thirst for a whole, the desire for an integrating experience that goes beyond all the contradictions and penetrates the evolving nature of the world. Faust longed to perceive how all things are interwoven into the same whole—"wie alles sich zum Ganzen webt." In one of the most famous fragments of the *Athenäum* (no. 116) of 1798, Friedrich Schlegel glimpsed the beginning of a poetry destined to be universal:

> Romantic poetry is a progressive universal poetry. Its destiny is not solely to reunite all the divided genres of poetry and to place poetry in contact with philosophy and rhetoric. Romantic poetry intends and should soon fuse poetry and prose, genius and criticism, artistic poetry and natural poetry. The Romantic form of poetry is still evolving; indeed that is its real essence, that it is forever evolving, and can never be completed. [19]

Under the emblem of poetry, the hunger for the integration of a disjointed world, a world fractured by historical knowledge and national consciousness, will be expressed in myriad ways. Literature serves to satisfy that hunger. Once more man will look to the arts to search out the microcosmos, the unity of humanity reconciled with itself thanks to the poet. This movement provided the impetus for organic or biological analogy, so prevalent at the beginning of the nineteenth century. For Oskar Walzel the concept of organism would be the keystone of the Romantic vision of life. [20] It was believed that the same laws rule both organic nature and the works of men, as in the case of a single work of art, comparable to a living being because of its unitary makeup, or in the case of vast cultural entities. In 1802 P. J. G. Cabanis had affirmed with complete conviction: "It is undoubtedly, citizens, a beautiful and great idea that considers all sciences and arts to be a part of an ensemble, an indivisible whole." [21] Adam Müller maintained in 1807 that works of art and genres were like the limbs and nerves of a large and beautiful body: "The single works of art and single genres were considered to be like limbs and nerves and muscle system of a large body, each one functioning independently in its own fashion and each one regarded as an obedient part of a beautiful and incomparable whole." [22]

Finally let us also note the transcendental function attributed by some to the arts as forces for integration during the pre-Romantic and Romantic years—"a visible apparition," Schlegel wrote, "of the kingdom of God on earth"; [23] the modality of systematic thinking in the sciences and philosophy, from Newton and Condillac to Kant and Laplace (*Exposition du système du monde*, 1796); and the efficacy of the belief in progress, applied from the time of the Quarrel of the Ancients and Moderns not only to scientific knowledge but also to artistic productions. Positive, hopeful, exalted visions of the literary or pictorial task that owe not a little to the emancipation of aesthetics that occurred about the middle of the eighteenth century and, as a consequence, the general recognition of the ontological peculiarity of works of art, now clearly differentiated from works of erudition, from the sciences, and from other branches of knowledge.

5

The Compromises of Positivism

The first steps of the new discipline are well known. Alexandru Cioranescu describes them very well in the first chapter of his *Principios de literatura comparada* (1964). In his view, two preoccupations stand out during the Romantic years: the reestablishment of the unity of literature (threatened, as we saw earlier, by the abandonment of traditional poetics) and the study of the relations between one nation and another, an easily accessible activity that gave rise to such important books and courses as those of Abel François Villemain, Philarète Chasles, or Jean-Jacques Ampère. The first comparatists were above all ambitious. Dazzled by the possibilities open to them, no horizon seemed unattainable.

Chasles (1798–1873) wrote more than forty volumes of criticism. Anglophile, with a sharp and facile pen, and possessing a good knowledge of Spain, he wrote about Rabelais, Aretino, Shakespeare, Alarcón, Antonio Pérez, Calderón, Carlo Gozzi, Hölderlin, Jean-Paul, Coleridge, Dickens, Oehlenschläger, Turgenev, and many others.[1] His preferred field of study was intellectual history, which he combined with poetical history. "I have little esteem for the word *literature*," he wrote once. "The word seems devoid of sense to me; it has been hatched out of intellectual deprivation."[2] His basic point of departure is the idea of national character. The Romantic dialectic sketched earlier, open as it is to the impulse for synthesis and the perception of national differences, is left diminished or mutilated. Chasles juxtaposes authors, countries, literatures. "The German should clarify his style, the French make his more solid, the English make his more organized, and the Spaniard calm his down."[3] As an example, we observe Chasles's characterization of the unmistakable French genius:

> Our country, as is well known, is the congenial country par excellence. France rejects nothing, not even folly. She has emotions for all emotions, and can understand all thoughts, even absurd ones. We have seen her in association with all civilizations since her beginnings . . . That central and nurturing mission of France sets us apart from all other peoples, while allowing us to understand them all.[4]

Ampère (1800–1864) likewise preferred to introduce and interpret countries and authors one by one, with as broad a perspective as that of Chasles. A Latinist as well as a Germanist, he was also interested in Oriental literatures (*La science et les lettres en Orient*, 1865), as well as those of Scandinavia and Czechoslovakia (*Littérature et voyages*, 1833). After his decisive meeting with Goethe (who talked about it with J. P. Eckermann on May 3, 1827), Ampère, a keener thinker than Chasles, would go on to develop a unitary conception of the two fields that he considered fundamental: *histoire littéraire* and *philosophie de la littérature*.[5] So it happened that his youthful ambition, expressed in a letter to his famous father, the physicist André-Marie Ampère, was not frustrated: "Oh, my father, my dear father, won't you understand my mission as I do? To trace the panorama of the history of the human imagination, discover its laws, isn't that enough to fill a man's career?"[6]

Other historians, equally ambitious, would scan entire literatures in books "from top to bottom," in Cioranescu's words.[7] It is "l'ère des grandes constructions,"[8] of diffuse synthetic panoramas, that today seem to us premature and hurried. Good examples of this tendency are the works of A. L. de Puibusque, *Histoire comparée des littératures espagnole et française* (1843); the lucid essays of Saint-René Taillandier in his *Allemagne et Russie* (1856); and E. J. B. Rathery, *Influence de l'Italie sur les lettres françaises, depuis le XIIIe siècle jusqu'au règne de Louis XIV* (1853). The two volumes of Puibusque offer a "parallel" with antiquity, no longer between poets but between literatures, characterized psychoethically: "In Spain all that is passion unfurls and is colored with the speed of electricity; in France all that is thought is summarized and formulated with a precision that one might call geometric."[9] This statement occurs in a long essay with a view of the whole, not at all similar to the analytic studies that some comparatists were beginning to cultivate.

In fact, the comparatists quickly go on to an examination of individual authors, or of one masterwork that reveals and pulls together a range of influences: J.-J. Jusserand's *Shakespeare en France sous l'Ancien Régime* (1856) and Pio Rajna's *Le fonti dell'Orlando furioso* (1876) reflect a scientific orientation and the triumph of studies of sources and influences, clearly characteristic of the second half of the nineteenth century. Rajna's book, superior to many others, is an authentic work of investigation, but its author does not get lost in details, since what he wants to highlight is the *invenzione* (fabrication) of the totality of the great poem. And after considering his sources, Rajna concludes that the essence of Arioso is the *contaminatio* (blend) that he achieved and the embellishment that he added.[10]

A new turn is taken by comparative studies around 1850, ushering in a period in which positivist theories and tendencies predominate. "Around 1850 the atmosphere changed completely."[11] René Wellek highlights two aspects of this shift that we must be careful not to confuse. In the first place, what Wellek calls *factualism* predominated: the triumph of facts, of tangible happenings, of copious "events" or supposed events. And in the second place, *scientism:* faith in the unlimited validity and general applicability of the exact sciences, above all the biological sciences, as a way of explaining literary history, how literature is produced and how it changes.[12] The science of psychology of this era—opposed by Freud—and the naturalism of contemporary novels would stress the hereditary origins of human conduct. Gustave Le Bon would emphasize patterns of mob psychology, the determinism of *La psychologie des foules* (1890). Nothing is more typical of this time than the obsession with causality. "Whether events are physical or moral does not matter," Hippolyte Taine maintained; "they always have causes."[13] Of the three best-known causes which Taine cites at the outset of his work on the history of English literature—*race, milieu, moment*— the idea of "race" is clearly of most concern to us here; that is, the concept of nationality that had been only one of the building blocks of Romanticism. The new direction taken by comparativism amounted to something like a pulling back, a retreat, or a serious impoverishment of those aspirations.

At the end of the century comparatists adapted Romantic internationalism and syncretism in this retreat in order to reconcile the two predominant tendencies of the time: the insistence on a national characterology and on the prestige of the biological sciences. It was believed that every literature exists, breathes, grows, and evolves like a living being, its roots anchored in a certain social subsoil and certain national idiosyncrasies. Expressed another way, here are the words of Joseph Texte:

In order that studies of the type we are discussing may be carried out, it is
in fact necessary that a literature be considered as an expression of a definite social state, tribe, clan, or nation, whose tradition, genius, and hopes
. . . it represents. In a word, such literature must constitute a well-defined
genre in the great *species* of the literature of humanity.[14]

The literature of a country thus became a biological variety, a subspecies of
universal literature; and the task of the comparatist was to be the elucidation of the cross-fertilizations and other grafts that link these subspecies and
give rise to their mutations, hybridization, and growth. The integrity of the
individual components of literature was not in doubt, owing to a firm belief
in the uniqueness of the character of each people. A considerable number
of historians who held to this belief kept silent about the evident unity of
medieval European literature. To quote the words of Fidelino de Figueiredo,
a "sort of all-absorbent spiritual imperalism prevailed over the past." [15] The
ideological conditioning of the concept of national literature was not understood at that time, nor the fact that the concept had been broadened retro-
actively: interests and designs of the nineteenth century were projected onto
the defenseless Middle Ages. Thus nationalism and Romantic internationalism were perfectly reconciled. Comparative literature combined all the
characteristics of compromise and halftones.

6

Weltliteratur

So it was that the idea of *Weltliteratur* was left far behind, its outlines blurred. It is well known that Goethe coined the term in his old age, in the year 1827, when a French adaptation of his *Torquato Tasso* appeared: "a general *Weltliteratur* is in the making in which an honorable role is reserved for us Germans." [1] Equally certain are the eighteenth-century origins of such an idea: Voltaire, J. G. Hamann, Herder. It was commonplace to use the term "the Republic of Letters," whose aim, according to the Abbé Prévost, would be "to bring together into one confederation all the individual republics into which the Republic of Letters can be divided up to the present time." [2] Note that the existence of individual republics is pointed out in passing. Indeed, in order for the concept of a world literature to develop it was necessary to describe first the diverse character of literature, that is, the insufficiently representative character of any one of its components alone, the limited nature of the contributions of any one nation or era to the culture in question. Something similar had happened in connection with the possibility of a universal history. Jacques Bénigne Bossuet in his *Discours sur l'histoire universelle* (1681) considered only those who in his judgment had raised their voices in song as part of God's design—the Hebrews, Greeks, Romans, and French. Not so Voltaire, who treated the Christian faith in a relativistic fashion in his *Essai sur les moeurs* (1753–1758), thus opening the door of the world community to China, India, and the Arab countries. [3]

37

The term *Weltliteratur* is extremely vague—or should we say in a more positive way, it is too suggestive, and is therefore open to many misunderstandings. Let us look at three accepted meanings. In German, the juxtapositions of two nouns can lend an adjectival function to the first noun. In such a case the range of meaning of the synthetic adjective can go so far as to imply that literature *itself* is worldwide, or that all literature is, or that only literature that is totally worldwide can be considered to be literature. What can one make of such an idea? The sum total of all national literatures? A wild idea, unattainable in practice, worthy not of an actual reader but of a deluded keeper of archives who is also a multimillionaire. The most harebrained editor has never aspired to such a thing.

As for the second meaning, one might think of a compendium of masterworks or of universal authors, if such words were understood to apply to those works that have been read and appreciated beyond the frontiers of their countries of origin: in sum, those authors hallowed either by a few respected critics, or by multitudes of readers. Quite a few historians have held this opinion, for example, Ferdinand Brunetière. Here is his definition of *littérature européenne:* "The works of a great literature belong to us only insofar as they have come in contact with other literatures, and to the extent that the contacts or encounters have had visible results."[4] At bottom he is speaking of European literature, and let us not call it world literature, a concept that, according to Luigi Foscolo Benedetto, came to be accepted in France. A disagreeable idea, in my opinion, and snobbish too, that recognizes success, and success only, together with its political, ephemeral, or contingent causes. It would be foolish of us to tell the history of our past in that manner, emphasizing its worst side: Vicente Blasco Ibáñez, Emil Ludwig and Erich Maria Remarque, Vicki Baum and Hans Fallada, Eugène Sue and Paul de Kock, Margaret Mitchell and Harold Robbins, Lajos Zilahy and Emilio Salgari and Corín Tellado. As far as our present-day evaluations of literature in Spain are concerned, it is more important that Juan Goytisolo admire and comment on the *Lozana andaluza* of Francisco Delicado, ignored in his own time, or on *Estebanillo González,* or the letters of Blanco White. Otherwise we find ourselves faced with the sad recapitulation of one trivial status quo after another, each one based on the influences and the influential writers of the past, and, of those, only those most visible and most widely known. That is what Guillermo de Torre, in an essay in *Las metamorfosis de Proteo* (1956), called "cosmopolitan literature," a literature that in many cases can hardly be considered even literary. Unfortunately this conception is still bothersome as relic and bad habit of the old attachment of comparatists to the study of influences.

But there is more. There is a third accepted meaning of *Weltliteratur* that cuts across the second one, limiting it to the works of writers of the first or very highest rank. With more reason, the proposal is made to select great universal classics, as Martín de Riquer and José María Valverde write in the prologue to their *Historia de la literatura universal* (1957–1974): "understanding as universal every literary creation capable of being of interest to everyone." The universities (in the United States, the Great Books program of Chicago or of St. John's College, the courses of general education) and certain publishers put this attitude into practice. I am not questioning their pedagogical virtues. The Cyclopean task of writing a universal history of literature has produced some valuable results, such as the *Historia* of Riquer and Valverde, livelier and closer to the original texts than others, although it does not include Oriental literatures; and then there are Giacomo Prampolini's overwhelming fat tomes stuffed with knowledge.[5] But one should reread or take note of Etiemble, for whom the adjective "world" or "universal" turns out to be hyperbolical most of the time.[6] Can one call the collection of "La Pléiade" classics universal? It is no less Gallic-centered than the inquiry carried out some years ago by Raymond Queneau, who asked sixty-one writers what their "ideal library" would be. Since fifty-eight of those asked were French, the results surprised nobody.[7] And looking back, the historical perspectives—that is, looking at the past from the past—on the whole have been narrow and restrictive. The works of neither Dante nor Shakespeare nor Cervantes were considered classics by many European readers until well after the beginning of the nineteenth century. Vittorio Alfieri was of the opinion that in his day it would have been difficult to find more than thirty Italians who had read the *Divina commedia*. The chapter "Curriculum Authors" in Curtius' great book, translated as *European Literature and the Latin Middle Ages* (1973), brings out unexpected facts. As an example of historiographic method, there are more commendable ways to examine the past. And we would not think of implying that our own era is exemplary. However difficult it may be to learn Hungarian, isn't the quality of the poetry of Endre Ady (1877–1919) amazing even in translation? Without going farther afield, why don't we read *Max Havelaar* (1860), the charming and powerful novel by Multatuli of the Netherlands?

The attitudes that we have been discussing have little or nothing to do with Goethe, who had in mind the peculiarities of his own time and above all was looking toward the future. To come closer to his meaning, perhaps we should translate *Weltliteratur* as "literature of the world." And we should

remember that Goethe started from the existence of some national literatures—thus making possible a dialogue between the local and the universal,
between the one and the many, a dialogue that from that day to this has
continued to breathe life into the best comparative studies. We are confronted then by three other groups of meanings. First: the presence of some
poets and some poetries that can be "of the world" and for all the world,
for everybody. Not limited to watertight national compartments, literatures
can be accessible to future readers of a growing number of countries. The
universality of the literary phenomenon is increasing. Second: works that
in their real itinerary, their acceptance or rejection by different readers, critics, or translators, have circulated throughout the world. These necessarily
include translations, transits, studies of reception aesthetics, close to what
the first French comparative studies would become, a theme intertwined
with the second accepted meaning of my previous paragraph but without
normative, valorative, or anthological intentions—without bells and
whistles. Bridges are built from country to country. János Hankiss once
asked himself whether a universal literature could exist in the organic sense,
in the truly unified sense of the term.[8] There is no such evidence for the idea
which we are discussing, whose foundation is pluralistic.

And the third meaning: poems that reflect the world, that speak perhaps
for all men and all women of the deepest, most common, or most lasting
human experiences: the romantic exaltation of the poet, his symbolizing
imagination, which may, as Coleridge wrote, "make the changeful God be
felt in the river, the lion and the flame," the dream of historians such as
Arturo Farinelli.[9] Thus we have three accepted meanings of "literature of
the world," in brief outline, two of an international nature, and the third
and last one better characterized as supranational.

In his conversation with J. P. Eckermann on January 31st, 1827, Goethe
sees "more and more" that poetry is the universal possession, or common
patrimony (*Gemeingut*), of humanity, and that poetry reveals itself everywhere and in all eras, in hundreds and hundreds of men. (Herder had already emphasized this fact: the romances, folk songs, and other forms conserved by the common people show very clearly the widespread nature of
this "poetry of the world," *Weltpoesie*.[10] That was the lesson of eastern
Europe, from Latvia to Serbia. Vuk Karadžić, established in Vienna since
1813, had begun to publish his collections of popular Serbian poems with
extraordinary success.) Translations and the study of foreign languages
make it possible for the writings of great poets to enrapture vast and diverse
audiences. In this manner—says Goethe—anyone can come out of his cor-
ner and breathe foreign airs: "National literature is now rather an unmean-

ing term; the epoch of world literature is at hand." A progressive expansion can be seen. The ancient Greeks did indeed fulfill an exemplary function. But it would be futile today to select a single nation or literature and try to convert it into a perfect "example"—whether it is "the Chinese, or the Serbian, or Calderón, or the *Nibelungen*," Goethe goes on to say. The earliest perfection remains in the past, the glory that was Greece. The future will be different. "All the rest we must look at only historically, appropriating to ourselves what is good, as far as it goes."[11] That is, the future will depend on a plurality of nations and their capacity for mutual understanding.

The starting point, Goethe explains elsewhere, consists of a national literature, but not of nationalism. "There is no patriotic art and no patriotic science." National literature is a beginning that will soon reveal its inadequacies. The reader, the critic, the curious man, the friend of peace and understanding between peoples are nourished more and more each day by works produced in myriad countries. So what the aged Goethe discovers and finds congenial is the growth of international exchanges. Note that Goethe emphasized what we call today the *reception* of literary works, a reception that becomes more and more international. He makes clear that increasing ease of communication is characteristic of modern times.[12] And he is interested in a class of phenomena that would later become a specialty of some comparatists: voyages and voyagers, magazines, reviews, and especially translations, such as those of Schiller into English, of Carlyle into German, or the French versions of *Faust*. There is the beginning of what Guillermo de Torre in *Las metamorfosis de Proteo* calls a "dialogue of literatures." There remains Goethe's hint of the connection between this dialogue of literatures and world trade, between the growth of economic relations and the expansion of cultural relations. Gerhard Kaiser emphasizes this connection with good reason: "The history of the concept of a literature of the world in the nineteenth century . . . can be understood only as a result of the change to which national as well as international thought was subjected in connection with the assumption of power by the bourgeoisie, a power that was, if not political, at least economic and social in nature."[13] But the increase of commercial interchanges and the growing power of the bourgeoisie are not considered here as threatening events. According to Goethe, they all contribute to peace and understanding—to the realization of the eighteenth-century ideal of a human community that was better informed, more tolerant, its components less isolated from one another. After the Napoleonic wars, achieving such a goal seemed more urgent than ever. The cannons of Waterloo still resounded in memory. The idea of *Weltliteratur* (like comparativism later) came out of a postwar atmosphere.

Such an idea would naturally become linked with similar, more innovative conceptions in the areas of politics and culture: with the Europeanism of Giuseppe Mazzini[14] and with the new socialist internationalism. As for Goethe's comments on the connection between literary and economic relations, *mutatis mutandis* Marx and Engels pick up the project of a *Weltliteratur* in the *Communist Manifesto* of 1848. The old economic self-sufficiency—they write—is giving way to international commerce. The same process is happening in intellectual as in material production. The spiritual products of individual nations are now "common property" (*Gemeingut*); and a world literature will be formed from the local literatures: "In place of the old local and national seclusion and self-sufficiency, we have intercourse in every direction, universal interdependence of nations. And so in material, so also in intellectual production. The intellectual creations of individual nations become common property. National one-sidedness and narrow-mindedness become more and more impossible, and from the numerous national and local literatures, there arises a world literature." [15]

Today the concept of *Weltliteratur* raises certain difficulties, as we have already seen. Perhaps the most interesting and suggestive one is the distinction between the international and the supranational. These two dimensions implicate each other and should not suppress but rather foster the encounter between localization and meaning, an encounter that gives rise to a certain literary impulse, as we pointed out earlier. The greatest distances, those that most impede communication and understanding, are perhaps not international but intertemporal. And yet, are there not metaphors, similes, forms that persist and, after thousands of years, still reach us and speak to us? We are still moved—thanks perhaps to a simile, a metaphor, a dynamic form in crescendo—by the expression of jealousy in a famous poem by Sappho, who was born in Lesbos around 612 B.C.:

> He seems as fortunate as the gods to me, the man who sits opposite you and listens nearby to your sweet voice and lovely laughter. Truly that sets my heart trembling in my breast. For when I look at you for a moment, then it is no longer possible for me to speak; my tongue has snapped, at once a subtle fire has stolen beneath my flesh, I see nothing with my eyes, my ears hum, sweat pours from me, a trembling seizes me all over, I am greener than grass, and it seems to me that I am little short of dying.[16]

This color green, between living and dying, cannot be simplified. The splendid verses of the Renaissance poet Garcilaso de la Vega come to mind, taken from his third Eclogue. The cadaver of a nymph lies beside the Tajo River:

Cerca del agua, en un lugar florido,
estaba entre las hierbas degollada
cual queda el blanco cisne cuando pierde
la dulce vida entre la hierba verde.

Near the water, in a flowery spot, she lay among the
grass with severed throat as the white swan lies when
he loses his sweet life among the green grasses.[17]

Going much further back in time, I will cite a passage from an Egyptian poem of the XIIth dynasty (1900 B.C.) with its symmetries and comparisons (the final rain, so ambiguous), the poem called by Adolf Erman "Gespräch eines Lebensmüden mit seiner Seele" (Dialogue of One Tired of Life with His Soul). The poet, eager for suicide, has a conversation with himself:

Today I have Death before me,
like the aroma of myrrh,
like someone resting beneath the sail on a windy day.

Today I have Death before me,
like the aroma of the lotus flower,
like someone feeling on the verge of drunkeness.

Today I have Death before me,
like a rain moving away
like someone returning to his house after a battle.[18]

It is well known that countless readers, not only westerners but Orientals also—for example, the Japanese—have read the works of Dostoevsky with passion. André Gide, who knew Dostoevsky's works well and admired them, declared that the most national writer is also the most universal. In our century, according to Harry Levin, no one fits that description as well as James Joyce:

If Joyce departs from nationalism to arrive at internationalism, he follows a path different from Dante's: if Dante particularizes the universals, Joyce universalizes the particulars. Dante had fulfilled the conditions for beauty, as they had been laid down by Saint Thomas Aquinas: *integritas, consonantia, claritas*. The problem, as it was presented to Joyce, was more complicated: starting from fragments to create a whole; from discords, consonance; and from obscurities, clarity.[19]

Although a fragment does not necessarily express the whole or a unified entity, let us agree that since we are speaking of literature, the fragment is at least no longer merely local or particular. In the context of literature, internationalism does not mean a triumphant heterogeneity. When fragment A and fragment B belonging to different localities come into contact, deeper and wider strata of sense are revealed, strata no longer confined to narrow spaces and moments, to a time *a* and a place *b*. Just as we leave the national sphere and approach a different one, we encounter not only the possibility of differences but also a confirmation of common values and questions. That is to say, matters of supranationality. Matters of transit and process that Goethe himself lived. Read again, for example, his 1828 review of Carlyle's *German Romance,* in which Goethe already supports the idea that it is the unique quality of the poet and of his nation that allows his literary work to illuminate *das allgemein Menschliche,* "the human quality in general":

> Evidently for a considerable time already the efforts of the best poets and best artistic writers of all nations have been directed toward the human quality in a general sense. In every particular aspect, whether historical, mythological, fabulous, or more or less arbitrarily invented, one will see that general dimension illuminating and shining through nationality and personality.[20]

The concurrence of these critical attitudes with the practices of Goethe the poet is evident—the poet who was interested in the rebirth of modern Greek literature, who translated one of the heroic Serbian cantos, "Lament for the Noblewomen of Asan Aga," who studied Czech during his summer vacations in Bohemia, and who—reader of Arabic, Persian, and Chinese poetry—wrote the *West-Östlicher Divan* (1819) and the "Chinesisch-Deutsche Jahres und Tageszeiten" (1830). As we will see later, the distinctions sketched by Goethe are fundamental to the theory of literary genres.

There is no doubt that most of his contemporaries held a narrower conception of cosmopolitanism or "universality" than he did. Quite frequently some of them adopted pan-European attitudes (Mazzini, Brunetière, Texte) or pan-Occidental stances. Or they perpetuated the hegemony of a half-dozen western European literatures. In the twentieth century the situation has changed appreciably; today writers confront literary groupings that include works and authors, procedures and styles originating in the most widely varying latitudes. As the Rumanian comparatist Adrian Marino explained so aptly, a unitary system of communication is functioning nowadays with ever-increasing force, a world colloquy quite similar to the one glimpsed by Goethe:

Time as well as space tends to expand more and more, to become super-imposed, transformed into a unified cultural consciousness of the world, permanent and simultaneous. Thanks to the universal system of communication that is literature, all literatures are on the way to becoming "contemporary" . . . Thus "universal literature" becomes the community of all literatures, past and present, no matter what their traditions, their languages, their historical dimensions and their geographical locations may be . . . The literary dialogue assumes a permanent and international character. Literary communication and community tend to merge.[21]

7

The French Hour

The irradiating center of comparative literature—the word (*mot*) as well as the object of study (*chose*)—was in France, where the term *comparative literature* began to be popularized and naturalized. After Joseph Texte looms the figure of Fernand Baldensperger (1871–1958), author of the archetypal volume *Goethe en France* (1904), professor at the Sorbonne from 1910 on, founder along with Paul Hazard of the *Revue de littérature comparée* (1921), and, in addition to his work on the *Revue*, editor of a series of specialized volumes (more than 120 when the Second World War broke out). Paul Van Tieghem published the first manual describing the new discipline in Paris in 1931. As is well known, his principal recommendation was the study of international literary influences.

It would be unjust not to recognize the determined pursuit of constructive, conciliatory, humanistic ends manifested by members of this circle of comparatists. By humanistic ends I mean an intention to gather and perpetuate not just some presumably unique revealed truths, but the noblest values discovered by men and women, derived from as many cultures and eras as we are able to know and appreciate. In this way the range of human experience will be enriched and restructured. It is worthwhile to reread Baldensperger's call in the inaugural volume of the *Revue* in 1921, in which he emphasizes that the very uneven reception accorded poetic works allows us to identify the most lasting ones:

> Add up the approvals and calculate the dislikes, note the changes of value accorded to a book, regarded as Attic by some, rejected as Byzantine by

others, so that a work disdained here is acclaimed there: these are all judgments that, better than certain postulates, would supply a dispersed humanity with resources less precarious than common values.[1]

Clearly, Baldensperger is referring to the mass of humanity uprooted or derouted as a result of the First World War. His allegation is a postwar act, as are the *Revue* itself and the spirit that inspired it.

The opposition between the "French school" and the "American school" in comparative literature is only too well known. And the conventional labels are as rudimentary as they are inadequate. Historically, there was no French "school" (an inappropriate term for the twentieth century), and of course no American "school" either. I prefer to speak of the French hour: a period of time—from the end of the nineteenth century to shortly after the Second World War—during which the example of the French comparatists predominated and was imitated by scholars of various stripes, all following certain orientations that can be reduced to a simplified conceptual model.

Theoretically, we find ourselves confronted by two opposing models, one international and the other supranational; but in practice, as I keep repeating, the two models are intertwined.

The French hour allowed space for investigations of very different types, but the studies were based on *national literatures*—on their preeminence—and on the connections between them. Major emphasis was placed on phenomena of influence, transmission, communication, transit (*passage*), or the link between activities and works belonging to different national spheres.

Among these, the study of influences is most typical: for example, the influence of Goethe in France, or Goethe in Denmark; Petrarch in Spanish; English or Polish poetry of the sixteenth century; Rilke, Valéry, Kafka in our century. The usual point of departure for this type of study is a great writer, or perhaps a thinker whose ideas have become widespread and generally known: for example, Nietzsche and the Generation of '98 in Spain (an influence thoroughly studied by Gonzalo Sobejano).[2] Sometimes the search for influences is combined with the history of ideas, as in Hazard's famous *Crise de la conscience européenne* (1934) or the chapter "Idées et sentiments" in Van Tieghem's manual. The two terms of this binary interrelation can be wide enough to take in constellations of writers, schools, movements—even including the stereotyped images that certain groups of people have built up about others by reading their writings. (The best known example is Jean-Marie Carré's *Les écrivains français et le mirage allemand*, 1947).[3] In general, these comparatists limited themselves to expanding one of the two terms of the equation that we have mentioned and nothing more. The proposition that a single author might be either the origin of an influence or its conclusion avoids excessive dispersion and makes it possible to bring together the numerous influences studied. Occasionally a study begins with the transmitter: Montaigne and his influence in England (Charles Dédéyan). Others begin with the receiver: Goethe and his assimilation of European literatures (Fritz Strich). Or a study may deal with interplay: Shelley and France, in their respective contacts (Henri Peyre).[4] The perspective is not changed if one of the two elements is a school, a movement, a national period: Juan de Ruysbroeck and the Spanish mystics; the Japanese *haiku* and the Mexican poets from the time of Juan José Tablada and Efrén Rebolledo; or William Faulkner and the *boom* of the Latin American novel. It was also appropriate to examine a part of the production of a group of poets of the same country: French poetry with bucolic themes from the end of the nineteenth century—Henri de Régnier, Albert Samain, Francis Jammes—and that of some poets writing in Castilian—Leopoldo Lugones, Julio Herrera y Reissig, Juan Ramón Jiménez. But in such cases the confines of the theme may appear arbitrary, since the scope of a movement or of a genre is usually international, and the most reasonable study is one whose boundaries coincide with the actual boundaries of the subject. The principal or most typical subject of study was the influence of one writer on another, as would be found in a binary interrelation. But in practice it is rare or difficult to limit oneself to the examination of a text A and a text B. In dealing with literary history, one must investigate how it was possible for A to arrive at B, having to overcome so many obstacles and such large distances to do so. That is to say, *tertium datur,* a third party mediating a matter of concord rather than discord: the translator, the critic, the theatrical director, the magazine. The collecting of countless biographical, sociological, bibliographic, or anecdotal details established a curious specialty within comparativism. A gateway to reading itself? A laboratory of preliminary *Hilfswissenschaft* (auxiliary science)? I am referring to the consideration of voyages and books about voyages, newspaper articles, magazines, all taken together, translations, dictionaries, companies of touring actors; and also the teaching of languages, critics, literary salons, and other components of the mesh of a great international literary network. From this point of view, wouldn't one say that those comparatists came close to being a part of "literary life"? From other points of view (such as the "aesthetic of reception"), must a modern literary historian be indifferent to information of this type? Cervantes in Naples, Voltaire in London (or Chateaubriand, or Blanco White), Andrés Navagero in Granada, Rubén Darío (or Hemingway) in Madrid, André Breton (or Marcel Duchamp) in New York, William Empson (or I. A. Richards) in Peking, Octavio Paz in

India are decisive links of a great chain; and also, centuries earlier, Ambrosio de Salazar, César Oudin, and other interpreters of the Spanish language in seventeenth-century France. At times the dictionary has been an invaluable instrument, even within a country: Giuseppe de Robertis, while revising *I promessi sposi,* proved that Alejandro Manzoni used the *Vocabulario milanese-italiano* of Francesco Cherubini. The writings of Robert Escarpit on the history of the book have caused us to reflect on the long and precarious course that makes it possible for a few poems or narratives to become a *book* at last;[5] and on the considerable influence—since we are talking about influences—of publishers and editors. Isn't it likely that the fact that Spanish literature became widely known in Europe during the sixteenth and seventeenth centuries was related in some way to the presence of Spanish publishers in Flanders, France, and Italy, a reflection of a strong military and political power? In our time, there are a number of clear examples: Gallimard, Feltrinelli . . . In Spain, beginning some twenty years ago, the active involvement of editors such as Carlos Barral and Jaime Salinas was undoubtedly decisive. Because the editor is also an *intermédiaire,* like the writer of articles, the interpreter, the bookseller (Adrienne Monnier, Sylvia Beach), and the professor. Somehow, something or someone makes the passage of text X to Y possible: someone edits X, translates X, gets Y interested, travels with Y, and so on. If Azorín had Gide's *Faux-monnayeurs* in mind when he wrote his novel *Félix Vargas,* it is likely that it was some pages of Unamuno, that tireless reader and exhorter, that inspired him to become better acquainted with Gide's work. The prestigious Georg Brandes was the critic who led Unamuno to Ibsen and Kierkegaard. José de Onís, in an interesting essay on comparative literature, evokes some such moments of the history of Latin American literature: José Martí and his articles about writers in the United States, Rubén Darío publishing *Los raros,* Hostos interpreting *Hamlet.*[6] And we would add today: Julio Cortázar translating Marguerite Yourcenar, and Octavio Paz, Fernando Pessoa, or Mario Vargas Llosa commenting on Flaubert. And we have not yet reached the place to speak of translations that, despite errors, have exerted a profound influence, such as the translations of Dostoevsky, Rilke, Valéry, or Faulkner. In fact, the three most interesting themes in this context are probably translations, the *intermédiaires,* and periodicals.

Later we will return to the study of translation (Chapter 15), beyond doubt a subject of fundamental importance to comparative studies. By *intermédiaires* we refer to certain types of persons, since translations and periodicals are also instruments of mediation. Think of an invitation to a literary voyage beyond one's own border, capable of inspiring writers such as Rémy de Gourmont,[7] Ezra Pound, Valéry Larbaud, Alfonso Reyes, Charles Du Bos, Ricardo Baeza, E. R. Curtius, or Edmund Wilson. François Jost very rightly distinguishes between a great writer, such as Milton (so Italianized, and whose *Paradise Lost* led also to Friedrich Gottlieb Klopstock), and minor figures such as Melchoir Grimm and Jacques-Henri Meister, whose famous *Correspondance littéraire* (1753–1770), as François Jost has observed, sought to link Paris with the rest of continental Europe:

> Intermediaries—which all writers are to varying degrees—if they are great, are named: Milton, Rousseau, Goethe; if they are minor, and if their role has been merely instrumental, they are simply styled intermediaries. In literary criticism the word "intermediary" has come to designate a rank, whereas it should only define a function.[8]

Referring to a certain function, it is useful to know who exercises it, and the distinction between a fine writer of articles of second rank and a renowned essayist or critic is not easily made. Ilia Milarov, of Bulgarian origin, who studied in Russia and later in Zagreb, introduced Russian literature and its critics (Nikolay Dobrolyubov, Nicolay Chernyshevsky) to a Croatian public during the 1880s. But writing from Paris up to the end of the century was Antun Gustav Matoš, a much more significant figure, also acting as intermediary for the same public.[9] And Goethe! And, of course, Voltaire, during the period when the different national literatures were in the process of separating, defining themselves, thereby enhancing the role of the mediator. The now-forgotten Charles de Villers, with his articles in the *Spectateur du Nord* of 1799—a decisive moment—revealed German literature to Madame de Staël. So we see that at times the great writer and the modest critic collaborate. Maxim Gorky made possible the translation into Russian of Imre Madách's *Tragedy of Man* (1903) after having had contact with a young Hungarian journalist, Akos Pintér,[10] who promptly disappeared from view. José María Blanco White, while exiled in London, introduced English poetry to the future Spanish Romantics and then fell into oblivion for a long time. But the value of his work was rediscovered by Vicente Llorens in the great *Liberales y románticos: 1823–1834* (1954).

I will cite only two more names, both from the sixteenth century: Damião de Goes and Leonard Coxe (or Cox). The renowned Portuguese humanist appears to us not as a fortuitous but as an essential "intermediary between Portugal and northern Europe,"[11] because of the special spirit that moved him. Damião de Goes lived and worked in Amsterdam, Vilna, Poznan, and Padua before returning to Lisbon in his old age to be sentenced to life imprisonment by the Inquisition. But what Marcel Bataillon emphasizes is the authenticity of his cosmopolitanism: "No doubt his spiritual importance rests in his cosmopolitanism itself, in the ties he knew how to knot between the Portugal of the great discoveries and the Europe of humanism, of the Renaissance and the Reformation."[12]

The case of the Englishman Leonard Cox, who did manage to avoid prison, is intriguing. Completely forgotten in his own country, he does not even appear in the *Encyclopaedia Britannica*. He is only mentioned in a summary as the author of the first treatise of rhetoric in English, *The Arte or Crafte of Rhetoryke* (ca. 1530), a book that owes everything to the *Institutiones rhetoricae* (1521) of Philipp Melanchthon.[13] A modern historian of the English Reformation, William Clebsch, tells in passing that the daring John Frith (who would die in the great London fire) returned to England in 1532 and was then arrested in Reading. In the Reading prison he talked with "one Leonard Cox": "He asked to talk with the local schoolmaster, one Leonard Cox, who had studied at Cambridge . . . moving Cox to seek and gain his release. [Thomas] More's orders frustrated, Frith escaped the country and returned to Antwerp."[14] Who could that obscure schoolmaster be, who was able to liberate the persecuted reformer?

If we travel eastward, we will discover that in earlier years Cox was a professor at the University of Cracow, where he published several books (*De laudibus Cracoviensis Academiae*, 1518; *Methodus studiorum humaniorum*, 1526) and developed a notably active career, according to József Waldapfel:

> The activity of the Englishman Leonard Coxe was of special importance in the intellectual life of Cracow as well as in the development of Hungarian civilization. It was he who first introduced the spirit of Erasmus to university teaching in the humanities. He carried on his work for scarcely ten years. During that period, he stayed in Hungary for some time . . . On his way to Cracow in 1518, he had passed through Paris, where he became acquainted with Henri Estienne, and then through Tübingen, where he had contacts with Melanchthon . . . His sojourn in Hungary lasted from 1520 to 1525, interrupted briefly several times. Coxe's inaugural lecture at the university was the first manifestation of the Erasmian spirit there.[15]

There are intermediaries who are bridges that, once used, seem to sink out of sight forever.

Baldensperger demonstrated the enormous role played by the press in the diffusion of Goethe's work in France. Others—comparatists or not—have

written and will continue to write about the high point of literary magazines, dating from the beginning of the nineteenth century, and the absolutely decisive role that literary periodicals played from the end of that century in forging innovative movements in poetry, prose, or thought. There is
no question about the prestige of great journals like *La voce* in Florence
(from 1908), *Nyugat* in Budapest (1908), the *Nouvelle revue française* in
Paris (1909), the *Revista de occidente* in Madrid (1923), or *Sur* in Buenos
Aires (1931). But magazines of comparable prestige could also be found
that in their day were more marginal or polemical—and even ephemeral—
publications of the avant-garde that exerted great influence, such as the two
in Coimbra, both aptly named, *Boémia nova* and *Os insubmissos* (1889).
The journal as carrier and intermediary of culture attained a new level of
importance in France during the second half of the nineteenth century. Like
literary gatherings, manifestos, or salons, the periodicals—varied, lively,
perhaps incoherent—are characteristic of the avant-garde, above all since
the time of Symbolism and other fin-de-siècle movements. Fritz Hermann
calculates that some two hundred *little magazines*—some not so little—
were spawned in Paris between 1880 and 1900.[16] It is useful to distinguish
between various polarities that characterize different publications. There
are magazines directed by a group of collaborators, and others, perhaps the
principal ones, that are inseparably linked to one outstanding personality:
thus it was with the old *Revue des deux mondes* of François Buloz (from
1831); Zenon Przesmycki and *Chimera* (1901), which brought together the
"modernist" writers in Warsaw; Teixeira de Pascoais and *Presença* (1910)
in Oporto; Ford Madox Ford and the *English Review* (1908), or the *Transatlantic Review* (1924), which gathered in the English-language expatriates
living in Paris: Joyce, Pound, Gertrude Stein, Hemingway;[17] José Ortega's
Revista de occidente; Victoria Ocampo's *Sur.* Then there are magazines
that, though innovative for the most part, serve as a meeting place for a
variety of styles and aims, such as the important *Revue blanche* (1891) or
The Dial (1920), or *Zenit* (1921) in Zagreb, or *Contimporanul* (1922) in
Bucharest. And finally there are still others that embody a movement or a
tendency of poetry, such as the Symbolist movement in Paris, or *Poetry* in
Chicago (1912), linked to imagism and the orientation of Pound, or *Ska-
mander* (1922) in Warsaw, post-Symbolist, almost neoclassical; and still
others that reflected an ideological inclination, magazines like T. S. Eliot's
Criterion (1922) or José Bergamín's *Cruz y raya* (1933).

But what is crucial here is the difference between the more "dignified,"
solid, or established publications and the marginal, experimental magazines

imbued with an unconventional spirit, such as the English *Yellow Book* (1894), with its covers by Aubrey Beardsley and its decadentist, ambiguous, "anti-Victorian," Frenchified contributions—*little magazines* that owed their existence to two motives: "rebellion against traditional modes of expression . . . and a desire to overcome the commercial or material difficulties which are caused by the introduction of any writing whose commercial merits have not been proved."[18] Finally, let's keep in mind two more criteria: the more or less important inclusion of plastic arts in publications such as *Blätter für die Kunst,* founded in 1892 by Stefan George, or *Pan* (1895), or Diaghilev's *Mir iskusstve* (World of Art) (1899), or the Dutch *De stijl* (1917) of Theo van Doesburg, publications that have a wide reach and include even subjects such as architecture and urbanism—as well as the luxury journals. Furthermore, we must consider to what extent room is made available to foreign writers. Some magazines have a marked cosmopolitan function, like the *Mercure de France,* which as early as 1897 opened its pages to Latin American literature through the articles (1903–1907) of E. Gómez Carrillo and the support provided by the personal leadership of Rémy de Gourmont.[19]

Perhaps of greatest importance for a magazine is not so much to be pleasing aesthetically, or pleasant, but to stir up, interest, inform, upset. Margaret Anderson, director of the *Little Review* (1914), recalled once what William Carlos Williams wrote her in a letter: "As always most of the stuff in the *Little Review* is bad, I suppose, but the *Little Review* is good."[20]

The examples I have presented in the last few pages fall within the scope and the themes of the comparativism of the "French hour"—that vast and curious laboratory that apparently regarded all facts as usable, and considered that everything has its place, and that every detail adds to the whole.

But to which whole? How can we avoid feeling overwhelmed by such a profusion of facts? Is Montherlant more interesting in Madrid than in Paris, or Navagero in Granada than in Venice? Well, yes: the meeting of Garcilaso with Navagero in Granada was and continues to be a sign of the fundamental relationship between Italian and Spanish poetry of the Renaissance. The whole in question can be either the historical-literary system of the moment or, as I prefer to think, our own critical-historical discourse: an integrating reflection of a history open to every nexus, to all contacts, including accidents that did in fact mark its path. History—social, economic, and political—merged with what can be regarded as merely literary, thereby making history more complete, perhaps more real. Let us not yearn for pure poetic analysis *in vitro,* the solitude of the study, where only texts are allowed. The study of literature, at least from that point of view and at that moment, is returned to the street, to the crossing of chance with idea, to confusion and diversity of events.

But there is still more. I have just mentioned the existence of that gateway to comparative studies, which is the intermediary's knowledge and his different personifications. At the same time, comparatists investigated what was called *la fortune d'un écrivain* (a writer's luck, or fortune). Instead of looking for the gateway, they went looking for the exit. Let's say that intermediaries made possible the passage of a text A to certain texts B, C, and D, before B, C, and D were published, by means of a factor *i*. A diagram of this process would then be:

$$A \longrightarrow i \longrightarrow B, C, D.$$

After the appearance of D, the final balance sheet of the consequences of a work—its influence, effect, success, diffusion, readership, and sale—was the writer's "fortune." The diagram then becomes:

$$A \longrightarrow i \longrightarrow B, C, D, \longrightarrow f \text{ of } A.$$

According to Pichois and Rousseau, fortune includes at the same time both a certain quantitative phenomenon called *succès* and some qualitative processes, less obvious, known as *influences:*

> Success can be calculated: it is measured by the number of editions, the translations, the adaptations, the objects inspired by the work, such as the number of readers who have presumably read it. The study of success is, then, one of the elements of the sociology of literary facts. To success, which is quantitative, we oppose influence, qualitative; to the passive reader, in whom the literary energy with which the work is charged is dissipated, we oppose the active reader, whose creative imagination will be stimulated, thereby revitalizing the work once more to be transmitted anew.[21]

Let's ignore the distinction between active reader and passive reader, information potentially too uncertain to be useful. (Is the writer the only active person? Isn't anyone who reads with maximum interest and sensibility also active?) But it is generally useful to differentiate between the class of phenomena called *succès* or *fortune,* collective and quantitative concepts, on the one hand, and *influences,* whose scope is individual and qualitative, on the other hand. Some time ago, Anna Balakian rightly suggested that the reception of an author or group of authors contributes to the definition of a period, of certain literary circumstances, that allow the most significant influences to survive later on.[22]

Rather than a disparity, we confront an opposition of concepts, *succès* versus *influences.* The fortune or success of a writer, genre, or movement is a process that follows the publication of a literary work. The extent of this process can be calibrated, measured sociologically. (The editor is perhaps a sociologist without realizing it, but only up to a certain point, if it is a question of writers in fashion.) Even those who do not read can be aware of a fashion, know who Byron was, use the adjective "Kafkaesque." The public is heterogeneous, and even in France one speaks of *succès d'estime.* Those who flocked eagerly to openings of Josep María de Sagarra in Barcelona during the 1930s were not readers of Carles Riba. In Budapest, the admirers of Ferenc Molnár were not best friends with Attila József. A poet's reputation can shrink to a small circle, perhaps to a very few of exquisite sensibilities, to a gathering of young writers, literary rebels. But that does not explain why a writer's reputation becomes widespread or lasting.[23] The renewed vogue of Luis de Góngora during the 1920s does not mean that the *Soledades* was the principal model for Federico García Lorca, Vicente Aleixandre, or Luis Cernuda. In his well-known letter of 1928 to René Taupin, Ezra Pound did not confuse the most prevailing influences of a literary period, such as the influence of Flaubert, with the most personal or intimate ones that the poet discovers by himself; in the case of Pound, the decisive discoveries were of the works of Jules La Forgue, Arnaut Daniel, and Catullus. Fortune and success, then, contribute to the establishment of what we would call today—along with Hans Robert Jauss—the readers' "horizon of expectations." The individual, genetic influences that most often preceded the publication of a text merit separate mention. We will return to them later, in Chapter 15. T. S. Eliot said that the most profound influences are those that transform a writer, or at least help form him, or confirm him in his identity.

At times, the unpredictable, capricious, and tangled events connected with literary influences lead the comparatist to ponder the complexity and peculiar character of the history of literatures. For quite a few years now, fortunes and reputations have taken on strange shapes. Stimulated by reading *Estudios hispano-suecos* (1954), a work by that true Spanish comparatist, Carlos Clavería, I wrote in an essay in 1962:

The influence of Cervantes during a century and a half was infinitely less than that of his contemporaries. According to Carlo Pellegrini, no French author fully appreciated Dante until the nineteenth century. Reread the pages in which Carlos Clavería . . . recounts the bizarre story of the translations of Fra Antonio de Guevara into Swedish, Hungarian, and Dutch. Alda Croce explains to us that the overwhelming presence of the Spaniards in Italy for so many years resulted in a scarcely noticeable influence of Spanish letters in that great country. Not long ago Alexander Gillies commented on two extremely fruitful mistakes: the influence of Shakespeare on Herder and that of Herder on Slavic Romanticism—both based on erroneous readings.

And I concluded, not without a certain feeling of exaltation:

A book is not simply a printed poem, but a literary creation that has penetrated the sphere of political or social history—that of wars, conquests, emigrations, social tensions, national antipathies, and so on. Poetry is not transmitted or diffused by a handful of righteous men in the best of all possible worlds. This curious marriage—not the one Prudencio sang of—of Literature with History leads us to sense what I would call the *contingency* of our literary past. This word is debatable, but what is important is that the concept is also debatable, and that the problem exists. Poetic phenomena do not constitute that world of pure "forms" or "development" that the critics amuse themselves by arranging, but one of the most mysterious and most arbitrary fruits of the vicissitudes of human life.[24]

Now, almost thirty years later, I would express myself in another way. But the problems I was referring to have given rise to a class of investigation, the theory of literary history, that as we will see later (Chapter 16) has become one of the most promising branches of comparative literature today.

Looking back, it is difficult now to explain the limitations of the particular phase of comparativism that I call the French hour. It is worthwhile to take note of the limitations in order to go beyond them, but I do not mean to be disparaging. It would be foolish indeed to reproach our predecessors for their ignorance of the future. There were three principal deficiencies, as I have already mentioned, that existed alongside the preeminence of national literatures. The first one concerns the positivist conception of *literary influences*. Mental or imaginative events, like physical, chemical, or biological ones, were thought to obey the principle of conservation of matter, of the transmutation of certain elements into others organized differently; the etymological image of flux, *flow—fluere—*would suggest that an influence represents an uninterrupted passage from one thing to another, and as a result that particular type of criticism tends to confuse influence as a biographical or genetic event with textual parallelism, or the reflection of one work in another. The presence of *Don Quixote* in Fielding's *Tom Jones* is indisputable; I mean, it is clearly visible; but it is not for that reason more significant than Poe's presence in French symbolism—manifested in a more theoretical than verbal form; nor more significant than the long shadow cast by Rousseau during the Romantic epoch, or that of Juan Ramón Jiménez among Hispanic poets who came after him. The spark can be provided by the persona and the example of a writer: that of the citizen of Geneva, or the bard of Moguer—or the example of Mallarmé, or of Breton. At other times, an influential work operates more than anything else on certain psychic states of the poet, or on moments in the life of the novelist, and thus becomes part of the process of genesis and creation, and so merits the name of influence. In such cases, perhaps the most interesting ones, it can be observed that a work B would not have existed *without* A, but that doesn't necessarily mean that A may be found *in* B. Amado Alonso explains, "Literary sources should be related to the act of creation as incitements and as motives for reaction." [25] Keep in mind also the necessary distinction between influences, intense and individual, and *conventions,* extensive and general—common premises, usages, the collective air breathed by writers of a era. Conventions belong to the literary system of a moment of history. Was it necessary for a Renaissance poet to read Petrarch in order to write Petrarchan sonnets? How many people were petrarching without realizing it? But if something of A is found in B, perhaps we have only an example of what is today called intertextuality. [26]

Second, the earlier interest in influences was not a manifestation of the *obsesión genética* that appears to us so typical of the nineteenth century. This obsession arose *inter alia* from a bad reading of Auguste Comte on the subject of positivism: he recommended the abandonment of absolute notions such as the causal explanations of a totalizing character when considering social changes. Comte wrote:

> Everyone knows that in positive explanation, even when it is most perfect, we do not pretend to expound the generative *causes* of phenomena, as that would be merely to put the difficulty one stage further back, but rather to analyze the circumstances in which the phenomena are produced, and to link them to one another by the relations of succession and similarity. [27]

These were admirably clear words. Nevertheless, other inclinations—like those of the most "vulgar" Marxism—would perpetuate antiquated notions of causality. Marc Bloch, more than a century after Comte, had to warn his historian colleagues against what he called *l'idole des origines,* showing that this idea is a result of a confusion beween origin and explication: "In popular usage an origin is a beginning which explains. Worse still, a beginning which is a complete explanation."[28] Many causes, even though necessary for the attainment of a certain type of effect, do not explain what such an effect might be, nor do they allow its concrete development to be foreseen. Henri Bergson made a distinction between different degrees of solidarity that exist between a cause and an effect. If the effect is invariable, like that of a billiard ball striking another one with a definite momentum, cause is an appropriate term; if the effect is not invariable, like that of a match placed next to a barrel of gunpowder, then without the ability to predict the exact nature or the consequences of the expected explosion, it would be better to speak of "occasion"—or of "condition."[29] But we would need God and all his angels to help us recognize whether the world of culture is a world consisting of occasions, or of conditions, or of conditionings, rather than of explicable causes.

In the third place, the tendency to isolate a singular work, converting it into a unique or sufficient object of study, has been called *atomism.* The critic is the successive interpreter of an Indian file of individualities. This current and almost irresistible tendency reflects an experience that should be known to every reader of poetry. There is a moment when the reading of San Juan de la Cruz, Stendhal, or Proust attracts us, hypnotizes us, *captures* us completely—to such an extent that we forget about the rest of the world, things, and people: a moment when the world is wiped out, everything is concentrated on that one object and on the emotions released by it. That moment is the aesthetic experience. The work has acted as a complete entity, absorbing and fascinating. The most disparate elements have contributed to it: references to things and people outside the confines of the work, to the world fragmented and turned upside down by it; allusions, explicit or silent, to contemporary history, to what has been shared existentially by the readers; echoes of other works, intertexts, refractions, transmuted forms, conventions, and generic expectations. But our personal experience of the literary work—singular and also diverse—is not solely aesthetic. The critic perceives on the one hand the unifying and centripetal will that makes the aesthetic emotion possible and, on the other hand, the multiplicity of relations that show the solidarity of the work with the structures of society and the directions of the historical future. For in addition to criticism, literary history and theory help illuminate these associations, leaving behind that unforgettable, dazzling moment that completes and reintegrates the work, the moment when the words stand alone and the world disappears. Otherwise, criticism—atomized, pulverized—would not be able to do more than simply add to the chaos of lore and libraries. Currently there are various theories such as neo-Marxism, the structuralism of the 1970s, and the aesthetic of reception, that have helped to rectify atomism, solitude, the dispersion brought about by certain traditional attitudes.

8

The American Hour

Both the practical and the theoretical limitations of comparative studies of French design were noted during the 1920s and 1930s by scholars on both sides of the Atlantic. The exclusive interest in the phenomena of influence was clearly drawing to a close. The Second World War accelerated this process along two main paths. That enormous human disaster brought an intensification of internationalist aspirations, a revulsion against the patriotic ideologies that had caused the massacre. A quarter of a century after the launching of the *Revue de littérature comparée*, there was a yearning for a more daring and more genuine solidarity, a denunciation of the prevalence of the investigation of influences in the principal national literatures. Instead, comparatists proposed a deeper humanism, a wider, more lucid perception of our own time.

Courses in comparative literature had been offered in the United States since the beginning of the century at Harvard and Columbia universities.[1] The fascism of the 1930s caused a massive migration to the New World of large numbers of esteemed artists, intellectuals, and scientists from all the latitudes and longitudes of Europe. The universities of North America, in contrast to their European counterparts, recognized degrees granted by institutions in foreign countries; they did not regard themselves as closed enclaves. As a result, they benefited to a remarkable extent from such a conjunction of spirits and learning, reaching new heights in specialties as diverse as the history of art, physics, sociology, psychology, psychoanalysis, architecture, political science, history of science, linguistics—and also comparative literature.

Some comparatists educated in the French tradition swelled the ranks of American faculties. But the really decisive element was the arrival of several generations of Europeans whose work in some cases attained maturity in America, demonstrating its quality and promise, like the work of René Wellek and Renato Poggioli; in the meanwhile, other scholars already eminent in their fields continued to develop their work and teachings; examples include Erich Auerbach, Roman Jakobson, and Américo Castro. The favorable conditions for comparatists in the universities of the United States and Canada were created in large part by the intellectual disposition of North American critics such as Harry Levin. Born comparatists, they were well educated in English literature and European culture, immersed in the polyglot and multicolored environment of a continent of immigrants. It is difficult for almost any European country to overcome the instincts of nationalism, whereas in America and above all in exile the concept of Europe arises naturally—from a distance—a vision of an entity, a break with the follow-the-leader mentality, apt innovations for the New World.

No wonder that at such a juncture comparativism would advance resolutely, overcome old habits and positivist vices, and prosper as a university discipline. The American hour signified the coming of age of the discipline through the work of a number of scholars of different origins, brought together on American soil. But as might be expected, not everyone was convinced. There was need for a clarification, for a decisive confrontation, which took place at the Second Congress of the recently established International Comparative Literature Association (ICLA), held September 8–12, 1958, at the University of North Carolina in Chapel Hill.

Numerous philogists and historians from both continents attended. Supranational categories, such as genres, forms, themes, styles, and movements, received the greatest attention. The high point of the severe criticism directed against traditional comparativism—still stubbornly clung to by some—was a masterly paper by René Wellek, "The Crisis of Comparative Literature." With his usual clarity and natural manner, he made a strong case for the indivisibility of criticism and history, of comparative literature and general literature, of the distinct strata of the work of verbal art conceived as a diversified totality and a structure of meanings and values. Wellek crossed the *t*'s and dotted the *i*'s regarding the old conception of the discipline, or rather subdiscipline, which consisted in collecting facts about sources and writers' reputations. And he added: "An artificial demarcation of subject and methodology, a mechanistic concept of sources and influences, a motivation by cultural nationalism, however generous—these seem to be the symptoms of the long-drawn out crisis of comparative literature." [2] Full of youthful enthusiasm, I took advantage of the opportunity to speak in the plenary session, reflecting on the concept of influence that many of us felt necessary for further progress. Among those attending the conference were Harry Levin, Renato Poggioli, Northrop Frye, Roland Mortier, Haskell Block, Anna Balakian, A. Owen Aldridge, and Walter Höllerer; the Hispanics were represented by Antonio Alatorre, Guillermo de Torre, Francisco López Estrada: all took part in formulating a definition of paths to be followed. In Chapters 11 through 16 I will sketch these orientations, pointing out five principal classes of comparative investigation. But it is appropriate to discuss some other questions first, such as the character of the diverse models of supranationality and the possible distinction between comparative literature and *littérature générale*, a distinction so vigorously rejected by Wellek in 1958.

9

Littérature Générale and Literary Theory

Outdated though it may seem to us today, it is worthwhile to recall the old argument that gave rise to the idea of *littérature générale,* and not simply because it still surfaces from time to time. The question is interesting for two reasons. First, the special tension existing between comparative literature and general literature helps us learn about the internal structure of an intellectual discipline—its polarities, resistances, and lines of force. What grades of theoretical abstraction are tolerated by this or that discipline? A very similar feeling of unease exists among comparatists today in connection with the flowering of literary theory. Second, we will soon find it necessary to distinguish between supranational categories that imply internationality and those that go, or tend to go, beyond international relations. The history of a problem often helps to place it and to bring subsequent questions into sharper focus.

The old distinction, characteristic of *l'entre-deux-guerres,* was formulated by Paul Van Tieghem in the following manner: Comparative literature would denote the study of relations between two or more literatures; binary contacts—between work and work, work and author, author and author—would assure these connections. However, a series of books about Schiller in France and Rousseau in Germany and Byron in Russia do not constitute a history of the Romantic movement. And thus an opening appears for *littérature générale,* a concept that, in a further attempt at synthesis, concerns itself with "les faits commun à plusieurs littératures," matters that are

63

common to several literatures. Genres, schools, styles, periods, and movements are all based on similar matters. "Of the domain of general literature," Van Tieghem concluded, "are matters of a literary nature that belong to several literatures at the same time."[1] As an example, Van Tieghem proposed three distinct contexts necessary for an understanding of *La nouvelle Héloïse*: first, that of national literature, that is, the place of *La nouvelle Héloïse* in the French novel of the eighteenth century; second, that of comparative literature, or the influence of Richardson on Rousseau; and third, that of general literature, or the sentimental novel in Europe influenced by Richardson and Rousseau.[2]

This strict tripartite division does not hold up on analysis, however, and turns out to be indefensible. The three classes of investigation are interlinked and interdependent. No single class can really be isolated and considered independently. On the other hand, saying that something cannot be isolated or stand alone does not cause it to disappear. I am not implying that there is absolutely no difference between a study of influences or sources and a study of literary genres such as the eclogue, the *entremés* (theatrical interlude or short farce), or the sentimental novel. The experiences of critics or readers are varied, successive, and encompass different moments: the moment, for instance, when I am perhaps fascinated by the influence of Scott over a certain novel of Balzac; or the debt Cervantes owes to the irony of Erasmus, to Renaissance dialogue, to the poetics of Tasso. As a momentary experience, any separate thing can be isolated. Then, if our objective is not a criticism fragmented by infinite atomizing but one that is integrated into the complexes that make up literary history itself, each solitary component must become a part of *an intelligible field of study*. And then we realize once more that the past itself, literary history in motion, *in illo tempore*, has always consisted in a constant interlacing of international relations (Balzac reader of Scott, Cervantes reader of Erasmus) with complexes and classes of a collective dimension: Renaissance irony and dialogue, neo-Aristotelian poetics, and so on. Going back to Van Tieghem's example, we need only read Rousseau's *Confessions* to verify that that great spirit lived and was acquainted with the most diverse texts and models. To project the narrow concept of French national literature over the complex and vast culture that he breathed is to perform an absurd surgical operation. One cannot analyze the relationship of Richardson to Rousseau without taking into account the earlier and later trajectory of the novel, or the character of subgenres such as the epistolary novel or the sentimental novel. Wellek untangled this confusion with masterly skill in his *Theory of Literature* and in "The Crisis of Comparative Literature." The example cited on both occasions was the influence of Sir Walter Scott outside England, an influence that cannot be separated from the itinerary of the historical novel in general: "One cannot make a valid distinction between the influence of Walter Scott abroad and the international vogue of the historical novel. 'Comparative' and 'general' literature merge inevitably."[3]

Some comparatists have been slow to recognize the inevitability of this convergence. For example, the reader of the well-known manual of Claude Pichois and André-Marie Rousseau (1967) stumbles on a *histoire littéraire générale* isolated from the *échanges littéraires internationaux,* and not much broader in its conception than the idea put forward by Van Tieghem; but despite its ambitious label, the idea that follows *littérature universelle* is reduced to the least interesting aspect of the *Weltliteratur* originating with Goethe—that is, to the catalogue of successes, the *Who's Who* of the most illustrious authors. Not so Gerhard Kaiser in his *Einführung in die Vergleichende Literaturwissenschaft* (1980; Introduction to Comparative Literature), which stresses the indivisibility of comparative literature and general literature: the fact that Jean-Paul and E. T. A. Hoffmann were assimilated with French Romanticism cannot be understood without the necessary references to styles, themes, and genres cultivated at that time by French and German literatures.[4] Nowadays, generally speaking, the term *comparative literature* is a conventional label encompassing both *littérature comparée* and *littérature générale.* The label is no doubt imperfect and antiquated, but precisely because it is so traditional it has the advantage of continuing to suggest the dialectic of unity and multiplicity more than the term *literature* alone or more grandiose ones such as *universal literature.* Without that dialectic, it would be difficult to understand or even conceive of the creation of poetry or its history, nor could a real idea of literature be developed.

I have already said that a discipline can learn much from the structures of its own history. We might ask ourselves now: What was the function of the opposition between *littérature comparée* and *littérature générale* in its day? When Van Tieghem published his manual, why did he specify *littérature générale?* I suggest two reasons. First, let us note that in the term he chose, the adjective, *générale,* yanks the noun, *littérature,* vigorously in its wake, signifying motion toward the supranational and the universal. As we saw earlier, comparative studies throughout the nineteenth century had capitulated to the prevailing concept of national culture or national literature. There was nothing halfway about it. National phenomena had assumed a very clear priority. But a muddying of values took place, and a bland, tepid, ineffective adoption of the Romantic ideals of synthesis and cosmopolitanism occurred. Van Tieghem sensed this weakness and tried to rectify it with his proposal of a *littérature générale.* And since he considered that the two fields were truly unequal (and keep in mind that the not-national or ultranational inclination is the authentic *differentia* of the comparatist), his call, though moving and lucid, implied its own dialectical autonegation, overwhelming *littérature comparée* by its own momentum. And he confessed:

> One would like to accept wholeheartedly the international point of view. Many works of comparative literature invite us there, but that's all: they show us the Promised Land, without guiding us to it, and even without pointing out the road. In order to enter, one has fix on other aims, employ other methods, and the point of view of comparative literature must be left behind.[5]

Second, the role of *littérature générale* was similar to the role of the theory of literature today; that is, it implicitly carried within itself a significant grade of "theoreticity." The path that must be followed to go from a study of Richardson's influence to the sentimental novel, or from the impact of Sir Walter Scott to the definition of the problem of the historical novel, presupposed a considerable effort of conceptualization. It is curious that those *comparatistes* were unaware of that fact. Remember that the meaning of "theory" or "theoretical" changes with the times, most particularly as a result of underlying epistemological premises.

The conception of knowledge of the *comparatistes* was a form of empiricism, based on a tranquil confidence in the objectivity of the declared literary critics. Conceived in such a way, comparative literature assembled and organized "facts." The influence of Richardson on *La nouvelle Héloïse* was simply a "fact." A national literature was not a selective framework of knowledge, guided by previous interests, but also a fact (as Simon Jeune put it: "A *littérature générale* does not exist in the sense in which one speaks of diverse national literatures").[6] In accordance with this image of the comparatist as collector or assembler of collections, as faithful receiver and mirror of things as they are, the larger dimensions spanned by *littérature générale* differ only in a quantitative sense from the different categories of facts at the comparatist's disposal.

According to W. V. Quine, there are various *grades of theoreticity* that respond to the different distances between observer and observable facts; accordingly, the different grades make possible individuation and other levels of interpretation.[7] For the reader of a work of verbal art, I do not believe that a zero grade of theoreticity—a totally innocent perception of interpretation—exists. But even if it did exist, an immense distance would separate such a perception from general constructions such as literary genres, themes, periods, or styles. This is what Northrop Frye explained for an entire generation of American students in his *Anatomy of Criticism* (1957):

It occurs to me that literary criticism is now in such a state of naive induction as we find in a primitive science. Its materials, the masterpieces of literature, are not yet regarded as phenomena to be explained in terms of a conceptual framework which criticism alone possesses. They are still regarded as somehow constituting the framework or structure of criticism as well. I suggest that it is time for criticism to leap to a new ground from which it can discover what the organizing or containing forms of its conceptual framework are.[8]

Today these words no longer need any elaboration. The genres, periods, and other terms of *littérature générale* constitute precisely what Frye called the "conceptual framework" of a reader's or critic's perception of basic observable facts. A few pages of Lope de Rueda or Luis Quiñones de Benavente can be read from the point of view of the concept of the *entremés,* or of the figure of the *jeune premier,* or of the Baroque style, whenever these tools of investigation seem to be adequate and sufficient; for an original investigation will call them to account or will replace them by others; that is, it will confront the conceptual framework consciously and constructively.

Today we understand very clearly that the definition of a literary genre such as the picaresque novel does not proceed from an inductive approach to a certain corpus of narrations—since the number of narrations considered picaresque depends on the earlier definition. It comes rather from the selection of certain general qualities capable of leading to particular results; or from erecting certain hypothetical models of description that we can continue to use in reference to all empirical situations or observable facts of interest to us. As for the components of literary history, such as periods or movements—the Baroque, Romanticism, expressionism, and so on, they are clearly not finished or prefabricated constructions. Comparative literature heightens our awareness of the high grade of theoreticity required by the *history* of literature.

For almost thirty years, literary theory has obviously enjoyed an astonishing boom—uncomfortable and disturbing for many. This is not the place to discuss the phenomenon. I will only say in passing that it is important not to mix up the property of the term *theory* with the occasions that arise to use the adjective *theoretical.* Today we need the adjective much more than we need the noun. That is, the profusion of theoretical writings that we read—writings that contain an intense theoretical charge, like so many electrified objects—is inversely proportional to the actually quite small number of produced or developed theories. What is striking is the enormous quantity of essays, articles, and books of a primarily theoretical character now appearing that propose no complete and coherent theories and do nothing to clarify a body of basic principles and fundamental criteria, without which there can be no such thing as poetics. They are theoretical precisely because they do not propose any theory whatsoever in a satisfactory fashion. We are dealing with a reactive activity. Today's theoretical disquiet comes out of a profound dissatisfaction. Many believe that the conceptual frameworks that the history and criticism of literature have at their disposal turn out to be precarious, deficient, hackneyed—in need of the most vigorous renovation.

With his usual perspicacity, Jonathan Culler has reflected on the relationship between literary theory and comparative literature, indicating that the new theoretical writings have transformed concepts such as influence into concepts basic to comparativism, attributing to them a way of operating applicable to any field of literary study:

> *Rezeptionsästhetik* and intertextuality are options in the study of any national literature, and as national literature departments have become less committed to the chronological study of a nation's literature—largely in response to new developments in literary theory—they have often gone further in their theoretical explorations than has Comparative Literature.[9]

There is little doubt that comparatists learn a great deal from noncomparatists. Certainly quite a few comparatists have maintained a conservative stance, and the most recent theoretical ideas usually come from other fields. But conservative or conformist, it would be rash to adopt and reflect immediately the actual status quo, no matter how innovative it might be. In addition, this hasty adoption puts us in a position of incoherence, in a chaos of perspectives, in an out-and-out marginal state. With a few important exceptions, such as Hans Robert Jauss, innovative explorations do not represent more than *approaches* to the singular text. Culler makes an effort to classify and reconcile the theoretical responses of the present day. But, responses to what questions? What system can a Scholastic of the present, today's historian of criticism, rely on? At the very minimum a prior and necessary condition of such a system would be the existence or continuity of some common problems. Comparativism at least knows the problems it faces. In confronting them, it is imperative that present-day comparatists admit that the theory of literature is a challenge for them at least as fundamental and necessary as general literature was for their predecessors. In sum, then, the internal structure of our discipline is the tension or polarity that exists between grades of theoreticity.

10

Three Models of Supranationality

As I understand it, three models of supranationality are presented to students of comparative literature. Here I will only sketch them briefly.

A. The most recent model is the study of phenomena and supranational assemblages that *imply internationality,* that is, suggest either genetic contacts or other relations between authors and processes belonging to distinct national spheres or common cultural premises. Examples of phenomena that imply a genetic relation include the picaresque novel and the theme of Don Juan. Alain René Lesage translates Mateo Alemán, Tobias Smollett translates Lesage, Dickens reads Smollett, Kafka (I am referring to *Amerika*) reads Dickens, and so on. Examples of a phenomenon involving common premises—antecedents of the same civilization—include the neo-Ciceronian style of certain prose works of the sixteenth and seventeenth centuries (Luis Vélez de Guevara, John Lyly) and the epic poem of the Renaissance. The conceptual framework that provides useful terms for studies of these types must be historically appropriate, either because the framework calls on the past lexicon of European poetics, on the itinerary of its self-awareness—in which case we will speak of tragedy or of elegy, of melodrama, or of free verse, of *doloras* (Campoamor) or of *greguerías* (Gómez de la Serna). Or perhaps new terms are adopted, terms applicable above all to definite historical phenomena—such as the concept of *anatomy,* developed by Northrop Frye, and applicable to Addison and Steele, to Spanish *costumbrismo* of the seventeenth century, and so on. Where I say "European" (European/American) read Chinese or whatever other suitable adjective you prefer, just so long as we always stay within the limits of one single civilization.

B. When phenomena or processes that are *genetically independent,* or belong to different civilizations, are collected and brought together for study, such an examination can be justified and carried out to the extent that *common sociohistorical conditions* are implied. One can easily see that investigations of type A, while not excluding an interest that might involve interactions between social history (or economic or political history) and literary history, did not arise necessarily from that interest but were circumscribed by exclusively literary categories. Not so for the second model, which postulates as its basis the existence of processes and common socioeconomic developments that permit political events pertaining to different peoples and civilizations to be linked and compared. As an example, think of the development of the novel in eighteenth-century Europe and in seventeenth-century Japan (Saikaku Ihara's tales of Osaka), considered from the point of view of their connections with the new middle classes or "bourgeoisie"; or the oral epic produced by different primitive or "feudal" societies (a theme I will return to shortly). The conceptual framework continues to have a predominantly historical character, although a certain theoretical awareness of the relation between social change and literary change is assumed.

C. Some *genetically independent* phenomena make up supranational entities in accordance with principles and purposes derived from the *theory of literature*. This model has the highest grade of theoreticity, since the conceptual framework, instead of being pragmatic or merely adequate in the face of the observable facts, usually provides a point of departure for the investigation or for the problem to be resolved. The theoretical framework suggests the statement of the problem. But as the framework evolves, a contrary motion can begin, and new knowledge or some unpublished facts can challenge any theoretical notion. An examination of diachronic processes and developments is by no means excluded, such as those provoked by periodological studies, by the appearance of modern genres, or by new styles (such as the "zero grade" of style), as long as the conceptual framework is a theory of literary history or a contribution to it. Obviously, today's East/West studies offer especially valuable and promising opportunities for investigations based on the third model. (But this perspective also encompasses works that agree with models A and B). In sum, model C permits the dialogue between unity and diversity that stimulates comparativism to focus on the open confrontation of criticism/history with theory; or, if you prefer, of our knowledge of poetry—supranational poetry—with poetics.

Naturally, there have been a number of other useful models, which we will discuss later. But first it is worthwhile to offer an example. Very interesting genres exist whose "universality" is debatable and a matter for investigation, such as the literary dispute or poem-debate (the medieval *débat,* the *Streitgedicht,* the Provençal *tensó,* the Persian *munâzarât*); but it would be more appropriate to consider them later, in the chapter devoted to genology. Instead let us examine a category of a formal type. I repeat that under model C comparative history tests specific theoretical formulations with the intention not of agreeing or disagreeing, but of harmonizing and enriching such formulations.

Roman Jakobson's thesis regarding parallelism is well known. According to him, parallelism is "the fundamental problem of poetry," [1] the essential dimension that characterizes the poetic phenomenon. Where does this formal characteristic come from? from the code of the language? from the cultural values of conventions typical of the literary system of a distinct historical epoch? Jakobson, in his "Poetry of Grammar and Grammar of Poetry," stresses the innate importance of syntactic forms or associations. The same piece of semantic material lends itself to distinct ways of connecting its components: "So dark the sky is," or the other way around, "The sky is so dark." This is what Gerard Manley Hopkins called *the figure of grammar.* Well then, if this figure is parallelistic, the possibility of poetry appears immediately, or to express it more accurately, the possibility of a "poetic function" appears. Over this bridge pass rhyme, morphological and semantic repetitions, prosodic symmetries, which all converge in one single poem. In "Linguistics and Poetics" and in other writings, Jakobson gives many examples of this phenomenon, taken from the popular Russian epic *(byliny),* the *parallelismus membrorum* of the Bible, the popular poetry of the Urgo-Finnish peoples (such as the *cheremis* studied by Thomas A. Seboek), and of the Turks and Mongols, the Vedic litanies, and so on. Without doubt the best examples come from folklore. "Folklore offers the most clear-cut and stereotyped forms of poetry, particularly suitable for structural scrutiny." [2] Here is the opening stanza of one of the *byliny:*

> A i vsé na pirú da napiválisja
> A i vsé na pirú da poraskhvástalis,
> Ulmnyj khvástaet zolotój kaznój,
> Glypyj khvástaet molodój zenój . . .

> Everyone at the feast was drunk,
> Everyone at the feast was boasting,
> The clever one boasts of his golden stock,
> The stupid one boasts of his young wife.

Clearly, the syntactic reiteration is tied to a series of parallelistic effects, on a semantic, phonic level (the accented vowels and anterior assonances and other forms of homophony; or rather, rhyme in its widest sense)[3] as well as on a morphological level (*zolotój/molodój*).

The *romancero* in Castilian offers many comparable examples,[4] such as the "Romance de doña Alda":

> Todas visten un vestido,
> todas calzan un calzar,
> todas comen a una mesa,
> todas comían de un pan,
> sino era doña Alda,
> Las ciento hilaban oro,
> las ciento tejen cendal,
> las ciento tañen instrumentos
> para a doña Alda holgar . . .

> All are dressed in the same dress,
> All wear the same shoes,
> All eat at the same table,
> All eat of the same bread,
> Except for Doña Alda
> A hundred were spinning gold,
> A hundred were weaving fine silk,
> A hundred were playing instruments
> for Doña Alda's pleasure.

The semantic and morphological iterations ("todas *calzan* un *calzar*") are arranged like a nest of boxes, each within another, slightly larger one; in this case, actually within the same syntactic figure. And notice that Doña Alda stands out from the surrounding unanimity, so that the news of the death of Roland at the end of the ballad breaks the harmony of the first part of the poem: "que su Roldán era muerto/en la caza de Roncesvalles" (that her Roland had died/in the battle of Roncevaux).

The effect of tension and interior collision appears very clearly in the romance "El prisionero":

> Que por mayo era por mayo,
> cuando hace la calor,

cuando los trigos encañan
y están los campos en flor,
cuando canta la calandria
y responde el ruiseñor,
cuando los enamorados
van a servir al amor;
sino yo, triste, cuitado,
que vivo in esta prisión,
que ni sé cuándo es de día
ni cuándo las noches son,
sino por una avecilla
que me cantaba el albor.
Matómela un ballestro;
déle Dios mal galardón.

It was Maytime, it was Maytime
when it grows so very hot,
when the wheat stalks grow tall
and the fields are in flower,
when the skylark sings
and the nightingale answers,
when those in love
go out to serve Love,
except for me, sad wretch
who live in this prison,
for I do not know when it is day
nor when it is night,
except for a little bird
that used to sing me the dawn.
A crossbowman killed it.
May God give him what he deserves.[5]

The grammatical framework operates as if it were a mnemonic device, a starter of the verbal motor, capable of provoking reiterations of distinctly different types that make up a series of variations. The first big success in this case is a marvelous dialogue between birds, with the alliteration of the *c* in the song of the skylark and the assonance of the *a* repeated seven times (the line has eight syllables):

cuando canta la calandria

and in the reply of the nightingale, with the coincidence of the two tonic accents with the vowel *o,* and also the alliteration of the *r:*

y respónde el ruiseñór.

The second part of the romance breaks the initial rhythm—the accents on the third and seventh syllables—beginning with the line in which the abrupt juxtaposition of two successive tonic accents jolts us:

> sino yó, tríste, cuitado . . .

The form of the romance is dynamic, changeable, and even conflictive: it contradicts itself.

After the first rhythmic design comes another that upsets and supplants it. Moreover, one might think that the initial design is there expressly to be overcome; and the parallelism is there to be refuted and dismantled. As we will see, this is what Michael Riffaterre calls *stylistic context*, whose contrast with a specific procedure produces the stylistic effect.[6] This transcending of the rhythm and the parallelism of the beginning affects the entire poem. ¡*"Sino yo . . ."!* (Except for me!) The protagonist does not take part in the general felicity. After the folkloric springtime, after the "Song of May" (which Gaston Paris considers the origin of all medieval lyric poetry),[7] after the fiesta of pagan origin, the rebirth and celebration of the senses, comes the lyrical-narrative expansion of the inner state of mind and solitude of the prisoner. The springtime, like the parallelism, is nothing more than a backdrop.

Something similar occurs in several Provençal poems, such as the famous one of Bernard de Ventadour, sad lover, alone and disconsolate, who sees "the lark stir her wings for joy/against the sunlight,/and forgetting herself,/letting herself/fall/with the sweetness that comes into her heart, . . .":

> Can vei la lauzeta move
> de joi sas alas contra.l rai
> que s'oblid'e.s laissa chazer
> per la doussor c'al cor li vai . . .[8]

Parallelism in such cases is nothing more than an opening and a framework for the development of a significant tension between the design of the poem and its single components. We do not have a *système clos*,[9] but an extremely complex multiplicity of interactions that make possible the mutual intensification of the different strata of the message: syntactic, prosodic, semantic, phonic, morphological.

This stratification is fundamental in poetry. Emilio Alarcos Llorach rightly stresses two strata that he calls syntactic sequence and rhythmic sequence, which may or may not coincide. "They will go in concert when the syntactic and the metrical pauses take place at the same point, with the result that the metrical unity—the line—and the syntactic unity—phrase or part of a phrase—correspond." Clearly, it happens again and again that the syntactic rhythm (Hopkins' *figure of grammar*) and the metrical or prosodic rhythm are different. The temporality of the poem is multiple. Alarcos writes:

> So then, in any poem we can discover four types of rhythm, more or less in concert, that constitute the inherent poetic rhythm: *(a)* a sequence of sounds, of phonetic material; *(b)* a sequence of grammatical functions accompanied by intonation; *(c)* a sequence, the metrical one, of accented or atonic syllables arranged according to a definite scheme; *(d)* a sequence of psychic elements (sentiments, images, and so on.[10]

That is why it is such a delicate task to read a poem aloud. We have to keep in mind more than one rhythm at the same time. If we make the pause at the end of the line too long, we favor the metrical rhythm. If we make it too short, we favor the syntactic rhythm. An exact equilibrium must be maintained between two contrary forces.

Our best critics of poetry have commented in an enlightening way on this plural mechanism of nexuses, oppositions, and superpositions: Osip Brik, on the tension between the rhythmic "series" and the syllabic series in Russian verse; Dámaso Alonso, on "the fantastic complex of relations within the poem;"[11] Francisco García Lorca, on the crisscross of rhythms with accentuations, of syntactic ambits with reiterations whose endless propagation acts even in the "most remote areas of sensibility."[12]

The poetic effect rests upon the tension, interaction, or contrast between the parallelistic and the antiparallelistic, or, if you prefer, the aparallelistic impulses. (This statement is made from Jakobson's point of view of the problem; I have no intention of defining a monolithic literary system here.) Later, when discussing morphology (Chapter 13), I will attempt to call attention to everything in a poem that is process, dynamism, transcendence of the poem by itself. Everybody knows that absolute order is intolerable, in the arts as well as in politics. Parallelism and aparallelism merge, and each needs the other in equal measure. The dialectic of the one and the many can also be found within the poem itself.

The parallelism that we perceive at one level of the poem is not necessarily found at another. Nor has anyone ever demonstrated that the syntactic order exercises any type of preference or priority. From every point of view, a totally complete *emboîtement* is incompatible with a stylistic effect that depends on phenomena of differentiation and alteration, according to what Riffaterre has shown.[13] In his book on biblical parallelism, James Kugel has analyzed with great elegance the limits of this relatively modern concept (from Robert Lowth, *De sacra poesi Hebraeorum*, 1753). Found most often in the Bible is a phrase composed of two clauses, with a minor pause between them and a major pause at the end of the verse:

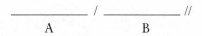

A   B

The passage from A to B is not mere reflection, nor repetition, nor variation, but something like an intensification that confirms and enhances in very different ways what was said previously.

> The briefness of the brief pause is an expression of B's connectedness to A; the length of the long pause is an expression of the relative disjunction between B and the next line. What this means is simply: B, by being connected to A—carrying it further, echoing it, defining it, restating it, contrasting with it, *it does not matter which*—has an emphatic, "seconding" character, and it is this, more than any aesthetic of symmetry or paralleling, which is at the heart of biblical parallelism.[14]

And Wolfgang Steinitz establishes some very useful distinctions in his fundamental presentation of the parallelisms of popular Finnish poetry. He points out that there are formal parallelisms and thematic ones, and the latter include those that can be in turn subdivided into contradiction, enumeration, and variation, either by way of synonymy or by analogy. He thus calls attention to the limitations of the procedure, although his descriptive term ("verses not parallel") is a bit clumsy.[15]

In view of this problem, the testimony of the multisecular poetic tradition of China is undoubtedly extremely valuable. Remember the interaction of the refrain and variations in the ballads of the ancient *Shih Ching* or *Classic of Songs:*

> Dry leaves, dry leaves,
> The wind tosses you about.
> Brothers, oh brothers,
> As you sing, so must I follow.
> Dry leaves, dry leaves,
> The wind blows you along.
> Brothers, oh brothers,
> As you sing, so must I also.[16]

This scheme is often used in Iberian poetry, from the Portuguese *cantigas de amigo*—in which the rhythmic unity is not a strophe but a pair of strophes,[17] with the strophes usually limited to two groups of two each—

to the later reelaboration of these traditional structures by Gil Vicente, Lope de Vega, and Federico García Lorca.

In China later, the genre called *sao* and its successor the *fu* would have in common the use of composed binaries and parallel phrases.[18] The usage became so common that it helped to blur the line between poetry and prose. "Balanced prose" (*p'ien-wen*) is characteristic particularly during the Ch'i and Liang dynasties, (479–556 A.D.), when the tendency of Chinese prose toward tetrasyllabic rhythm developed, according to James Hightower. But Hightower adds:

> When pairs of these are deliberately reduced to a common grammatical pattern the result approaches Parallel Prose. A more subtle kind of rhythm is possible in Chinese, based on the sequence of tones, a phonemic element in the language. Grammatical parallelism, reinforced with strict syllabic correspondence, may be further refined by a similar or contrasting pattern of tones in the parallel phrases.[19]

Obviously the phonemic function of the tones in Chinese permits a very complex formal counterpoint, not limited to the parallelistic framework, and also used in the so-called regular verse (*lü shih*) of the great poets of the T'ang dynasty.[20] Thus it is worthwhile to distinguish between different genres, styles, and historical periods if we do not intend to subordinate the variety of poetry to the unity of one poetics to an exaggerated extent.

From such a point of view, the absence of a distinction between traditional oral poetry and cultivated poetry is also debatable. What is striking in this connection is the use of the recourse—mnemonic? rhetorical-persuasive?—in the most ancient poetry of Eurasia and America—of what Angel María Garibay calls diphrasis, which consists simply in saying the same thing twice.[21] The most ancient myths and hymns of Sumer offer many examples. Here is a myth of the Creation, translated by Samuel N. Kramer:

> In primeval days, in distant primeval days,
> In primeval nights, in far-off primeval nights,
> In primeval years, in distant primeval years . . .
> When bread had been tasted in the shrines of the land,
> When bread had been baked in the ovens of the land,
> When heaven had been moved away from the earth,
> When earth had been separated from heaven . . .[22]

And so on in the same vein many poems translated by Garibay in his great history of Nahautl literature, where the lines are like links of reiterations and concatenated variations:

Nada cierto decimos sobre la tierra:
oh dador de la vida, cual en su sueño dormitamos
cual si durmiéramos hablamos,
nada cierto decimos sobre la tierra.
Aunque esmeraldas se nos dieran,
aunque perfumes tuviéramos,
con sartales de flores te rogáramos,
nada cierto decimos para él . . .

We say nothing certain upon the earth.
Oh, giver of life, we slumber as though in your dream.
We speak as though we slept.
We say nothing certain upon the earth.
Though we were given emeralds,
though we had perfumes,
we would beg you with chains of flowers;
we say nothing certain for him.[23]

The line that separates diphrasis from parallelism is not easy to trace in Nahuatl poetry (nor in the Finnish *Kalevala*),[24] and Garibay proposes some very useful shades of meaning in this regard. The Nahautl diphrasis would consist in "pairing two metaphors, which together give the symbolic medium for expressing a single thought." Parallelism would consist in "harmonizing the expression of one thought in two phrases that either repeat the same idea in different words (synonymic), or contrasting two thoughts (antithetic), or completing the thought, by adding a variant expression that is not pure repetition (synthetic)."[25] Despite the supposedly unbridgeable distance from ancient Mexico to Finland, Garibay's three types of analogy match the three forms analyzed by Steinitz.

In the face of these distinctions that imply historic change as well as the step from oral to written poetry, aren't we missing a diachronic reflection? That is what V. M. Zhirmunsky suggests in his brief but masterly study of parallelism (written in homage to Steinitz) regarding the old epic *cantares* of the Asiatic peoples of the Turkic linguistic family (Kirghiz, Uzbek, Kazakh, Karakalpak). It is a pity that there is no room here to present his examples and reasoning in detail. I will have to confine myself to his conclusions, which are as important as they are suggestive.

Zhirmunsky examines the historical development of diverse poems from the early Middle Ages to the sixteenth century. The most ancient form of versified rhythmic structure is the simple repetition of the line followed by a freer syntactic parallelism. Later, rhyme appears, first interior or initial, and then final also (the latter frequently based on syntactic analogies), and sometimes alliteration. Finally two things triumph: syllable count and end rhyming, more varied, or rather, morphologically diverse. At the same time, parallelism loses ground, as though a choice had been made between "parallelism or syllabic form with rhyme." Zhirmunsky concludes: "The installation of the end rhyme as an autonomous and obligatory means of metrical linkage leads evidently at the same time to a retreat of parallelism and alliteration." [26]

This confrontation between two great Russians—Jakobson and Zhirmunsky—suggests what might be called a *diachronic structure*.[27] (We are not dealing with the historical poetics called for by a third Russian, A. N. Veselovsky, since it is usually not possible to employ a merely historical-inductive method.) The speculative hypothesis of a Jakobson was necessary for Zhirmunsky's clarifications to emerge (all actually based on Steinitz, as was Jakobson's work, and of course mine also). The diachronic structure arises from temporality but points to a fundamental option: a repertoire or lexicon of forms, configured by interrelations. Therefore, let us ask ourselves: If we regard rhymed syllabism and parallelism as two structural poles, can we conclude that the use of free verse and the retreat of rhyme and quantitative counting in general in certain modern poetry, from Walt Whitman to Vladimir Mayakovsky, have been linked to a strengthening of the parallelistic procedure?

Remember the reiterated verbal waves in Saint-John Perse's *Exil* (1942):

> Toujours il y eut cette clameur, toujours il y eut cette grandeur,
> Cette chose errante par le monde, cette haute transe par le monde, et
>   sur toutes grèves de ce monde, du même souffle proférée, la même
>   vague proférant
> Une seule et longue phrase san césure à jamais inintelligible . . .
> Toujours il y eut cette clameur, toujours il y eut cette fureur,
> Et ce très haut ressac au comble de l'accès, toujours au faîte du désir, la
>   même mouette sur son aile, la même mouette sur son aire, à tire-d-
>   aile ralliant les stance de l'exil, et sur toutes grèves de ce monde, du
>   même souffle proférée, la même plainte sans mesure
> A la poursuite, sur les sables, de mon âme numide . . .

> There has always been this clamor, there has always been
>   this grandeur,
> This thing wandering about the world, this high trance about
>   the world, and on all the shores of the world, by the same
>   breath uttered, the same wave uttering
> One long phrase without pause forever unintelligible . . .
> There has always been this clamor, there has always been
>   this furor,
> And this tall surf at the pitch of passion, always, at the

peak of desire, the same gull on the wing, the same gull
under way, rallying with spread wings the stanzas of exile,
and on all the shores of the world, by the same breath
uttered, the same measureless lamentation
Pursuing across the sands my Numidian soul . . .

I will also quote the first and last stanzas of a poem from Vicente Aleixandre's "Sierpe de amor" (Serpent of Love). Carlos Bousoño points out that
the stanza contains hendecasyllabic and heptasyllabic interior rhythms.[28]
But the metaphoric variation and syntactic parallelism are also prominent
features in most of the stanzas:

Pero ¿a quién amas, dime?
Tendida en la espesura,
entre los pájaros silvestres, entre las frondas vivas,
rameado tu cuerpo de luces deslumbrantes,
dime a quién amas, indiferente, hermosa,
bañada en vientos amarillos del día . . .

Boca con boca dudo si la vida es aire,
o es la sangre. Boca con boca muero,
respirando tu llama que me destruye.
Boca con boca siento que hecho luz me deshago,
hecho lumbre que en el aire fulgura.

But tell me, whom do you love?
Stretched out in the undergrowth
among the sylvan birds, among the living fronds,
your body patterned by a daze of light,
tell me whom you love, indifferent, beautiful,
bathed in the yellow winds of day . . .

Mouth against mouth I doubt if life is air
or blood. Mouth against mouth I die
inhaling your flame that destroys me.
Mouth against mouth I find release, transformed into light
transformed into flame that flashes in the air.

In Walt Whitman the recuperation of the primitive parallelism is somewhat
overwhelming. It is enough to recall his "Song of Myself" (*Leaves of Grass*).
From the anaphoras and the dualisms of the beginning:

I celebrate myself, and sing myself,
And what I assume you shall assume,
For every atom belonging to me as good belongs to you.

> I loafe and invite my soul,
> I lean and loafe at my ease observing a spear of summer grass.

We encounter here something very similar to the *seconding effect* found by James Kugel in the Bible—a process that emphasizes, reinforces, enhances.

> There was never any more inception than there is now,
> Nor any more youth or age than there is now,
> And will never be any more perfection than there is now,
> Nor any more heaven or hell than there is now.

Since rhyme and strict syllable count are abandoned, it seems as though the verbal and thematic reiteration might be replacing the absent forms and interrelations:

> Twenty-eight young men bathe by the shore,
> Twenty-eight young men and all so friendly;
> Twenty-eight years of womanly life and all so lonesome.

The enumerations of Finnish poetry come to mind, commented on by Steinitz, as well as those of the Hispanic *romancero;* that is, we notice a return not only to ancient parallelism but also to oral poetry, even including the synthetic repetitions or variations typical of the *byliny* cited by Jakobson. Once again, from "Song of Myself":

> The city sleeps and the country sleeps,
> The living sleep for their time, the dead sleep for their time,
> The old husband sleeps by his wife and the young husband sleeps by
>   his wife . . .

These few examples amount to only a brief experiment. We will end with two corroborations. In the first place, Benjamin Hrushovski points out the return of parallelism as a characteristic of certain modern Hebrew poetry, the poetry that came after Avraham ben Yishak and was influenced by Alexander Blok or Anna Akhmatova; he sees these forms as being close to free verse, whose forms, he says, "are too varied to be discussed . . . Basically they depend on syntactic patterns, strengthened by parallelism and sound orchestration."[29]

Moreover, after writing these pages, I had the satisfaction of finding that Fernando Lázaro Carreter had reached similar conclusions, developed with exactness and clarity in an essay titled "Función poética y verso libre." Lázaro, commenting on some observations of Amado Alonso regarding repetition in Pablo Neruda (a procedure that Alonso attributed to the art of the Chilean poet alone), emphasizes that without the poetic function—defined by him elsewhere as a *structuring* function—free verse, stripped of the rhythmic instruments belonging to traditional metrics, would not be viable; and that finally *"repetition is in the very heart of free verse, as its fundamental constitutive principle."*[30] Many people will think that one should elucidate the various functions of parallelism in different sociohistorical contexts. In his critique of Jakobson's basic ideas, Jonathan Culler finds the separation of formal reading from thematic relevance to be unsatisfactory: "It would seem not unreasonable to suggest that patterns discovered are relevant only when they can be correlated with some experience that they explain."[31] It is indeed so, and also from a comparative point of view. The magical, liturgical, affective, rhetorical functions of the parallelistic procedures are without doubt worthy of reflection. I have examined here only their existence and delimitations in accordance with a basic proposition of comparativism.

It goes without saying that there are other models of supranationality of concern to the comparatist. I have emphasized type A because it is the one that best describes a good part of current work; type B, because a series of investigations that are under way in the Soviet Union and in eastern Europe approximate it (I am referring to the historical-typological analogies of V. M. Zhirmunsky and Dionýz Ďurišin). Type C is important not only because of the appropriate and promising growth of East/West studies but also because its emphasis on theoretical premises bring to the forefront the role of literary theory as generator of models for investigation. Clearly, the elements of the literary theory cultivated so zealously by so many today and the propositions of comparative literature need one another, aid one another, and are involved with one another; it is possible that they will be even more closely intertwined tomorrow. The Slavic scholar Dionýz Ďurišin, in one of the best presentations of our discipline, rightly considers this double relationship as a joint destiny, "a reciprocal process of collaboration"—and brings to mind the historical poetics that A. N. Veselovsky called for at the end of the last century. But Veselovsky wanted a poetics that was merely inductive, an "explanation of the essence of poetry through a study of its history,"[32] and not the reciprocal questionings and substantiations that, in my opinion, give life to model C.

I am of course aware that other conceptual frameworks can predominate in the definition of a supranational whole and become its center of gravity. Thus we encounter models that we could call D, E, F, and so on, each corresponding to the conceptual framework in question, and just as numerous as the following, to suggest a few: theory of religion, theory of culture, mythology, cultural or social anthropology, theories of personality—for example, psychoanalytic theories of personality—sociological schemata, and, of course, linguistic theories as well.

In my opinion, the most significant difference for comparativism between types A and C of supranationality is not so much the grade of theoreticity, on the increase in every respect, but the degree of universality. Or is it possible that the two terms merge in comparativism? Isn't it true that the phenomena that constitute model C already suggest a conception of the universal? not a total, but a relative conception, that is to say, one that has definitely gone beyond spatial and temporal differentiations? Thus we return to the confrontation of the one and the many. The passage from A to C reveals the tenacious search for ultralocal entities that would signify not universality or maximum spaces but coherence and unity. At the same time, a contrary impulse comes into play, the attraction of the singular, of the inimitable, of real events. And then it is the unitary scheme that must undergo the test of diversity, of dispersion, of spatial and temporal disparities—from country to country, from period to period. No scheme more so than the one elaborated by the literary theorist, whose task cannot be limited to mere speculative exercises or to a *cognito ex principiis*. Unity that has not been tested is of no interest, and neither are matters such as the neo-Platonic Form, ingenuous essentialism, the establishment of categories that are primarily intellectual. That would amount more or less to what was earlier called a theory of the literature of the moon—half a dozen tales and poems in two or three languages that vindicate perennial concepts, neoclassical absolutes. Since the Renaissance, the tension existing between poetics and poetry in Europe has been a well-known fact. It would be naive, then, to ignore it, to disregard its temporal evolution. The poetics of today, like the poetics of earlier years, has to be stripped of its pretensions of essentiality, become flexible, and mold itself to fit what has in fact happened in history and in human societies. This molding, this difficult equilibrium between humanity and dissimilarity, hypothesis and testimony, theory and creation, is the unavoidable challenge facing literary studies today.

It is seldom easy to define a comparative investigation, to assign fixed limits to it. For example, think of the study of a "theme." In order to define such a study, what grade of generality can we allow ourselves? To what extent are we interested in grasping historical particulars without losing the taste of the differences? A treatment of the theme of Don Juan from the point of view of comparative literature is usually focused more or less on model A: concentrating above all on some theatrical, operatic, or poetic texts that appeared in Europe in the seventeenth to twentieth centuries. Its attributes (the Commendador, Stone Guest, and so on) and literary origins

(Tirso de Molina, the Italian theater, Molière) are visible and quite distinct. Since the publication of G. Gendarme de Bévotte's *La légende de Don Juan* (1911), the folkloric sources of the theme have also been examined, but with the intention of sketching a prehistory of the authentic theatrical art of the seventeenth century. The inquiry flows along with evident coherence as we pass from one author to another, from one version of the figure of Don Juan to another, one that in many cases confirms the existence and even knowledge of earlier versions. We are not dealing with a newly invented term or a critical abstraction, but with a long itinerary that gradually became conscious of itself. In an impeccable manner, the sinuous evolution of the theme and its international character are in harmony with each other. There are moments and events in the itinerary that can be identified with complete certainty. For example, a Frenchman, Henri Blaze de Bury, Germanist, facile writer, translator of Goethe, was the first who dared fabricate a happy outcome, that is, to convert the hero. Thanks to the "eternal feminine," to *das ewige Weibliche,* Don Juan, like Faust, is saved.[33] It would be difficult to imagine a theme possessing a historical supranationality more rooted in space and time, or more sharply outlined.

The vigor characteristic of Don Juan has paradoxical consequences. Think of the commentaries of Kierkegaard, Camus, Ortega, Otto Rank, Micheline Sauvage, Montherlant, Gregorio Marañon, José Bergamín, and so many others.[34] What is of foremost importance now is not a series of transmutations, often historical and national, or rather the perception of change, but a fundamental figure suggesting meanings of many types, including the phenomenological, existentialist, mythical, philosophical, psychoanalytic, or sexological. Certainly such global interpretations would be inconceivable without a bare minimum of familiarity with the avatars of the theme according to model A. But the predominating factor is the unanimity required by a conceptual framework—of a type D or E, let's say, to go back to our scheme. However, no matter how broad the interpretation may be, its point of departure will not have been a universal figure, but a Don Juan who is European, Spanish, even Sevillan. The possible universality will have to start from model C, from an archetype, a man who is an inveterate woman-chaser, an untiring and incorrigible lover, who is found in the most widely varied cultures and literatures: in Africa, India, China, Japan. We would find ourselves face to face with a Seducer, of which Don Juan is no more than the European variety. We should not be surprised then to find that this primordial Seducer, once removed from his poetic or dramatic situation, also lends himself to multiple psychological-philosophical explications; and in that way, we run across the Indecisive One, the Adolescent, the Insecure One, the one Sacrificed by his mother, the Adventurer, the Seeker of the Absolute. The ambiguities and the mistakes would be foreseeable, so that little difference would remain between the primordial Seducer and the Skirt-chasing Prankster of Seville. But an opening of such proportions could or ought at best to lead to new explorations and reflections.

In other contexts the distinctions are clear-cut, and the models do not become confused. I have before me some investigations of texts from Indian America, pre-Hispanic or non-Hispanic. Because it goes without saying that comparativism is interested not only in the great, rich literatures of Asia, such as those of China, India, and Japan, but also in the poetic testimonies of the equally ancient cultures of Mexico, Guatemala, or Peru. For example, José María Arguedas and other scholars have translated into Castilian the beautiful Quechua elegy "Apu Inqa Atahuallpaman," which mourns the death of and yearns for the rebirth of Inkarrí—mythical fusion of the last two Incas, Atahualpa and Túpac Amaru, both executed by the Spaniards.[35] What usually strikes us in either Peru or Mexico is not so much the persistence of a literary genre (such as the the elegy) but the abundant mythological imagination: myths of creation or cosmologies, cataclysmic myths, heroic myths, ritual myths, and so on. This leads Mercedes López-Baralt to base her comments on the myth of Inkarrí and on the elegy "Apu Inqa Atahaullpaman" in particular on works of Mircea Eliade (the cyclical character of sacred temporality), Norman Cohn (the psychic roots of millenarianism), and Victor Turner (the liminal moment, or moment of transition, in the *rites de passage*). It is clear that in this case an appeal is made to models D or E, whose conceptual basis is the theory or anthropology of religion. Nor would it be wrong to say that at the same time a historical comparison, or model B, is also taken into consideration, inasmuch as López-Baraut indicates that the myth of the millennium functioned as a reply to or defense against the assimilation imposed by the Spaniards in distinct places and periods.[36]

In regard to model C, it has taken a long time to clear the way for joint studies of genetically independent phenomena. This type of investigation would not have been regarded as legitimate thirty or forty years ago. Comparativism was then dedicated to international relations, to what Jean-Marie Carré called, unforgettably, *rapports de fait*.[37] And even today quite a number of scholars tolerate nongenetic studies of supranational categories with great distaste or scant enthusiasm. Hugo Dyserinck is inclined toward the integrity of the *Kultureinheit* (cultural unity).[38] Ulrich Weisstein, in his *Comparative Literature and Literary Theory* (1973), explains that "we hesitate nevertheless to extend the study of parallels to phenomena pertaining to two different civilizations," and he adds: "For it seems to me that only within a single civilization can one find those common elements of a consciously or unconsciously upheld tradition in thought, feeling, and imagination which may, in cases of a fairly simultaneous emergence, be regarded as signifying common trends."[39] And in their manual, Claude Pichois and André-Marie Rousseau vacillate and express reserve in face of the evident necessity of making room for similar phenomena that cannot be justified as resulting from binary influences: "One finds in different literatures analogous flowerings that cannot be entirely explained by the play of influences." For example, according to the authors, the Italian, French, German, and Slavic baroque periods did not mutually engender each other according to a rhythm of chronological succession:

> To understand them, it is necessary to go back to a common ancestor, Petrarchism, the sentiments and ideas of which were again taken up toward the end of the sixteenth century, along with its structures and forms, by integrating them into works of a very different spirit. That spirit is not only the famous and too vague *Zeitgeist,* the spirit of the time; it is the reflection, or rather, according to the Marxists, the product of socioeconomic determinism, the superstructure of an infrastructure that postulates and reflects it, or the product of opposing religious tendencies at the time of the Reformation and the Counter-Reformation.[40]

From this one deduces nothing very clear except the survival of what Marc Bloch called *l'idole des origines,* as we saw earlier.

The target of such objections is René Etiemble and his 1963 book *Comparaison n'est pas raison,* which in its day was an event and remains one still, as proved by the slow pace of the acceptance of its propositions. Written with brilliance and a lively polemical talent, this book advocates the knowledge and study of the most diverse literatures, of the most varied poetic testimonies of the human condition. Etiemble vigorously attacks European or Eurocentric chauvinism (a chauvinism that is also false, since it reduces Europe to four or five literatures). But that is only the beginning. For Etiemble it is not enough that we take an interest in Chinese, Japanese, or Indian poetry—in Hindi, Urdu, or Tamil—in Arabic and Persian poetry. It is senseless to keep on ignoring the Urgo-Finnish languages that have given us the *Kalevala,* Mihály Vörösmarty, and Endre Ady. Think of the admirable Victor Zhirmunsky, who learned several of the languages of Central Asia in order to carry out his studies of the popular heroic epic; and

Albert B. Lord, exceptional expert in Balkan languages, as shown in his *Singer of Tales* (1960).

> What is more, when one is French, how can one boast about one's accomplishments in comparative literature while neglecting the question of bilingualism among the Madagascan, Arab, or Vietnamese writers, the analogies between the *hain-tenys* of the people of Madagascar and the poetry of Eluard, the influence of French poetics on the Vietnamese poetry of today, the influence of colonial literatures, or the literatures of colonized countries on the mother country and its literature, and so on.[41]

And even more:

> The institute of which I dream would naturally include Hellenists and Latinists, but also Sumerologists and Egyptologists, also Slavists, specialists in Hindi and Bengali, Sinologists, Germanists, and Romanists, as well as Semitologists, those versed in Finno-Ugric, Turko-Mongolian, and Dravidian literatures, and I am not forgetting the Japanese! Everything exists in the history of literatures, and it will never be possible to understand a single one, I mean understand, without possessing more than just a few insights into a sufficiently large number of the others.[42]

Dream? Utopia? In agreement with Etiemble, I would add one fact. In the area of Oriental literatures or others less well known to us, we are now beginning to have access to what has been available for a long time in the field of Hellenic and Latin literatures: translations, histories, critical studies, and other intermediary instruments. For example, I have pointed out the possible value of a comparative investigation of the fictitious letter or the poetic epistle on a worldwide scale. In 1925 Adolf Erman published a collection of ten literary letters that were school exercises in his edition of the *Papyrus Lansing*. These were Egyptian papyri found in a tomb of Thebes going back to the twentieth dynasty in the twelfth century B.C. And as for the Sumerologists mentioned by Etiemble, Adam Falkenstein has analyzed a Sumerian letter dating from before 1500 B.C. and directed to Nonna, goddess of the moon; and O. R. Gurney has analyzed an epistle found in Sultantepe and fictiously attributed to the hero Gilgamesh.[43] Examples even more ancient and remote are not rare. Be that as it may, I am not speaking of practice here, not even the work of Etiemble himself in his *Essais de littérature (vraiment générale)* (1974). We must thank Etiemble above all for his energetic affirmation of a spirit, some proposals, and his resolute humanism.

Perhaps the most promising tendency in comparative literature is the one "that considers that even when two literatures have not had historical contacts, it is nevertheless legitimate to compare the literary genres that they have elaborated, each one alone." And this tendency, more than a dream, is a sign of a social and political disquiet, of a preoccupation with the real world—a world that encompasses the Third World—of our time.

> Under the pretext of an apparently technical dispute, it seems to me we are gambling with the future of our humanism. Will we keep on rotting away proudly, provincially, within a narrow culture, very French and very historistic, or will we instead sweep away prejudices, routine, and accept the opening of our faculties of letters to the world, to the aesthetic, so that our students may be prepared to become finally persons in a real world, a world in which black Africa, yellow China, or India, Japan, or Spanish America, Brazil, and the Arab culture will have more than one word to say to us?[44]

These preoccupations are obviously not foreign to the socialist countries of eastern Europe (the blindness with which Aleksandr Fadeev in 1950 denounced the "bourgeois cosmopolitanism" of Georg Lukács having been overcome).[45] In 1960 the Gorky Institute of Moscow, devoted to the study of world literature, dedicated a congress to the interrelations and interactions between national literatures. In 1962 the Academy of Sciences of Budapest organized a large international colloquium of comparatists with Western scholars in attendance; in 1967 the ICLA met in Belgrade, and so on.[46] Since then contacts and meetings of comparatists from eastern Europe and the West have increased. The Gorky Institute (like other institutes in the Soviet Union) has published at least eight histories of very diverse national literatures. The vast *History of World Literature* is especially significant. This nine-volume work, still in progress, begins with the origins of literature and goes to the outbreak of the Second World War.[47] Along with other volumes of literary theory, this ambitious project presupposes a historiological concern that some of us critics in the West sincerely share, as I hope to show later in this book.

Diverse models of supranationality can be recognized in the works of the comparatists of eastern Europe, and it would be awkward to simplify them. Some models of very great value coincide with what I have called model A, and with C as well. But it should be noted that on more than a few occasions model B has also been accepted. First of all, let us consider the mature works of V. M. Zhirmunsky, in particular one book and an easily accessible summary, the 1967 article "On the Study of Comparative Literature."

Sometimes Zhirmunsky respectfully follows the example of A. N. Veselovsky (1838–1906) and his "paleontology of plots."[48] Zhirmunsky does not deny the existence of influences in the itinerary of literatures—Veselovsky called them "countercurrents" in battle against peculiar currents of a national history—that crisscross with the analogous supranational lines of development. But the task of the comparatist consists in discovering these analogous and parallel processes, which result from social preconditions and the laws that rule literary history—"the general laws of literary development."[49] Events and literary movements considered as international phenomena are stimulated by analogous historical developments in the social life of peoples as much as by reciprocal cultural and literary contacts between them. The idea of a general evolution of human societies—unique and in conformance with its own regulations and laws—is the indisputable point of departure of such observations.

> Comparative study of literature in this sense presupposes as its basic principle the notion of unity and regularity in the social evolution of mankind in general. Similarities in the realms of ideas between peoples at similar stages of historical development are based on parallelisms in their social organization—parallelisms which can be traced even between Western European and Central Asian peoples during the age of feudalism. Typological analogies or convergences of the same kind between literatures of distant peoples, not in direct contact with each other, are far more common than is generally supposed.[50]

Zhirmunsky, who knew not only the principal European languages but also the literatures of Iran, of the Arabic countries, of Turkey and Central Asia (Kalmuk, Uzbek, and others), as well as of Mongolia, gives examples of what he calls "typological analogies." He seems to have three favorite genres: the Western *roman courtois* of the twelfth and thirteenth centuries in relation to Persian literature—such as the similarity of *Tristan et Iseult* to the Persian poem of Fakhroddín Asʿad Gorgānī *Vīs-o-Rāmīn* (eleventh century), or that of Chrétien de Troyes to that of Abu Mohammad Elyās Nezāmi; the traditional epic poem; and traits shared by the art of the troubadours and the *Minnesänger* with Arabic love poetry such as *The Ring of the Dove* by Ibn Ḥazm, a much-debated matter that the Russian historian cannot explain genetically, but for which he does indeed find analogical validity: "not an indication of literary influence, but of typological analogy—even granting cultural intercourse between Arabic Spain and the South of France."[51]

The similarities that Zhirmunsky finds between the different and numerous forms of the "heroic epic" are especially interesting. These elements,

summarized in his 1961 book *Vergleichende Epensforschung,* are sufficiently well known: for example, the miraculous birth of the protagonist
such as that of the Serbian hero Marko Kraljević, or the same event occurring in Scandinavian sagas and so many other epics; the heroic deeds carried
out during infancy—*enfances* of Charlemagne, of Vivien—to which Zhirmunsky assigns a somewhat later date in the evolution of the genre, when
speaking of the Russian *byliny,* of the *Song of the Three Children* in Kalmuk, or the deeds of Nurali and Rawshan in Uzbek; and the magical invul-
nerability of the hero: Achilles, Siegfried, Isfendiar (of the *Shāh-nāma* of
Firdausī), the Turkish and Mongol warriors *(Alpamysh),* among others.
Zhirmunsky's presentation is usually diachronic (as all three models described here can be) and leads him to emphasize a law of development (*En-
twicklungsgesetz*) of an interior character in the case of the epic. Zhirmunsky confronts the genetic explanations of these analogies (such as Nikola
Banašević's thesis about the French-Italian sources of the Yugoslav *cantares,*
or that of M. Chalanski regarding the Germanic origin of the Russian epic)
in order to refute and reject them in no uncertain terms. The interrelationships that the scholar must stress are the typological ones: "Traits in accord
with one another in the heroic epics of different peoples almost always have
a typological character."[52]

These analogies are revealed in all their breadth through the exceptional
erudition of Zhirmunsky. And no comparatist today would dare to attribute
them to the play of international influences. Many of the analogies are
found in the area of "oral literature," or folklore, a field studied by contemporary narratologists since the time of Vladimir Propp, and an area whose
compatibility with historical differences has been a problem brought out by
structuralist discussions.[53] In my opinion, what is valuable in Zhirmunsky's
stance and that of his successors as far as written literature is concerned is
the effort to find supranational typologies in the itineraries and the evolution of literary history itself. Up to now, these propositions do not seem to
have differed from those that we assigned to our model C.

And what about model B? Is the ideology in this case more than a backdrop? In practice, as far as I know, Zhirmunsky's sociohistorical or socioeconomic considerations are hasty and sketchy, making us feel that they are
inadequate. For example: "*Heroic poetry* of an essentially narrative kind
(epic songs and poetry) emerged independently among different peoples at
an early stage of social development (the so-called 'heroic age')." Or regarding the historical novel: "Typical of the age of romanticism is, for example,
the historical genre (historical novel and drama): its international vogue
was due to the rise of historical and national consciousness during the social

and international conflicts of the French Revolution, which were associated with a growth of interest in science and art, and in the national past." [54]

These explications by someone who wrote an excellent book on Herder are surprising. In this context, in fact, the social preconditions are more a premise or an axiom than the object of study that we would need—precise, complete, detailed. I say knowledge of this type would be necessary because the analogies that we find at first glance among similar literary phenomena, such as the Spanish picaresque novel and the tales of Saikaku Ihara (of seventeenth-century Osaka) are much clearer and more convincing than those that could be established between seventeenth-century Spanish and Japanese society. The resemblance of Japanese or Chinese love poetry to the Provençal or Portuguese is striking. It is essential to test or at least to analyze carefully the existence of common social preconditions. These preconditions are at least as debatable as the analogies and poetic affinities. Nevertheless, instead of presenting them, Zhirmunsky takes them as understood and demonstrated, so that the supposed causes—base of the integrity of the theme under consideration—remain relegated to a tacit subtext or are displaced to a discourse that differs from the one pronounced by literary history.

I do not say nor do I think that we must reject model B. Palpable, provable cases of social similarities undoubtedly existed and were in play. The *sociocritique* has much to say to us now, above all when it is a microcriticism attentive to precise and concrete situations, such as prison or exile, the convent or slavery. [55] I do not reject but rather find lacking in our field the thorough analyses of economic history associated with the trajectory of literary history. The typologies collected by Zhirmunsky are enormously suggestive. In order to investigate them, one does not have to bow down to a philosophy of history that is unique and definitive. Nothing would be more inaccurate or further from the life experiences of men and women of the twentieth century. The historical novel that confronts that experience is of course no longer Tolstoy's, so serious, so self-satisfied, but is instead *The War of the End of the World* (1984) by Mario Vargas Llosa, with his disturbing and also debatable perception of the moral ambiguity, violence, and theoretical precariousness of our time.

Perhaps it would have been appropriate in this context to discuss the so-called East/West Studies of interest to so many people now, but I will return to them in Chapter 12. [56] I do not believe that a combined study of, say, Chinese and European texts is likely to bring up different theoretical questions. In this chapter I have concerned myself with only one example—arduous, promising, with a plethora of possibilities—of supranationality, to which we can apply the general models and conceptual frameworks that I have sketched.

Every conceptual framework is provisional and has to be tested, if it is to be a scientific one—it has to be "refutable," as Karl Popper insisted. The principal task of comparative literature is the confrontation of poetics with our knowledge of poetry, that is, of the theory of literature, always in motion, making use of the vast and constantly increasing deployment of knowledge and of interrogations made possible by comparativism.

11

Taxonomies

A peculiar trait of comparativism, for good or for ill, is the problematical awareness of its own identity, and the resulting inclination to rely on its own history. Like certain peoples and religions, comparativism defines and recognizes itself not dogmatically but historically.

In the past many comparatists have arranged and classified their materials and fundamental objectives by proposing taxonomies, hierarchies, and other subdivisions of their field of study. More than likely as the years go by the card game stays the same, but the deck changes, so any card could be a winning one depending on the rules of the game at any given moment.

In a 1943 article Renato Poggioli concluded that at the end of the nineteenth century there were four primary directions of investigation in comparative literature: first, the thematic, or study of folkloric themes, the origins and transmigrations of legends and medieval tales (referring to the French school of Gaston Paris and above all to the German *Stoffgeschichte*); second, the morphological direction, or study of genres and forms, which at that time meant above all the Darwinian theory of *l'évolution des genres*, a posture maintained by Ferdinand Brunetière; third, the identification of sources, or *crenología*, from the Greek *krene* (spring); and, fourth, the examination of the *fortuna* (fortune, luck) of a writer, which in turn meant paying attention to intermediaries involved in the *fortuna*—journals, translations, and so on.[1]

From our present vantage point what is lacking in this classification is a reflection on literary history (to which Poggioli contributed so much in practice), and lacking also are the configurations of literary history: periods, movements, currents. In addition, the same questions are still with us today, but phrased differently and with very different results. The theme or the genre is defined, focused, or interpreted differently (since Brunetière's theory collapsed very quickly). But the starting point can still be the birth of the hero or the epic poem in general. As far as sources and fortune are concerned, Poggioli performed a great service by pointing out the wide scholarly acceptance of each of these categories toward the end of the past century—the causes and effects, so to speak, of an individual literary work. Today we would put them into one category, that of literary international relations, but we would also underscore the history and theory of translation, as well the phenomena of reception.

As for the French hour of comparativism, consider Paul Van Tieghem's manual *La littérature comparée* (1931), in which he placed great emphasis on sources, influences, reputations, and international relations. Van Tiegham presented six categories of *littérature comparée:* "genres et styles"; "thèmes, types, et légendes"; "idées et sentiments"; "les succès et les influences globales"; "les sources"; and, finally, "les intermédiaires." As might be expected, the last three categories treat the phenomena of influence in detail. The first two reserve a place of honor for two of Poggioli's major orientations—the thematic and the morphologic. Notably, Van Tieghem also assigned an outstanding role to the history of ideas or "sentiments": or rather, to religious, moral, and even philosophical ideas—cosmovisions and *Weltanschauungen.* No other method recommended by Van Tieghem has aged so rapidly, not even the search for sources. Today the history of ideas—as practiced by Lovejoy in America or as cultivated by José Luis Abellán in Spain—approaches or is included in the study of philosophy or of thought. It is no longer considered necessary for literary critics to concern themselves with ideas or an unadorned vision of the world—uprooted from form, wrested from style, ripped from theme, from period, from movement, that is, from the classifications of comparativism proper. I will not comment in detail here on other works that keep Van Tieghem's spirit alive, such as those by M.-F. Guyard (1951) and Simon Jeune (1968),[2] or that of Alexandru Cioranescu (1964) in Spain, a book that distinguishes among "relations of contact" (the presence of an individual literary nexus), "relations of interference" (multiple interpenetration of ideas or of currents), and "relations of circulation" (timeless themes). Nothing of importance exists beyond these relations as far as Cioranescu is concerned.

Ulrich Weisstein's well-known *Einführung in die vergleichende Literatur-*

wissenschaft (1968; translated into English as *Comparative Literature and Literary Theory*, 1973) serves as a transition or bridge between America and Europe and confirms the currency of Poggioli's four categories, though they are brought up to date: "influence and imitation," "reception and survival," "genre," and "hematology." And Weisstein rightly adds a fifth category: "epoch, period, generation, and movement." But his most original contribution is the important role that he assigns to one category: the "mutual illumination of the arts," or rather, what Paul Maury in 1934 called *arts et littératures comparées*, as cultivated later by Jean Seznec in France, bringing to mind the *Wechselseitige Erhellung der Künste* (Mutual Enlightenment of the Arts) that Oskar Walzel, inspired by the great Heinrich Wölfflin, had already called for in Germany in 1917.[3]

Henry Remak's definition of comparative literature is even more controversial. At the beginning of N. P. Stallknecht and Horst Frenz's *Comparative Literature: Method and Perspective* (1961), Remak wrote:

> Comparative Literature is the study of literature beyond the confines of a particular country, and the study of the relationships between literature on the one hand and other areas of knowledge and belief, such as the arts (e.g., painting, sculpture, architecture, music), philosophy, history, the social sciences, religion, etc., on the other. In brief, it is the comparison of one literature with another or others and the comparison of literature with other spheres of human expression.[4]

I have no objection to the first words of this definition—up through "the confines of a particular country"—but I do object to the rest, for three reasons. Remak chooses comparison itself as a constituent factor, although it is not exclusively nor even especially characteristic of comparative literature, as we have already observed.[5] As a result, we are forced to emphasize not supranationality, but national literatures ("the comparison of *one literature* with another"); and above all we are obliged to widen the field excessively, thereby assigning too great a value to every element, every cultural activity that might be included in comparative studies. I acknowledge that interdisciplinary imagination is and has been extremely fruitful; without such imagination, it would not be possible to comprehend the history of the natural sciences, for instance. But what we are concerned with here above all are the identity and existence of a discipline, one that cannot be defined to begin with as a *mens ab alio*.[6]

Other definitions, proposed by Weisstein, A.-M. Rousseau, and other specialists, seek to incorporate *arts et littératures comparées* into comparativism, a suggestive, complex question, confused at times, one that more than one theorist has tried to clarify. The observations of Wellek and Warren in chapter 11 of their *Theory of Literature* are very useful in this regard. Here, however, I will merely summarize this jurisdictional dispute before completing our taxonomic review.

Two questions emerge that I will try to answer without delay. One, does interartistic investigation lead to criticism and to the history of literature as well? To put it another way, does the study of relations between literature and the other arts lead to and become integrated with literary comparativism proper, the subject of this book? In some cases I think it does; but we must keep in mind that a change of jurisdiction is possible, and that such a change might encompass a different real or theoretical space where an interartistic equilibrium is maintained. The center of gravity continues to be literature. And then there is no lack of additional classifications or "excursuses." I am referring to any foundation, or inspiration, or origin, pictorial or musical, of a work of pure literature, as well as to the study of sources, practiced so assiduously in this field, themes, and even forms.

A plastic image, a pictorial motif, a musical form give rise to pages of Proust, Thomas Mann, or Alejo Carpentier. The result is a unique literary entity whose origin, as always, is something else. *Tutto fa brodo;* and the artistic signs form part of the world—the worlds—to which the word of the writer responds. The belltower of Martinville—is it art?—the windows of a church of Combray, the pavingstones of a street, a cup of tea, some flowers—is there anything more culturally "marked" than a flower?—a sonata by Vinteuil, all strike Proust's sensibility with equal force, without any intermediary. Remember the chapter about Clavileño, the magical wooden horse, in the second part of *Quixote* (XLI): Don Quixote compares the wooden charger with the Trojan horse ("If I remember rightly, I have read something in Virgil . . ."); and the narrator compares Don Quixote to a pictorial image: "he looked like nothing so much as a figure in some Roman triumph, painted or woven upon a Flemish tapestry." But there is clearly no novelistic work in which the artistic invention and humble and common everyday objects elbow each other as much or are so closely intertwined as in *Quixote*. Here is another example from closer to home. Being at home in the world and in life was the point of departure of Jorge Guillén's *Cántico* (1950); then he published *Clamor* (1963), a book situated in (and subtitled) "Tiempo de historia," historical time. *Homenaje,* a book devoted largely to cultural experiences and memories, appears later. But music and painting appear already in *Cántico,* in poems such as "Música, solo música," "El concierto," "Estatua ecuestra," "Amiga pintura." Bird and statue, concert and friendship, air and painting share the same vital process, without any *ontological gap,* without radical differentiation of realities. One could say the same about the admirable poems of Rafael Alberti, *A la pintura* (1942–1952), or about Pablo Picasso. We encounter not so much a transmutation of signs—as if the poet did not exist, or were limited to the task of transferring a work of art from one mold to another—but rather we witness the communication of a vital experience, a judgment or exercise of taste, which taken as such signifies a difference, a critical posture or a stance of personal consciousness.

This stance or posture is very clear as far as art criticism in particular is concerned, when we consider works of Diderot, for instance, or of Stendhal, Baudelaire, or Eugenio d'Ors: reflections, diaries, thoughts, glosses, a type of essay meant to be descriptive.[7] There are pages about Goya that are merely moments in the history of the reception of his work, and other pages, in the writings of André Malraux, for instance, that are also literature. The description of the visible allows for the perception of a sculpture, a painting, an amphora, or a Greek urn, the object forged by man—called *ekphrasis,* from the shield of Achilles in Homer and the line of busts that Christodorus tries to characterize in the *Greek Anthology* of the tenth century, or, in our own time, the use of the same method by Miroslav Krleža.[8] Certainly the *découpage* of the world by artists of the past, or the prestige of certain fabulous images, can direct the attention or awaken the imagination of a writer. Aside from ruins and gardens, the pictorial landscape is older than the poetic. One of the most intense landscape painters of our century is the extraordinary Catalan prose writer Josep Pla, who admired many artists (Santiago Rusiñol, Manolo) but above all looked, saw, and wrote with passion, with inexhaustible capacity for attention to life. Read again the surprising diary of adolescence, the *Quadern gris* (Gray Notebook), which evokes and recreates the instant when a young boy from the provinces discovers and explores the Barcelona of 1918–19—its streets, architects, poets, pedants; its gatherings, institutions, picture galleries. The great European capital is a crossroad of epochs, artistic styles, ways of living in the world, all of which make possible or inspire the creation of new works of art. The great city displays a plethora of signs superimposed on one another, in constant motion.

Up to this point we have given a brief indication of a kind of comparativism centered in literature but open to the entire gamut of the arts. This polygeneity—this superabundance of origins, from distinct levels of the real—is characteristic of the literary phenomenon. It is not our task here to examine the inspirations that come from a contrary direction, inspirations that have verbal beginnings, such as the iconography in religious art of the Middle Ages, studied so admirably by Emile Mâle. Language becomes image. Biblical texts and legendary tales are turned into capitals of cloisters, Romanesque porticos, Gothic tympanums. Rita Lejeune and Jacques Stiennon have devoted two volumes to the presence of the *légende de Roland* in medieval art.[9] Biblical, mythological, or historical figures and narrations dominate a good part of painting up to the time of David and Delacroix. Impressionism utterly stripped painting of its literary content. But it is curious that at that same moment—when Van Gogh was painting his shoes—composers of music came closer to the verbal and plastic arts. "Program music" appeared, Moussorgsky and his *Pictures at an Exhibition;* Debussy and *L'après-midi d'un faune,*[10] the formidable influence of Wagner. As is well known, during the last of the nineteenth century and the beginning of the twentieth, synesthesia, the relations between the arts, and the musicalization of narrative art were in fashion—including the obsession with time (Proust, Mann, Pirandello, Machado, Pérez de Ayala). So perhaps these transmutations may be better subjects for a rigorous analysis than literary polygeneity.

In an interesting article Dionýz Ďurišin refers to a model taken from communication: as we pass from work A to work B, each belonging to a different art, all the information coming from the world, from reality, from the extra-artistic sphere, serves only to condition the production of work B; but according to Ďurišin that is not the case concerning information coming from an artistic context (AC):

> In information from an artistic *context (AC),* during the process of inter-artistic communication an essential change takes place in the relationships among items of information of the artistic order *proper (p)* and those of the extraliterary area *(e)* and this unequivocally in favour of the latter. The mutual relationships between these two types of information of an artistic context may not be neglected.[11]

I agree with the last sentence, and, if I understand it correctly, the importance lies in opposing *p* with *e* to prove that the function of *p*, the artistic information, in the production of the work B, is not trivial, nor partial, but of a totalizing nature. This seems to happen if we analyze a painting by Poussin, a piece by Debussy, or the *Todesfuge* of Paul Celan. But returning to literature, the same thing rarely occurs in the opposite direction. Remember the subsection of *The Magic Mountain* by Thomas Mann, titled "Fülle des Wohllauts" (Fullness of Harmony), when the protagonist, Hans Castorp, listens to a series of records (Verdi, Debussy, Bizet, Gounod). These records (operas, relatively literary, and *L'après-midi d'un faune*) simply summarize the earlier phases of Castorp's education, and that's all. There is no "epiphany," no formal radiation; only the thematic use of some musical pretexts. In this case, there is no primacy of *p* over *e*.

And now for my second question: Does the comparison of arts or of works of art with one another constitute a field of special investigation? Yes, no doubt it does, but to avoid misunderstandings, let us not call them *arts et littératures comparées*, as if we were engaging in "interdisciplinary" or "interartistic" studies, analogous or similar to the interliterary studies that properly belong to comparative literature. The difference is not merely quantitative, since the class of investigation of arts with one another moves freely in a theoretical direction. And it is customarily called aesthetics, or semiology, the theory of communication, the history of criticism, or poetics, or something else. With good reason Pierre Dufour stresses that *"the aesthetic point of view is necessarily imposed as the directing point of view of a transdisciplinary comparative analysis"* and asks for *"a differential aesthetic analysis."*[12] Very often we see a work of art described in the press and even in conversation using concepts and a vocabulary belonging to a different art. People speak or write of perspectives in Cervantes, or the lyricism of Vermeer, or the chiaroscuro of Zola, and so on. In antiquity they already spoke of *colores rhetorici*, and since the time of Horace of *ut pictura poesis*. We should not be surprised by these interartistic metaphors. But things get more complicated when we use words such as *variation, counterpoint, polyphony, crescendo, modulation, texture, fabric, warp, framework*, or *arabesque* in referring to poems and novels. In Aldous Huxley's *Point Counter Point* "the musicalization of fiction" was carried to an extreme.[13] And what can one say about such basic concepts as repetition or contrast? At a certain level of abstraction we may conceive of a morphology capable of encompassing various arts simultaneously (or a thematology, as we shall see later). But such ideas cannot be interesting or fruitful unless we first clarify our thinking about the structure of each single form of art in question, its stratification, limitations, and so on. That is, we must enter the terrain of aesthetics.

That is the conclusion of André-Marie Rousseau at the end of his recent review of the question:

> Instead of clinging to the traditional idea of a multiplicity of autonomous systems of creation and communication, sensorial and linguistic, half closed in upon themselves and communicating only in a marginal way with one another, we prefer to postulate a global universe of signs appealing

simultaneously to sensation and to significance, manifested by diverse *media* that overlap partly through form, content, and design.[14]

The works of a Louis Marin or a Jean-François Lyotard must indeed be placed in the fields of semiology and aesthetics.[15] Just as the theory of literature, beginning with Aristotle, started out as a theory of genres, aesthetics no longer inquires what art is but what arts are. How do they differ from one another? What are their common dimensions, their various levels, their structural incompatabilities? We see already in Gotthold Ephraim Lessing that the contemplation of a singular work of art, the ancient Greek sculpture depicting Laocoön, implied an important distinction between the temporal arts and the spatial arts. As a result, H. P. H. Teesing, a historian of literature, made a great effort to apply to other arts the ideas of Roman Ingarden regarding the stratification of literary works.[16] When Louis Marin reads at one and the same time the biblical story and the painting of Poussin, *Les Israélites ramassant la manne dans le désert,* his aim is not to find sources, as Jean Seznec would do, or to elucidate thematic effects. His intention is to reflect in general on structural transformations that are verified when a narrative-verbal system of representation yields to another system that is of necessity narrative-pictorial, as a result of the use of planes, empty spaces, and figure groupings. And of course Marin is very familiar with Poussin's letters, with aesthetic ideas of the seventeenth century, and the controversies regarding line and color that would later lead to the theoretical writings of Roger de Piles and the abbé Dubos.[17] It is in the context of such reflections that the traditional allusions to *ut pictura poesis* and other interartistic comparisons reach their most interesting level, for example in the aesthetic meditations of Delacroix, Zola, Hofmannsthal, or Valéry.[18] What remains, as I said a little while back, continues to be literature.

Between these two poles, the literary and the aesthetic, many isolated encounters, crosses, reciprocal commentaries can be found that do not give rise to supranational entities or to historical continuities but to a voluminous amount of erudition, often beautiful, even elegant, but erudition and nothing more, with a propensity toward anecdote, diffusion, and marginality.

Of course an anecdote is a curious biographical trifle. Rilke was Rodin's secretary. Flaubert writes, "Je suis amoreux de la *Vierge* de Murillo de la galerie Corsini."[19] But the aim of the anecdote is usually to elucidate the genesis of a work, or rather, a psychological approach to a literary creation that more often than not leads to studies of sources and influences, as we saw earlier.[20] While investigating the origins of the opulent *Tentation de*

Saint Antoine, Seznec could discover no substantial difference between book sources, figurative sources (Brueghel), and childhood recollections.[21] But we do indeed gain a better understanding of Flaubert the man, the one who inspires his biographers with so much passion. Studies of a more personal and unique nature are those concerning the multiple creator, the one who cultivates several arts—*Künstlerische Doppelbegabungen* (artistic double talents), "double vocations," according to the title of a book by Herbert Guenther. Guenther's study is limited to German artists: Clemens Brentano, E. T. A. Hoffmann, Annette von Droste-Hülshoff, Ernest Barlach.[22] Most people are familiar with the best-known double or multiple artists in history: Michelangelo, William Blake, Eugène Fromentin; in modern times, Hans Arp, Almada Negreiros, Henri Michaux, Mário Cesariny, and many artists of the avant-garde. In Spain we find Gustavo Adolfo Bécquer, Santiago Rusiñol, José Moreno Villa, Rafael Alberti, Salvador Dalí, and Federico García Lorca. Indeed, certain surroundings seem to favor such convergences: Renaissance Florence, avant-garde Paris. And China of the T'ang dynasty: Wang Wei. But in the West at least, the idiosyncratic side of the multiartist prevails and is regarded as more interesting than the outcome. Federico the poet, and above all the dramatist, cannot be well understood without keeping in mind his love for music and drawing. And there is nobody more multifaceted than Pablo Picasso. Why was it that Picasso, who in general resisted surrealism in his painting, resorted to it in his Spanish poems (such as *Trozo de piel,* 1959)?[23] Whatever the answer might be, nothing connected with that genial, brilliant creator should surprise us.

Later I will devote some pages to historiology and the problem of periodization. It should be made clear that the pluralistic model and the concept of the dialectic of a period, favored by many today, are in conflict with the homogeneous and interartistic concept of the cultural epoch. And we do not say in conflict with the idea of the "simultaneous flow" or synchrony of the arts (*Gleichlauf der Künste*), to use Kurt Wais's term.[24] Each art has its own rhythm, itinerary, and development. The automatic application of Wölfflin's categories of the visual arts to literary history (categories that formed a varied assemblage of conceptual *models*) has brought about much vagueness and oversimplification. Again I agree with Wellek when he writes:

> The various arts—the plastic arts, literature, and music—have each their individual evolution, with a different tempo and a different internal structure of elements . . . It is not a simple affair of a "timespirit" determining and permeating each and every art. We must conceive of the sum total of

man's cultural activities as of a whole system of self-evolving series, each having its own set of norms which are not necessarily identical with those of the neighbouring series.[25]

Certain artistic manifestations or channels of communication of a "complex" character, such as opera, cinema, and ballet, merit separate mention. These classes of art are neither pure music nor mere literature, neither simple movement nor plain photographic image. But neither can they be considered mixtures or juxtapositions of the traditional channels of artistic expression. Let us suppose that what is involved is the molding of a new art, *sui generis*, and not simply a work of collaboration, or synergy, or some other element pasted on. In such a case, why speak of literary comparativism, of "Literature and X," to use the well-known formula, except from the genetic point of view? Song, ballad, romance, *emblemata*, or emblem of the sixteenth century,[26] *masque* of the seventeenth, royal fiestas, the *autos sacramentales* of Pedro Calderón de la Barca, the illustrated book, cantata, motet, opera, oratorio, operetta, *Lied, Singspiel,* ballet, zarzuela, *calligramme,* cinema, *collage,*[27] concrete poetry,[28] conceptual art, mixed media, television series . . . The primary task in each case is to distinguish between a simple juxtaposition and an original complex fusion of different classes of signs meant to give rise to *other* semiotic systems or polysystems; in other words, the creation, more or less, of a *Gesamtkunstwerk,* the "conjoined work of art." And when such a conjoined work is examined, we may find that the role literature plays may not be as important as we had imagined.

One of the most inspiring creators of art, one who came closest to perfection in our century, was George Balanchine, who removed the literary component from Russian ballet. Teesing is completely right when he maintains that just as criticism rejects the divorce of form from content in a poem, a libretto cannot be torn out of an opera for the purpose of branding the libretto alone as mediocre. A *leitmotiv* of Wagner is successful to the extent that it is both thematic and melodic.[29] It is useless to attack a libretto that is not text but pretext,[30] that is not literature but simply a tool used for the construction of the *Gesamtkunstwerk.* Why did so many good writers consider themselves failures in Hollywood? Such a thing doesn't happen in other places, with directors who write their own scripts, directors like Carlos Saura. In a work like *Elisa, vida mia* (1976), Saura brings about an astonishing and definitive convergence of action, dialogue, narrative commentary, image, landscape, and even the rhythm of a delicious piano piece by Erik Satie.

I agree in general with Teesing's criterion that it is also improper to assign to the illustrated book the place of privilege and rank granted it by A.-M. Bassy. In an ambitious article, Bassy says that the book would be "the ideal place for the observation of the variations of the connection between the thing written and the thing seen, the changes in interpretation and in the attitude of the readers, and for the exercise of a psycho-sociology of the arts." [31] In fact, from the dawn of printing to our days, the illustrated book (cultivated by the best artists—Braque, Chagall, Picasso, Eduardo Chillida, Antonio Tàpies, Xavier Guerrero) usually represents an interpretation that comes after the appearance of the original work. It is more like a commentary, or a relatively personal homage. The illustrated book includes text, metatext, and a beautiful juxtaposition, enhanced perhaps by the excellent quality of materials and elements used to produce a luxury book, things involving another form of art and one of the most exquisite at that (paper, ink, typeface, binding, and so on). Seznec has made an elegant study of the history of French illustrations of *Quixote,* which usually reveal a sensibility reflecting the critical attitudes of each era: a farcical tendency in the seventeenth century, tragic during the Romantic period, grandiose in the illustrations of Gustave Doré, and so on. [32] And the result is a history of the reception of Cervantes in France. [33]

Returning to taxomonies, let us recall that shortly after the Second World War certain clear changes in emphasis were already apparent. In surveying comparative studies in America, Henri Peyre noted in 1952 that thematology, ignored by the French school, was being revived as a result of renewed interest in myths and symbols in anthropology and psychoanalysis. This same tendency was also evident with regard to literary genres—and translations, whose function in the history of culture should not be underestimated. [34] Soon afterward Harry Levin came to similar conclusions while placing special emphasis on the study of translations, traditions, and movements; the transformation of genres throughout history; and the elaboration of a "repertoire of themes," [35] following ideas of Gaston Bachelard and Stith Thomson. Indeed, as we shall see later, Harry Levin has demonstrated a tenacious loyalty to thematic studies.

So within the confines of a certain repertoire of possibilities, we observe the vicissitudes of the same few inquiries, *essentially contested concepts,* to use Wellek's term. [36] The players change more often than the play, and preferences more often than the terms that make up the options. I have assembled and accept in general the classifications that A. Owen Aldridge applies in his *Comparative Literature: Matter and Method* (1969), a selection of articles published in the journal *Comparative Literature Studies.* Aldridge does not rely on speculations but on the practice of a fair number of comparatists. He lists five principal areas of investigation: (1) "literary criticism and theory," (2) "literary movements," (3) "literary themes," (4) "literary forms," and (5) "literary relations." As might be expected, Poggioli's two basic classes of investigation survive: the thematic (Aldridge's 3) and the morphological (4). Sources and influences, less interesting to scholars today, are condensed and grouped under "literary relations." The revival of literary history, its components and configurations, is acknowledged (2). These four categories are also identical with the ones presented by François Jost in his very useful *Introduction to Comparative Literature* (1974): (1) "relations: analogies and influences"; (2) "movements and trends"; (3) "genres and forms"; (4) "motifs, types, themes."

The following pages will present a slightly different order, reflecting my goal in this book. I have maintained from the beginning that comparative literature has been and is an intellectual discipline characterized by the posing of certain problems that only comparative literature is in a position to confront. The encounter with these problems, these questions, some that we have not yet discovered, is what reveals the specific nature of comparative literature and vindicates its historical continuity. The present book is *not* an introduction to the investigation of literature in general, nor a theory of literature. Here I am not asking the Sphinx about the interpretation of a unique or isolated text, although such texts have intrigued me in the past and continue to do so, but only insofar as I ask myself how the idea of an individual style, for instance, is related to a collective concept of style. I will not be presenting different "approximations" to the study of texts, or genres, or forms, so numerous and all based in general on a series of interrelations—with society on a socioeconomic level, with the personality of the writer, analyzed psychoanalytically,[37] and so on. Instead, like my predecessors, I prefer to study above all how texts, forms, or genres are presented and organized, keeping in mind the constant to and fro between the unity sought by our discourse or our human consciousness, and the countless historical-spatial differentiations, so real and so tangible in the field of literature, so alluring and fascinating. At this point, merely to mention the need for interrogations will suffice. *What* do we approach when we speak of literature, as a result of the historical *découpage* of the comparatist?

Owen Aldridge adds a fifth category to the four basic ones that we have already noted: criticism and literary theory. Certainly René Wellek's *History of Modern Criticism: 1750–1950* (1955–1965) remains one of the great monuments of comparativism today.[38] A critical exercise does not exist if it does not presuppose theoretical knowledge and postures more consciously all the time. Wellek himself has always insisted on the indivisibility of criticism, history, and theory. A consciousness of theory—as I hope to show—is part of and adheres to every category of comparativism. For example, the investigation of a literary genre would be exceedingly ingenuous if it failed to ask at a certain moment: What are genres? What functions do they fulfill? We shall see very soon.

Indeed, this question appears so relevant to me now that I tend to distinguish between genres proper and proceedings that are primarily formal, including those that I will call "channels of presentation." Since we are using here a traditional neo-Aristotelian lexicon, based on the opposition of matter and form and their mutual dependence, I consider it justified to distinguish between the critical exercise (or the moment of reading) that identifies or isolates a formal aspect of the text (such as the rhymed octave); the distinguishing characteristic of the theme (such as the voyage of discovery); and that which brings the genre into question (such as the epic paradigm of *Os Lusíadas*). The elucidation of the genre should not veer too far either from the theme or from the form. The most attractive difficulty is found in that middle ground. I am not overlooking the fact that a pure form or a pure theme is hardly conceivable. We are faced with mental models that later become methods of analysis, highly relativized in practice.

Like the earlier chapters, those that follow will attempt to be allusive. Sometimes my purpose in elaborating will be to make room for examples that clarify ideas and make the presentation more palatable. My aim is not to enumerate books or authors, but to point out directions, highlight problems, and offer useful information to the curious student and reader. I will refer to five classes of investigation. One, the genres: *genology*. Two, the formal proceedings: *morphology*. Three, the themes: *thematology*. Four, literary relations: *internationality*. Five, the historical configurations: *historiology*.

Part II

―――――

The Basic Issues

12

Genres: Genology

The matter of literary genres is one of the *essentially contested concepts* that has played a leading role in the history of poetics since the time of Aristotle. This problem is tenacious and interminable, neither resolved nor dissolved, because after we ask: "What are literary genres?" or "Which genres are there?" other questions await us: "What is literature?" or "What is poetry?"; and definitive answers to the last two would probably imply the inevitable death of literature and poetry. Here is an obviously fruitful problem that every age, every school, and every critical approach must confront circumstantially; that is, the problem must be considered from the vantage point of or in relation to other questions or queries that make up the historical environment of the time.

In my opinion six aspects of the question condition our approach to literary genres. I summarize them briefly below.

1. *Historically,* genres were thought of as occupying a terrain whose components evolve over centuries, as ever-changing models for which we must find a place in a literary system or polysystem that sustains a definite moment in the evolution of poetic forms. An individual model may also be embodied in different works such as the picaresque novel, exemplified during the seventeenth century by *Lazarillo de Tormes* and Mateo Alemán's *Guzmán de Alfarache,* and later by Alain René Lesage's *Gil Blas* (1715–1735). This historical and dynamic perception of genres prevailed until the Romantic or pre-Romantic age—for example, in Schiller's "Über naive und

sentimentalische Dichtung" (1795; About Naive and Sentimental Poetry) and Friedrich Schlegel's "Gespräch über die Poesie" (1800; Conversation about Poetry). After the foundering of Ferdinand Brunetière's Darwinian theory (*L'évolution des genres,* 1890), the most influential conception of our century has been that of the Russian Formalists, who saw in each era the progressive exhaustion of the principal prior models, which were then relegated to the sidelines to make room for the rise of genres previously considered secondary or popular—for example, in nineteenth-century Russia, the letter, the personal diary, and the serialized novel. The Formalists were very closely allied to the avant-garde poetry of their time and concentrated almost entirely on the study of only one literature, the Russian, whose late appearance on the literary scene coincided with the transition from wornout neoclassicism to rebellious Romanticism. Therefore, it is hardly surprising that their theses were not germane to the entire complex of Occidental literary history. As we shall see later, however, certain aspects of their agonistic vision are very valuable. Viktor Shklovsky himself pointed out that the superseded components were not permanently eclipsed but continued to be "pretenders to the throne" or were passed along to be integrated into new systems.[1] Jurij Striedter confirms that the other Formalists agreed with the idea of a literary evolution that is neither organic growth nor a series of revolutions.[2]

Not so Mikhail Bakhtin, who plowed his own furrow all his life and shared with the Formalists only a conflictive conception of the relations between literary genres, or rather between two large classes of literature: on the one hand, the elevated genres, the established culture; and, on the other hand, everything that signified change, the future, parody, laughter, proximity to popular and contemporary life. This double vision is useful; however, Bakhtin could not or did not wish to apply it to a diversity of genres with a view to being historically precise, but insisted on calling "novel" the totality of genres and subgenres opposed to the important or dominant culture (Tzvetan Todorov points out that Schlegel had done the same thing),[3] in the sense of either belonging to the sphere of the novel, or being a predecessor, or being related to it. So we find ourselves faced after all by a category that is excessively broad and "transhistorical,"[4] that on the one hand includes works as far from being unusual or perturbing as the Byzantine novel (Heliodorus, Achilles Tatius), or the Baroque novel of the seventeenth century (Gautier de Costes de La Calprenède, Casper von Lohenstein) and, on the other hand, passes over and undervalues—a serious failing—genres such as the Latin love elegy, the Greek and Renaissance eclogue, and nothing less than lyric poetry and the essay (Montaigne). If

Bakhtin had grasped the idea of function (a concept that I will comment on later), he might have been able to find a place in history for the opposing categories that preoccupied him, and perhaps to overcome the practical difficulties presented by such oppositions.

In addition, the Formalists' perspective—historical-evolutionist and agonistic—encompassed not only the genres, the methods, styles, and even the concept of literature itself (the literary/nonliterary polarity) but also the premises on which we base our reading; and therefore, even the study or the science of literature. The historicity of critical terms, to the extent that they affect reading, is what Roman Jakobson emphasized in "On Realism in Art" (1987; originally published in Czech in 1921). And Jurij Striedter notes: "If one says that Tynyanov proceeds from an investigation of literary evolution to the evolution of the concept of literature itself, Jakobson's path leads in the final analysis to an evolutionary, historically relativized conception of literary scholarship."[5] As a result, the question "What is a literary genre?" ceases to exist, as happens so often today with the questions "What is literariness?" or "What is fictionality?"—purely ultrahistorical and speculative queries. In fact, those formulating questions of this type are merely inserting themselves into the cultural circumstances of their own time, by choosing one response or another. Striedter's commentary is important because it assures us that in recording the history of literary genres that make up poetry itself, we also record the history of poetics, which was to a large extent a theory of genres; and we also incidentally place our own theory within a certain phase of a temporal evolution. I do not believe this means giving in necessarily to a total relativism; but it does indeed mean a revival of the confrontation of unity with multiplicity in time, a confrontation that we will encounter again later.

One should of course examine more closely the nature, rhythm, and outline of the historical evolution of literary genres. Fernando Lázaro Carreter formulates various useful and suggestive proposals in this regard. "In the first place, the dissatisfaction of a writer of genius with the established genres is an appropriate attitude," as, for example, in the case of Lope de Vega. The brilliant writer is thus the forerunner of the development of a genre of known origin. Second, a genre arises when a writer "finds in a prior work a structural model for his own creation." Third, this structure consists of functions recovered "by means of certain significant elements, characters, behavior, scenes of action, emotional attitudes." Fourth, the epigone utilizes the inherited generic scheme, but not without modifying certain functions or introducing significant changes. Fifth, the generic relationship of two works depends on the use of certain common functions, not on mere similarities in themes or plots. And, finally, each genre has a fixed, more or less extended "época de vigencia" (period of viability or efficacy), but a period that Lázaro is inclined to limit quite rigorously in time.[6] These six approaches to literary genre, summarized too briefly here, constitute a necessary point of departure for a reflection of a diachronic sort. How does a genre come about? And also, how does it disappear? (In effect, only imitation, reiteration, or remodeling establishes a genre, and the innovator does not necessarily have to be a genius—the epigones of Montaigne established the essay, and compare Aloysius Bertrand with Baudelaire in regard to the prose poem.) What elements make possible a structure of functions? If we do not limit ourselves to the argumental and thematic functions of Vladimir Propp, we must assume that the formal and the thematic functions are identical. I will return a little later to the very delicate matter of the temporal duration of a genre.

2. *Sociologically,* at least since the time of Madame de Staël—or, in our day, Harry Levin—we have been aware that literature is not only an institution but genres as well: subgenres, if you prefer, or *istituti,* as some Italian critics say.[7] I am not referring here to a sociology *of* literature, but to the components and classes of literature itself considered as established and conditioned social complexes. Because they are so well known, it is easy to forget the really astonishing antiquity and persistence of genres such as comedy. In spite of so many avatars and very substantial changes, a spectator at a modern performance of one of Aristophanes' plays has no doubt that he is watching a comedy. In the early days of the French Revolution, Saint-Just proposed the creation of a prize reserved for the ode and the epic.[8] (Today publishing houses and ministries of culture are firm believers in the concept of genre.) The classical Chinese genres cultivated by Mao Tse-tung come to mind; and I also recall the admiration I felt one day when I discovered that the *qasida,* the quintessential classical genre of Arabic poetry, had survived an upheaval as profound as that experienced by muslims during the emergence and propagation of Islam. How was a pre-Islamic genre able to survive and grow in vigor after the seventh and eighth centuries, especially in conquered territories such as Syria and Iraq, where not only a new faith but also important social changes were suddenly imposed?[9] It is not necessary to explain that the extraordinary resilience of genres is equally tolerant of change and of opposition to change, innovation and attachment to roots, the audacity of a Rimbaud, who did not invent the prose poem, and the nostalgia of a Giuseppe Tomasi Lampedusa, a Llorenç Villalonga, or a Solzhenitsyn. Genres are the most obvious manifestations of the crisscross and superposition of continuity and discontinuity that mark the peculiar itinerary of literature.

Fernando Lázaro Carreter explains that a genre assumes the permanence of a "structural model," which an esteemed epigone alters in various ways (even by omissions). Thus we have permanence and change at the same time. We observe here the difficult problem of the nature of change in the history of literature, or at least of change in what we call genres. The problem will be simplified if we keep in mind my fifth aspect—that a genre often functions as a conceptual model, and what evolves then is a mental paradigm, generally consisting of some canonical works, while at the same time individual imitations of the model obey their own rhythm of evolution. Lázaro does not concede that histories of genres might be "like continua that extend through the ages," as for example the development of the novel since *Don Quixote:*

> The history of the novel is composed of more or less continuous lines . . .
> and one cannot see which could be a direct continuation of *Don Quix-*
> *ote*—and of "births" as a result of other genres. Eighteenth-century nar-
> ration emerges like a comment on the philosophical essay; the nineteenth-
> century novel, like a complex amplification of the sketch of manners, in
> the same way that the sixteenth-century novel had been born of clever and
> complicated developments of other existing genres. If we look for common
> traits among works as different as those which are labeled "novel," we will
> see that the common traits become scarcer and tend to disappear as we
> consider more titles and a wider temporal compass.[10]

It is curious that this variety of "births"—and rebirths—should be evident above all in Spain (since in England the Cervantine model of the novel had already borne fruit by the middle of the eighteenth century). But Lázaro's comments are generally apt. Genres interact and are modified endlessly. That is what the perspective of the reader or the critic brings to light at the moment he accepts what Fernand Braudel calls *moyennes durées* (medium durations). At the appropriate time, and simultaneously, the *longues durées* (long durations) are expanded and extended, and very clearly too, like the High Road of the novel leading from Fielding and Balzac to Galdós, Tolstoy, Mann, and Proust. Later, when we are considering themes (Chapter 14) and historiology (Chapter 16), we will have occasion to reflect on this superposition of evolution and continuity, a superposition that to my mind is not resolved by the fact of mere motion.

3. *Pragmatically,* or from the point of view of the reader (or, more accurately, readers: the public), genre implies not only contact but contract.[11] It is what Hans Robert Jauss has named deftly and successfully "horizon of expectations" (*Erwartungshorizont*). The reader has expectations of certain genres. If these are popular, oral, or commerical artistic forms—the story,

the epic poem, the detective novel, the horror movie, the Western—the matter is very clear. Think of the comedy of Lope de Vega, who certainly knew how to create a public following. Was this a more important factor when Lope was improvising a comedy than when he was composing a polished epic such as *Jerusalén conquistada* (1609)? Seldom does the "receptor" take up a book or go to the theater or listen to a story without previous and ultraindividual expectations and hopes. The innovative writer understands this and often relies on it to fabricate his surprises.

4. *Structurally*, since the time of Schiller's famous essay, genre has been considered not only as an isolated element but also as a part of a whole—that is, of a complex of options, alternatives, interrelations. Confronting the ideal space of the models of an era, the writer chooses a particular genre from the range of models available at a certain time; since some classes are thus excluded, the chosen one is differentiated from the others—a difference deliberately made that can become a link. Some genres are contragenres, or works whose origin is contrageneric.[12] The protonovel of Cervantes is in part a response to the picaresque narration that *Quixote* and various "exemplary novels" tried to leave behind. The difference that connects one genre to another can be defined as the exercise of a determined function. For example, is it not true that some great Latin American novels today fill the slot occupied by the traditional story in earlier times? The structuralism of the 1970s and the mental scheme attributed to Ferdinand de Saussure have undoubtedly helped us to understand better the idea of the genre at the core of a system of functions; but nevertheless an idea that Yuri Tynyanov had already formulated with complete clarity in a famous essay, "De l'évolution littéraire" (1927). "The study of genres," wrote Tynyanov, "is impossible outside the system within which and with which it is correlated. Tolstoy's historical novel is correlated not with Zagoskin's historical novel, but with the prose of his time."[13]

Earlier I suggested that the absence of the idea of function is what obliged Bakhtin to designate as novel, or to relate to novel, all those writings that fulfilled the same role in the history of literature. Bakhtin wrote with regard to ancient Greek literature and the mutual interaction of genres within it: "the whole of literature, conceived as a totality of genres, becomes an organic unity of the highest order."[14] But it is necessary to go one more step, the one that takes us from the neo-Romantic notion of the organism to that of system—an assemblage of interrelations, interactions, options, but also of certain functions carried out by its components.

One could say the same thing about the idea of tradition expressed by T. S. Eliot in *The Sacred Wood* (1920): an assemblage that continues to grow and be transformed harmoniously, thanks to the intervention of the individual talent. Eliot stated that in any historical period whatsoever European literature "has a simultaneous existence and composes a simultaneous order"; that the truly new writer changes that order and our way of seeing its principal monuments; and that it is not possible to judge a work without contrasting and comparing it with its predecessors. Francisco Rico, in a recent gloss, has gone further. The individual talent not only alters but also is altered by tradition, or more accurately, modifies the tradition intrinsically within the new text. The formal features of a sonnet by Quevedo are linked to a literary system whose recollection echoes between his lines. Thus every poetical moment conserves and imparts force (intertextually) to the image of earlier moments. Rico sums up by saying, "Literature today is the awareness of the environment in which those phenomena [of linking] have been produced and continue to be produced: the historical awareness of itself, the history of literature." [15] This accurate vision does not omit but rather takes in an awareness of the divergences that link writers, the choices made between generic streams that make writing possible, and the function that one genre fulfills during a specific period in contrast to all other genres.

In sum, the concept of function links not only the single work but also the genre with the whole, evolution with continuity, and the critic's historical and structural perspectives.

5. *Logically,* from the point of view of the writer above all—but that of the critic as well—the genre acts primarily as a mental model. This ideal or conceptual aspect of genre is what the critic loses sight of as soon as he limits himself to saying "X's book is a novel" or "Y's work is utopian"—as if one were allowed to say that a horse is of the equine species. If a roan can be described only as belonging to the equine species, a poetic production can "belong" without any difficulty to more than one genre. A few years ago, speaking of Garcilaso, I used the following simile:

> A ship crosses a strait at night and determines its course with the aid of two powerful beacons that follow it with their beams from the heights. The beacons do not suppress the navigator's freedom to maneuver; on the contrary, they presume such freedom and favor it. The beacons dominate the position of the ship but do not coincide with it. Who would dream of maintaining that the course followed by the vessel "is" one of the beacons? Or that its exact destination "is" one of the lights that guide it? [16]

Here we find an example, a guide, a concept-summary, that collects and reconciles the predominant traits of a plurality of works, authorities, and canons. The *qasida*, a classical genre of Arabic poetry, arises not from some great poem of Imru'-al-Qays, for example, but from a mixed model derived from the totality of an influential anthology such as the famous *Mu'allaqāt* (Seven Odes) of Hammad al-Rawiyah (eighth century), in which the paradigm of Imru'-al-Qays is indissolubly mixed with others.[17] From this point of view, it becomes necessary to confront the problem posed by *genera mixta* and the great hybrid works—border markers, milestones—far from scarce in the history of literature.[18] Genological investigation, more than the elaboration of an inductive taxonomy (although I do not deny that such an approach might also be legitimate and suggestive, like Northrop Frye's "four forms of prose fiction"),[19] is the outlining of certain complex, paradigmatic mental spaces and of their changing historical trajectory.

6. *Comparatively,* the question arises of the "universality" or relative limitations of each genre or system of genres in space and in time. In how many languages, how many cultures, how many civilizations has genre X appeared? The question is especially pertinent to comparative literature.

The examination, of necessity comparative in nature, of the range of a genre is both delicate and decisive. Even though a critical reading of a single work from the point of view of the genre or genres to which it belongs can be very effective, genology clearly cannot be limited to that one procedure. An analysis of Baudelaire's poetic work cannot serve as basis for a theory regarding the prose poem. Only historical time is capable of demonstrating that a model has indeed attained the status of a genre. For the comparatist, then, only the passage of years and centuries can manifest and display the structural riches and options of a specific genre. For this reason, a researcher conscious of such a perspective cannot permit himself the luxury, more poverty than luxury actually, of remaining circumscribed within the bounds of a few western European literatures. An isolated and solitary poem within a literature can seem unusual, or even marginal, if not supported by other poems that demonstrate the existence of a common genre or subgenre. Lázló Hadrovics proceeds from this point of view regarding the *Planctus* of Maria in Hungary (ca. 1300), by linking it to analogous works in Bohemia (*Pláč Panny Marie*) or to the motif of the hagiographic hymn (the Magyar *Canto de Lázló,* ca. 1470).[20]

Think of the prestige of the pastoral drama, which enjoyed considerable popularity and diffusion during the last years of the sixteenth century and throughout most of the seventeenth. In Spanish, the bucolic mode gave rise to narrations of the first rank—Jorge de Montemayor, Gaspar Gil Polo, Cervantes—although of course it is not proper to describe the corresponding genre without taking into account Sir Philip Sidney and Honoré d'Urfé.

As for the dramatic current, the eclogues of Juan del Encina, Gil Vicente, and Lucas Fernández have been performed since the first third of the sixteenth century. But it was a particular model that became successful at the end of the sixteenth century.

The pastoral drama of the European type emerged in Italy, nested like a promise, so to speak, in the eclogues of Theocritus and Virgil (to such an extent that it would be hard to differentiate pastoral drama from eclogue in dialogue), starting with Angelo Poliziano's *Orfeo* (1471). Two masterworks, Torquato Tasso's *Aminta* (ca. 1573) and Giovanni Battista Guarini's *Il pastor fido* (ca. 1583), were combined and interlaced in the "ideal space" of the generic system of the era that allowed the development of a mixed model. Two decisive circumstances surrounded the presentation and identification of this mixed model. The long polemic stirred up by the censures of *Il pastor fido* and by Guarini's responses heightened the level of theoretical consciousness about the definition of the genre.[21] And actually the genre was presented as a "pastoral tragicomedy." One of its English imitators, the dramatist John Fletcher, came close to repeating a commonplace when he wrote in the prologue to *The Faithful Shepherdess* (ca. 1609): "It is a pastoral tragicomedy . . . so called in respect it wants deaths, which is enough to make it no tragedy, yet brings some near it, which is enough to make it no comedy."[22] It is clear in this case that the two modes determining the tragicomedy are the pastoral and the satirical, as Susanne Stamnitz accurately points out in her book *Prettie Tales of Wolues and Sheepe* (1977). And allegory makes its appearance as well. So then, only a vision of the whole can allow us to perceive these structural options clearly, when we also consider that few works of the first rank have been written in this genre outside Italy. The French *bergeries*, for example, do not go beyond the discrete quality of Jean Mairet's *Sylvie* (1628), as Daniela Dalla Valle has shown in a valuable study.[23]

Tasso's *Aminta*, adapted repeatedly in the principal European languages,[24] was immediately translated into Serbo-Croatian by Dominko Zlatarić (Padua, 1580; second, corrected edition, Venice, 1597, under the title *Ljubmir*).[25] Among subsequent imitations in Serbo-Croatian, one stands out as a masterpiece: the *Dubravka* of Dživo Gundulić, which appeared in Dubrovnik and had its premiere in 1628. This work raises the Ragusan language to the level of a mature instrument suitable for great poetry. In his book about Gundulić, Wsevolod Setschkareff points out all the satirical and allegorical elements of *Dubravka*, not without betraying a note of surprise.[26] The greatest Magyar poet of the Renaissance, Bálint Balassi, without leaving eastern Europe and by going back to the beginning of the sixteenth century, in 1589 adapted a pastoral drama by an author of second rank, the *Amarilli* of Cristoforo Castelletti, and called it *Szép magyar komédia* (Beautiful Hungarian Comedy). It is a relatively free adaptation; although he respected the conventions of the genre (such as verses with "echo" rhymes),[27] he toned down the fanciful bucolic elements (there were no nymphs) and allowed some characters to use popular, vernacular speech.[28]

Finally, another work should be mentioned that appeared well along into the seventeenth century, *Daphnis drzewem bobkowym* (1638; Daphne Changed into a Laurel Tree), by the Polish writer Samuel Twardowski. This work brilliantly extended and dramatized the erotic obsession common to Renaissance eclogues. (Think of the complaints of Garcilaso's first Eclogue, the besieged chastity of Tasso's and Guarini's protagonists, or the shepherdess Marcela in *Quixote*.) In the ancient and pagan world of Twardowski's mythological drama, Apollo's intense desire has as dénouement neither life nor death but complete frustration: the metaphormosis of Daphne into a laurel tree. The tyranny of love, which in the pastoral world is beyond discussion—"on n'en a jamais honte," Claude Backvis comments[29]—is resolved into a yearning for spiritual elevation. We are in the midst of the Baroque. The courtly fiesta coincides with the theatrical space, with a stage-set that is an "enchanted island," as Jean Rousset writes, and the place where man encounters the illusory nature of his own life. Human life is an *illusion comique*—to use a title of Corneille. The pastoral drama is a spectacle because the world is. And within the sphere of theatrical truth, love is a tragicomedy.[30]

This last example does not go beyond the bounds of European poetry—of the *littérature (vraiment) européenne,* as René Etiemble would say. Its roots are international, according to the model A sketched in Chapter 10. As we proceed to examine genres of a clearly supranational type, matters grow more and more complicated, and above all, important modifications are introduced. Here we have a class of investigation still in its incipient stage, vacillating, insecure about its theoretical premises. The mere choice of a genre for investigation promptly turns into a problem in our hands. Earlier I insisted on the usefulness of a radically historical posture in matters of genology, but not with the intention of giving up our own taxonomies in certain contexts. For example, we have on the one hand the concept of pastoral tragicomedy that Guarini began to define in his time and, on the other, the concept of *anatomy* (narration based on ideas more than on lives, like the utopian or the philosophical stories of the eighteenth century). *Anatomy* is the term used by Northrop Frye in an original way in his great book to designate one of the "four forms of prose fiction" that he was proposing. Do we then feel an urgent need to emulate Frye, but with the determination to widen the perspective, to take into consideration Asiatic, African, Indo-American, and other literatures? I have already expressed my agreement with Etiemble's view, but I have also stressed that the alternative "either History or Theory" is a seriously inept proposition. I have refused to choose between historical knowledge and purely speculative theory, as I pointed out in my comments on Jakobson's notion of parallelism in poetry. Then we saw that the diachronic structure was derived from Zhirmunsky's comparative and historical investigations; that is, it was historical knowledge that enabled a plausible renewed theory to surface. For now, it suffices to mention the interest aroused by problems brought to the fore by supranational genology, above all in the field of East/West studies, where intriguing questions keep emerging in a vigorous way. It is appropriate at this point to take a look at two principal paths being explored in East/West studies. The first applies terms proceeding from European poetics to other peoples, other civilizations, other climates. Certain Chinese comparatists, principally in Formosa, are carrying out such studies with quite interesting and efficacious results. Have there been epic heroes in Chinese literature? asks Ching-hsien Wang.[31] Did they write tragedies? And what about the *aubade* (lament of lovers at the coming of dawn)? A. T. Hatto's book continues to demonstrate the supranational nature of the *aubade*,[32] which means we may well ask: "Does the *aubade* also occur in the *Shih Ching*?" The danger of this kind of investigation rests, of course, in the perpetuation of Eurocentric attitudes, by transposing concepts of Chinese or Japanese poetry onto Western forms of thinking, as one might convey titles of nobility. Edward W. Said ripped off the cultural masks of colonialism with vigor and skill in his *Orientalism* (1978). With good reason, Heh-hsiang Yuan denounces the comparatists who project their Occidental models onto the literature of the East, only to discover superficial resemblances.[33] The adoption of Oriental genres or forms by American or European writers also calls for careful scrutiny—without casting doubt on the value of such stimuli: from the *haikus* and *tankas* written in Mexico by Juan José Tablada (*Un día*, 1919), to Carles Riba in Catalonia (*Del joc i del foc*, 1946) and, in San Francisco, the poems of Kenneth Rexroth (*The Morning Star*, 1974), or rather those of his heteronomous Marichiko. In my view, facile and hasty worldliness is as erroneous as the excluding attitudes of Sinologists and other specialists who remain walled up in their exotic and arrogant science, as if there were no common ground, analogous themes, comparable forms; as if the human race were irremediably and absolutely divided into watertight compartments. A Pindaric hymn is neither more accessible nor less remote than a song of Li Po—to be sure, only for those who possess the necessary linguistic and cultural preparation.

A short while after the fateful instant in his conversation with Eckermann when Goethe pronounced the word *Weltliteratur* for the first time, he spoke admiringly of a Chinese novel that he was reading. "Very remarkable," he called it. "That must look strange enough," the good Eckermann commented. "Not as much as you might think," replied the already illustrious poet. "The Chinese think, act, and feel almost exactly like us . . . except that all they do is more clear, pure, and decorous, than with us." Then Goethe noted a relationship—in true comparatist fashion—between the Chinese novel and those of Richardson, and also with his own *Hermann und Dorothea:* "With them all is orderly, citizen-like, without great passion or poetic flight; and there is a strong resemblance to my *Hermann und Dorothea,* as well as to the English novels of Richardson."[34]

The second path of the two mentioned earlier starts from the generic concepts offered by poetics throughout its historical trajectory. The goal here is not only to confirm the traditional concepts or to broaden their areas of applicability but also to refine, correct, and modify them. Otherwise, new facts and knowledge would be superfluous, and the task of acquiring them vain. Ideas should be broken in, Unamuno said, just the way shoes are. At the time time, the generic spaces of poetics will have to be enriched, renewed, the schemes split apart, after undergoing the test of supranationality—the test that will reveal common meanings as well as ineradicable differences. Earl Miner describes this double condition at the beginning of his book about the "linked poetry" of Japan (*renga* and *haikai*):

> Like all other literature that may be thought truly important, the linked
> poetry of Japan makes a dual claim: to sameness and difference. Its claim
> to sameness means that it offers us a valued kind of knowledge of ourselves
> and our world that is recognizably like that provided by other important
> literature . . . Its claim to difference means that the knowledge it gives is
> also determined by, appreciated for, the distinct terms on which it gives . . .
> In all important literary matters we seek the valued sameness, importance,
> or we would not seek at all. But we discover it only through difference.[35]

A difference actually so suggestive, in this Japanese example, that four contemporary poets cloistered themselves for a week in a hotel in Paris to try it out: Octavio Paz, Jacques Roubaud, Edoardo Sanguineti, and Charles Tomlinson together composed *Renga* (1971). "Difference also tends to be a subtle fulfillment of a mystery or a doubt," Gracián noted.[36] How is it possible not to think of difference and a model of writing that inspires some of Octavio Paz's best verses? And let us not forget the example set in Paris by the collective "Cadavre Exquis" (Exquisite Corpse) of the Surrealists.

Our second model is experimental and dynamic. Wai-lim Yip's theoretical essay "The Use of 'Models' in East-West Comparative Literature" emphasized that, faced with the example of a Chinese style A and a European style B, the concepts proposed by criticism do not have to omit the unique quality of the original sources:

> The answers to these questions must come from the understanding of both the historical morphology and the aesthetic structure of both models. Besides pointing out common elements between the two circles, the overlapping *C*, we must reach back to the indigenous sources of Circle *A* and *B*. Thus and only thus can we avoid the pitfalls of "commonplace comparisons" of the early East-West comparatists.[37]

Our second model tests the most widely known generic paradigms by returning to "indigenous sources." In that way it brings together and gradually transfigures theoretical thinking and historical knowledge, taken as a phase of a dialectical process (historical knowledge being a term that encompasses both spatial and temporal dissimilarities). The stylistic and periodological categories that some critics assign to Asiatic literatures may be considered from the same point of view. Tak-wai Wong and other comparatists have attributed the properties of the Baroque to the poets of the T'ang dynasty (seventh and eighth centuries), to be sure not without some misgivings and changes. And as might be expected, the famous Parry-Lord theory would inevitably be tried out in this area.[38]

According to the interpretation of Milman Parry and Albert B. Lord, the nature of "oral literature" (neither primitive, nor epic, nor popular) depends on the various uses of certain "formulas" (according to Parry's definition, "a group of words which is regularly employed under the same metrical conditions to express a given essential idea"). The discovery of the continued use in South Slavic songs of techniques of oral composition and execution found by Parry in Homeric poems led Lord to elaborate not only the idea of *formula* but also that of *theme* and, later, *type-scene*.[39] Well then, shouldn't these definitions be applicable to information coming from other eras and other latitudes? Joseph Harris, specialist in medieval Anglo-Saxon and Scandinavian poetry, thinks so. Yet neither the "theme" nor the "type-scene" can be easily found in the areas that he knows:

> It is a commonplace of the history of linguistics that the concepts and terms of Latin Grammar both stimulated and perverted the description of the

European vernaculars. In an analogous way we owe to the prestige of the "grammar" of oral poetry derived from the South Slavic heroic epic some difficulties in the analysis of other traditions, but also the very existence of the attempt.[40]

Ching-hsien Wang makes such an attempt in the area of Chinese poetry in *The Bell and the Drum: Shih Ching as Formulaic Poetry in an Oral Tradition* (1974). His meticulous analysis of this extremely ancient anthology, or "Book of Songs," dating from just before 600 B.C., has interesting results. The poems of the *Shih Ching* are presumed to have gone through a period of transition or transmission, from a first "formulaic" stage to the one we know today, suffering changes at the hands of scribes and later compilers. Perhaps this stage cannot be verified in Yugoslavia, but it can be observed in Anglo-Saxon compositions such as those of Cynewulf (ninth century): "The case of Cynewulf, for instance, may become less problematic after the study of a similar Chinese case, where it is shown that lettered poets once had recourse to oral formulas during a 'transitional period.'"[41] And going in the opposite direction, Wang maintains that the idea of composition by formulas and themes throws new light on the concept of *hsing* (an image or element that produces emotive effects),[42] an idea so often disputed by the classical Chinese theorists. What is important is that the initial proposals have evolved. The two terms of the comparison come out enriched.

Something similar is achieved by Anthony C. Yu in his study of the thematic or subgeneric dimension, shared by two monumental creations, the *Divina commedia* and *Journey to the West* (probably written in the sixteenth century by Wu Ch'êng-ên): the religious pilgrimage. Viewed from such a vantage point, the Chinese *Journey* proposes three levels of reading: as a tale of travel and adventure, as the itinerary of karma and Buddhist redemption, and as an allegory of a way of perfecting philosophical and alchemical understanding.[43] In this study, Yu successfully presents an ample and finished conception of the pilgrimage as a structure of experience common to two "worlds" as different and mutually remote—Marco Polo and Fernão Mendes Pinto notwithstanding—as were late medieval Europe and the China of the Ming dynasty. Isn't that the "dialogue of literatures" called for by Guillermo de Torre?

The usual practices and *idées reçues* of our genology are thus subjected to a severe test. To end this section, I will now mention briefly not an example—that would require knowledge that I do not possess—but a desideratum or possible scheme of reflection. A while ago, we saw that the origin of the pastoral tragicomedy of the Renaissance was the Greek and

Latin eclogue. From that eclogue (together with other sources, such as the Aesopic fable, the *synkrisis* and the *certamen,* essential in Greece and Rome, or the Lucianic dialogue) arose also the *conflictus* or medieval Latin debate and its kin in the Vulgate—*Certamen rosae lilique, Conflictus hiemis et estatis, Débat du vin et de l'eau,* and so on. The kinship with the verse debates of the Provençal troubadours—*tensó* and *joc partit*—is clear, but the relation to polemical poetry or "in two voices" forms in other languages is not so obvious. In the nineteenth century, Fauriel had already cited possible Oriental sources; and other scholars have suggested with more detail the Arabic *Munazarat* and above all—Hermann Ethé—the Persian debates.[44] Modern scholars have rejected these theses, inasmuch as the positivist idea of influence has gone into decline. And in fact the differences are enormous between a dialectical debate of an abstract or didactic type and a poem composed conjointly by two troubadours. But all this—the breakdown of the genetic theses, which at least were not provincial—does not mean that the question has to be abandoned, that is whether or not a polemic or polyphonic poetry exists in various literatures. A question that subdivides into three or four questions.

In the first place, isn't it true that poetical contests are celebrated in different cultures, above all in primitive cultures? I am referring to a real rivalry or competition, in which flesh-and-blood versemakers confront one another. Such contests, *Dichterwettstreite* or poetical competitions, did indeed exist in Greece, according to Hans Walther[45] (Menander and Philemon, who, according to legend, loved the same woman). The great Chinese writer Han Yü recounts that in January of the year 813 the Taoist Mi-ming challenged Liu Shih-fu and Hou Hsi, provoking them to improvise verses about a stone tripod that happened to be nearby (with results similar to Japanese "linked poetry").[46] I realize that such a confrontation should not be confused with the situation of two or more writers who compete by sending compositions back and forth, each intending to respond to and to outdo the other, as in the examples of certain Provençal *cuestiones de amor* (matters of love) or of the *sirvientes* that pitted Marcabru against N'Audric;[47] and, above all, some of the great Arabic satirical poets, such as Djarir (died 729) and al-Farazdaq (640?–732?), who insulted and detested each other cordially for forty years. The common dimension is the primitive belief in the magic and even lethal power of words.

Unquestionably, no culture in the Iberian peninsula is more ancient than that of the Euskadi, or Basque. Nor is there one of more extended continuity; the immemorial figure of the Basque *bersolari,* or bard, produces a form of poetry not easy to define, according to Koldo Mitxelena:

In one of its forms, perhaps the purest, it consists in witty and live improvisation. To improvise verses in Basque is not very difficult, since the language—basically suffixal—offers in certain endings an unlimited series of consonants and assonants that, if needed, are acceptable as very poor rhymes. Nevertheless, the skill that some *bersolaris* have shown in improvising on the spot is truly marvelous. The tradition goes back at least to the improvised verse dramas of the fifteenth century that Garibay talks about.[48]

In 1801 Juan Ignacio de Zabala and Txabalategui (José Joaquín de Erroicena) competed with each other in the plaza of Villabona before an audience of more than four thousand. Villabona was a neutral location, since Zabala was from Amézqueta and Txabalategui was from Hernani. Each one chose a judge; the mayor of the village was the arbitrator. According to the contract agreed upon with town officials, they sang for a set time—two hours—and the contest ended in a tie, since Fernando Amezketarra, who was also a *bersolari,* decided that "we should leave them even so that all Guipúzcoa can be glad":

> Utci bear ditugu
> Biac berdin berdin;
> Guipuzcoa guciac
> Ardezan atseguin.[49]

Both poets were illiterate. The challenges of the famous *bersolari* Vilinch (1832–1876) to Joxepa de Fuenterrabía are well known, as is Patxi Balallo's challenge to the even more famous and legendary Xenpelar (1835–1869), who used more different strophes and melodies than any other Basque versifier and knew how to steer his competition toward themes less advantageous to them. Father Antonio Zavala commented, "It is possible that between then and our own days the spirit of rivalry and aggression has diminished among the *bersolaris.*"[50]

With this polemical exercise of the poetic word as backdrop, perhaps we are in a position to understand better the *tensó* (the "debate between two troubadours," in the words of Martín de Riquer, "in which each one defends what he believes to be most just, proper, or most in accordance with his preferences,")[51] the *joc partit* or *partimen* of the Provençal troubadours (true dialectical game and tournament of poets, as in the Scholastic debates of the Middle Ages), and even those eclogues of Theocritus, of Virgil (*Eclogues* 3 and 5), in which two shepherd-poets contend with each other. The verbal altercation proper to the sagas and other works of the Scandinavian skalds—*flyting* or *senna*—belong to another category, along with the

Anglo-Saxon and Germanic cantos *(Beowulf, Nibelungenlied)*, since the contenders in these works are characters, not poets. But the *senna*—"a stylized battle of words"[52]—preserves the force as well as the formal structure of combat based on the magic or devastating and lethal power of the poetic word. So then, is it an exceptional or rather an average attitude that leads two poets to collaborate and contend with each other at the same time, participating in the composition of the same poetry? The backdrop in this case could be "choral" work, in which the voices do not express individual traits, but represent groups, ages, or sexes, as in the ancient Greek epithalamia; or the pretroubadour lyrics sung by alternating choruses, and also certain ritual songs of the Incas. In his book about Quechua poetry, Jesús Lara presents the dialogue-poem called *wawaki* that is sung in fiestas in honor of the moon or to celebrate the season of planting: "A chorus composed of individuals of one sex would begin the song, and another of the opposite sex would respond."[53]

Be that as it may, the purest examples of polyphonic poetry, written sequentially by various authors, were found in the French Midi and in Japan. Earl Miner's study of the *renga* clearly demonstrates the incomparable originality of this Japanese poetic tradition. The Provençal poems in dialogue are debates. The long sequences of the *renga* are not; although there is sometimes competition, participants in *renga* compositions try not to outshine each other; that is, they try not to sacrifice the narrative sequence or the concatenation of strophes to the brilliance of a few unique verses.[54] Then what can two arts so dissimilar have in common? I would say an extraordinary formal tension. Polemical poetry, like the polyphonic, can manifest a satirical or a didactic inclination, but also a formal one, and that to the highest degree. Everything is deduced from the knowledge of a few rules of composition shared by various writers, of the demands of a meticulous art, and of the difficulty of such a challenge. In the best Provençal poetry, as perhaps also in the Japanese, we are stirred by the verbal discipline and the unusual audacity of the form, in themselves staggering.

Goethe, puzzled by the kinship of the Persian and Arabic poems that inspired his *West-östlicher Divan*, wished to know what is lasting and persistent in the field of genres, and what evolves and disappears. His list of what he called *Dichtarten*, genres or ways of writing—allegory, ballad, song, drama, elegy, epigram, epistle, epic, tale, fable, heroic poem, idyll, didactic poem, ode, parody, novel, romance, satire[55]—was incoherent, too "external" and dependent on historical chance, Goethe thought. These categories were not to be confused with the *Naturformen der Dichtung*, natural forms of poetry, which for him continued to be the three basic ones: the epic (or narrative), the lyric, and the dramatic.

At this point it is worthwhile to draw a distinction between four basic concepts. The terminology varies and is debatable; and in practice the classes touch and intertwine, as an example will soon demonstrate. In the first place certain "radicals of presentation" (Northrop Frye's term)[56] continue to predominate; or call them radicals of communication, if you prefer, like the three that Goethe considered as natural: narration, the sung poem, representation or simulation. This tripartite mental model or theoretical scheme does not include monologic discourse, not the rhythmic, nor the sung, that is, more concretely, oratory. What is involved is a channel of communication—rhetoric—that also belongs to the sphere of orality, although its historical function consisted in providing a link between the art of speaking and the art of writing. Whether there are four channels of presentation or perhaps a larger number, they no longer seem "natural" to us today: they do not strike us as immutable and independent of cultural circumstances. However, a primordial circumstance as ancient as our first concept, narration, that through the years allows different and specialized treatment, based on a related selection of themes and forms—that is, of genres—arises from historical conditions (*longues durées,* we could say, with Fernand Braudel), conditions clearly visible from the sociological or anthropological point of view. We may then ask ourselves in the case of a specific society: What are the real paths, the viable, established radicals of communication?

On the whole, it is proper to keep postulating the most ancient channels, going back to their origins: the song accompanied by rhythm or a musical instrument, the tale told around the communal hearth, imitations or mimetic representations, persuasive discourse. But literary prose is not a modern phenomenon. Quintilian maintained that Plato was worthy of Homer because of the divine gift of his style, "eloquendi facultate divina quadam et Homerica" (*Institutio oratoria,* X.1.81). In his *Poetics* Aristotle took the "Socratic dialogues" into account (1.447b10)—that is, their manifestations in the *writing.* Some other channels, such as epistolography, historiography, philosophical or scientific reflection, would correspond to different social, didactic, or political functions of writing. One might say as much of later eras.

Modern conditions of communication, such as the printing press before Cervantes and the press since the 1700s, facilitated the development of new genres, such as the novella, the essay, and the journalistic article. Frye observed that Joseph Conrad's novels combined two unequal channels, the oral tale and the solitary act of reading the written word. In connection with "complex" arts such as opera, cinema, and television, we have already seen that the techniques of presentation and communication continue to evolve and to be enriched. What new channels might not come from technological discoveries as yet unforeseeable? Perhaps this is the moment to consider briefly the considerable space occupied today by journalism in our society and in the world of letters. Journalism provides room for a multitude of genres and subgenres: reporting, the chronicle, the background article or editorial, the interview, the "column," the brief note (or *billet*), the review. Do the prose writings of a journalist of the caliber of Francisco Umbral (Spaniard and great writer as well: inventor of anti-literature) differ from Montaigne's essays other than in the literary form? or rather, by its peculiar access to the public, by the manner in which we must read it, by its possible effects? Journalism can be as much paraliterary as authentically literary. Thus from our point of view it is characterized by its precarious nature, the frontier zone in which it operates. Writing is irreversible; and traditional literary channels favor not only reading but, above all, rereading. But it doesn't matter that journalistic writing may be irreversible, because in fact it is unrereadable. It maintains a maximum degree of reference to a specific moment, to a time that passes and flows by, and that journalistic writing cannot rise above, as a poem or a novel can. What resembles journalism most is a certain kind of oral expression (the rebuff, the defiant remark, the sermon), and so it is that a newspaper like *El país* in Madrid becomes a large daily national gabfest.

As for the second concept, *genres* proper exist—tragedy, the epic poem, the eclogue, the essay—which I will begin to describe shortly. They are all relatively specialized from the point of view of form as well as theme; however, we can still designate them with an article, thus conceding to them a substantive value: "X is *a* tragedy" or "*an* essay." Or the other way around, like Diderot: *Ceci n'est pas un conte.*

The third concept: there are certain *modes*, often as ancient and enduring as genres, but whose characters are adjectival, partial, and not adequate to encompass the entire structure of a work. They are aspects of the work, qualities, principal slants, veins that traverse it. The function of a mode is usually thematic, although the intertextual intention can also be relevant, as when we say: "This is a pastoral tragicomedy" (that is, not a poem and not a pastoral novel). Other examples of modes are irony (an almost intangible quality of a way of telling, the tone of a prose writer, of a system or period such as Romanticism), satire, the grotesque, allegory, or parody—practiced in connection with different genres.[57]

Finally, our fourth concept: it is customary to designate as *forms,* in the most generally accepted use of the term, the traditional methods of inter-relation, arrangement, or limitation of a piece of writing, such as conventions of versification, division into chapters, disposition of the chronology, use of scenes or summaries in a narration, intercalation, repetition, dynamic, or circular structures. The next chapter will be devoted to these topics. Some readers may think that the morphology mentioned here is often confused with genology or with the thematic dimensions of literature. And I concede that such confusions do indeed occur throughout a spectrum of differentiation that only critical analysis—being also successive—compels us to simplify. For example, where should we place the structures of narrative arguments (the basic *plots,* studied by Peter Brooks)?[58] The passage of a form to a genre, or of a genre to a form, is in itself a historical event, as in the case of the development during the Renaissance of the dialogue and the sonnet, which later evolved into genres. When is a sonnet something more than a form, a highly arranged invitation to brevity, a tightened complex of tensions, always ready at hand? During the Renaissance the love sonnet, or cycle of love sonnets, definitely became a genre. Antonio García Berrio has shown that the thematic space of a sonnet, like its formal space, can be defined structurally.[59] And, *mutatis mutandis,* when a thematic mode adheres to a formal mold in a relatively stable manner, engendering a prestigious model, a genre appears and takes root. Such is the trajectory of the satirical *sermo* in Rome (the satire in verse), whose flip side, the moral epistle, we will observe now. Here is a class of divagation or development that can be clarified only by meticulous historical study.

Let us note right away that in effect forms are usually partial. That is, they are what one might call "formal elements," such as the dialogue that emerges as one more component in a specific time or place of this or that genre: in an epic poem, a romance, a ballad, a tale, a novel, an essay, even in a theatrical work (which does not always coincide with the dialogue). But when the dialogue becomes a totalizing form, it can perhaps be said that we have a form in search of a genre. That was what happened during the sixteenth century after Baldassare Castiglione, Erasmus, or León Hebreo, or in Spain after Juan de Valdés, Pero Mexía, or fray Luis de León. In reality, at such times we are dealing with intraformal elements: relations that surface in the midst of other relations.

When reading the verse epistles of the Renaissance—probably the most brilliant moment in the history of this genre: Clément Marot, Sir Thomas Wyatt, Garcilaso de la Vega, Sá de Miranda, Francisco de Aldana, John

Donne, "La epístola moral a Fabio"—we must keep in mind two constituent circumstances: the letter in verse is in Horace a contragenre of satirical
poetry; and we find at one and the same time a genre and a channel of
presentation.

These two characteristics mark the itinerary of epistolary poetry in Europe. Alfred North Whitehead once said that European philosophy was a
footnote to the thought of Plato. It is hardly an exaggeration to say that the
letter in verse is a footnote to Horace's accomplishments and influence. For
the writer of these lines, the interesting part of the matter is that something
so elemental, so widespread, so omnipresent as the writing of letters should
turn into epistolary poetry, the only one that we have and know about, not
as a result of some inexorable law of the human brain, but because of the
precise influence of a Roman writer born in Venusa in 65 b.c. It is not
necessary to choose between necessity and contingency: everything happened the way it happened rather than in a different manner, thanks to this
contingency.

What is characteristic of the genre developed by Horace is the persistent
and functional social practice of sending and receiving letters, already so
important in the Mediterranean world before Christ; to say it in another
way, letters were a channel of presentation. There are an infinite number of
poems—in the West and in the East—that might be called "dedications";
that is, they evoke a vivid image of someone: a person admired or remembered, a powerful person, an enemy; obvious examples are the mouth of
Cassandra, the eyes of Elsa, and the waves of Lisi's hair. But the poetical
letter is presented just like a letter, as something *written*. We are dealing
with a poem that does not pretend to be anything other than an act of
writing—what is more, nothing but the humble, primitive transition from
oral communication to writing, exemplified by the composing of a letter.
Perhaps for this reason the literary epistle, cultivated in two of the ancient
civilizations of the Mediterranean, might in later eras seem to us like a
survival of the decisive hinge that joined and also separated the spoken
word and the written word. The verse epistle would preserve (with very
lively and lucid theoretical awareness) the conventions of this channel of
communication.[60] Think of the epistles of the Renaissance, like the "Epístola a Arias Montano" by Francisco de Aldana (1537–1578), perhaps the
best of the Castilian epistles. A verse epistle is *not lyric* poetry; it was never
"sung," nor could it be sung. Even so, Aldana, who is an uneven poet in the
best sense of the word, has moments when his language rises and even
soars:

Aquellos ricos amontonamientos
de sobrecelestiales inflüencias
dilatados de amor descubrimientos . . .
aquellos, ¿qué diré?, colmos favores,
privanzas nunca oídas, nunca vistas,
suma especialidad de bien de amores,
¡Oh grandes, oh riquísimas conquistas
de las Indias de Dios, de aquel gran mundo
tan escondido a las mundanas vistas!

Those splendid accumulations
of ultraheavenly influences,
far-flung discoveries of love . . .
Those—dare I say?—overwhelming favors,
unheard-of boons, unknown till now,
supremely special goodness, especial love.
Oh the great *conquistas,* richest of all,
of God's own Indies, of that cosmos vast,
concealed so long from mortal eyes!

But the most successful verses are perhaps those in which the poet confirms that he has written an epistle by signing the poem as if he were signing a letter:

Nuestro Señor en ti su gracia siembre
para coger la gloria que promete.
De Madrid a los siete de setiembre
mil y quinientos y setenta y siete.

God in thee His grace implant,
So mayst thou reap His promised heaven.
Done at Madrid, this seventh of September,
fifteen hundred and seventy-seven.[61]

Final curtain of unquestionable poetic efficacy. Something so fleeting, unique, perhaps without any significance, like a date, a city that one happens to be passing through, a farewell—mere *événement,* Lévi-Strauss would say—is preserved forever. The localization is indeed meaningful. The poem as a declared written communication, antilyrical, is still poetry. The tension and the skill of the best verse epistles rest on that fact, on their approximation to prose, as well as on other aspects, also substantial, of the letter as a form of individual and social relation as suggested, for example, by the first line of Donne's epistle "To Sir Henry Wotton":

Sir, more than kisses, letters mingle souls . . .

A line that Pedro Salinas cited in his stupendous "Defensa de la carta misiva" (In Defense of the Letter; the first chapter of *El defensor*, 1948).

One should also point out the antigeneric character of the verse epistle; it has intertwined irresistibly with satirical poetry since the time of Horace. Read again with care the first of Horace's *Epistulae*, and you will see that the contrast satire/epistle will affirm all his human feeling. I will quote only the beginning. As in the initial poems of his earlier works, the odes and satires, the poet's words are directed to Maecenas:

> Prima dicte mihi, summa dicende Camena,
> spectatum satis et donatum iam rude quaeris,
> Maecenas, iterum antiquo me includere ludo?
> Non eadem est aetas, non mens.

Addressed in my first song Camena [the muse who dedicated the remaining books to Maecenas] and being addressed in my last song, do you, Maecenas, seek to involve me once again in the ancient game, after I have been satisfactorily approved as a gladiator and have already been granted a wooden rapier upon retirement? My age is not the same as it was then, nor my mind.[62]

Essential, and of an impressive simplicity, the partial fourth line: "Non eadem est aetas, non mens." That is, don't ask me to go back to my old tricks, because my age is different, and my mind as well . . . From this confession or attitude comes not only the first Epistula but also all that follow. Maturity—in those days, old age—was no longer content with the condemnation of the errors and foolishness of others, the negative gesture, the pride implicit in making fun. In other words, man cannot live by satire alone. The mature poet must seek the good and the true, undertaking the road of moral philosophy. The author of the Epistula is the ex-satirical poet.

> Nunc itaque et versus et cetera ludicra pono,
> quid uerum atque decens, curo et rogo et omnis in hoc sum.

And now I put down both my verses and my other foolish sports. What I care for, inquire after, and am totally involved in is whatever is true and morally fitting. (Lines 10-11)

Elias Rivers in his fundamental study of Garcilaso's "Epístola a Boscán" (1534) elucidated the general characteristics of the "moral epistle" originating with Horace, above all the extremely important role of friendship: framework, situation, and relation with an addressee that permits and requires the joint search for the "good and the true" on a relatively intimate and concrete plane.[63] It concerns masculine friendships. Horace writes to a young male friend—not a female friend—whom he tries to guide without giving him too much advice, saying "we" whenever possible. The moral epistle infuses real or existential life into abstract ideas through friendship, making ethical thought accessible to the addressee, the reader, to the limited existence of a single person. But friendship also suggests, at least in Horace and his successors, what remains outside, ambiances and places that the friends reject. The search for truth responds to something that is not truth. The transcendence of satire through friendship must be repeated in every new poem. And perhaps in order to reach moral truth, awareness of the lie is absolutely necessary, the memory of social scandal and of that minimum of anger needed to keep wisdom from veering too far from the world of men.

At the core of each of the *Epistulae* there is usually one of those satirical counterblows. Countless readers will have appreciated those seesaw motions, the contrasts, the relapses that characterize the art of Horace and his tradition (the form called "climactic and anticlimactic" in the odes of fray Luis de León, to use Dámaso Alonso's description).[64] The poetic phenomenon is presented like a chain of opposites and polarities. The contrast "satirical principle/epistolary principle" is nothing more than the broadest of the polarities that constantly configure the *sermo* (talk or conversation) of Horace as well as that of his Renaissance imitators. I have already pointed out elsewhere the surprising appearance of some satirical verses in Garcilaso's "Epístola a Boscán."[65] A poet of the same generation, Sir Thomas Wyatt (1503–1542), introduced some compositions in *terza rima* into English, inextricably mixing satire and the moral epistle, as in "Mine own John Poins . . . ," itself a reworking of one of the satires published in Luigi Alamanni's *Opere toscane* (1532–33):

> I am not now in France to judge the wine,
> With sav'ry sauce those delicates to feel,
>
> Nor yet in Spain where one must him incline,
> Rather than to be, outwardly to seem.
> I meddle not with wits that be so fine . . .

And Wyatt ends with a smooth allusion not only to a "retiring life" in the style of Horace, *cum litteris*—with books and good friends—but also to an England that, quite distinct from the Catholic countries, is merely Christian:

> But here I am in Kent and Christendom,
> Among the Muses, where I read and rhyme;

Where, if thou list, my Poins, for to come,
Thou shalt be judge how I do spend my time.[66]

The epistles of Clément Marot (1496–1544) are well known; they brim over with wit, naturalness, and vivacity. But Marot is much more than a facile poet. And the poetry of his maturity displays a classicism of real excellence. Read, for example, *Epître* LVI, "A un sien ami" (François Noël, gentleman of Bellegarde), where, "Loin des tumultes et loin des plaisirs courts" (Far from the tumult and far from fleeting pleasures), the principal motifs of the genre meet: friendship, stimulus, and framework of the poem; disdain for the court; attachment to a group of literary friends; the *aurea mediocritas;* and the praise of poetry that will make the name of the author eternal and conquer death, "la fausse lice" (that false bitch):

Et tant que oui et nenni se dira
Par l'univers, le monde me lira.
Toi donc aussi, que as savoir et veine
De la liqueur d'Hélicon toute plaine
Ecris, et fais que Mort, la fausse lice,
Rien que le corps de toi n'ensevelisse.

For as long as yes and no will be said
Throughout the universe will I be read.
You too, then, who have knowledge and a vessel brimming
with the elexir of Helicon
Write, and do such that Death, the false bitch,
Bury only your body.[67]

The theme of friendship surrounding the whole poem affects its tone, style, and pace. Indeed, some conventions are usually connected with a distinct genre that announce it, mark or identify it—conventions of a formal type, such as the easygoing tone and apparent improvisation of the *sermo* in the epistle, as well as its thematic character, as we just saw.

And now let us make two more observations before concluding this brief sketch of the poetical letter. First, let us ask ourselves: How wide a stylistic latitude does it take in? From ancient times on, the letter covers a whole range, from the familiar to the exalted. That is, it is innovative and heterodox inasmuch as it fails to adhere to the stylistic specialization (*Stiltrennung*) that operated until the eighteenth century, according to Auerbach. And second, what function does it fulfill? (Theory obliges.) I would say, a prenovelistic function. But let me make clear that I am not referring to sources or filiations. During the Renaissance the epistle followed impulses that would later converge in the novel: the infusion of individuality, autobiographical desire, the theoretical awareness of its own course, the profusion of things, openness to the humble and the daily circumstances of life.

From such a point of view the comparative critic approaches the perspective of the writer who is free to choose between the models of his time and of earlier times, while keeping in mind a plurality of paradigms. There is no reason for a comparatist to be someone who merely classifies and simplifies. Ilse Nolting-Hauff calls Quevedo's *El sueño de la muerte* (The Dream of Death) a "narrated comedy." And in addition, "into the *Sueños* have entered elements of dialogue of the dead, of humanist discourse, of comedy (of the *entremés*, but above all the autosacramental), and, finally, of the sermon and the ascetic tract."[68] To which one could add satire and vision. It is true that the plurigeneric talent of Don Francisco de Quevedo (a *poeta "largo"* if there ever was one) is exceptional in Western literature. (Another exception would be Goethe.) Quevedo tried his hand at an almost infinite variety of forms. What genres and what forms did his insatiable writing *not* allow? Not the epic poem (but burlesque, yes), not tragedy (but its tone and style, in the glosses of Jeremiah's *Lamentations*, yes), and not the pastoral novel (but poetry, yes).

Aside from these omissions, Quevedo cultivated in verse nothing more than *canzone, silva, octava, décima,* romance, *jácara* (ribald street song), satire, epistle, fable, epigram, rondel, gloss, eulogy, epithalamium, dirge, elegy, epitaph, threnody, idyll, madrigal, hymn, Pindaric ode, psalm, riddle, sonnet cycles, and so on; and, in prose, treatise, discourse, dialogue, Menippean satire, sermon or homily, biography, aphorism, picaresque novel, and more. In addition, Quevedo opened writing to as many avenues of communication as were available in the society of his time: laws, documents, decrees, interpretations of laws, briefs, lists of tariffs, capitulations, pacts or treaties—all that language copies from the power of the state and its principal institutions. Because it is a matter of language, above all. Quevedo was faithful to the classical concordance of a certain level or verbal class that goes with a distinct genre. The multiplicity of generic models provided Quevedo with the spur he needed to persist in his tireless exploration of the language, to wrest himself violently from the inertia of the given and the lived; thus freed from a detested reality left far behind, he embarked on his long and fabulous verbal voyage.

Intertextual contextures are also found in Quevedo, multiple allusions occurring in the same literary work, a phenomenon becoming more common with each passing day in contemporary literature. Of course the intergeneric creation par excellence is the novel, as was already pointed out years ago by Friedrich Schlegel in "Gespräch über die Poesie." And that was true from the very beginning when Cervantes included in *Don Quixote* poetry, discourse, the Italian-style novella, the traditional tale, pastoral ambience, the story with a Moorish theme, the exotic voyage (such as *Viaje de Turquía,* 1599), the precepts of conduct (proper for *Galatea:* the advice to Sancho, II.42), the allusions to the picaresque, the dialogue about poetics (I.47), the letter, the vision (the cave of Montesinos, II.23), and if I am not mistaken, even historiography (certain pages of the story of the captive captain, I.39).

This generic pluralism of the novel is evident and well known. What characterizes Bakhtin's view is not merely the amplitude that he concedes to such diversity, but also the inclination to find something like an opening to the external and real world in it, a gateway for forms that are not considered literature, or at least not cultivated literature. For Bakhtin the relevance of genres that he calls extraliterary—confessions, diaries, letters, articles—arises from this attitude. Since a novel is constructed in an area bordering on contemporary society, it takes on the look of the society, becomes multicolored and inconclusive, as we read in his essay "Epic and Novel." The novelist often crosses the frontier separating fiction from real historical experience; and so a way is opened allowing frank political declarations, or confessions as "a 'cry of the soul' that has not yet found its formal contours." [69] In Rabelais, powerful popular, playful, and critical currents mingle, those at home in the street, the plaza, the fairs, or in Carnival celebrations. The polygeneric element of the novel, we read in Bakhtin's "Discourse in the Novel," is linked to its essentially plurilingual expression:

> [Inserted genres] serve the basic purpose of introducing heteroglossia *into* the novel, of introducing an era's many and diverse languages. Extraliterary genres (the everyday genres, for example) are incorporated into the novel not in order to "ennoble" them, to "literarize" them, but for the sake of their very extraliterariness, for the sake of their potential for introducing non-literary language (or even dialects) into the novel. It is precisely this very multiplicity of the era's languages that must be represented in the novel. [70]

The concept of heteroglossia is perhaps Bakhtin's most interesting idea, one that can without doubt be applied to the novel, either to the core of a single novel (Benito Pérez Galdós) or to the whole of the work of a narrator (I am thinking of the temper and mastery of Miguel Delibes, who assigns different registers to different works). Well then, is heteroglossia not also to be found in other genres? not only in the plays but also in the poetry of Lope de Vega? And can we not include Quevedo as well?

The reader will know of modern, even ultramodern examples that open the narrative to the entire range of channels, forms, styles, and genres that have been or are to come—even the collages of William Burroughs and Julio Cortázar's narrations, which can be arranged according to the whim of the reader. But there are also poetic collages, as we have already seen: Eliot's *The Waste Land,* Pound's *Cantos.* This breaking away from norms and the search for a nonliterary, extraofficial language: isn't the end result surrealism? One of Cortázar's characters in *Rayuela* (1963; translated into English as *Hopscotch*), expressing an attitude close to surrealism, points out the limits of a liberating strategy reduced to language:

> It's not a question of the job of verbal liberation. The surrealists thought that true language and true reality were censored and relegated by the rationalist and bourgeois structure of the Western world. They were right, as any poet knows, but . . . Language means residence in a reality, living in a reality . . . Wanting to free it from its taboos isn't enough.[71]

That is, not many more things are lacking except "to arrive at something else," "to touch a more authentic bottom," as Jaime Alazraki explains in his study of the poetics of the "neofantastic" in Cortázar. "Understood in this way, the fantastic no longer represents an evasion or an imaginative digression of reality but, on the contrary, rather a form of penetrating reality at a point beyond the systems that fix it in an order that in literature we recognize as 'realism,' but that in epistomological terms is defined in our rationalistic apprehension of reality."[72]

We are beginning to see that it is difficult to practice generic, stylistic, and thematic criticism simultaneously, as Bakhtin did. Does the plural character of the novel bring us closer to the world? But to what world? what worlds? The intergeneric element of the modern novel (or its plurality of languages and dialects) does not necessarily imply a critical or extraofficial vision of society. But the surrender to the imagination, in Julio Cortázar or Gabriel García Márquez, for example, can indeed carry us to a true subversion of our regular way of seeing things. The thematic influence of the genre has its limits. There exist, indeed, a realistic poetry, and a theater of the absurd, and fantastic stories, and, now, neofantastic novels.

Years ago Romanticism, as exemplified in works by Goethe, Byron, and Pushkin, had already combined narration, drama, and poetry. Frederik Paludan-Müller, who knew the work of Goethe and Byron well, presented in his *Adam Homo* a novel in Danish *ottava rima*. Bakhtin always considered *Eugene Onegin* to be a novel, without paying much attention to the verse in which it was written. In effect, criticism is treading on very shaky ground here. Note that linking genres (such as the novella and the pastoral tale) or fusing channels of presentation (such as narration and drama) is not the same thing as writing in verse or not, or writing in prose or not. (Aristotle already emphasized that the only thing that Homer and Empedocles had in common was that they wrote in verse; *Poetics* 1.447a18). This last distinction is not of primary concern to us here; since ancient times, drama as well as narration could be composed in either mode. Alfonso Reyes, a great and authentic comparatist, makes a very useful distinction between the "formal" functions in literature—drama, narration, poetry, or rather Goethe's *Naturformen der Dichtung*—and what he calls "material" functions, that is, prose and verse. According to his terminology, either of the two material functions could be related to the three formal functions; and thus we have a novel in verse (*Hermann und Dorothea,* Byron's *Don Juan, Eugène Onegin, Adam Homo*); drama juxtaposing prose and verse (Shakespeare); story juxtaposing prose and verse (al-Hamadani's Arabic *maqāmāt*) (anthologies), *Aucassin et Nicolette,* Jacobo Sannazaro, Cervantes' *Galatea*); poetry juxtaposed with prose and verse (Dante's *Vita nuova,* according to Reyes); prose poems; and so on. According to Reyes, José de Espronceda's *El estudiante de Salamanca* (1840) is a story in verse in no way comparable to the authentic conjunction of narration and dramatic dialogue present in the cycle of the *Celestina* and in Lope's *Dorotea*.[73] These examples are debatable, but it is indeed clear that the relation between genre and prose or verse is an extremely variable historical convention.

After the liberation brought about by Romanticism, these conjunctions would again be put into practice, as we have just observed. The narrative channel tends to be confounded with the dramatic in some of the later novels of Galdós, such as *El abuelo* (1897; The Grandfather), a novel in dialogue, but not meant to be staged since the author would have been obliged to reduce the number of characters and scenes for the theater of 1904. In the prologue to his novel, Galdós wrote the following words concerning genres:

> Although by its structure and division into acts and scenes *El abuelo* seems to be a theatrical work, I have not hesitated to call it a novel, without giving to the terms an absolute value; in this case, as in all that belongs to the infinite realm of Art, the most prudent course is to flee from catalogue-type classifications of genres and forms. In each novel where the characters speak throbs a dramatic work. A theatrical work is nothing more than the

condensation and coupling of all that which in the modern novel consists of actions and characters.[74]

Today, examples of multigeneric communication are legion, though not always interesting. One such work that is indeed very interesting is Maria Velho da Costa's *Casas pardas* (1978; Dark Houses), in which the channels are constantly changing, being juxtaposed vertically, including poems in English and in Castilian, a three-act comedy, as well as fables, monologues, and a piece called *Little Women* that has the following footnote: "Title of a romance for young ladies-in-waiting by Henrik Ibsen." In his *Introducción a la literatura* (1979) Andrés Amorós recalls various examples of works he denotes as *fronterizos* (frontier works) that are characteristic of the tendency nowadays to blur the dividing lines between the genres: the poetical novel of Ramón Pérez de Ayala, the *greguería* of Ramón Gómez de la Serna, the "new journalism" (close to fiction), as well as the *Jardín de las delicias* (Garden of Delights) of Francisco Ayala, which brings together stories, memories, and prose poems.[75]

It is also useful to keep in mind that there are authors who fight, so to speak, against the genre they are using by injecting it with antibodies. Not all genres live peacefully in the center of a single work unless the integrity of the whole is called into question—or literature itself as tradition and institution. That is precisely what the avant-garde seeks to do. There are conventions and traditions that crash and collide with one another. Then the genre includes a contragenre within itself. In the itinerary of the novel of the nineteenth century—starting with Balzac himself—it is not rare to discover a certain incompatibility between the "existential" inclination of the genre on the one hand and, on the other, an obstinate taste for the "essentialism" of gnomic writing, of moral aphorisms or maxims, in the manner of Vauvenargues, Saint-Simon, or La Rochefoucauld.[76] In the tradition of the novel, ideas are usually occurrences—in more than one of the accepted meanings of this word—inseparable from the sinuous and changing evolution of certain concrete personalities. For example, how can one reconcile the posture of Cervantes with that of Baltasar Gracián in the same work? The Portuguese novelist Agustina Bessa Luís constantly deals with this challenge in narrations such as *A sibila* (1954; The Sibyl) and *Fanny Owen* (1981), works so morally tense and intense. A tension above all between real-life men and real-life women—not at all models—and our necessity to understand Man, or to know Woman, through this novelist's art so brimful of wit and ingenuity. One might make a similar comment about the last stories of Albert Camus.

This disturbing presence of antibodies within the novelistic body is a generic phenomenon. What happens when the channels of presentation are intermixed? An event far from rare, as we have just pointed out: dramatic dialogue (but not theater) and story, epistolography and story (the epistolary novel), reportage and narration (Euclides de Cunha), lyric poetry and essay (the "prophetic" poet: T. S. Eliot), and even theater and cinema: a brief movie is projected at the end of Carlos Fuentes' *Orquídeas a la luz de la luna* (1982; Orchids by the Light of the Moon),[77] though within the framework of a theatrical representation, that is, with complete subordination of one channel to the other. Is such a subordination the norm when the channels are combined?

Milan Kundera's novel *Kniha smíchu a zapomnění* (1978; translated into English as *The Book of Laughter and Forgetting*) invites such questions. The book begins as follows: "In February 1948, Communist leader Klement Gottwald stepped out on the balcony of a Baroque palace in Prague to address the hundreds of thousands of his fellow citizens packed into Old Town Square."[78] Next we encounter a subsection of the chapter that is a brief commentary or historical essay. The next subsection introduces a fictitious character called Mirek, and so on. A historical-political essay and fiction follow one another, in alternating fashion, throughout the length of the aptly named *Book*. The experiment is surprising and fascinating because it is not a matter of moral maxims or of the mere intervention of the narrator, in the manner of a Dickens or—with special intensity—of a Robert Musil in *Der Mann ohne Eigenschaften* (1930; translated into English as *The Man without Qualities*). In the first place, Musil's narrator-moralist talks to us about the fictitious characters of the novel (his commentaries are not "extra-diegetic," we could say with Gérard Genette); and in the second place, it seems that in this case there is no insoluble conflict between the narrative voice that tells a story and the gnomic voice that comments on human behavior. But what Kundera is searching for affects the voice of the narrator to such a degree that we usually consider the postures of the storyteller and of the historian to be radically different. Neither the traditional historical novel, à la Manzoni, nor the partially political novel, as in Malraux or Sartre, or the Cortázar of *Libro de Manuel* (translated into English as *Manual for Manuel*) allows such amplitude to the writer's voice from the very beginning. Kundera's characters do not have to hold political opinions, because their behavior is the result of a political atmosphere that dominates and corrupts everything. And at the same time, things happen today that are so unbelievable, grotesque, brutal, laughable, and unforgettable that, when we are faced with them, our conception of what constitutes fiction collapses.

In a word, genology enjoys good health at the present time.[79] The misgiv-

ings of Benedetto Croce, whose writings we still read with the greatest interest, have lost their efficacy inasmuch as our methods today (the six points
sketched at the beginning of this chapter) open a path for us that was
blocked for him. And in my judgment, nobody is better equipped than the
comparatist to examine certain collective categories—genres, channels, and
modes—which for the most part are of an international or supranational
type. The most ancient genres, such as tragedy,[80] and the more enduring
modes, such as the pastoral—a river of literature that goes underground
and then comes to the surface again later, as Renato Poggioli demonstrates
in his exemplary commentary *The Oaten Flute* (1975)[81]—keep providing
room for significant studies. Under the auspices of the ICLA, several volumes are being published that configure a *histoire comparée des littératures
européennes*. Groups of specialists, working in all European languages, are
thoroughly investigating precise fields and genres. For example, the theater
from the end of the eighteenth and the beginning of the nineteenth centuries
has been studied under the direction of Roger Bauer.[82] Not surprisingly the
scholars are concentrating above all on those "new" genres whose growth
and development from some centuries ago to the present day pose the most
suggestive questions from a historical and theoretical point of view. I am
referring to those most predominant genres, exemplified by Montaigne and
Cervantes, that emerged during the essential era of renovation of models in
the sixteenth and seventeenth centuries: the essay, ignored by critics for a
long time;[83] and naturally the novel, whose theoretical delimitation has
been a stimulating metacritical theme by itself for some sixty years now.[84]
Georg Lukács' *Theorie des Romans* was published as a book in 1920. And
equally valuable is the large array of genres, for the most part developed
after the sixteenth century, that contemporary criticism is able to present to
us, such as tragicomedy, the epistolary novel, the book of maxims, the idyll,
the didactic or descriptive poem, the utopian novel, the gothic novel;[85] and
also autobiography, the historical novel, melodrama, the story or novella
(called in Spain *costumbrismo*, in France *roman à thèse*), the intimate diary,
the detective story, the fantastic story, and the prose poem.[86]

13

Forms: Morphology

We have just seen that genres are conventional models, and that in order to examine them we must pay equal attention to thematic as well as to formal elements. For example, the picaresque novel in general entails not only the life of an orphan, inwardly estranged from society and outwardly a coward or opportunist, but also the autobiographical form; the *pícaro* himself is the one who tells the tale. That being so, it is quite clear that any action of a reader-critic carries a certain degree of duplicity embedded within. On the one hand, we declare that the thematic and the formal aspects are inseparable; at the same time, we in fact separate them so that we may formulate statements of some sort or another about them. The autobiography of the *pícaro* is not like any other, since it evokes the ancient aporias of Chrysippus the Stoic (Epimenides the Cretan states that all Cretans lie, and so on): the picaresque novel is the confession of a liar. We may entertain such a thought because at a certain moment in the reading we isolate the pseudoautobiographical form and at the same time recall what the form has in common not with the picaresque novel in general but with the *Confessions* of Saint Augustine, the *Fiammetta* of Boccaccio, or the *Life* of Saint Theresa. We simultaneously tear apart and put back together, cut and sew, ravel and reweave. The vision of the reader is double: partial and at the same time unifying.

The complete freedom of the reader rests on the exercise of such a vision, even though it is necessarily often only partial throughout a series of perceptions. And the disagreements that confront critics—each attached to his or her respective restrictions—tend only to suppress this freedom of the reader, and, more than freedom, that kind of free will that Cervantes so generously offered to the "Idling Reader" in the prologue of *Don Quixote,* not asking the reader to excuse him for the faults of ". . . this book . . . the child of my brain":

> . . . you are neither relative nor friend but may call your soul your own and exercise your free judgment. You are in your own house where you are master as the king is of his taxes, for you are familiar with the saying, "Under my cloak I kill the king." All of which exempts and frees you from any kind of respect or obligation; you may say of this story whatever you choose without fear of being slandered for an ill opinion any more than you will be rewarded for a good one.[1]

In the history of literary criticism, what critics are rewarded or slandered for usually changes in accordance with various eras, schools, and passions. But it seems that the subject of this chapter, forms, or, more accurately stated, the moments when we isolate, identify, and judge them, has often had a bad press—even a bad conscience—in various eras and civilizations. And yet, what attentive or sensitive reader has not experienced such moments? E. R. Curtius recalled that innumerable students learned Latin by translating Virgil's first Eclogue. When we come to the fifth line, "formosam resonare doces Amaryllida silvas" (teaching the woods to echo "Amaryllis" beautiful), how many have not been deeply stirred by such a prodigy of vowel harmony? Here we have, without any doubt, one of the incentives for translation; for example, that of Clément Marot (1532), who managed to reproduce some of Virgil's assonances, based on the *a* and the *i:* "la tienne amie Amarillis la belle."[2] But closer examination would surely show also that Virgil's harmony, like any other supposedly pure form, is naturally not lacking in meaning.

There are no pure forms. That is, there are no insignificant forms. Let us take a brief look at one example: digression. In a certain work a writer produces a text of type A, then suddenly interrupts himself and goes on a detour, before returning to A or going on with some coherent transition to B. The digression as such, the author's decision to present to us, suddenly or even capriciously, an *x* alien to the context of the work we are reading, might seem merely a shift in direction with no special significance. But, no sir! Whoever starts going around Robin Hood's barn has felt the urge to do so. Even before asking ourselves what might be the *x* content of the digression or diversion that cut and abandoned text A, we surmise that the intention alone of the digression to free itself from A, to go off on a tangent, to trans-form itself, is meaningful. How many meanings might be attached to such a desire for change! It is no less true that change in such a case is an open phenomenon, whose real resolution we do not know and which may lead to the most varied outcomes. And this accessibility is characteristic of forms. It is also true that if digression may signify many things, it may not signify *nothing*. The ancient rhetoricians understood this fact very well when they recommended digression as a procedure that provokes "distraction," *ex taedio aliquid detrahere,*[3] and much though digression might entertain the audiences in the Forum, it could also help to persuade. That is Cicero's explanation in *De oratore* (III.3). Swift's use of digression is without doubt rhetorical in *A Tale of a Tub,* in which digressions take up various entire chapters. In one, titled "A Digression in Praise of Digressions," Swift writes: " 'tis manifest, the society of writers would quickly be reduced to a very inconsiderable number, if men were put upon making books with the fatal confinement of delivering nothing beyond what is to the purpose." Swift enjoyed the freedom digressions gave him in his writing; he used them in the face of the classical canons of continuity and decorum, which places him in the company of the "Moderns." However, digressions are ineffective if a coherent structure is not in place on which they can rest, or from which they can differ. A chaotic collection of fragments cannot be called digression. Sheldon Sacks has shown that Fielding's digressions may be regarded as true digressions from the point of view of the action narrative, but not if they are seen as apologues or commentaries based on moral ideas—"as ethical comment on the actions of the important characters in the novel."[4] In sum, digression is semi-independent; it may also fulfill a number of other functions, depending on the occasion; but it is never a vacuum, an indifferent formula, an outline without body or volume.

Forms exist in the same way that themes and genres exist. If we call the moment when we perceive and study forms "formalistic," no serious, integrating reading could forgo such a moment. Geoffrey Hartman writes: "There are many ways to transcend formalism, but the worst is not to study forms."[5] The reason is that formalism has often been taken to mean a tendency to investigate forms of an excluding, exclusive type, apparently a more reprehensible activity than specialization in themes (called in Italy *contenutismo*), inasmuch as such formalism is thought to separate us from reality in a precious and excessive manner. Later we will see to what extent the same thing happens with themes as well. Here it may suffice to recall that an interest in forms does not necessarily imply the complete autonomy of a single work of art in relation to other works, or to society. In the

Aristotelian tradition, to which we owe everything in this field, there is no form without matter; and the relation uniting them is dynamic, temporal, "processual." In other words, we would regard such a relation today as inconceivable without active and willed human intervention. Forms do not divide but unite. Within them pulses the history as well as the "evolution" of literature, as Yuri Tynyanov wrote. That is the idea articulated by the Russian Formalists with such exceptional keenness.

In his celebrated essay "Art as Process," when the idea of "defamiliarization" or estrangement (*ostranenie*) was launched, Viktor Shklovsky was already suggesting that the characteristic procedures of a work of verbal art did not only simply configure that art but also transformed, deformed, or reformed earlier usages. The context of the phenomenon of defamiliarization seemed to be triple: the work itself, the vital or habitual experience of the contemporary reader, and the customs of earlier literature. According to Shklovsky, Pushkin's contemporaries, for example, were surprised and even shocked by the contrast between the relaxed manner of his poetic language and Deržavin's elegant style. The order of the columns of a Greek temple, never exactly even, "disorders" the earlier arrangements in a way impossible to systematize, as rhythm "disorders" poetry: "since in reality it is not a matter of complicating the rhythm but of disordering it—a disorder that cannot be predicted."[6] In his important article "The Literary Fact" (1924) Tynyanov insisted that any attempt to isolate a literary work is absurd. What catapults a work into a "literary fact," from an earlier status as marginal document, is the new relation established with a different historical system. "If we isolate a literary work or an author, we will not be able to penetrate the individuality of the author."[7] And in "On Literary Evolution" (1927), Tynyanov added that the "constructive function" of the components of a work has two tendencies: in the "autofunction," components establish relations with a similar series belonging to other systems; while the "synfunction" inclination connects with other elements of the selfsame system and work.[8] The dynamism of the literary evolution thus remains involved in the construction of a unique poem. Fredric Jameson explains that in this way a path is opened for a new conception of literary history:

> Not that of some profound continuity of tradition characteristic of idealistic history, but one of history as a series of abrupt discontinuities, of ruptures with the past, where each new literary present is seen as a break with the dominant artistic canons of the generation immediately preceding . . . The formalists saw this perpetual change, this artistic permanent revolution, as being inherent in the nature of artistic form itself, which, once

striking and fresh, grows stale and must be replaced by the new in unfore-
seen and unforeseeable manners.[9]

According to Jameson, this formulation was already latent in the idea of
ostranenie.[10] Certainly the thinking of the Formalists themselves evolved
and—while possible—was enriched over the years. A significant modification of this itinerary is represented by the step from the concept of "procedure" (*priem*)—from the mere cataloguing and amassing of procedures—
to the concept of "function," integrated into a complex of functions. From
this second point of view, Douwe Fokkema writes, "a work of literature is
not an accumulation of devices but an organized whole, made up of factors
of varying importance."[11] Thus we find here the beginnings of a *historical
structuralism* based on the perception of the innovating force of forms.

Now turning our attention to forms and themes, let us undertake a type
of analysis that implies partiality. The partiality, however, does not appear
all of a sudden, but instead is usually a disjunction that occurs during the
act of reading. Dámaso Alonso rightly describes this choice of focus as a
progressive approximation that can follow opposite paths: toward the form
from the theme, or toward the theme from the form. It is what he calls
"exterior form" and "interior form" in *Poesía española* (1950):

> The "form" does not affect only the signifier, nor only the signified, but the
> relationship of the two. It is, then, the concept that from the side of literary
> creation corresponds to the Saussurian "sign." The analysis . . . allows us
> to see in the "form" two perspectives. We understand by "exterior form"
> the relationship between signifier and signified, in the perspective from the
> first toward the second. That same relationship, but in the perspective from
> the signified toward the signifier, is what we call "interior form."[12]

The most recent theoretical paradigms help to clarify these age-old problems to the extent that they emphasize the moment of reading. Especially
since the appearance of Michael Riffaterre's *Essais de stylistique structurale*
(1971) and his subsequent books, a great deal has been written concerning
the decisive contribution of the reader to the molding of stylistic and formal
effects, or what Riffaterre calls "conventional forms."[13] It is important here
to guard against assigning a closed, massive, "ontological" value to such
elements, oppositions, or interrelations. The *permanence du message* indeed
exists.[14] But reading and criticism are acts; and the decision, necessarily
partial, to focus on definite stylistic and formal phenomena falls within the
scope of those acts. To quote Gérard Genette regarding the narrative categories emphasized in his *Narrative Discourse:* "We will be careful, however,

not to hypostatize these terms, not to convert into substance what is each time merely a matter of relationships."[15] As for relations, there is only one thing to be done: make a choice. And then—who chooses? The exercise of that freedom that Cervantes offered to his readers becomes inescapable.

The field of forms is immense, and here I can give only some general indications. We face an entire gamut of projects and procedures, situated at different points along certain lines of force whose extremes we are able to recognize. First of all, how much territory does a form encompass? For example, the distinction between linear form and circular form tends toward one pole, the macromorphological. If I think of a story such as *Lazarillo de Tormes,* I ask myself: Is the disposition of *Lazarillo* linear or circular? Or is it instead both, at different levels? The examination of "formal elements" or intraformal elements, such as the division of a novel into chapters and sections, requires a more detailed investigation. R. H. Willis dedicated a worthwhile book to the study of such divisions in *Don Quixote*[16] (whose *princeps* edition, of 1605, is subdivided into four *partes,* a separation that most modern editions and translations do not respect).[17] In such cases, the linguistic components do not structure or define, but rather make possible the formal elements that provoke critical reflection. That is, the analysis of the language is also partial, inasmuch as the total ordering of a work is interwoven with the syntax of a phrase or a paragraph but does not coincide with it. On the other hand, there are analyses of a micromorphological nature, studies such as those of Leo Spitzer or Riffaterre, that link as closely as possible the verbal contexture of a poem with the stylistic elements. I know of no study of this type more meticulous than the "Análisis de dos versos de Garcilaso," by Francisco García Lorca, who in effect spends a good number of pages examining with extraordinary attentiveness only two stanzas of the third Eclogue.[18] And think of the attention—very ancient and yet modern—paid to the figures of rhetoric: such as syllepsis in Renaissance tales, from Boccaccio to *Lazarillo,* or paranomasia, and *amplificatio* in Quevedo and other poets of the seventeenth century.[19]

Studies based on the widest perspectives usually imply premises concerning the nature of forms,[20] giving rise to the opposition between static form and dynamic form. Jean Rousset, in *Forme et signification* (1962), defines what criticism tries to understand in a literary work as "the simultaneous flowering of a structure and a thought, the amalgam of a form and an experience in which genesis and growth are joined."[21] The most important words are "flowering," "genesis," "growth." The work germinates, flowers, grows. Rousset aims to go beyond the old dichotomies (form as mere abstraction, or as *dispositio* of earlier materials; material as theme without outline or figure), and so stresses that evolution is *formation* before it becomes form. This formation is a willed process, a series of deliberate acts, a process of making and coming into being in the course of which the poetic conception, language, and even author and reader of the poem are conjoined. Rousset emphasizes to advantage the self-creation present in the work of the writer. "Before the paper the artist makes himself," said Mallarmé. The poet or creator alone—*poiétēs*—makes himself, molds himself, influences himself, creates himself, as Donald Fanger demonstrates in *The Creation of Nikolai Gogol* (1979). Carlos Blanco Aguinaga rightly stresses the will of the writer in his presentation of a collection of poems by Emilio Prados: "poetic will is order imposed on time, choice of the maker: definitive action." [22] Bakhtin thought that the author's intervention in the work was tangential, but less so from the point of view of form: "We meet him (that is, we sense his activity) most of all in the composition of the work: it is he who segments the work into parts (cantos, chapters, and so on) that assume, of course, a kind of external expression—without however directly reflecting the represented chronotopes [that is, spatial-temporal complexes]." [23] The idea of form as formation, as an active process, is clarified if we think of it as "order imposed on time"—successive temporal becoming over which a will toward identity is at work: refutation of time from the vantage point of time. From this perspective, we gain a better understanding of the concept of fable or argument in Aristotle's *Poetics*—"composition of events" or "structure of events" (1.450a15: *pragmatōn systasis;* notice that Aristotle uses *systasis,* not the opposition form/matter, which in fact does not appear in the *Poetics*) which is "like the soul of tragedy" (1.450a35). Or consider the concept of recognition, *anagnorisis,* in which tragedy turns on itself and recapitulates the path traveled (1.452a30); and the concept of climax and denouement (1.455b26–28), which, like recognition, implies a conciliation of structure with time. We also understand better the "word in time" of Antonio Machado; the Jakobsonian projection of an equivalence principle of the "axis of selection" over the "axis of combination"; and Riffaterre's notion of *stylistic context,* with which the singular element collides in order to produce a stylistic effect. [24]

I agree very happily with Jakobson that the poem is a cohesive system of equivalencies that nevertheless contain tensions and interactions, as we saw in the earlier discussion in connection with parallelism. But that does not make the poem into an atemporal thing. Very often the poem is also a process (not because of contagion by the novel, as Bakhtin thought), an adventure that keeps revealing little by little the qualities of a system. Who can forget that writing is a constant risk, a challenge ever renewed and ever

changing? And that imminent triumph—always imminent as we read—of
the system over the process is itself a process. The dialectic of the one and
the many—system and difference—is what gives continuing life to the literary form. This emotion of the reader is what I have tried to express regarding Antonio Machado's *Campos de Castilla*.[25] At the same time, Jean
Rousset comments with keen insight on the "triple joint movement" of the
action of Corneille's *Polyeucte,* with its upward spiraling movement, "mon-
tée en vrille." [26] On the other hand, there are certainly verbal constructions
of a static, visual, or circular type; for those it is not so important to under-
line the changing transformations and tensions. In a classic article, Joseph
Frank showed how to find "spatial" forms even in the nineteenth-century
novel.[27] But in any case we must always keep in mind the dynamic, "processual," and diversifying tendencies of a work of verbal art, underestimated
for so long by rhetorical conceptions of structure as *ordo* and *dispositio*.

    I am not referring just to the old rhetorical idea of *ordo,* clearly obsolete,
according to which the poet merely rearranges, places, and combines earlier
materials (the Scholastic conception of the relation between matter and
form, which, as we noted earlier, did not come from Aristotle, but was often
so interpreted by the Renaissance poets, in accordance also with their reading of Horace, as well of Tasso's *Discorsi sull'arte poetica,* 1587). That
concept of order is inadequate because it is too linear (here we are speaking
of the chronological, alphabetic, and other such orders). It is better to return with Saussure to the concept of *system:* a unified whole that implies
multiple interrelations. It is not enough to observe that the poem arranges
the successive elements of a temporal discourse, no matter how important
that might be. The work of art reconciles all sorts of differences, every type
of diversity, and achieves unity. In the visual arts think of collage (Kurt
Schwitters) and its literary equivalents (Eliot, Pound). The form reveals, in
chancy fashion, more or less tangibly, a volition toward system.

Some studies of forms tending to frame or even encompass entire works
undertaken by those interested in what were earlier called channels of communication (or *radicals of presentation*) are likely to take a more macromorphological point of view, although such studies also involve style. It is
a matter of the elements that make up all narration—narratology—more
than an examination of a certain genre, such as the novel, the short story,
the novella, or the short novel; a question of the requisites of dramatic
representation rather than comedies, tragedies, or *entremeses*. This does not
mean, however, that we are necessarily dealing with unifying forms. I continue to think that in the majority of cases what we observe is a plurality of

"formal elements," or criteria that help us understand them, similar to the procedures put forward by Genette and Dorrit Cohn, for example, as we shall see later when we also consider one of the principal contributions of Franz Stanzel: the "dynamization" of the narrative: the forms of narration are modified as the novel advances. Certainly some narratologists are intent on discovering and excavating the universal bases of the totality of all stories, the primeval Story; but then we would be dealing with structures, or more accurately, metastructures, in the "structuralist" sense of these terms, or rather with the components of a mental repertoire, of an imaginative system of an ultrahistorical character, exposed to distinct transformations and combinations—analogous up to a certain point to the *langue* of Saussure.[28]

I do not know if the attempt to find formal characteristics common to all channels of communication and all genres is fruitful or advisable. Roman Ingarden, in his famous *Das literarische Kunstwerk* (1931), tried to determine the order of strata or levels proper to a work of verbal art. He identified three principal ones: a phonic level, composed of sounds; a level of unities of sense, or semantic stratum; and the level composed of represented objects, characters, and other elements of the "world" of the work. (Ingarden added two more, but Wellek rightly comments that they can be included in the third level: the focus or point of view of the presentation; and certain "metaphysical" qualities: the sublime, the tragic, the sacred, and so on).[29] Then it is obvious that the levels or sequences that configure a poem do not coincide with the three reduced strata of Ingarden: the metrical sequence of a poem does not usually coincide with the sequence of sounds, and this discrepancy is of utmost importance. Ingarden's monolithic scheme lacks temporalization, and thus does not leave room for the distinction between "fable" and "subject," or between the sequence of the story and the chronology of the action, a distinction that has thrown light on the theory of narration from the time of Shklovsky to Genette. The signs that come together in a theatrical representation are of a very different type: word, decor, gestures, and so on. What the different channels of presentation do indeed seem to have in common is the *stratification* itself—similar to the phenomena of *tension* and interaction between one stratum and the others. But this abstraction turns out to be too far removed from the real diversity of the channels of communication.

Stratification, a general condition of the literary phenomenon in its concrete realizations, becomes extremely complex and specialized at a certain moment, as if in fact the properties of a certain channel of communication were accentuated. The tension between the phonic and the grammatical levels, and between these two and the prosodic level, is typical of poetry. It is curious that Ingarden accepted the phonic level in his basic model but did not make room for the other related strata in a poem. What happens when one analyzes a narrative poem, that is, a creation in which two channels, the narrative and the poetic, merge? Diego Catalán, editor of a new *Catálogo general del romancero,* an undertaking of exceptional importance and breadth, accepts as the basis for the cataloguing and understanding of the Iberian romances the four levels of narratological analysis proposed by Cesare Segre in *Le strutture a el tempo* (1974): the *discurso,* or "significant narrative text"; the *intriga* (*intreccio;* the English *plot,* or "subject" of the Russian Formalists), considered as the signified of the discourse; the *fábula* (fable), composed of the cardinal elements of the story in logical and chronological order; and the *narrative model* ("modelo actancial" for Diego Catalán), or the sequences of functional structures that connect, on a more general or abstract level, with the dramatis personae. Later on we will consider Vladimir Propp—from whose work this fourth level is derived. But first let us look for a moment at Segre's scheme because of its attempt to connect one stratum of a work to another by means of signification: the intrigue (plot) is the signified of the discourse. Everything contributes to narrativity, but if the process of signification of a narration is considered to the exclusion of all the rest of the work, all other elements are relegated to the position of mere cogs in a wheel. The sense implicit in the figurative or metaphorical elements of the story, or the "world" of invented objects and spaces constructed by the narrator, is entirely subordinated or shoved aside, to say nothing of the tensions proper of the poetic phenomenon, in the case of a narrative poem.

Once again we see that critical analysis is necessarily selective; and if various channels or different forms converge in a work or in a genre such as the romance, the most fitting model of stratification will depend upon the priority conceded earlier to a specific channel or form. The fruitfulness of the work that Catalán and his collaborators are carrying out derives from this circumstance. In the first place, some extremely refined models of stratification can be applied as well to oral or traditional poetry as to written literature; second, the study of the *romancero* can become a privileged field for understanding the mutual relationships among the distinct levels of narrative poetry and how they affect one another. According to Catalán, the romance is an open model, a virtual "program" that allows different individual versions to merge in distinct sociohistorical surroundings. The effect achieved by the unique version assumes three levels of "articulation": the first level converts the plot into discourse; the second, the fable into plot;

the third, the narrative model into fable. This triple articulation is manifested synchronically in any and all examples of traditional romance, and it is prominent above all when one analyzes the structures of the "program" throughout its many changes and avatars. The dramatic and metaphoric qualities of a version also derive from inherited cultural values, but they do not constitute the basic scheme of the program.[30]

I have already pointed out the general characteristics of stratification in poetry (Chapter 9), and I have referred more than once to works of comparative prosody, from Zhirmunsky's great book about rhyme (*Rifma*, 1923) to the investigations of Jakobson, Craig LaDrière, and Benjamin Hrushovski. LaDrière applies to versification the distinction between the particulars and the whole: "To be in verse or in prose is a feature of the microstructure of a speech; to have or have not units of the size and character of strophes or cantos—or *cantiche*—is a feature of the macrostructure ... It is because in the *Divina commedia* there is equal elaboration of microstructure and larger design that Dante is universally regarded as so great a poet."[31] LaDrière argues strongly that the prosodic examination of the structures of the line is necessarily comparative in nature. All prosody is a theory. But if that theory is based on the corpus of a single literature or one linguistic tradition, there is a risk that it may be inadequate. Only a prior inventory of the principal prosodic systems gives clear access to their relationships with languages or families of languages. Because of the absence of rhyme, Japanese poetry resembles the Latin more than it resembles the Chinese. The Celtic languages have in common an abundance of phonetics and alliteration, but Welsh, the richest of all in this regard, has some types of rhyme not found in Irish.[32] And LaDrière adds:

> The classical Sanskrit, Greek, Latin, Arabic, and Persian verse-systems are similar in that their rhythms depend principally upon temporal duration, as does also Turkish verse of what may be called the "classical" period. But classical Greek or Latin verse is as a whole not at all like Arabic, or even Persian, since the Greek and Latin make no regular use of patterns or other aspects of sound and meaning which are exploited habitually in the Near East, where rhyme for example is essential and semantic parallel very conspicuous. In these respects, therefore, Arabic and Persian verse are more like Chinese—or Welsh or Icelandic or even Provençal—than they are like Greek or Latin, or Sanskrit.[33]

That is, any descriptive system will be defective if it fails to take into account the variety of types that comparative prosody reveals, or if it ignores the distinct strata that configure the poem—phonic, syntactic, semantic, and so on. So then, as far as prosody is concerned, performance of the phonic operation is of course the most important.

At the beginning of his analytic summary of Hebrew prosody, Benjamin Hrushovski states that "the term form . . . refers to all poetic patterns which employ sound elements for the organization of the language material of the poem, such as rhyme, acrostic, meter, stanza, and other principles of composition."[34] Since for centuries Jewish poets have almost always lived in intercultural situations, or in relation with writers in nations alien to their own, Hrushovski reviews not much less than the entire spectrum of known prosodic systems: poetry based on accent (the Bible); or on the number of accents (postbiblical); or on the number of words (liturgical); or on a quantitative meter, in which the short syllable contrasts with the long (Spanish medieval poetry, based on the Arabic); or on syllable count (in Italy since the Renaissance, and in eastern Europe since the nineteenth century), or on a syllabic-accentual meter (modern poetry); or on an accentual meter with a limited number of syllables (in Israel after the First World War); or on forms of modern free verse (rhythms of phrase groups). The only system missing appears to be the meter based on the tone or pitch of the voice, as in China. In sum, Hrushovski's exemplary study displays all the comparative knowledge that LaDrière asked for, and that turns out to be necessary in order to trace the exceptional trajectory of Hebrew poetry.

As a result of the analysis of other channels of presentation—the theatrical and above all the narrative—a large number of interesting investigations have emerged during the last thirty years and have changed our way of perceiving such forms of art. I do not possess the necessary knowledge to provide more than a few indications here. In regard to drama, it is important to remember how the development of a new semiology of the theater has revealed the many ways of representation that converge in a theatrical function. It is no longer a question of deciphering the essence of the dramatic, as an entire aesthetic tradition originating in the Romantic period kept trying to do, paying attention for example to a certain synthesis of "epic objectivity" and "lyrical subjectivity" (Friedrich von Schelling, G. W. F. Hegel, F. T. Vischer) or to a basically conflictive structure (Hegel, Brunetière).[35] Numerous explorations during our century (abstract theater, or epic, or ritual, or absurd, and so on), together with the theoretical statements of an Adolphe Appia, a Gordon Craig, a V. E. Meyerhold, a P. Witkiewicz, or an Antonin Artaud, have excised the literary from our conception of the aesthetic of the theater. The investigations of Pyotr Bogatyrev and Roman Ingarden[36] have shed new light on the polyphony of representation that Barthes characterized in his *Critical Essays* (1972): "What is theatricality? It is theatre-minus-text, it is a density of signs and sensations built up on stage starting from the written argument; it is that ecumenical perception of sensuous artifice—gesture, tone, distance, substance, light—which submerges the text beneath the profusion of its external language."[37] In the excellent characterization of J. M. Díez Borque, the theatrical representation is a "despilfarro semiológico," a semiological extravagance.[38] Its elements (or strata) are known to all. Tadeusz Kowzan enumerates the following ones: word, tone, facial mimicry, gesture, movement of the actor on the stage, costume, accessories, decor, light, music, sound, makeup, hair style.[39] And to these thirteen fellow guests, one can easily add others. How many things can a gesture signify? And in how many ways can it be combined with the voice and the movement of the actor? It is what Umberto Eco calls "paralinguistic": "intonations, inflections of voice, the specific significance of an accent, a whisper, a doubt, a 'toneme,' even a sob or a yawn."[40] As for the stage set, the decor, isn't it important to distinguish between the objects in it and the space in which they are situated? The objects also become signs—as Barthes observed about the raincoat and other articles of clothing or materials common in social life whose use is converted into a "sign of that use";[41] but there is a special degree of density and coordination in a stage set. The configuration of the set signals the outlining of a space and the beginning of its interpretation; in addition, the fact that it is placed apart from everything outside, away from it, links it to the exterior world (Chekhov's character who contemplates the fields, and dreams of traveling to Moscow). The set organizes the space just as the argument of the work organizes the time. The dramatic piece assumes also an argument or sequence driven by events—for the most part always divided into scenes, into brief segments that intermingle or crisscross, as Segre explains in his reflection on the narrative forms of the theater.[42] The module "enter/exit" is constant within the theatrical space, as is the dialectic "inside/outside" or "present/absent," mentioned by C. Pérez Gállego,[43] and the connection "present/past" or "present/future." Concentrated spatially and temporally by necessity, the dramatic work expands and contracts at the same time. Think of the famous "Récit de Théramène" in Racine's *Phèdre*, or the description of Lisbon in Tirso de Molina's *Burlador de Sevilla*: what the characters describe and tell us as seen from the limited enclosure of the stage set, what Díez Borque calls "verbal scenery."[44] And we must add two characteristic phenomena: contradiction and simultaneity. It is important to remember that the different classes of signs are not a perfect fit, but often create tensions and superpositions. Some gestures are concomitant with speech, but others, such as those studied by L. García Lorenzo,[45] prolong, replace, or refine it, as if two distinct opinions were being expressed at the same time. As Díez Borque observes, "in the theater it is possible to have simultaneity of signifiers at the same moment, but in language not."[46]

The nature of the theatrical sign—like that of cinematography[47]—is extremely complex. In the first place, we observe concrete, perceptible, present, apparently real signs, but in fact they are fictitious. Umberto Eco (in a brilliant and also very charming essay, *mirabile dictu* in the theoretical field) explains it this way: "The theatrical sign is a fictitious sign not because it is a feigned sign or a sign that communicates things that do not exist . . . but because it pretends not to be a sign."[48] That is, the representation is ambiguous with respect to its own possiblity of signification. Do the visible and the audible always have to be significant? Like the set, the costumes, the music, the actor has to "be" and "signify" at the same time. In other words, the spectator not only understands what the music and the actors mean but is himself implicated in the literal ambit of the performance, a participant in it. When we read at the beginning of the story entitled "El inmortal" that the Princess of Lucinge acquired the six volumes of Pope's rendering of the *Iliad* in an antiquarian bookstore and that the last volume contains the manuscript that we are about to read, we don't believe for one second in the narrator's artifice. On the contrary, it is perfectly clear that we are about to read one of the fictions of Borges (in *El aleph*, 1957). But when María Casares sheds streams of tears on the stage, as if she were not pretending, the effect is more complicated. It is not a matter of asking ourselves whether her tears are real or not—they obviously are—or of believing that María Casares is really Phedra, but of feeling that we are witnessing a passionate woman who weeps, not *the* passionate woman, the rejected lover. The tears are converted into a sign that belongs to a total complex of signs. The theatrical performance *shows* us the actress—as Eco would say—in her exact place, in the middle of a stage set, a spotlight focused on her, as if we were being told: here you have a human body that *signifies* the weeping of a passionate woman. In order to signify, it is necessary first to exist with considerable intensity—and with the veiled design of being significant. I say "intensity" without meaning to imply excessive or exuberant gestures. Spencer Tracy could move his head a bare two centimeters, and the public would be fascinated. Or—more than that—Spencer Tracy could do absolutely nothing and nevertheless the spectator would understand completely the latent sense. Dámaso Alonso has explained that in poetry signs become necessary that would be arbitrary in other forms, according to Saussure.[49]

The great actor achieves something similar by means of his movements, gestures, his own body.

With regard to the theatrical sign, the distinction between systems of communication and systems of "significant manifestation" (or simply "signification)" is basic.[50] Anyone who studies the functioning of language, for example, or the highway code, is dealing with authentic systems of communication, based on codes, messages, and certain signs that some semiologists call "signs" (*signaux*). The signs are conventional symbols that the sender produces on purpose, thanks to a code understood by the receiver. But when Barthes makes a semiological study of the kinds of clothes we choose to wear on social occasions, it is no longer a matter of clearly and purposefully communicated signs. In these cases, one can observe only a significative manifestation, based on other indications or "indices": actions or things that give us the opportunity to know *other* traits—not perceptible perhaps on other occasions—of the actions and persons in question: "Indices are interpreted . . . signs are decoded."[51] Well then, in the theater it is presumed that the *indications* are fundamental. As Georges Mounin suggests, "Author and director, designer, actors, costumer, scene painter are all intent not on 'saying' something to the spectators . . . but on producing an effect on the spectators."[52] The stimuli received by the audience cannot be reduced to a scheme of communication; Mounin concludes that one should therefore not analyze theatrical phenomena by methods suitable for analysis of linguistic statements. Are we then obliged to understand theatrical events as we try to understand everyday events, ones that we participate in or witness? "Quite simply, the theatrical spectacle is constructed (in general) like a very particular genre of a sequence of events produced intentionally in order to be interpreted."[53] The signs become "hypersigns" and the indices "hyperindices," requiring interpretation.

Such a manifestation is unusually indirect. Eric Buyssens throws light on this characteristic of the dramatic presentation when he states: "The actors in the theater pretend to be real people who communicate with each other; they do not communicate with the audience."[54] That is certainly a theatrical convention most of the time, but with quite a few exceptions that are themselves conventions. Think of the Greek chorus, the asides in Latin comedy, the narrator in Thornton Wilder's *Our Town* or Arthur Miller's *A View from the Bridge*, to give just a few examples. The Brechtian actor often directs his words to the audience. At the beginning of Carlos Fuentes' *Orquídeas a la luz de la luna* (1982; translated into English as *Orchids in the Moonlight*), the author instructs the actress who plays Dolores Del Rio (or rather plays the actress Dolores del Río) in the following way: "Dolores looks intently at the audience for thirty seconds, first with a certain defiance, arching her brows; but she slowly loses her composure beneath the look." Then Dolores explains this look: "They didn't recognize me," she says sadly.

But the principal convention in the theater is the *double intent* of the dialogue. The spectators are "eavesdroppers" on the words that the characters direct to one another in the first instance (using what is indeed a system of communication in this case), and at the same time spectators are "second observers" (or voyeurs) of the gestures and actions carried out on the stage. Some will say that we are pointing out here nothing more than a trait characteristic of all dialogue, such as occurs in the novel, and I also understand that to be so. Don Quixote and Don Diego de Miranda converse in Don Diego's house (II.18); the words are not actually directed to the reader, who simply overhears the discussion. But the analogy is only a beginning. Don Quixote is not aware that we are listening to him; and it would be fairer to compare the position of the theatrical spectator with that of Sancho and Doña Cristina, Don Diego's wife, who are present but do not take part in the conversation.

Recall instead the situation described by Sappho in the famous poem mentioned in Chapter 6. The poet sees that the woman she loves is talking with a man "fortunate as the gods" who sits beside her and "listens nearby to your sweet voice and lovely laughter." We assume that the poet also hears those words; and, furthermore, that her lover knows it and perhaps for that reason speaks sweetly and smiles at her masculine partner in the conversation and allows him to sit so close to her. We might ask ourselves not what the observing woman feels—that is very clear: unbearable jealousy—but, interpreting this very brief encounter as a small dramatic action, what is the *indication* of the conduct of the loved woman? Flirtation? Boredom? Freedom? Provoking jealousy on purpose? Bisexuality?

Up to a certain point this describes the situation of the spectator in the theater, free interpreter, to whom the words of the dialogue are not directed but who is, more than the character spoken to, the final objective of everything said and acted on the stage. The spectator of a theatrical presentation (in contrast to motion pictures) shares the same uninterrupted space with the actors, who are both fooling him and devoting themselves to him. The author prepares and the actor puts into practice this double intent, this duplicity, so similar to what we experience every day in our social life that we have to overcome a certain instinct of caution in the theater in order to allow ourselves finally to feel emotion, indignation, empathy, and, in the case of tragedy, even pity and terror. The word, in sum, is *sign* for the actor who listens, *index, indication,* for the spectator.

I would not wish to quarrel either with the duplicity of the dialogue or that of the actor, for two more reasons. First, in general the character on the stage directs his attention only to the other character to whom he is speaking, but the spectator places the verbal signs within an entire complex of indices. The character dwells only in the space circumscribed by the set. But for the spectator, this space has extra meaning, since it reveals the designs of author and director—very capable no doubt of manipulating the actor. And obviously the same arguments hold true for monologue as for dialogue. In both cases the spectator is an additional or accomplice listener. Dialogue therefore involves not two but three participants; and monologue not one but two: what Cesare Segre calls "oblique" communication in his book *Teatro e romanzo* (1984), in which he analyzes beautifully and in depth some semiotic dimensions that I have been able only to suggest in this brief commentary.[55]

During the 1960s the structuralist mode of thought had a major effect on the knowledge and study of narrative forms. Theoretical analyses by A.-J. Greimas, Claude Bremond, and Tzvetan Todorov appeared, all based on the work of the Russian Formalists (Viktor Shklovsky, Boris Tomashevsky), on Vladimir Propp (*Morfologija skazki,* 1928; first translated into English in 1958), and also on the work of Etienne Souriau. From a hundred Russian fairy tales Propp had extracted thirty-one functions and seven basic characters. (The function is "the action of the character, defined from the point of view of its significance in the unfolding of the plot.")[56] Now the attempt was made to construct a science of the story in general.[57] The structuralist approach, methodologically ambitious, attempted to identify not only internal structures (oppositions, options, and so on) limited to one or more narrations, but also a vocabulary of virtual metastructures, available to *every* story, overarching unique works and historical changes.

That is what Todorov attempts to do in his *Grammaire du Décaméron* (1969). Here he employs, astutely and systematically, a linguistic model, or better, a syntactic model. In a narrative statement, the *agent* corresponds to the proper noun; the "state" (such as being in love), the "property" (such as pride), and the "status" (such as being of Jewish origin, for example) all correspond to the adjective; the action corresponds to the verb that leads to the modification of a situation, and so on. Does one perceive the *Decameron* more clearly as a result of such a reflection? No, absolutely not; but it would be wrong to reproach the critic for that, since his objective is completely different. Let us leave aside the literary qualities of the unique work in question and its structure of values. "The work is not the object of study but the potentialities of literary discourse that have made it possible."[58] Let us say that what the critic is looking for is the narrativity. A unique, abstract narrative scheme has to reflect the unity (curiously enough without options or structural polarities) of the grammar and the language in general: "Grammar is one, because the universe is one."[59]

In this first phase of the structural analysis of a story, we hit a snag concerning the elimination of those properties of language that cannot be reduced to syntactic relations: vocabulary, figures, style, and so on. For example, without taking into account the words themselves, how is it possible to differentiate between the narrator's intervention in a novel and that of a character, or to discern whether or not a description is incorporated into the time of the action? The nuances of narrativity depend on the context of the language. The *Grammaire du Décaméron* distinguishes between the syntactic aspects of the story, the semantic (what is represented and evoked), and the verbal, passing lightly over the last two. But Todorov also declares: "Bocaccio himself pointed out the road to follow: he did not INVENT these stories, he said, but he WROTE them. In effect unity is created in the writing; the motifs that the study of folklore makes known to us are transformed by Bocaccio's writing."[60] So here we have it: narrativity will be crossed with writing—and, fortunately, with literature as well.

With this encounter as a starting point, Roland Barthes in *S/Z* (1970) emphasizes the plurality of meanings made possible by the convergence of a diversity of codes. Barthes thus transcends the excluding considerations either of the plot or of the actions themselves (the "fable" and the "subject" of the Formalists), on which Claude Bremond concentrates (in *Logique du récit*, 1973: a narration is a discourse that gives form to some actions). Later narratology would assume the indivisibility of these two levels of the story, called by Genette *récit* and *histoire* (the narrative statement itself, the concatenation of events: the *fábula* of Cesare Segre), and the interpenetration of both with the words (as, for example, in "indirect free style").

The works of Yuri Lotman, Cesare Segre, Gérard Genette, Franz Stanzel, Dorrit Cohn, and Seymour Chatman belong to this second phase of narratology, which has generated an unceasing flood of publications.[61] These contributions represent a notable advance in our understanding of narrative forms. In the next few pages I will comment briefly on two or three general characteristic traits.

First, in a study of exceptional richness, *Narrative Discourse* (1980), Gérard Genette undertakes an enormously suggestive analysis. The method employed is not unistructural, but pluristructural, or more simply, pluriformal. The search for the one narrative, the mother of all narratives, tale of tales, the *Urerzählung,* that Greimas and his circle dreamed of, is abandoned. A uniform universe simplified by the categories of the human brain is not postulated. The richness of the poetic imagination is not forced to conform to the supposedly general or universal laws of grammar. Faced with a story, Genette begins from the simultaneous perception of the three superimposed strata that configure it: *récit* and *histoire*—the narrative discourse, the logical series of happenings—and also *narration,* that is, the act of telling. The story usually chosen by Genette is Proust's masterwork, a work of extreme formal complexity that Genette as critic undertakes not so much to simplify as to know thoroughly as an individual creation. That endeavor requires a constant passing back and forth between criticism and literary history, or rather between the reading of Proust's novel and recapitulating the forms manifested and fully displayed by the multisecular itinerary of Western narrative art. The three strata in question touch and intertwine at every moment. These interrelations give rise not to countless but certainly to an abundance and diversity of forms: the story is *polymorphic.*

Certain fundamental questions arise from the contact of the story with the narration: What is the temporal disposition of a work? its rhythm? What is meant by the frequency of narrated events (are they singular, or repeated, and so on)? And also, no longer speaking of temporality but of degrees or modes of information: What degree of knowledge is imparted to the reader about the action and the characters? Which character's perception of the others and of the action governs the narrative field? And the degree of information or knowledge—linked naturally to the extent that time in the story is compressed—cannot be appreciated without an awareness of the language itself, since the language chosen can affect any phrase or any word of the narrative statement.

Every elucidation of the voice that tells us the tale corresponds to the contact between the level of narration and the story—of the telling with the told. How many voices are there, and how are they mutually related? Are there interpolated stories (*métarécits,* or metanarratives)? How is the time of narrating related to that of the story: later (most common), or simultaneously (in the case of a diary, an article, or an epistolary novel)? Is the act of telling located within or outside the represented world or diegesis, "the spatial-temporal universe designed by the narrative"?[62] How is the narrator linked to the story he tells (is he hero, friend, peripheral character, creator, or another)?

These very rudimentary indications suffice to demonstrate the extremely important place of temporality, not just in Proust but in every configuration of a story. They also help in understanding *Marxism and Form* (1971), by Fredric Jameson, for example, who rightly associates the temporality of a story with historical time. To narrate is to live and to make time live—to channel it, mold it, fill it, hand it over to the happy caprice of the reader (as in Julio Cortázar's *Hopscotch*) subjugate it, perhaps save it . . . Alejo Carpentier very properly called one of his collections of short stories *Guerra del tiempo* (1958; translated into English as *The War of Time*). Time is so important that it seems impossible to separate temporality from narrativity. But clearly we must remember that not everything is narration in a novel (or in a novelistic romance of the fifteenth century, or in an epic poem, neither in *Faust* nor in *Eugene Onegin*). Concerning pauses in the narration, true suspensions of the tick-tock of time, Genette points out that not all of them are descriptions, nor are all descriptions pauses. That is true in Proust, whose descriptive passages, vital in *A la recherche du temps perdu*, coincide with the exercise of the hero's sensibility. To look, to admire, to penetrate the visible is also to live, also a form of activity. In the case of Proust, it is the protagonist who describes.[63] But neither is the passage of time necessarily interrupted if the person describing is a narrator who does not participate in the action. Let us look now at an example of description that incorporates the diegesis into temporality.

The first sentences of *La regenta* (1984), by Leopoldo Alas, or "Clarín," introduce us right away to Vetusta, the fictitious city where the entire novel takes place:

> The city of heroes was having a nap. The south wind, warm and languid, was coaxing grey-white clouds through the sky and breaking them up as they drifted along. The streets of the city were silent, except for the rasping whispers of whirls of dust, rags, straw and paper on their way from gutter to gutter, pavement to pavement, street corner to street corner, now hovering, now chasing after one another, like butterflies which the air envelops in its invisible folds, draws together, and pulls apart. This miscellany of leftovers, remnants of refuse, would come together like throngs of gutter urchins, stay still for a moment as if half asleep, and then jump up and scatter in alarm, scaling walls as far as the loose panes of the street lamps or the posters daubed up at street corners; and a feather might reach a third floor, and a grain of sand be stuck for days, or for years, in a shop window, embedded in lead.

Not as lazy as the people, the wind does not take a nap. The narrator, with the wind's help, describes not the static aspect of a few things, but their movement. Verbs abound, almost all of them active or implying activity—

and time. Very humble, minuscule objects (as in the picaresque novel) seem to be personified and symbolized. Only two characters in the novel (Ana Ozores and Fermín de Pas) will share this tendency to transcend the inertia of matter in vertical ascent. Everything else in the sleepy city is mediocre or hypocritical. Like the birds—very significant in *La regenta*—the scraps, the crumbs, and papers rise, ascend, soar, if only ephemerally; except for an almost bodiless grain of sand, sticking to a shop window "for days, or for years." In sum, the represented world is indivisible from temporality. There is neither pause nor tranquillity, but dynamic diegesis.

If space—between the one and the many—separates, time unites or re-unites people, things, events. Everything is temporalized by the art of the storyteller: by the interaction of story, history, narration. An absolutely isolated event, one totally removed from the course of time, is inconceivable. From the moment an event is inserted into a story, it occurs "after" or "before" or "suddenly" or "usually," or "a single time" or "for the last time," and so on. I cannot resist quoting here a few words of Genette concerning what Vladimir Jankélévitch has called the *primultimité*, or "pri-multimateness" of the first time, of whatever occurs for the first time: "That is, the fact that the first time, to the very extent to which one experiences its inaugural value intensely, is at the same time (already) a last time—if only because it is forever the last to have been the first, and after it, inevitably, the sway of repetition and habit begins."[64] He is speaking of Proust, who certainly expresses these phenomena of temporalization with special intensity, but we find the same thing in Homer. The consciousness of time lays the foundation for the narrative channels. And it is not at all surprising that these channels occupy a privileged position in modern literatures and in the responses that these literatures propose to historical saturation, to the incessant change and the plurality of the worlds we live in—mobile, dispersed, unfinished.

I have called this type of narratology polymorphic for more than one reason. As for the *tempo* of the story (the pace of the verbal statement, in contrast to the time of the action), Genette points out the existence of four canonical forms of novelistic duration: the "ellipsis" ("three years passed": pure chronology; or at times with a single indication: "after three years of divine happiness . . . ": Stendhal); the "pause" (description without time; or the narrator speaks for himself: Sterne); and between these two extremes, the two most frequent forms: the "scene" (usually in dialogue, in which the time of the narration and that of the story are the same) and the more rapid "summary," which usually serves as a transition between scenes, or also as retrospective recapitulation, two functions in which Cervantes is a past master.[65] Here is the beginning of *Celoso extremeño* (translated into English as *The Jealous Hidalgo*):

> Not many years ago an hidalgo of a village in Extremadura, the son of well-born parents, left home and, like that other Prodigal, he wandered—throughout different parts of Spain, Italy, and Flanders, squandering his years as well as his patrimony. After long travels (his parents now being deceased and his estate dissipated), he finally came to the great city of Seville, where he found ample opportunity to fritter away the little he had left.[66]

There is neither gap nor suspension of the story but a vertiginous characterization of an entire life. So then, in practice, as we read a certain novel this scheme *suggests* to us observations not contained in the initial scaffolding. The categories proposed by the critic are combined and in that way engender a variety of forms. Chapters 4 and 6 of *Lazarillo de Tormes* (translated int English as *The Life of Lazarillo of Tormes*) are "summaries," yes, but with obvious elliptical traits; as when the narrator says of the fray de la Merced, his master: "He gave me the first pair of shoes I ever wore, but they didn't last me a week. And I wouldn't have lasted much longer myself trying to keep up with him. So because of this and that and some other little things that I don't want to mention, I left him" (Chapter 4). In this case the narrator confronts two problems at the same time: that of the tempo and that of the degree or mode of information. These two conditions intersect and affect each other in a novel such as Carmen Martín Gaite's *Ritmo lento* (1963), in which the truth yearned for by the hero demands the difficult rejection of the speed of life that prevents us from knowing the people we love most, and who remain fatally unclear to us; and a character confesses: "For some time I have kept up a relationship with my son, and last year we stopped it. It is very difficult to explain what that relationship was like, and I would need all that time that you mention to go into this explanation, time to tell without hurry a whole life. And also I would have to find someone who might wish to listen to me." [67]

A further suggestion would be the study of another procedure of a temporal type in the story: *prediction.* I am referring to what a character of a novel or story says or predicts, announcing or foretelling events to come—not the formulated prognostications of the narrator, which very commonly belong to the "anachronisms" analyzed by Genette, that is, to the discordances between the order of the events in the story and its order in the narration: retrospection and anticipation. Genette calls them *analepsis* and *prolepsis.* An earlier event in a story is evoked, or a later event is announced beforehand.[68] A recent example carried to the extreme of anticipation, or prolepsis, by the narrator—soon to become a classic—is the first sentence of *Chronicle of a Death Foretold* (1982), by Gabriel García Márquez: "The day they were going to kill him, Santiago Nasar got up at five-thirty in the morning to wait for the boat the bishop was coming on."

And Santiago Nasar will not die before the narrator's last words, fulfillment of the first words, pinnacle of the great canopy that the initial anticipation allows to rise over the entire novel. The narrator predicts nothing, since he knows what happened, *a posteriori,* and he tells it all as though it were a traditional story and not a novel (a risky undertaking that doesn't mean that we are not reading a novel after all). In reality, practically all the inhabitants of the village except Santiago Nasar suspect that he is going to be assassinated: "many of the people in the port knew that they were going to kill Santiago Nasar." But clearly they didn't know it for certain; and the narrator doesn't let them speak, or rather doesn't give them the opportunity to predict the crime (and perhaps to prevent it). In this type of story the illusion of freedom is markedly diminished and the illusion of fatality becomes enormous—"a certain load of 'predestination,'" as Genette writes regarding Abbé Prévost's *Manon Lescaut,* the outcome of which we know from the beginning, and of Tolstoy's *The Death of Ivan Ilich,* which also narrates a predicted death. (From Spanish literature Rico would add to this list Lope's *Caballero de Olmedo.*)[69]

These cases differ from predictions made by *a character,* a prediction that complicates the freedom of the other characters, inasmuch as such a personage still has to base his prediction on conjectures, observations, astrological beliefs, and his supposedly prophetic powers, since the character is basically ignorant of the future, no matter how omniscient he might believe himself to be. It is true that the inclination toward prediction and easy prophecy—easier than understanding the present, to say nothing of the past—is very common in daily life and is therefore not at odds with the possible or longed-for realism of so many novelists. But I refer here to those predictions that indeed come true. And it is worthwhile to ask: What is the function of such a prediction in a story? The prediction obviously serves to string together disparate events and thus to make the work more unified. A potential, hypothetical future happening is glimpsed, without any feeling of "weight of predestination," because the prediction, to exist as such, does not have to be true. As the story goes along it is enough to verify whether it was a foolish prediction or not. In effect, only the narrator can announce the future. Or, as in detective novels, the narrator can fake a clue that turns out to be a hoax. The prediction by the character mysteriously interweaves today with tomorrow and so creates the phenomenon of *suspense,* as in Hitchcock-type movies and also in a certain kind of jazz—Duke Ellington, Billie Holiday, Errol Garner—which subjects the listener to an almost unbearable tension between two times: the present and the future.

Then there are characters of a prophetic lineage, such as the blind man of *Lazarillo of Tormes,* the blind seer (Tiresias, Oedipus, King Lear), the "great master" who in matters of understanding of life guides the boy who is supposed to guide him, instructing the boy in the preeminence of the invisible over the visible. "I tell you," predicts the blind man in *Lazarillo,* "if there's one man in the world who will be blessed by wine, it's you." Foresight that the hero (street vendor of wine) could corroborate: "but the blind man's prophecy wasn't wrong . . . he must have had a gift for telling the future." [70] And there are many other versions, with different nuances, of this formal figure: the prediction by a character. Remember in passing one of the best known predictions of this type, the words of the abbé Blanès in *The Charterhouse of Parma* (Chapter 8), who predicts and paves the way for prison for Fabrizio del Dongo and for his final years as a Carthusian monk: "warned by my voice, your soul can prepare itself for another prison, far different in its austerity, far more terrible! . . . You will die like me, my son, sitting upon a wooden seat, far from all luxury . . ." (and then adds: "on a wooden seat and clad in white"). It can be seen that Blanès does not suppress the freedom of his young friend, since he permits and recommends that he live—stoically—with inner independence. One can also observe that Stendhal's irony moves the reader to ask himself if knowable destinies might not exist between heaven and earth, between divine providence and individual improvisation, knowable destinies; and that the character of Fabrizio himself is especially sensitive to portents, to a dissatisfaction with the inertia of life, or to that almost pleasant inner suspended state that gives rise to presentiments about the future. "Thus it was that, though not lacking in brains, Fabrizio could not manage to see that his half-belief in omens was for him a religion, a profound impression at his entering upon life. To think of this belief was to feel, it was a happiness." [71]

To bring this brief collection of samples of narratological propositions to an end, I would like to mention two interesting and relatively recent books: one by Franz K. Stanzel and one by Dorrit Cohn. Stanzel devotes a good part of *A Theory of Narrative* (1984) to outlining different types of "mediacy" (*Mittelbarkeit*) that are important discoveries in the art of the novel. Certainly every narration is mediatized—distanced, shaped, evaluated, perceived, felt—by a narrator. It is curious that Stanzel considers this dimension a characteristic of the narrative genre (as the title of his first chapter proclaims), a proposition that seems debatable to me. According to Stanzel, the degrees of mediacy in a novel are relative and varied. The same thing happens in poetry that begins with the activity of an observing, contemplative, and evaluating voice or sensibility, not to be confused either with the "object" (or "concept," as the precepts of the Renaissance would call it) of the poem or with the flesh-and-blood poet. It becomes difficult to maintain the Platonic-Aristotelian distinction (*Republic* 392d–394d; *Poetics* 1.448a) between works in which the writer "imitates" others or "assumes another personality," and those in which he speaks for himself, as "his own person." Must we think that the poet imitates himself? The model of communication available to us at present does not include the real author, whether novelist ("The narrator of a novel is never the author," says Vargas Llosa, like Proust in *Contre Sainte-Beuve*),[72] dramatist, or poet, but includes instead the voice that impels and gives life to what happens between reader and words, shaping them and in that way mediatizing the object represented. Perhaps what Stanzel says about one of the three archetypal narrative situations might be proper for poetry, the "personal" situation (the one who mediatizes is not the narrator, who hides from view, but a "reflector" character in the core of the story: the *point of view* of Henry James): Stanzel says that the aim of going beyond mediacy by means of the *illusion of immediacy* is a characteristic of the "personal" situation.[73] Going beyond and illusion: are they not also achieved in a good number of poems? But it is not necessary to settle this dispute here. Nevertheless, here are difficulties that could be resolved if narratologists would be more attentive to the theory of genres— that is, if they would distinguish between the novel, the story, or the novella, on the one hand, and, on the other, the *radicals of presentation* or channels of communication, such as narration, which occupy such a prominent place in poetry as well as in the theater.

Stanzel describes three principal types of mediacy. In addition to the personal situation (the *figural narrative situation*) there is the pseudoautobiographical story (*Ich-Erzählung*, or *first-person narrative situation*) whose narrator is a character included in the depicted world, and the *authorial narrative situation*, in which the narrator remains outside that world. Stanzel's analysis, so rich that it is difficult to summarize, has three important merits in general. In the first place, we are not dealing with a taxonomy of forms, or classification of objects that are present. He writes: "The nineteen-fifties mark the end of the Linnaean age of the theory and criticism of the novel . . . [Now we are interested in] the variations and modulations of these forms, in their combinations and fusions just as they appear in a particular novel or short story."[74] For example, one cannot evaluate the interventions of the authorial narrator (Dickens, Galdós, Musil) if we insist on separating a few apparently "superficial" structures from others that are "deep," as in generative grammar.[75] In the second place, this type of reflection leads to an enhanced *historical* vision of the evolution of narrative forms (as discussed also by Genette). It is obvious that since the end of the nineteenth century the use of the "reflector" character, and thus the use of "indirect free style" (*erlebte Rede*) has intensified.

Finally, the way is opened for the examination of what Stanzel calls *dynamization* of the unique narrative phenomenon, or rather, of the intensification of mediacy through the use of certain formal tactical changes throughout a novel.[76] This third perspective, a consequence of the first two, helps us perceive the changes in rhythm and focus ("altérations," Genette calls them)[77] that enrich and vitalize a story such as Goethe's *Werther,* to give a classic example, or, among contemporary writings, Vargas Llosa's *La ciudad y los perros* (1963; translated into English as *The Time of the Hero*). Stanzel points out that these processes in turn become conventions themselves. *Pepita Jiménez* (1874), by Don Juan Valera, adapts—and complicates—the scheme of *Werther.*[78] (The two Spanish novels that I keep citing most often, *Quixote* and *La regenta,* are enriched and modified to a high degree as the story unfolds.) Often the final section of a novel reanimates or surprises the reader through these formal dynamisms. For example, take the case of the so-called peripheral narrator (who belongs to the narrated world and knows the principal character but does not take part in the action: an observer, like Watson next to Sherlock Holmes; or one not fully accepted by the main characters, like the gossipy and indiscreet fellow countryman in *The Brothers Karamazov*), but who in the end becomes an almost central character, as in Nabokov's *Pnin* (1954), not however without posing certain stimulating questions for the reader: What sort of relations could the narrator—exiled Russian also—have with the wife of the disgraced Pnin? and a number of others. Something similar occurs in Carlos Fuentes' *The Hydra Head* (1978), in which the thematic puzzle is heightened by the fact that the narrator on the sidelines turns out to be the chief spy (like John le Carré's "Control"), who tries to direct the actions of the protagonist.

The felicitous choice of title, *Transparent Minds* (1978), makes the aim of Dorrit Cohn's book transparent: to present a typology of the narrative modes of knowledge of the inner natures of the fictional characters. Here at last is a rigorous attempt to analyze the vast exploration, so paradoxical, carried out by the modern novel. The art of the novelist tends to bring about the illusion of recognizable life, the "air of reality" that Henry James had in mind. The paradox rests on the fact that "narrative fiction attains its greatest 'air of reality' in the representation of a lone figure thinking thoughts (referring to *The Portrait of a Lady*) that she will never communicate to anyone."[79] That is, the psychic transparency of the novel assumes and suppresses the opacity, the inexorable mutual ignorance, that we face in our daily lives. The vaunted realism of the novel ends in an imagined recreation of the intimate meditative conscience of the characters. That infusion of interior clarity—which goes beyond the self-knowledge of the I— is a contribution of the author, from Cervantes to Joyce, a contribution that does not merit the name of irreality either. What Bergson called *attention à la vie* leads not only to oneiric alternatives but also to the novelistic effort to penetrate the surface of the visible. From the moment a supposedly not invented narration—like the "nonfiction" of Capote or Mailer, which reports on the lives and deaths of known criminals; or a quasiautobiographical chronicle (Carlos Barral)—tells us what someone thought while alone, for himself alone, we are clearly entering the terrain of novelistic fiction.

In the Hispanic world we have available a very clearly contrasting element, namely the genre called *costumbrismo* (Estébanez Calderón, Mesonero Romanos, Ricardo Palma), akin to the Romantic vignette (Victor Joseph Etienne de Jouy), and the eighteenth-century "sketch of manners" (Joseph Addison, Sir Richard Steele), the old satiric tradition (the *Narrenschiff* of Sebastian Brant, the *Mundo por de dentro* of Quevedo) and the no less ancient "characters" (Theophrastus, Jean de La Bruyère). The most famous example of *costumbrismo* is the *Diablo cojuelo* (1641) of Luis Vélez de Guevara (reworked by Alain René Lesage), clever busybody who uncovers the roofs of houses in order to spy on the occupants from above.[80] And what if he were to uncover thoughts? No, never; the *costumbrista* limits himself to *seeing* the "world from outside" in order to sketch types of humanity and behavior: professions, ages, sexes, vices, customs, "traditions." But as Pere Gimferrer writes in an intentionally specular story—the protagonist is a painter—*Fortuny* (1983): "one eye refuses to let another eye look into its own depths." Seven centuries earlier Ramón Llull had said in the *Arbol ejemplifical* (VI.3.10): "No man is really visible." The Hispanic affinity for outward appearance in literature was not overcome until after Galdós and Clarín.

So then, in regard to the novel proper, Dorrit Cohn clarifies his different forms of imagined psychology. There are three basic ones. First, *psycho-narration*: discourse of the narrator from the outside, discourse that reveals the conscience of the character, his inner state. Second, *quoted monologue*: mental discourse of the character from within, in the first person and simultaneous with the action, including the traditional soliloquy and—when that became unconvincing in the nineteenth century—the so-called interior monologue, from Edouard Dujardin to Joyce's *Ulysses*, where it is scarcely separate from the flow of the narration itself. Going even further along this line, we have a less conventional, perhaps more incoherent verbalization (which has come to be called *stream-of-consciousness*): an uninterrupted string of impulses, associations, digressions—and stylistic effects. (Antonio Prieto has demonstrated that the degrees are extremely varied throughout such a spectrum,[81] as shown in Spain by Miguel Delibes in *Cinco horas con Mario* [1966] or by the very rich shadings of Rosa Chacel in *Acrópolis* [1984].) Dorrit Cohn's third form is the *narrated monologue:* a mental discourse of the character reproduced by the narrator from the outside and in the third person. These three forms are modified in cases of pseudoautobiographies, or "first-person" works, in which a period of time separates the narrator from the *self-quoted monologue*.[82] These analyses cannot be simplified, and I cannot do more than suggest something of Dorrit Cohn's valuable contribution to the subject of narrated monologue (called in French *style indirect libre* and in German *erlebte Rede*).

Jane Austen cultivated such a procedure, introducing into her novels written in the third person a type of introspection proper to the confessional or epistolary story; this technique was perfected by Flaubert, Zola, and Henry James, as is well known.[83] Narrated monologue is situated midway between psychonarration, on the one hand, spoken by the narrator in his own language and from the point of view of his own knowledge, and, on the other hand, the pure, or "quoted" monologue presented by the narrator in the words of a character. It goes without saying that a number of intermediate positions exist between these two extremes.

In Clarín's *La regenta*, the person telling the story often comes close to true narrated monologue, to the meeting of two states of mind, only to veer away later, in a changeable, unstable, and even equivocal manner. The pure monologue (of such ancient lineage: the asides of *Lazarillo;* Sancho's monologue, actually a self-dialogue: *Quixote*, II.10), is very rare in *La regenta*. It is identified by the use of the first person; for example, when the gallantries of Don Alvaro Mesía offend Ana Ozores (Chapter 9): "Ana immediately forgot everything else, thinking about the pain she felt as she heard his words. 'Might I have been imagining things? Might this man never have looked at me with love in his eyes? Might seeing him everywhere have been a simple coincidence? Might the eyes which gazed at me have done so in mere indifference?'" The questions and indecisions expressed in the first person show that the passage is a soliloquy; however, its origin shows through; that is, it comes out of psychonarration, through the use of "if" that would be applied in such a case ("Ana asked herself if seeing him everywhere might be . . .").

The opposite extreme is psychonarration in the third person, most often found in *La regenta* (from Chapter 10): "She felt cries of protest in her very bowels, cries which seemed to call upon her with supreme eloquence, cries inspired by justice, by the rights of the flesh, by the rights of her beauty . . . Ana, almost delirious by now, could see her own destiny in the night sky: she was the moon, and the cloud was old age, terrible old age, where there was no hope of being loved." We recognize the contraction of the summary in the third person; the temporal flexibility of the psychonarration that Dorrit Cohn speaks of, "a kind of panoramic view" of the psychic state of the heroine.[84] And that assumes the use of words that would not be hers; it would be strange if she were to say: "I feel cries of protest in my very bowels . . ." And since a person in delirium rarely knows it, the adjective "delirious" can only be a contribution of the narrator.

On other occasions psychonarration expands, slows, and seems to merge with Ana's thoughts, as when she recalls her confession to the Magistral (Chapter 13):

> She remembered everything they had said to each other; and she also remembered that she had spoken to him as she had never spoken before, her ears and her heart rejoicing at his words of hope and consolation, at his promises of light and poetry and of a life full of meaning, a life dedicated to something good, great and worthy of what she felt within herself, of all that lay in the depths of her soul. She had occasionally read something of the sort in books, but where was the Vetustan who knew how to speak like that? Furthermore, reading such good and beautiful ideas in books was very different from hearing them from a man of flesh and blood with gentle warmth in his voice, soft music in his speech, and honeyed sweetness in his words and gestures.

We have entered the mental and sentimental world of Ana, the frustrated poet, the reader of San Juan de la Cruz and Chateaubriand. Only she could say that the Magistral's words were "honeyed."

Psychonarration in the third person is like a base, while the numerous and extensive monologues narrated in this novel form an overarching canopy. To avoid misunderstandings, Clarín puts these psychonarrated passages inside quotation marks, as in the following (Chapter 10):

> "But that wasn't the point. She was dying of boredom. She was twenty-seven years old, her youth was slipping away, for twenty-seven years, in a woman, were the threshold of old age, and she was already knocking at

the door . . . Love is the only thing worth living for, she had often heard and read. But what love? Where was this love? She had never experienced it. And she remembered, half in shame half in anger, that her honeymoon had meant no more than futile arousal, a false alarm for sensuality, a cruel practical joke. Yes, yes, why try to keep the fact hidden from herself when her memory was shouting it at her?"

The quotation marks are the typographic convention used to introduce Ana's private thoughts. The third person of the verb is the grammatical convention that protects the rights of the narrator and of the writing, which cannot coincide with a mental state, but can symbolize it and at times even interpret it. The narrator translates and abbreviates when he writes that Ana was "half in shame half in anger." The absence of commas, the para-tactic juxtapositions, the repetitions, the quick sketches—-"Where was this love? She had never experienced it"—that summarize longer durations, the self-dialogue shows that what is symbolized here is a state of consciousness not limited to a verbal complex. More important perhaps is the need to communicate the rhythm of that state. That is what Dorrit Cohn explains when referring to Joyce's *Portrait of the Artist as a Young Man:* "By leaving the relationship between words and thoughts latent, the narrated mono-logue casts a peculiarly penumbral light on the figural consciousness, sus-pending it on the threshold of verbalization in a manner that cannot be achieved by direct quotation." [85] There is no attempt to reproduce the words of the character in his or her most luminous and vigorous moments of self-expression, the hallmarks of pure monologues, but to cross the threshold of a remote inner state. That threshold is also the threshold of verbalization—with its aura, gestures, and shadows. The narrator's discretion is what best defines the difficulty of the challenge the author sets for himself: that of an encounter between two states of mind.

Perhaps the statement made at the beginning of this chapter may be clearer now: that forms are always meaningful, and that their perception does not imply the complete autonomy of a unique work in relation to other works. It has not been possible for me to gloss some narrative categories without referring to our sense of time, or to our doubtful knowledge of the con-sciousness of another person. As far as the tension between a unique work and collective forms is concerned, the comparatist naturally tends to be interested in the latter. But it is abundantly clear that such tension exists, as much because of the modern conception of the poet as because of the vigor of some inherited forms. The "narrated monologue" of the past century makes it possible for Clarín's discretion to be different from Flaubert's, and the difference cannot be discerned except from a historical perspective.

Later we will discuss some recent studies of intertextuality that show that there are eras when a multiplicity of models propels certain writers—Virgil, Petronius, Cervantes, Joyce—into a period of creative crisis. That helps us understand Laurent Jenny when he says that literature cannot exist without the acceptance, realization, transformation, or transgression of several archetypal models.[86]

In his lectures at Harvard University a few years ago, titled *The Witness of Poetry* (1983), Czeslaw Milosz, speaking from the vantage point of one with very special reason to know, discussed the division in the writer's mind between two inclinations, one mimetic and the other "classic." Milosz' theme is the circumstance of the modern poet, subject to the "logic of an incessant *movement*," which expels him from the "orbit of a language ordered by conventions" and condemns him therefore to risk, to danger, while he nevertheless remains faithful to his "passionate pursuit of the real."[87] For no present system of philosophy will ever convince him that the world does not exist, that its riches are not incalculable, and that it cannot or should not be apprehended by poetry. From this belief comes the "internal tension between imperatives" that Milosz describes:

> I affirm that, when writing, every poet is making a choice between the dictates of the poetic language and his fidelity to the real. If I cross out a word and replace it with another, because in that way the line as a whole acquires more conciseness, I follow the practice of the classics. If, however, I cross out a word because it does not convey an observed detail, I lean toward realism. Yet these two operations cannot be neatly separated, they are interlocked.[88]

The curious thing is that this tension, this boundless quest for a slippery and partial truth is characteristic of the modern cultivated poet; or rather, of *written* literature, whose formulation is usually definitive after it is given to the printer, but whose earlier composition allows erasing, correcting, change of mind, rewriting. Written words are, to a greater or lesser degree, rewritten words. And the rewriting born as a result of the gestation of a cultivated poem represents for a Milosz what he calls a passionate pursuit of the real. For the *oral* or traditional poet, such a reality already exists, for the most part. For the oral poet there is usually nothing that contains more truth—often historical—than the history sung by his elders, taught by his masters, the truth that he endeavored to record, recreate, or perform, from one moment to another, with essential faithfulness. With this observation I approach the immense field of oral poetry, a field that I don't mind calling oral literature, if we agree not to stumble over the "letter" enclosed in the word "literature" but rather decide to keep in mind the indisputable literary quality of such elevated poetry: Homer, the medieval European epic, or the Hispanic *romancero*. A different tension proper to this type of poetry has primordial consequences of a formal type.

Diego Catalán's investigations have stressed emphatically that a basic property of the Iberian romance is its *apertura* (openness): "Each romance is not a closed fragment of discourse (like the poems or stories of nontraditional literature) but rather a virtual 'program,' constantly subject (though very slowly) to transformation as a consequence of the very process of memorization and reproduction of versions by successive (and simultaneous) transmitters of traditional lore." [89] The apertura/openness of the signifier and the signified "accompanies every medieval work—such as the *Libro de buen amor* of the Arcipreste de Hita—in the course of its transmission, either oral or written, and conditions the manner in which the model is reproduced." [90] That trait of oral poetry no longer exists since the advent of printing and of the uniform reproduction of consumable and—as far as their production is concerned—closed texts. On the other hand, the essential flexibility of the traditional open poem merges with the necessity to update again and again the underlying design that allows the form to continue to flourish in very different sociohistorical contexts. Earlier we saw the scheme of stratification proposed for this genre of poetry. Catalán concludes that it is "the existence of those different levels which create the dynamism of the model, which permit the constant readaptation of the narration to the medium in which it is reproduced." [91] That is, some simultaneous articulations of a poetic type (comparable in language itself to A. Martinet's "double articulation") present the performer or recreator with a variety of thematic and formal options. Thus the openness of the romance is manifested "in the search for forms of expressing the signifieds with more efficacy." [92] For example, some variations or possible amplifications of a relatively macroformal character, such as the setting of scene and dramatization, exist within the limited space of the romance. The transmitter tries to visualize an action by placing it in a scene or a set. This "setting of a scene"—carried out on the level of the discourse, not of the narrative plot—can be very brief, as in certain versions of "Tarquino y Lucrecia," where, surprised by the presence of the King in the house,

> Cuando en su casa le vido   como a rey le aposentaba
>
> When they saw him in their house   like a king they received him

only one line is added:

le metió gallina en cena,   cama de oro que se echara.

offered him a chicken for supper,   a bed of gold to sleep on.

But a Moroccan version delights in description:

Púsole silleta de oro   con sus cruces esmaltadas,
púsole mesa de gozne   con los sus clavos de plata,
púsole a comer gallinas,   muchos pavones y pavas,
púsole a comer pan blanco,   y a beber vino sin agua;
con un negro de los suyos   mándole hacer la cama:
púsole catre de oro,   las tablas de fina plata,
púsole cinco almadraques,   sábanas de fina holanda,
púsole cinco almohadas,   cobertor de fina grana;
siete damas a sus pies,   otras tantas le demandan.[93]

they gave him a golden stool   with enameled crosspieces
gave him a table with hinges   fastened with silver nails,
gave him hens to eat   many peacocks and hen turkeys,
gave him white bread to eat   and unwatered wine to drink
one of their black servants   was ordered to make the bed:
they gave him a cot of gold   with slats of fine silver,
gave him five mattresses   sheets of fine Dutch linen,
gave him five pillows   a coverlet of fine scarlet cloth;
seven ladies at his feet,   as many others as he might wish.

Obviously dialogue is the principal form used in dramatization, dialogue of highly variable length, since one of the basic formal recourses of traditional art, on the plane of discourse as well as of plot, is ellipsis or omission.[94] Also on the level of discourse, seen now from a microformal point of view, the use of formulas and formulaic expressions is much in evidence, both in the brief Hispanic romances as well as in the long epic cantos that gave rise to the theoretical observations of Parry and Lord.

Already in 1935 Milton Parry set out to find a precise definition of the formal peculiarity of oral tales: "the principles of oral *form.*"[95] His discovery of the function of some *formulas* in the Homeric poems, a concept accepted by almost all specialists, is beyond discussion. Albert Lord, in *The Singer of Tales* (1960), chooses as an example the first fifteen lines of the *Iliad* and shows that 90 percent of this passage employs either *formulas* (short groups of words used regularly to express the same idea)[96] or *formulaic patterns:* a line or hemistich erected over the structure of a formula. In addition Lord's long and detailed work in the field of Yugoslavian oral poetry proves that until very recently the art of the *guslar* or South Slavic bard continued to rely on identical procedures—that is, on what Paul Zumthor, in his recent *Oral Poetry: An Introduction* (1990), also calls *micro-formes*.[97] Other microformal characteristics also mark these traditional, oral tales, such as the absence of the necessary enjambment—the basic element is the line or the hemistich, as also in the *romancero*[98]—and what Parry calls the *thrift* of formulaic art ("each position in the verse tends to allow one way, rather than many ways, of saying any one thing,"[99] if we are speaking of a single bard), a quality also found in Hesiod.[100]

As mentioned earlier, the fact that the discretion of traditional poetic art includes ellipsis and omission is well known by every hearer or reader of the *romancero*. But Diego Catalán is totally correct when he points out that the economy employed in oral poetry also implies its opposite, or rather, a freedom of choice between the two.

> The oral tradition, in its continuous search for an efficient expression of the narrative contents that it transmits, oscillates between two extremes: giving priority in the communication to economy, or emphatically stressing the message to make it reach the audience more incisively. Thus the various subtraditions of a romance may in each case tend to reduce a sequence to the mere enunciation of its nuclear phase or enrich it with adjectival, adverbial, and other modifiers.[101]

According to Catalán, this is where the formulas and formulaic turns of phrase come into play in the romances. For him the formulas are above all tropes and belong to the figurative language of the *romancero*. That is not so in the case of the Homeric epics, according to Lord: the second half of the first hexameter of the *Iliad*, "Achilles, son of Peleus," functions as a formula seven times in the poem.[102] Diego Catalán points out that the formulas bridge the space between the intrigue or basic plot of the tale and the poetic discourse itself, a conclusion that seems correct to me; and he shows that in practice the tropes in question are sometimes the most literal and least figurative ones, such as the *amplificatio*, the concrete epithet or a mere description—by which the action "he led her" is transformed (in "La Condesita") into

> La ha agarrado de la mano   y la ha puesto en el portal.[103]
>
> He took her by the hand   and placed her at the doorway.

The essential lesson of the South Slavic bards, again according to Lord's investigations, is that the authentic oral poet composes at the moment he is singing for a particular public on a precise occasion, and that he sings as he composes. The performance and the composition are indivisible. The true popular poet, as much as he may intend to do the opposite, never repeats himself exactly; nor is it proper to confuse him with the mere transmitter, relatively passive, who limits himself to memorizing a few particular poems. Faced with a theme or a series of themes that make up a story, the oral composer enjoys considerable freedom in the use of some formulas that are in themselves flexible: "His art consists not so much in learning through repetition the time-worn formulas as in the ability to compose and recompose the phrases for the idea of the moment on the pattern established by the basic formulas."[104]

In fact we face two extremes, and more than a few intermediate positions lie in between. On one end of the scale is the *aoidos* (bard-creator), a term applied to the Homeric and Hesiodic poems: an authentic oral poet who recreates as he composes, under the circumstances and using the methods described by Lord. On the other end is the *rhapsoidos* (rhapsode), a performer who memorizes and reduplicates entire poems. Regarding the era of the *romancero,* Don Ramón Menéndez Pidal also distinguished between a period "bardic or flowering when poetic narration, born either among the lower classes or in those higher, was propagated throughout all the people and actively repeated," and another period "rhapsodic or decadent, when the tradition was limited almost entirely to reproducing what had been created earlier," remaining limited "to the most common and most rural populations, as happened with the romances beginning with the thirteenth century."[105] In order for traditional songs to stay alive and not lose their artistic value and vigor, present-day singer-transmitters must be able to combine the different possible models, or variable and dynamic patterns, offered by the romances to create a distinct version-object, or to reproduce a single model with poetic-craftsmanlike sensibility: "the various performances of a romance differ among themselves as do the different reproductions made from models of a potter's 'water jar' or a 'gazpacho' recipe or a farm community's model of 'farmhouse.'"[106] *El romancero tradicional de las lenguas hispánicas* collected more than 900 versions of the romance of "Gerineldo." In Chapter 10 I commented on an ancient version of the romance of "El prisionero." To show that the capacity to create formulas still exists today, Diego Catalán cites an Andalusian version, in which the solitude of the prisoner is expressed this way:

> Preso pa toda la vida   sin oír ruidos de coche,
> sin saber cuándo es de día,   sin saber cuándo es de noche.[107]

> Prisoner for life   without hearing noises of cars
> not knowing when it is day   not knowing when it is night.

In other places and historical periods we observe no absolute distinction between the true bard and the rhapsode/reciter. Gregory Nagy points out that the diffusion of the Hesiodic and Homeric poems throughout Greece was clearly not based on written versions but on their recitation by rhapsodes at the pan-Hellenic festivals, which allowed certain values and beliefs of local origin to be disseminated to the entire nation. The creating and recreating nature of these recitations would diminish only very slowly: "By way of countless such performances for over two centuries, each recomposition at each successive performance could become less and less variable. Such gradual crystallization into what became set poems would have been a direct response to the exigencies of a Panhellenic audience." [108]

I do believe that it is necessary to hold to Lord's ideas regarding the microformal effects of oral composition. The closer our examples approach his model of bardic recreation, in which the acts of imagining and of singing are one, the more urgent and indispensable becomes the use of procedures such as the formula or the formulaic configuration. The oral circumstances of recreation give priority to the particular. With regard to Yugoslavia, we must keep in mind that we are dealing with very long compositions, ones that extend over many hours. Even in 1950 the great *guslar* Avdo Mededović could produce a narrative of 12,000 lines. Never written down, never seen as a whole, the tale could be made longer or shorter at any moment of its composition. The themes keep coming along one by one, being expanded or contracted—all within the general framework of the plot—being enriched with a greater or lesser amount of detail and ornamentation, depending on the strength of the singer and the interest of his audience. But what is essential is the immediate word, the response to the challenge of the decasyllablic line with the caesura occurring normally after the fourth syllable. The pressure of the moment takes precedence over all other considerations. I do not mean to imply that other elements of the whole composition were unimportant, but merely that they conformed to a less rigid, much more flexible scheme. In Spain the common fragmentation of the romances is very well known. They occur in greatly varying lengths, some frequently very short and therefore easy to memorize. "La Virgen se está peinando" (The Virgin Is Combing Her Hair), a most beautiful romance from the province of Valladolid that appeared in a recent collection, has been found in three different versions: one of seven lines (of two octosyllables each), one of fourteen, and one of eleven. [109] What is one to make then of a poem of 12,000 lines? Lord says that the Homeric epics are "oral dictated texts," composed in oral circumstances by a recreator who was called Homer and transcribed by one scribe or several scribes. It would be absurd, Lord adds, to ask the poet to keep in mind concepts of unity, in the style of Aristotle. In that case he would not have been Homer, nor would he have composed the *Iliad* and the *Odyssey*. Allow me here another, longer quotation of Lord, since I prefer not to summarize his words:

It is on the story itself, and even more on the grand scale of ornamentation, that we must concentrate, not on any alien concept of close-knit unity. The story is there and Homer tells it to the end. He tells it fully and with a leisurely tempo, ever willing to linger and to tell another story that comes to his mind. And if the stories are apt, it is not because of a preconceived idea of structural unity which the singer is self-consciously and laboriously working out, but because at the moment when they occur to the poet in the telling of his tale he is so filled with his subject that the natural processes of association have brought to his mind a relevant tale ... Each theme, small or large ... has around it an aura of meaning which has been put there by all the contexts in which it has occurred in the past.[110]

Unity that certainly, from the point of view of the audience, depends on the memory of the listeners, on what they heard sung by the bard earlier as well as on the contexts that might have conferred an aura of meaning to his themes on other occasions.[111]

To avoid confusion I wish to limit myself here to two aspects starting from a concrete point of reference: first, the concept of the oral poet, applicable to Homeric epics and other great modern tales "improvised" by singers while they are singing (the verb "improvised" is inadequate, but what I have just said will explain my quotation marks); and second, certain formal aspects of works produced by these singers and by the transmitters of the Spanish *romancero*. I am aware of the fact that poetic orality in general, as opposed to literary writing, encompasses much wider areas that are of special interest today to observers of the mass media and the mechanized transmission of the human voice, since the time of Marshall McLuhan and Walter J. Ong;[112] and I have not forgotten that a sociology not just of writing but also of orality must exist: analyses of audiences, of the radiation of certain themes, of the social, national, or political functions of the spoken or sung word. The field is unquestionably vast and extremely varied. But there are occasions when the critic should consider its entire compass, as Paul Zumthor has done in *Oral Poetry*. Today there is no doubt that just as during the Renaissance printing tilted the balance toward writing, nowadays songs, recordings, radio, concerts performed for audiences of thousands inject new life into oral communication. Today there are many countries of Europe as well as of Africa where three channels of communication are found juxtaposed—written literature, traditional oral poetry, and the modern media—and a number of other important ones as well.

Among these latter, I have in mind the protest song, of such significance in the Hispanic world: in Argentina, Chile, and Spain; the Catalan *nova cançó,* following the example of Raimon and Pi de la Serra. The singer-author, in general well-informed about the best poetry, does not improvise but performs his own texts and also the writings of others (Pablo Neruda, Miguel Hernández); his audience is not the vast multitude that might be commercially desirable, but groups of flesh-and-blood people, sharing certain critical feelings of unease about society or some revolutionary aspirations; and the role of the music is so important in their compositions that it is really a matter of interartistic creation. Zumthor, in commenting on such varied manifestations, is right to insist on the fact that the *voice* is more than the spoken word or even the intonation.[113] The voice introduces an unmistakable timbre that reveals the involvement of a real person (as in the theater, of course, or in undubbed movies), the commitment of the performer to his listeners, the breathing of a body that does not coincide completely with the language.

But this recovery of the voice through new channels of mass communication, with their illusion of immediacy—the opposite of the *Mittelbarkeit* (mediacy) that Stanzel was concerned with in the case of written narration—does not imply a return to a state of primitive innocence. A voice that can also deceive and seduce often provides that ancient link between orality and writing: rhetoric. I don't know if apologists for the modern techniques of communication are aware of the degree to which a recorded reproduction diminishes and mutilates the integrity of a live performance that brings singers or reciters together with their listeners. Isn't that precisely the essential nature of a live performance—in concert, speech, poetry reading, theatrical function, bullfight? Isn't that what makes such events singular, unique, and unrepeatable?

After all, for these and other reasons, and in face of such a jumble, it is important not to lose sight of two considerations. We should not blur the obvious dividing lines that separate different present-day vocal genres from the oral poetry of a bardic type described by Lord, or from what Menéndez Pidal called traditional poetry, a poetry recognized for centuries by a wide public for its capacity for constant recreation or variation.[114] Zumthor assumes this distinction when he differentiates between *oral transmission* (which includes phenomena of *transmission* and *reception*) and *oral tradition* (which links *production, storage,* and *repetition*);[115] but his scheme does not make very clear that storage and repetition may in certain areas and moments continue to be creative and productive. The tradition studied by Menéndez Pidal, Catalán, and Lord demonstrates beyond any doubt that the creation of a poem of this type is not something that happens only one single time, destined to be merely transmitted, conserved, or repeated later on.

And I consider it obvious that a certain iconoclastic or demythifying attitude before the institutionalization of literature (institution and attitude very characteristic of France, less marked in other nations) should not cause us to renounce all value judgments concerning oral literature. "Despite current trends I disregard quality as a criterion because it is too imprecise," Zumthor writes.[116] Whether we wish it or not, we apply that criterion whenever we approach the romances and tales of Spain and Yugoslavia as well as the songs disseminated today by the mass media, whether with interest, admiration, boredom, or repugnance. Precisely because they are not within the framework of the institution of literature, I am free to accept them—pass them on and repeat them in my memory—or to reject them. No scientific pretense obliges me to confuse the very intense quality of the songs of Raimon or the delicacy of "La Virgen se está peinando" with the vulgarity of the vocalizations, tacky and feeble, of some famous singer whose name I prefer not to remember.

Between the wide, integrating or totalizing, forms on the one hand and the verbal microforms on the other are found many procedures whose definition is really empirical and relative. Every figure of the empirical and relative type, no matter how limited its reach may seem at first glance, is worthy of interest because of its function as part of a whole. Each of the verbal microforms is obviously and positively part of a formal complex; thus their reach is partial, and their impact is rather more relational than relative. We have already seen that digressions are of necessity meaningful, simply because they are different from what went before. Many forms exist that also arise from modification, inversion, or discrepancy: interruptions, silences (white space, suspension points), narrative and moral intercalations. They are so common that their apparent absence, namely reiteration, whose acceptance in its broadest sense already preoccupied Kierkegaard, has given rise to quite a number of critical reflections.[117] (I say "apparent" inasmuch as the anaphoric series paradoxically also brings about a process of change. As Todorov says, whoever repeats himself cites—and modifies[118]—himself). Genette has classified the different types of intercalated narration that he calls metadiegetic story (relative to the world of another tale within the tale), found so frequently in the epic, from the *Odyssey* to Tasso, in the ancient novel (Apuleius, Petronius), in novels of the seventeenth and eighteenth centuries (Mateo Alemán's *Guzmán de Alfarache* and the works of Paul Scarron, Laurence Sterne, Denis Diderot), and naturally in *The Thousand and One Nights*.[119] When the telling of the enveloping tale with the story embedded within it does not tend toward divergence or contrast but rather analogy, we find ourselves before the interior duplication or *mise en abîme,* pointed out by André Gide in his day and noticed quite often recently.[120] Once more we see that the critic's formal categories are provisional, or rather that in practice they are shaded, combined, and multiplied. The analogy, the specular image, of the *mise en abîme* can be larger or smaller: explicative as it refers to plot, or thematic (the medieval *exemplum*). And that by itself can become both enigma and allurement for the reader.

The same thing happens with respect to intercalated narration, from Cervantes to Proust, that is, in the modern novel—an open complex of forms, polyphony, plurality of styles, devouring plasticity of other genres, as Bakhtin's critical meditation points out. The author of the "One Who Was Too Curious for His Own Good" in *Quixote* is not a character in the novel (like the captive captain) nor an extradiagetic narrator. His identity is unknown. Nothing more Cervantine: surprise, mystery. From the beginning the relation of the part to the whole turns into a problem. And this complication of forms by intratextuality obviously appears also in other civilizations and in other artistic spheres, such as in the very rich narrative of Japan, from the time of Lady Murasaki and Saikaku Ihara to Natsume Soseki, Yasunari Kawabata, and Yukio Mishima.

I have in mind now an admirably constructed novel by Mishima titled *Runaway Horses,* which revolves around an intercalated tale, "The League of the Divine Wind," and the decisive influence that the reading of the tale had on the protagonists. The main action takes place at the beginning of the 1930s: the rebellion of the young traditionalists of the League, narrated and praised in the intercalation (which itself encloses various brief interposed texts), occurred in 1876 and 1877; and the person who narrates is an extradiegetic author, Tsunanori Yamao. The young hero, Isao, transformed in a quixotic manner by the reading of "The League of the Divine Wind," tries to imitate and revive the values and deeds presented on those pages—even going so far as to commit the essential *seppuku,* or ritual suicide. Throughout the novel the reader of Mishima, who has also read the same text read by Isao, never stops asking himself whether the deeds and values of the rebels of 1876 can or ought to be emulated sixty years later. The puzzle of the possible connection between the diegetic and the meta-diegetic tale becomes mixed with the plot and the meaning of the novel. Keep in mind that Isao's point of view is not the only one expressed. A short while after reading the story of the League, in a copy given to him by Isao, Judge Honda writes a letter to Isao in which he tries to explain that one cannot interpret past events without a sufficiently wide perspective:

Learning from history should never mean fastening upon a particular aspect of a particular era and using it as a model to reform a particular aspect of the present. To take out of the jigsaw puzzle of the past a piece with a set form and attempt to fit it into the present is not an enterprize that could have a happy outcome. To do so is to toy with history, a pastime fit for children.[121]

There is then a confrontation—something like a dialogue in the figurative sense of the word—at the core of Mishima's story between the juxtaposition of opinions regarding the pertinence of the intercalated narration. The dialogue in its strict sense is incorporated into that plurality of languages and styles mentioned by Bakhtin. The plot with its dénouement is narrower than the diversity of values that continue to reverberate in the mind of the reader until after the narrator's last phrase, which describes Isao's suicide. Remember the death of Alonso Quijano: in both cases the novel goes beyond the dénouement.

Dialogue (as we indicated in Chapter 12) is a form common to many genres: the moment when two or more persons make direct use of words in a story, poem, description, essay, interview, or philosophical, critical-literary (Friedrich Schlegel), or scientific reflection (Galileo). We have already noted one of its characteristics: the double intent. Dialogue is a "formal" or "intraformal" element, whose potential depends upon numerous associations and connections with the history of ideas and social institutions. In the Renaissance, for example, dialogue came to be totalizing—that is, tended to become a genre—because of its possible contacts with Aristotelian logic or dialectic on the one hand and with Socratic modes of thought on the other. The dialectic discussion uses as its point of departure what Aristotle calls in his *Topics endoxos:* the admitted idea, the idea of general acceptance, what people say. Out of this, putting aside its more technical or Scholastic uses, comes the familiar or "realistic" aspect of the ancient dialectic and its possible application to drama or the novel. Nothing is more lively than the need to refute, to top what someone else said, to persuade others of the error of their opinion, of what's said and heard in a conversation. That is not the case in a certain type of dialogue cultivated during the Renaissance to the extent, always debatable, that it followed the Socratic tradition of Western thinking: process in various voices, continuing and dynamic quest that enchannels, as Paul Foulquié writes, "a movement of the mind, an impetus of conquest, a going beyond the first given."[122] Movement of the mind not limited to the exercise of a few logical procedures, and, what is more, difficult to imagine unless supported by a certain moral, social, or political stance. In this way intellectual dialogue lends itself to many varied inclinations, from the simulacrum of a confrontation of attitudes (the fact being that only one can flourish), or a static contrast of appearances, to an exchange between two minds, a continuing encounter of two persons, or better yet, of two lives, that makes possible the discovery of concepts that cannot be attributed to one intelligence or another but to the fruit—co-intelligence—of the interchange maintained between them.[123]

Remember that after the Council of Trent the movement known as the Counter-Reformation encompassed a general plan of codification. Numerous codes were adopted in general unitary and monological agreements having to do with the most diverse fields: jurisprudence, politics, guides of moral conduct or of social etiquette, anthologies, and also treatises on poetics. In face of the superabundance of models, the norm was extolled. Here is another polarity that characterizes the era: the normative treatise, on the one hand, and the Socratic dialogue on the other.

Dialogues written by Lope de Vega, Racine, Voltaire, Dickens, Oscar Wilde, Hemingway, Sartre! The differences are so great that only with difficulty do they escape historical-typological limits. Gerhard Bauer describes four types of dialogue in his *Zur Poetik des Dialogs* (1969). First, a closed and conventional mode of interchange in which some persons take as a point of departure some common social and linguistic premises—*gebundenes, konventionstreues Gespräch* (bound conversation, true to convention—the classical French theater). Second, dialogue that is open and free of conventions, in which the characters manifest themselves impulsively, or without reaching full reciprocal communication: *konventionssprengendes Gespräch* (conversation that discards convention—Cervantes; Turgenev: silences and equivocations). Between these two extremes Bauer places authentic experimental and dialectical interchanges, in which a basic desire for understanding unleashes a succession of changing opinions and the possibility of attaining a wider synthesis, *dialektisches Gespräch* (dialectical conversation). And finally, a simple *Konversation,* no longer a channel for a few well-marked ideas or individualities, but use of language with no other aim than to conform to certain modes of conviviality.

This scheme is only a beginning. In practice we find ourselves obliged to add to it. There is a type of novelistic dialogue, for example, in which two or more persons share common premises (Gerhard Bauer's model 1), or rather they don't talk in vain, nor impulsively, but with the intention not so much of understanding one another and reaching an agreement (model 3), as for each one to explain himself to the other, for each speaker to explain himself better to himself, as in the case of Don Quixote's dialogue with the Knight of the Green-Colored Greatcoat (II.620–628), the peak of the confrontation of values in the Cervantine novel. Neither of the speakers proposes to vanquish the other, to refute him or surpass him dialectically. They define two incompatible systems of values. The two hidalgos agree not to agree, to respect each other's convictions. There will be no violence, no combat, no tragedy, but the differences between the two contrasting systems will not be resolved. The "second hearer," the reader, is the one who measures the psychic space where dialogic opposition can develop and mature. The reader is the stage where the full dialectical confrontation is played out.[124] And similarly Bakhtin regards as erroneous the idea that Dostoevsky proposes a dialectical synthesis of the thesis of Alyosha and the antithesis of Ivan in *The Brothers Karamazov*:

> For Ivan is disputing not with Alyosha but above all with himself, and Alyosha is not disputing with Ivan as an integral and unified voice but rather intervenes in his internal dialogue, trying to reinforce one of its rejoinders. And there can be no talk here of any sort of synthesis; one can talk only of the victory of one or another voice, or of a combination of voices in those places where they agree.[125]

I am still referring to dialogue in its literal, dictionary sense—"conversation between two or more persons." But the term tends to exceed the limits of such a strict definition. Socrates explains in the *Theaetetus* (189e): "I suspect that when the mind thinks, it is conversing with itself, asking questions and answering them, and saying either yes or no." Who would hesitate to say that at that instant the mind *dialogues* with itself despite the absence of a second person and of the spoken word? A few years ago I wrote in regard to the last dialogue *sensu stricto* of *Quixote,* the dialogue between Sancho and Alonso Quijano, who is dying (not Don Quixote): "The dialogue, implicit, totalizing, deposited in the memory of those who read it, remains unfinished."[126] Like superimposed layers, this implicit and incomplete dialogue preserves the numerous oppositions of values that have been accumulating throughout the novel, not literally somewhere in the book, but in the reader's memory. But how can implicit and explicit dialogue be reconciled? At that time I was not yet acquainted with the work of the admirable Mikhail Bakhtin, who wrote regarding the author of *The Brothers Karamazov:* "In Dostoevsky's novels, the life experience of the characters and their discourse may be resolved as far as plot is concerned, but internally they remain incomplete and unresolved."[127]

The relational and reactive structure that is dialogue *sensu lato* acquires in Bakhtin's writings a very special breadth, function, and intensity of sig-nificance. (Some of these writings were unknown until very recently, even in the Soviet Union.[128] As Todorov rightly points out, it is true that other thinkers, more or less allied to existentialism, have also assigned a central place to dialogue and to the ontology of alterity: the Sartre of *Being and Nothingness* (1962); and above all Martin Buber.[129] In 1956 Stephen Gil-man published *The Art of "La Celestina,"* in which he based the originality of Fernando de Rojas on the use of the word as a vital and dynamic trajec-tory that an "I" directs to a "you," converting the dialogue into "the axis of spoken life": "the word in *La Celestina* is a bridge between speaker and listener, the meeting place of two lives."[130] Gilman (whose book owes some-thing to Buber) discovers in Fernando de Rojas a dialogic virtue entirely comparable to what Bakhtin praises in two other great writers of the Ren-aissance (*sensu lato* also), Rabelais and Cervantes. Well then, two things are characteristic of Bakhtin: the application (during forty years of untiring and passionate meditation) of a dialogic principle to the entire history of West-ern literature, to linguistics, and to philosophical anthropology; and the extreme agility that allows him to pass from the literal use of a term to its figurative use, concerning dialogue or also the novel. (With regard to such mobility Todorov prefers to speak of intertextuality rather than of dialogue, intertextuality being a concept launched by Julia Kristeva precisely because of Bakhtin;[131] a stance that runs the risk of muddling the critical terrain and of not distinguishing clearly enough between internal and external relations in a text, the external being its responses to other spheres and languages.)

For Bakhtin dialogue, *sensu lato,* essentially defines man. "The single adequate form for *verbally expressing* human life is the *open-ended dia-logue*. Life is by its very nature dialogic."[132] In effect, man is heterogeneous; and this essential diversity of his (close to the "heterogeneity of being" that Machado wrote about) corresponds to the need for verbal expression that at all times manifests the presence of the other in a being, the consciousness of the other, the response to the words of the other. In 1970–71 Bakhtin wrote, "I call *sense* what is a *response* to a question. Whatever does not respond to any question is senseless."[133]

The heterogeneity of man, bordering on the other, and involved in a con-stant dialogue with the other, is confounded with the plural character of language, whose unifying tendencies strive without success to overcome the abundance of tongues that surrounds every expressive and meaningful sit-uation: what Bakhtin calls "heteroglossia" (*raznoiazychie, raznorechie, raz-norechivost'*).[134] "The word in language is half someone else's."[135] Like the novel, the human being is a "mixture of all . . . kinds," as Todorov says,[136] an unfinished process, inasmuch as dialogue that forms the basis for the process implies a multitude of alien words:

> The word, directed toward its object, enters a dialogically agitated and tension-filled environment of alien words, value judgments and accents, weaves in and out of complex interrelationships, merges with some, recoils from others, intersects with yet a third group: and all this may crucially shape discourse, may leave a trace in all its semantic layers, may complicate its expression and influence its entire stylistic profile.[137]

Or also:

> In language, there is no word or form left that would be neutral or would belong to no one: all of language turns out to be scattered, permeated with intentions, accented. For the consciousness that lives in it, language is not an abstract system of normative forms but a concrete heterological opinion of the world. Every word gives off the scent of a profession, a genre, a current, a party, a particular work, a particular man, a generation, an era, a day, and an hour. Every word smells of the context and contexts in which it has lived its intense social life; all words and all forms are inhabited by intentions. In the word, contextual harmonies (of the genre, of the current, of the individual) are unavoidable.[138]

Is the use of "dialogue" *sensu lato* in Bakhtin rather metonymic? Well, it is a matter of truncated interchanges, "versations" instead of conversations, replies to past contexts or absent speakers, on the one hand; and, on the other, a sum or open series of infinite stimuli and countless reactions that make up an immense dialogue if we put the parts and particles together. What we really experience is a parceling out or atomization of that unseizable, unfinished whole, accumulating from a past and above all moving toward a future. For a word too much or a word too little, truly meaningful dialogue escapes us, between memory and intention.

Bakhtin is so coherent that he is not blind to the fact that this great dialogue is not realized completely in the novel—promise of future readers—and naturally does not coincide with the literal exchange between his characters:

> The internal dialogism of authentic prose discourse, which grows organically out of a stratified and heteroglot language, cannot fundamentally be dramatized or dramatically resolved (brought to an authentic end); it cannot ultimately be fitted into the frame of any manifest dialogue, into the frame of a mere conversation between persons; it is not ultimately divisible into verbal exchanges possessing marked boundaries.[139]

Bakhtin says on one occasion (when it seems that the eighteenth-century phantom of *innere Form* might reappear) that the Socratic dialogue was "the first step in the history of the new genre of the novel . . . but . . . little more than an external form of dialogism."[140] In Dostoevsky that deepest "dialogism" is found not in the "manifest dialogues" but rather at the core of a supposed monologue like the legend of the Grand Inquisitor, which Ivan Karamazov recounts:

> A more detailed analysis of this dialogue [of Ivan with Alyosha in the tavern] and of the "Legend of the Grand Inquisitor" itself would show a profound participation of all elements of Ivan's world view in his internal dialogue with himself and in his internally polemical interrelations with others. For all its external proportionality, the "Legend" is nevertheless full of interruptions; both the very form of its construction as the Grand Inquisitor's dialogue with Christ and at the same time with himself, and, finally, the very unexpectedness and duality of its finale, indicate an internally dialogic disintegration at its very ideological core.[141]

But unfortunately we cannot keep on quoting Bakhtin. I believe that the problem is clear for the student of literature. What relations can we find between the "dialogism" of a work and the "manifest dialogues" that appear in it? Donald Fanger proposes a reading of the dialogism of *Quixote* that is without doubt accurate and valuable:

> A Bakhtinian analysis would show dialogue to be . . . its medium and constitutive principle. It would note how the first sentence of Cervantes' prologue already announces this by engaging the reader in a half-tacit dialogue that will be sustained through the entire text . . . And it would study the dialogic relations between all the "historians" of don Quixote who appear in the text, from the hypothetical Cide Hamete to the historical Avellaneda. Beyond this, a Bakhtinian analysis would consider the *impersonal* dialogues in the book, between and among genres of discourse . . . It would do so, moreover, by relating them to the medium in which character is made manifest and dynamic. This is the medium of dialogue in the more restricted sense, for it is in dialogue, in that border area where two consciousnesses interpenetrate, that meaning is created. The Bakhtinian analysis of *Don Quixote*, accordingly, would trace the mutually defining relations of don Quixote and Sancho with virtually the entire population of the book, and—most importantly—with themselves . . . *and with each other*. Bakhtin's theoretical model of the novel . . . would also show its utility by providing a method for considering the most important features of this book in their interrelatedness—the better to characterize the dynamic universe of their meanings.[142]

The cloth is cut. To my way of thinking it is important not to disdain its most obvious scraps: what people say *when they talk*—and also what they don't say or only imply. The relation between a broader dialogism and concrete verbal exchanges could thus be turned into a real object of study. Or in another way we might give in to more than one temptation at a time: to the disdain of the verbal surface, or of the spoken word; to the search for a remote unicorn, of a hidden or absent dialogism like the Platonic Idea; and to a hyperbolization of dialogue that may be converted into a synonym of opposition, interrelation, or structure.

In the case of dialogue, examples and historical knowledge offer more than an enrichment of the problem: we would find it difficult to consider the problem without them. That is not the case for the micromorphological procedures mentioned at the beginning of this chapter, whose definition comes from the traditon of rhetoric: syllepsis, amplification, zeugma, oxymoron, and so forth. Their use is usually particularizing and mean to distinguish unique styles, or rather speculative and ahistorical ones, above all as a consequence of Jakobson's opposing poles—the metaphoric and the metonymic, whose abuse is astonishing to those of us who never thought that Jakobson's idea, applicable to Boris Pasternak and other writers, was universally valid. I am in agreement with the worthy collectors of popular Castilian romances, who write the following, without any pretense whatsoever:

> It is an overly common error to consider that metaphor constitutes the indispensable unity and substance of a poem; such a theory is denied by the exquisite compositions of a Gil Vicente:
>
> > Mal haya quien los envuelve
> > los mil amores,
> > mal haya quien los envuelve. . .
>
> > Damned be he who weaves
> > those thousand love affairs,
> > damned be he who weaves them . . .[143]

I have already emphasized that literary theory concerns itself with the problems of comparative literature only insofar as it remains historically (that is, temporally and spatially) flexible. In this area, that of rhetorical microforms, the theoretical context is usually logical, semantic, philosophical, or merely linguistic. Or rather what is proposed, along with Paul de Man, is a general theory of literary communication, characterized by an awareness of gesticulation, duplicity, exaggerated signs of emotion, the vanity of the figure and the procedure, or rather, by its failed rhetorical transparency.[144] Like his object, the critic of rhetoric claims universality. On the other hand, it is curious that a speculative and ultrahistorical bent is not usually apparent in the study of *styles,* perhaps because from the beginning, starting with their descriptions in the ancient precepts, styles have been diverse or different and have allowed poetical and unlike genres to be differentiated.

The great success of the masterwork of Erich Auerbach, *Mimesis* (1946), is that each chapter begins with a micromorphological reading. Moreover, the analysis of brief passages is based on the opposition between two collective styles (hypotaxis and parataxis) and on a historical approach to the application of the rhetorical theory of the three styles to literary genres (Quintilian, *Institutio oratoria,* XII.10: *subtile, medium, grande*). Auerbach tests his theoretical scheme at each step, confronting it with a long series of precise inquiries. The general verbal categories that in this context are called styles belong to historical poetics and are only hypothetical models that every textual analysis tries to refine. I insist on the efficacy of this linkage of the peculiarity of a unique work with style conceived as collective model, because that linkage is at the root of the interest of this procedure for comparativism.

This dualism—or ambiguity—seems to be a constituent and functional element for any understanding of the concept of style, so broad that it takes in both the perception of the idiosyncrasies of a work or of a writer and the vision of a complex of collective and historical models: styluses, gravers, inherited tools, recourses that existed earlier. Style (like theme, as we shall see now) is a multiple nexus. Our best critics show, as Auerbach does, that style is a certain kind of relation between the two poles—social and individual—of the concept, or of the stance before them. I allude to an important critical tradition that has produced work of the highest prestige in the Hispanic sphere: what was called *Stilistik;* stylistics. The authorities and the dates are very well known: Karl Vossler, Leo Spitzer, Helmut Hatzfeld, Giacomo Devoto, S. Ullman, the classes of Amado Alonso in Buenos Aires in the 1930s and 1940s, the masterly books of Dámaso Alonso, and—since I must necessarily limit myself to only a few more names—the exemplary prose writings of Raimundo Lida, the lectures of Angel Rosenblat, the critical and theoretical inquiries of Carlos Bousoño.

Forty years have gone by, and we have a very different situation. I have tried to summarize in another place the severe attacks that the concept of style has suffered since then, and the challenges that its rescue will entail.[145] I refer to the reservations of Barthes in 1967 in *Writing Degree Zero* (style, intimate and biological imperative of the individual, "resides outside art, that is, outside the pact which binds the writer to society"; the "writing" that seals this pact "is always rooted in something beyond language"), in 1974 in *S/Z* (where one reads the famous sentence: "The work of the commentary, once it is separated from any ideology of totality, consists precisely in *manhandling* the text, *interrupting* it"). And I refer also to Kristeva, whose use of the term *discourse* proclaims, with more clarity than the writing of Barthes, a return to the social or collective dimension of the word, or rather to the premises of ancient rhetoric; to Jakobson in the no-less-celebrated "Linguistics and Poetics" (1960), where the poem exemplifies only a general "poetic function"; and to the hermeneutics of E. D. Hirsch: "the words ... institute a spiritual process which, beginning with the words, ultimately transcends the linguistic medium." [146]

In my opinion there is much to learn from these reservations. One could say as much of those that have appeared in other latitudes. I am referring to the distinction that Bakhtin proposed between style and stylization. In that distinction (already evident in Roman writers, apprentices to their Greek forerunners) the consciousness or representation of the alien word has its effect: "Stylization differs from style proper precisely by virtue of its requiring a specific linguistic consciousness (the contemporaneity of the stylizer and his audience), under whose influence a style becomes a stylization, against whose background it acquires new meaning and significance." [147] In this way the Croatian Slavist and comparatist Aleksandar Flaker endeavors to suppress the atomism of individual and isolated styles through the idea of "stylistic formation": continuous evolution of large unities, of verbal proclivities, that connect a majority of writers. [148]

I will summarize very briefly some of the misunderstandings or obstacles that a certain kind of stylistics comes up against. One: the confusion of the writer with the work: "Can we define the soul of a certain French writer by his particular language?" Spitzer asked. [149] The most recent schools of stylistics reacted against this neo-Romantic biographism (for example, in Belgium). [150] Two: *no*, the style is not all the literary work; nor does the poem coincide exactly with its language; nor the science of literature with linguistics. [151] This false panlinguistic premise has been disproved by excellent studies of style: Amado Alonso, who tried to discern the evocative and suggestive power of words, the aura and the silence that surrounds them; [152] and others for whom gesture and thrust are "much more than what is expressed in words," to quote Fidelino de Figueiredo. [153] And with abundant reason René Wellek concluded: "We have to become literally critics to see the function of style within a totality which inevitably will appeal to extralinguistic and extrastylistic values, to the harmony and coherence of a work of art, to its relation to reality, to its insight into its meaning, and hence to its social and generally human import." [154] In the third place: the noninsularity of the text was never clearly perceived; rather, it was thought that the text was raised above its antecedents, and thus a completely autonomous and solitary architecture was erected. Now we understand better the intertextuality of the poem, that it is a cross of unsuppressed origins, carrier of cultural and social codes: in sum, like the human being, original confluence of ancient itineraries. [155] Four: the uniqueness of a style was often defined as a deviation or divergence from the ordinary norms of language. Such a *petitio principii* is not acceptable. Neither are the supposed norms invariable, nor does every innovation necessarily bring with it a stylistic effect. And there are stylistic effects that are not considered abnormal. [156] And finally: Barthes was partly right when he denounced the ideology of totality (without guarding against the idea, also ideological, of the primacy of disintegration). The religion of art, the adoration of the text as sacred icon, also an inheritance from Romanticism, is neither useful nor necessary. I believe that the choice of form as a subject for the work of a literary critic is a fruitful premise and one that is historically justified; but it would be foolish to use it as a weapon to engage in an exquisite fencing match with the discords of history.

The ambiguous attitudes toward language have been typical of our time and our critical fervor. Octavio Paz writes: "Critical passion: excessive, impassioned love of criticism·and its precise devices for disconstructions, but also criticism in love with its object, infatuated with the very thing it denies." [157] However, sooner or later we return to the words, to the words of the great poets, which are also ours. And the study of literature returns to the detailed and constructive investigation of language, exemplifed today by the excellent work of Michael Riffaterre.

14

Themes: Thematology

Comparatists of the French hour like Paul Hazard did not have a high regard for the study of themes, so assiduously cultivated by medievalists, folk-
lorists, and other investigators at the end of the nineteenth century.[1] This
lack of interest among the French comparatists is not surprising if we take
account of what most annoyed them: the scant attention paid to the direct
and clear influence of one writer on another. In effect, thematology at that
time usually consisted in assembling or summarizing the diverse treatments
of a single topic or figure in its global manifestations, or in tracing the
itinerary of a traditional myth, procedures injurious to the binary relations
dear to Paul Van Tieghem. On the other hand, many comparatists were
irritated by the piling up of facts, the abundance of minor works, the positivist catalogue of titles and materials. As is well known, the reaction
against positivism was characteristic of the best criticism of the first half of
our century[2]—Russian formalism, for example, the New Criticism in the
United States (R. P. Blackmur, John Crowe Ransom, Cleanth Brooks), or
German and Spanish stylistics. But the last few decades have witnessed a
rebirth of various thematological investigations, both practical and theoretical, studies not in conflict with genological or morphological studies but
rather linked to them.[3]

A few pages back, with Dámaso Alonso as our guide, we saw that some
critical discourses follow a single path for the most part, starting from different points or bound for different destinations: from the form to the

theme, or from the theme to the form. We also emphasized at that time that the critic must constantly choose, extract, cite; in other words, we saw that forms and themes, more than discrete entities, are partial elements brought together by the intervention of the reader. Concerning thematology, such intervention will be more or less important depending on the breadth and richness of the historical panorama available to the comparatist, and on the relevance of the phenomena of intertextuality capable of identifying a theme through recall of earlier representations. I am reviewing these observations to help us confront the frightful dispersion that these assemblages present, and none more affected by the scattering than the many-branched subject of thematics. In face of the jumble, the tangle, the *totum revolutum* of literary themes, mirror of the confusion of life itself, a selective attitude becomes indispensable. I am not advocating that comparatists return to the chaos that literature in general tries to remedy.

"Not enough forms . . . ," wrote Flaubert, "and too many things."[4] Forms—between the one and the many—tend to come together; things tend to split apart. But on the other hand, it is worth noting that it is often a theme that helps a writer deal with the superabundance and profusion of real existence, by drawing a line between experience and poetry. In practice, theme becomes synonymous with "significant theme" and above all with "structuring theme" or "inciting theme." The thematic element, like the formal element I mentioned a short while ago, thus fulfills a utilitarian function: it reconciles literary writing and reading. As Manfred Beller observes, the theme is an element that structures a work in a perceptible way.[5] In a letter to Goethe, Schiller explained that the poetical task starts from a dark, almost unconscious idea, *Totalidee,* which needs an *Objekt* in order to be realized.[6] Similarly, T. S. Eliot thought that an emotional starting point is necessary, as well as an *objective correlative,* to make it concrete—perhaps an image or a motif.

Not what the poem says, but what it uses to say it. Such a concretion takes on different formal profiles. Unique thematic elements exist that cannot be repeated within a work, as for example in the case of the descent to the underworld typical of epic poetry, which prefigures—and thereby thematizes—the episode of the cave of Montesinos in *Don Quixote* (II.23). Don Quixote's dream, spatially circumscribed, affects in a metonymic fashion the entire second part of the book. The limits of a theme, if it is a theme, are very relative. All this becomes clearer when a theme is modified, broadened, or repeated. The *Motiv* thus becomes *Leitmotiv,* based on the dynamics of reiteration. Think of the use of theme as similar to variation in music, as Thomas Mann recognized when he characterized his own work as *thematisch.*[7] Think of Ramón Gómez de la Serna's *Senos* (1923), one of the most erotic books of modern Spanish literature, with its endless playful variations on one synecdoche: breasts = woman.

Or think of the *Suites* (1920–1923) of Federico García Lorca: "Suite del agua," "Suite de los espejos," "Canciones bajo la luna" (which bring to mind Leopoldo Lugones of the *Lunario sentimental,* 1909); and other series of works held together by the pretext of a common motif, about which André Belamich writes as follows:

> It is known that "suite," in the seventeenth and eighteenth centuries, indicated a series of dances all written in the same key as that used in the first. The link that here joins each poem to the first one is more narrow: it is the one that exists between a theme and its variations, the "differences" of the vihuelists of the sixteenth century such as [Antonio de] Cabezón, Luis Millán, [Alonso] Mudarra . . . These series appear like the facets of a same object or like the phases of a meditation that keeps probing the same motif.[8]

Theme here implies form; and from this point of view the differences and explorations that unite a handful of poems closely resemble the successive moments of a single composition, above all the parallelisms and reiterations characteristic of a certain type of popular poetry: songs, as brief and concentrated as those of Rafael Alberti in his *Baladas y canciones del Paraná* (1976):

> Cuanto más chico, más chico,
>   se le adentra más el sol,
>
> Cuanto más chico, más chico,
>   se oye mejor,[9]
>
> The smaller, the smaller,
>   the more the sun enters,
>
> The smaller, the smaller,
>   the sharper the ears,

Few Spanish readers will not be acquainted with Lorca's "Baladilla de los tres ríos," with its variations that turn on two opposing motifs (the one river of Seville and the two of Granada) and a double refrain as well; it serves as a good example:[10]

> *¿Ay, amor*
> *que se fue por el aire!*
>
> Para los barcos de vela
> Sevilla tiene un camino;

por el agua de Granada
sólo reman los suspiros.

¿Ay, amor
que se fue y no vino!

Ay, the love
that went off on the breeze!

For boats under sail
Seville has a road;
on Granada's waters
only sighs row.

Ay, the love
that left and didn't return!

Or the "Serenata" constructed around two themes already sketched in the first stanza (night, with the river and the moon; the desire of Belisa):

Por las orillas del río
se está la noche mojando.
Y en los pechos de Belisa
se mueren de amor los ramos.

Down on the riverbanks
the night has gone wading
and against Lolita's breasts
for love, bouquets are fading.

These internal changes also bring together intertextual echoes, such as the delicate tensions that usually characterized the Portuguese *cantar de amigo*. Consider the "Cantiga de roda" by Jorge de Sena, where the circular dialogues with his own soul lead finally—and like in medieval times—to a Dance of Death:

Minh'alma, não te conheço
minh'alma, não sei de ti,
oh dança, minh'alma, dança,
por amor de quanto vi.

Não te conheço, minh'alma,
e nunca te conheci,
oh dança, minh'alma, dança,
dança por mim e por ti.

Conhecer é possuir
e eu nunca te possuí:

oh dança, minh'alma, dança,
por amor de quanto vi.

Tu sabes tudo de mim,
eu nunca te conheci:
oh dança, minh'alma, dança,
dança por mim e por ti.

Eras luz simples e pura
acesa dentro de ti:
oh dança, minh'alma, dança
por amor de quanto vi.

Na dança morremos ambos
tão longe e perto de aqui:
oh dança, minh'alma, dança,
dança por mim e por ti.

I know thee not, my soul,
naught I know of thee . . .
Dance on, oh soul, dance on,
For love of all that round us be.

No, I know thee not, my soul,
nor ever did I knowledge have of thee,
Yet dance, oh soul, dance on apace,
Dance for thyself and dance for me.

To know indeed is to possess,
And never yet didst thou belong to me,
Then dance, dance, yet dance my soul,
Dance for the love of all I see.

All things in me thou knowest well,
But never did I knowledge have of thee.
Oh dance, oh dance, my dancing soul,
Dance for thyself and dance for me.

Light wast thou, light plain and pure,
Light lit within the heart of thee.
Then dance, my dancing soul, dance on
Dance for the love of all I see.

This dance is for both our Dance of Death,
So far, and yet so near we cannot flee:
Dance on, my dancing soul, dance on,
Dance for thyself, and dance for me.[11]

Intertextual and intratextual at one and the same time, the thematic element in such cases links the poem with other poems and with the successive moments of the poem itself.

The terms and materials in question are highly varied: theme, motif, myth, situation, type (or character, or *actant*), scene, space, commonplace, topos, image? Images, significant visual entities, such as color—the whiteness of *Moby Dick*—which according to Borges gives away the secret of the story.[12] *Topoi* and commonplaces, of varying lengths, such as the invocation of the muses, or the "pleasant place," conceived as channels of expression, scaffolding, or poetical schemes.[13] Characteristic spaces and settings, like a garden, or, in the case of novels, the great modern city—Paris, St. Petersburg, Madrid, Berlin, Buenos Aires—catalysts of extensive narrative creations.[14] Episodes or scenes required by certain conventional genres—the descent to the underworld in the epic, and also the conclave of the gods, the flattery of a seductress[15]—or what are inseparable from specific well-known fables—the last moments of Faust, Don Juan's supper with the Stone Guest. Moral, social, or professional types, such as the miser, which present-day criticism (Propp, Souriau, Greimas) teaches us to differentiate from two things: the *actant,* or basic function of the story or drama (the protagonist), and the specific character (Harpagon, Grandet, Pliushkin, Torquemada).[16] The great *thèmes des héros,* whose level of personification supports and stimulates the writer's concrete modulation, according to Raymond Trousson:[17] Ulysses, Oedipus, Medea, Antigone, or, later, Troilus and Cressida, Alexander, El Cid. In general, the motif is considered to be less extensive than the theme. But some specialists use the terms the other way round, as we shall see later. In the face of such diversity, the reluctance of some comparatists to take on thematology is understandable.

There is no doubt that a quantitative criterion is in order, but it is useful only in the descriptive sense. Microthemes, macrothemes, minimotifs? According to Borges, what is curious in this case is that the fleeting appearance of a color, a flower, a tree, the smallest object, can be as important, as revealing, from the point of view of its function, as the entire argument of the work. In poetry as in the other arts, less is more. A "monograph of blue" would be necessary, Rilke said. Bernhard Blume has shrewdly observed the role played by water in several great German poems.[18] We keep observing that theme (in the wide sense of the word, including the variations outlined earlier) brings together and structures the successive parts of a work by providing links with life and with literature. Triple linkage, therefore, of the poem: with poetry, with the world, with itself.

The condition of a theme is active and passive at the same time: a provoking, integrating factor, on one hand; object of modification, on the other. Coming out of the world, from nature and culture, the theme is what the writer modifies, modulates, overturns, not what he says but what he uses to say with, whatever its extension, as we noted. Take for example the traditional plot of one of Racine's tragedies.

On November 17, 1667, the young Racine presented *Andromaque* before the king and his court for the first time. On the next day the same actors performed the play for the general public in a theater of the Hôtel de Bourgogne. The role of Andromache was played by Mademoiselle du Parc, an outstanding actress who had been lured away from Molière's company by Racine. The success of the play was exceptional, as was also the *querelle* that followed, comparable to the one that followed Corneille's *Le Cid*. Philippe Quinault, Michel Leclerq, Nicolas Pradon, Thomas Corneille, all the minor poets and poetasters confronted the young author. In May 1668, Perdou de Subligny staged his *Folle querelle ou la critique d'Andromaque*, in which he reproached Racine for his infidelity to history, his distorted argument, the brutality of the character of Pyrrhus, the excessive attention given to amorous sentiments, that is, Racine's treatment of certain ancient materials, of a *theme* that a good part of the audience of the Hôtel de Bourgogne recognized. Racine himself later pointed out his sources: the *Iliad* (books VI, XXII, XXIV), which gave him the figure of Andromache, widow and mother; the *Aeneid* (III.294–343), where Andromache appears along with Pyrrhus, Orestes, and Hermione; Euripides, with the account of the heroine in captivity, subject to Pyrrhus and the jealousy of Hermione; Seneca (*The Trojans*), which emphasizes Andromache's inner struggle, her conflict between the memory of her dead husband and the necessity of saving her son, Astyanax. The critics had also called attention to the influence of Corneille's favorite dilemmas (*Pertharite*, III.1) and of the erotic entanglements of Jorge de Montemayor's *Diana enamorada*. Racine's play—notwithstanding the indifference of his contemporaries and colleagues—has given rise to countless different readings, depending on generations and schools. But the major literary interpreters agree that the significance of Racine's drama goes well beyond its theme, nor is it limited to the most obvious treatment of his characters and their vicissitudes.

Read again Roland Barthes' dazzling *Sur Racine* (1963): what stands out in *Andromaque* is not the events proper of the classical theme, but the relations with authority, heightened by passion, the obsessive memory of past love (Andromache), the unfortunate loyalty to the old order (Hermione), the awareness of the glance, the menace of death, the verbal aggression, the inner schism of the tragic character, the frustrated hope, the inescapable final settling of accounts.

A very useful exposition of comparativism, *Comparative Literary Studies* (1973), by S. S. Prawer, divides themes into five groups: first, the literary representation of natural phenomena (the sea), fundamental conditions of human existence (dreams), and *perennial human problems;* second, the recurrent motifs of literature and folklore (the three wishes, the magic ring); third, recurring situations (the conflict of son with father); fourth, social types, or professional and moral ones (the gentleman, the criminal, the traveler); and finally, characters derived from mythology, legends, or literature itself (Prometheus, Siegfried, Hamlet).[19] Clearly the cards are not usually dealt until the game is about to begin. The Oedipal conflict, for example, could also be considered a perennial human problem. But to summarize, two principal paths of investigation can be inferred from Prawer's arrangement.

The first is of a historical nature. A short while ago we commented on the social and intertextual aspect of certain themes in connection with songs with a strong traditional flavor such as Jorge de Sena's "Cantiga de roda." But that is not enough. A global investigation of a theme must differentiate between what is "perennial" (useful hyperbole, having nothing to do with botany) and what is not; or, as we phrased it earlier, the continuing evolution of the theme, disentangling and revealing, if it can be done, a structure of possibilities that can be manifested and discovered only by history. Trousson is absolutely correct when he says that thematology, far from ignoring literary history, serves rather as an instrument to help us understand it and write it.

As for Prawer's second path, a very clear polarity stands out at first glance: the polarity that distinguishes between a natural phenomenon like a stone, a river, or a flower, and an imagined prefiguration like the fire of Prometheus or the dream of a Golden Age. Tempting, elusive polarity that soon turns into essential questions for us: Where does nature end and culture or society begin? How are they intermixed? How do they affect one another? What mediators facilitate these interrelations? Would a poetic theme not be one of the mediators?

Perhaps the two paths converge at certain moments—when a historical situation *thematizes* a natural phenomenon. Let us investigate a few brief examples.

A man contemplates the sea. It is the poetic voice of Pedro Salinas, facing the sea at San Juan de Puerto Rico: *El contemplado* (1946; translated into

English as *Sea of San Juan: A Contemplation*). The Spanish subtitle reads:
Tema con variaciones (Theme with Variations). Actually the poet is contemplating life itself with wonder, its most profound part, exploring it, seeking its value, returning to discover it. But the theme is the sea; the poet meditates on the sea, holds a dialogue with it, throughout fourteen variations. And two primordial moments stand out, two stances, intermeshed and re-iterated.

On the one hand, the contemplated object is born and reborn as pure nature before the poet's eyes, not as object but because the poet sees it as though for the first time, free of all patina, with no trace of bitter aftertaste:

> Vuelve el mar a su tiempo el inocente,
>   ignorante de quillas,

> The sea returns to the time of its innocence,
>   all ignorant of keels,

as if the language were also that of the poet, nothing more—spare, true, simple, free of dross, and as though time might not exist.

> Dentro del hombre ni esperanza empuja
>   ni memoria sujeta.

> El presente, que tanto se ha negado,
>   hoy, aquí, ya, se entrega.

> Within the man, neither hope pushes onward
>   nor memory holds fast.

> The present that has denied him so much,
>   today surrenders all.

But this innocence is not definitive. What is being contemplated is now intermeshed with culture, the sediment of centuries, collective humanity. "The Spanish poet," says Juan Marichal, "feels linked to the sea and to the men who have contemplated it before him."[20] It is the double, or even more, the triple connection that we saw earlier: that of the theme with life, with the history of the culture, with its own variations. The sea is now the one of our origins, the one of our myths and epics, the sea that comes from Greece.

> Estas esbeltas formas que las olas
>   —apuntes de Afroditas—,

> inventan por doquier, ¿van a quedarse
>   sin sus dioses vacías? . . .

¿Olas? Tetis, Panope, Galatea,
　glorias que resuscitan.

Resurrección es esto, no oleaje,
　querencia muy antigua.

These delicate forms that the waves invent
　these hints of Aphrodite

everywhere, are they going to remain
　empty, without their goddesses?

Waves? No: Thetis, Panope, Galatea,
　glorious beings reborn.

This is resurrection, not surging sea,
　a very ancient striving.

It is no longer the faraway glance that emerges but the awareness of a common multisecular search (Variation 13):

Ahora, aquí, frente a ti, todo arrobado,
aprendo lo que soy: soy un momento
de esa larga mirada que te ojea,
desde ayer, desde hoy, desde mañana,
paralela del tiempo.
En mis ojos, los últimos,
arde intacto el afán de los primeros,
herencia inagotable, afán sin término.

And now here, all enraptured, before you,
I learn what I am. I am but a moment
of that long vision that gazes on you
from yesterday, from today, from tomorrow,
parallel with time.
In my eyes, the latest,
burns intact the eagerness of the first,
endless ardor, inexhaustible heritage.[21]

Back and forth between nature and culture is also to-and-fro between originality and tradition, between individuality and history. Poet of the twentieth century, Pedro Salinas leaves personal anecdote behind and delves into
the theme that moves him and helps him to go beyond the personal.

　José Manuel Blecua has devoted a beautiful anthology to the sea in Spanish poetry, the poems arranged historically.[22] The "diachronic structure" of

the theme, if there were room to encompass it, would have to start from some historical investigations, so that one could choose from among various options, various basic polarities. For Salinas, for Juan Ramón, for Rafael Alberti, for the poet of today, perhaps the principal opposition may be between a world of the present, enveloping or near, and its absence or loss, the quest or longing for it—the circularity of the question that A. Romero Márquez aptly describes:

> The sea that surrounds us with waves and foam gives rise to a vague thirst of faroff places, a restlessness for the unknown. But it always returns to us what we put into it: our own mystery. In it we can interpret ourselves; that is, through it we can do away with the suspicion that we cannot be really interpreted, that we become, floating and open in the immanence of a chance being to the immanence of the Whole, of Silence.[23]

Once more historical sense here means knowledge of collective and definite differences in time as well as in space.

So the to-and-fro between a "natural" flower and a "cultural" flower is very well known in European civilization, from Ausonius to Baudelaire; but shouldn't the structure of options be tested by other civilizations, to be altered and enriched in the process? In Nahuatl poetry, flowers occupy an important place, one of a consummate, very delicate polysemy. And there also, flowers embrace contrary notions: the imminence of death, the urgency to live. The "Song of Flowers" (*Xochicuicatl*) tends toward reflection, with death near at hand. The "flower of the field" denotes spring and life; the "flower of our flesh," corn; the "flower that dances," the warrior. The poet himself is the flower that blooms, and his song a garden of flowers. Here is a poem from Chalco, translated by Angel María Garibay (the yearning flowers are the captives who will be immolated):

> Ya llegaron las flores, las flores primaverales;
> bañadas están en la luz del sol;
> ¡múltiples flores son tu corazón y tu carne, oh Dios!
>
> ¿Quién no ambiciona tus flores, o dios dador de la vida?
> Están en la mano del que domina la muerte;
> se abren los capullos, se abren las corolas;
> se secan las flores si las baña el sol.
>
> Yo de su casa vengo, yo flor perfumada;
> alzo mi canto, reparto mis flores:
> ¡bébase su néctar, repártanse las flores!
> Abre sus flores el dios, de su casa vienen las flores acá.[24]

Now the flowers have arrived, the flowers of spring;
they are bathed in the light of the sun;
many flowers are your heart and your flesh, oh God!

Who would not aspire to be your flowers, oh God giver of life?
they are in the hands of the one who rules death;
the buds open; the corollas open;
the flowers will dry up if bathed by the sun.

I come from your house, I perfumed flower;
I raise my song, scatter my flowers:
drink your nectar, scatter the flowers!
The god opens your flowers, from his house come the flowers here.

Still today in different places the process of naturalization gives rise to motifs based on modern inventions. The first chapter of *Sanchiro* (1908), by the excellent Japanese novelist Natsume Soseki, introduces one such motif, a journey by railroad—and above all, the tendency that such a journey may awaken erotic fantasies. The protagonist, Sanshiro, leaves his home village for the capital to begin studies at the university. He is a timid soul, more than anything else. An attractive woman approaches him on the train—"her mouth was firm, her eyes bright." The train has to make an overnight stop in Nagoya, where the woman asks Sanshiro to help her find an inn. The inn is a very modest one, and before he can protest, it turns out that they must share the same bath, the same room, and the same bed. During the night Sanshiro doesn't dare make a move or utter a word. Finally the two say goodby in the station before continuing their respective journeys:

> The woman gave him a long steady look, and when she spoke it was with the utmost calm.
>   "You're quite a coward, aren't you?"
>   A knowing smile crossed her face.[25]

And the reader understands that what upsets Soshiro, in Nagoya as well as later in Tokyo, is not only the sexual initiative of the woman but also the many changes that Japanese society is undergoing.

The same journey-by-train theme may be treated in a more personal way, as in a story by Josep Pla, *El que es pot esdevenir: res* (That Which It May Become), collected in *Bodegó amb peixos* (1950; Tavern with Fish). This time the journey is at night. The train crosses central France en route to Barcelona, to which the narrator is returning. Black night, silence, boredom, while the train speeds along. The narrator goes out into the corridor.

A young woman emerges from another compartment, with a bluish dark light showing inside; she is blond, elegant, and injects a few drops of perfume into her cigarette. It seems she has been crying. The two strike up a conversation. Since the woman can't sleep, she will get off and stay overnight in Limoges. They discuss various things, such as love and marriage, in an apparently lighthearted way. The narrator, attracted, extremely interested at bottom but held back by fear of seeming ridiculous, pretends a cynical wisdom. It's three in the morning, and she asks him to keep her company in Limoges. She explains that her husband is deceiving her and that perhaps she could deceive him in turn—the narrator believes he is dreaming. In the Hotel del Comercio they separate for a moment. The narrator returns to his companion's door, left ajar, hesitates, tormented, for five minutes: "I didn't turn the key. I looked at my watch. I could tell she was getting into bed . . . I took out my hand holding the cloth and wiped my forehead. Later, I went back to my room, my mouth feeling dry." The next day they say goodby at the station:

> "Why are you always looking for explanations: Do you think it's really worth it?"
> "Won't we ever see each other again?"
> "Well, who knows?"
> "Hope you have a nice trip."
> "Same to you."
> That woman . . . I was in love with her for a year or so. Later on, little by little, it all began fading away, and the memory of her was lost in the gray fog of the weeks and months and years.[26]

Sometimes fiction is more revealing than autobiography. In the case of Josep Pla, the story of the alluring woman on the train shows that he is renouncing a direct search for individual happiness, that is, for an inner satisfaction provided by self-delusions.

There are themes of long durations, *longues durées,* that last by being transformed over many centuries; others have a briefer span, like the railway reverie that I just mentioned, a theme that has already grown old; and still others, *moyennes durées,* let us say with Braudel, are dominant in a certain historical period or at a certain moment become part of our cultural heritage, perhaps permanently.

Among the first type is the theme of water—river, sea, pool, fountain, spring—in poetry and in thought, so widespread its study would be endless. Are there perhaps eras when the function of the theme of water was particularly prominent? According to Erik Michaëlsson, water is "the center of metaphors and of metamorphoses in French literature from the first half of the eighteenth century." [27] In Spain the same could be said of the Renaissance eclogue—Garcilaso and his successors. Gisèle Mathieu-Castellani has analyzed the "poetic of the river" and its place in the pastoral code of seventeenth-century France: springs, fountains, meadows, fields, woods, and groves, streams and banks; also mythical spaces—nymphs—where death intrudes. [28] These investigations focus on a particular model, Jean Rousset's masterly book *Circé et le paon* (1953) and its anthology of baroque poetry, based not on authors but on motifs, images, and myths such as Proteus or inconstancy; illusion and metamorphosis (dreams, disguises); the spectacle of death, the nocturnal knowledge of transcendence (night and light); images of instability, movement and flight (bubbles, birds, clouds, winds, fireflies); and water and mirrors, worlds that flow and pass by, *eaux miroitantes,* fountains and rivers that reflect inverted figures, running waters, or also sleeping waters, as in Tristan l'Hermite ("Plaintes d'Acante"): "Visitant d'un étang la paresse profonde . . ." (Visiting a pond's deep sloth . . .). [29] Once again we are in the middle of the baroque. And it is clear that the images are simply channels of a sensibility and a way of perceiving life.

To perceive something as a possible fruitful pretext, making it into a theme, is to use a specific focus, rooted in history and conditioned by it. Let us take mountains as an example. Who discovered their latent values? In antiquity and the Middle Ages mountains were the dwelling places of the gods, mythical or malicious peaks, allegories, biblical illustrations. In Mont Ventoux Petrarch indeed found a Horatian-style refuge, but in general the elemental, antibucolic force of the mountain was not favorable to the *locus amoenus.* The mountain becomes capable of interpretation, humanly valuable and attainable with the advent of the Renaissance and succeeding centuries, above all during the pre-Romantic eighteenth century. I am referring to Konrad Gesner (1516–1565), who observed the Stockhorn (Berne) and wrote *De montium admiratione;* to the scientific interest in phenomena and disorders caused by altitude—Father José Acosta before the great peaks of Peru (*Historia natural y moral de las Indias,* 1590); or to the experiments associated with the vacuum designed by Florin Périer at Puy-de-Dôme (1648), [30] which aroused the interest of Pascal; and now with a completely literary sense, to Jean-Jacques Rousseau. A brilliant article by Américo Castro shows that the Saint-Preux of *La nouvelle Héloïse* sees in the Alps not a remote element of nature but a symbol very close to the inner conflicts that agitate his own being. [31] Little by little, from Gesner to Rousseau, mountains were secularized.

Colors also have their temporal mark and their situation. "L'art, c'est l'azur" (Art, it's azure), Victor Hugo declared; and in *Les châtiments:*

> Adieu, patrie!
> L'onde est en furie.
> Adieu, patrie,
>   azur!

> Farewell, homeland!
> The waves are in fury.
> Farewell, homeland,
>   azure![32]

Romanticism granted a privileged place to azure, blue, color of the ideal, of the longed-for and remote, of evanescent illusion.[33] In other words, the tendencies to extol symbols and specific colors merged. Because it is not the color itself that is significant, but the attitude toward the color. In Germany a symbolizing chromaticism enables blue (*traumblau,* literally, *dreamblue,* the color of dreams) to prevail in a highly visible way. Jean-Michel Palmier writes: "No doubt the blue that dominates all of Novalis' novel *Heinrich von Ofterdingen* is synonomous with what is pure, divine, heavenly, like that mysterious 'blue flower' that has marked all of the young German Romanticism."[34] That attitude is perpetuated in German poetry up to the very numerous polarities of Georg Trakl, as in "Kindheit":

> Ein blauer Augenblick ist nur mehr Seele.

> A blue glance is only more Soul.[35]

Trakl was acquainted with the group *Der blaue Reiter* (title of a painting by Vassily Kandinsky), first exhibited in Munich in 1911. In the meanwhile, the character of the poetic symbol had been undergoing transformations in ways that cannot be summarized here. Anna Balakian explains it very well in her book on symbolism. Since the poet's direct discourse is displaced by the indirect discourse of the Symbolists, the symbol ceases to designate or represent emotions and begins to suggest enigmas and multiple virtualities in an Orphic manner.[36] Before the tedium and futility of life, before the abyss (*gouffre*) of existence, Mallarmé glimpsed a totality that was *azur*—heaven and blue at the same time. In the sonnet of the same name, the call of the *azur* is like an illusory obsession:

> Où fuir dans la révolte inutile et perverse?
> Je suis hanté. L'Azur! l'Azur! l'Azur!

Where to flee in my useless and perverse rebellion?
I am haunted. Azure! Azure! Azure![37]

Balakian points out that from then on the word became a part of the Symbolist code.

In Spanish *azul* would be a translation that simplifes the word, if not the concept, but not when Rubén Darió says "el azul" (meaning *cielo;* English sky, ceiling, heaven). José Martí used the symbol as early as 1875.[38] "El pájaro azul" (1886) is the earliest story of Rubén's *Azul;* Don Juan Valera comments on the title in his prologue. In *Historia de mis libros* (1909), Rubén returns to the subject: "But blue was for me the color of reverie, the color of art, a Hellenic and Homeric color, oceanic and firmament color, that in Pliny is the simple color that resembles the heavens and sapphire."[39] Maeterlinck's *L'oiseau bleu* (1908) is quite a bit later than Rubén Darío. But the curious thing is that the chromatic adjective came to predominate over the noun, creating beings and things that symbolize desire, the ideal, purity or art, from Picasso to Franz Marc's blue horses and Wallace Stevens' blue guitar that transformed everything:

> The day was green.
> They said, "You have a blue guitar,
> You do not play things as they are."[40]

Toward the end of the century the possibility seemed at hand that a single color would penetrate or occupy an entire work as in certain paintings by Van Gogh. What caused this monochromaticism? Perhaps a heightened awareness of color, very typical of the era, of its symbolic value (Rimbaud), of the interartistic "correspondences" mentioned in the previous chapter. Since color is intensely meaningful, is it perhaps enough to choose a single one?

Wilhelm Wundt had reflected on the psychological effect of colors. Natsume Soseki refers to his work in a 1907 essay ("Bungaburon"): "White gives an impression of florid beauty, green of serene pleasure, while red expresses forcefulness."[41] Kandinsky thought that each color held a spiritual potential within (*Über das Geistige in der Kunst*, 1912). For him the "typically earth" color was yellow.[42]

Certainly yellow was a very *fin-de-siècle* color, at times with decadent connotations. Tristan Corbière had published his *Amours jaunes* (1873). Once again, the origins were romantic. Albert Sonnenfeld quotes Charles Augustin Sainte-Beuve's "Les rayons jaunes," from *Poésies de Joseph Delorme:*

La lampe brûlait jaune, et jaune aussi les cierges;
Et la lueur glissant aux fronts voilés des vierges
   Jaunissait leur blancheur.

The lamp burned yellow, and yellow also the candles;
And the gleam slipping across the veiled brows of the virgins
   Yellowed their whiteness.[43]

As for magazines, let us recall *The Yellow Book* of London, which reflected a fleeting but overwhelming fad. Yellow stood for the daring, the impertinent, the strange. William Morris painted sunflowers on the walls of the Oxford Union—flowers praised by Oscar Wilde. The best posters were yellow. Sir Richard Burton, the famous Orientalist, gave yellow breakfasts in his rooms:

> Yellow had assumed significance before the dawn of 1890. It gathered importance during the decade . . . A favorite color with the Pre-Raphaelites, with Rossetti and Burne-Jones, it was also affected by Whistler, whose yellow breakfasts with orange nasturtiums or darting goldfish in a flat blue bowl inspired Lily Langtry . . . whom he painted so gorgeously in a yellow robe . . .[44]

Then it should not come as a surprise to find monochromaticism used in poetry. Juan Ramón Jiménez, who blazed many trails and who dared in one poem to stake everything on a single card, included this "Primavera amarilla" in his *Poemas mágicos y dolientes* (1909):

Abril venía, lleno
todo de flores amarillas:
amarillo el arroyo,
amarillo el vallado, la colina,
el cementerio de los niños,
el huerto aquel donde el amor vivía.
   El sol ungía de amarillo el mundo,
con sus luces caídas;
¡ay, por los lirios áureos,
el agua de oro, tibia;
las amarillas mariposas
sobre las rosas amarillas!
   Guirnaldas amarillas escalaban
los árboles; el día
era una gracia perfumada de oro,
en un dorado despertar de vida.
Entre los huesos de los muertos,
abría Dios sus manos amarillas.

April came, all
full of yellow flowers:
the yellow stream,
the yellow fence, overflowing,
the children's cemetery,
the garden where love was living.
　The sun anointed the world with yellow,
with falling lights;
ah, through the golden lilies,
the warm golden water;
the yellow butterflies
above yellow roses!
　Yellow garlands were climbing
the trees; the day
was a grace perfumed with gold
in a golden awakening of life.
Among the bones of the dead
God opens his yellow hands.[45]

Open road, this poem, for the poets who followed. For Federico García Lorca, with his concise "Campana" (Bell), from *Poema del cante jondo*:

En la torre
amarilla,
dobla una campana.

Sobre el viento
amarillo,
se abren las campanadas.

En la torre
amarilla,
cesa la campana.

El viento con el polvo
hace proras de plata.

Up in the yellow tower
tolls a bell.

Over the yellow wind
it opens its knell.

Up in the yellow tower
the bell is ceasing.

The wind with the dust,
is shaping prows of silver.[46]

And here a "Canción" by Rafael Alberti, from his Argentine exile *(Baladas y canciones del Paraná)*:

> Los amarillos ya estarán llegando
> a aquellas tierras de por sí amarillas.
> Quiero oírlos llegar cantando
> tan lejos de las dos Castillas.
>
> Amarillos color de la pobreza
> y la desgracia, hermanas amarillas.
> Cantarlos quiero en su grandeza
> tan lejos de las dos Castillas.
>
> Amarillos de otoño, helado umbrío,
> que les hiere las manos amarillas.
> Cantarlos quiero en este río
> tan lejos de las dos Castillas.

> The yellows will now be coming
> to those lands themselves yellow.
> I wish to hear them come singing
> so far from the two Castiles.
>
> Yellows, color of poverty
> and misfortune, yellow sisters.
> I wish to sing their grandeur
> so far from the two Castiles.
>
> Yellows of autumn, frozen shade,
> which wound the yellow hands.
> On this river I wish to sing their praises
> so far from the two Castiles.[47]

The unique color, such a novelty in its day, is converted little by little into a procedure at the service of a modern vision of the poetic symbol, thus adding to the repertoire of available recourses. Perhaps we have witnessed the birth of a continuing process. Something similar had happened centuries ago with flowers and with mountains; they were read and mythified or rather written by literature, within the framework of distinct historical societies. An object or a personal experience can be naturalized and thematized within the structure of a society, through its channels of communication, and in that way directed toward its readers or hearers.

For these reasons and in view of the penetration of the natural by the cultural, we cannot avoid pondering the usefulness of a theme or a thematic element for practitioners of literary history. Later we will consider historiology (Chapter 16); but for the moment, theme poses more basic questions, which will perhaps remain unanswered forever, such as the intermingling of permanence with change—of the one with the many in time—throughout the history of culture. Themes, so literary and social on the one hand, so close to nature on the other, that is, to continuity in time and to unity in space—the unity that the exact sciences postulate—give rise to many perplexing questions.

Walter Kaiser, in his book *Praisers of Folly* (1963), tries to show that the "fool"—or booby, or buffoon, or rogue (the meaning of "fool" in English is quite complex)—fills an essential role in the works of three of the great creative figures of the Renaissance: Erasmus, Rabelais, and Shakespeare. Moreover, Kaiser affirms that the fool is one of the *personnages régnants* of the Renaissance; that is, the fool was the embodiment of one aspect of an age and the articulation of a pattern of thought characteristic of that age. (Hippolyte Taine made a case for the idea of the *personnage régnant* in *De l'idéal dans l'art*, 1867.) Each era has its literary protagonists who appear to symbolize the premises, aspirations, and nostalgias of the moment: during the Middle Ages we have the pilgrim, the perfect knight, the enamored warrior; or in the nineteenth century, the young ambitious man from the provinces who, spurred on by Werthian or Napoleonic dreams, seeks his fortune in London or Paris. By the time of the appearance of Erasmus' *Stultitia* (his *Moriae encomium* dates from 1509) and Rabelais's *Panurge* (ca. 1545), readers were already familiar with the basic figure, which had by then been thematized, or at least sketched as theme, during the fifteenth century. At the beginning of his study Kaiser notes: "The Renaissance authors whom we shall be considering assumed that their readers had a certain image of the fool in mind."[48] Think of the *Narrenschiff* (1494), by Sebastian Brant, with his daring representation: a ship rowed by fools. But the Renaissance would go further than the satirical depiction of vices, classes, or professions. The pretensions of reason itself would be questioned and undercut by the ironies of Erasmian humanism.

Two things made this new theme possible: a social fact and a cultural process. In medieval villages and cities, simpletons, fools, and harebrained types were found everywhere. They were tolerated by society for different reasons: they were held to be under the protection of God, and the Christian faith, according to Saint Paul, valued their simple natures. Actually, fools did not follow the codes of community behavior; they enjoyed a certain freedom, standing on the sidelines and mocking every established convention. Princes granted this liberty to jesters in their courts and palaces, or rather the license was granted to an "artificial fool" whose job consisted in imitating the "natural fool":

Thus the license of the natural fool was appropriated for the artificial fool: his nonconformity was turned into iconoclasm, his naturalism into anarchy, and his frankness into satire. Whether in the court or on the stage, he was able to criticize the accepted order of things and to voice daring indictments of the church or the throne or the law or society in general.[49]

It is important to point out that a theme with such an intellectual or philosophical aspect as Erasmus' *Stultitia* was not a mere intellectual invention or a linguistic abstraction, but rather came from real life, from events witnessed and experienced. Once again the distinction between a natural and a poetic motif seems relative to us and hardly historical. The clown, the fool's apprentice, seemed the same in the theater as in life. The transformation of the natural fool into an artificial rogue really took place and had many names and shadings: the buffoon of kings, princes, and prelates, for instance, those of Pope Leo X in Italy at the beginning of the sixteenth century;[50] in Spain the jester, the semibuffoon (Charles V's Dr. Villalobos), Don Francisco de Zúñiga, Soplillo, Pabillos of Valladolid, the boobies and dwarves of Velázquez.[51] From Shakespeare to Ben Jonson, the fool stands out in the English theater with vast radiations of meaning (Feste, Touchstone) that affect kindred characters like Falstaff and, in *Henry V,* as Kaiser suggests, even the young Prince Hal. King Lear goes really crazy in the company of a fool who pretends to be. These disturbing counterpoints come out of cultural and social phenomena typical of the fifteenth and early sixteenth centuries. Kaiser emphasizes the "holy simplicity" of Thomas à Kempis and the "learned ignorance" of Nicholas of Cusa, who, like Erasmus years later, studied in the halls of Deventer.[52] Bit by bit the way would be opened for the problematization of rational thought, the praise of folly, and the mixing of jests and truths that the Licenciado Vidriera, or Master Glass, and Don Quixote would carry to their ultimate consequences.

To be sure, what is offered here is a taste, a sample, and not a complete explanation. A single theme cannot function as synecdoche, because a historical period, defined as such by our critical discourse, in the last analysis is not a verbal entity or a work of art. Walter Kaiser points out the relevance of other dramatis personae of the Renaissance, such as the *pícaro,* whom Harry Levin places alongside the fool—"across Europe, along the drift from Renaissance to Reformation . . . stride two gigantic protagonists, the rogue and the fool"[53]—and even the enamored fool (Ariosto); or, we could also add, the enamored shepherd. (All these characters are brought together on the Cervantine stage.) Moreover, the plurality of signifieds revealed by the investigation of one theme is beyond dispute, within a single period.

As we noted a short while ago, this polysemy can be found in motifs of visibly natural origin as well as in representations of a type that is primarily mythological, religious, fantastic, or intellectual. A. Bartlett Giamatti has disentangled the wealth of utopian aspirations expressed by the best epic poets of the sixteenth century, up to the time of Tasso and Camoëns, by examining the theme of earthly paradise; and also, in the same era, the multivalence of the image of Proteus.[54] Keep in mind that the Renaissance poet felt the ancient mythologies and literatures to be something apart, and therefore distant. María Rosa Lida de Malkiel sums it up this way: "When the excision between present and past occurs that separates antiquity and shows it as remote and exemplary as the Golden Age, it means that the Renaissance has arrived."[55] Then allusions to mythological gods are made in a more conscious manner. Thematized, the gods and their "marvelous" avatars are instruments of self-interpretation, like the heroes, inscriptions, adages, and maxims that Montaigne would ponder and test.

Thus the multiform Proteus—*vates,* seer, son of Thetis and Ocean—can become a convenient and related symbol for many thinkers and poets, as Giamatti demonstrates. The symbol is so rich, so malleable that it allows the most varied and even opposite thematizations. On the one hand, Giovanni Pico della Mirandola and Juan Luis Vives (*Fabula de homine,* 1518) use the marine god in order to praise the limitless capabilities of man: free, adaptable, imaginative, perfectible, creator of innumerable works and cities. Mutability, indetermination, versatility are protean.[56] Montaigne thought that everything in man was change, mobility, and inconstancy: "Les plus belles âmes sont celles qui ont plus de variété et de souplesse" (The fairest souls are those that have the most variety and adaptability; III.3). And also: "Certes, c'est un sujet merveilleusement vain, divers et ondoyant, que l'homme" (Truly, man is a marvelously vain, diverse, and undulating object; I.1).[57] But Giamatti stresses here the use of the adjective *vain;* because, on the other hand, Proteus is for many no longer the prophet (*Odyssey,* IV.360–571) or the artist, but a deceiving and malevolent *magus,* manipulator of words and lies (Plato, *Euthydemus,* 288c), expert in masks and disguises. Has a structure of possibilities been uncovered here? Giamatti comments: "[Proteus] appealed to the Renaissance for many reasons, but above all two: because he could reconcile all differences and opposites, and because he embodied the principle of illusion as a mask for reality, appearance at once concealing and leading to vital or to deadly truths." Indeed, an opposition arises, even a contradiction. It was Shakespeare who opened the entire compass and admitted the contradictory possibilities of the theme in *Two Gentlemen of Verona.*[58] Something like our view of the symbol of the flower: from the urgency of life to the imminence of death.

Perhaps Proteus might not be the only motif able to "reconcile all differences and opposites." Are the most enduring themes those that, like refrains, are capable of contradicting themselves?

The fool evoked by Kaiser and the Proteus outlined by Giamatti, both figures dating from the fifteenth century, are *moyennes durées,* let us say once more in the words of Fernand Braudel, medium durations, which coincide with a historical period and help us understand it. Georg Brandes, in his monumental history of European letters of the nineteenth century, threw light on some themes that flourished during the Romantic period: childhood, incest, suicide.[59] Even when considering topics from antiquity, such as those sketched by Curtius that span so many centuries—the invocation of nature, the affectation of modesty, the old child *(puer senex)*, the model as image of virtue, arms and letters *(sapientia et fortitudo)*, the pleasant place, praise of the powerful, the solace found in the memory of exemplary men, the great theater of the world, and much more—there is no doubt that a focus that illuminates temporality and change is appropriate.

Sadly enough, such a focus at times reveals the fatigue of some themes, how quickly they become worn, the automatization insisted on by the Russian Formalists—in sum, the mortality of themes. Northrop Frye took pleasure in stressing that social life consists of conventions as well as literature; that is, without conventions, literature could not be distanced from life or distinguished from it.[60] Frye was right except that he did not judge literary conventions as severely as he did those of everyday life. From a historical point of view, one not adopted by Frye, are there not conventions that become doubly conventional at a certain moment? In this regard, I remember (criticism is also autobiography) the emotion I felt one day when I read some lines of Antero de Quental—in my opinion, the most powerful and interesting Iberian poet of the nineteenth century. Let us endeavor now to put aside Antero's death—one of those suicides whose memory follows us to our own death. The lines are from "Hino de manhã (1989; Hymn to Morning):

> De que são feitos os mais belos dias?
> De combates, de queixas, de terrores?
> De que são feitos? De ilusões, de dores?
> De misérias, de mágoas, de agonias?
>
> What are they made of, these loveliest days?
> Are they made of struggle, moaning, bated breath?
> What are they made of? Of hopes, pangs of pain?
> Of wretchedness, anguish, throes of death?[61]

Antero's despair is so extreme, so irrational, so inescapable, that we find one thing in it: authenticity. Pessimism as a theme in literature reached its true peak during the past century: Arthur Schopenhauer, Eduard von Hartmann, Antero de Quental. That force, that total conviction, almost innocent, causes many novels and poems of our century to pale by comparison: routine central European works, secondhand nauseating creations, tedious redos, domestic agonies, such conventional raptures as the sixteenth-century amorous sonnet praising the eyes of Amaryllis. The reader will undoubtedly recall other themes that have became automatic, such as adultery, an inseparable part of the naturalistic novel at the end of the nineteenth century, and which Joris Karl Huysmans confessed in his 1903 preface to *A rebours* made him want to retch.[62]

Philippe Ariès has shown that attitudes toward death evolved slowly, staying invariable for centuries, then falling apart in a rapid transformation within a short time. During the Middle Ages, all men and women died, that is, *they themselves* died: no one was unaware of his own mortality. Medieval man awaits Death with foreknowledge, in a state perhaps similiar to that described in Jorge Manrique's *Coplas por la muerte de su padre* (Verses on the Death of His Father):

> y consiento en mi morir
> con voluntad placentera
> clara y pura.

> and I consent to my death
> with a joyful clear
> and pure will.

Don Rodrigo Manrique died in a familiar and public ceremony, "surrounded by his wife / his sons and brothers / and servants."[63] Ariès says that with the end of the eighteenth century, it was *the others* who began to die. From this new attitude came the Romantic dramatization of death, protests against solitary death, an increase in mourning rites, the cult of tombs and cemeteries, as in these well-known lines by Bécquer (LXXIII):[64]

> ¡Dios mío, qué solos
> se quedan los muertos!

> Dear God! how alone
> are left the dead!

Finally even the theme of the cemetery would disappear. Now when life ends it is absolute rupture, the void and nothingness, the nonexistence of someone, like Ignacio Sánchez Mejías, who has "died forever." Jorge Guillén writes:

> No te entristezca el muerto solitario.
> En esa soledad, no está, no existe.
> Nadie en los cementerios.
> ¡Qué solas se quedan las tumbas!

> Do not be saddened by the lonely dead.
> In that solitude, he is not, he does not exist.
> Nobody in the cemeteries,
> How alone the tombs remain![65]

Ariès, along with Geoffrey Gorer, comments on the ban imposed by modern industrial society on the most obdurate enemy of happiness.[66] The taboo of sexuality, very much a nineteenth-century product, has been replaced by the taboo of mortality.

In the thematic field a consciousness of change predominates. Faced with long durations and topics, Don Rafael Lapesa says the comparatist tries to

> emphasize the constant modification that enlivens the traditional transmission and prevents it from becoming fossilized. Secular themes, commonplaces, ready-made formulas of expression, ideas proceeding from a cultural heritage, can change meaning when put at the service of a new conception of the world or of a different vital attitude ... In reality, all study of comparative literature, or of one author's influences upon another, carries within itself the need to point out contrasts.[67]

Américo Castro recommended also what he called contrasted literature in an essay on the medieval interpretations of the figure of the Sultan Saladin. The contrasts to which he refers are a result not so much of temporal evolution as of spatial differences between nation and nation: the unequal modes of valuing life and of putting into practice the values that make up the *moradas vitales*, existential spaces, of the Spanish, the Italian, and the French.[68]

For the same reasons as Calderón, a modern sociologist like Erving Goffman does not think that the world is a stage and that life consists in role-playing. Life is a dream: what would these words not suggest to a Romantic or a Surrealist? We could say the same thing of fratricide and the figure of Cain (John Webster, Schiller, Byron, Unamuno). The country fellow who seduces a refined woman in mythology (Polyphemus and Galatea) or in a pastoral poem has little or nothing to do with Lady Chatterley's lover. The theme in such cases is thematization with historical roots that sprouts anew over and over again.[69]

And yet . . . we cannot regard as a mere *boutade* Borges' observation regarding the privileged quality of a few metaphors, such as the coupling of dream and death, stars and eyes, woman and flower, old age and dusk, time and water.[70] At the center of the most lasting motifs—natural phenomena that were naturalized one day—a sphere of culture endures, pulses, and remains tangible, one that is actual tradition, continuity present and alive. Persistence and change are inextricably interwoven in a process whose complexity should not be simplified by applying a dialectic, logical-rationalist, or idealized model, that is, a model that by main force crams everything into the crucible of change. In the history of literature some norms and proposals have endured and remained functional and have, through their tenacity, made possible discoveries and innovative variations. On other occasions, merely skin-deep formulas and topics are also perpetuated. An arduous task of selection is then imposed on thematology: to distinguish between the trivial and the worthwhile. And to our surprise we find that the process of selection can be understood more easily when radically cultural themes are examined, as for example the myth of the Golden Age, the idea of man as microcosmos, or the fictional meeting of two lovers.

The *topoi*—topics, commonplaces, stock expressions, handed-down turns of speech, brief images, or representations—usually denote lasting traditions, memorable recollections, *longues durées,* of very unequal importance. Manfred Beller, Walter Veit, and other present-day historians have pondered the meaning and function of these persistent elements with valuable results.[71] The exceptional erudition of María Rosa Lida de Malkiel has thrown light on some topics that have been present in the classical tradition in Spain for centuries. We are dealing with a cultivated traditionality that in the Middle Ages often was the outcome of the practice of a scholarly discipline, but at other times, particularly during the Renaissance, represented attempts at recreation and reworkings. Lida de Malkiel is alert to the nightingale of Virgil's *Georgics* (IV.511–515), literary bird above all others: to Philomena, who weeps for her lost little ones; to the wounded deer of the Psalms and the *Aeneid* (IV.67–74); and to the mythological dawn, formula repeated countless times in Homer as well as in works after him: "when the young, rosy-fingered Dawn appeared again . . ." (*Iliad*, I.477; *Odyssey,* II.1, and so on). Well then, considering a motif in depth, we clearly encounter both a living rethematization, "mythical expression of a natural event," of wide radiation within a single work, and a "conventional requisite for a literary genre": simple carryover of scant usefulness. Because, as Lida de Malkiel herself writes regarding the mythological dawn, "the value of such a long biography, of course, does not lie in the mere endurance through a static time, but in the almost pathetic tenacity with which that thread of tradition interlaces such an old culture with a new one, surrounding its incredible diversity within the golden circle of Greco-Roman tutelage." [72] In effect, we have already had occasion to see that reiterations are seldom static. Whoever quotes something values what he repeats. It is not a tracing but a retracing, or rather, evidence of an impulse toward continuity so tenacious that it becomes pathetic. So the *topoi* are not of interest as textual reality—because they may be banal and hackneyed—but they are interesting as signs, that is, as the acknowledgement of a cultural complex of *longue durée* to which a writer is partisan and in which he is actively involved. A good example is the mythological Aurora, with rosy fingers and golden hair.

And as centuries go by as much homage is paid to the norm of Aurora as to its inverse or its mockery. The mocking attitude, so bookish—what is a Berni making fun of, if not a literary tradition?—is found in Cervantes of course ("Day had barely begun to appear upon the balconies of the east . . . ," I.13), in Lope's *Gatomaquia;* in Góngora, in Quevedo's *Necedades y locuras de Orlando el enamorado* (II.6):

> Ya el madrugón del cielo amodorrido
> daba en el horizonte cabezadas . . .

> Already the earlybird of the drowsing sky
> was nodding its head on the horizon . . .

and also the reverse side, now serious, terribly serious in Quevedo:

> Risueña enfermedad son las auroras . . . [73]

> Dawns are a smiling sickness . . .

Was the enemy topos necessary to justify Quevedo's bitter vindication? Everything happens as if the poet, liberated at last from convention, or from an orphan automatization deprived of sense, could now begin to feel and think the dawn anew; at first, either with Quevedo's visceral loathing, or years later in our own time with the equally unusual concurrence of Jorge Guillén, so many times renewed in *Cántico*—as in "Amanece, amanezco" (It Dawns, I Dawn):

> Heme ya libre de ensimismamiento.
> Mundo en resurrección es quien me salva.
> Todo lo inventa el rayo de la aurora,

Here I am now free of introspection.
World in resurrection is what saves me.
Everything is invented by the dawn's ray,

and that in *Cántico* also presupposes a force of will at certain times, in the face of the current negative convention, as in "Los balcones del Oriente" (The Balconies of the East):

Amanece
turbio . . .
¿Y la aurora? ¿Dónde mora
la doncella que es aurora?
Con una luz casi fea,
el sol—triste
de afrontar una jornada
tan burlada—
principia mal su tarea . . .

Dawn comes
turbid . . .
And dawn? Where does she dwell
the damsel who is dawn?
With an almost ugly light,
the sun—sad
at facing a workday
treated with such derision—
makes a poor start at his task . . .

But it is not only the exhaustion of the formula that allows discovery. Although Lida de Malkiel limits herself to the Hispanic Golden Age, she mentions no less than twenty-five occurrences of the symbol of the wounded stag that craves water and goes down to a stream, examples from Juan Boscán Almogáver ("Historia de Leandro y Hero") to Sor Juana Inés de la Cruz, who appropriates the theme and secularizes it, "Liras que expresan sentimientos de ausente" (Expressing the pangs of separation):

Si ves al ciervo herido
que baja por el monte acelerado,
buscando, dolorido
alivio al mal en un arroyo helado,
y sediento al cristal se precipita,
no en el alivio, en el dolor me imita.

See how the wounded hart
goes streaking down the mountainside,

desperate to find relief
in icy currents of swift water brooks;
behold his thirsty plunge into the streams:
his wounds, not their relief, like mine will seem.[74]

As the Renaissance drew to a close, Boscán had achieved the decisive *con-taminatio*, joining two motifs: the psalmist's stag thirsty for God—"As the hart panteth after the water brooks, so panteth my soul after thee, O God" (Psalms 42.1)—and Virgil's simile in the *Aeneid* (IV.67–74), in which un-happy Dido "in her madness" roamed through the city like a wounded doe ("coniecta cerva sagitta") that the shepherd had pierced with his arrows. During the Renaissance the biblical tradition (given scant attention by Cur-tius in his book) and the transmission of profane motifs merge: the yearning for God and the pain of love. But there is a third element: the Galician-Portuguese lyrics of the Middle Ages had seen an allegorical figuration of Christ in the wounded stag. Peak of such rich convergence is the "Cántico espiritual," by San Juan de la Cruz, who twice introduces the theme of the wounded stag.[75]

Already in the first stanza this convergence is verified:

> ¿Adónde te escondiste,
> Amado, y me dejaste con gemido?
> Como el ciervo huíste
> habiéndome herido;
> salí tras ti clamando y eras ido.

> Where have you hidden yourself,
> my love, and left me moaning?
> Like the stag you have fled
> having wounded me;
> I came out, crying, after you, and you had gone away.[76]

As in the medieval song of the friend, the beloved weeps because of the absence of the lover. As in Virgil, the enamored and wounded woman goes out in search of her lover, and her clamor evokes the divine affection of the psalmist. All this gives rise in the "Cántico" to a highly complex and sug-gestive—mysterious—web of motifs that function simultaneously as sym-bols. And Francisco Ynduráin explains, "And as such they function in the culture to which their work belongs: they expand in all directions, harmo-nize and provoke harmonic resonances in many traditions at the same time."[77] The main thing here is the inversion that San Juan dares to imagine. The stag itself, like the hunter, is the one who wounds. The poet's own commentary leaves no room for doubt:

The Bridegroom is compared to the stag because here the stag means himself. And it is known that the nature of the stag is to climb to high places, and when he is wounded he hastens to seek coolness in cold waters, and if he hears his mate complaining and feels she is wounded, then he goes with her and pampers and caresses her. And that's what the Bridegroom is doing now, because, seeing the Bride wounded by his love, he also, hearing her moan, comes wounded by her love. This feeling of charity and love of the soul makes the Bridegroom come running to drink from that fountain of love of his Bride, as cool waters cause the thirsty stag to come for a cooling drink.[78]

As Lida points out, the Virgilian image predominates throughout the poem, the yearning of the enamored woman, wounded like the stag.[79] But at the same time God is the wounded stag who shares the suffering of the animal and, being thirsty, longs for the relief of cold water. That is confirmed by stanza 12, whose last lines introduce the voice of the Husband for the first time:

> ¡Apártalos, Amado,
> que voy de vuelo!
>   Vuélvete, paloma,
> que el ciervo vulnerado
> por el otero asoma
> al aire de tu vuelo, y fresco toma.

> Take them away, Beloved,
> for I am soaring
> Bridegroom: Come back, dove,
> for the wounded stag
> shows himself on the hill,
> in the breeze of your flight,
> and cools himself.[80]

Impossible to analyze here the skill of the supreme poet. I would only like to note, in agreement with Lida de Malkiel, that this skill is truly poetic. In the first place, it is visual, concrete, material, and therefore capable of shaping symbolically the reality of the transcendental. God, the wounded stag that appears on the hill dominating the plain. The woman, the dove that cuts through the air in rising flight. "The stag, supernatural apparition . . . accentuates its divine character, outlined on the mountaintop, tangent of sky and earth where all epiphanies are fulfilled." [81]

There are themes whose reach is measured by their depth, like the wounded stag of San Juan, and other themes whose human value can be appreciated longitudinally because they have endured for more than two millennia. As mentioned earlier, resolutely cultural or imaginative representation perhaps reveals best those elements that permit us to speak of a human condition—clearly without having in mind the existence of any particular woman or man. We may admire or be unmoved by the grandeur of mountains, symbolize or pity the wounded stag, understand or incarcerate the mad; but is it conceivable that at any time of our history, we did not feel a yearning for a less painful life or a more just world? Not what actually exists but what is missing is perhaps the most enduring. Manfred Beller's brief summary of studies devoted to the vast but coherent thematic field of celestial or terrestial paradisaical myths is very suggestive: happy gardens, Arcadias, and other pastoral daydreams, El Dorados, strange and fortunate islands, the memory of the Golden Age, and other ideas that together or separately have embodied and sustained the utopian aspirations of humankind.[82]

The Myth of the Golden Age in the Renaissance (1969), by Harry Levin, is not really limited to the Renaissance. The myth comes from far back. Its historical vicissitudes should not be disdained. Levin points out the relative absence of such a myth during the Middle Ages for two reasons: first, lost perfections of the past were thought to reside in the biblical paradise; and second, longing for a Golden Age was not deemed conducive to strengthening Christian belief in the possible perfectibilty and salvation of men. On the peak of Mount Purgatory, the protagonist of the *Divina commedia* discovers the truly terrestial paradise, perhaps the one, as Dante insinuates, that the ancient poets dreamed about from Parnassus (*Purgatorio,* XXVIII.139–141):

> Quelli que anticamente poetaro
> L'etá dell'oro e suo stato felice
> forse in Parnaso esto loco sognaro.

> They who in olden times sang of
> the Age of Gold and its happy state
> perhaps in Parnassus dreamed of this place.

And that brings two related concepts into exact correlation, except for the distances between poetry and faith. Levin's book sheds light not only on the continuity of the image of the Golden Age but also on its diverse uses through many centuries, as well as its affinity to other myths and beliefs. A theme of long duration that cannot be isolated persists perhaps because it intersects with others within the lattice of the imagination.

The applicability of such a theme is demonstrated above all by those *conquistadores* and colonizers who "discovered" the most-longed-for daydreams of Europe in the *terra incognita* of America, and who substituted a temporal distance for a geographic one. During his first voyage, Columbus believed that there was an island in the Caribbean populated by Amazon women who used "bows and arrows" (letter to Luis de Santángel). His curiosity was understandable: "along that route would be found the island of Matinino, which they say was populated by women without men, from which they say the Admiral would like very much to take five or six of them to the King and Queen" (January 15, 1493).[83] Vasco de Quiroga, translator of Thomas More's *Utopia* and bishop of Michoacán, wrote that the Indies deserved to be called New World because everything in it seemed to belong to the Golden Age.[84] Pierre Ronsard, in "Les îles fortunées," praised the Indians, who, without lawsuits or attorneys, shared the same goods:

> Et comme l'eau d'un fleuve, est commun tout leur bien,
> Sans procès engendré de ce mot *tien* et *mien*.[85]

> And like the waters of a stream, all their goods are in common,
> Without lawsuits engendered by the words *yours* and *mine*.

That is indeed the myth of the Golden Age, when men lived in peace, enjoyed the fruits of the earth without exploiting it, and were ignorant of private property; a myth that today we would label communistic and ecological if such societies existed; a myth so old that it is astounding to realize that its significance may be based on the memory of a past even more remote in time. The civilized world felt itself old already in ancient Greece. In the eighth century B.C. Hesiod imagined five generations or races in a descending order of metals (later reduced to four: gold, silver, bronze, iron). More than a thousand years later Torquato Tasso wrote:

> Il mondo invecchia,
> E invecciando intristisce.

> The world grows old,
> And growing old, grows sad.[86]

Quevedo, settled in an age that later would be called decadent, could only make fun of the conventional image:

> Tardóme en parirme
> mi madre, pues vengo
> cuando ya está el mundo
> muy cascado y viejo . . .
> De la edad de oro
> gozaron sus cuerpos;

pasó la de plata,
pasó la de hierro
y para nosotros
vino la del cuerno.[87]

She was slow in giving birth to me
my mother, since I come
when the world is already
very worn out and old . . .
In the golden age
they enjoyed their bodies;
the silver one went by,
the iron one went by
and for us
came the one of horn.

There are many ties on either side. Levin devotes a number of pages to different areas of Renaissance literatures: to l'Abaye de Thélème in *Gargantua,* the pastoral novel—Jacobo Sannazaro, Sir Philip Sidney—the third and fifth cantos of Spenser's *Faerie Queene,* the tragicomedy of Tasso and Giovanni Battista Guarini, *As You Like It* by Shakespeare; and also *The Tempest,* where Gonzalo ascribes to an imaginary kingdom the qualities that Montaigne would praise in the New World ("Des cannibales"), or rather, the inversion of the defects of Europe (act II, scene 1):

I' th' commonwealth I would by contraries
Execute all things; for no kind of traffic
Would I admit, no name of magistrate . . .
No occupation; all men idle, all;
And women too, but innocent and pure.

And also:

I would with such perfection govern, sir,
T' excel the Golden Age.

At that moment the Golden Age and the idea of a utopia in the political-social sense merged: the former was projected toward an immemorial past; the latter modeled an absent space and an unknown future. Already in Eclogue IV, Virgil had converted the Golden Age into a prophetic vision. This decisive turnabout would lead to the semantic field for which Levin endeavors to find a structure. From the here and now, the visionary sets out toward other spaces and other times. The desired space may be remote but is of this world or else ultraterrestrial: celestial paradises. If we reject the present, the exemplary time can be a retrospective Arcadia or a utopian future. Certainly these categories are intermixed or superimposed on one another.[88] Utopian dynamics usually presupposes the creation of another place or the development of virgin territories, with eyes fixed on a better future. Etienne Cabet, author of a socialist utopia, *Le voyage en Icarie* (1840), tried to found a revolutionary community in America. It is also fitting that revolution transfigures an ancient existent space, if possible. Levin can only allude to the itinerary of this theme in modern literature. The historical novel, the futuristic or utopian novel, science fiction, the fantastic or neofantastic tale jumble together remote or imaginary times and spaces. Many things fit into science fiction—tale or movie—satire, as in Stanislaw Lem; play in what Susan Sontag calls "the imagination of disaster"; and even science. But also the material or logical transformation of known reality that Lem calls "travel in time." And in such contexts, references to the Golden Age do not completely disappear: from the quixotic first sentence of Georg Lukács' *Theorie des Romans* (1920), in his pre-Marxist phase ("Happy are those ages when the starry sky is the map of all possible paths . . . "[89] until, in the midst of surrealism, *L'age d'or* (1930) of Luis Buñuel.

Two thousand years also encompass one of the ideas most characteristic of the culture that was Greco-Roman and later became European, namely, that of man conceived as a microcosmos, an abbreviated world. The ramifications of these ideas were examined by Francisco Rico in *El pequeño mundo del hombre* (1970). This idea will seem to many today more widespread than the myth of the Golden Age, in view of the fact that it had a great many contacts with very diverse areas of knowledge for two millennia, as Rico shows. A unifying idea, then, on more than one level. First, because all its meanings, which evolved along with different schools of thought, implied and maintained the same conception of the cosmos—the tautology is worth mentioning—as a whole "one and several, ordered and adorned . . . spherical, beautiful, clean, the one the scholars find reflected or condensed in man, small world, *microcosmos.*"[90] Tradition, not content with perceiving the unity of the exterior world, placed man in it, bound him to it, extolled the affinity, concordance, or sympathy of man's own human constitution with the parts and order of the universe. In addition, this theme brought together, for example, the sciences of physics and medicine—the famous parallel between the four humors and the four elements—and was shown to be "essential in the elaboration of a plenary science of reality: science that not only fuses medicine and astrology, cosmography, and chronology, but also takes equal account of aesthetic appreciation (of music or architecture, let us say) and of the beginnings of politics."[91]

For the Pythagoreans or Aristotle, or fray Luis de Leon, the soul is linked musically with the body—mixture and synthesis of contraries—and vibrates in consonance with the music of the spheres. For Vitruvius and certain later theorists of architecture, the human proportions provided the symmetrical guidelines for every edifice, civil or religious. It is known that abstract concepts can become part of literature provided someone experiences them intimately and can infuse them with definite life. Here we find an idea that is more like an available structure, a form of thinking, rather than a metaphysical conception *sensu stricto:* "too imprecise and vulnerable to technical analysis of the *prima philosophia,* the notion should appear as a useful hypothesis for the minor sciences (medicine, for example) or as a simple metaphor, matter of literature." [92] In effect, a form of thinking that by its capacity for association and its instantaneous breadth could be regarded as a promising metaphor for poetry: Lope de Vega, Shakespeare, Calderón. Shakespeare's works, which create an ordered and hierarchical world, insist on analogy, for example political analogy, which includes not only harmony but also moments when the storm of passions threatens disorder and misrule (*Julius Caesar,* act II, scene 1):

> Between the acting of a dreadful thing
> And the first motion, all the interim is
> Like a phantasma or a hideous dream.
> The Genius and the mortal instruments
> Are then in council; and the state of a man,
> Like to a little kingdom, suffers then
> The nature of an insurrection.

Little world, or rather, "little heaven," Calderón calls woman—as in this flattery from *La vida es sueño* (II.7):

> Oye, mujer, detente;
> no juntes el ocaso y el oriente,
> huyendo al primer paso;
> que juntos el oriente y el ocaso,
> la lumbre y sombra fría,
> serás sin duda síncopa del día.

> Stop, woman—listen to me!
> Coming and going so fast, you push
> sunrise and sunset together.
> With the dawn and the dusk colliding
> that way, you cut short my day. [93]

A figure of diction called syncope (the abbreviation of a word: "Espe" for "Esperanza" in Spanish, for instance, or in English contractions such as "ne'er" for "never"), like the idea of microcosmos, reduces the larger to the smaller. Both conventions would form part of that repertoire whose literary essence Francisco Rico brings to light:

> What we sometimes reject nowadays as a commonplace, sin against art, could have been years ago something definitively literary, artistic. Books such as this one . . . are, I would say, contributions to a "historic grammar" of literature, of the traditional language of literature. As readers, perhaps we are more interested in the unusual and whatever goes against the norm; as historians, our duty is to make a record of the generic and whatever is subject to the rule.[94]

The orthodoxy of the perfect parallel between man and the Periclean cosmos, on one hand, and the eighteenth century and empiricism, on the other, as for example in Diderot's *Encyclopédie,* where one reads: "but if man is the sum of the perfections of the universe, one can also say that he is the sum of its imperfections."[95] But in Rico's collection, one keeps hearing echoes of the old idea as expressed by the Krausists, Benito Peréz Galdós, and Rubén Darío. Julián Sanz del Río wrote: "Just as man is organized in spirit and in body, so also society is organic"; and for Don Francisco Giner de los Ríos, "each person is of necessity constituted like a State."[96] But aside from these isolated instants, unsupported by tradition, are not man and the world already in contrast with one another?

Although some of the answers may fall into disuse, the questions endure. None less banal than the one proposed by the theme investigated by Rico: the question of the relation between man and the world. The *Encyclopédie* opened a new path: imperfection as basis of a happy analogy. Freud divided men into three parts, later reduced to two: the conflict between Eros and the death wish. In Chapter 3 of this book I quoted various testimonies of what Machado called the heterogeneity of being. Here is Octavio Paz: "In a universe that breaks up and separates from itself, a whole that has ceased to be thinkable except as absence or a collection of heterogenous fragments, the self also breaks apart."[97] In the words of the Mexican poet, in his precise formulation—"whole that has ceased to be thinkable"—throbs the memory of a lost norm. Is it diversity that holds us together? "The self also breaks apart . . ." Perhaps the dark chaos of the individual reflects a great general incoherence. Man continues to be a little world, now by way of fragmentation.[98]

I will point out one more example of what clearly seems a norm to us, a "generic" event and "subject to the rule," found in literature as well as in life impregnated by literature, in the midst of a civilization that soaks up poetic and plastic values. Jean Rousset has devoted a book, *Leurs yeux se rencontrèrent* (1981), to a theme familiar to everybody: the encounter of two lovers, or of persons who from the first moment are destined to become lovers. Is there a single norm? No, of course not. But there are indeed some clues, some archetypal and extreme scenes: the simplest, briefest, most intense ones. Thus, above all, the act of falling in love suddenly, mutually, decisively. The inexplicable shot of the arrow, fatal, almost passive (Eros is the archer). The interchange of glances, a very frequent motif.

Ordinarily the first amorous contact is visual, "love at first sight," already a conventional formula for Christopher Marlowe in "Hero and Leander":

> The reason no man knows, let it suffice,
> What we behold is censur'd by our eyes.
> Where both deliberate, the love is slight;
> Who ever lov'd, that lov'd not at first sight?

Fatality of the first, which determines and condemns the last. Here is the the meeting of Rousseau with Madame de Warens (*Rêverie*, 10): ". . . this first moment determined my whole life, and by an inevitable chain of events shaped the destiny of the rest of my days." [99] It is something like a conversion with which Dante begins *Vita nuova:*

> a li miei occhi apparve prima la gloriosa donna
> de la mia mente, la quale fu chiamata da molti Beatrice . . .
>
> There appeared before my eyes the now glorious lady
> of my mind who was called Beatrice . . .

The apparition of Beatrice, prepared for by an earlier encounter in childhood and revived later, in symbolic form, in a dream. The apparition, with its supernatural connotation, is repeated innumerable times; as in Flaubert's long description in the first chapter of *Sentimental Education,* a drawn-out variation on the theme, which I can only abbreviate: "What he then saw was like an apparition . . . Never before had he seen more lustrous dark skin, a more seductive figure, or more delicately shaped fingers than those through which the sunlight gleamed . . . He assumed she must be of Andalusian origin, perhaps a creole . . . Their eyes met." [100] What happens is that the first encounter represents the end of a wait, the concrete presence of an earlier, idealized image. The encounter is a re-encounter. As in Balzac (*La vielle fille*): "The glance is fascinated by an irresistible attraction, the heart is moved, the melodies of happiness resound in the soul and in the ears, a voice cries: *It is he* . . . A lightning flash of true love scorched the weeds flourishing in the breath of libertinage and dissipation." [101]

The *locus classicus,* to which Rousset also returns, is Heliodorus' *Ethiopica* (fourth century). The souls of the enamored pair will be seen attached to one another by innate affinities of divine origin:

> As soon as those two young people looked on one another they fell in love, as if from the first encounter the soul recognized its like and hastened to its proper domicile. At first they stood in sudden amazement, and then, very slowly, she handed him the torch. He received it, and they fixed each other with a rigid gaze, as if they had sometime known one another or had seen each other before and were now calling each other to mind . . . In a single moment, in short, their countenances betrayed a thousand shades of feeling; their various changes of color and expression revealed the commotion of their souls. [102]

Basing his study on this and other similar texts, Rousset collected the characteristic traits of the archetypal meeting: instantaneousness, amazement, commotion, muteness, reciprocity, manifest destiny, praise of the beauty of one or both partners, the annihilation of space, the festive or unusual place where the meeting occurs . . . Naturally, the variations are countless; many involve silences, omissions, what doesn't need to be said. If there is a narrative "point of view," for instance, we know only what one of the protagonists feels. Or also certain aspects of the encounter are developed in detriment to others, such as their visual character: the light, colors, a detail or part that concentrates all the sensuality of the moment or the person. Read again the scene in *Tirant lo blanc* (1490), when for the first time the hero sees Carmesina, daughter of the emperor of Greece. The empress and the princess are in mourning, enclosed in a dark room hung with black drapery. As Tirant enters, lighted torches are brought in. Finally the knight can see the maiden lying on a bed with a black canopy, the maiden "clad in a black satin dress and mantle," but sufficiently open at the throat so that Tirant is irremediably caught by her crystalline breasts:

> As Tirant listened to the emperor's words, his eyes were fixed upon the fair princess. It had been so hot with all the windows closed that she had half unbuttoned her blouse and he could see her breasts, which were like two heavenly crystalline apples. They allowed Tirant's gaze to enter but not to depart, and he remained in her power till the end of his days. [103]

But in amorous literature, falling in love is also often progressive. If the *Ethiopica* provides a model of the instantaneousness and sudden reciprocity of love, another Greek novel, *Daphnis and Chloe,* presents a pattern of the slow growth of love between two adolescents who have known each other since childhood, like Pyramus and Thisbe, Floire and Blancheflor, and, in Spanish literature, Abindarráez and the beautiful Jarifa in *Abencerraje* (ca. 1560). Must we conclude, therefore, that one of these two poles constitutes the norm, and the other a deviation? Rousset comes close to this point of view when he speaks of *écarts* and *transgressions* in his chapter on the plentiful variations that Balzac's work develops around this motif: "I will end this Balzacian inventory by several examples of deviation, less provacative no doubt but which also break with the tradition to which all narrators subscribe; in pointing out the discrepancies, one becomes aware of certain unwritten laws of the romantic tale." [104]

Balzac, who tried and depicted everything, from sudden passion to the slow maturation of love, was less interested than Stendhal in the temporal process of love as a progressive imaginative construct. "Love does not spring up as suddenly as one might think," said Stendhal in *De l'amour*. And in a note on the manuscript of *Lucien Leuwen:* "No sudden passion," [105] which clearly indicates that according to Stendhal the shot of the arrow was a commonplace, the ordinary norm, what people thought and accepted. Obviously this is in the midst of Romanticism. From a historical perspective, wouldn't it be better to follow the trajectory of a topic, its alternatives, its enrichment, its exhaustion—its structurable diachrony?

Jean Rousset, mentioned various times already, an unquestionably elegant critic, is indifferent to Hispanic literatures and does not even quote Cervantes. That is a pity. In Cervantes all mental habits, all norms, all codes are put to the test. Multiple variations on the theme that concerns us here are to be found in Cervantes: the pre-encounter, the portent, the wait, loving each other without knowing each other, love by letter, the woman half-seen or sleeping (the "very white hand" of Zoraida in the episode of the captive captain, *Quixote,* I.39). We have no space to analyze these variations here. But it seems to me that the loves that ripen slowly predominate for more than one reason.

Certainly the call of violent desire exists (*La fuerza de la sangre*), the showy seduction of fleeting consequences (Leandra in *Quixote,* I.51). However, time must test the authenticity of love (*La Gitanilla; The Gipsy Maid*) and its insertion into reality. The literary side of idealized or Petrarchan love must suffer the storms of experience. The declaration "I am dying of love for you," if true, leads to suicide (Grisóstomo). Plastic description and visual sensuality are decisive, and the encounters often take place at night, by the light of a few candles, like the scene in *Tirant lo blanc* quoted earlier. Thus when the naive Cardenio satisfies Fernando's desire to see his own beloved, Luscinda (*Quixote,* I.24):

Most unfortunately, I yielded to his wishes and showed her to him one night by the light of a candle at a window where we were accustomed to converse. As she appeared to him in her loose-flowing robe, she at once caused him to forget all the beauties that he had thus far seen. He was struck dumb and stood there in a daze as if he had lost his senses. In brief, as you will see in the course of my story, he had fallen in love with her.[106]

But note that a phase of mental preparation came first, an imagined pre-encounter. The desire preceded the meeting. The typically Cervantine addition is the awareness of an earlier imaginative scheme, for example, in *La ilustre fregona* (translated as *The Illustrious Kitchen Maid*), in which one of the two heroes, Avendaño, begins by imitating the model of the picaresque novel—Mateo Alemán's *Guzmán de Alfarache*—and ends by emulating the enamored knight. Before arriving at the Inn of the Sevillan in Toledo, the *pícaro's* apprentice hears the praises of the serving girl: "the simple description that the muleteer had given of the beauty of the kitchen maid awoke in him an intense desire to see her." Already in the inn the wait drags out, until finally, at dusk, the girl comes out into the patio "with a lighted candle in her hand . . . Avendaño paid no attention to the girl's attire, gazing only at her face, and it seemed to him like those in the paintings of angels. He was struck speechless by her beauty, and could think of nothing to say, so bemused and carried away was he." [107] The commotion and muteness are conventional, as in Heliodorus. Less so the earlier, verbal phase, and the stage of subsequent confirmation. The postponement and delay of the consummation of love—which last for years in Galdós' *Fortunata y Jacinta*—serve only to heighten the original desire.

If a norm exists, a counteranorm usually arises. The two together maintain a structure of possibilities that the writer confronts in order to weave his changes and differences. And his intensifications, since they are partial, presume some omissions. Thus the emotion of the hero of *David Copperfield* (1850) is so immoderate, so hyperbolical—like Dickens' narration itself—at his first meeting with Dora that the hero tells us neither what he sees nor what he hears—only what he feels. It is as though sound and image were interrupted in a movie. At the invitation of her father, David crosses a garden and enters the room where Dora is waiting (Chapter 26):

And I heard a voice say, "Mr. Copperfield, my daughter Dora . . . !" It was, no doubt, Mr. Spenlow's voice, but I didn't know it, and I didn't care whose it was. All was over in a moment. I had fulfilled my destiny. I was a captive and a slave . . . I loved Dora to distraction! She was more than human to me . . . I was swallowed up in an abyss of love in an instant. There was no pausing on the brink; no looking down, no looking back; I was gone, headlong, before I had sense to say a word to her.

We have here one of the longest of the *longues durées,* a structure of possibilities that persists up to Thomas Mann, André Breton (*Nadja*), modern cinema, sentimental romantic novels; and one that is also found in the best love poetry, that is, that of Pedro Salinas: *La voz a ti debida* (1933; translated into English as *To Live in Pronouns*). To know oneself is to recognize oneself; an instantaneous vision happens at a moment and in a place, but in such a way that love may later transcend the space and time of the visible:

> Conocerse es el relámpago . . .
> Te conocé en la tormenta,
> en ese desgarramiento
> brutal de tiniebla y luz,
> donde se revela el fondo
> que escapa al día y la noche.
> Te vi, me has visto, y ahora,
> desnuda ya del equívoco . . .
> eres tan antigua mía,
> te conozco tan de tiempo,
> que en tu amor cierro los ojos . . .
> a ciegas, sin pedir nada
> a esa luz lenta y segura
> con que se conocen letras
> y formas y se echan cuentas
> y se cree que se ve
> quién eres tú, mi invisible.

> Finding each other is a lightning-flash . . .
> I found you in the storm . . .
> in that brutal rendering
> of darkness and light,
> where depths are revealed
> that escape from day and night.
> I saw you, you've seen me, and now
> stripped bare of ambiguity . . .
> You've been mine from so long ago,
> I've known you for such a long time,
> I close my eyes in your love . . .
> [and walk] without wavering,
> blindly, without asking anything
> of that slow sure light
> by which letters are recognized,
> and shapes, and accounts are kept
> and people think they see
> who you are, my invisible one.[108]

Yes, the thematic structure persists in order to be changed; but to persist and to change over and over again, that is, throughout the course of a history that is not completely resolved in inconstancy.

I said a little while back that the most arduous and delicate task in the field of thematology is to distinguish between trivial and worthwhile elements; or, if you prefer, between the superficial and the profound. It would be absurd to regard all details as equally significant in a modern novel, so filled with objects and events, some of which serve only to advance the action or make it completely comprehensible. In *The Charterhouse of Parma*, Fabrizio's shoes and even some of his actions don't interest us as much as other things do, things that readers notice and critics comment on with attention. Stephen Gilman chose towers and elevated places as outstanding Stendhalian symbols. In an earlier chapter I talked about formal elements and aggregates of forms. We are inclined to view or to represent the intermeshing of these forms in a longitudinal fashion. The thematic complex of a literary work consists of various elements, including relations or distances that are transversal, spatial, rather than longitudinal, that go from the most visible to the most profound. Alexandru Dutu, in studying certain Rumanian books of entertainment, speaks of *superposition de thèmes,* a useful phrase: "the study of superimposing can show how the image of Alexander the Great was overlaid by that of Chosroes"; and he gives other examples.[109] In effect, everything happens as if the thematic elements were placed, grid-fashion, one on top of another. We are already familiar with superposition as an aspect of Racine's work.

So we are required to observe a work of verbal art from the point of view of depth perspective, a common occurrence when viewing painting. A visitor to Venice is able to admire many of Tintoretto's paintings, which treat identical themes such as the Last Supper. The variety of effects that a single painter can draw out of the same event is astounding, the vast gamut of meanings that come out of a relatively limited repertoire of Bible stories. From Heinrich Wölfflin to Erwin Panofsky, the great scholars of art have kept these iconographic distinctions very much in mind. Wölfflin explains that a Renaissance or Baroque artist who depicts Saint Jerome, for example, with his lion, his shelves, and his folios, is painting immobility as well as change, nearness as well as distance, mass as well as outline of objects and persons.[110] So Pierre Dufour distinguishes between motif, a broader concept, and theme, inseparable from individual and concrete realization. How many different realizations have not been provoked by the motif of the Virgin and Child? Botticelli's virgins, or Mantegna's, Renoir's *Mère et enfant,* Picasso's *Maternidad azul* . . . Dufour writes:

A given theme, such as "Maternity," unique because it concerns an elemental anthropological level, has been able to find expression in extremely different motifs: mother nursing her child or carrying it in her arms, pregnant women, mother pictured in the midst of her children, or mother exhausted by daily tasks, mother holding her dead child in her arms, or every other scene imaginable.[111]

Dufour turns to Louis Hjelmslev's linguistic terms and calls the motif *forme du contenu:* "A sort of Kantian scheme, presumption of form, mental form, sociocultural model or *pattern*, archetype, 'structure of the imagined,' the motif is not yet a concrete form of expression, as long as it has not given way to the material realization, by necessity aleatory, that is the work of art or the literary work."[112]

This is a question pondered by the best scholars of literary thematics. Elizabeth Frenzel, to whom we are indebted for reflections and inventories of great usefulness in this area, distinguishes between primary theme, such as the material collected or utilized by the author, and principal motif, or significant situation elaborated by the author.[113] The primary theme is not identical with its individualized treatment, product of the incorporation of thematic discourse with the other types of discourse that make up the configuration of the finished work. Frenzel's terminology is different from Dufour's, but she has a similar perspective. Raymond Trousson, who presented theoretical arguments for thematology, also follows the path from wide concept to personified theme. For him, as for Dufour, motif precedes theme:

Let us choose to call this way a backdrop, a broad concept, designating either a certain attitude—for example, rebellion—or a basic situation, impersonal, whose actors have not yet become individualized—for example, the situation of a man between two women, or the conflict between two brothers, between a father and son, the abandoned woman, and so on . . . What is a theme? Let us agree to call it then the particular expression of a motif, its individualization, or, if you prefer, the result of a passage from the general to the particular.[114]

Trousson, who is interested in "heroes" and legendary characters—*thèmes des héros*—shows in practice that the theme of Prometheus crisscrosses with other themes to give expression and life to the same motif or general conception. Rebellion, favorite motif of the *Sturm und Drang* movement and of Romanticism, is personified not only in the figure of Prometheus but also in the figures of Cain, Satan, Faust, and Byron's Manfred. At the same time, during the Romantic era the polysemic figure of Prometheus is subdivided, so to speak, giving rise to Balzac's brilliant artist, many a poet's heretic, the precursor of Christ in Quinet, among others. I see here three phases, the first two of which Trousson emphasizes and calls motif and theme—Frenzel names them in the opposite order. What is involved is something like a process, or rather something like a complex made up of surfaces superimposed on one another that the critic is perfectly free to analyze or dismantle in any way he sees fit.

The terminological confusion, though irritating, is not of great importance. What matters is that a deep perspective is opened. I do not believe that a genetic examination of the elaboration of a work, of its sources and growth, would produce the same result. A number of years ago, reflecting on the theme of seduced innocence, a theme studied by Hellmuth Petriconi, I emphasized the great distance between the conceptual configuration of a theme, or a preliterary sketch, perhaps an idea or an extremely schematic situation, and the final poetic treatment that succeeds in capturing and realizing the theme aesthetically.[115] For we are dealing with two things not simply separated by distance that are unlike and incomparable. The pretheme, the sketch, is a conceptual model, the simplified residue of various readings. "The motif, ancient or modern," wrote Américo Castro, "is mere possibility of a new creation; what is important in that creation is its function, its power as style, and as human value, but not the formal skeleton that ties it to something else that is not it."[116] In Trousson's example, the theme of rebellion and the figure of Prometheus are found simultaneously in certain Romantic authors. It is useless to ask which enjoys priority: the theme and the motif are superimposed; or—in the selfsame way—the motif and the theme.

The reader perceives both. For the biblical Last Supper *is* in Tintoretto's paintings; Iphigenia *is* in plays by Racine and Goethe; Prometheus, in Calderón and Shelley. Samson, in Joost van den Vondel and Milton. Following the recommendation of Américo Castro, it is important to observe how a theme functions within a work that brings together a plurality of values. It goes without saying that these values can be extremely diverse. The great polythematic works, from Dante to Proust, cannot be easily forgotten. Many times the *Themen-Verflechtung*, or knitting together of themes, is primordial, as Curtius pointed out in a brilliant essay on the novels of Hermann Hesse. Often found in Hesse's work are songs of birds, wounded animals, fish—fish linked symbolically with the unconscious. Water is temptation and danger. Hesse's diverse and favorite motifs are combined in his mature masterwork, *The Glass Bead Game* (1969). Curtius concludes that mixing motifs with themes is unsound. For him *Motiv* is what makes the argument possible objectively, what invites its composition: the intrigue, fable, or *mythos* of Aristotle. *Thema* is the personal and subjective attitude of the writer face to face with what life and literature suggest to him. "Es ist dem Dichter mitgegeben." (It is bestowed on the poet).[117] Motifs are given, found, or invented; and without them it is difficult to find an approach to a drama or a novel. The theme is the inescapable destiny of the writer. It is what leads to a valuable, more profound work. Since a single theme is not common to the different works of one writer, one must conclude that a theme does not lie in the work, or that it may be discovered only genetically.

Curtius' essay dates from 1947. Pedro Salinas expressed similar thoughts in 1948 in *La poesía de Rubén Darío*. Remember one of the definitions of theme in Miguel Covarrubias' *Tesoro de la lengua castellana* (1611): "every fool with his theme, because they always have some special pet phrase, and mostly what was the occasion for losing one's wits." Every great poet, according to Pedro Salinas, who was unquestionably a great poet himself, has a "vital" theme within him that prevails over the "literary" themes (the motifs of Curtius) and that a repertoire of symbolic and imaginative recourses puts at his disposal, helping him to give concrete form to his irresistible inclination. The theme as an irrepressible obsession, completely anterior to the discovery of concrete forms of expression, is "the most profoundly human" of everything involved in the creative act:

> The theme of the poet to be projected onto poetry is sought for in the topics that, in each case, seem most to his liking. In general the theme is not finished or exhausted in one work, in one affair. Since it is found in a state of continual interior flux, hardly made concrete in a new form—the novel or poem hardly finished—restful and calm periods of the creative impulse of the theme, awakes anew and is put in motion, demanding a future realization. A work is made, finished, but the theme, no. When a writer regards himself as finished, it is not for lack of topics or executive skill; it is that his vital theme lost its impulsive energy.[118]

It is very clear that Salinas distinguishes between two senses of the term. One is the vital theme, which leads to the work and underlies its concrete molding. In Rubén Darío, the erotic inclination:

> Guióme por varios senderos
> Eros.

> He guided me by various paths
> Eros.[119]

The "literary" theme (Curtius' motif, Trousson's theme) is the channel for such a molding: in Rubén, the centaur, the swan, the garden with peacocks.

It is not a matter of a meditation on an earlier theme or a topic derived from the rhetorical tradition, *donnée,* that we are pondering, but a largely irrational impulse that becomes part of the poet's task:

> The theme is not the thing that the artist wishes reflexively, what he proposes to do in his work; it is what he does, it is what he adds to the proposition, in the process of execution. It is what is posed—by inexplicable means—over the proposed. The theme determines in mysterious fashion the final being of the intentions, as the sun by its height governs the length of the shadows.[120]

If sun and shadow exist, if superimposed levels of definitely different depths exist, then as a practical matter the task of thematology is to select among them, and if possible to link them together. If we were speaking of painting, we would say that the most figurative levels are presented on one side and the most abstract ones on the other. Some critics are content with the first levels. This point of view has given rise to a singular work by J. P. Weber, *Domaines thématiques* (1963); Weber believes that clocks provide the key to the whole of Alfred de Vigny's work. A joint study of literature and the plastic arts, to which we are often lured by thematology, usually stresses the figurative aspects: the looks of Polyphemus; the face of Narcissus, in Il Domenichino and Lope de Vega, Giambattista Marini, and Nicolas Poussin; the appearances in fables of Apollo and Daphne, collected by Yves Giraud.[121] The extreme opposite attitude, that of being interested only in the deepest strata, is in my opinion a riskier procedure. For then the artistic creation can easily evaporate, vanish. Not only the personal obsession of the artist mentioned by Pedro Salinas arises, but also the complex of imaginative orientations that lead to a community or a cultural tradition. The propensities of the imagination rather than what is imagined, the subsoil or the idea rather than the finished work, the archetype or the myth founded on a hypothesis that cannot be proved true or false, like those of C. G. Jung, are the phantoms that lie in wait if one loses sight of what Harry Levin calls the natural links that connect the imagination with the work of the poet:

> What matters are the natural ties that relate a twice-told tale to its archetypal source, the recognizable store of possibilities to which the world's fictions can be retraced, the continual recombination and ramification of traditional features to meet the onset of fresh experience. The universal custom of fabulation repeats itself in cross-cultural paradigms. How deeply the iceberg of culture itself subtends beneath the surface we have been coming to realize more and more. The sophisticated processes of a self-conscious literature do not differ as much as we used to think from the subliminal processes of folklore.[122]

In such cases it is important to glimpse the universality of the poetic imagination, its most common fables, its images and constitutive arguments. Oral literature provides a privileged terrain of study: for example, Albert Lord has found that epic themes, such as the conclave of rulers and the scene in which a hero prepares and arms himself for war, are the same in the *Iliad* or the *Chanson de Roland* as in the great popular cantos of Yugoslavia.[123] Thus complexes that are supranational are undoubtedly linked, but on a theoretical basis the linkage may be extremely variable—ranging from model A to D and to the others mentioned in Chapter 10. The point of departure is not always the theory of literature. I think of illustrious works such as those of Georges Poulet on time and space, and also on the circle, as expressed in different eras and by various authors; or even closer to home, the works of Jean-Pierre Richard and Victor Brombert. The four elements are the subject of Gaston Bachelard's books, based on a personal bouquet of literary citations.[124] Gilbert Durand's orientation, also tending toward unification, is based on a conceptual anthropological framework; Charles Mauron's "psychocriticism," on the obsessions that torment certain writers.[125]

The challenge presented by mythography is of special interest. Literature "endlessly redistributes myths,"[126] Natália Correia said not long ago, in referring not only to the literature of antiquity but also to modern literature. James Joyce, André Breton, Octavio Paz: the poets and critics of our century show that poetry redistributes dreams when linked with myths. I have already mentioned Mircea Eliade. However, it is also true that mythography can stray off into vague conjectures, reflecting history in a mediocre sense—neither present nor absent—a practice denounced by Roy Harvey Pearce[127] ("the cause of Enlightenment has been better served by the effort to demythologize," Levin observes);[128] or, on the other hand, it may drift into transparently ideological demystifications: the falsely obvious of popular culture (Barthes, *Mythologies,* 1957) or the institution of literature itself (Barthes, *S/Z,* 1970). Not so the mythographic proclivity found in works from Maud Bodkin to Northrop Frye that has given rise to one of the most original currents of criticism in the English language.[129]

Ironic, ambitious, pleasant, keener than most, Frye published some books—*Fearful Symmetry* (1947), *Anatomy of Criticism* (1957), *The Educated Imagination* (1968), and various others—whose critical quality surpasses the persuasive force of the theoretical schemes on which they are based. For him as for T. S. Eliot, literature constitutes a universal order, a complete world.[130] "All themes and characters and stories that you encounter in literature belong to one big interlocking family."[131] What is the integrating principle for such a vast whole? The persistence of ancient myths. Understand by myth not only a collective fantasy that incarnates ideals and memories (as defined by Levin)[132] but an effort of the imagination to unite the world: "A myth is a simple and primitive effort of the imagination to identify the human with the nonhuman world, and its most typical result is a story about a god."[133] Literature and myth do not describe or measure the surroundings in which we live but absorb them and shape them, converting them into our space, more human, more intimate, and also more bearable, through the psychic distance that we maintain before poetic inventions. As in the eighteenth century, for instance in Schiller, a high value is placed on the authenticity of the spirit of primitive man, its ingenuous and childlike quality.[134] Frye, so sophisticated, so complex, so refined, at bottom comes close to the poets and artists of our century who have tried to recover an ancient and playful innocence. But what he develops is an intricate, inexorable, theoretical scheme, that has a "fearful symmetry" and an overwhelming systematization. For the survival of Greco-Latin myths does not necessarily presuppose history. Frye does point out the gap between the heroic magnitude of the great poetry of antiquity and the ironic mediocrity of the modern antihero, or the level of realism that he calls *low mimetic*.[135] "In Shakespeare we can still have heroes who can see ghosts and talk in magnificent poetry, but by the time we get to Beckett's *Waiting for Godot* they're speaking prose and have turned into ghosts themselves."[136] Basically, however, Frye skirts around historical evolution and constructs a vast atemporal space, that of a literary anthropology based on categories taken from rites, myths, and tales of folklore, whose trajectory is not necessarily successive:

> We next realize that the relation between these categories and literature is by no means purely one of descent, as we find them reappearing in the greatest classics—in fact there seems to be a general tendency on the part of the great classics to revert to them . . . Here we begin to wonder if we cannot see literature, not only as complicating itself in time, but as spread out in conceptual space from some unseen center.[137]

There is an elemental myth, a matrix narration that Frye defines at times as the loss and reconquest of the identity of the hero ("the story of the loss and regaining of identity is, I think, the framework of all literature");[138] and at others as a *quest-myth* (as in Greimas, the story of a desire): itinerary of a search, a yearning, a pursuit, that leads from death to rebirth, through the four seasons of the year. To these correspond also the literary genres: the springtime of the romance, the summer of comedy, the autumn of tragedy, the winter of satire.

The irrefutable postulate of this thematic idea in Northrop Frye is universality. Everything gives way to it. Eugene Ionesco's *The Bald Soprano* presents a respectable gentleman and a lady who converse and discover gradually, not without surprise, that they are husband and wife. Frye notes the reappearance of two ancient conventions: the situation of two persons who have contact with each other but don't know each other; and the scene of recognition (one assumes that it is the *anagnorisis* of Aristotle).[139] But what about Ionesco's peculiarly absurd situation? his humor and unique verbal technique? his affinity for historical allusion? Before the dialectic of the one and the various, nation and world, continuity and change, Frye turns to the primacy of theory. Jakobson said that the objective of criticism is not literature but literariness. Frye thinks that just as the physics student does not study nature but an organized body of knowledge, the critical apprentice must study not literature but a body of knowledge relating to it.[140] He is partly right. A familiarity with some conceptual frameworks is without doubt indispensable. But the analogy with the natural sciences has its limits. The chemist may shut himself up in his laboratory because what he sees when he goes out in the street has little or nothing to do with the scale of his investigations, but the critic/historian can and must turn to individual poetical works (a little like the geologist who studies the Arizona desert), observing and correcting in that way his theoretical hypotheses. Or rather, the critic proves the existence of those natural ties that Levin spoke of, the ties between myth and motif, motif and poem.[141] As much as thematology inclines toward unity, it does not manage to suppress, but rather to structure, the diversity of literature.

15

Literary Relations: Internationality

In Owen Aldridge's anthology, *Comparative Literature: Matter and Method* (1969), composed of articles published in the journal *Comparative Literature Studies,* 20 percent of the contributions are contained in the section titled "Literary Relations." Clearly, what is meant is international literary relations. Aldridge deals honestly with a real situation: both international literary relations and studies concerning them indeed exist. Colloquia and conferences dedicated to such topics as "Spain and French Literature" and "Oriental/Western Literary Relations" are constantly taking place. However, not many new ideas have emerged from such projects. It is difficult to respond to such venerable questions from the point of view of a contemporary sensibility. Questions—like literary genres, according to the ideas of the Russian Formalists—wear out and become automatic. In the field of sources and influences, it would be surprising to find someone writing a book today as brilliant as Pierre Villey's *Les sources et l'évolution des Essais de Montaigne* (1933), or John Livingston Lowes's *The Road to Xanadu* (1927), which Mario Praz praised thus: "I know of no aesthetic analysis of Coleridge's *Rime of the Ancient Mariner* more penetrating than J. L. Lowes's excellent study of its sources."[1]

In Aldridge's collection, for example, Robert Shackleton reexamines Montesquieu's debt to Machiavelli. (The attempt had been made earlier, in 1912, by E. Levi-Malvano in his *Montesquieu e Machiavelli.*) There are numerous borrowings in Shackleton's article, especially those of a fragmentary type. The first chapters of *L'esprit des lois,* which define the nature of a monarchy, of despotism, of a republic, make use of a number of Machiavelli's explanations, particularly those concerning the history of Rome. However, Shackleton concludes that Montesquieu's fundamental thought and basic design are quite far removed from Machiavelli's. "The great synthesizing principles of the masterpiece owe little to the Italian."[2] The harvest is as poor as it is predictable. Was that baggage really needed for that trip?

In Chapter 7, dealing with the French hour of comparativism, I tried to provide information and methodological facts concerning the more traditional classes of internationality. I will add a little more at this point, before considering three problems that appear to be of greater interest to us currently: intertextuality, multilingualism, and translation.

The study of international influences is a task bristling with obstacles, pitfalls, and all possible misunderstandings. For that reason, it would be unjust not to recognize the merits of those who have succeeded in such an difficult undertaking. So let me recall here as model an exemplary essay by Mario Praz, "Rapporti tra la letteratura italiana e la letteratura inglese," first published in 1948. The essay begins in masterly fashion with what is already a summary of the work. Praz writes that there was neither reciprocity nor simultaneity of any kind in the trajectory of the mutual influences between Italian and English literature:

> From this comes the Italian ignorance of literary works, even renowned ones, of that marginal province that was England in European culture until the eighteenth century, and English ignorance of Italian literary works from the nineteenth century on, when Italy's position becomes, in large measure, peripheral . . . The Italian influence on English, after a high point in the second half of the fourteenth century (with Chaucer), pervades all the fields of culture and of fashion during the Renaissance, only to fade away, by degrees, in the seventeenth, after one last gleam in the case of Milton, who, for intensity, presents a case parallel, in its decline, to the fourteenth-century precursor of the tide. The English influence in Italy does not proceed so clearly and visibly: Italy undergoes that influence almost indirectly, through the center of Paris, and the imitation of works and of English attitudes will be sporadic, provincial, and will never enter strongly into the creations of a genius, as was the case in England with Chaucer, Shakespeare, Milton.[3]

The "Italian adventure" of Chaucer must be told first of all. He went to Italy in 1372–73 in order to negotiate with Genoa the selection of an English port where Genoese merchants might enjoy special privileges, and also to obtain a loan from the Florentine bankers for his king. Chaucer was not only his own *intermédiare*, all by himself; his financial dealings with the Bardi or the Peruzzi families came before his discovery of Dante, Petrarch, and Boccaccio. That being so, Praz takes note of both the socioeconomic conditions underlying literary developments and the historical differences from one period to another insofar as they concern the dialectic of the local and the universal. During the Middle Ages there was only one single literary culture: "Chaucer and the great fourteenth-century Italians spoke different languages, but their culture was the same." [4] Furthermore, the works of the great Italians were as easily accessible to the English poet as the *Roman de la rose* and other French texts had been in the past. Chaucer's assimilation of the Italian writers is noticeable in the *House of Fame,* more so in the *Parliament of Fowls,* and plain to see in the *Canterbury Tales.* Praz stresses that Chaucer owes a marked debt to the Italians in the development of his prosody, but through analyses and comparisons he tries to make clear the differences between the detailed and fragmentary influences, on the one hand, and those differences affecting the general conception of a work, on the other. Chaucer is heavily indebted to various episodes from the *Commedia* ("The Monk's Tale" and the story of Ugolino) and to Boccaccio's characters and probably also his use of the narrative *marco,* or framework; but in essence, Chaucer's principal model was Dante. [5] And the same distinction is made in the cases of other authors. The similarity between Spenser and Ariosto is superficial, because Spenser allegorizes, that is, medievalizes, Ariosto's epic *romanzo.* [6] For Praz the most relevant affinity is that of the *forma mentis,* but also the stylistic similarity that manifests and gives poetic reality to the concept. Thus John Lyly in his *Euphues* (1579)—so influential in its time—"allowed his work to be permeated by the most profound kind of Italianism, to the extent that it influenced his style." [7] As for Milton, Praz decides in favor of his debt to Tasso, not only for the theory of the Christian epoch but also for the paradigm of gravity, exaltation, and magnificence of language, which the English poet carried quite a bit further: "how much closer to the Tassoesque conception of the 'magnificence' and the 'music' is Milton's epic verse than that of Tasso!" [8] Here is a phenomenon that has occurred over and over: the case of an imitator who surpasses the original. The "Italian" tragedies of John Webster (*The White Devil,* 1612) were far superior to the Seneca-type Italian melodramas that inspired them, just as Shakespeare's *Othello* definitely overshadows a certain story by Giraldi Cinzio. Some traditional categories of comparativism come into this context as well—if we are careful not to confuse circumstances with results: categories such as the negative "image" of Italy—violent and corrupt—fundamental to the English theater and other genres until the 1700s;[9] and the role of intermediaries like John Florio, author of manuals and dictionaries of the Italian language (*A Worlde of Wordes*, 1598) and admirable translator of Montaigne.

The term *international relations* is usually understood to include cultural, social, and political relations at the same time. Hence the human, complex, lively, and even painful interest of international relations, for more than one country and one era. Without going further afield, think of Europe as it is today—and as it may be tomorrow. Concerning comparative studies in Hungary, ranging from the past century to the present day and the nexus that they represent with Western nations, György Vajda wrote in 1964:

> one found—as generally in the soul of all cultivated Hungarians for a century or a century and a half already—the nostalgia for Europe, the desire to be adopted by it or to be able ouselves to adopt the "virtual Europe," which stubbornly refused to take account of our language, our culture, our literature. In the chaos of war of the first half of the forties and in the fear of annihilation, spirits were dominated by the feeling of solitude, expressed by the motto *egyedül vagyunk* ("we are alone").[10]

This isolation of a national literature, the very isolation that comparativism fights against, is to a greater or lesser extent a frequent and generalized condition. The Magyar intellectuals evoked by Vajda were not in essence alone in their aloneness. International relations, in their cultural as well as political aspects, presuppose an incessant confrontation with ignorance, misunderstandings, provincial prejudices, mental inertia, and of course with economic and military power. I will not pause now to gloss this difficult tangle, a task that I attempted earlier in my *Literature as System* (1971). The itinerary of influences and literary relations is a contingent, if not irrational, matter and obeys no order of qualitative justice. The diffusion of a writer's work and a region's literature demands, at the very least, that the knowledge of the language be widened and that the work arouse the interest of some translators. There is often an enormous gap separating a great poem—and we are not speaking of its execution, printing, and distribution as a book—from the remote reader born to read it.[11]

Is the most powerful nation the one whose culture and literature predominate? So goes more than one catechism. But historical blends are indispensable. Naturally, imperial power brings with it the extension of a language, carried along irresistibly by the predominant force and accepted avidly by self-interested parties. However, a culture consists of different levels, and often what is brought along by a stronger economic and military power may be the most elementary or utititarian level of its culture, serving only to spread over the host country a visible but superficial glaze of predominance, without any intellectual substance. The prestige of the French and of France during the eighteenth century and a good part of the nineteenth did indeed encompass all levels, as the influence of the *Encyclopédie* demonstrates very well. On the other hand, the Germany of Kant, Goethe, Fichte, and Hegel, writers whose highly merited prestige was quickly recognized everywhere, lacked political leadership. In our own time, the diffusion of the works of the great Latin American writers is inversely proportional to the economic prosperity of their countries of origin. Italianization, the *sine qua non* of the Renaissance of sixteenth-century Europe, grew in tandem with the weakening of the Italian states. Spain's military and political presence in Italy for many years did not favor but rather prejudiced the acceptance of the poets and prose writers of the Spanish Golden Age; they were considered the "barbarians" of the era, looked on with mistrust by a supposedly superior culture. Alda Croce concludes that in the sixteenth century "Spanish literature was, in general, regarded with great disfavor by our writers." [12] Benedetto Croce expresses the opinion that Spanish literature did not exercise the profound influence that only ideas can offer—since "the power of culture has its fulcrum, and, at the same time, its tool in thought and in philosophy." [13] This observation could well be applied to other periods in the cultural history of Spain.

The concept of *intertextuality,* developed some twenty-five years ago, is especially useful for comparatists. We believe that here we have at last a way to dissipate the many ambiguities and errors such as those brought along in the wake of the notion of influence.

When someone said "Dickens influenced Kafka," we never knew for certain whether it was a matter of vague repercussions of a personal or biographical nature, perhaps profound, but with heaven knows what precise consequences; or whether it meant the confirmation of the presence of *Martin Chuzzlewit* in *Amerika.* The statement "*Martin Chuzzlewit* has had an effect on *Amerika*" would not turn out to be very clear either, since we would not understand whether the form and incidents of Dickens' novel were indeed recognizable in Kafka's, or whether the statement referred to something that happened earlier, during the gestation of the work, or whether Dickens' story had only transmitted a mental model of a picaresque novel, as other works could also have done, such as *Lazarillo de Tormes* or Tobias Smollett's *Roderick Random.* The superficial, visible, merely detailed character of the influence was also very seldom elucidated, in contrast to impulses toward the deeper or more universal strata of the work. Different connections were not structured but were left isolated, in no hierarchical order. But the decisive ambiguity, a component of the old idea of influence, was undoubtedly the superposition of biographical and textual elements.[14]

Basically, we found ourselves facing once more the kind of prestige accorded in the nineteenth century to biological schemes and the *idole des origines,* to such an extent that the terrain of influences in the genetic sense seemed no longer immense but boundless—as unlimited as our knowledge of the life of an author, including the most intimate details as well as the most external facts. Goethe observed to Eckermann (December 16, 1828), "I owe much to the Greeks and French; I am infinitely indebted to Shakespeare, Sterne, and Goldsmith; but in saying this I do not show the sources of my culture—that would be an endless as well as an unnecessary task."[15] The limitless, the boundless—*das Grenzenlose*—is the terrain of influences not only in the quantitative sense, but also because precisely there life merges with literature to an infinite extent in pursuit of the root of roots, the origin of origins, hoping to find at last the source of sources—"le fonti delle fonti," as Croce suggested.[16]

The term *intertextuality*—analogous to "intersubjetivity"—was proposed by Julia Kristeva in a 1966 essay, "Le mot, le dialogue et le roman" (translated into English as "Word, Dialogue, and Novel"), concerning the work of the then relatively unknown Mikhail Bakhtin. For Bakhtin, man is a dialogic being (see Chapter 13), inconceivable without the other, impregnated with alterity; and the novel is "heteroglossia," a crossroads of many languages. It might just as well have been suggested that the text of a literary work is heterotextual, penetrated by alterity, by words other than its own. Kristeva writes: "Any text is constructed as a mosaic of quotations; any text is the absorption and transformation of another. The notion of *intertextuality* replaces that of *intersubjectivity,* and poetic language is read at least *double.*"[17] The word is not a "point," something fixed, a given sense, but an "intersection of textual surfaces," a "dialogue among several writings."[18] This dialogue takes place among three languages: that of the writing subject, that of the addressee (whether outside or inside the work), and that of exterior texts, or cultural context, present or past. Thus the word, which is double, "one and other" at the same time, can be considered from a horizontal or a vertical point of view: horizontally, the word belongs equally "to writing subject and addressee";[19] and vertically, to the text in question and to other prior or different texts.

The literary word loses all of its own substance, becomes static, is shorn of its aptness, becomes unraveled. More than that, the concept of text also turns heterogeneous and dynamic. The text no longer *is* something, nor does it encompass any value that might be there, before the reader's eyes, needful of perception or interpretation. The text must be produced, elaborated, or rather continue to be elaborated, since it started with a dialogue: "Bakhtin was one of the first to replace the static hewing out of texts with a model where literary structure does not simply *exist* but is generated in relation to *another* structure." [20] We encounter, then, the search for a theory of the text that leads Kristeva and her contemporaries to propose in other essays more terms (such as *géno-texte* and *phéno-texte,* referring to origin and productivity, respectively).[21] Thus agreeing in principle with the spirit of Bakhtin in a certain sense (literature as transgression, questioning, carnival), these authors attack the presence in the text of relations of authority, of all interdiction in the diction, of all prohibition in the explication. The semiotic of Kristeva rejects the idolatry of the sign. Throughout a dynamic process that goes from 0 to 2, it is noted "that the linguistic, psychic, and social 'prohibition' is 1 (God, Law, Definition)," [22] and that poetic discourse is the only verbal practice capable of escaping such a prohibition.

Roland Barthes, elaborating on these ideas, explains in passing that the "intertext" has nothing to do with the old notion of source or influence:

> Every text is an *intertext;* other texts are present in it, at varying levels, in more or less recognizable forms; earlier cultural texts and those of the surrounding culture; every text is a new texture of past citations. Passing over into the text, redistributed in it, are bits of codes, formulas, rhythmic models, fragments of social language, and so on, because language always exists before the text and around it. Intertextuality, the condition of every text, no matter what it is, is obviously not limited to a problem of sources or influences; the intertext is a general field of anonymous formulas, whose origin can seldom be located, of unconscious or automatic citations, given without quotation marks.[23]

The benefit of this point of view for comparatists is considerable. When speaking of intertext, without any doubt we would like to denote something present in the work, something that exists in the work itself, not a long genetic process whose main interest rests in its passage, its growth, thus relegating the origin as well as the result of the work to a second level. We comparatists made an effort to distinguish between the influence and a certain X, free of ambiguity; and that X is what is now called intertext. The concept of influence tended to individualize a literary work, but without success. The idea of intertext emphasizes the social aspect of literary writing, whose individual character, up to a certain point, is located at a specific junction of earlier writings.

However, other problems arise. In the first place, the authoritarian and monolithic character of the pronouncements of Kristeva and Barthes is notorious. If the best theories are in error by being fallible and rectifiable in the future, as the philosophers of science explain, then absolute theories must be absolutely in error. A speculative construction *ex principiis* can be recognized by the use of the statement "All A is B" or "All A consists of B," as, for example, "Every text is an intertext" or "Any text is constructed as a mosaic of quotations." My comment is inspired by Kristeva's expressed intention to impose the force of a prohibition on literary language, on the idolatry of the sign. Why then—one may ask—the idolatry of theoretical language? Perhaps that is what happens when a theory, instead of confronting reality, confronts another theory, or departs from one, or bases itself on one.

The second difficulty, not far removed from the first, is practical and perhaps more serious. It would not be surprising if the idea of intertextuality were in fact reduced to a general conception of the poetic sign, a theory of the text, rather than to a method for the investigation of relations existing between different poems, essays, or novels. That would be a door opening onto a path of reading, rather than the path itself. In the quotation above, Barthes speaks of the text as a texture of citations. This phenomenon is well known—Gil Polo, for example, in *Diana enamorada* (1564), quotes entire lines of Garcilaso—and has the advantage that the lines are easily identifiable. But obviously the allusions of one text to another are not always so explicit, particularly when the allusion often refers not to a phrase or an expression, a formula or a topic, but to a verbal structure, a poetic or narrative form, or a generic paradigm. Does the investigation of intertexts presuppose the primacy of the linguistic act? of verbal microforms? We have already seen the limitations of such an approach regarding stylistics (Chapter 13). But no, what Barthes seems to have in mind is rather the anonymous and automatized conventions: "a general field of anonymous formulas, whose origin can seldom be located, of unconscious or automatic citations." So that we are circumscribed by conventions and commonplaces, that is, by an existing field but one hardly suitable for the perception of a phenomenon of indisputable relevance to literature: individuality. Comparativism will make very little progress by following this road. Our objective is to do away with the vagueness and the interminable list of facts that characterized the studies of sources and influences. But vagueness and limitlessness return at a gallop if intertextuality means anonymity and generality. How can the quantity of conventions, formulas, and commonplaces that make up the language of literature be limited, even for a single era? We would never be able to reach the end—"es würde ins Grenzenlose gehen"—to quote Goethe's words again.

The idea does not lack antecedents, since we are speaking of formulas and topics, and some of these antecedents are as ancient as rhetoric itself. Yuri Tynyanov emphasized the role of what he called the *synfunction* of a work, or rather the function that links it to a different cultural series. Northrop Frye, in his well-known article "Literature as Context: Milton's *Lycidas*," shows that Milton's elegy contains numerous conventional pastoral elements: "every poem is inherently connected with other poems of its kind."[24] It is true that Frye was concentrating more on the premises of the genre than on the verbal density of the poem. The term *context* does not stress the interweaving of the language of one poet with the language of others as forcefully as the term *intertext*.

Once again it is Michael Riffaterre who reconciles theory with criticism of poetry in a more balanced way. In Chapter 7 of *La production du texte* (1979), he examines the intertextuality of the fourteen sonnets that make up Joachim du Bellay's "Songe" (1554). These sonnets, which close the cycle of *Les antiquités de Rome* and *Les regrets,* repeat a significant structure from Petrarch (*canzone* 42): a beautiful or admirable object is destroyed before the eyes of the reader, exemplifying the vanity of all things. With a precision that we cannot reproduce here, Riffaterre analyzes the superimposed codes of sonnet VII of du Bellay's "Songe." The immediate theme is an eagle, although the theme is only alluded to (lines 1–4):

> Je vy l'Oiseau, qui le Soleil contemple,
> D'un foible vol au ciel s'avanturer,
> Et peu à peu ses ailes asseurer,
> Suivant encor le maternel exemple . . .

> I saw the bird, contemplating the sun,
> venture toward the sky in feeble flight,
> and little by little firm up its wings,
> still following the maternal example . . .

After a majestic flight to the sun, the bird is reduced to fire and finally to ash (lines 12–14):

> Je vy son corps en poudre tout réduit,
> Et vy l'oiseau, qui la lumière fuit,
> Comme un vermet renaistre de sa cendre.

I saw its body reduced to dust
and saw the bird which flees the light
and like a larva be reborn from its ashes.[25]

For Riffaterre *semantic indirectness* is the general rule of literary discourse: the work does not mean only what it says. A first reading, of a mimetic nature, accepts what the text represents and a certain stylistic order, basic conditions for a uniform perception of the work on the part of readers. A second stage, the semiotic one, takes the process apart in a freer manner, allowing the mimetic events to mean something more than or something different from what the words say. The vertical and intratextual relations that link the signifier and the signified give way to a series of horizontal and intertextual relations with words and cultural codes external to the sonnet being read. These intertextual connections are multiple: linking the sonnet with the other sonnets of "Songe" and the joint reading/interpretation of *omnia vanitas;* with the myth of Phaëthon (certainly so important in the *Divina commedia,* where it is connected by way of contrast with the successful ascent of the hero toward "il sole e le altre stelle"); with the Phoenix; with one of Petrarch's sonnets that links animals and light ("Son animali al mode de si altera . . ."); and with the "Roman discourse"—the majestic eagle—of *Les regrets* and *Les antiquités:* the grandeur and decadence of Rome, and so on.

To Riffaterre's observations, I dare to add the "narrative discourse" of *Les regrets:* the story of a (fictitious) exile that is above all the inverse of Ovid (the poet in Rome, no longer a central and triumphant city but a marginal and corrupt one, leaving the poet longing for his native France); but at the end the exile, in a complete turnabout, ends up disillusioned by his return (now we have an antithesis of the Ulysses myth), who even goes so far as to express ironic admiration for the city earlier unprized: "Adieu donques, Dorat, je suis encor Romain . . ." (Adieu then, Dorat, I am still Roman . . .). So here we have du Bellay proclaiming himself Roman like Ovid. All of du Bellay is sinuosity, paradox, and formal play. The scheme grandeur/decadence does not satisfy him permanently, nor does exile/return. If the fourteen sonnets of "Songe" allude intertextually to Petrarch's *omnia vanitas,* the seventh introduces a cyclical structure. The vanity of all things has a subspecies: mutability. Mutability also has a subspecies, more paradoxical: inversion, which opens the perspective of a renewed cycle—a rebirth of the majestic bird that resembles the birth of a larva (*vermet,* close to *ver*—worm—and *vermine*—vermin): "Comme un vermet renaistre de sa cendres."

Riffaterre opens a considerably broader compass, since his conception of intertextuality includes words, thematic structures, forms, and cultural codes. All these elements require that the reader rewrite what has been half-stated, or unsaid, the rewriting being based on the term *overdetermined*, charged with symbolic power, as in the case of Phaëthon (suggested by the eagle): "This is cited in a certain way, because it is possible for us to reconstitute it mentally from the overdetermined word: thus the effect of the phantom citation is due to the active participation of the reader, to his rewriting of the unspoken—such is the practice of intertextuality." [26] But is it necessary to rewrite a symbol that is so suggestive, so understandable? For the reader it is more a matter of completing, of continuing to feel and think and associate memories, to keep on "writing" in the mental sense of the word: to talk to oneself, link quotes, thus establishing intertextual boundaries. We are in the realm of the tacit, the mute, the stylistics of silence. The frontier between things seen and things imagined turns out to be extremely blurry.

In a very effective essay, Jonathan Culler attempts to deal with the unlimited nature of the field of intertextuality. The principal critics he comments on are Barthes, Kristeva, Laurent Jenny, and Harold Bloom. (I will speak later at a more appropriate place about Bloom's ideas, which deal primarily with the theory of history.) Culler recognizes that what we are dealing with here is a general conception of conditions that govern literary discourse. These conditions, like conventions, have the property of leaving behind and transcending a clear consciousness of some origins: "it is a part of the structure of discursive conventions to be cut off from origins." [27] How can one distinguish between a simple allusion and an intertext that is a condition of the sense of a poetic work? Culler turns to Edward L. Keenan's notion of *presupposition*[28] in linguistics. The logical presupposition of a sentence is the previous or tacit statement that makes it possible for a later statement to be true or false. The sentence "Adolph has stopped lying" presupposes the previous statement "Adolph lies." Well then, in poetry it often happens that a semantic structure assumes a number of prior presuppositions that form the basis for an intertextual space; knowledge of this space affects the reading in a decisive way. As an illustration, Culler cites the beginning of Baudelaire's "Bénédiction":

Lorsque par un décret des puissances suprêmes
Le Poète apparaît en ce monde ennuyé . . .

When by a decree of the supreme powers
The Poet appears in this jaded world . . .

The Poet's boredom seems like a decree or circumstance or myth existing from earlier times that Baudelaire will confront in order to define his own attitude, as will the reader. From a logical point of view, this type of presupposition suggests a significant pre-text. Culler distinguishes it from a pragmatic presupposition, one that assumes objective surroundings ("The door opened" implies the existence of a closed room), as happens in so many novels that begin more or less *in medias res*. Many novelists try to sketch the scene of the action from the very first sentences. Not so in poetry, which gives us the impression that it comes from nowhere, from the hollow of the white page, to go secreting little by little its own reality from its own substance. Emilio Alarcos Llorach stressed this peculiarity of the poetic text, which does not make words defer to things, but things to the words:

> That is, there is no *situation*. That should emerge from the poem itself. It seems, then, that the ultimate purpose of the poem—at bottom, creation— is neither creation of language, nor creation of an objective entity called poem, but rather *creation and fixing of a situation*, unique, unrepeatable, but capable of being evoked (precisely thanks to the poem).[29]

Without doubt the intertexts, palpable, modest, but significant, that Culler tries to demarcate add to this progressive growth of the poem.

If—leaving aside the general conventions that are the means and resources common to an entire era—we limit ourselves to the aspects of intertextuality just mentioned, then a series of coordinates that would serve to determine the uses of intertextuality seem appropriate. In my opinion, there are two coordinates that stand out. In the first place, let us keep in mind a line whose two extremes are *allusion* and *inclusion*. Certainly many intermediate positions exist. But in practice, it is clearly one thing to make a simple allusion or reminiscence, necessarily implying a memory from the past, or the externality of what is alluded to, and to include in the poetic fabric of the work itself—adding to its verbal surface, one might say, words or forms or foreign thematic structures. Such an act, by its explicit nature, should by no means be disdained; it is rather a tangible manifestation of the openness of individual poetic language to a plurality of languages—the heteroglossia so dear to Bakhtin. But it is also necessary to distinguish between the two extremes of *citation* and *significance*. (Allow me to remove from the word *citation* here all relevant substance or function.) The intertext is limited to citing when its exclusive effect is horizontal, that is, when it consists in evoking authorities or establishing related links (or polemics) with past figures and styles, without intervening decisively in the vertical semantic structure of the poem. In such cases the function of the intertext is rather more contextual. Significant allusions, of high symbolic tension, exist, some of them mentioned by Riffaterre in connection with du Bellay's sonnet; and there are also inclusions that are primarily citations of a contextual import.

T. S. Eliot said that bad poets imitate and good ones steal. Clearly the larceny, admiring or affectionate, takes place in broad daylight. A poem from the last years of Pedro Salinas, "Confianza" (from the book of the same name), begins this way:

> Mientras haya
> alguna ventana abierta,
> ojos que vuelven del sueño,
> otra mañana que empieza.
>
> Mar con olas trajineras
> —mientras haya—
> trajinantes de alegrías,
> llevándolas y trayéndolas.
>
> Lino para la hilandera,
> árboles que se aventuran
> —mientras haya—
> y viento para la selva.
>
> Jazmín, clavel, azucena,
> donde están, y donde no
> en los nombres que lo mientan.
>
> As long as there may be
> some open window,
> eyes returning from a dream,
> another morning commencing.
>
> Sea with bustling waves
> —as long as there may be—
> shuttling gladness,
> taking it and bringing it.
>
> Flax for the weaver,
> adventuring trees
> —as long as there may be—
> and wind for the forest.
>
> Jasmine, carnation, lily,
> where they are and are not
> in the names that belie them.

Our attention is immediately caught by the musical use of "Mientras haya", *leitmotiv* repeated thirteen times in a poem of sixteen stanzas, as well as by the cultural character of quite a few of the enumerated things and images:

> Mientras haya
> quien entienda la hoja seca,
> falsa elegía, preludio
> distante a la primavera.

> As long as there may be
> someone to understand the dry leaf,
> false elegy, distant
> prelude to the spring.

Beneath the baton of the *leitmotiv*, everything becomes temporalized; what is suggested to the reader is that the curve of time is not negative, that today is open to the morning, that the future will bring more life. I say what is suggested but not stated. *As long as there may be* . . . The subordinate clause in the subjunctive, "Mientras haya," does not lead to a principal clause—not even in the last stanzas:

> Susurros de estrella a estrella
> —mientras haya—,
> Casiopea que pregunta
> y Cisne que la contesta.

> Tantas palabras que esperan,
> invenciones, clareando
> —mientras haya—,
> amanecer de poema.

> Mientras haya
> lo que hubo ayer, lo que hay hoy,
> lo que venga.

> Whispers of star to star
> —as long as there may be—
> Cassopeia who asks
> and Cygnus who answers.

> So many words await,
> inventions, growing light
> —as long as there may be—
> dawn of poem.

As long as there may be
whatever was yesterday, whatever is today,
whatever may come.

As long as there may be light, music, language—the names of the constellations—what are we to think? That there is confidence in temporality?
willingness to tolerate all the rest? acceptance of death itself? A hundred
years earlier Gustavo Adolfo Bécquer had written (*rima* 39):

Mientras haya unos ojos que reflejen
    los ojos que los miran;
mientras responda el labio suspirando
    al labio que suspira;

mientras sentirse puedan en un beso
    dos almas confundidas;
mientras exista una mujer hermosa,
    ¡habrá poesía!

As long as there may be some eyes that reflect
·   the eyes that look at them;
as long as the lip responds sighing
    to the lip that sighs;

as long as may be felt in a kiss
    two mingled souls;
as long as a beautiful woman may exist,
    there will be poetry!

It is not necessary to recall Bécquer's verses in order to perceive, or comprehend, or feel those of. Pedro Salinas. To understand them, obviously not,
since the conclusion is not "habrá poesía," there will be poetry. And not
only because the penultimate stanza of "Confianza" allows "amanecer de
poema" (dawn of poem) between the hypothetical beings, in the subjunctive
mood, but because we have no conclusion of any kind; and whatever could
be deduced about the enduring nature of such beings is granted or relegated
to the reader's imagination. One of Bécquer's syntactic structures as well as
a temporal adverb axis ("mientras," as long as, but not "mientras haya, "
as long as there may be) is indeed included in Salinas' poem. But the significance of the poem in essence does not encompass elements of Bécquer's
poem. The intertext is a poet's use of a device employed earlier, one that
has become part of a repertoire of means available to modern writers. And
in addition—as we said earlier regarding certain traditional themes—the
contextual citation is a sign of gratitude on the part of an exiled poet, living

in America but also dwelling in his language: a gesture of solidarity with the Spanish poetic tradition.

There is another verse of Bécquer (*rima* 67) that ends with these words:

> En donde esté un piedra solitaria
>   sin inscripción alguna,
>   donde habite el olvido,
>   allí estará mi tumba.

> Wherever there may be a solitary stone
>   with no inscription whatsoever,
>   where forgetting may dwell
>   there will be my tomb.

Luis Cernuda retrieved the penultimate line in the title poem of *Donde habite el olvido:*[30]

> Donde habite el olvido,
> En los vastos jardines sin aurora;
> Donde yo sólo sea
> Memoria de una piedra sepultada entre ortigas
> Sobre la cual el viento escapa a sus insomnios.

> Donde mi nombre deje
> Al cuerpo que designa en brazos de los siglos,
> Donde el deseo no exista.

> En esta gran región donde el amor, ángel terrible,
> No esconda como acero
> En mi pecho su ala,
> Sonriendo lleno de gracia aérea mientras crece el tormento.

> Allá donde termine este afán que exige un dueño a imagen suya,
> Sometiendo a otra vida su vida,
> Sin más horizonte que otros ojos frente a frente.

> Donde penas y dichas no sean más que nombres,
> Cielo y tierra nativos en torno de un recuerdo;
> Donde al fin quede libre sin saberlo yo mismo,
> Disuelto en niebla, ausencia,
> Ausencia leve como carne de niño.

> Allá, allá lejos;
> Donde habite el olvido.

> Where forgetting may dwell
> In the vast gardens without dawn;

Where I alone may be
Memory of a stone buried among nettles
Over which the wind flees from its insomnias.

Where my name may leave
the body it designates in the arms of the centuries,
Where desire may not exist.

In that great region where love, terrible angel,
May not hide like steel
Its wing in my chest,
Smiling full of airy grace while the torment grows.

There where this urge that demands a master in its own image may
    end,
Surrendering its life to another life,
With no more horizons than other eyes face to face.

Where pains and pleasures may be nothing more than names,
Native sky and earth surrounding a memory;
Where at last I myself may be left free without knowing it,
Dissolved into fog, absence,
Light absence like the flesh of a child.

There, far off over there,
Where forgetting may dwell.

Here we also have an unconcluded clause in the subjunctive that stops the
reader in his tracks. *Where forgetting may dwell* . . . Except that this time
the absent conclusion is not a complete void. There is absence, yes, but also
the presence of the intertext from Bécquer: ". . . allí estará mi tumba" (. . .
there will be my tomb). We have not only inclusion, but significant inclusion. Without doubt the challenge represented by the intertext is functional,
not contextual. But, let us be very careful! The significant inclusion does
not give us *one* sense. It goes further; the silent intertext turns the reading
problematical, complicates it, requires the intervention of the reader, who
is obliged to choose, to decide: where *this* forgetting may dwell—not Bécquer's—will the tomb of the poet be found there or will it not? All of which
shows how close in feeling Cernuda comes to the Romantic poet, only later,
finally, to retreat from him. Because Bécquer definitely distinguishes between life and death, imagines his tomb, anonymous: solitary rupture with
a vain existence—but a tomb after all, erected as such in the fiction of the
poem. It could not be more different from Cernuda's atmospheric, diffuse,
open symbolism. Yes, the beginning of Cernuda's poem does seem to indicate a tomb: there is a garden, a buried stone, a name without a body. The

closest Cernuda comes to the description of a tomb is "buried stone." But this stone is found in a wide space, not a garden but gardens, unreal world, dynamically conceived, which changes little by little into symbolic vision. Note that the syntactic inconclusion is less decisive than in the Salinas poem. The "while there may be" of Salinas presupposed the addition of a time and a future, some events or feelings left unspoken. But the "where" of Cernuda—repeated seven times—does not transport us to any space other than the one designated by the poem, as when one says: right there. Or rather, far away, far, far away. The poet desires a place without desire, the other side of existence, negative photograph of the world, or perhaps positive picture of a sphere of experience where the choice between life or death might not exist, but where one might dwell in absence, fog, dream. Dream of a minimum life, light, sonambulant, airy. A world ruled by omission and inhabited, more than anything else, by forgetting. The first line of the poem, which is also the last, expresses the essential part. The rest—like the tomb—is an addition.

Perhaps scholars of intertextuality can one day outline its trajectory, as proposed by Laurent Jenny. Coordinates similar to those sketched a moment ago, or more refined ones, could serve to characterize one period or another. The extensive degree of intertextuality found, for example, in the Rome of Horace and Virgil, in the era of du Bellay, or in that of Joyce, is very striking. Once again it can be seen how much the Renaissance and the twentieth century have in common, particularly since the First World War: both periods are more fruitful in doubts than in beliefs, both overwhelmed by a superabundance of literary models.

The trajectory of intertextuality will have to take account of the history of genres and also that of reading. The confluence of the two is precisely what Stephen Gilman illuminates in *Galdós and the Art of the European Novel: 1867–1887* (1981). Gilman's reflection is centered not on the term *intertextuality,* which he could have used (but mentions only in passing),[31] but on the "colloquy" of novelists—or "dialogue," or "double dialogue." Well then, the fundamental condition of such colloquy is the unusual intensity of the act of reading novels during the nineteenth century: the constituent function that Albert Thibaudet was to call *le liseur de romans.* That reader, that peruser whose personal experiences encompass life as well as literature, and literature as well as history, is a character who appears and exists in the novels themselves—Don Quixote, Emma Bovary, Ana Ozores, and Víctor Quintanar in Clarín's *La regenta,* Maxi Rubín in Galdós' *Fortunata y Jacinta,* and others. Clarín reads Balzac, Flaubert, Zola, or Eça de Queiróz; and Galdós reads all of those as well as Clarín; and finally the

ordinary reader, who remembers and compares many of the writers mentioned, according to circumstances. The great original novelist sheds new
light on the predecessors who made his work possible, no longer within a
"tradition" without limits, one in which everything might find a place (as
T. S. Eliot thought), but within the formal and thematic dimensions that a
specific group of stories have in common. If those novelists were avid readers more than anything else, as Gilman argues, then the boundary between
experiences of real life and those that come from reading is blurred and
even useless. And this consciousness that is inseparable from reading seems
essential to us—awareness of character, reader, author: "the Cervantine
equation of consciousness with reading." All are sensitive to what Américo
Castro called the "incitation" of literature.[32] In that way a double dialogue
is opened between incited novelists. First, the dialogue of the author with
himself, that is, with his earlier works. Galdós' *Doña Perfecta* reconstructs
the schemes—the responses to the national historical problem—posed in
La fontana de oro, just as *La desheredada* goes beyond *Doña Perfecta,* so
that *Fortunata y Jacinta* can later overturn the formulas of *La desheredada.*
And then one novelist responds to another: *Doña Perfecta* to Balzac's *Eu-
génie Grandet* and *Les paysans;* of *La desheredada* to Zola's *L'assommoir;*
and *Fortunata* to various other works, such as *Le ventre de Paris,* studied
by Gilman in detail, naturally without forgetting Clarín's *La regenta.*[33]

    The chains linking these stories are of many different types, and their
nature cannot be simplified. We contemplate points on a line traced between
two extremes: the gestation of a work and the experience of a reader. The
genetic substrate of intertextuality is difficult to sidestep, in Gilman as in
Riffaterre, and occasionally the critic finds himself obliged to transport himself mentally to the writer's workroom. At the same time, between the two
extremes there are points that are nothing more than a visible coincidence
of one writer's methods with those of another, as regards genetic stimuli;
for example, the presence in *La desheredada* and later in *Fortunata* of two
usages of Zola, narrated monologue (or indirect free style) and colloquial
language from the "lower depths" of the city.[34] But Gilman also emphasizes
the function of certain significant allusions to precise situations and characters of Zola and Clarín found in some scenes of Galdós. The title of the
first chapter of *La desheredada,* "Final de otra novela" (End of Another
Novel), which recounts the death of Rufete, makes an irresistible allusion
to Coupeau's delirium in *L'assommoir* (and also to the death of Alonso
Quijano). And there is a scene in *Fortunata* (II.4.4) that is like a parodic
commentary on an episode in *La regenta,* that of Rosa Carraspique (Chapter XII), which shows Fermín de Pas behaving in as criminal a fashion as

did his predecessor Carlos Herrera, the name assumed by Vautrin in *Splendeurs et misères des courtisanes*.[35]

On such occasions there is little difference between an intertext that alludes and one that includes, as long as we start out—and this is a decisive point—from the history of reading, and more concretely from the peculiar conditions of the modern *liseur* or reader of novels, who becomes as immersed in the worlds created by the great writers of narrative fiction, from Balzac to Proust, as in a personal life experience. Fictitious worlds converge and touch each other and become intertwined in different ways according to different readers, but the process of convergence is indubitable and unavoidable. The colloquy that writers engage in among themselves is only a phase of this process, expanded by the reader in later phases into a still wider diversity of imagined worlds. In the last analysis, the intertextual dialogue is verified and brought to completion in the consciousness represented by the psychic space of the reader.

Is there a reader, no matter how forgetful, who has not glimpsed the gestures and words of one novel through the transparent pages of another? Since dialogues of this type can be extensive, I will only point briefly to the suggestive final paragraphs of the masterwork of José Maria Eça de Queiróz, *Os Maias* (1888; translated into English as *The Maias*). Two lifelong friends talk, recapitulate, draw conclusions. Carlos Maia, the protagonist, and João da Ega make a pact with comfortable mediocrity, recognizing calmly, without bitterness, *all passion spent,* their respective failures. Ega says:

> "We've failed in life, my friend!"
> "I believe so . . . But so do most people. That is, they fail insofar as they never attain the life they planned in the imagination."[36]

The plot and its dénouement are left behind, together with their failed romantic notions. And it is impossible not to recall the end of *Sentimental Education*, which is all recapitulation and which gives an account, in a somewhat conventional manner, of what has become of the various characters of the novel. Frederick Moreau and his friend Deslauriers, ex-romantics also, talk next to the fire, recalling their disillusionments without any anguish:

> And then they each proceeded to summarize their lives. They had both failed in their objects—the one who dreamed only of love, and the other of power. What was the reason of this?
> "It's perhaps from not having taken up the proper line," said Frederick.[37]

And they search for other causes and excuses. Finally, the best memory is one of unfulfilled juvenile desire, a visit to the brothel of *la Turque*, from which the two adolescents fled. These are the last words of the book:

> "That was the best time we ever had!" said Frederick.
> "Yes, perhaps so indeed! It was the best time we ever had," said Deslauriers.

That's not the way it is for Carlos Maia and Ega, who agree on a conception of existence, a "philosophy of life," a fatalistic attitude, indifference, a dissolving of oneself in the universe: the tranquillity of one who does not search, does not desire, *does not move*. The two friends go out into the street, and there they see, receding into the distance, the lights of the tram that they need to catch. Here is how the long novel ends:

> And once more Carlos and João felt a hope and would make an effort:
> "We'll make it!"
> "We'll make it!"
> The red lantern began to move. And to catch the tram, the two friends had to run desperately down the hill and along the Aterro under the light of the rising moon.

A scene that denies and leaves behind the earlier theory of the two friends, like Flaubert's ending, so retrospective and coherent. Eça de Queiróz, not satisfied with a conclusion that concludes, with a form that closes, leaves the door open for contradiction, time, the reader's imagination. All around the two men, the world continues, trams go by, the moon rises. Does life, like the novel, not end completely? That is the question that emerges from the dialogue between the two great novels and stays in the memory of the reader.

In the literary field, international relations often mean relations that a writer maintains with himself. The class of dialogue that we just saw—by Eça de Queiróz, a master of the Portuguese language, who also not only knew but loved the French language, an idiom very much alive for him—often presupposes other languages; and in such cases, unbridgeable distances do not exist between them. The second idiom, not mastered by the poet to the same extent as his own, but with which he holds a dialogue that finally became part of the growth of his spirit, does not imply the same degree of externality or of separation characteristic of the history and atmosphere of modern national states. The *littérature comparée* of the end of the nineteenth century and the beginning of the twentieth, based partly on an excluding and centralizing nationalism, and partly on a Romantic conception of the soul or of the unmistakable genius of each language, did not pay enough sympathetic attention to the phenomena of *multilingualism,* so important throughout the literary history of the West.

Most obvious is the multilingualism (limited on occasion to bilingualism) of those writers who in fact expressed themselves in more than one language, writers like Ramón Llull, who cultivated Catalan, Latin, Arabic, and Provençal. But there is another kind of multilingualism, latent in character, typical of societies, cities, or entire nations, such as that of the poet, dramatist, or prose writer for whom the contact with more than one language formed the humus of his culture and the condition of his unilingual work— no matter whether the multilingualism came from his surroundings, or was acquired and therefore an individual trait. In such cases, and according to different eras and societies, the patent phenomenon seems to be a visible sign of the latent one of relations existing between a writer and his surrounding, or rather, surroundings—different concentric circles—in which it fell to his lot to live and learn. It is certainly true that a person who ventures to write in two or three languages is very different from one who writes in only one. But that does not mean that a writer of several idioms knows the languages better or feels them more intensely than one who limits himself to writing in his mother tongue. As a constituent condition, it is enough to read or understand or cultivate assiduously another language. Because it is well known that "equilingualism," or the identical mastery of two linguistic means of communication, is extremely rare, save in exceptional cases such as Samuel Beckett. And we should note that Beckett is not primarily a poet.

Leonard Forster's indispensable book, *The Poet's Tongues: Multilingualism in Literature* (1970), reviews a considerable number of patently polyglot writers and works, ranging from the bilingual poems of the Middle Ages (in German and Latin, in the fifteenth century, and the Iberian *jarchas*) to the experimental writings of Dadaism (like the writings in *alimón* by Hans Arp and Tristan Tzara).[38] I am not overlooking a possible objection to his book: that many of the authors discussed were of second rank. In the case of Yvan Goll, for example, a poet who was German and French at the same time, perhaps the most interesting aspect might be precisely his inner split, his uprootedness, his anxiety of perpetual exile, manifested plainly in the lyrical cycle *Jean sans terre* (1936); something of what Eva Kushner calls "l'ubiquité de sa souffrance":

> Est-ce mon coeur qui tonne?
> Est-ce mon pouls que bat?
> J'ai mal à Barcelone!
> j'ai mal à Guernica![39]

> Is it my heart that booms?
> Is it my pulse that beats?
> I feel bad in Barcelona!
> I feel bad in Guernica!

But what about Milton, Stefan George, Rilke? Milton, the incredibly agile artificer, who also wrote in Latin and Greek, published four sonnets and a *canzone* in Italian that were praised by Giosue Carducci. However, even if he had not written in those other languages, Milton's fame and merit would have been the same. What is of primary importance is the indication of the literary system within which Milton worked and his conception of language as a complex of conventions and recourses that was very typical of baroque art, according to Forster's summary: "There is no mystique [for Milton] about languages; they are simply media in which a poet can work—and can be expected to work."[40] At the same time the multilingual work of Stefan George is skimpy; only a few poems in French and English remain. But he did leave a highly revealing indication suggesting a dissatisfaction with the situation of German literature, and showing his love for the Latin tradition of western Germany, by elaborating a curious *lingua romana,* quite close to Castilian: "La sera vola circa me con alas taciturnas . . ." (the evening flies near me with taciturn wings).[41] Post-Symbolist elaboration, basically, of a highly personal poetic language, very remote from the *mots de la tribu.*

Rilke did indeed compose exquisite verses in French during his old age in the Valais. There, surrounded by a language familiar to him for a long time, he returned to writing it very naturally, often using some of his favorite procedures, such as highlighting a simple word or a preposition:

> Le pain naïf, l'outil de tous les jours,
> l'intimité des choses familières,
> qui n'est capable de les laisser pour
> un peu de vide où l'envie prospère?

> The humble bread, the tool used every day,
> the intimacy of familiar things,
> who is not capable of leaving them for
> a snatch of nothingness in which envy prospers?[42]

Or in the sonnets written with complete ease in honor of the word *verger,* orchard:

> Pauvre poète qui doit élire
> pour dire tout ce que ce nom comprend,

un à peu-prés trop vague qui chavire,
ou pire: la clôture qui défend.

Poor poet who must choose
in order to say all that this name comprises,
an all-too-vague approximation that collapses,
or worse: a closure which defends.[43]

In the case of George, as well as those of Joyce and Ezra Pound—I am thinking mainly of those extraordinary polyglot constructions *Finnegans Wake* and the *Cantos*—the multilingualism of this century reveals certain hermetic, post-Symbolist, or modernist attitudes toward the problematical aspect of language in general.

With his usual talent and vigor, George Steiner emphasizes and examines this problematical aspect in *Extra-territorial* (1971). Steiner regards Heinrich Heine as one of the first modern "dualists," so different from the bilingual humanists of the Renaissance, like Petrarch, whose entire work rests on a secure, confident veneration of language. The realistic novel of the nineteenth century, such as those by Henry James, used as a starting point the fitting of verbal activity to reality. The author was rooted in his native tongue; it was little less than an integral part of his being and his destiny as a writer. Beginning in the first decades of this century a feeling of disquiet toward the word culminated in a crisis of language, especially evident in central Europe: Hugo von Hofmannsthal, *Der Schwierige* and the famous *Letter of Lord Chandos* (1902); Karl Kraus, Fritz Mauthner (*Beiträge zu einer Kritik der Sprache,* 1901); the philosophy espoused by Wittgenstein, which is really a critique of language; silences, fragmentation, the antiliterary frugality of Kafka. This is the condition I referred to when speaking of Rilke and Joyce and the aspirations of the Symbolists. Finally, Steiner highlights three writers: Beckett, that eloquent skeptic of words, Borges (I believe mistakenly: the international diffusion of his work is a result not of any potential multilingualism or of any verbal disquiet, but of the force of his imagination); and Nabokov, whose strange linguistic modes would demand new investigations: "They would clarify not only his own prodigious talent, but such larger questions as the conditions of multilingual imagining, of internalized translation, of the possible existence of a private mixed idiom 'beneath,' 'coming before' the localization of different languages in the articulate brain."[44] This concept of interior translation, or "internalized translation," which Steiner has also applied to Paul Celan, seems fitting.

Once again a historical perspective is imposed, but one that may not lead to fusion. Multilingualism and a skepticism regarding the possibilities of language cannot be forced to join hands. It is not the case of Nabokov, a writer—in that he practiced the craft of writing—who was prolific, exuberant, happy. An awareness of the limits of words has emerged more than once in the past—it is enough to recall the Greek Cynics, some of whom chose to express themselves by means of signs; the mystics of the Middle Ages and of sixteenth-century Spain; or the fragmentation of the Romantic period. At the end of the eighteenth century and during the nineteenth, the sentiment of loyalty to a mother tongue reached its peak and inspired the reproach directed by Schiller to those who surrendered to any language (not excluding the dictates of one's own): "You think you have already become a poet because you have succeeded in writing a poem in a cultivated language that thinks and writes poetry for you."[45]

Turgenev (who was besieged by his French friends, or so I imagine, to write in French) stated in more than one letter that it was dastardly not to write in one's own language.[46] And yet multilingualism is an important aspect of the nineteenth century. M. P. Alekseyev stresses that polyglotism was common in Russia in the 1700s and 1800s, and there were also numbers of bilingual writers: in French from Dmitri Kantemir to Feodor Ivanovich Tyutchev, in German from Hemnitzer to Count Tolstoy. (Soviet linguists have concluded that bilingualism will be an unavoidable necessity for future societies).[47] Let us not forget that not only individuals but territories and states are multinational: "we forget that there were entire epochs when it was not natural to express oneself in writing in the mother tongue."[48]

That observation is fundamental. In countless places and times, multilingualism is the characteristic feature of a society and consequently determines the posture of a writer toward that society. Multilingualism is also common among primitive peoples; most aborigines of Australia, for example, know two or three languages or dialects.[49] But the advent of writing caused a rift and required a choice of language. Think of the Rome of Epictetus and Marcus Aurelius, philosophers in Greek; and of the first Christian churches of Rome, whose liturgy evolved in Greek; of Saint Paul, brought up in a strongly Hellenized city, Tarsus, but who spoke Aramaic with his parents. Think of the city of Lucian that Bakhtin loved to remember: Samosata, junction of many tongues and cultures, crisscrossed by the languages of Mesopotamia, Persia, and even India. Its inhabitants were Syrians who spoke Aramaic, but the educated classes wrote in Greek, and the administration was Roman.[50] Today think of Belgium, Luxembourg, and, of course, Switzerland, about whose literature, with its enigmatic and shifting boundaries, François Jost says: "instead of being one and indivisible, the literature [of Switzerland] is one and diverse."[51] Think of Spain, in the tenth and eleventh centuries, when a secular Hebrew poetry flourished for the first time, with splendid brilliance, apparently as a result of one of those pivotal moments in the history of the Sephardi when Arabs, Christians, and Jews lived together, competed with one another, and became friends. Otherwise, how could one account for Judah ha-Levi, who was from Tudela (a multilingual town at the time), and Solomon ben Judah ibn-Gabirol, from Malaga? Ibn-Gabirol composed his *Reparación de las cualidades del alma* (1045) in Arabic and was famous in his day for a neo-Platonic treatise written in Arabic that was translated into Latin under the title *Fons vitae;* and in addition to his Hebrew poetry—amorous, religious, satirical—he wrote in Aramaic.[52]

I leave to the specialists, that is, the sociolinguists, the task of distinguishing among the different kinds of interrelations between idioms, dialects, or linguistic levels within a single society—"languages in contact," to use the title of the well-known study by Uriel Weinreich (1963). It is recognized that unequal levels of prestige, culture, or functionality may correspond to different social classes or intraregional zones. As Tolstoy taught us, the aristocracy in nineteenth-century Russia took pride in speaking French.[53] But diglossia is typical above all of countries in which the speech of common people is subjugated and devalued by another dominant language, as in Bohemia at the beginning of the eighteenth century, where only the common people spoke Czech, and in Prague it was a sign of elegance to speak Czech with a German accent.[54] Equally characteristic is the simultaneous existence of two types or levels of the same language or family of languages, like the two versions of German in Switzerland, or the classical and the dialectical idioms in Arabic countries. The course of history sometimes drives a wedge between the written and the spoken languages of a region. During the nineteenth century—apex of the rebirth of European nationalities—this gap necessitated a difficult search for adjustments, half-tones, and other solutions. Taking for example the neo-Hellenic literature that, not content with the *Katharevousa*—purist compromise—of the end of the eighteenth and the beginning of the nineteenth centuries, would admit the hybrid language of an Andreas Calvos, the initiative of Kostes Palamas, the development of the demotic, and also the stylistic peculiarities of Constantine Kavafis, so different from his predecessors.[55] This matter demands the diligent efforts of comparatists trained as linguists. But at first glance it seems to me that these various connections share quite a number of common traits: among them the fact that a person may live intellectually in a language other than his most familiar one; the porosity of a language surrounded by others; the function of alterity or "heteroglossia" that Bakhtin so insisted on. The case of Kavafis brings to mind the post-Symbolist urge to elaborate a new poetic language, mentioned a short while ago in connection with Stefan George. And thinking of the attempt made during this century or at the end of the last to infuse new life into marginal languages by writers such as Eduardo Pondal and Ramón Otero Pedrayo in Galicia,[56] or Hugh MacDiarmid in Scotland, we conclude that the challenges they assumed provided an efficacious and important literary stimulus, particularly on the verbal and formal levels. The analogies with the rise of French, Spanish, and German literatures during the sixteenth and seventeenth centuries are plain to see.

Faced with such a complex of problems, we scholars of western Europe will have to make the same effort recommended earlier with regard to genres: study the literatures of eastern Europe. There, especially in the Balkans, numerous ethnic-linguistic enclaves *(Sprachinseln)* can be found. Weinreich emphasizes two things regarding these *Sprachinseln:* the decisive influence of divisions along religious lines (the Germanic enclaves are usually Lutheran), and the obvious strong feelings of linguistic loyalty (*linguistic allegiance*) that result. Such linguistic loyalty is also common in border areas of large countries.[57] Paul Celan was born in Bukovina, which is in Rumania, as was the fine Israeli poet Dan Pagis. The many multilingual writers who flourished during the sixteenth and seventeenth centuries in areas where Croatian was spoken are much in evidence, writers such as S. Bobaljević-Mišetić from the end of the sixteenth century, who cultivated not only Latin and his own language but also Italian; the trilingual poets of Dubrovnik, the island of Hvar, Split. We should note that although Venice was the dominating power in Dalmatia from 1409 to 1797, Ragusa remained almost autonomous. Marko Marulić (1450–1524), who was born in Split and studied in Padua, composed didactic and historical works (*De institutione bene beateque vivendi*, 1506), wrote poetry in Latin, and composed the epic *Judita* in Croatian, the very first book published in that language (1521).[58] Two circumstances are worth emphasizing: the persistence of Latin as a living instrument of culture; and the mediating role played by certain cities of southern or central Europe, for example, the influence on Croatia of some Italian cities: Venice, Padua, Siena (where the great Ragusan dramatist Marin Držić studied).

Similar circumstances prevailed for the writers of Hungary, where Latin was cultivated very widely and continued for centuries to provide the link with different centers of culture. The connection was with Florence during the time of Matías Corvino (fifteenth century), Venice and Padua during the sixteenth, Cracow also, and, at the end of that century, Wittenberg. Holland and England were central for Protestantism in the seventeenth century, and

Vienna during the century of Enlightenment. When Erasmianism was established, during the first half of the sixteenth century, "Cracow was the native home of Hungarian books, of printing in the Hungarian language."[59] But at the end of the eighteenth century and the beginning of the nineteenth it was through the mediation of German that Hungarian readers became familiar with the works of neighboring countries, such as Serbian poetry.[60] Earlier, Latin translations had predominated, such as fray Antonio de Guevara's *Reloj de príncipes* and François de Salignac de La Mothe Fénelon's *Télémaque*. Obviously, multilingual Magyar writers were legion, although it is worthwhile to distinguish between explicit and latent multilingualism. Bálint Balassi, the great Renaissance poet of pastoral tragicomedy, knew Italian, German, Croatian, Czech, Polish, Rumanian, and Turkish. He translated or adapted texts from several of these languages, such as Turkish and Italian, but he wrote only in Hungarian. Later I will discuss other multilingual writers in more detail, such as Francisco Rákóczi (Ferencz II, prince of Transylvania, 1675–1735), who wrote in Hungarian, French, and Latin; Mihály Csokonai Vitéz (1773–1805), outstanding poet in his native tongue, but who owed much to the facility with which he translated from Greek, Latin, Castilian, and French; and Mihály Vitkovics (1778–1829), attorney in Pest, son of parents of Serbian origin, who cultivated both languages and made fashionable a certain style of Magyar poetry that was similar to Serbian songs. How could these various levels of multilingual aptitude—knowledge of languages, translation, poetic creation— avoid mutual interpenetration? Clarifications of these questions could probably give us a better understanding of the writers of Ireland, Wales, Switzerland, as well as Catalonia, some of whom write in Catalan and some in Castilian.

At this point it seems appropriate to recall another poet of Hungary, or rather of Croatia, Miklós Zrínyi (1620–1664), captain-general of Croatia during the Hungarian domination, known above all for his epic, *Szigeti veszedelem* (1646; The Siege of Sziget). His family, of Dalmatian origin, had been settled in Zrin Castle of Croatia since the fourteenth century and were influential in Magyar political affairs during the sixteenth century (in particular during the siege of Sziget, in 1566) as well as the seventeenth. An eminent specialist writes about the family as follows:

> Since those times the Zrinyi were Hungarians and Croatians, depending on which of the family estates they inhabited, the Hungarian or the Croatian . . . Whereas Niccolò Zrinyi wrote his literary works in the Hungarian language, his younger brother, Pietro, became a Croatian poet. Niccolò, however, composed his great Hungarian epic poem, the *Obsidio Sigetiana*,

under the influence of Croatian works and heroic songs. Pietro, in contrast, translated his brother's Hungarian poems into Croatian.[61]

In addition, Miklós Zrínyi—the older brother and epic poet—inspired by Machiavelli, interested himself in literature "for reasons of state." He translated the Italian version of Baltasar Alamos de Barrientos' *Tácito español* and wrote a work called *Vitéz hadnagy* (ca. 1650; Virtuous Captain), which, like the verse epic, seems to reveal influences from abroad in its schemes or patterns; his language, however, shows no signs of foreign influences and contains no Slavic elements.[62]

Zrínyi, like Balassi, though latently multilingual, remained unilingual when writing poetry and other literary works, despite the bilingual society that surrounded him and that enabled his brother Pietro to follow another path. It is important to distinguish between writers whose multilingualism—effective or not—is a personal destiny, result of avatars of their singular life story, like Joseph Conrad, and those who became multilingual in response to the peculiarities of their social surroundings and the particular historical moment handed them by fate. Great differences, both spatial and temporal, obtain between these innately polyglot circumstances, and the critic attempting to evaluate a bilingual writer should be acutely aware of these differences, since they provide both a starting point and background necessary for any analysis. Consider a community where one language is spoken in the street, among tradesmen or family members; a second in government offices, schools, and the institutions of the church—Latin; and a third is not spoken there at all, but only in other places, and is employed only in a stylized manner for a certain genre of literature. This model is quite a close description of the situation of the Catalan troubadours who wrote in Provençal from the twelfth to the fourteenth centuries. According to Josep Nadal and Modest Prats, their use of an acquired language, like the technical procedures of poetic composition, demonstrates their cultivation of an exemplary art and their response to the challenge posed by the difficulties involved. It is for these reasons that the authors of the first treatises on Provençal versification were not Occitanos, where *langue d'oc* was spoken, but Catalans, such as Raimon Vidal de Besalú and Jofre de Foxa. Nadal and Prats write:

> We should not be surprised by the fact that . . . the "Italian" and Catalan troubadours adopted . . . a language foreign to them; moreover, this is a fact to which they were already accustomed, considering the history of use of Latin as a literary language, this language that wasn't their own—Provençal—was endowed with all those features that allowed it to be considered as an *art*: an artificial language, distinct from Latin but, like Latin, fixed in time and space.[63]

Except for the distances involved this situation might seem to anticipate the modern multilingualism of an Ezra Pound or a Stefan George, but matters look different if we move to the Balearic Islands, where the creator of Catalan prose, Ramón Llull, was educated. In this case we remain within the bounds of the same language, Catalan. Llull was born in Mallorca between 1232 and 1235, that is, shortly after the reconquest of the island (1229), and thus was able to grow up in "direct and lively"[64] contact with the Arab population still living there. (The Arabization and Semitic experience of a good number of the medieval Catalan states was similar to that of other Iberian communities. Menorca was reconquered later than Seville.)[65] Llull's major language of expression was his mother tongue, Catalan,[66] but he also wrote in Latin and Arabic in order to reach a specific audience. The verses that he composed in Provençal as a youth were also written for practical reasons. The kings of Mallorca also held the barony of Montpellier and—as Martín de ·Riquer suspected—the Catalan of Mallorca and the *langue d'oc* of Montpellier were spoken in both courts. Moreover, Llull was in residence in Montpellier on many occasions.[67] That little circle of courtiers was, then, bilingual to some extent.

There have been of course many urban areas in both ancient and modern times that were (and are) bilingual or multilingual. A few of these are the Vilna in which Czeslaw Milosz grew up and studied, the Alexandria of Kavafis, Kafka's Prague, and the too-neoclassical Strasbourg that disappointed the young Goethe to some extent in 1770. I mentioned in Chapter 7 some examples of an *intermédiaire*, one of the traditional figures of comparativism. Clearly, often the intermediary is a multilingual city. We have already noted the important role played by Venice and Vienna in this regard for eastern Europe. In Budapest itself—or rather, in Buda and Pest, not yet united—Hungarian did not become the official language until 1844. During the first three decades of the nineteenth century the atmosphere of the city was notoriously polyglot. Earlier we mentioned Ján Kollár, the Slavic poet who advocated pan-Slavism; and Mihály Vitkovics, the bilingual writer in whose house intellectuals of very diverse origins often gathered. Numerous Serbs, Greeks, Slovaks, Rumanians, and Ukranians lived side by side with Magyars and Austrians in the capital city and published their books and journals there.[68] No wonder that at the end of the century it was a Hungarian, Hugo Meltzl, who would publish the first European journal of comparative literature, *Acta Comparationis Litterarum Universarum* (1877–1888).

Faced with such sociohistorical circumstances, comparativism would have to determine a typology of individual responses. Here I can give only a few examples. When one culture not only dominates but humiliates and annuls another, those who cling tenaciously to their own language must be regarded as exceptional figures. One such example from Latin America is Wallparrimachi (1793–1814). His life was so brief, and yet his poems, written only in Quechua, survive intermingled with folklore.[69] A somewhat similar case is that of a solitary Celtic writer, Jean-Pierre Callach'h (1888–1917), a Breton poet born on the island of Groux, author of *A genoux* (*An er deulin*, 1921), which includes a verse that says:

> It approaches with haste, the last day of our perishable flesh, the day of
>   the Last Judgment,
> The day of the death of the nations . . .
> Our bards sing "the other Brittany," but they know very well that there
>   is no Paradise for nations . . .[70]

Other writers living under foreign domination may find it necessary to cultivate the acquired language, preponderant and alien, fully aware of the fact that it is so, as was the case of the Inca Garcilaso de la Vega. Enrique Pupo-Walker has pointed out the use of intercalated stories, Incan myths, mixed materials in the *Commentarios reales* (1609–1616; translated into English as *Royal Commentaries of the Incas*): a work that is a poetical crossbreed comparable to the author himself, born in Cuzco eight years after the Conquest. His mother was a niece of Huayna Cápac, whose words are remembered thus:

> The long account of the origin of our kings was given me by the Inca, my
> mother's uncle, of whom I asked it. I have tried to translate it faithfully
> from my mother tongue, that of the Inca, into a foreign speech, Castilian,
> though I have not written it in such majestic language as the Inca used, nor
> with the full significance, the tale would have been much more extensive
> than it is. On the contrary, I have shortened it, and left out a few things
> that might have been odious.[71]

The equal domination of two languages, or true equilingualism, occurs very rarely. The patently polyglot writer will be neither equilingual nor equipoetical. Leonard Forster's comments in this regard are interesting concerning the work of a Dutch poet of the Renaissance, Jan van der Noot, who published two bilingual collections, *Lofsangh van Brabandt* (1580) and *Cort Begrijp van de XII Boecken Olympiados* (1579), with the Dutch versions and the French texts *face à face*. In French, van der Noot was no more than a discreet imitator of Ronsard; but when he said the same things in Dutch—since he apparently translated himself—a text of a superior quality resulted. This was not just because Dutch was his mother tongue (he was a native of Amsterdam), but because he was obliged to forge a new poetic instrument.[72] It is more difficult to compare the work of a bilingual poet who does not translate his own work from one language to another, but writes different kinds of compositions in different languages. In such cases it is not surprising that a historical *décalage* may be noted, inasmuch as the author in one of the languages belongs to a temporal evolution that is not in sync with the evolution of the other language. Milton writing in Italian is a poet of the end of the sixteenth century (or rather, he did not know Marino).[73] But the native language does not always provide the best means of linkage to contemporary writing. Magyar poetry of the fifteenth century is still medieval; but Janus Pannonius, bishop of Pécs and later chancellor to the queen of Hungary, was an excellent neo-Latin poet: *poeta doctus*, like others of those times. So we may well ask ourselves: If one poet writes in two languages, is a condition of doubleness probable? Is more than one personality involved, as though we were dealing with more than one writer? Taras Shevchenko, the great Ukrainian poet, writes also in Russian— poems, plays, even a diary. His Ukrainian compositions, for which he is famous, are without doubt his best. But according to George Gravowicz' explanation, Shevchenko's division goes deep and is to be found at the level of personality. In such cases bilingualism is the consequence rather than the cause of a dualism of attitudes or of values. In Shevchenko this duality is not always intermixed with bilingualism. When writing in Russian, he looks at the problems of his country rationally and from a distance, within the framework of the imperial society. When he turns to Ukrainian he is the unadapted man, emotional, who identifies with underdogs and outsiders and evokes the Ukrainian past in order to transform it into a repertoire of poetic symbols.[74]

Whatever the impulse, situation, or attitude, no encounter with a specific language can be indifferent. Language is more than tool; it is history, inheritance, fund of wisdom, system of conventions, as neo-Latin poetry makes clear. What abundant riches are available for someone writing in Latin! An entire world of themes, forms, moral shadings, conceptual distinctions, borne along by the literary language. Janus Secundus of Holland introduced modern expressions and neologisms into his *Basia* (1539). According to Fred Nichols, the curious part of this affair is that the best neo-Latin writers, like Giovanni Pontano and George Buchanan, composed some poems of a very personal nature.[75] And what about the bilingual author who cultivates both Latin and the vernacular language at the same time? Wiktor Weintraub makes some interesting observations about the great Renaissance poet Jan Kochanowski (1530–1584). Kochanowski studied in Cracow; then in Padua, where Francesco Robortello was teaching rhetoric; and also in Paris, where he knew Ronsard. He wrote first in Latin and later went on to Polish, but never abandoned the Latin muse. Of course, each language possessed its own schemes—"two separate sets of conventions"—such as the Roman elegy (Tibullus) and the love sonnet (Petrarch), or specific styles. But in addition, as Weintraub explains, the fictitious I of the poem, the persona that conditions and channels the writing, tends to be different: "The Latin poet seems to look at the world with different eyes than does the Polish one, and he expresses opinions which are in conflict with those uttered in Polish." In Latin the poet, more lighthearted, more playful, relying on archetypal situations, directs his words to an audience of connoisseurs. In Polish the poet cultivates an idealized Petrarchism but also treats civic and religious subjects—he translates the Psalms—to reach a wider audience. Every felicitous expression in Polish more or less amounts to his own discovery. In Latin he has at his disposal a cultural inheritance of formulas and descriptive adjectives—colors, lights, shadows—that help him see things and people. In Polish he has no choice but to rely on his own capacity of observation, bound to be more limited than the resourses available to him in Latin prosody.[76]

These phenomena of radical bilingualism have little to do with the so-called *Sprachmischung,* if by that we mean the transitory use of other languages inserted into the dominant language of a comedy, a novel, or poetry. In such cases, the added words are essentially foreign ones and appear as such in the works in question. That describes Shakespeare's use of French, for example, in *Henry V;* or the moment when Panurge answers Pantagruel in seven languages, two of which are nonexistent;[77] the language of Góngora's Moriscos, Negroes, gypsies, and children;[78] Lope's characters who mangle various tongues, like the Italian who is ridiculed in *El anzuelo de Fenisa,* the incomprehensible Fleming of *El asalto de Mastrique,* the Moorish blunders and gauche rhymes of *San Diego de Alcalá;*[79] or, in our own time, the German voices that Marina Tsvetaeva introduces into some of her poems.[80] In Rabelais one might well imagine that the games played by Panurge reflect a creative unease before the conventional limits of the language, which in turn mimic the games played in the society. But Lope de Vega's polyglot passages, like those written earlier by Gil Vicente, Torres Naharro, or Francisco Delicado, are merely signs of the actual historical circumstances in which Spanish writers of that time developed. What is important is to determine whether or not these accidental mélanges reveal a true multilingualism, even a latent, genuine one, as in the best Basque novels of Pío Baroja. Although Camilo José Cela inserted more than three hundred Galician words into his *Mazurca para dos muertos* (1983), Cela's prose, unmistakeable in its flavor, undergoes no significant modification, and his bilingualism does not go beyond a superficial and picturesque level, like the image of Galicia elaborated by the novel.

Finally, the most profound problem is perhaps represented by the latent multilingualism of a writer who unifies his own diversity, or obliges himself to be a more or less osmotic unilingual writer, or forcibly simplifies himself, or transcends his original bilingualism, or keeps vacillating between two languages all his life. (I say *perhaps* because of the complexity of the problem that I mention here so briefly.) This type of situation can lead to a marked degree of technicality or affectation, an excessive correctness of speech mentioned by E. M. Cioran ("The disadvantage of using a borrowed language is not having the right to make too many mistakes"),[81] the francophilic games of Algernon Swinburne and Oscar Wilde, or the more tiresome pages of Nabokov's later writings. But I think also of the suffering of Yvan Goll, a perennially uprooted man as we recalled earlier, and of the inventor of the man without a shadow, *Peter Schlemihls wundersame Geschichte* (1814), Adalbert von Chamisso, born French and exiled by the Revolution, a writer in German always accompanied by the shadow of another language, neither forgotten nor recovered, as Madame de Staël remarked in her straightforward manner: "You have a good mind but you neglect your accent. You know all languages and are ignorant of your own."[82] The extremely correct language of a more fortunate narrator, Conrad Ferdinand Meyer, is a Swiss tradition.[83] But according to one critic, one can also observe in his style the typical coloration of the writing of someone hearing certain French expressions "in the ear": "'je nie que cela soit' lies still in my ear," he said regarding "ich leugne, dass das ist" (I deny that that could be).[84]

In this context the example of a brilliant poet of our century stands out, Fernando Pessoa, who like Kavafis learned English as a child, but in addition cultivated it poetically (is there anyone who has felt the colloquium of the one and the many in a more dramatic fashion?) before returning to Portuguese, to Portugal, to the Sebastianistic nationalism of *Mensagem* (1934) and finally to a multiplication of the poetical I.[85] At the very least, Pessoa's heteronyms reveal a vivid awareness of alterity, an urge toward being other, or more accurately, others. And wouldn't the liberation of a hoped-for integrity of the I be based on a prior transcending of linguistic unity? In both cases the poet breaks the ties of certain norms and circumstances not of his choosing while going about his labor of creation. This double process of liberation—in face of the identity of the person open to alterity and the supposed isolation of a single language—brings Bakhtin's theory of language, mentioned earlier (Chapter 13), irresistibly to mind. That is, at the core of a single language one would have to take into account the contact of the words "of the others": relics of the past, signs of a countless plurality of experiences, professions, ages, social strata, spoken or written levels, and so on, or rather, the multilingualism encompassed by a supposedly unique language.[86] Pessoa's latent multilingualism, which he carries to its ultimate unilingual consequences with his heteronyms: would it not have to be related to Bakhtin's heteroglossia? In both cases certain centrifugal forces fight against the coherence of literary and social conventions.

The to-and-fro between unity and multiplicity is what links the controversial theory of the Russian thinker to the difficult psychic nature of the great Portuguese poet. The prodigious multiplicity of words—codes, idioms, psychic areas, verbal worlds—is the spur for both, as for so many others. I have tried to review here some of the numerous responses to such a challenge. Among them, the cultivation of multilingualism. Or limiting oneself to a single instrument of communication; channeling oneself into a single verbal stream. Writing novels that are of necessity polyglot, according to Bakhtin. Becoming one—linguistically—and many at the same time, like Pessoa. Or also translating one's own work, either in a hidden manner—while preparing or elaborating a work—or as openly as did Jan van der Noot and Samuel Beckett.[87]

The theoretical study of *translation* is intricate and has many ramifications. We saw earlier that the principal classes of comparativism—genology, morphology, thematology—are based on theoretical reflections directly or implicitly, but we also saw that their pretensions to universality are as hypothetical as they are provisional, and that we find ourselves obliged to question them, prune them, test them at every step. In contrast to scholars of national literatures, comparatists not only broaden the fields or objects under consideration but also question their validity as synecdoches or adequate symbols. This dialogue also takes place in the field of translation: between *traductology* and *praxiology,* according to the terms used in a 1982 conference of the International Comparative Literature Association.

We see translation as a form of ternary communication encompassing different segments in time and in space. The communication starts from some existing signs belonging to a segment I, and goes on to establish another group of signs destined to function within a segment II belonging to another linguistic system and destined for a new audience. The process is composed not of four but of three basic elements. If segment I presumes that some words A are directed to an audience B, and segment II consists of some words C destined for an audience D, what happens in the process of translating is that the second component, B, disappears and we are left with only three elements: the original text A, the translated C, and the new audience, D, which replaces the original readers. In general, there is a radical change of the linguistic-cultural system and of readers as we go from nation to nation, but also from period to period, the essential element in both cases being the duality of spatial-temporal segments:

$$\underbrace{A \longrightarrow [B]}_{I} \ / \ /\underbrace{C \longrightarrow D}_{II}$$

The process that goes from A to D presupposes an effort to extend the latent communication of a text beyond its remote original contours, while trying to annul differences and suppress distances. George Steiner sums up by saying: "The schematic model of translation is one in which a message from a source-language passes into a receptor-language via a transformational process." [88] Traductology endeavors to clarify the nature of this process, often intercultural as well as intertemporal in nature.

The ramifications of this definition are many, since translation as verbal communication, seemingly so unique, shares a considerable number of traits with other forms of communication. Moreover, translation can illuminate the challenges and difficulties for those dealing with language in general. This circumstance has inspired a number of truly brilliant pages by George Steiner in his extensive reflection, *After Babel* (1975). According to Steiner, every reading of a text implies an attempt to comprehend a language different from one's own, since meanings, allusions, tonalities, and rhythms change inexorably and swiftly. A complete reading of a text requires the comprehension of a verbal world that differs from ours (also different from the various worlds depicted in Quevedo's *Buscón,* or *Fortunata* by Galdós, Ramón María del Valle-Inclán's specters, certain of Francisco Umbral's articles, or *La ciudad y los perros,* translated as *The Time of the Hero,* by Vargas Llosa). A good reader, like an honest critic, editor, or responsible actor, must interpret a text overflowing with allusions to an unfamiliar linguistic-cultural complex. In life itself the relation of a man with a woman at the moment of the sexual act can contain more and greater verbal misunderstandings than erotic ones.[89] To sum up, *translation* and *to translate* (like *dialogue* and *to dialogue,* as we have been able to confirm more than once in this book) are terms that lend themselves easily or inevitably to extension and metaphor, and come to mean comprehension, interpretation, understanding.

The theme of translation, as Steiner knows and points out, has preoccupied a multitude of thinkers, philologists, and writers since ancient times: from Cicero and the authors of rhetoric to John Dryden, Goethe, Friedrich Schleiermacher, Benedetto Croce, I. A. Richards, and Ortega.[90] But the scientific analysis of translation has increased markedly in the last thirty years, so that the question is rather if this type of investigation, generally regarded as marginal and specialized, is to be incorporated at last into the theory of literature. Steiner has his doubts:

> The field is made neither formally rigorous nor continuous by an increase in the number and transparency of individual samples. It stays "subject to taste and temperament rather than to knowledge." The inference, unmistakeable in [William] Arrowsmith's and [Roger] Shattuck's programme, of a progressive systematization, of an advance from local inventory and insight to generality and theoretic stability, is almost certainly erroneous.[91]

A long tradition, from the Jewish talmudists and cabalists to Walter Benjamin ("Die Aufgaber des Übersetzers," 1923; The Task of the Translator) has pondered the problem presented by the overwhelming variety of human languages (at least four thousand at the present time), aftermath of the mythical misfortune of the Tower of Babel. Benjamin thought that the great classical texts—above all the sacred writings—contain their virtual translations within their own words. That is to say, to translate is to delve into the apparent disparity of languages until the unique and universal language of truth is found. This search for deep structures is repeated in varying ways in Gottfried Wilhelm Leibniz, Johann Georg Hamann, Wilhelm von Humboldt, and Noam Chomsky. But Steiner's principal inclination, like my own, is the understanding and study of literature. The study of translation, which appears to be specialized, leads to other areas as well, one of the most interesting being the theory of language and analytic philosophy. A linguist like Roman Jakobson finds in translation a particular example of general semiological conditions, and distinguishes between "rewording," "translation," and "transmutation" (of verbal signs into others nonverbal).[92] For an analytic philosopher like W. V. Quine, translation sheds light on the mysterious connection between language and sense, or between word and object.[93]

I believe, along with Steiner, that our path is a different one. It is advisable not to mix the problem of translation in general—sensu lato—with the study of literary translations properly speaking in history and criticism. An understanding of literary translations turns out to be extremely difficult if the social and historical context in which translation's arduous task of communication was carried out is not taken into account. Steiner writes: "I question whether any context-free system, however 'deep' its location, however formal its *modus operandi* [the allusion is to Chomsky], will contribute much to our understanding of natural speech and hearing."[94] An expert in the theory and praxiology of translation, André Lefevere, who has a clear historical orientation—as is also true of Gideon Toury and José Lambert— calls at the same time for going beyond the linguistic obsession that in turn goes back to the Romantic belief in the identification of every people with the genius or soul of its language:

> The genius of a nation would find its creative expression in and through language. This conviction is incompatible with the fact that language is only one element in the generation of the literary text, among others such as genre, theme, motifs. The establishment of national philologies has created a gulf between literatures written in different languages on the one side, and the "language" of literature, on the other side. The creation of a scholarly discipline called comparative literature can be interpreted as an attempt to bridge that gulf.[95]

The sociologist of literature finds an ally in the traductologist. To translate honorably means to be alert to the fact that the language of every poetic work contains countless historical allusions and social conditionings. These factors become enormous when the semiotic system and the audience are changed. "Translation takes place within a social and political context," say Arrowsmith and Shattuck.[96] Basically there are two contexts, the originating one and that of the receptor, and Arrowsmith and Shattuck very rightly emphasize the second, since the process of communication is directed to it. Clearly, conditionings of a wide variety of types can be implied, ranging from those aiming for mere intelligibility to servile copying. This is proved more than ever by authoritarian regimes of our century which, like the inquisitors of long ago (fray Luis de León and the *Cantar de los cantares*), imprison some translators and enrich others (or force poets to be nothing more than translators). The different versions of the Bible (in thirty-three languages when printing was invented, and in more than eleven hundred today) are without doubt intertemporal, but they are also intersocial, according to Eugene Nida: "It is quite impossible to deal with any language as a linguistic signal without recognizing immediately its essential relationship to the cultural context as a whole."[97] For Eskimos the biblical sign "lamb" is from the outset as strange as the theological and historical premises of the ritual of the paschal lamb, and one must either speak to Eskimos of the "paschal seal" or opt for descriptive circumlocutions. Jakobson explained that every language has adequate resources to remedy the absence of any word whatsoever.[98] The theorist can reject this idea, but in practice the translator cannot. As said earlier, we are required to reiterate a message devised for an audience B and direct it to an audience D. This accounts for the importance of everything that may make access to D possible: prologues, presentations, publicity, critics, professors, and other intermediaries similar to those discussed earlier (Chapter 7). Historically speaking, translations that endure, for good or for ill, those that are real and efficacious, and in effect successful and continue to be successful, are the translations that are published and read, no matter how transparent their ideological, religious, or political ends, or how many "betrayals" they might have committed.

In this field the fecundity of error, what Robert Escarpit has called *trahison créatrice,* is well known. According to him, the history of literature is an evolving process begun by a writer but not ended by him. It is not possible to leave out the time that passes between the poet's labor and the reader's feeling, but writing fixes forever the words torn from the surroundings that gave them meaning. That is how the infinite number of misunderstandings arise that, traitorous as they may be, have nevertheless infused great texts with enduring life and engendered works by subsequent authors.[99] The best example is perhaps the history of the theater, where the greatest latitude of interpretation is not only allowed but desired. The text is twisted, interpreted, altered so it may reach the public. When I. Eliade-Radulescu in Rumania translated Voltaire's *Mahomet,* he stressed the hatred of tyranny, like other men connected with the theater in eastern Europe, where dramatic works have contributed significantly to an awakening and an awareness of national consciousness.[100] Anna Balakian observes that a number of movements appropriate earlier writers as precursors and standard-bearers, remodeling them in their fashion: the pre-surrealists associated with André Breton; or William Blake, whose eighteenth-century language was changed, between 1922 and 1947, by André Gide and other translators into the language of a French poet modeled on Arthur Rimbaud and Alfred Jarry.[101] That's how it stands: no one is less of a traitor than a good translator, and no one more so than a Pierre Menard, in Borges' famous story, who burns the midnight oil in order to reproduce Cervantes' words exactly.

The "genres" of translation are numerous and do not lend themselves easily to simplification. It is absurd to judge a specific version without keeping very closely in mind the period when it was written, the criteria observed, the function that the author sought to fulfill. Arrowsmith and Shattuck recognize the following genres:

> Identifiable "genres" come easily to mind: the literal "trot" (or "transposition," as Mr. Carne-Ross calls it); the scholarly-genteel or belletristic translation; the "free" version; the "adaptation"; the "recreation"; the "imitation" (in Robert Lowell's sense); and so on. Each of the different "genres" reflects a basic difference in function; each is good or bad according to its mode, and it is as idle to blame, say, a free version for not being literal (and vice versa) as it is to blame chalk for not being cheese.[102]

For instance, think of Quevedo, whom some would flunk in classical and modern languages for the liberties he took in translating Epictetus, Anacreon, or Saint Francis de Sales. Quevedo was faithful to his purpose, namely, to infuse new life into ancient texts, modernizing them, carrying them to an extreme, using them as paths of action for his time; and therefore his translations are no less rhetorical than his original poems.[103]

Faced with such a myriad of functions and criteria, let us keep in mind a dynamic model, contained between a pole X and a pole Y. For D. S. Carne-Ross the two poles are *transposition*—chalcography to the letter like the original, word for word, on one side—and on the other, *recreation*—like the work of the Romans praised by Nietzsche in *Die fröhliche Wissenschaft* (*The Gay Science*), the Romans, conquerors of countries as well as thinkers and poets, being created anew in them, merging with them.[104] Kimon Friar calls pole X *interlinear transliteration* and pole Y *paraphrase*.[105] Translation itself is located between these two extremes and is—for Friar or for Ortega y Gasset[106]—neither more vain, nor more utopian, nor more hopeless than many other forms of human endeavor. In this respect the summary of Marilyn Gaddis Rose is useful: she points out that these various classifications can usually be reduced at bottom to the binary opposites "literary" and "nonliterary" (Schleiermacher already distinguished between *dolmetschen* and *übersetzen*) or "literal" and "free," if one assumes that there is no literary quality without freedom. Gaddis Rose recommends that attention be paid to the changing character of a communication depending on the importance attached to the target audience, the choice being between writing that is *reader-oriented* or *text-oriented,* to use Lefevere's terms. The translator tends to orient himself toward the autonomy of the orginal text *(source text autonomy)* or toward the requirements of the audience *(target audience needs).*[107] The difficulty of translation rests on a reconciliation of these two demands that do not necessarily exclude each other. Moreover, the translator is precisely the poet who sets out to reconcile them, provided we leave aside consideration of translators who merely "transpose" or "re-create."

Certainly every concept or word carries with it peculiar associations typical of distinct communities. Consider a concrete and simple term like *bread*, or such a basic abstraction as *justice*, or *liberty*, or *peace*. To translate is to introduce. To translate is to bring over verbally, from one space to another, not only texts but patterns, elements, things, fragments of dissimilar cultures. It involves an act, a cultural initiative, as innovative as any other as far as the receptor public is concerned. In translating Pessoa, Octavio Paz succeeds in bringing the Portuguese writer into the sphere of Hispanic letters. Translation of the Bible into the vernacular, sometimes a risky undertaking, gave impulse to the Protestant Reformation, just as the translations of Greek classics into Latin, an equally hazardous enterprise, hastened the coming of the Renaissance. Thus poetical movements are expanded, by means of certain texts and authors who launch them or symbolize them, texts based not on the originals but on foreign versions.[108] The style of the writers of the German *Sturm und Drang* movement owed more than a little to J. J. Bodmer's translation of Milton's *Paradise Lost*, and its influence on Friedrich Gottlieb Klopstock. Nabokov recalled that for the Russians of Pushkin's time there was only one Byron, the one known in Amédée Pichot's French version.[109] Ibsen's plays entered Europe by way of the *Volksbühne* of Berlin, and the dramas of Strindberg came through Paris, in French translations,[110] as did the great Russian novelists at the end of the century. As time goes on, translators have come to collaborate on the proposal for a more profound internationalism, as Gide wished:[111] the imminence of the common, the shared, the supranational.

The important translator, never merely a passive figure in that he does not limit himself to reflecting or reproducing, is one of the motors of change and of the history of literature. Let us agree with George Steiner that the translator is an interpreter: of themes, attitudes, values, of cultural contents, and also, in certain cases, a meticulous critic, who explains distant words and helps us understand them better. Think of what a good modern version of a classical Chinese poem can require. Achilles Fang explains it in detail. The translator must be aware of certain stylistic traits, such as paratactic structure, the evocative power of great Chinese poetry, and must possess other indispensable knowledge.[112] Obviously Fang is placing us within the sphere of the best translators of our time: the sphere comprising knowledge, rigor, enthusiasm. E. R. Curtius confessed that he translated as a labor of love, as a consequence of his excitement provoked by the discovery and admiration of certain authors. Jorge de Sena, in "Envoi" (in *Visão perpetua*, 1982), describes this need to come close to a poet by translating him into one's own language "so that he may exist in my language, the one that belongs to me":

> Se vos traduzo para vós em mim,
> não é porque vos use para dizer o que não disse,
> ou para que digais o que não haveis dito,
> mas para que sejais da minha língua,
> aquela a que eu pernenço e me pertence,
> e assim nela eu me sinta em todo o mundo e sempre,
> por vossa companhia . . .

> Poets, if I translate you for the you inside of me,
> it's not really because I'm using you to say something
> I never really said,
> or to make you say what you never really said,
> but it's so you may exist in my language,
> the language I belong to and which belongs to me,
> so that in it I may feel myself in everyone and forever,
> by being in your company . . .[113]

Renato Poggioli, a fine interpreter of Russian poets, in one of his articles described honestly the current idea of what a translator is. More sentimental than naïve, in Schiller's use of both words, today's translator responds subjectively to his chosen enthusiasms and affinities. The forms come later. Today's translator, who is identified with certain themes cultivated by others, is, according to Poggioli, "a literary artist looking outside himself for the form suited to the experience he wishes to express."[114] That is similar to what Haskell Block points out regarding Baudelaire and Gide. Poe did not "influence" Baudelaire because at bottom, according to Block, the two were very similar: "Do you know why I have translated Poe with so much patience? Because he resembled me."[115] That is, Poe confirmed him in his inner nature, helped Baudelaire to be more Baudelaire.

Not so in other eras and other places. When discussing multilingualism a few pages back, I mentioned Jan van der Noot, polyglot like many of the great writers of the Netherlands Golden Age: Jacob Cats, P. C. Hooft, Joost van den Vondel, Constantijn Huygens. In Hooft's multilingual circle translating was a natural and frequent occupation.[116] Nobody more polyfaceted than Huygens (1596–1687): statesman, diplomat, composer, admirer of Rembrandt. The eight-volume collection of his poetry that I have seen (*De Gedichten*, 1892–1898) includes, in addition to a voluminous production in Dutch, a considerable number of pieces in Latin and French. Some are games, occasional verses, epigrams, brief and rapid compositions (*Sneldichten*), and translations; for example, an epigram of Ben Jonson, or one of Petrarch's sonnets translated into Dutch and French. There is a poem from 1627 titled "A des Yeuxs. De l'espagnol." I have been able to identify the original: some anonymous "Redondillas" that appeared in the *Primavera y flor de los mejores romances,* collected by Pedro Arias Pérez in 1621. Writing about the success of this anthology, which had seven further editions before 1627, José F. Montesinos says "to judge by the number of editions, it must have literally been in the hands of everybody during almost half a century." [117] I copy here only three stanzas:

Ojos, cuyas niñas bellas
esmaltan mil arreboles,
muchos sois para ser soles,
pocos para ser estrellas.

Beaux yeux, qui de dessous vos voiles
tirez des traits si nonpareils,
vous êtes trop peu pour des étoiles,
vous êtes trop pour des soleils.

No sois cielos, ojos raros,
ni infierno de desconsuelos,
que sois grandes para cielos,
y para infiernos muy claros.

Vous n'êtes ni des cieux de grâce,
ni des enfers de cruauté,
car les cieux tiennen plus d'espace,
et les enfers moins de clarté.

No sois dioses, aunque os
   deben
adoración mil dichosos,
pues en nada sois piadosos
ni justos ruegos os mueven.

De vous nommer dieux adorables
c'est profaner la Deité,
vous voyant si inébranlables
à la prière et la pitié.[118]

Starting from the initial "concept," the two poets develop several variations that we lack space to analyze here. It is evident that Constantijn Huygens, once he has cleared the hurdle of the first stanza by means of various commonplace expressions, introduces effective rhymes with assurance, rhymes not as hackneyed as the Castilian ones (stanza 2), and a grammatical fluency (stanza 3) of a certain elegance. The question of the criterion followed by the translator is intertwined here with that of baroque multilingualism, mentioned earlier. Huygens translates from one foreign language into another, his attitude identical with that of an artist who passes from working in one medium to a second. It is not the intensity of the theme that attracts Huygens, but the challenge represented by its form—antithesis, brevity, ingenuity—and the possibility of carrying it off with real style. Form comes first for the artisan working in a language that is not his own. And perhaps for that reason Huygens' adaptation of the subject seems technically superior to the original Castilian.

To sum up briefly, a historical approach to translation is highly recommended. The traductologist must be a historian, and a most accomplished one, because no genre of writing can bring out the theoretical, social, and ideological basis of the literary phenomenon to such an extent. Don Francisco de Quevedo, Constantijn Huygens, Baudelaire, Jorge de Sena represent a few of the milestones in the long evolution of the stance assumed by the translator before his task. It is evident that scholars have begun to study the greatest successes of the past. F. O. Matthiessen devoted his first book, *Translation: An Elizabethan Art* (1931), to the great interpreters without whom certain works of Shakespeare could not have been conceived: Sir Thomas Hoby's Castiglione (1561), Sir Thomas North's Plutarch (1579), John Florio's Montaigne (1603). In Spain we know that Boscán (1534) was as important as Hoby, and that no version of *Aminta* surpasses that of Juan de Jáuregui (1607). But do we really know the principal translations read by Cervantes? Antoine Berman writes in *L'epreuve de l'étranger:* "There is a fabulous irony in the fact that the greatest Spanish novel [*Don Quixote*] should be presented by its author as a translation from Arabic—that is, of a language that had been dominant in the Penisula for centuries. That fact most certainly could tell us something about the Spanish cultural consciousness. But also about the link of literature with translation." [119] This link, this horizon of translated texts, is what Berman calls *transtextualité* in his book, devoted to an examination of the theoretical attitudes of German Romanticism—Novalis, Friedrich Schlegel, A. W. Schlegel, Schleiermacher—and even to their varying relations with the translations of Goethe, A. W. Schlegel, and J. C. F. Hölderlin. No system of poetics determines all aspects of poetry; that being so, a comparison with contemporary translators would be interesting: Plutarch by Jacques Amyot and North; Proust by Scott Moncrieff and Pedro Salinas.

The history of translation thus branches off into two parallel paths. In the first place, a historical poetics of translation is elucidated: the itinerary of its ethic, its proposals, its directive criteria. But on the other hand, it is not enough simply to understand translations from a historical point of view. Even more important, *mutatis mutandis,* is to integrate translations into the history of literature for several reasons. I suggested years ago, in *Literature as System,* that the history of literature cannot be reduced to a series of novelties, innovations, discoveries ("a tale of modernity in the making"). I said then that in order to study the literary system of a given moment, one must also take into consideration earlier writers whose works are reissued and read once again, dramatists whose works are still presented, classical works that still live and those that do not, forgotten works that some try to rescue: writers, genres, translations. The integration of all these elements is what makes up a historical system.[120] Currently, André Lefevere, José Lambert, and other investigators from Belgium and the Netherlands go quite a bit further: they are attempting to incorporate a knowledge of translations into a determination of specific historical systems, and to do so in a rigorous and no less than exhaustive manner. At present this seems to me to be the most useful, coherent, and reasonable method of approach. Lefevere distinguishes between "literary translation" (the one nearest to the "literary" pole within the graduated spectrum sketched earlier) and "translated literature," the decisive point being that the readers and writers at a given historical moment are the ones who make the distinction. The enveloping system determines whether a translated work may be received as literature (or may be regarded as an event, a "literary fact," as Tynyanov thought):

> I would only like to affirm that the specificity of literary translation should not be looked for on the level of the process, but on the contrary, in the way in which the product, the translation, functions in the receptor literature and culture. The analysis of translated literature could, in that way, contribute not only to the study of translation, but also to the study of literature in general.[121]

Translation is a component of a historical literary system whose function and determination, in the last analysis, depend on its relation to the other components that make up the system.

I must certainly agree with the development of the concept of system—in its general characteristics—by Lambert, Lefevere, and other critics today such as those working in Israel (Itamar Even-Zohar, Gideon Toury). Naturally much remains to be done. One must elucidate which specific *functions* allow a translated text to become part of a historical system, thus enabling certain authors to transcend the boundaries of nation and language. Think of the current diffusion of works by Jorge Luis Borges, Julio Cortázar, Gabriel García Márquez. The imaginative power of these three writers cannot be overlooked—and in fact, their works find a ready audience in a time of impoverished imagination. It is curious that traductology shows, or rather confirms, that language is not everything in a work of literary art.[122] At the same time, it goes without saying that we must keep in mind the differences between genres and channels of communication as well as the difference between the use of verse or prose. In the novel, the "discourse of things" is fundamental—actions, characters, fictitious worlds—or rather the diegesis of the narratologists. *Amadís de Gaula,* Ariosto, Cervantes, Byron, Dostoevsky, Kafka, like the great Latin Americans later, furbish their works with absurdities, surprises, extravagances, irrational acts, madness. Won't the translatability of a narrative creation, of specific moments and systems, depend on the level of diegesis, on an imaginative or fantastic function? Let us than take account of the functions of the works within certain systems and also the stratifications of diverse genres.

As far as poetry is concerned (see the discussion of stratification in Chapter 10), it is immediately clear that the translatability of the phonic stratum does not have the same character as that of the syntactic, prosodic, morphological, and semantic strata. For instance, let us look at these well-known lines by Rafael Alberti,

> Se equivocó la paloma;
> se equivocaba,[123]

with the obvious difficulty of the two assonances contained in each verb (*o*-*o* of "equivocó", *a*-*a* of "equivocaba"), much, much harder than the change of the verb tense. As an example of a possible translation, let us say:

> Elle se trompe, la colombe;
> elle se trompait.

Or perhaps, "She made a mistake, the dove; / she was mistaken." In any case, the syntactic stratum—the *figure of grammar* of Hopkins and Jakobson—is reproducible in other languages. Not so if the phonic stratum is the principal and primary element in a poem. For instance, take the famous quatrain by Matthias Claudius (1740–1815). I find the bewitchment and power of physical attraction evoked by the sensual quality of the words indisputable—-"Oh!, it is so dark in Death's chamber, / How sad it sounds, when he moves / And then raises his heavy hammer / And strikes the hour."

> Ach! es ist so dunkel in des Todes Kammer,
> Tönt so traurig, wenn er sich bewegt
> Und nun aufhebt seinen schweren Hammer
> Und die Stunde schlägt.[124]

One can point out the triple initial alliteration of the consonant *t* ("Todes," "Tönt," "traurig") and the triple final alliteration of the *s;* and the interior assonance of the third line ("aufhebt," "schweren") that echoes the vowel of the rhyme ("bewegt," "schlägt"). But this kind of analysis yields scant results, since these four lines make up an indivisible phonic tangle. And what the ear perceives above all in the two first lines—since the last two in effect concentrate on the vowels *e* or *ä*,—is like a slow unfurling of the vowel richness of the German language, held and made more intense by the gravity of the tone and the accentuation of the line over the span of at least seven vowels:

> Ach! es ist so dunkel in des Todes Kammer,
>   Tönt so traurig, wenn er sich bewegt . . .

As for the semantic level, one could perhaps apply what was pointed out a moment ago in regard to narrative diegesis: that even though the semantic level is in principle the most accessible feature, the translatability of everything in a poem that tends toward visionary image or metaphor is what prevails. Here is a *haiku* of Matsuo Basho:

> The mountain temple
> its stones are struck and pierced
> by cicadas' cries.[125]

An idea—as powerful as it is—of Judah ha-Levi is not sufficient to give two of his lines the force of a poem:

> Los esclavos del mundo son esclavos de otros esclavos;
> el esclavo de Dios es el único esclavo que es libre.

> The slaves of the world are slaves of other slaves;
> the slave of God is the only slave who is free.

And also perhaps not the ingenious discovery of a half-real situation:

> . . . me besó entre risas los ojos,
> pero no besó en ellos sino su imagen.[126]

> . . . amid laughter she kissed my eyes;
> but kissed in them only her own image.

Another visionary image—because such images existed during the Renaissance and the Baroque period—is the celebrated final line of the "Epístola moral a Fabio": *antes que el tiempo muera en nuestros brazos* (before time die away in our arms). Time personified? Time not only deadly but mortal at the instant when it is not the two friends—Fabio and the poet—who die in it, but is it time itself that may die in and with them? Does the image of a heartbeat bring us down us to a physiological sphere? Are we present at our own death, as if we were protecting it? The possible readings of this line by A. Fernández de Andrada are multiple, if we attach a + sign and a − sign to "time," "die," and "in our arms" and arrange these six positive or negative visions of the same few intertwined realities in different ways:

Ya, dulce amigo, huyo y me retiro
de cuanto simple amé: rompí los lazos:
ven y sabrás al grande fin que aspiro
antes que el tiempo muera en nuestros brazos.

At last, sweet friend, I flee and withdraw
from everything which in my simplicity I loved; I have broken the
    bonds:
come and you will see the great purpose to which I aspire,
before time die away in our arms.[127]

Incredibly rich image and as such, nevertheless,

   tant que le temps ne muere dans nos bras,

perhaps translatable.

This brief discussion will suffice to suggest the relation between stratification, the imaginative function, and translatability. On other occasions and in other systems the outstanding functions will be different. But with that conclusion we will undertake—thanks to translation—the field of historiology and our final chapter.

16

Historical Configurations: Historiology

The fundamental components of literary historiography, the large entities—periods, currents, schools, movements—that provide the structures, make it understandable, and order its temporal evolution, are rarely restricted to single nations. There are indeed some terms that apply to specific countries only, such as *Sturm und Drang* and *Biedermeier*,[1] and others that describe movements or submovements that are more or less local in character, such as Italian *Futurismo,* Russian *Aceísmo,* Catalan *Noucentisme,* Hispanic *Creacionismo.* Also, in some cases concrete adjectival expressions used in national manuals fall within the context of wider concepts, such as *Elizabethan drama, Restoration comedy, Decadentismo,* or *Generation of '98.* (The idea of generation is usually, though not always, limited to one nation—one of its drawbacks.)[2] But obviously these smaller units have to be incorporated sooner or later into larger entities that describe the development of Western literary history. The internationality of the principal stages of this development are conspicuous and imply contacts between different languages and traditions. At the same time the stages of development act as indices of supranational eras and historical tendencies that include both the history of the natural sciences and the history of political or philosophical ideas, true for example in the case of the Renaissance. As practice proves, such interweavings and superpositions are complex and cannot be simplified. In Germany the era called *Klassizismus,* which coincided with Goethe's old age, is usually placed after Romanticism. And the transition from the

Renaissance to the Age of Enlightenment—two eras or currents whose existence is rarely challenged—is quite confusing from a European point of view, above all in regard to the extent of the spread of the Baroque and its relation to French *Classicisme* and its boundaries. But no one can dispute the sheer vastness of the field covered by the terms generally used to trace the itinerary of literature written in European languages. I refer to such concepts as the Baroque, Romanticism, realism, and symbolism—to limit ourselves to those discussed by René Wellek.[3]

But the character, aptness, and precise use of each of these concepts, and the manner in which they may be interlaced or joined diachronically—even the very nature of the idea of period, current, or movement—all these aspects are indeed debatable. Moreover, in my opinion these concepts should be regarded as what Ferrater Mora called "debatable questions." But this is not the case in some countries. In Spain, for instance, scholars—with some illustrious exceptions like Joaquín Casalduero[4]—devote all their energies to literary criticism—or nowadays to literary or linguistic theory—but for the most part continue to accept the conventional historical configurations with strange intellectual parsimony, as if they were dealing with concrete objects or *faits accomplis*. Why does plagiarism have to be the norm in the field of historiography? Why do we have to depend on the theory of history—historiology—of others? As an example consider those scholars who question and agonize over relations that exist or have existed between literature and history, or between literature and social history. But from the outset these are not sensible questions. We cannot strip all historical content from literary criticism, separating the notions of literature and history, and then yearn later for the rectification of such a serious rift. In actual fact, we are looking at distinct genres—yes, *genres*—of historiographical thinking and writing, genres such as literary history, social history, political history, and so on, that correspond, would have to correspond, to distinct levels or sectors of the pluralistic world, or worlds, in which we live. These subdivisions are in themselves subjects for the study of history; that is, they are historiable. To verify how different levels touch, include, or mutually affect each other is an arduous task of philosophical (and literary) dimensions. I am indeed aware that a prior—or simultaneous—condition for a response to these ambitious questions is the intelligibility or integrity of literary history itself. What are the constituent principles at work? What are the intertemporal forms that determine the continuities and discontinuities? the originality—or difficulty—that the peculiar survival of the poetic implies ("sign of a history, and resistance to that history," as Roland Barthes said)?[5] What classes of relating or what narrative tactics do literary histories draw on, and what do they have in common with fictitious or invented "histories"? What is a poetical "event" (*événement, Ereignis*), and what type of interactions are there between such an event and the surrounding system of an era? In earlier chapters we confirmed that the diverse investigations proper to comparativism all assume a theoretical consciousness. At the same time it should be noted that theoretical or historiological reflection in this field is on the increase.

The scholar who takes on the history of literature as his task will find that the basic vocabulary available is much more limited than that available in the field of criticism; a natural and logical state of affairs, since criticism can still rely on the legacy of poetics and rhetoric, which antedates the historical preoccupation of modern times. Even today one need only page through any specialized dictionary to become aware of the paucity of vocabulary for literary history. Joseph T. Shipley's *Dictionary of World Literature* (1943, 1953), one of the best, includes the terms *period* and *tradition*, the latter having been in frequent use in Anglo-American criticism since T. S. Eliot and John Livingston Lowes.[6] A more recent and substantially more complete work, Alex Preminger's *The Encyclopaedia of Poetry and Poetics* (1965), lists only "tradition."

Under such circumstances, Renato Poggioli felt obliged to define the ideas of "movement" and "school" at the beginning of his *Teoria dell'arte d'avanguardia* (Bologna, 1962). Poggioli uses the concept of school to include the principal artistic and literary groupings before Romanticism: the *neoteroi* of Alexandria, Provençal troubadours, *Minnesinger,* Petrarchists, the *Pléiade,* and so on. A school presupposes some teachers, continuity, a tradition that is respected and studied, certain skills that are acquired, a group of students who believe their own experience to be inadequate—*ars longa, vita brevis.* On the other hand, *movements* with polemical and immanent intentions have flourished ever since Romanticism. A movement is directed toward the future, or rather, away from it—what Octavio Paz would later call the "tradition of rupture."[7] Certainly in practice the matter becomes complicated and we find movements that are blends or survivals of earlier ones, like Mallarmé's *lundis,* the tower of Vjačeslav Ivanov in Russia, the *Kreis* of Stefan George. But the polarity represented by movement/school is no doubt useful:

> Where the school presupposes disciples consecrated to a transcendent end, the followers of a movement always work in terms of an end immanent in the movement itself. The school is inconceivable outside the humanistic ideal, the idea of culture as a thesaurus. The movement, instead, conceives

of culture not as increment but as creation—or at least as a center of activity and energy.[8]

Some years later Aleksandar Flaker would add that a movement depends on the effect of a system of criticism, or simply on the activity of a critic—like Nicolay Chernyshevsky, who invented the term *Gogolian movement* used by critics of the 1970s. This movement of Gogol (*gogolevskoe napravlenie*) would later be called "realism." "'Movement,'" Flaker writes, "should be applied to those tendencies within the processes of literary history that are manifested at a particular time in literary criticism and other forms of literary *consciousness*."[9] I believe this characteristic was included, or at least implied, in Poggioli's definition, and that a theoretical consciousness was also important in certain schools of antiquity, or during the sixteenth century for forerunners like Ronsard or Fernando de Herrera. In both cases, theoretical consciousness is a unifying factor of obvious efficacy that the historian must keep in mind when distinguishing, as Flaker says, between his own typological analogies and the groupings that have been defined in the past through manifestos, for example, so typical of the avantgarde. Here we have two conceptual models—school, movement—whose distinctive characters determine at one and the same time certain practices and postures, conventions or theoretical self-definitions.

In 1967 I prepared a paper for the International Comparative Literature Association conference held in Belgrade on the idea of literary *period*—my choice of subject had actually been stimulated by the polemic of Lévi-Strauss with Sartre at the end of *La pensée sauvage* (1962; translated into English as *The Savage Mind*), in which Lévi-Strauss stressed the conventional nature of the chronological schemes on which history relies. I felt compelled to call attention to the fact that the bibliography on the theme of period was very skimpy, with some few exceptions such as the writings of René Wellek.[10] But I was indeed able to refer to the debate between Karl Heussi and Georg von Below during the 1920s; to the proposals of Fernand Braudel; to the trajectory of the concept of Renaissance, or rather to the reflections of historians themselves regarding the problem of periodization.[11] Clearly the peculiar character, *sui generis*, of literary history demands marked modifications and adaptations in order to pass from one class of historiography to another. Since 1967, studies concerning periodization have become more frequent, and today it is one of the basic themes of comparativism. To mention one example, the recapitulation by Ulrich Weisstein, *Vergleichende Literaturwissenschaft, 1968–1977* (1981), includes a chapter on *Periodisierung*.[12] The colloquium held at the Academy of Sciences of Budapest in 1972 was also significant in this regard. The *acta* of the conference make up the first volume of the journal *Neohelicon* (1972). And—what is perhaps more important—the volumes that have been published since 1978 under the title *Histoire comparée des littératures en langues européennes* demonstrate the existence of a consensus, both theoretical and practical, concerning the problem of periodization on the part of the comparatists collaborating on this massive project.[13]

In considering the particular problem of how to structure historical time—the need to subdivide or determine development, to interpret cultural evolution, to order a nonfictitious story—it is also appropriate to point out two opposing points of view, or if you prefer, two complementary models. What we will call model A stresses discontinuity. Its dominant values arise from and dominate temporality and prevail during a certain number of years, seeming to like principal and characteristic values of one period as well as another. Such values construct something like small worlds—"moradas vitales" or "existential spaces," Américo Castro would say—societies from the past that nevertheless still live in the present, made available once again to the sensibility of a modern reader through the efforts of some historian. These *moradas vitales* can be clearly distinguished from what happened earlier or later. One example of this type of axiological world would be Jacob Burckhardt's idea of the Renaissance. Whereas Jules Michelet and his predecessors had viewed the Renaissance as the dawn of the century of Enlightenment and of the belief in progress, placing most stress on the historical dynamics and the interrelation between different phases or eras, Burckhardt isolated the special ambiance of the Italian cities and treated it as an almost autonomous cultural ideal.

In contrast to model A, model B stresses continuity, underlines the flow of time, the contact between before and after; and within each period, well blended in its individuality or autonomy, the diversity of its components is made manifest. This second model emphasizes the plurality of values—and of styles, conventions, themes, forms—that come from the study of confrontations and disagreements common to every age. We perceive in the past what many of us have experienced in the present: options and struggles, the interaction of continuities and discontinuities, the contrast between singular events and venerable institutions, the superposition (as in Fernand Braudel) of distinct rhythms and durations, corresponding to distinct classes of literary, artistic, or cultural activity.[14] Such a multiple and polemical model accepts contradiction and change as structures typical of every developed nation or civilization. For this reason, Francesco De Sanctis, who in his splendid *Storia* de-emphasized conventional periods, turned whenever possible to a noninterpretative chronology (*Trecento, Quattrocento,* and so on), and while interweaving the diverse moments of the evolution of Italian literature, came back as often as he could to the exemplary and even prophetic value—as we shall see now—of certain essential protagonists (Boccaccio, Machiavelli, Manzoni).[15] And there is also Johan Huizinga, who saw in the Renaissance only one aspect of the culture of the sixteenth century, and stressed those forms of the medieval world that kept meandering and remaining effective throughout the century, going counter to the Reformation and other innovative events, as if the Middle Ages and the Renaissance should be seen as flowing together side by side, or superimposed one on the other, throughout many years, and not as two periods severed by a vertical line.[16] Also Georg Brandes, who in his *Hovedtromninger*—or *Hauptströmungen:* principal currents—forcefully emphasized the great dynamic, reforming, and revolutionary impulse that moves and animates the entire nineteenth century, against all odds, overwhelming obstacles and setbacks, such as the failures of the liberal uprisings of 1848.[17]

Viewed from such an angle the notion of *current* (or whatever analogous term one might wish to use, that is, something markedly "horizontal" and diachronic) turns out to be indispensable. The idea is perfectly compatible with the dialogic and pluralistic model of period. More than that, period presents itself as superposition or structured interrelation—or rather, as system—of fundamental and constituent currents, some of which are derived from the earlier period, while others keep flowing and evolving toward the future. This describes the consensus I referred to a few pages back in regard to the *Histoire comparée des littératures en langues européennes,* which includes volumes devoted to a complete temporal space (such as *Le tournant du siècle des Lumières. 1760–1820,* edited by G. M. Vajda for genres in verse, and by Jacques Voisine for prose) and other works concentrating on currents (like *The Symbolist Movement in the Literature of European Languages,* edited by Anna Balakian). Other contemporary movements are also included, for instance *Naturalisme,* to which Yves Chevrel devoted some volumes in the the same series. Uses and meanings of related terms, such as *generation,* are classified from a similar point of view.[18]

The method of arranging by generations, cultivated in Spain by José Ortega y Gasset and by Julián Marías, sheds light on a certain historical dynamism through the dialogue that takes place between generations and between those who share certain common experiences; in that sense, it comes close to the polemical model B just sketched, by means of the diachrony constructed by the succession of generations. But in essence, like its opposite, this method emphasizes the homogeneity of a synchronic grouping, underestimating differences and disagreements between groups, currents, and movements made up of persons of the same age—the very diversity allowed by model B. Generation is a synecdoche, a partial slice of too limited a reach for those of us inclined toward model B in general, or more concretely toward a wider and more totalizing concept of literary or cultural system, to which we shall now return.[19]

According to István Sötér, literary periods are polyphonic: "Within a historical period there exists a *polyphony* of trends and events in literature and the arts."[20] This polyphony permits variations and differences not only between tendencies and new or novel events, but also between the new and the old, or rather between the new and the revitalized values that the old assumes through contact with the new. Alberto Blecua observes that in considering eras in which great cultural changes come about, critical analyses must perceive how old signs and new ones crisscross each other: "in general, in these kinds of studies there is usually a tendency toward simplistic dichotomies that contrast the old with the new, without shadings and without considering that a sign maintained throughout centuries could only with great difficulty keep the same meaning in each historical moment."[21] In effect, acceptance of this plurality has a great advantage in that it helps us to discern clearly the conditions and forms of *change* in the temporal itinerary of literature. A monolithic model of era runs into serious difficulties when trying to comprehend the transition from one era to the next.

The temporal itinerary of literature is a complex and selective process of growth. Literary systems evolve in a very special way, characterized by the continuity of certain components, the disappearance of others, the awakening of forgotten possibilities, the swift irruption of innovations, the tardy effect of others. Great reputations, not mere passing fads, sink out of sight; genres and subgenres vanish, like *La Celestina* and its imitations at the end of the sixteenth century, or the sonnet in modern Italian poetry. There are *recuperations* and rescues, influential and spectacular at the same time in all spheres of the arts and culture, like the efforts of the Rumanian linguists and humanists of the second half of the eighteenth century—S. Micu, G. Sincai, P. Maior—to investigate the Roman origins of their language and culture, thus paving the way for the future affirmation of the identity and national unity of Rumania; or the attempt to stimulate the regrowth of African roots in Latin America and later in the United States through cultivation of different genres of African American art. Think of the return to ballads and romances after Herder and the brothers Grimm; to the motifs of Greek vases and the Greco-Roman taverns in painting; to the *Popol Vuh* and the indigenous poetry of Peru and Mexico; to great forgotten artists like El Greco, Vermeer, or La Tour. These cultural phenomena of specific durations that are not definitively interrupted are what George Kubler in *The Shape of Time* (1962) calls *intermittent durations,* a term meant to denote the peculiar discontinuities of historical-cultural time. Pierre Vilar points out that such discontinuities cannot be reduced to curves, growth, and decay, or other ideas taken from mechanical or biological models.[22] Biological time, Kubler writes, consists of uninterrupted sequences; historical-cultural time, of actions that are intermittent rather than continuous; between these lie intervals that are highly variable in extension and content.[23] From this circumstance comes the need for constant reevaluation of the lost and underestimated past: Nerval and Lautréamont reinterpreted by the surrealists; John Donne and the English metaphysical poets by T. S. Eliot; Góngora by Dámaso Alonso and his poet friends. Recuperations are characteristic of all or nearly all eras. "Reaching into the past," in Wellek's words, is a fundamental coordinate of the history of literature.[24] And in order to encompass its richness and peculiarity, not only is a pluralistic conception of period or era necessary, but also a diversified and complex vision of temporality, subdivided and multiplied into currents, rhythms, and different durations.[25]

These flexible and multiple conceptions of periodization allow historians to include or even to bring to the fore one or another important current— that is, whatever catches the interest of historians—without having to reduce an entire temporal space to that particular current. In that way, schemes propounded by criticism regarding terms such as the *Baroque, Romanticism,* or *symbolism* are no longer totalizing or excluding. The vicissitudes of the criticism of the Baroque confirm two things: one, that the history of European literatures is much more intricate than the path of the plastic arts, which in general is successive and unilineal (and whose system of periodization literary critics try to follow, above all since Wölfflin); and two, that such complexity entails special difficulties when one examines the centuries between the twilight of the Middle Ages and the triumph of the Enlightenment. So we can observe the introduction of another term taken from painting a few years ago, namely *Mannerism,*[26] and the tendency nowadays to study the Baroque analytically and cautiously, without neglecting national disparities, starting from a neutral chronological space, the seventeenth century, a period that takes in the principal Baroque works and schools. As Wellek says, what is decisive in each case is the choice of the dominant current. The periodological terms—period terms—are "names for systems of norms which *dominate* at a specific time of the historical process."[27] Wellek's own survey of Romanticism is above all a recapitulation of the critical usages of the adjective "romantic," from its origins in the seventeenth century to the investigations and proposals of Albert Béguin, Albert Gérard, Henry Remak, and Geoffrey Hartman in our own day.[28]

And so we return to a historical perspective, this time vis-à-vis the avatars of structuring, implying evaluation, of the past. I will give two brief examples. Roger Bauer has shown that the discovery of the rococo during the second half of the nineteenth century goes hand in hand with the vogue in Paris of the word *décadence* and of decadentism. *Decadentia* is a late term that does not belong to classical Latin. Its vulgar derivations are used occasionally during the seventeenth and eighteenth centuries—by Montesquieu, in regard to the Roman Empire, but less frequently than *corruption, dégénérer, luxe, mollesse*—and appear very infrequently in the Romantic period. Baudelaire used it in referring to Poe (1857); Théophile Gautier, in his funeral elegy of Baudelaire (1868). The term, actually introduced by Paul Bourget and the Goncourt brothers, was enormously popular during the 1880s and 1890s (Huysmans' *A rebours,* 1884, not an innovator in this regard; the journal *Le décadent,* 1886; the ironies of Paul Verlaine; the accusations of Zola) and was instantly adopted in other places as an intellectual gallicism. Nietzsche first used it spelled in the French fashion in *Ecce homo,* 1888: "need I say that in questions of *décadence* I am someone with experience?".[29] Well then, the return to the rococo (argot derived from *rocaille*) is a parallel process, like the fascination with moribund Venice, the theme of the androgyne (from Gautier to Thomas Mann), the Carthage of *Salammbô,* Lesbos. The twilight of the *ancien régime* is recovered, along with all possible disdain toward the bourgeoisie—clearly by some members of the bourgeoisie who were rebelling against themselves, according to Jules and Edmond de Goncourt, who wrote in their *Journal* (August 24, 1860): "the bourgeois . . . revolts against himself and seeks the rococo." Watteau is rediscovered, pleasure parks, masques, carnivals, the fabulous voyage to Cythera, the favorites of Louis XV. There are Verlaine's *Fêtes gallantes,* and those of Rubén Darío. According to Roger Bauer, "Every age is betrayed by its nostalgias."[30] My other example is Donald Fanger's first book, *Dostoevsky and Romantic Realism. A Study of Dostoevsky in Relation to Balzac, Dickens, and Gogol* (1965). Impossible to use a term so debated and debatable as *realism* with Fanger's originality without first being aware of its historical trajectory. That is the intent of his first chapter, titled "Realism, Pure and Romantic." How can one delimit realism, that tremendous *petitio principii?* On one hand, we have a particular modality ("a discrete *mode*") that has existed since antiquity; on the other hand, we find "the product of a more recent historical *moment.*" This moment consists of the years before 1850 when, in connection with the painter Courbet, and later Champfleury, Philippe Duranty, and other writers, *réalisme* proclaimed its existence in a critical and defiant tone (thus becoming a movement, according to Aleksandar Flaker). The ancients had assigned the daily and ordinary aspects of life to the realm of the comical, whereas the "pure" realism of the second half of the nineteenth century assigned them to areas that their predecessors, the Romantics, had not known how to perceive or evaluate. The impulse toward realism of those "reformed idealists," as they were called by Harry Levin in his monumental book, *The Gates of Horn* (1963), coincides with a "literature of opposition," which Fanger sees as a legacy of the comical tradition. Situated between these coordinates, the realists of the first half of the century, not pure realists but indeed writers of exceptional interpretative breadth—Balzac, Dickens, Gogol (who made the work of Dostoevsky possible)—are outlined much more clearly. In the midst of Romanticism, these visionaries of the visible, rhapsodes of the real, pursue and discover the characteristic, the symbolic, the grotesque, the melodramatic, the ironic, and, above all, the pronounced individuality of their characters, among which incessant contrasts appear. For these *mythopoets* the city is the favorite field of mythical exploration. Dostoevsky, certainly a mythopoet of the city, discovers in St. Petersburg an inexhaustible nightmare.[31] But I wish to point out here only what is pertinent to the present topic: that within the period called Romanticism Donald Fanger identifies a current, romantic realism, that does not coincide with the entire period—not everything in Romanticism is realism, nor is realism completely circumscribed by Romanticism—realism as "mode" existed earlier and later. The current isolated by Fanger is intraperiodological and extraperiodological at the same time.

It is important to stress this dimension, one of the principal virtualities of what I earlier called Model B. The structuring of historical time does not raise unbreachable barriers. The division into eras, periods, or phases does not lead to a kind of historical atomism. As we saw earlier (Chapter 14, in regard to thematology), the diversity offered by historical evolution does not have the last—or only—word. The avant-garde movements are a good example of this extraperiodological dimension. Renato Poggioli's *Teoria dell'arte d'avanguardia* (1962; translated into English as *The Theory of the Avant-Garde*) is a great book. Its originality and also the method employed can be better appreciated today than thirty years ago (although the first version appeared even earlier, in the journal *Inventario* in 1949 and 1950). In fact during those years the so-called structuralism of the 1960s would denounce the limitations of historical curiosity restricted to the before and after, content with a recitation of *événements,* of unusual and fragmented happenings. Remember the final sentence of Lévi-Strauss's *From Honey to Ashes:* "to be valid, any investigation which is entirely aimed at elucidating structures must begin by submitting to the powerful inanity of events." [32] An atomism of temporality does indeed exist (also for artists, above all for novelists: "epiphanies," sudden illuminations, in Joyce, Faulkner, and Rosa Chacel). One of the most powerful thinkers of our time (and one of the least understood), Claude Lévi-Strauss, proposes a hypothesis: the existence of vast universal entities or codes of potential signs (of structures, or rather, to avoid confusion, metastructures). The relations of coherence found in a single entity—like a unique myth of a specific society—would be structures only if they appear to be local transformations of a latent, transhistorical repertoire of meanings, after study of elements of other comparable entities from different cultures. [33] This hypothesis, however, so suggestive and so fruitful in the field of myth and folklore, is difficult to apply to written literature, with its changeable individual and social roots. Do we then have no other way out except a sense of uniqueness?

Let us now take note of the existence of at least one other path, the one followed by Poggioli. For nearly two centuries an entire gamut of poetical movements have shared certain psychic, social, and ideological conditions (such as *Antipassatismo,* Nihilism, Agonism, Futurism, Decadence, Alienation, Experimentalism, Scientificism, Humorism, metaphysic of the metaphor, mystic of purity), always provided we consider them *as movements of the avant-garde.* Here is an authentic example of diachronic structure, historical and recurring at the same time. It is not surprising that the originality and also the wide spatial extension of this example have attracted the attention of numerous critics in the past few years, particularly in eastern Europe, such as Miklós Szabolcsi, Adrian Marino, and Aleksandar Flaker. [34]

What we have here can be called a diachronic structure. It is not necessary to appeal to extraliterary or extracultural causalities in order to localize and analyze it. No doubt some common social conditions are factors to be considered, but when we regard them as a source of explanation, we not only shift our reasoning to another genre of historiographic discourse; we also lose the opportunity to recognize the dialectic of the one and the many in literary history itself. The question proposed here is the possibility of a nonatomized literary periodization, and an inquiry regarding the forms employed in order to link one moment of such an itinerary to another—pointing toward certain forms of interhistoricity.

One of the most brilliant attempts to forge links of this type—intertemporal and interpoetic—was made by Harold Bloom, even though his attempt has little or nothing to contribute to the comparative study of poetry. Bloom's essays (or rather his own literature, quite close in vigor and tone, a cheerful pathos, to the style of certain Yale deconstructionists) start with an affirmation of the vanity of all correct or accurate literary criticism, and in effect corroborate in practice the viability of such a posture. Bloom no longer cultivates either criticism or history—in the minimally exact sense of that word—but in return offers us a theory of the Modern Poet, or rather, to express it in his own terms, of the poet after the Enlightenment. The modern poet of the first rank, whom Bloom calls "the strong poet" (not in the style of Nietzsche, it seems to me, but rather in the style of Hemingway, like a North American tourist running with the bulls in Pamplona), suffers anxiety—I refer here to *The Anxiety of Influence* (1973)—caused by a life-long confrontation with the Father, or rather the previous Great Poet, whom he emulates: veering away from him, correcting him, assimilating him, or *misreading him*. It is a matter of a form of intertextuality (whose Freudian aspect only confirms its compulsive character). Bloom enumerates a series of phases that are revisions and utilizations of varied types, of which the first, or *clinamen* (the swerve that, according to Lucretius and the ancient atomists, permitted one atom not to follow the path of another), stands out. To read is to misread; all reading is a misreading; but the mistakes of the great poet are deliberate.

> Poetic Influence—when it involves two strong, authentic poets—always proceeds by a misreading of the prior poet, an act of creative correction that is actually and necessarily a misinterpretation. The history of fruitful poetic influence, which is to say the main tradition of Western poetry since the Renaissance, is a history of anxiety and self-saving caricature, of distortion, of perverse, wilful revisionism without which modern poetry as such could not exist.[35]

These ideas do not take us by surprise. We already commented on Escarpit's *trahison créatrice*, the agonistic diachrony of the concept of generation, influences, and intertextuality.[36]

The drawbacks to these ideas are only too evident. One of them is ingenuous logic:[37] If, as Bloom claims, every reading is a misreading, there are no accurate readings; but if correct readings do not exist, how is it then possible to be mistaken? Another is the lack of an authentically historical vision. Bloom postulates that since the Enlightenment the poet's destiny has consisted of a subjectivism leading to anxiety, rancor, and parricidal struggle. If we accept this premise, its principal diachronic consequences lead to the gradual exhaustion of poetry. Then how can we help recalling the many prophecies during the last half-century announcing the demise of the novel? Yet novelists as authentic as Mario Vargas Llosa and V. S. Naipaul keep on emerging. One can expect the same thing to happen with regard to Bloom's prediction of the demise of poetry, inside or outside English-speaking countries. Furthermore, Bloom's perspective is notoriously narrow: it addresses only Anglo-American poetry, to the exclusion of poets writing in other languages, the great Greco-Latin and Oriental classics, prose or nonoffical prose, painter or musician friends, the voyage to Italy, Greece, or Mexico, international movements; and even, from a synchronic point of view, the rivalry not with the Father but with the Brothers, that is, contemporaries. But the most serious defect of Bloom's thesis is biographism: the psychologizing of intertextuality. Bloom falls into the trap of the *comparatistes* of half a century ago or more: conjectures regarding psychic relations between writers. We return to the ambiguities of the old concept of influence (discussed in Chapter 15). I have already stressed the promising nature of the passage from influence to intertextuality. Harold Bloom proposes that we follow the same path but in the opposite direction.

The most fruitful interhistorical conceptions are other ones, such as those discussed by Claus Uhlig in *Theorie der Literarhistorie* (1982)—a most suggestive, erudite, well thought-out work, brimming with information. Uhlig's starting point is a criticism of Harold Bloom. In his second chapter, he analyzes three "theoretical principles" of literary history that are naturally intertemporal relations, to which he assigns Greek names: *palingenese,* or regeneration: yesterday reborn in today; *ananke,* or necessity: yesterday determines today; and *palimpsest,* or rewriting: today rewrites and reintegrates yesterday. (The interrupted sequences and recuperations of George Kubler mentioned earlier can be assimilated in the first principle.) In the next chapter Uhlig adds to this first descriptive approximation a qualitative analysis, in which the principal element is no longer the direction that governs the intertemporal relation or the measure of determination that it brings with it, but the degree of historicity in general, and the intensity of recall and use of the artistic past *überhaupt.* Man lives between the need to forget and the urgency to remember; and at the same time the writer lives between contemporaneity and reminiscence (*Reminiszenz*)—voluntary recall of the past—or *Repristination,* "rejuvenation"—intent to renew the ancient. Is the writer who regards himself as a modern writer also the same one who yields to the urge to forget? No, Uhlig argues shrewdly, modernity is precisely the consciousness, positive or negative, of historicity. What appears debatable to me is the idea—not too far from Bloom and from Walter

Jackson Bate in *The Burden of the Past and the English Poet* (1970)—that the historicity of a literary text, its density of allusions and layers proceeding from the past, keeps increasing with the passing of centuries. Among Spanish poets, for example, Góngora does not include fewer reminiscences or rejuvenations than Lorca.

Uhlig's reflection leads to an interpretation of the historicity of poetic texts—of the history *in* the poetry—more than to a study of historiographic structures. But it is also necessary to read the histories *of* literature, whose essential narrative character it is now time to consider. As is well known, when we say history we have to denote two things, as though they were perhaps separable: a prior event and a body of knowledge (*Geschehen* and *Kunde,* according to Uhlig). A history of Rome creates a picture of a remote space and time that cannot possibly be confused with today's space and time. But such a history is also current historiography, knowledge about the past without which that particular time and space would disappear from our consciousness. Such a body of knowledge is organized like a story. History is a narration of a lived experience of earlier times. An example will help clarify the indivisibility of both aspects: what can be called *prophecy from the past.*

Consider the stock character of burlesque comedy who comes onstage saying, "Now I am leaving for the Thirty Years' War." It's comical that one person pretends to be actor (or agent) and historian at the same time. We feel it logical and desirable that the two roles be distinct. As far as time is concerned, a contemporary witness can know no more than some of the past and some of the present. In Stendhal's *Charterhouse of Parma* Fabrizio del Dongo, who was only an inexperienced and youthful participant, didn't have the faintest idea that he found himself in the middle of what would later be called the Battle of Waterloo. Well then, according to the historiographer Arthur C. Danto, a correct example of historical statement is: "The Thirty Years' War began in 1618."[38] It is understood that on reaching the year 1618, a chronological narrative has every right to include that obviously prophetic sentence, from the point of view of that year.

What differentiates literary history from other historiographic genres is the fact that its components or entities are literary works and writers, or rather, systems, codes, poetical events, and horizons of expectations on the part of readers and critics, as we shall see later. Also, these works—*scripta manent*—are still today accessible and legible: different receivers have read them and may continue to read them. But the same cultural heritage of narrative forms is shared by all the genres of historiography. The task of every literary historian consists in reconciling some of these forms with those distinctive components.

Each and every moment, system, reception, element must be incorporated into an active series, a sequence, with the aim of constructing a story. Every element must add to the impulse of narration to make it go forward. At a minimum, each component must be related to others. That is what we called earlier intertemporal connections or conceptions. Nothing could be less historical than atomism carried to the extreme, the description of single facts, isolated from any context. That was the method used in the ancient genre of "ephemerals," such as the Sevillan *Anales* of Don Diego Ortiz de Zúñiga (Year X: "So-and-So was named bishop"; Year Y: "There was a great flood of the Guadalquivir").

Relations make a certain meaning possible; a net is extended between different temporal points, as R. G. Collingwood would say. One document tells us for certain that on a definite day Caesar was in Rome, and another says that a short time later he was in Gaul. There is no proof that Caesar took a trip; but "we interpolate this with a perfectly good conscience." [39] That is a basic, rudimentary connection, legitimate without doubt. Apparently no causes or consequences are involved. But why is the voyage of interest to us? What makes us think that Caesar's entry into Gaul is an interesting event, worthy of being introduced into the story by the narrative link of the voyage? More than likely the historian is keeping in reserve other events and the gradual construction of significant processes. Let us suppose that no pretense is made to offer explanations, or to identify the necessary conditions for a certain development. Even so, the historian's act of relating is a beginning of meaningfulness. William Dray writes: "The operative notion is less of discovering necessary and sufficient conditions than of relating parts, at first not seen as such, to a whole of some kind. Thus the historian interprets a host of occurrences in fifteenth-century Italy as a 'Renaissance'; he explains a series of incidents in eighteenth-century France as a 'Revolution.'" A. C. Danto sums up this type of observation as follows: "We are to think of events as having a 'meaning' with reference to some larger temporal structure of which they are components." [40]

In effect, this is an essential dimension, *sine qua non*, of the task of the historian. There is no sense without intertemporal relations. What is not necessarily implied is the construction of a *plot*, characteristic of fictitious stories; nor an unwarranted development, nor a teleology; nor does the intervention of an observer presuppose the abandonment of a volition for objectivity. On the contrary, the volition for objectivity is precisely what is exercised and tested on such occasions. Let us suppose that a document attests to the reality of an event A in the sixteenth century and another proves the existence of an event B three centuries later. No human being could participate in both events, but the historian is indeed capable of discovering the latent properties—the "sense"—that A and B have in common. On the basis of such properties, the historian constructs connections that could not be revealed without his intervention, things that no person could experience in reality. These connections are bridges spanning the flow of temporality (or metaphors—the comparison is difficult but inevitable). The historian and the poet discover new and nevertheless "real" relations, since the relations are not found outside reality but within it, and since all their components have "taken place" in the world. Hayden White has written an important book on the principles of narrative composition that he calls "tropologic," in a rhetorical sense.[41] In addition to the historian's metaphors that give spatial form to the flow of time, highlighting its dominant traits—a repeated event like civil war, a certain type of writer or thinker as we saw in De Sanctis—, the most traditional narrative forms such as repetition, amplification, or parallelism are fundamental. Fundamental also are Genette's *analepses* and *prolepses*—Eberhard Laemmert's *Rückwendungen* and *Vorausdeutungen*,[42]—or rather retrospective glances; as well as predictions, which I mentioned a short while back. Now fortunately Danto has pointed out their historiographic function.[43]

The historian's use of both perspectives—looking backward and forward—is undoubtedly legitimate, as in the sentence we quoted earlier: "The Thirty Years' War began in 1618." An equally valid statement would be: "Garcilaso wrote the first *lira* in Castilian between 1533 and 1536." From the point of view of Garcilaso, or of the crossbowman of 1618, these pronouncements would have been prophetic and unintelligible. In his own time Garcilaso was a great poet and innovator who, in addition to other things, introduced into Spain a five-line stanza, the one used in "A la flor del Gnido," which begins thus (*canción 5*):

> Si de mi baja lira
> tanto pudiese el son, que en un momento
> aplacase la ira
> del animoso viento,
> y la furia del mar y el movimiento . . .

> If the sound of my lowly lyre
> were so powerful, that in one moment
> it could placate the wrath

> of the vigorous wind,
> and the fury and movement of the sea . . .[44]

This most felicitous combination of heptasyllables and hendacasyllables went on to be called much later, after the poet's death, by the last word of the first line of the ode, a *lira,* not because this ode was one of Garcilaso's best poems, which in the opinion of many it is not, but because during the second half of the sixteenth century the *lira* came to be the favorite prosodic channel for two of the greatest poets in the Spanish language, fray Luis de León and San Juan de la Cruz. The union of meter, rhythm, and syntax that Garcilaso might have proposed did not find fruition in his own work, during his life's brief span. But we cannot place him within a history of Spanish poetry without mentioning his introduction of the *lira,* just as we also cannot read his poems without keeping in mind Fray Luis and San Juan. We cannot "tell this history" without alluding to a certain future, or rather without the type of relation that I have called "prophecy from the past."

Because the moment we speak of the future, the question arises: whose future? Let us go back to our two events A and B that happened several centuries apart and let us add a third: C. It goes without saying that the historian has a perfect right to go back and forth among the three events, establishing intertemporal connections in both directions. But is it necessary to exclude the point of view of the agents or actors—or authors—who participated actively, or creatively, in the history in question? History is at one and the same time a retrospective focus and the telling of a series of events *in fieri,* in the making, in the course of which *after* does not erase the perspective of *before;* that is, memory and the capacity for anticipation— for a vision of the future—of the actors or authors themselves. Clearly it often happens that a poet located at point C may return first of all to A. The archetype of such a posture was Petrarch, who placed the writers of his immediate past—the Middle Ages—in a subordinate position to writers of antiquity. José Ortega y Gasset explained that in human life the past is always accessible to a person living in the present, and therefore the past is a fixed, inexorable component of his being. But since all of us must go forward, since our life, in anti-Eleatic fashion, cannot be static, we find ourselves obliged to choose between the options of the past, not only in order to emulate them but also to become "what has not been." [45] That is, in the choice of a particular past lies the seed of the future—just as man himself, or the actor of history, experiences it. I know of no one who has seen or felt this circumstance more deeply than Antonio Machado in a passage from *Juan de Mairena:* "The philosophy of history has been facetiously defined by some as the 'art of prophesying the past.' In point of fact, the more we reflect on the past and penetrate to its depths, the more we uncover the sum of the world's hopes, neither realized nor yet wholly realized: in short, that sense of futurity which has always been the legitimate content of prophecy." [46] Machado was meditating on what the past carried within itself, or rather on the past as such, *in illo tempore,* and as carrier of certain virtualities or some projects: of an accumulation of hopes that came to mean the future. The future of the actor of history is an accumulation of hopes not realized—how were they to be realized at all? How could they be realized without ceasing to be a future, or without coinciding with the historian's future?—but also, and here is the decisive intuition, not failed either. In the first place, hopes cannot fail *completely,* cannot lead to a totally negative balance. And moreover, what may look like a failure to us will have helped propel a moment of history forward, along with its disappointments and successes.

The future of the agent or participant—the accumulation of hopes of the warrior of 1618—cannot coincide with the future of the historian—the one who writes that the Thirty Years' War began on that date—without losing its quality and force of futurity. For the future, from the point of view of life itself, of one who conceives it and glimpses it, is never what will come to pass, nor a present that awaits us tomorrow; but as Karl Rahner states, it is the unknown, what is not reduced to evolution or plan:[47] a desire for differences, an accumulation of wisdom and ignorance, or projects and hopes. In sum, it appears that Machado suggests to us and predicts the ontological utopianism of Ernst Bloch, for whom man is the restless being par excellence, carrying within himself the drive (*Trieb*) desirous of future improvements, the incomplete being whose consciousness of a lack, of having a history that is also incomplete, makes hope and utopia the principal constituents of our existence.[48]

History-as-it-happened must fuse with history-in-the-making. Our knowledge of the former should not inhibit our ability to comprehend history *in fieri* as volitional activity, tension, invention, freedom, frustration, failure. It is not enough to require that a historical narrative be true, if by true we mean only narratives faithful to what in fact occurred. In order to capture the context and quality of a past experience, it is necessary to be open to the complexities of certain processes that encompass varieties of options, accumulations of hopes, and the interactions between them, as well as social and material conditionings—whose results and outcomes might have been *different.* The dialogue between history from the perspective of the present and history from the perspective of the past uncovers a third dimension: that of the virtual, of what-might-have-happened. Going back to Ranke's well-known terms, historical narration takes in not only how it actually was, *wie es eigentlich gewesen war*, but also how it might have been, *wie es hätte sein können*.

One book of this type is *La España posible en tiempos de Carlos III* (1963), by Julián Marías, and there are a number of others as well. In the area of literary criticism we come up against a stumbling block, the famous *intentional fallacy* ridiculed by W. K. Wimsatt and Monroe Beardsley and the New Criticism group of the United States in general more than thirty years ago.[49] Can there be any doubt that it is a mistake to confound a writer's intentions with his works? More than once in this book we have rejected the ambiguous vagueness of facile critical biographism in regard to the old concept of influence, or the new concept of Harold Bloom. But the time has come to go beyond atomism also, the chaos of solitary and isolated words, a notion that owes more than a little to the narrow idea of a connection between activity and work, production and product. If, as often happens, the intention—free of anecdotal psychologizing—and the work do not coincide, an interesting disparity results, in itself a part of history.[50] In Italy Luigi Russo and Walter Binni have tried to develop an investigation of the "poetics" of writers, particularly since the time of Binni's *La poetica del decadentismo italiano* (1936).[51] According to these critics, poetics implies a creative tension—*tensione expressiva*—which changes continually as it intersects specific moments in the continuity and evolution of the poet's career. From a neoclassical point of view, such a poetics is not circumscribed by a series of rules or a normative aesthetic program. The functioning of such a system of poetics that is not merely intellectual (in spite of Valéry) starts from an *attiva coscienza*, aware consciousness. That awareness demands the total effort of the poet, the determined orientation of his own work, and not only are the individual hopes of a single poet in play, but also the literary system of the era and the vast array of desires and contradictions that configure the whole of a society or a culture.[52] Thus it is not a matter of mere intentions. In considering a sequence of works by the same poet—Garcilaso's eclogues, the innovation of his epistle to Boscán, his elegies, and the prosody from which the *lira* emerged—the historian tries to capture in an objective way the élan, the impulse, that links the different works, projecting them toward what was to be the author's future.

Histories of the literature of various nations are usually mediocre, except in the case of Italy. A notable Spanish exception is a relatively short manual written specifically for North American students, Angel del Río's *Historia de la literatura española* (1948; enlarged edition 1963). Lack of space prevents me from commenting on this book here with the care that it deserves, but I wish to make two observations concerning historiographic structures referred to earlier. In the first place, the book uses traditional narrative procedures such as repetition, parallelism, amplification, and the highlighting or praise of exemplary figures. A typical sentence might be: "Benito Pérez Galdós, creator of modern realism in the Spanish novel, was born in 1843." Del Río points up the rise of the novel during the nineteenth century: "The most important literary phenomenon of the second half of the nineteenth century is the rebirth of the novel." [53] The notion of rebirth presupposes a complex conception of temporality, inasmuch as it implies something like a process of growth that reiterates or reflects earlier growths as well as a descending interval or an interruption. The process culminates in Galdós, who recovered ancient works—Cervantes—and at the same time laid a foundation for the achievements of his successors—Clarín, Doña Emilia Pardo Bazán—without whom there might not have been the "complete artistic cycle" [54] that del Río extols. On arriving at Romanticism a few pages later, his *Historia* becomes denser in the use of parallelisms and also—my second observation—in the use of predictions and presentiments of a virtual Spain, what the future Spain might become one day. One exemplary figure looms large among others, Juan Martín el Empecinado, who personified the intervention of some social classes no longer willing to continue to be passive objects of history. "Then an unexpected phenomenon comes into play, typically Spanish: the somewhat anarchical awakening of the people." [55] This time what is typically national entails a new form of life for the entire country: a vision of a future, of certain hopes not yet reached or failed; "there is no doubt but that in these years, carried along by the agitated and dark events of the reign of Ferdinand VII, a new way of life was being hatched." [56] The retrospective vision of the historian alerts us to the fact that the Napoleonic Wars deepened the open divisions of society of the previous century—"The popular traditionalism, much deeper than that of the theoretical defenders of Calderón in the eighteenth century and the liberalism of the spokesmen of the Central Junta and the Cortes (Parliament) of Cádiz, much more aggressive and radical than that of the ministers of the enlightened despotism of Carlos III." [57] All of which clearly applies to the history of literature. In Europe the Romantic period had already begun. Once again influences from abroad caused Spaniards to rediscover their own past. "We saw it already in the seventeenth century. It is repeated in Romanticism." [58] But ultimately Romanticism in Spain gives way, recedes, is frustrated. Except for Mariano José Larra and José de Espronceda, the future that was glimpsed earlier did not come to pass. What happened to the hopes of the francophiles, the liberals, the exiles of 1815 and 1823? "The renovating process begun in the second half of the eighteenth century was interrupted and the promising harvests of almost a whole generation were ruined."[59]

The history of literature, then, shares some partial forms with invented narrations—in both directions of time—forms like joints that connect successive parts and thus assure the integrity of the diachronic whole. But the history of literature has neither beginning nor end. Not even a national history has such bounds, since no matter how much one concedes an inaugural value to the Middle Ages or the Renaissance, nobody is unaware of the extremely ancient origins of all poetry.[60] The historiographic genres are found at points of a triangle whose vertices are religion, the novel, and journalism. In contrast to the believer, the historian does not start out a priori from a faith in an inevitable meaning and a final destiny. The historian should not capture the present from the live perspective of the present, like the journalist (or the author of the ancient "ephemerals" and chronicles). And to the questions posed by readers of novels—What will happen next? How will it end?—the historian, prophet of past futures but not of our own,[61] offers no answer at all, because his story has no plot.

Earlier we considered the problem of periodization, with results that were rather general, more or less macrohistorical, and in a number of cases applicable to extensive spans of time, such as the eighteenth century for the Enlightenment or the sixteenth century for the Renaissance. We examined a plural or polyphonic model based on a multiple temporality. The period turns out to be a superposition and interrelation of constituent currents, some coming from an earlier period and others evolving toward later times. The dynamism of this model has the advantage of not suppressing the future. But also needed are more exact, relatively microhistorical determinations that permit analyses of precise moments. Other concepts of recent use are helpful in carrying out such a task: concepts such as *system* (see Chapter 15), code, and horizon of expectations. Some theorists believe that system, as well as code, coincides with period. To my mind, these terms indicate concentrated, brief focuses, as if we were to make a slice in the future at any point or date we might wish to perceive more clearly. In Israel, Itamar Even-Zohar has worked vigorously to develop the idea of system—or rather, to use his own word, *polysystem,* a term that takes into account the heterogeneity of the entities under consideration. This idea originates in the work of the Russian Formalists, whose spirit is perpetuated by Even-Zohar. In effect, the interrelations that structure a polysystem are conflictive and hierarchical. A series of terms designates these opposites and subordinates: central/peripheral, low/high, primary/secondary, canonical/noncanonical. The starting point is the place of contact between official and extraofficial genres, the area emphasized by the Formalists in their studies of the great Russian literature of the nineteenth century, and that today is focused on the distinction between trivial literature (*Trivialliteratur*) and literature proper.[62] But "intersystemic" contacts are also examined, that is, the contacts between national and supranational systems, and those between literary polysystems and cultural megasystems.[63] Notwithstanding the difficulties of such terminology, this method can undoubtedly be very well adapted for use in comparative studies proper. Even-Zohar shows that just as within a polysystem noncanonical genres or authors depend on established ones with which they compete, national literatures often depend on the literatures of other nations, by way of either emulation or subordination. During the nineteenth century, for example, literature in Yiddish occupied an inferior position relative to literature in Hebrew, while both depended on Russian (and Polish) literature.[64] Even-Zohar has tried to demarcate a typology of contacts between diverse literatures, comprised of two principal classes: contacts between relatively established and therefore relatively independent systems, and those between nonestablished or "fluid" systems partially or completely dependent on other systems.[65] For a dependent literature, the relation with a foreign culture over many years can become an indispensable condition of its existence. So it is with Ukranian literature (versus Russian), Flemish (versus French during the nineteenth century), Hebrew (versus Arabic in Spain), Norwegian (versus Danish, from the sixteenth to the nineteenth century), Czech (versus German until the twentieth century), and so on.[66] Even-Zohar and other scholars must also be credited with incorporating translations into polysystems, as I pointed out earlier (Chapter 15).

According to José Lambert, a system can be identified at the moment when the following elements are observed to be more or less coherent within it: "the literary norms—the models corresponding to these norms—the oppositions between high and low literature, peripheral and central, and so on—the relations with the surrounding systems."[67] And Lambert also proves that this method can be applied to national literatures, "self-organizing entities" whose components can—*to a certain extent*—also be part of either regional subsystems or other powerful and centralizing literatures.[68] From this point of view, it is easier to gain a better understanding of the position of a "marginal literature" or one that falls into an "intermediate zone," as in the case of Belgian literature. The expressed desire to create a distinct Belgian literature is commonplace in the nationalistic criticism of the nineteenth century. But what really happened was that authors writing in French and those writing in Flemish maintained a passive and eclectic attitude toward the prevailing literary movements in France and the Low Countries. And this passivity, this relative dependence, is characteristic of the Belgian system: "thus, one could accept that there does indeed exist a literary system typical of Belgium in the nineteenth century, to the extent that writings in Dutch and in French behave in similar fashion vis-à-vis the surrounding systems."[69] It is evident, almost tautological, that a conception of a system based on the opposition canonical/noncanonical is going to be extremely practical in helping us understand the functioning of norms and authorities, canons and prestigious models, those that become established and those passed over, those belonging to central as well as to marginal zones. But in regard to the theory of genres of the Russian Formalists, we already saw that this method is especially apt when applied to a nineteenth-century literature (with movements but no schools, we could say with Poggioli), one possessing no cultivated poetic tradition other than the neoclassical—literature and theory based on Romantic and neoromantic postures. Is there no other class of relation between the components of a system? It goes without saying that I accept the idea of polysystem. But I also believe that, along with the Russian model, it would be worthwhile to retrieve something of the Saussurian concept of system: the notion of differential value, mentioned earlier in reference to the structural approximation to genres (Chapter 14). A writer chooses a certain genre, thus excluding some and distancing himself from others; there are genres that are contragenres; and poetical genres offer ideal spaces, since they consist of options and differences. I take Tynyanov's famous statement—"the historical novel of Tolstoy is correlated not with the historical novel of Zagoskin but with the prose of his time"—to mean not only that Tolstoy stands out in comparison to his predecessors, but also that his work is differentiated from other nonhistorical novelistic forms of contemporary writing, and is correlated with them by way of contrast and through its superior dialectic, through an *Aufhebung* that up to a certain point subsumed its opposite. Let us remember a classical Spanish example: the Spanish picaresque novel. Mateo Alemán competes with the knightly novels and pastoral novels that were bestsellers—particularly the former—but also expresses different and antithetical values found at times in picaresque narration, such as honor or love. *Guzmán de Alfarache* (1599) is distanced from the knightly and pastoral norms by means of antithesis, and from *Quixote* by means of parody. In sum, I think that a "horizontal" slice, that is, a slice of differential and axiological character, could be added to the "vertical" slice—agonistic, hierarchical—used by Even-Zohar in his polysystem.

In regard to the idea of code, the recent investigations of Douwe W. Fokkema are both useful and suggestive. With sharpness and theoretical vigor, Fokkema applies to the history of literature the semiological concept of code that Roland Barthes, Umberto Eco, and Yuri Lotman had already incorporated into the study of the literary text.[70] To comment briefly on this work, I would point out that three things must be taken into consideration here: one, the idea of historical code; two, its use in practice (the works of Fokkema regarding modernism and postmodernism); and three, a certain constituent attitude or methodological posture regarding the science of literature. What concerns us here is the first. The second is evolving, and its results may not be as new or surprising as the theoretical models that make them possible.[71] In this book I agree, moderately or modestly, with some aspects of Fokkema's methodological posture,[72] but not with its general desire for rupture (see Chapter 13). In the Low Countries—think of Rien Segers[73]—as well as in France and certain universities in the United States, the desire for rupture is a sincere expression of boredom with the academic tradition or with the *antipassatismo* that Poggioli attributed to the avant-garde and movements of the neo-avant-garde, but that cannot be attributed to postmodernism, which has a completely contrary character.

According to Fokkema, the three principal modes of conceiving the object of literary studies are: (1) as a text accepted as literature by groups of readers at a certain time; (2) as a situation or process of communication (*communication-situation*) in which a sender transmits to a receiver what the receiver accepts as literature; and (3) as the code used by the sender and accepted as such by the receiver for the purpose of communication.[74] Based both on the semiological theory of communication and on reception theory, this triple definition assumes some important premises. The literary text is not an unchanging "monument" but "an assembly of signs that in differing contexts can be interpreted differently."[75] It is essential to keep in mind the social and historical conditions of the process of communication, that is, the context of the reception and the historicity of the reader. It is not the historian's task to decide that this or that interpretation is proper or mistaken, since every interpretation belongs to a specific reception and its context. This means that the historian's own critical evaluations—his own interests—are excluded from his work.

It would be anomalous if a theory did not encounter difficulties (challenges and incentives for the determined thinker), and the paradigm proposed by Fokkema and other theorists is no exception. I ask myself three questions, the first of which was formulated by Fokkema himself. How can one limit or identify the receivers—individuals, genders, classes, and so on? In regard to the three definitions of the object of study, how can one deny the historicity—proclivities and interests—of the scientist of literature? As for the third definition, how can the historian-scientist avoid functioning also as critic, or simply as reader, when analyzing the components of a code—choosing, emphasizing, citing, and so forth?[76] Leaving these perplexities aside, let us see how codes are incorporated into historiography. Yuri Lotman looks at the poetic, semiological, and structural codes simultaneously and makes a distinction between the codes used by the sender to execute a communication and those used by the reader to receive or decipher the message. A plurality of codes is characteristic of the artistic phenomenon, so when different codes are applied to a unique text, the text divides itself in different ways into operative signs:

> The difference of interpretation of works of art is a daily phenomenon, and in spite of current opinion, it does not result from just any accessory or easily eluded causes, but is organically proper to art. It is, at least visibly, precisely to this particularity that is linked the capacity, noted earlier, that art possesses to enter into correlation with the reader and to give him exactly the information he needs, the perception for which he is prepared.[77]

No communication can take place if the codes of the reader and those of the author do not intersect. According to Lotman, the codes in both cases belong to two principal categories: the linguistic, inseparable from every verbal communication; and the literary, or rather, the literary art considered as a special language composed of special conventions—genres, styles, or specific artistic tendencies—that "are inserted into the complex hierarchy of the artistic languages of a given era, a given culture, a given people or a given humanity." [78] Well then, how are these codes to be arranged? Fokkema suggests that five stand out; however, there may be more, which would increase the possible richness of the message and at the same time oblige both sender and receiver to choose between the multiple options of codification and decipherment. Fokkema's five codes are: (1) the linguistic code, which makes it possible for a reader to receive a text written in English, for example, as such; (2) the literary code, which prepares a reader to read the text as literature, or rather, as a text shaped by a desire for coherence, by connotations of a certain type, by metaphors and other procedures; (3) the generic code, which instructs a reader in advance regarding certain expectations and omissions belonging to the genre selected;[79] (4) the code appropriate to the period and the group (*group code*), on the basis of which the reader applies his knowledge of the conventions of a particular semiotic period or a particular community; and (5) the author's idiolect, which also functions as code to the extent that it possesses some recurrent and distinguishing traits.

Fokkema points out that in choosing among the options offered by one of these codes, the author limits the possibilities of the others—for example, the selection of a genre conditions the uses of the linguistic or the literary code. Fokkema also observes that the historicity of some codes is greater than that of others, meaning that the continuity of generic conventions is conspicuous in these cases, as are many procedures belonging to the literary code. For this reason, the characteristic code of a period or group, the *sociocode*, lends itself best to historiography. The historian must concentrate on determining the dominant sociocode of a specific period, such as modernism:[80] "the code forged by a group of writers often belonging to a particular generation, a literary movement or current, and accepted by its contemporary or later readers."[81] Some outstanding inclinations differentiate modernists from one another: the conception of the text as indefinite (Valéry), epistemological doubt, the example of the metalinguistic commentary (Gide), the role conceded to the reader. It is understood that this dominant code has to be inserted into "the succession of literary systems," as well as into the succession of periods, whose internal multiplicity remains beyond doubt.[82]

This semiological approach to the system of conventions employed by movements, schools (going back to a more remote past), and literary currents is perfectly compatible with the broader idea of polysystem, and also with the polyphonic concept of period. In effect, by emphasizing the sociocode, or code of the innovator group, that is, the newness or original contribution of the dominant movement or current, Fokkema leaves the relation to conventions originating in the past to be defined later, along with the recuperations and intermittent durations that we discussed earlier in this chapter, including the history of translations, the reissue of books, and theatrical revivals; the definition of these connections is precisely the task of the polysystem. Without doubt within every polysystem and every period the functioning of two dialectics must be clarified. The first is the one existing between the innovator code of the group, or sociocode, and the remaining codes (linguistic, literary, generic), which are no less proper as history because they follow slower rhythms of change. The second is the one found between the totality of codes employed by the sender or author (because the system of conventions studied by Fokkema is essentially limited to them) and the repertoire of codes employed by the highly diverse group of receivers or readers—of different types, according to Lotman—some of whom continue to read and interpret with the aid of codes belonging to earlier currents or periods, which are thus superimposed during the act of reading. Not only do we often read the old with a focus projected by the new, but we read the new following habits retained from the practice of the old.

I have always considered it evident that the history of literature cannot be reduced to the itinerary of novelty, the innovations of the moment. (Innovation often perceived by later generations and not by contemporaries. Rimbaud's contemporaries were reading Verlaine.) This objection becomes irrefutable if such a history consists in large part of the memory of what was read. (Who knows whether Tristan Tzara read Montaigne on the sly? or whether André Breton secretly read Agatha Christie?) By allowing room for countless readings and readers we risk opening chasms between the ones and the others, shattering periods and systems.

The foundations of reading—that is, the historical environs that make it possible—indeed maintain their integrity in the seven theses proposed by Hans Robert Jauss in his celebrated programmatic essay of 1967 (translated into English in 1982). *Erwartungshorizont* can be translated as "horizon of expectation" (or expectancy) and also "of expectations." The genitive can be plural, but not the nominative: "horizon of expectations," the most prominent integrating term among those proposed by Jauss in writings that have decisively influenced our conception of the history of literature. Without attempting to summarize them here I would like to comment primarily on the concept of *event,* whose absence can be noted in the proposals just presented—movement, current, system, code—all of a periodological character. These terms configure the evolution, order the multitude of authors, works, and even literatures; but they seem to float above the string of events, offering parallel structures, as if historical discourse were not able to approach the past as past, *in fieri:* the past of those who lived it not only as authors but also as readers, as Jauss demonstrated in masterly fashion.

The process of communication that is a manifestation of the literary phenomenon is also a process of increasing historicity.[83] The passage from the sender to the receiver assumes two things: first, that the text is made concrete and becomes real in the reading. After the work of Roman Ingarden and Wolfgang Iser,[84] we understand more clearly today that it is the reader who fills in the blank spaces, compensates for silences, completes allusions, responds to questions, refuses or agrees to be persuaded, listens to the two speakers of a dialogue, restores norms, explores meanings; in sum, the reader himself engages in a dialogue with the text. But the reception cannot end there. The reader, gradually changed by what he has read, which may not coincide at all with his previous cultural disposition or set of conventions, goes on to discover a different horizon of expectations. A writer is obliged to take this change into consideration. New works emerge that manipulate, rectify, or refute the complex of conventions accepted by readers. So subsequent processes, evolutionary and proper to history, are joined with the process of the unique reading (always assuming that we use the word *evolutionary* without teleological intent and keep in mind the collisions and ruptures as the Russian Formalists did). A series of productions and of receptions—of works produced, read, and so on—make up the links of this constant relation, always renewed, between the works and their receivers.

An act of reading that took place in the past, *in illo tempore,* when a certain work first appeared, implies contact with the horizon of expectations then in view—a system of prior knowledge of genres, forms, themes, and "the opposition between the poetic and the practical function of language" (the second thesis of 1967).[85] Such a horizon did not remain at a distance or on the outside, but on the contrary was incorporated into the aesthetic life experience of the work, participating in its perception in ways often foreseen by the author. There is a changing and successive connection between reading and horizon that affects and modifies both. The contact of the innerness of a work with the outerness of the system encloses an "aesthetic distance" (third thesis) that is not limited to the surprise of innovation. Jauss knows very well (fifth thesis) that innovation alone cannot assure artistic value (as the Russian Formalists insisted). The aesthetic distance is due to the dimension that distinguishes the world of the reader from the work he reads—work conceived not as a simple reflection of the given, as a certain branch of neo-Marxism maintained, but as a process of shaping realities and levels of consciousness. The historian reconstructs the horizons and the aesthetic distances contained in some past era—which are not merely subjective but rather collective or transsubjective—while keeping in mind the resulting critical judgments and evaluations. He always works with a clear understanding of the hermeneutic abyss that separates that past from his own present and from the conditionings of his own capacity for evaluation. The conventions, poetics, and norms of the past era made certain interpretations possible, but not others. The others came later, extending the virtualities of the text as it came into contact with new horizons. Without putting aside forgotten and resurrected works, earlier called intermittent durations by George Kubler, this succession of differences sketches the history of reception, which is both a past process in motion (not *post festum,* Jauss says) and the recapture of that process from the standpoint of the ineluctable, functional, and primary difference of the present.[86]

Does the horizon of expectations coincide with the system? Jauss himself tries to link them in the sixth thesis of his 1967 essay. It must be possible, he said, to study a phase of a literary evolution by taking a synchronic cross-section, to arrange the heterogeneous multiplicity of contemporaneous works in equivalent, opposing, and hierarchical structures, and in that way to discover an overarching system of relationships in the literature of a moment of history. The moment a synchronic cross-section is made, this system (or better, polysystem, precisely in view of its heterogeneity) is opened to a variety of works that may be real or unreal, premature or late, because the cross-section, the slice, reveals the coexistence of distinct temporal curves. Earlier in this chapter, I commented on this multiplicity of durations.[87] Thus Jauss incorporates the horizon of expectations into a totalizing historical system. I accept Lotman's distinction between the code of the author and that of the reader. No matter how familiar the reader may be with the latest poetic creations, his horizon of expectations obviously cannot be the same as that of a writer of the first rank, neither an innovator like Joyce nor an epigone like Lampedusa: in both cases there is disparity. This *décalage* can be investigated with the help of the differentiations proposed by Fokkema. Since the process of communication is based on a plurality of codes, the reader's horizon of expectations can be assimilated, *grosso modo*, to Fokkema's first three codes—the linguistic, the literary, and the generic—and the writer's system of conventions to the last two, the sociocode and the idiolect. Clearly both sets of codes are integrated into the same polysystem.

Of course these historical totalities are not events. The event, or happening, without which there would be no narrative history but only description,[88] occurs within the enveloping polysystem. But the term *event* is not used to designate just anything that happens. An event is not a fact or simply a bit of historical data. From among the many things that occur, the historian selects and brings to the fore the ones that seem significant and worthy of being linked to what happened before or later; in this way he assumes the role of a narrator. Choosing involves excluding whatever does not seem to have been an event (*nonevent*), as Roger Bastide's definition makes clear:

> The outline of the event is detached from that gray background and that uniformity, it is a "cut" in the discontinuity of time, it is what takes on importance either for us (marriage, birth of a child, sickness, and so on) or for a social group (war, revolution, crowning of a king), in brief, in the temporal continuity, whatever seems sufficiently "important" to us to be cut out, put in relief, and capable later of being if not commemorated, at least memorized.[89]

Jauss, who promised a history of literature consisting of events—"eine er-
eignishafte Geschichte der Literatur" [90]—has reflected on this problem in a
splendid essay published in 1973. Jauss notes that the origin of the term—
the Latin *eventus*, from *evenire*, "to take place" or "to take place finally"—
indicates "the not obvious, unexpected outcome of something": "den nicht
selbsverständlichen, unerwarteten Ausgang einer Sache." [91] The event implies the realization and result of a process whose conclusion seems to us
right away as uncertain. The Castilian *evento*—"suceso imprevisto" (un-
foreseen event) says the Dictionary of the Royal Academy—still retains this
dimension of eventuality or uncertain realization, in expressions such as *a
todo evento*, (in any event), which means the same as *pase lo que pase*
(whatever happens/ come what may).

Returning to what we said earlier, a poetical work carries the future
within itself—viewed from the angle not of history *post eventum* but from
history on the move, *in illo tempore* (according to Jauss, *geschehene Geschichte* and *geschehende Geschichte*) history happening and history that
happened. Well then, the activity of the writer—the impulse or élan that
links his works objectively and moves his writing forward—makes possible
a process of communication in which the writer himself, as a person of flesh
and blood, no longer intervenes, but a process whose dénouement lies in
the hands of his readers. The unequal systems or codes of conventions spanning the successive moments of the process lead eventually to the visible
outcome represented by the literary event or happening. In the first instance
as well as the last, the happening results from the work's encounter with the
codes of the readers.

Last but not least, it is worthwhile to keep in mind a very important
aspect in the reception and path of a literary work: its critical and social
effects. Jauss devotes the final (seventh) thesis of his 1967 program to these
effects. It is not enough to find in the literature of all epochs a "typified,
idealized, satirical, or utopian image of social existence." [92] The social function of literature is fulfilled later, again and again, constantly, when the
process of reading reaches and penetrates the horizon of expectations of
man in his everyday life and thereby affects his behavior. That is what Béla
Köpeczi calls the "ideal" effect (*ideelle Wirkung*)—through ideas—of literature: "everything that happened in the socialist countries in the last few
decades—whether in a positive or a negative sense—proves that literature
exerts an effect in the sphere of ideas, an effect that is still larger during the
period of socialist construction than was the case earlier in bourgeois society." [93] Is there any doubt that this effect is a consequence of the aesthetic
experience of the work itself, a critical experience that calls the world about
us into question?

For those who emphasize the later phases of the process, the modified sense of existence that literature refracts is not as interesting as the modification that literature imposes on life itself. That is true for different reasons: the reaction against positivism and biographism; boredom with the interminable labyrinth of causality; and the use of semiological models that focus on the contact between the message and the receiver. But the earlier phases did exist, and so does the appearance of changes in the established images of social existence. Comparativism is not limited to an immanent criticism of literature. The categories that we have glossed here, such as genres, formalizations, thematizations, translations, all presuppose some classes of past and future historical activity. This activity occupies the space of an aesthetic distance—no longer between reader and work, but between work and society—whose theoretical elucidation is a task for linguists and analytic philosophers. The analysis of causality, refined by Louis Althusser, more than anything else continues to preoccupy one strain of Marxist criticism that sees itself in the position of demythifying art as an *ideological* function, having at last abandoned the notion of a work of art as reflection or example.

This function belongs to history, and its effects can be investigated. John Beverley shows that the "production of solitude" by Luis de Góngora, whose final success was especially notable in Latin America (thus colonized by letters), is linked with a view of nature that the court of the Castilian Philip IV (ruled 1621–1665) could assimilate, "because it eludes the comprehension of the vulgar and is situated outside the arena of the market and of money as a means of possession and a determinant of status and power."[94] Góngora, who belonged to a marginal circle of Andalusian aristocrats, managed to *avivar el ingenio,* to exercise wit—as he claims in his "Carta en respuesta" (Letter of response): "one has to admit that it was useful to exercise wit, and this emerged from the poet's obscurity"[95]—and to shape a form of heroic discourse all the more admirable in view of the total decline in heroic action by the Spanish nation of that time. Beverley's essay can be seen as a contribution to the history of reception or *utilidad* (usefulness) of a supreme poet, through direct examination of texts and documents of the period.

Not so for a certain criticism that has a purely and exclusively polemical character or intention: struggle, refutation, combative criticism, at times valuable as a subgenre of literary essay writing but whose coherence is narrowed to criticism of a political *praxis.* It would be naive to try to weigh the rational value of a type of criticism that is second rate because of its reliance on debatable postures. Such occasional essayism (in the sense of

occasional verse) passes judgment on the documenting culture, as Marshall
Sahlins shows (*Culture and Practical Reason,* 1976), and incidentally documents itself.

This type of criticism often does not recognize the specific nature of the
literary phenomenon, one which is not didactic, which presents not disem-
bodied ideas, but rather ideas that are dramatized or expressed in dialogues,
personal experiences, and values. Above all criticism of this kind does not
recognize the specific nature of the history of literature. The specificity of
the history of literature exemplified by the writings of Jauss and so many
others has been convincingly demonstrated.[96] I do not deny the existence of
broad periods and macrohistorical developments encompassed by literary
processes, but an exclusive devotion to such configurations and relations,
subordinating the processes again and again, would suppress all differences
and finally annul the history of literature.

The old concept of ideology as false awareness—the concept held by the
early Marx of *The German Ideology* (1845) or as expressed in Engels' famous letter to Franz Mehring (1893)—that when carried to the extreme
asserts that the literary word is a lie, has given way since Althusser's time
to the idea of ideology as a structural limitation. This limitation is no longer
an illusion, but is among other things the representation and use by an
individual or a social group of an imaginary conception, deformed or inadequate, of the relation of individual or group to the total conditions of
existence.[97] This mutilated vision of the relation of the part to the whole
clearly presupposes the priority of the whole. There is no synecdoche without a prior whole, nor ideology without enveloping totality.

With his usual acumen and generosity of spirit, Fredric Jameson in *The
Political Unconscious* (1981) does not reject outright·a good number of
different methodologies in their entirety but holds them to be usable, inasmuch as his own methodology aspires to be totalizing, integrating, unlimited. An initial postulate is the idea of totality in Lukács or of totalization
in Sartre and Althusser, ideas that allow us to confront the hermeneutic
contradictions of historiography (such as the fusion of horizons proposed
by Hans-Georg Gadamer and Jauss), as well as the "mystery" understood
only with the aid of such a postulate. From the very first, Jameson affirms
the vast macrohistorical unity of the "human adventure":

> This mystery can be reenacted only if the human adventure is one; only
> thus—and not through the hobbies of antiquarianism or the projections of
> the modernists—can we glimpse the vital claims upon us of such long-dead
> issues as the seasonal alternation of the economy of a primitive tribe, the
> passionate disputes about the nature of the Trinity, the conflicting models

of the *polis* or the universal Empire, or, apparently, closer to us in time, the dusty parliamentary and journalistic polemics of the nineteenth-century nation states. These matters can recover their original urgency for us only if they are retold within the unity of a single great collective story.[98]

This multisecular combat—to sweep up the kingdom of Liberty into the kingdom of Necessity, according to Marx in *Das Kapital*—is presented here as theoretically privileged precisely to the extent that it stands out as a unique theme, erasing differences, linking periods and societies through presentation of a total story, directed by a single argument; that is, by appealing to the recourse of unity as the solution a priori of the aporias of hermeneutic history. This struggle, whose reality I do not doubt, does not call for only one interpretation of the past, or one vast narrative conception. Its theme coincides with an ontological intuition—confluence of Being and Time, the Whole and the Part. It is an intuition of the constituent and fundamental totality, and nevertheless absent, ungraspable, invisible, like the face of the Hebrews' God: "Indeed, in some paradoxical or dialectical fashion, Lukács' conception of totality may be said to rejoin the Althusserian notion of History or the real as an 'absent cause.' Totality is not available for representation, any more than it is accessible in the form of some ultimate truth (or moment of Absolute Spirit)." [99] If ideology implies ignorance of this totality, a new word would be needed—totalogy?—for the attitude that condemns any division into parts, and that sacrifices the parts for the sake of a conjecture.

Perhaps the time has come to abandon Schillerian nostalgia for a lost totality. What Fernando Savater resolutely calls the Passion for the Whole—a Whole that would of course be empty were it lacking diversity—perhaps now might be put to rest or left in suspense:

> The Whole is not monochord nor monolithic, except wherever it strictly needs to be so. *The Whole is plural and one: it needs plurality in order to function, unity in order to eternalize its order.* Of the one purely one, of the being without a spark of difference—of not being—one can say only that it is, in its spherical immobility, in its round static state, unproductive, just as Parmenides taught.[100]

Clearly, Jameson's theme is not static. It is enough that his theme does not pretend to be *completely* static to be acceptable and recognizable, bearing much resemblance to what I keep calling a diachronic structure, that is, an option or opposition, or aggregate of options or oppositions, that order certain significant entities over and over again. A diachronic structure is totalizing; it encompasses vast areas, like a very wide span, but without coinciding completely with whatever it structures, or with any totality. Such a structure allows historical and cultural diversity, since it is repeated diachronically. As I have tried to make clear, the best comparativism contrasts totalization to diversification by means of structures that must be discovered, constructed, and continually renewed and enriched as time goes on. Jameson's unique theme can be dominant and primary—determination of such a hierarchy is a privilege and perhaps a duty of the historian—without being the structure of structures or the premise of premises, perfectly complete and accessible. The fact that it is fully interhistorical is sufficient.

The structures revealed by literary comparativism are varied, partial, incomplete; like the history of man and like narrative literature, which, according to Bakhtin, comes nearer to human history as it becomes more open; like the sectors and levels of the worlds in which we live, each of which offers a particular level of integration, depending on the place and the moment, as for example a cultural climate, a community, an institution, a harmonious or quarrelsome family, a peaceful society, or one in a state of war.[101] Totality, integrity, or entirety are not *données,* givens, but the results of human endeavor.

I said in the beginning that comparative literature deals with the systematic study of supranational entities. After our long journey, we can now add that comparativism culminates in a study of the supranational complexes that are diachronic structures—or of diachronic structures that are supranational complexes. In my opinion, the major task of comparative literature is the investigation, explanation, and ordering of *diachronic and supranational structures.*

This triple term—for the sake of brevity shortened to diachronic structures—in each case must make sure that the theme under consideration has passed two initial tests: that of cultural difference (or spatial difference, as I called it earlier) and that of historical (or temporal) difference. A genre, for example, is not a diachronic structure if it has not persisted throughout various historical periods, allowing change to occur. Change is used here in the sense of historical evolution, or—and here I use the concepts of Claus Uhlig (*palingenese, palimpsest, ananke*)—in the senses of being regenerated, rewritten, affecting works that come later. And what is more, a genre is not a diachronic structure if it has not been cultivated in more than one civilization (see Chapter 12) or in various divergent and dissimilar cultures.

The two dimensions taken together—the historical and the cultural—signify the conjunction of the one and the many in the literary field. It is not enough to single out the occurrence of a certain event or a series of events at one definite moment in the past. Otherwise we would become enmeshed in the old atomism that all of us active in the field today are trying to leave behind. A unique event could undoubtedly be important as a moment of history *in illo tempore* (Jauss's *geschende Geschichte*). But in the last analysis, comparativism can be only a current reflection on the history of literature. Just as a meaningful event from the past is separated from the *grisaille* (according to Roger Bastide) of minor incidents, or of trivial *Fakten* (according to Wolf-Dieter Stempel) that go no further,[102] current historical reflection must identify events and other elements, conventions, norms, and values that are intrinsic parts of interhistorical structures, clearly distinguishing them from the inveterate confusion, the unavoidable diversity.

Any genre, any form, any theme—such as those described in Chapters 12–14 of this book—can be considered and analyzed as diachronic stuctures. I am proposing modes of questioning the vast body of knowledge that comparativism now possesses rather than any new ideas. Certainly such questioning brings with it one requirement: the task of structuring. A theme under study must pass three tests: the cultural, the historical, and the structural. Once we identify a genre, form, or theme that seems to be a supranational diachronic structure, we must of necessity investigate those options, relations, semantic, and formal spaces that encompass or link different periods and places: the structures that without coinciding entirely with a period or a place—with some term of an option, some outstanding component of a relation—subsume, or better yet, sum up the multiplicity of facts. Structure is the conceptual desideratum, the historiographic plan that reconciles the one with the many. Diachronic structure is not just the one, and neither is it just the many, but an interhistorical complex.

Without doubt the typological analogies dear to V. M. Zhirmunsky, examined in Chapter 10 under model C of supranationality, can be assimilated to these configurations. But diachronic structure is a more flexible scheme, even though limited to few terms and options. It is wider, since it is not limited to relations based on likeness. Analogy describes common or similar elements. Structure takes in opposite or dissimilar elements, only one of which may appear at a certain moment, while the contrary element may stand out and dominate in another era or nation. In this way, Zhirmunsky could show that parallelism, the predominant poetic form in the heroic poetry of certain peoples of central Asia, gave way after several centuries to metrical count and rhyme. Like others, I have observed that modern free verse has abandoned metrical count and rhyme in favor of parallelism (Chapter 10). In this case, structure is not a descriptive analogy but a conceptual model inferred from history, that is, a theoretical option encompassing dissimilar manifestations. On such occasions, literary theory cannot be allowed to do what I have condemned at various times in this book, namely, to fly off heedlessly toward a universal model based only on knowledge of a single nation, a single writer, or a single period, thereby creating an absolute from the lesson of a single example. The structure of possibilities encompassed by the trajectory of a genre is stretched to the fullest extent when the diverse spaces occupied by it are taken into consideration, a point emphasized earlier in the discussion of pastoral tragicomedy, whose satirical and allegorical value was predominant in eastern Europe. Literary polysystems allow room for contrasting genres—genres and contragenres, as we called them regarding works of Mateo Alemán and Cervantes—works that intersect, allude to each other, or implicate each other back and forth. At the same time, the study of narrative form (for instance, the different attitudes that a narrator may assume vis-à-vis the narrated attitudes ordered typologically by Genette and Stanzel) and the study of semantic spaces that cover in such a contradictory fashion the most enduring themes (like falling in love; Chapter 14) sum up the constellation of responses that make up a diachronic structure throughout the centuries. What Jauss pointed out as happening in poetic work also occurs in the case of themes, forms, or genres: the artistic character and semantic possiblities cannot be immediately perceived from a single horizon of expectations. Jauss, following Gadamer, applies the "logic of question and answer" (*Logik von Frage und Antwort*) to historical tradition,[103] just as diachronic structures owe their continuity—relatively speaking—to the persistence of questions posed by social existence and cultural heritage.

I refer, of course, to reiterations, parallels, affinities, or inversions of a highly varied nature. Some typological analogies allow room for extensive historical developments, whose resemblances must be discovered in a first phase of study and then be analyzed from the point of view of a logical inquiry of questions and answers. I suggest that a study of the emergence of national literatures, an important and complex supranational process, can be an interesting desideratum for a similar type of investigation.

One might think that all emerging literatures follow the same process that in the West includes two fundamental stages: first, the Renaissance (Italy, Spain, France, Portugal, England, Poland, the Low Countries, Germany); and second, the latter half of the eighteenth century and all of the nineteenth for the literatures of the Nordic and eastern European countries (Scandinavia, Hungary, Russia, Yugoslavia, Rumania, the Baltic region, and so on) and of different European nationalities (the Flemish and Catalan, among others). But the differences between the two phases are decisive. It is one thing that a literature exists and quite another that it wishes to come into existence, propelled by a political or cultural plan. This plan—and here is the first question: Does it exist or does it not?—affects the appearance as well as the disappearance of a national literature, like that of the Spanish Moriscos of the sixteenth century, whose desperate will to resist Luce López-Baralt described this way: "the Moriscos were gradually ceasing to be authentic Muslims although—fanaticized by the historical pressures to which they were subjected—to continue to be so was precisely what was of most importance to them." [104] During the nineteenth century the efficacy of a concept of nationality symbolized by the great writers, by a collective consciousness that recognized itself in them, accelerated the birth or rebirth of new or marginal literatures at that time, and thus hastened the twilight of the normative and unifying poetics that had prevailed until the eighteenth century. The existence of an Arcipreste de Hita or a Chaucer would not have been enough: a consciousness of literary nationality would come later for the countries that participated in the Renaissance and the baroque. [105] Other options exist jointly with this alternative, owing to the multiple co-ordinates—linguistic, geographic, political—that affect the process. Does the maturity of a national literature go hand in hand with a country's use of its own language, or does it presuppose the use of a language cultivated in other places (German, in the case of Austria)? Is there opposition to the continued use of the language of colonizers (Castilian in America, French in Africa)? Or, in the case of marginal nationalities, is there resistance to the predominance of the national tongue (Occitania, Catalonia)?

Furthermore, in the case of literatures interrupted after the Renaissance, the two principal phases that I just mentioned are superimposed, making room not for a first but a second awakening (*Wiedererweckung*) of Provençal and Catalan poetry, as well as poetries of various nationalities of eastern Europe during the nineteenth century. Of course, this development is gradual. The revolt of 1821 in Rumania did not suddenly bring about any great cultural improvements, and even after 1848, advances in journalism and the theater preceded the slow maturation of an elevated poetry by several decades. [106] In the countries of eastern Europe, patriots, scientists, and journalists were the first to become prominent; but the most authentic poets "appear only in the second or third generation of the reawakening." [107] The moribund Aljamia-Moorish poetry of the sixteenth century (Spanish written in Arabic script) "consists mostly of utilitarian and prose-litizing texts." [108] But such a process also assumes different forms according to various political, geographic, and linguistic coordinates. In Estonia, Ivar Ivask says, the first unique poet whose given name and surname are known, after centuries of oral literature, is Kristjan Jaak Peterson (1801–1822); but only in the 1930s does a generation of poets appear, who had been educated entirely in Estonian, the generation of Betti Alver.[109] In the Philippines a decisive confrontation and rivalry existed between languages in use there: Balagtas (Francisco Baltazar, 1789–1862) wrote *Florante at Laura* in Tagalog, and at the same time a promising literature in Castilian was emerging (José P. Rizal, *Noli me tangere,* 1887), spoiled by the introduction of English. All of this contributed to the push for cultural independence and enabled writings in the predominant native Philippine language to emerge.[110] Let us also remember the role played by literary magazines (the *Sydney Gazette,* which initiated Australian literature in 1803);[111] the role of critics and theorists; that of great and prominent writers (A. D. Hope, Patrick White in Australia); and that of painting and other forms of visual culture, as Alexandru Dutu brings out in the case of Rumania.[112]

To end this reflection on supranational structures, let me now propose another brief example, also offered as desideratum, or plan of study.

Let us look at the anthology. To what category—generic, formal, thematic—can it be assigned? An anthology is a collective intratextual form that presumes the rewriting or re-elaboration on the part of a reader of already existing texts by making them part of new entities. Reading is its starting point and its destiny, since the author is a reader who assumes the right to direct the reading of others, intervening in the reception of multiple poets, modifying the horizon of expectations of his contemporaries. Writer of the second rank, the anthologist is a superreader of the very first rank. Without doubt anthologists fulfill an indispensable function, since we find them in the most diverse cultures and civilizations, including primitive and exclusively oral ones. Moreover, it is difficult to conceive of the existence of a culture without canons, authorities, and instruments of autoselection. I mentioned earlier the famous *Mu'allaqāt* of Hammad al-Rawiyah (eighth century), which shaped the paradigm of the *qasida,* preceding many other collections of Arabic poetry. The most ancient poems of the Dravidian communities of southern India (from the first to third centuries) are conserved in eight anthologies, which followed the example of earlier Sanskrit collections.[113] This type of emulation has occurred quite frequently, the affirmation of one culture in face of a more powerful or prestigious one. The first anthologies in Japan, the beginning of true Japanese poetry, starting with the *Man'yōshū* of the eighth century, represented something like a *défense et illustration* of a national art in face of the illustrious and established models collected in the most ancient anthologies of China. We could say the same regarding the first important collection of Persian poetry, the *Lubāb al-albab* of Muhammad 'Aufi (ca. 1221), which appeared side by side with the poetry and the *ars poetica* of the dominant Arabs, to whom Persian writers owed a great deal.

So then, after recapitulation and study, a diachronic structure should offer a series of options and variations. As for anthologies, I would immediately propose the following (without going into great detail: the reader can add his own examples):

1. The anthologist is interested in the past (including the origins of a culture, mythic or religious, such as Ki No Tsurayuki, referred to in the prologue of *Kokinshu*, dedicated to the emperor of Japan in 905) or else in the present (the Provençal collections; *Tottel's Miscellany*, 1557; in Spain, Gerardo Diego and J. M. Castellet).

2. The anthology is either collective or is limited to a single author (to a Provençal troubadour; to the subject of an Arabic *diwan*).

3. The anthologist omits historical time, spatializing it, converting it into present time, or else relies on chronology as the principle of presentation. Some collections are purely thematic—or, until the eighteenth century, divided into rhetoric and poetics. In general, simple chronological arrangements, not apparent in Europe until well into the nineteenth century, have remained in a minority.

4. The anthologist can choose not to be restricted to a national culture, and opt instead for a genre, a particular thematic approach (*humour noir*, feminism), and so on. In general, nationalism, or simply the need felt by a culture to erect its own canons and authorities, has been by far the principal motive for anthologies. There have been two fundamental moments in modern Europe: first, the Renaissance, above all in Italy, which was faced with a superabundance of classical models and also the feeling that its own great poets were already *antichi* (very ancient). With *I fiori delle rime de' poeti illustri* (1558), Girolamo Ruscelli made the compilation into what Agostino Gobbi would call a small library, *piccola libreria*, thanks to printing.[114] In England during Shakespeare's time, the commercial motives of the anthologists are evident. The second moment for anthologies was the eighteenth century, when the Herderian concept of national culture would lead sooner or later to the confection of "Parnassuses" and "Treasuries" through which a nascent literature could proclaim its value and independence. In Spain this trend began with Juan José López de Sedano's *Parnaso español* (1768) and Antonio de Capmany's *Teatro histórico-crítico* (1786).

5. Anthologies tend to be militantly conservative; through them, past achievements are converted into models for the future. They can even be thought of as a kind of microcosmos reflecting the structures of a society.

For example, *El libro de las banderas de los campeones* (The Banners of the Champions), compiled in 1243 by Ibn Sa'id al-Magribi, who was from Al-calá la Real, arranges 145 poets by geographic zones—Spain, North Africa, Sicily—and within each of those segments by social and professional rank, according to the following hierarchy: kings, ministers, noblemen, lawyers, grammarians, men of letters, and poets. For Granada an even more humble class existed: women.[115] But the opposite may also occur, and the anthologist may go against the current. In China the anthologist was usually a defender of tradition, but James Hightower points out that a sixth-century erotic collection, the *Yü-t'aihsin-yung* of Hsü Ling (506–583), freed itself not only from the classics but also from the conception of literature as guide to behavior.[116]

6. What are the criteria of selection? Fame? artistic perfection, the precepts of art? pedagogical usefulness, ideological function? Many scholarly texts of the late sixteenth and the seventeenth centuries pillage an earlier selection, the *Epigrammata Graeca* of Johannes Soter (1525), expurgating it and using it—in the case of the Jesuits—for the teaching of Latin.[117] One of the most astute observations on this subject was made by Agostino Gobbi in the prologue to his *Scelta de sonetti e canzoni de' più eccellenti rimatori d'ogni secolo* (fourth ed., 1744–1749). Gobbi does not exclude the well-known poems recognized by others but also does not limit himself to the perfect ones, "since in poetic matter, the beauty does not consist so much in its being flawless, as in its having some excellent virtues." Gobbi includes the source-poems, those that made possible later and better ones; but when dealing with Petrarch, his favorite poet, he finds himself obliged to choose between *lo bueno e l'ottimo,* the good and the best. Even when they are merely good, Petrarch's poems are superior to the best ones written by others. But Gobbi's posture is not arrogant, nor does he forget the "rule of art laid down by others" in accordance with "our own age," nor does he fail to consult with others.

7. To what extent are the single pieces of an anthology integrated into a whole? The degree of integration or of intertextuality does, of course, vary; however, a unifying intention is almost always present, above all when the anthology, like the Japanese ones, is arranged thematically or in accordance with a conception of national originality; or if a Goethean idea prevails, like that of Francis Turner Palgrave in his *Golden Treasury* (1861), reissued countless times, and for whom the different poems compose one single great Poem, written in collaboration with all its authors;[118] or if the selection represents a recommendation and praise of brevity, like the *Anthologia Graeca,* which contains mostly epigrams.[119]

8. Is the anthologist also a critic? When the diverse parts have already been gathered and arranged, a vision of the whole and a theory are almost irresistible. Sometimes the anthologist leaves the words to the poets, and we have a collection that is a collaborative effort. On other occasions, the compiler disclaims any knowledge of poetry and concentrates on practical aspects, like someone who says, "This is what it is." But definitions are quite common, as for example the one found in the prologue to the Japanese *Kokinshu* of 905: "poetry exists to let the heart express itself through things seen and heard. The song of the nightingale is in the flowers; in the water is the voice of the frog." [120] Or the didactic concept of literature that Wei Hung (first century) demonstrated in his prologue to the *Shih Ching*: poetry is "the emotive expression of self-willed thought." [121] The anthologist acts not merely as a mirror of the past, but as someone who expresses or puts into practice an idea of what is literary, fixing genres, emphasizing models, affecting the reader's sense of the present, and, above all, directing the reader's eyes toward the future. In that case we find that the anthologist is also simultaneously a critic and a superreader: a critic who characterizes and defines what is given; a superreader who arranges and redisposes the given, making contemporary systems real, giving an impulse to what will be. The option then is to be or not to be an anthologist, that is, an "I" who ceases to be a private person and aspires to be a "we."

Thus the experiences of unity and diversity, continuity and change, touch and intertwine. I said that the goal of comparativism is to identify, order, and study supranational and diachronic structures. I call them structures because the complexes under consideration make it possible to bring out not just single terms but options, alternatives, oppositions, discrepancies, and other interrelations made up of dissimilar elements, all within the same field. These structures are patently supranational if they result from the examination of more than one civilization or a sufficient number of divergent cultures, and to the extent that they span different historical periods, they strike us as also diachronic. For instance, we just noted the astonishing supranationality of the anthology. And earlier we saw that the theme of falling in love, as investigated by Jean Rousset, should have made possible an elucidation not only of norms but also of counternorms; not only detours and infractions *(écarts et transgressions)* but also options open to equally valid terms *(Daphnis and Chloe* as opposed to *Theagenes and Chariclia).* We noted how the alternative parallelism/antiparallelism derived from Zhirmunsky's work enriched the radical reductionism of the Jakobsonian thesis by way of diachrony.

I am reviewing this evidence in order to make very clear that a perception of the one and the many, a perception that differentiates and structures at the same time, is incompatible with two tendencies of critical thinking: reductionism and ahistoricity. In this connection I would like to mention René Etiemble's *invariants* and Yuri Lotman's culturology.

Etiemble's *invariant* is "a universal and common element of literature and/or of literary thought." [122] An element whose global extension and temporal reiteration are manifest—a genre such as the elegy, a theme such as the flower—can be seen as universal. But that is only the first phase of discovery and confirmation; normally the next phase consists in attempting to structure the differences. That is in fact what Etiemble himself often tries to do, after first going in search of precursors and parallels: the Arabic encyclopedists of the tenth century were forerunners of Diderot; the Hegelian dialectic of the master and the slave appears earlier in Lesage; the idea of Rimbaud's *Sonnet des voyelles* goes back to the eighteenth century; and so on. [123] I do not deny that universals exist in comparative literature as well as in linguistics, but they cannot be circumscribed to the terrain of analogies. We run the risk that a "simultaneous reading" [124] of these universals might strand us in an atemporal and classisist order à la T. S. Eliot. And above all I hold the option universal/particular to be excessively simple, or simplifying. *Tertium datur:* what I keep calling here diachronic structure, that is, a complex of relations linking change with continuity, difference with analogy, particularity with generality.

In the writings of Yuri Lotman the semiotic model of culture leads to critical consequences that are greatly superior to the theoretical schemes of earlier writers. In my opinion, a typology of cultures, viewed as modalities of information, leads either to structural anthropology, of very doubtful applicability to written literature, to say the least, or to a reductionist periodization that, like Michel Foucault's intellectual archaeology, looks a great deal like the old *Geistesgeschichte*. Lotman is of course aware of the inadequacies of reductionism, and so tries to drag in by main force centrifugal and marginal codes, such as Bakhtin's Carnival, through "the very beginning of alternativeness." [125] Let us read from "On the Semiotic Mechanism of Culture" (written with B. A. Uspenski):

> The affirmations "Everything is multiple and cannot be described with any general scheme" and "Everything is unique, and we do nothing more than face the infinite variations of an unvarying model" in one form or another are continually repeated in the history of culture, from Ecclesiastes and the ancient dialecticians down to our own day; and it is not by chance: such assertions describe different aspects of the unifying mechanism of the culture and are inseparable, in their recriprocal tension, from its essence. [126]

So then the unifying mechanism of a culture absorbs everything, and the way to transcend its limits is more or less what Lévi-Strauss postulates: diverse cultures integrate the components of a vast universal repertoire. I have already said elsewhere that this conjecture (either neo-Kantian or neurological) is neither debatable nor necessary.[127] Between the unifying mechanism of culture and the human brain we lose sight of the differential force of real events and the abrupt, unpredictable, discontinuous, intermittent contour of the history of literature and other arts. Christian Delacampagne wrote concerning Lévi-Strauss: "The risk of such an approach is to forget that a myth is also a slice of the real that can transmit knowledge, translate a vision of the world; that an 'isolated' myth is is any case an abstraction, since myths exist only in a situation, being inserted in a natural and social context." [128]

Not so the historical and supranational entities that comparatists bring to light. These entities encompass elements—themes, forms, genres, movements, systems—that have actually existed. But the entity itself is a structure of relations, entirely typical of the activity that William Dray held to be proper for the historian, as we saw earlier ("the operative notion is less of discovering necessary and sufficient conditions than of relating parts, at first not seen as such, to a whole of some kind").[129] Some people have experienced an event A; others, many years later or far removed in terms of cultural space, have experienced an event B; and it is the historian who discovers the structure that shelters both events. I do not say that the historian reveals a common structure, because as a matter of literature the significant entity can imply both isomorphism—the typological analogies of Zhirmunsky—and heteromorphism—man is a "little world" as harmonious as the cosmos, or man is a little world as contradictory and fragmented as the context of modern life. Discrepancies are as revealing of structure as are analogies. In neither case is the historian of literature limited to a single period, to the codes that govern a single culture, or to a chain of successive moments. For example, the avant-garde movement in the widest sense of the term, the one developed by Poggioli, embraces different periods and currents from Romanticism to the present, including intermissions and interruptions. The emergence of national literatures whose study I sketched some pages back takes on a different coloration after the Renaissance and after the appearance of the idea of cultural nationalism in the eighteenth century. Comparativism relates, structures, constructs, without yielding to that degree of mental violence (or of pseudo-pre-Socratic simplification, as in Saveter's statement, "Everything is water") that usually implies reductionism.[130] Because, of course, historical structures are erected.

Confronted by the groupings that investigation brings to light, the comparatist elaborates a complex historical model, and I do not feel it necessary to recapitulate the rightness of this approach. Neither limited to some invariables nor dependent on absent or conjectural totalities, the model requires the construction of provisional and rectifiable schemes. Like all working hypotheses, the model is not merely inductive, since in practice we erect provisional structures of description that guide later observations and investigations, relating the structures to empirical situations that we wish to connect.[131]

Despite the vogue of certain theories of an absolutist cast, I do not believe that the perspective presented here is a minority one today. The volume *Sur l'actualité des lumières. Aufklärung heute* (1983), for example, includes a number of contributions that emphasize the diversity of the eighteenth century. Roland Mortier, an expert and eminent comparatist, has written:

> As a whole, the Europe of the Enlightenment offers the spectacle of an extraordinary diversity, in which intellectual oppositions and historical imbalances create a prodigiously complex mosaic. Liberals, revolutionaries, adepts of enlightened despotism are strange bedfellows, just as atheists, deists, and believers are. The variety of the Enlightenment is precisely one of its most typical characteristics: it possessed neither dogma nor credo, but rather a certain number of ideals, sufficiently supple to be adapted to very diverse mentalities.[132]

Certainly Mortier tries to comprehend some real dimensions of the century of Enlightenment, but his success results from a differential model of comparatism that I would call a structural model also: open to the interrelations encompassing not only uniformities and analogies, but also oppositions and dissimilarities. The perspective of the present and the object of investigation of the past touch each other and are mutually enriched. Perhaps this is the "fusion of horizons" extolled by Gadamer and Jauss.

This differential and structural model, either of literary history or of literature itself, undoubtedly arises from a real historical situation and fulfills significant functions at the present time; otherwise, the compenetration of horizons would not have occurred. It is not easy to analyze functions relating to our own environment and certain problems that are so close to us. And yet a minimum of hermeneutic rigor requires that we question such functions and problems, and that from the vantage point of our horizon, we ask ourselves what forms literature assumes today. To describe a system of the past, using suitable methods, is very different from trying to understand the system operating in our own time; or rather, since we are not speaking of autohistory, to perceive the primary positions, the bases, from which we interpret literature, "the curve drawn by our existence and our experience," as the hermeneuticists say.[133]

In his old age the great Erich Auerbach wrote a wise and melancholy essay, "Philologie der Weltliteratur" (1952), in which he attempted to divine the future of a philology that would be devoted to the literature of the world. The idea of *Weltliteratur*, he said, presupposes a plurality of distinct cultures. But life is becoming uniform throughout the planet. Even the newest and most active nationalist movements tend toward technological ends and similar forms of existence. This process of concentration leads to a single literary culture, "and with that the idea of a world literature would be both realized and destroyed." At the same time the idea of an inner history of man, our principal myth, is endangered or seems to be unrealizable: to understand man through his history, through "a history of a humanity that has attained self-expression." Indubitably we know more every day and dispose of a superabundance of materials that span many centuries and more than fifty literary languages; but that does not mean that we understand the common destiny of peoples any better. Actually, the degree of specialization is increasing. Methods, collateral bodies of knowledge, the influences of related disciplines, all abound. "In any case, our philological home is the earth; it can no longer be the nation . . . but only in separation, in overcoming can it become effective." [134] Between nation and world, distinct cultures and unique nascent culture, the synthesis that we will need becomes more urgent and more arduous, more remote and unreachable every day.

   We do not know what Auerbach have thought forty years later. I do know that an awareness of history linked to a common preoccupation with man's destiny has neither diminished nor disappeared; on the contrary, it is spreading and being expressed today in literature, the arts, and thought, perhaps producing the best fruits of our age. But this awareness no longer looks back, as Auerbach did in following the long road of his *Mimesis,* in order to trace the trajectory of uninterrupted progress, or to total up the advances of a self-satisfied civilization. The disillusionment felt during the postwar years by those who earlier had viewed the future with optimism will not recur, because optimism as a general atmosphere hardly survives; nor is the future regarded simply as a logical consequence or desired outcome of the integrity of history. In the absence of such historical integrity, the task of a writer, an investigator, or a scholar does not involve undertaking vast and ambitious syntheses. Our projects are usually analytic and partial; partial like the vision of some worlds that we no longer perceive as synthesizable wholes. It is not a question of accumulating more knowledge but of structuring what we have, of taking in not quantity but diversity and richness, of being open to ever-wider spaces with the purpose of discovering not uniformities but significant relations, problems that can be analyzed in depth, options available before an uncertain, unknown, different future. In this way, the knowledge and experience of literatures become a differential tool for enriching our lives and a method for resisting or transcending technological standardization and political subordination.

Today we find that we are as far removed from nineteenth-century nationalism as we are from the easy cosmopolitanism of the eighteenth-century variety. Literature catapults us suddenly and unexpectedly into supranationality: that is, into our real environment, the one that is, that exists, for the reader as well as for the listener and the spectator of the other arts; in other words, an environment that is completely contrary to the internationalism practiced by states, statesmen, the superpowers, by regional or world institutions. That kind of internationalism is a realistic compromise, a political policy, a strategic manipulation, or a defense of national interests. From the historical point of view, the term *nationalism* is an invention of the nineteenth century.[135] As Francisco Ayala explains, the theory of nationalism formulated by Fichte and the thinkers of the Romantic era at the beginning of that century was a reaction against Napoleon's domination, and at the same time the use of the revolutionary spirit he engendered in order to promote the unification of distinct European countries.[136] That unification, once achieved, often led states to simplify violently the cultural diversity within their own borders as well in other countries. But the supranationality of art and of thought is not a hoax. Art, asserted Croce—like Goethe—expresses what is individual and generally human, but not that spiritual pseudocategory called nation: "art *qua* art being always individual and always universal, and therefore always above nationality."[137] We already saw (Chapter 2) that, as Claude Esteban puts it, poetry ascends to the immense boughs of a single tree from some local roots. Artists live the adventure of the continuous search, the exploration of otherness, the discovery of the not seen and not heard because they are, in the words of Eduardo Chillida, "men who question, who maintain an attitude of wonder before the unknown."[138] That being so, supranationality, the object of our search, does not offer us completed totalities, nor does it place us in a familiar, comfortable, well-arranged environment. The exploration of the richness of the world, the worlds, is an open process that does not immediately yield to a stable and intelligible cosmopolitanism, because the prescient cultural cosmos, as opposed to the scientific one, is yet to be structured; that is, as a total order, it does not yet exist. Guy Scarpetta declares eloquently that today's cosmopolitanism is going through a period of dispersion, of changeable interrogation, of multiplication, and of the rebellion of literature against its origins, myths, archetypes, radical bonds.[139] Rather than being drawn to an eighteenth-century utopia, we feel ourselves akin to the peregrination prized by medieval thinkers such as Hugh of St. Victor, who wrote the following words (*Didascalicon* III.20): "It is the great founding principle of virtue that the mind gradually trained learns first to alter entirely these things of a visible and transitory nature, that the mind then is able even to abandon them. That mind is still tender for whom the homeland is sweet, but brave for whom the whole world is a homeland, and truly mature for whom the entire world is a place of exile."[140]

To sum up, the antithesis national/universal does not come into question. The dialectic part/whole is essentially what concerns us and engages us as readers, historians, critics, theorists. We enter the circle of the dance, the *Zirkel im Verstehen* or interpretative circle, more or less knowingly; and the hermeneutic approach affects our own concept of literature and perhaps of life itself.

In examining the realities around us, or those in which we live, José Ferrater Mora speaks of three notions: systems, levels, and continua. A system is a composite of elements tightly and precisely connected to one another, such as the system of the atom or that of whole numbers. So although, according to what we know, literary entities brought together by comparativism are interrelations endowed with a systematic character, Ferrater Mora's term *level* is more apt for literature:

> In contrast to "system," I understand by "level" an assemblage of elements and structures formed by those elements, so that the properties and functions of these elements and of structures are explicable within a determined conceptual framework, that is, by means of ideas applicable only to the level or to some part of the level. Thus, a conceptual framework formed by ideas such as the "elementary particle," "force," "field," "resistance," "velocity," and so on is applicable to the level, and only to that particular level, of the physical elements and structures.[141]

We already saw with regard to Northrop Frye's theoretical plan (Chapter 9) that literary genres as well as periods and other general terms make up conceptual frameworks within or from which the reader and the critic perceive basic observable facts.[142] We also saw that these concepts are instrumental models that help us perceive facts but that are at the same time themselves modified by the facts. Perhaps certain microforms, such as rhetoric and other traditional forms resistant to change, could be likened to elementary particles on the level designated by physics. But it is not only the conceptual framework that changes when we are dealing with literature; the determination of the basic elements depends on the notions that make up the framework. For example, if we adopt Jauss's perspective, the horizon of expectations simultaneously intervenes in the reading of a work and is changed by it, in a constant movement of action and reaction. This to-and-fro, this knitting and unraveling of the consistency and coherence of the level, is fundamental and inevitable. We do not find a stable reality in the cultural terrain. From the point of view of a reader who experiences and interprets texts and notions available to him, reality is a process, critically renewable, tested repeatedly, open to additions, negations, and other transformations. Rather than remaining static, the level encompasses an intermittent process in which historical as well as individual forces are in play. After the experience of unity—of any conceptual framework whatever, or of the totality of known frameworks of a certain moment—comes a perception of differences that in turn contributes to the process, challenging and rejuvenating our unifying vision of the level.

In fact the analysis of this process is what Jauss and his group of collaborators of "Poetik und Hermeneutik" practice when tackling a problem such as modernity.[143] In a brilliant essay, Enzo Caramaschi demonstrates to what extent the proposals of hermeneutics pare and at the same time propel and enrich the actual history of literature: "at the heart of every critical process we find again the 'circle,' like a force of propulsion that conditions us at the same time."[144] Hermeneutic criticism is a lesson in authenticity. Literature as All, as whole of wholes, is ungraspable and unreachable. Our idea of literature is a preconception that intervenes in a series of personal experiences, and evolves, changes, even if only slightly, throughout the span of a wider process; part of the process always remains in our mind's eye as we read or do research. Between the "perceived part" and the "conceived whole," between the facts and the hypotheses, between what is read and the systems of reference, between one's personal life experiences and those of another, we discover that the authenticity of our experience of culture depends on the lucidity we maintain during our immersion in the perilous interpretative sea. Adrian Marino, in a suggestive article, "In Favour of a Hermeneutics of the Idea of Literature," tries to find Ariadne's thread. Every definition of literature involves the activation of some presuppositions (*Voraussetzungen*). Two dialectically related planes intersect these presuppositions: the personal conception of the interpreter, that is, his own body of knowledge, his individual reflections, cultural experiences, aesthetic and ideological ideals; and the historical-cultural tradition—and I would add also the social circumstances that shape the idea of a specific literature at a particular moment. Obviously, for a historian another plane must be added: the past horizon, made up of the dominant conceptions of the era under consideration. Marino asks that the numerous past and present meanings be catalogued historically. In effect, from the point of view of poetics, one must be familiar with a wide array of concepts; but that does not mean that they cease to function as preconceptions or presuppositions, or that the to-and-fro between presupposition and the actual experience of reading, or between general intuition and perception of the fragment, fostered by the interpreter's historical as well as personal situation, is suppressed. What is important in such a context is the awareness of that uncertain convergence pointed out by Marino between socio-collective presuppositions and personal ones, present within the confines of a fruitful unfinished process of interrogation.[145] The reader contributes actively to the unfolding. Literature can be considered simultaneously as a *level* of reality and as a *creative process* that is continually renewed by the encounter between the reader and the writer with a plurality of preconceptions.

In this way impersonality remains excluded. The process of literature—its existence and survival—requires the intervention of the total, critical individual, even one who is rebellious and disobedient in the face of prevailing norms. Such a person must not be asked to synthesize what cannot be synthesized, or to hold to fixed and pedantic totalities. The entities change, are enriched and transfigured, as a result of the tension created as the socio-collective preconceptions evolve; and the imagination of the individual is set free. Such a person starts from the curve of his own existence and actively strives to extend its span. The confluence of the two planes indicated by Marino is also a process, tense, potentially resistant to impersonality. Within this confluence, the good reader forges his own conception of literature.

Modern man is "condemned to recreating his own universe," said Oskar Kokoschka. Carlos Castilla del Pino, when speaking of the ideas of modernism and postmodernism, quotes these words to emphasize that the individual in the context of modernity lives in a state of rebellion against inertia and uniformity, in the sense not of noncooperation but of "creativity." That does not represent in any way the *quiebra de la razón,* breakdown of reason, but the construction of the world *desde cada razon,* from every reason—"that world that has little to do with its materiality, with its physicality, that contains much more of the imaginary, or, if you prefer, of the mental, and is not erected by each one and then perishes, obviously, with each one." [146] Most of the time this mental, personal world obviously cannot be separated from the levels and systems of culture, by which I mean above all the arts, which refer us back to what was elaborated and shaped by others in different places and at other times. I am not excluding subjective caprices and oneiric alternatives. But in my opinion the vocation of comparativism is completely different, like that of the artistic and intellectual condition that we have labeled, for good or for ill, postmodernism. Literature invites us to a personal experience of the many worlds that transcend the limits of individual imagination. If no theory is permanently true, if the visions of the levels of reality are multiple and discordant, an individual selection and structuring by an exercise of personal discretion is inevitable. But the quality of such discretion depends today on our capacity for what could be called critical empathy, or perhaps creative empathy, with events felt and suffered by men and women in diverse spaces and times.

After this long recapitulation, I venture to think once again that comparativism is not alien to the literature of postmodernism, above all when it elaborates diachronic structures. What they have in common is *interhistoricity.* "The struggle of man is the struggle of memory against forgetting," Czeslaw Milosz has said [147]—a double struggle characteristic of the writers of our time. Postmodernism encompasses an original sense of history. I will mention only a few names by way of example: Günter Grass, Carlos Fuentes, Leonardo Sciascia, Gabriel García Márquez, Agustina Bessa Luís, Manuel Mujica Lainez, Jorge Ibargüengoitia, V. S. Naipaul, Peter Handke, Juan Benet, Mario Vargas Llosa. Even those among them who write the history of the present or of the immediate past (such as Juan Benet) pose the same questions. They do not portray a society placed at an unmistakable point in a unilineal and successive time span. They do not describe events as such but present them as possible intersections with the present. The past is neither the merely similar nor the simply remote and unique. The reiterations of time are like the throbbing of a life that is also our own.

The past is thus a powerful moral metaphor of modern life. Some element of human criminality escapes the net of a history supposedly unrepeatable. Like Oskar Matzerath at the end of Grass's *The Tin Drum,* we find that we are accomplices in what made and makes possible the injustices around us. Only after the loss of innocence can the language of history, as rich a language as that of the imagination, question itself. (By history we mean both cultural and temporal differences.) Modernism and its avant-garde movements cultivated rupture, play, criticism of bourgeois society, and a certain vision of the future, even though an apocalyptic one. Today the hazards of the future make ritual rupture seem irresponsible, and the mere rejection of the contemporary seems inadequate and superficial. "We are what we are and what we will be." Twenty-five years ago Harry Levin wrote that modernism "thought of itself in the present tense, separating modernity from history." [148] Even ancient myths were transported, as in Joyce, to a timeless present. The decentralized world of today that cannot be reduced to an ahistorical unity esteems myths because they are ancient. Intertextuality, as evident in literature as in architecture—the citations, allusions, the use of earlier forms—is also a sign of interhistoricity. Every language is aware of other languages, and all of them are aware of how far they are from real things. The techniques of distancing used by novelists, who again take pleasure in telling a tale (such as García Márquez), can be compared to the estrangement felt by some characters (as in Naipaul and Handke) from the earth they step on. The completely amazing nature of our social and political experience turns all distinctions between the believable and the fabulous blurry and enigmatic. The neofantastic narrative questions this amazement and this uncertainty. Postmodernism uses both present and past indicative tenses simultaneously to shape queries and thought. In that way the present is joined to history: We are what we are and what we have been.

Abbreviations

CL	*Comparative Literature* (Oregon)
CLS	*Comparative Literature Studies* (Illinois)
CRCL	*Canadian Review of Comparative Literature* (Edmonton)
CREL	*Cahiers roumains d'études littéraires* (Bucharest)
ICLA	International Comparative Literature Association
NLH	*New Literary History* (Virginia)
Proceedings II	*Comparative Literature. Proceedings of the Second Congress of the ICLA*, 2 vols., ed. Werner P. Friederich. Chapel Hill, University of North Carolina Press, 1959.
Proceedings III	*Actes du IIIe Congrès de l'AILC/Proceedings of the IIId Congress of the ICLA*, ed. W. A. P. Smit. The Hague, Mouton, 1962.
Proceedings IV	*Actes du IVe Congrès de l'AILC/Proceedings of the IVth Congress of the ICLA*, 2 vols., ed. François Jost. The Hague, Mouton, 1966.
Proceedings V	*Proceedings of the Vth Congress of the ICLA/Actes du Ve Congrès de l'AILC*, ed. Nikola Banašević. Amsterdam, Swets & Zeitlinger, 1969.
Proceedings VI	*Proceedings of the VIth Congress of the ICLA/Actes du VIe Congrès de l'AILC*, 2 vols., ed. Michel Cadot, Milan V. Dimić, David Malone, and Miklos Szabolcsi. Stuttgart, Kunst und Wissen, Erich Bieber, 1975.
Proceedings VII	*Actes du VIIe Congrès de l'AILC/Proceedings of the VIIth Congress of the ICLA*, 2 vols., ed. Milan Dimić and Eva Kushner. Stuttgart, Kunst und Wissen, Erich Bieber, 1979.
Proceedings VIII	*Proceedings of the VIIIth Congress of the ICLA/Actes du VIIe Congrès de l'AILC*, 2 vols., ed. Béla Köpeczi

and György M. Vajda. Stuttgart, Kunst und Wissen, Erich Bieber, 1980.

Proceedings IX	*Proceedings of the IXth Congress of the ICLA/Actes du IXe Congrès de l'AILC,* 4 vols., ed. Zoran Konstantinović et al. Innsbruck, Verlag des Institus for Sprachwissenschaft der Universität Innsbruck, 1980.
PT	*Poetics Today* (Tel Aviv)
RLC	*Revue de littérature comparée* (Paris)
Syn	*Synthesis* (Bucharest)
Tr	*Tamkang Review* (Taipei)
YCGL	*Yearbook of Comparative and General Literature* (Chapel Hill, N.C.; Bloomington, Ind.)

Notes

1. First Definitions

1. On the history of the term, see Wellek, 1970, pp. 3–26. In 1832 J.-J. Ampère gave a course in Paris called "Histoire comparative des littératures." But the passive form of the past participle, *comparée,* used by Villemain (see Vauthier, 1913), is an unfortunate creation copied in the other Romance languages (Italian, Portuguese, Rumanian, Spanish) in place of the active adjective used in English (*comparative*) and German (*vergleichend*), as well as in Dutch, Hungarian, Russian, and others. By the same token it makes sense ·that it be the knowledge or the science of literature to be compared—*vergleichende Literaturwissenschaft*—and not the object of the knowledge, that is, not literature itself. As for the French usage of the term, two points should be kept in mind: in the first place, there was early acceptance of labels such as *anatomie comparée* by Cuvier (1800), *grammaire comparée des langues de l'Europe latine* by Rayounard (1821), and *principes d'anatomie comparée* by Ducrotay de Blainville (1822); in the second place, the use of "literature" in the sense of "literary culture" persisted until the end of the eighteenth century and the beginning of the nineteenth. (Thus the *Diccionario de Autoridades,* 1726–1739, gives the definition as "the knowledge and science of letters.") Voltaire writes that "Chapelain avait une littérature immense." Thus as "anatomy" did not designate the human body itself but knowledge of it, "literature" signified the science or knowledge of letters. As for my own definition, I agree with Hugo Dyserinck, 1977, p. 11: "[wir können] die Komparatistik spezifisch *supranational* nennen" ([we can] call comparativism specifically *supranational*).

2. See Marino, 1982a and 1982c, p. 7: "this discipline is called upon to adopt a critical and combative position, to become directly involved in the great ideological controversies of our era."

2. The Local and the Universal

1. Paz, 1983, p. 21.
2. Paz, 1973b, p. 245.

3. Esteban, 1979, p. 43.
4. Borges, 1964b, p. 203.
5. Borges, 1989, p. 172.
6. Cervantes, 1967, II, p. 61. All subsequent translations of *Don Quixote* are taken from Cervantes, 1967.
7. Marcel Bataillon, "Relaciones literarias," in Avalle-Arce and Riley, 1973, p. 226.
8. Márquez Villanueva, 1973, p. 331.
9. Hrushovski, 1972, p. 1.198a.
10. Dante, 1973b, p. 16 (Spanish), 17 (English), ll. 61–63.
11. See Kirschbaum, 1966; and Jechová, 1982, pp. 146, 311.
12. Anderson Imbert, 1967, p. 81. See also Marasso, 1941.
13. Quoted in Anderson Imbert, 1967, p. 58.
14. Paz, 1967, pp. 16, 18.

3. The One and the Many

1. Borges, 1964a, p. 104.
2. Quoted in G. Bonnot, "Le Temps retrouvé du professeur Prigogine," *Le nouvel observateur,* 10 Dec. 1979, p. 77.
3. Cioranescu, 1964, p. 18.
4. Quoted in ibid., p. 23.
5. Ortega y Gasset, 1957a, I, pp. 68–71.
6. See Torre, 1957, p. 39; the article by Ortega appeared in *El sol* (2 Feb. 1919) and is an expression of what Josep Pla calls "moment de supreme felicitat" in his *Quadern gris* (Barcelona, 1977), p. 491.
7. Unamuno, 1895, pp. 47–144.
8. I refer to the well-known axiom of René Wellek; see Wellek and Warren, 1956, chap. 4.
9. Pessoa, 1982, p. 175; translation, 1991, p. 145.
10. See C. Guillén, 1978a.
11. See Croce, 1923, p. 71. "You can't judge except by comparing," Mme. de Staël wrote in *De la littérature.* See Fanger, 1962, p. 155; Malone, 1954.
12. See Vossler, 1928, p. 203.
13. Cambon, 1979, p. 161.
14. A. Alonso, 1940, p. 2.
15. Fuentes, 1976, p. 93.
16. Calvino, 1986, p. 101.
17. A. Machado, 1957a, p. 1.233.
18. Idem, 1957b, p. 1.134; translation, 1963, p. 6.
19. Montale, 1975, p. 371; translation by Ruth Feldman.
20. Cited by Amorós, 1979, p. 201.
21. Ibid., pp. 198, 201.

22. See Escarpit, 1966b. At the same time the accepted meanings of the traditional term *literature* are naturally differentiated and subdivided. See Wellek, 1966; and Hernadi, 1978.
23. Paz, 1973a, p. 240.
24. See Pavel, 1980.
25. Quoted in Todorov, 1984, p. 73. Transcription from the Cyrillic alphabet to the Latin presents difficulties and occasions for confusion. This book usually follows the English transcription.
26. See Paz, 1973b, p. 136.

4. Romantic Ideals

1. See Wellek, 1970, p. 10; Vauthier, 1913.
2. On the origins of comparative literature and its history in general, see Pichois and Rousseau, 1967, chap. 1; Weisstein, 1968, 1973; and Kappler, 1976. Weisstein, historian and major chronicler of the discipline, has published a supplement (1981) for the period 1968–1977. The publications of Pierre Brunel, Pichois, and Rousseau (1983) are significant. Of interest not just to Hungarians is the extensive article by Vajda, 1964. Like my predecessors, I stress the initial French contribution of about 1830; but it is also a fact that there were parallel attempts in Germany and other countries. In Holland Willem de Clercq studied the influence of Italian, Spanish, and German literature on the literature of the Netherlands, *Verhandeling over den invloidden invloid welke letterkunde . . . gehad heeft op de nederlandsche taal en letterkunde* (Amsterdam, 1823).
3. See Kappler, 1976, p. 129; and Focke, 1923.
4. See Kappler, 1976, pp. 122–128; and Wellek, 1970, p. 21.
5. See Kohut, 1973; and Maravall, 1966.
6. Gsteiger, 1967, p. 7.
7. Jost, 1974, p. 7.
8. See Cioranescu, 1964, p. 14.
9. See Kappler, 1976, p. 81.
10. See ibid., pp. 174–177.
11. Wellek, 1970, p. 25.
12. Texte, 1898, p. 12.
13. See Herder, 1957, pp. 72–95.
14. Ibid., p. 63; translation by Wolfgang Franzen.
15. Ibid., p. 130; translation by Wolfgang Franzen. See also Mayo, 1969.
16. Texte, 1895, p. 453.
17. Ibid., p. xiv.
18. De Sanctis, 1952, I, p. 263.
19. Schlegel, 1967, I, p. 182.
20. See Walzel, 1912, p. 12.
21. P. Cabanis, *Rapports du physique et du moral de l'homme* (1802), 1824, III,

p. 35; translated as *On the Relations between Physical and Moral Aspects of Man* (Baltimore: Johns Hopkins Press, 1981).

22. Müller, 1807, p. 44.
23. "Die Kunst ist eine sichtbare Erscheinung des Reichs Gottes auf Erden"; quoted by Wellek, 1955, II, p. 349, n. 61.

5. The Compromises of Positivism

1. See A. Levin, 1957 (selection of essays by Chasles about French literature); and Pichois, 1965.
2. Chasles, 1847, p. 28.
3. Chasles, 1867, p. 128.
4. Chasles, 1847, p. 13.
5. See Ampère, 1867, p. 3; and Schlocker-Schmidt, 1961.
6. Quoted in Haufe, 1935, p. 60.
7. Cioranescu, 1964, p. 21.
8. Pichois and Rousseau, 1967, p. 18.
9. Puibusque, 1843, I, p. 14.
10. See Rajna, 1900, pp. 252–256, 608.
11. Wellek, 1970, p. 31.
12. See ibid. and Vajda, 1964, p. 531.
13. Taine, 1866, I, p. xv.
14. Texte, 1898, p. 3.
15. Figueiredo, 1935, p. 16. The author goes on to say: "Spain exerts it extensively when including in the history of *Spanish* literature the names of Roman authors born in Hispania, such as the two Senecas, Lucan, Martial, Quintilian, Pomponius Mella, and Columella." Regarding the so-called national literatures in medieval times, see Klaniczay, 1966, p. 189.

6. Weltliteratur

1. Goethe, "Duvals Tasso," 1902–1907, XXXVIII, p. 97.
2. Quoted in Marino, 1975, p. 71.
3. See Merian-Genast, 1927; and Bender and Melzer, 1958.
4. Brunetière, 1900, p. 23.
5. See Prampolini. 1959–1961. On universal histories of literature, see Brandt Corstius, 1963. The Dutch comparatist makes a distinction between the historical surveys arranged by eras (like that of Riquer and Valverde, 1957–1974) and the juxtapositions of national literatures (such as the three volumes edited by Queneau, 1955–1958). Brandt Corstius was not able to read the meritorious (and aptly named) eight-volume *História da literatura ocidental* of Carpaux, 1959–1966. Martínez Estrada, 1946, is a lively personal essay.

6. For example, Etiemble, 1966.
7. See *Pour une bibliothèque idéale. Enquête présentée par Raymond Queneau* (Paris, 1956). Obviously these conceptions of universal literature leave aside or are unaware of the literatures of nations less studied or translated. See the commentaries of Ďurišin, 1972, pp. 39–43.
8. See Hankiss, 1938.
9. See Farinelli, 1925.
10. See Strich, 1946, p. 25. On *Weltliteratur,* see, in addition to the authors cited in earlier chapters: Vossler, "Goethe als Kritiker" (1928), in Curtius, 1950, pp. 25–58; Auerbach, 1952; Schrimpf, 1968; Jost, 1974, chap. 2; and G. R. Kaiser, 1980a, chap. 2.
11. Goethe, 1984, p. 133.
12. Goethe, "Maximen und Reflexionen," 1902–1907, XXXVIII, p. 272; notes on the German translation of Carlyle's *Life of Schiller* (1830); see ibid., p. 211. Translations by Wolfgang Franzen.
13. G. R. Kaiser, 1980a, p. 19. See the summary of Vajda, 1968.
14. See Griffith, 1932; Foa, 1956; and Benedetto, 1953.
15. See Vajda, 1964; translation from *The Marx-Engels Reader* (New York: W. W. Norton, 1972), pp. 338–339.
16. D. A. Campbell, trans., *Sappho and Alcaeus* (Cambridge, Mass.: Harvard University Press, 1982), pp. 79–81.
17. Rivers, 1988, p. 76.
18. Erman, 1896, pp. 67–68; and Donadoni, 1957, p. 81.
19. Levin, 1958, p. 284. See also H. Levin, 1975–76.
20. *Goethes Werke* (Weimar, 1903), XLI (2), p. 305; translation by Wolfgang Franzen.
21. Marino, 1975, p. 68.

7. The French Hour

1. Baldensperger, 1921, p. 29.
2. See Sobejano, 1967.
3. These investigations, which might be characterized as more or less paraliterary, of "images" and national preconceptions, without doubt real as events or historical conditionings, have not fallen into disuse at all; on the contrary, there has been an attempt to resurrect them and make them more modern. See Pichois, 1957; Dyserinck, 1966 and 1977, pp. 125–127; Pageaux, 1971, 1981; of A. M. Machado and Pageaux, 1981, chaps. 1, 3; and Dutu, 1976, 1979.
4. Dédéyan, 1944; Strich, 1946; and Peyre, 1935. A more recent example is Weisgerber, 1968.
5. See Escarpit, 1966a, and 1966c. There is a good bibliography in Darnton, 1982.

6. See Onís, 1962, p. 65. (This was one of the first essays in Spanish about comparative literature. Along with Gicovate, 1962, on the problem of influences, see C. Guillén, 1962; and Cioranescu, 1964.)

7. See Sieburth, 1978.

8. Jost, 1974, p. 35.

9. See Grahor, 1977.

10. See Waldapfel, 1968, p. 360.

11. Bataillon, 1952, p. 191.

12. Ibid., p. 156.

13. See Cox, 1899.

14. Clebsch, 1964, p. 101.

15. Waldapfel, 1968, pp. 17–18.

16. See Hermann, 1959; also Jackson, 1960; and Martini, 1956.

17. See Poli, 1967.

18. Hoffman, Allen, and Ulrich, 1946, p. 4.

19. See Samurović-Pavlović, 1969.

20. M. Anderson, 1953, p. 11. On Diaghilev's magazine, see *Mir iskusstva: La cultura figurativa, letteria e musicale nel simbolismo russo* (Colloquium in Turin, 1982) (Rome, 1984).

21. Pichois and Rousseau, 1967, p. 73.

22. Balakian, 1962.

23. See Weisstein, 1973, p. 48.

24. C. Guillén, 1962, p. 66.

25. See A. Alonso, 1954, p. 383; see also A. Alonso, 1952; and the bibliography of literary influences, Chapter 15, note 14.

26. See C. Guillén, 1971, chaps. 1 and 2. On the concept of convention, see H. Levin, 1966, pp. 31–61; Brandt Corstius, 1968, chap. 4; and Frye, 1957 and 1968, pp. 86–91. On the idea of intertextuality, see Chapter 15 in this volume.

27. Comte, 1974, p. 24.

28. M. Bloch, 1953, p. 30.

29. See H. Bergson, *L'évolution créatrice* (Paris, 1911), pp. 79–80. On causes and conditions, see Nelson, 1980, p. 217; and Uhlig, 1982, pp. 74–86.

8. *The American Hour*

1. On the history of comparativism as a university discipline, country by country, see Weisstein, 1973, pp. 167–252.

2. R. Wellek, "The Crisis of Comparative Literature," in *Proceedings II*, I, p. 155; reprinted in Wellek, 1963, p. 290.

9. Littérature Générale *and Literary Theory*

1. Van Tieghem, 1951, pp. 174, 175.

2. Ibid., p. 175.

3. Wellek and Warren, 1956, p. 49.
4. See G. R. Kaiser, 1980a, p. 157.
5. Van Tieghem, 1951, p. 170.
6. Jeune, 1968, p. 11.
7. See W. V. Quine, "Grades of Theoreticity," in Foster and Swanson, 1970, pp. 1–17.
8. Frye, 1957, p. 15. Today almost no one denies the inevitability of this theory. As Meregalli, 1983b, p. 88, wrote, "a refusal of theory is impossible because the very refusal is a theory."
9. Culler, 1979, p. 177. See also L. Nyirö, "Problèmes de littérature comparée et théorie de la littérature," in Sötér and Süpek, 1964, pp. 505–524. See also A. M. Machado and Pageaux, 1981, chap. 8, which emphasizes the insertion of literary theory as well as literature into a process of social communication, "de simbolização do mundo" (p. 116). Highly visible indeed are the ideological conditionings of our theorists, as these authors show very well with Portuguese examples: Teófilo Braga, António Sérgio, António Sardinha—and also, in his different phases, António José Saraiva. In spite of the will toward abstraction, is there anything that hovers over our interests, instincts, and passions more than theory? See also Mooji, 1979; and Fokkema, 1982, pp. 2–4. In criticism itself diachronic structures seem to exist: the resemblance between certain theoretical attitudes of today and those of the end of the nineteenth century (Jules Lemaître, Oscar Wilde) is extremely interesting. On this point see Caramaschi, 1974 and 1984, p. 31, where that fin-de-siècle criticism is described: "The tendency to blur, in the name of an autonomous essayism, the boundaries between creation and criticism . . . a mocking or anarchistic refusal to bow down before the authority of the author of a text . . . These seem to be the most striking characteristics of the European literary fin-de-siècle."

10. Three Models of Supranationality

1. See Jakobson, 1987c. Jakobson repeats his thesis in other places, such as 1987a and 1987b. See Buxó, 1978.
2. Jakobson, 1987b, p. 83; the example that follows can be found in Jakobson, 1987c, p. 125. See Seboek, 1974.
3. This is the sense that V. Zhirmunsky chooses in his *Rifma* (reprinted in Munich, 1970, p. v): "every repetition of sound required by the functional meaning of the metrical composition of a poem."
4. Diego Catalán gives examples of a class of extreme parallelism that he calls twinned formulas, or doubles; see Catalán, 1984a, p. 193. The following example, "Romance de doña Alda," is found in Menéndez Pidal, 1969, p. 79; translation by Christopher Maurer.
5. "Romance del prisonero," in Menéndez Pidal, 1969, p. 192; translation by Christopher Maurer.

6. See Riffaterre, 1971, chap. 2, on "stylistic context." See the explication of Yllera, 1974, p. 34.

7. See Frenk, 1979, p. 34; Paris, 1892, pp. 12–13.

8. Bernard de Ventadour, "Can vei la lauzeta mover," in Riquer, 1975, I, p. 384, ll. 1–4; translation Paul Blackburn, *Proensa: An Anthology of Troubadour Poetry* (Berkeley: University of California Press, 1978), p. 76.

9. A *système clos* and a *système ouvert* are intertwined in Baudelaire, according to Jakobson and Lévi-Strauss, 1962, pp. 18–19.

10. Alarcos Llorach, 1976, pp. 237, 238.

11. See O. Brik, "Rhytmus und Syntax," in Striedter, 1969, pp. 163–222; idem, "Contributions to the Study of Verse Language," in Matejka and Pomorska, 1971, pp. 117–125; and D. Alonso, 1950, p. 50 and passim.

12. Francisco García Lorca, 1984, pp. 55–56.

13. See Riffaterre, 1971, chap. 2.

14. Kugel, 1981, p. 51.

15. See Steinitz, 1934; his terms are: *formal* or *inhaltlich; synonymparallel* or *analogparallel; gegensätzlich, aufzählend,* and *variierend.*

16. Watson, 1962, p. 215.

17. See Saraiva and Lopes, n.d., pp. 47–49.

18. See Watson, 1962, p. 206.

19. Hightower, 1966, p. 38.

20. See C. Guillén, 1971–72, p. 412.

21. Garibay, 1953–1954.

22. Kramer, 1979, p. 23.

23. Garibay, 1953–1954, I, p. 194; translation by Christopher Maurer.

24. See F. P. Magoun, Jr., Introduction to *The Kalevala* (Cambridge, Mass., 1963), p. xix.

25. Garibay, 1953–1954, I, pp. 19, 65.

26. Zhirmunsky, 1965, p. 390.

27. Adrian Marino analyzes literary "ideas" that are both synchronic and diachronic, 1974, p. 207: "history submits to the scheme, lets itself be called to order; the scheme submits to history." On diachronic structures, see Chapter 16.

28. See Bousoño, 1956a, p. 233. The following example is from Aleixandre, 1977, pp. 177–178.

29. Hrushovski, 1972, p. 1.234a.

30. Lázaro Carreter, 1979, p. 60; on the structuring function, see ibid., pp. 63–73.

31. Culler, 1975, p. 67.

32. Ďurišin, 1972, pp. 37, 44.

33. See Henri Blaze de Bury, *Le souper chez le commandeur* (Paris, 1835; reprinted in *Poésies complètes de Henri Blaze* [Paris, 1842]), in which the author says (Prologue, p. vi) that he has been heavily reproached for his conversion of Don Juan. (The work appeared first in the *Revue des deux mondes,* [1834], 497–

558, under the pseudonym Hans Werner.) Of the work of Blaze de Bury, see *Le Faust de Goethe* (Paris, 1840); *Ecrivains et poètes de l'Allemagne* (Paris, 1846); and the very interesting "Mes souvenirs de la Revue des deux mondes," *Revue internationale* (Rome), 17, 18 (1888), in installments. See Jacques Voisine, "Voyageur ou plagiaire? Blaze de Bury au pays de Jean-Paul," in *Connaissance de l'étranger: Mélanges offerts à la mémoire de Jean-Marie Carré* (Paris, 1964), pp. 515–524.

34. See Kierkegaard, 1944; Said Armesto, 1908; J. Ortega y Gasset, *El tema de nuestro tiempo,* in *Obras completas,* vol. III (Madrid, 1947), pp. 174–179; O. Rank, *Die Don Juan-Gestalt* (Vienna, 1924); R. Cansino Assens, "El mito de don Juan," in *Evolución de los temas literarios* (Santiago, Chile, 1936); G. Marañón, *Don Juan* (Buenos Aires and Mexico City, 1942); A. Camus, "Le donjuanisme," in *Le mythe de Sisyphe* (Paris, 1942), pp. 97–105; H. de Montherlant, *Don Juan* (Paris, 1958). For works nearer to literary history and criticism, see Gendarme de Bévotte, 1906–1929; Weinstein, 1967; Singer, 1965; Poyán Díaz, 1966; and Márquez Villanueva, 1983, which has a useful bibliography on the origins of the legend.

35. See *"Apu Inqa Atahuallpaman": Elegía quechua de autor cuzqueño desconocido,* ed. T. L. Meneses (Lima, 1957). According to Lara, 1947, it is a *wanka,* which is "a genre that has a surprising affinity with the European elegy" (p. 91).

36. See M. López-Baralt, 1979, pp. 65–82, and 1980, pp. 79–86.

37. J.-M. Carré, Foreword to Guyard, 1951, p. 5.

38. Dyserinck, 1977, p. 149.

39. Weisstein, 1973, pp. 7–8; worthwhile as an example of a certain posture. Weisstein later went on to interest himself in typological analogies; see Weisstein, 1975 and 1981, pp. 130–135.

40. Pichois and Rousseau, 1967, pp. 43, 94.

41. Etiemble, 1963, p. 37. See A. Marino, 1982a; Block, 1970, p. 25.

42. Etiemble, 1963, p. 19.

43. See Erman, 1925a, 1925b; Gurney, 1957; Falkenstein, 1959; Kraus, 1980; and P. Michaelowski, "Königsbriefe," in *Realexikon der Assryologie und vorderasiatischen Archäologie,* ed. D. U. Edzard (Berlin and New York, 1981), pp. 51–59.

44. Etiemble, 1963, p. 65 and back cover.

45. See Etiemble, 1963, p. 12; and Struve, 1955, pp. 1–20 (updated in *YCGL,* 6 [1957], pp. 7–10, and 8 [1959], pp. 13–18).

46. On comparativism in eastern Europe, quite a number of summaries and anthologies have appeared since István Sötére's *La littérature comparée en Europe orientale* (1963); see Ďurišin, 1967, 1972; Ziegengeist, 1968; G. R. Kaiser, 1980b.

47. The Institut mirovoi literatury, or Gorky Institute of Moscow, has published books, along with other institutes of the Academy of Sciences of the U.S.S.R., about Dante and world literature (1967), Czech-Soviet relations (1965), and

about different national literatures: history of English literature (1943–1976, 5 vols.), American literature (1947; an enlarged edition is in progress), and so on. The Institute of Oriental Studies prepares basic histories of Oriental literatures; one on Vietnamese literature appeared in 1977. The Gorky Institute has published quite a number of works of literary theory, or of history broadly comparative, such as L. I. Timofeiev's *Bases of Literary Theory* (1976) and E.M. Meletinski's notable study *The Medieval Novel: Origins and Classic Forms* (1983).

48. Zhirmunsky, 1967, p. 4; on Veselovsky, see Erlich, 1959, pp. 33–36.
49. Zhirmunsky, 1967, p. 2.
50. Ibid., p. 1.
51. Ibid., p. 5. There is a German version of this article in G. R. Kaiser, 1980b, pp. 77–89. Essentially the same ideas are expressed in Zhirmunsky, 1969 (in German in Ziegengeist, 1968, pp. 1–16). Concerning the concept of typological analogy, the comments of Ďurišin, 1972, pp. 47–50, are very valuable. See also Seidler, 1973; and Weisstein, 1981, pp. 130–135, which has a bibliography on the idea of analogy. On the East, see also Markiewicz, 1980; and Jrapchenko, 1968.
52. Zhirmunsky, 1961, p. 117, and 1969.
53. See C. Guillén, 1978b.
54. Zhirmunsky, 1967, pp. 2, 6.
55. See Lowenthal, 1948; Hauser, 1951; Rosengren, 1968; Orecchioni, 1970; Schober, 1970; Weimann, 1971; Williams, 1973; 1977 (bibliography pp. 213–217); Cros, 1976, 1983; Duchet, 1979; Naumann, 1980; also Leenhardt, 1973; Strelka, 1973; and Cornea, 1976.
56. I have already presented some bibliographic recommendations. It is useful to consult the proceedings of congresses and colloquia dedicated to East/West studies, first, those of the University of Indiana: Frenz and Anderson, 1955; Frenz, 1959; and *YCGL:* 11 (1962), 119–236; 15 (1966), 159–224; 20 (1971), 57–88; and 22 (1975), 57–103. See also the colloquia held in Tapei, Formosa, published in *TR*, 2–3 (October 1971–April 1972) and 6–7 (October 1975–April 1976); the first colloquia in Hong Kong, in *New Asia Academic Bulletin* (Hong Kong), 1 (1978); and Deeney, 1980. (The colloquia of Taipei and the second one of Hong Kong have very useful summaries and commentaries by Owen Aldridge.) See the bibliographic articles of Deeney, 1970, 1978. From a theoretical and methodological point of view, see Witke, 1971–72; Yu, 1974; Liu, 1975b; Yip, 1975–76, and Yuan, 1980.

11. Taxonomies

1. Poggioli, 1943, pp. 114–116.
2. Dyserinck, 1977, comes close to Van Tieghem in some proposals, such as that of general literature, pp. 150–155, but not in others.

3. See Maury, 1934; Seznec, 1949; Seznec and J. Adhémar's edition of Didérot's *Salons*, 4 vols. (Oxford, 1957–1967); Seznec, 1980; Walzel, 1917.

4. H. H. H. Remak, "Comparative Literature, Its Definition and Function," in Stallknecht and Frenz, 1961, p. 3.

5. See Croce, 1923, p. 71. Zhirmunsky, 1967, p. 1, goes further: "it seems to me that in literary research, as well as in other social studies, comparison has always been—and must always remain—*the basic principle* of historical interpretation." On the other hand, in 1961, p. 7, Zhirmunsky adds that comparison is a method but not a methodology; that is, it does not coincide with an assemblage of theoretical principles derived from a conception of the world. See the commentaries in this regard by Ďurišin, 1972, pp. 30–36. Also see Sötér, 1974, p. 10.

6. See the criticism formulated in Wellek, 1970, p. 18.

7. See Fosca, 1960; Castex, 1969.

8. See Hagstrum, 1953; Bergmann, 1979; Dubois, 1982. For the ekphrasis of Keats, see Spitzer, 1955b; and for another of Rilke, Clüver, 1978. On these and other points touched on in this section, see Amorós, 1979, pp. 78–89. Regarding Christodorus (end of the fifth and beginning of the sixth century) see P. Waltz, ed., *Anthologie grecque*, vol. I, *Anthologie Palatine* (Paris, 1928), bk. 2, pp. 55–65. The characters of Krleža's *Banket u Blitvi* (1939) describe some sculptures numerous times; see *Banquet en Blithuanie*, tr. M. Sullerot-Begić (Paris, 1964) pp. 100–105, 114, 127, 129, 133, 184, 204, 244, 246. On Spain, see Orozco Díaz, 1947.

9. See Lejeune and Stiennon, 1965; and E. Mâle, *L'art religieux du XIIe siècle en France*, 5th ed. (Paris, 1947).

10. See Scher, 1982, pp. 225–250 (bibliography pp. 242–250). On the relations of music with literature, the contributions of Calvin Brown are fundamental, particularly 1948, 1970a, 1970b, 1978. At the same time, see the special number of *CL*, 22 (1970); Weisstein, 1977; Barricelli, 1978; Rodríguez Adrados, 1980; Célis, 1982; and Scher, 1984.

11. Ďurišin, 1977, p. 127.

12. Dufour, 1977, pp. 164, 156.

13. Scher, 1982, p. 231.

14. A.-M. Rousseau, 1977, p. 50.

15. See Marin, 1972a; Lyotard, 1971; also Dijkstra, 1969.

16. See Teesing, 1963, pp. 27–35.

17. See Marin, 1972b.

18. On *ut pictura poesis*, see Lee, 1940; Schweizer, 1972; Trimpi, 1973.

19. Quoted in Seznec, 1949, p. 92.

20. See ibid., pp. 78 and 309.

21. Compare ibid., p. 2: "I made every effort, absolutely . . . to discover the points of contact and of coincidence between the documents and his life."

22. See Guenther, 1960.

23. See King, 1953. Picasso's poetry, so powerful, can also be characterized, according to Torre, 1962, pp. 98–106, as abstract, not figurative, that is, as an attempt to rob words of their "capacity for meaning." I don't know: the words of *Trozo de piel* (Piece of Hide, referring to the shape of Spain as a bull's hide; translated into English as *Hunk of Skin,* 1968) without any doubt evoke memories of a Malagueña childhood. What he tries to weed out is rather "literary language"—and, through that, literature itself. See Jiménez Millán, 1983. For more on literature and arts in Spain, see Gallego Morell, Soria, and Marín, 1971; and on literature and music, Sopeña Ibáñez, 1974.

24. See Wais, 1936.

25. Wellek and Warren, 1956, p. 134.

26. A subject studied in detail by Karl Selig; see the summary of Selig, 1963; and Henkel and Schoene, 1967.

27. See Weisstein, 1978.

28. See Solt, 1970.

29. See Teesing, 1963, p. 29.

30. Shown very convincingly by Voisine, 1976. See P. J. Smith, 1970.

31. Bassy, 1973, p. 18.

32. See Seznec, 1948.

33. On literature and the arts, see in addition to the previous notes (7–32) the special numbers of *CLS,* no. 4 (1967); *CL,* 22, no. 2 (1970); *Cahiers de l'Association internationale des études françaises,* 24 (1972) on the eighteenth century; *Neohelicon* (Budapest), 5, no. 1 (1977); *YCGL,* 27, (1978). See also Kerman, 1956 (on opera); Bluestone, 1957 (cinema); M. Gaither, "Literature and the Arts," in Stallknecht and Frenz, 1961, pp. 153–170; Praz, 1970; Hunt, 1971; Seznec, 1972; Stiennon, 1973; and the bibliography of Weisstein, 1982. The Modern Language Association of America, which published the volume of Barricelli and Gibaldi in 1982, also published Thorpe, 1967, which includes the music-literary study of B. B. Bronson, pp. 127–148. From the French point of view of today, see F. Claudon, J. Body, and C.-F. Brunon in Pageaux, 1983, pp. 111–119. Vol. III of *Proceedings IX* is dedicated to "Literature and the Other Arts."

34. See Peyre, 1952.

35. See H. Levin, 1953. On the idea of *tradición,* see also H. Levin, 1958, pp. 55–66. Another very valuable recapitulation of the comparativism of the era is Remak, 1960; and, twenty years later, Remak, 1980.

36. Wellek, 1973, p. 439.

37. On literature and psychology or literature and psychoanalysis, see Ruitenbeek, 1964; Yllera, 1974, p. 172; Serpieri, 1983; Felman, 1982; and the very useful bibliography of M. M. Schwartz and D. Willbern in Barricelli and Gibaldi, 1982, pp. 218–224. See Chapter 10, note 56, above; and the bibliography in Sammons, 1977, pp. 106–230.

38. The statement about Wellek's great *History* is applicable to other valuable

works of the history of criticism/theory, such as Folkierski, 1925; Bate, 1946; Russo, 1946; Abrams, 1953; Weinberg, 1961. More recent works of particular importance are Culler, 1975; and Fokkema and Kunne-Ibsch, 1977.

12. Genres

1. In his article on Rozanov, cited by Boris Eijenbaum in his "Teoría del método formal." See Striedter, 1969, p. lxv.
2. See Striedter, 1969, p. lxvi.
3. See Todorov, 1984, pp. 85–87.
4. See Ibid., pp. 85, 90–91.
5. Striedter, 1989, p. 68. On Russian formalism, Striedter, 1969 and 1989, and Stempel, 1969–1972, are of fundamental importance. See also Matejka and Pomorska, 1971. Belonging to an earlier phase and written from the Western point of view are Todorov, 1965; and Lemon and Reis, 1965. See also the five volumes of *Russian Poetics in Translation* (Oxford, 1975–1978), devoted above all to the recent "structuralists" of Moscow and Tartu (Yuri Lotman) but also including essays by O. Brik and B. Tomashevsky (vols. IV and V) and a glossary of terms used by the Formalists (vol. IV). See the historical study of Hansen-Löve, 1978, following the now classic work of Erlich, 1969; and, for the semiologists of Moscow and Tartu, Eimermacher and Shishkoff, 1977. See the summary of Fokkema and Kunne-Ibsch, 1977, chap. 2; and notes 11 and 13, below.
6. "Sobre el género literario," in Lázaro Carreter, 1979, pp. 116–119.
7. See H. Levin, 1963, pp. 16–23; Anceschi, 1968; Corsini, 1974; the bibliography of C. Guillén, 1971, p. 506, n. 46. On the genre as institution, see C. Guillén, 1977a and especially, 1978a.
8. See J. Gaulmier, in Adam, Lerminier, and Morot-Sir, 1972, II, p. 6.
9. See C. Guillén, 1978a, p. 540.
10. Lázaro Carreter, 1979, p. 118.
11. See Jameson, 1975, reprinted in Jameson, 1981, pp. 103–150.
12. See C. Guillén, 1971, pp. 135–158.
13. Tynyanov, in Todorov, 1965, p. 128. See also García Berrio, 1973.
14. Bakhtin, 1981, p. 4.
15. Rico, 1983, p. 16.
16. C. Guillén, 1972, p. 232.
17. See Richter, 1938.
18. On the Renaissance, see Colie, 1973. For nineteenth-century and Russian examples, see Morson, 1981.
19. See Frye, 1957, pp. 303–314.
20. See L. Hadrovics, "Rapports de la poésie hongroise ancienne avec celles de l'Europe centrale," in Sötér and Süpek, 1964, pp. 105–127.
21. See Weinberg, 1961, II, chap. 21.

22. John Fletcher, *The Faithful Shepherdess*, ed. F. W. Moorman (London, 1897), p. 6.

23. See Dalla Valle, 1973; Cremona, 1977.

24. See Beall, 1942; Simpson, 1962; J. de Jáuregui, *Aminta*, tr. T. Tasso, ed. J. Arce (Madrid, 1970); Arce, 1973; Stamnitz, 1977.

25. See Trogrančič, 1953, p. 114.

26. See Setschkareff, 1952, pp. 54, 61; and, on the pastoral drama by Gundulić, M. Držić, and other South Slavic writers, Birnbaum, 1974, p. 349; Kadić, 1962; Torbarina, 1967.

27. See Dalla Valle, 1980.

28. See *Balassi Bálint szép Magyar komédiája*, ed. J. Misianik, S. Eckhardt, and T. Klaniczay (Budapest, 1959); Waldapfel, 1968; I. Bán, "Il dramma pastorale italiano e la 'Bella commedia ungherese' di Bálint Balassi," in Horányi and Klaniczay, 1967, pp. 147–156.

29. Backvis, 1968, p. 321.

30. See ibid., p. 353; Rousset, 1967; and Warnke, 1972, pp. 66–89.

31. See Wang, 1975.

32. See Hatto, 1965.

33. See Yuan, 1980, p. 1.

34. Goethe to Eckermann, January 31, 1827, in Goethe, 1984, p. 132.

35. Miner, 1979, p. vii.

36. Gracián, 1987, p. 146.

37. Yip, 1975–76, p. 123.

38. See Wong, 1978; and McLeod, 1976.

39. Quoted in Lord, 1960, p. 30; see ibid., chap. 4; Fry, 1969; and Parry, 1971.

40. Harris, 1979, p. 65.

41. Wang, 1974, p. 127. On the question of transitional text, see Jabbour, 1969; and Campbell, 1978.

42. See Owen, 1975 and 1977, p. 98.

43. Se Yu, 1983. On East/West studies, see Chapter 10, note 56, above. On the possibility of determining some universal categories of literary criticism or metaliterature, Occidental as well as Oriental, see Yip, 1969, 1975–76, 1976; Lefevere, 1978; and Marino, 1982a.

44. See Ethé, 1882; Selbach, 1886; Jones, 1934, chap. 1. Fiore, 1966, has good information but returns to the idea of direct influence.

45. See Walter, 1920, p. 8. It is certainly true that in the pan-Hellenic festivals the rhapsodes competed with one another, but they did not respond directly to one another.

46. I am grateful to Stephen Owen for his translation of "Linked Verse of the Stone Tripod," (which is not included in Erwin von Zach's *Han Yü's poetische Werke* (Cambridge, Mass., 1952).

47. See Riquer, 1975, I, p. 66.

48. Mitxelena, 1960, p. 24.
49. Zavala, 1964, p. 12.
50. Ibid., p. 83.
51. Riquer, 1975, I, p. 67.
52. Harris, 1979, p. 66. See also Clover, 1980, p. 444.
53. Lara, 1947, p. 83; On the *wawaki,* see ibid., pp. 83–85, 181–182. On medieval choral poetry, see Frenk, 1979, p. 44, quoting P. Le Gentil: "la poésie lyrique romane a eu très vraisemblablement à l'origine un caractère choral."
54. See Miner, 1979, pp. 62, 157.
55. "Noten und Abhandlungen zu beserem Verständnis des West-östlichen Divans," in Goethe, 1902–1907, V, p. 223; translation by Wolfgang Franzen.
56. Frye, 1957, pp. 246–251.
57. On irony, see Knox, 1961; Booth, 1974. On allegory, see Fletcher, 1964; de Man, 1969; Quilligan, 1979; Bloomfield, 1981. On the grotesque, see Kayser, 1957; O'Connor, 1962; Iffland, 1972. On parody, see Bakhtin, 1981, pp. 51–53, 61–68, 76, 309–315; Genette, 1982, pp. 17–19. On satire, see Highet, 1962; Elliott, 1960; Paulson, 1967; Kernan, 1959.
58. The concept of argument/plot (the Russian *siuzhet*) presupposes the organization of certain thematic materials—sequences of acts and events—by means of a simultaneous choice of form and sense. As I will explain later, (Chapter 13), Peter Brooks starts from the idea of form as formation, as intervention by the author (and by the reader), and in that way defines the argument/plot in Freudian terms, as dynamic shaping/transference of desire. This adventure of desire, often failed or cut short, is for Brooks (like the melodramatic gesture, see Brooks, 1976) a merely individual effort, free of established models, from the beginning of the nineteenth century and the disappearance during this century of a global, providential, divine argument/plot. (Historically, Bakhtin would not agree with this view; he would perceive the argument/plot, not indispensable in the epic, as typical for every novel. See Bakhtin, 1981, pp. 31–32.) This attempt by Brooks, not lacking in grandiosity, to link the desire for realization or sense in the novelistic argument/plot with that of persons treated by Freud or with the process of psychoanalysis goes awry only because of the limits of any model that postulates the universality of the procedure in question (above all transference) as an image of human life. See Brooks, 1978, 1982, 1984. See also Skura, 1981.
59. See García Berrio, 1978a, 1978b, 1981. On the sonnet see also Mönch, 1954; Moisés, 1968; Jost, 1974; and Scott, 1976.
60. For examples of the antiquity of the literary letter, including the fictitious and students' exercise compositions, see Chapter 10, note 43. It is well known also that the Greeks reflected on the nature of the letter: its relation to dialogue, its connection to friendship—peripatetic tradition—its openness to specific themes, to more than one style, and so on. This theory of the letter—Cicero,

Quintilian—is found in Demetrius of Phaleron, *De elocutione* and crops up even in the "Epístola" of Garcilaso a Boscán (1534). In this respect see Koskennemie, 1956.

61. Aldana, 1978, pp. 70–71, 76; translation by Fritz Hensey. The most famous antecedent of the use of the date is Petrarch's sonnet 211: "Mille trecento ventisette, a punto / Su l'ora prima il dí sesto d'aprile, / Nel laberinto intrai; né veggio ond'esca."
62. *Epistula* I.1–4; translation here and below by Steven Scully.
63. See Rivers, 1954; and Morris, 1931.
64. See Stégen, 1960, p. 6; and D. Alonso, 1950, pp. 149, 198.
65. See C. Guillén, 1972.
66. See Thomson, 1964, chaps. 6 and 7.
67. Marot, 1964, pp. 272–276; translation by Jeffrey Mehlman.
68. Nolting-Hauff, 1974, pp. 95, 104.
69. Bakhtin, 1981, p. 33.
70. Ibid., p. 411.
71. Quoted in Alazraki, 1983, p. 98; translation from J. Cortázar, *Hopscotch*, tr. Gregory Rabassa (New York: Avon Books, 1969), p. 450.
72. Alazraki, 1983, pp. 86, 84. Is there a realistic poetry? See Urrutia, 1983, pp. 85–114.
73. See Reyes, 1963, pp. 447–480.
74. Galdós, 1954, p. 10.
75. Amorós, 1973, chap. 5.
76. Fink, 1934; C. Rosso, 1968; and Brody and Spitzer, 1980.
77. Attempts were already made at the beginning of the century. See Kowzan, 1975, p. 57.
78. M. Kundera, *The Book of Laughter and Forgetting*, tr. Michael Henry Heim (New York: Alfred A. Knopf, 1980).
79. And I do believe (in contrast to Lázaro Carreter, 1979, p. 114) that the approach from genres as instruments of literary criticism, with regard to single works and authors, has been fruitful. Without going further afield, I think of the writings of Américo Castro about Cervantes, Stephen Gilman about *Celestina*, Amado Alonso about the historical novel, Francisco Rico and Lázaro Carreter himself about *Lazarillo de Tormes* or *Guzmán de Alfarache*. On the problem of literary genres, see, along with those cited in notes 6, 11, 13, and 56 above, Viëtor, 1931; Poggioli, 1959; Elliott, 1962; Reyes, 1963; Jauss, 1970b; Todorov, 1970, 1976; Weitz, 1970; Tókei, 1971; Hernadi, 1972; Riffaterre, 1972; Fubini, 1973; Hempfer, 1973; Liu, 1975a; Genette, 1977; Strelka, 1978; Dubrow, 1982; and Fowler, 1982. The journal *Genre* (University of Oklahoma) has been appearing since 1968.
80. On tragedy, see Weisinger, 1953; Krieger, 1973; Steiner, 1961; Szondi, 1964; Krueger, 1973; Vickers, 1973; Lenson, 1975; Omesco, 1978.

81. In addition to Poggioli, 1975, see Gerhardt, 1950; Empson, 1960; Rosenmeyer, 1969.

82. The proceedings of the colloquium published as *Das Ende des Stegreifspiels: Die Geburt des Nationaltheaters,* ed. Roger Bauer and Jürgen Wertheimer (Munich, 1983).

83. On the essay, see Schon, 1954; Marichal, 1957; Torre, 1962, p. 316; Berger, 1964; Lima, 1964; Haas, 1969; Terrasse, 1977; Loveluck, 1982.

84. The bibliography on the novel is excessive, brimming over, extremely copious. For the most recent "narratology," see Chapter 13, notes 61 and 76. Going further back (after Henry James, Percy Lubbock, E. M. Forster), I would stress: Fernandez, 1926; Thibaudet, 1938; Petsch, 1942; Laemmert, 1955; Watt, 1957; Booth, 1961; Freedman, 1963; Stanzel, 1963; Scholes and Kellogg, 1968; Goldknopf, 1972.

85. Some examples. Tragicomedy: Herrick, 1955; Guthke, 1966; Styan, 1968. The epistolary novel: "Une forme littéraire: Le roman par lettres," in Rousset, 1962b; Versini, 1979. The maxim: Fink, 1934; Aldridge, 1963; Mautner, 1966; Rosso, 1968. The idyll: Nemoianu, 1977. The didactic poem, description: Riffaterre, 1972; Hamon, 1981; issue no. 61 of *Yale French Studies* (1981). Utopias: Elliott, 1970; Biesterfeld, 1974; Manuel and Manuel, 1979. The gothic novel: Nelson, 1963; Klein, 1975; and Punter, 1980.

86. On autobiography and the autobiographical novel, Rousset, 1973; Démoris, 1975; Lejeune, 1975, 1980; May, 1979; Beaujour, 1980; Yllera, 1981. Historical novel: Wehrli, 1941; A. Alonso, 1942; Lukács, 1955. Melodrama: Brooks, 1976. Tale, short story, *novelle:* Malmede, 1966; Gillespie, 1967; Wiese, 1963; Hell, 1976; Serra, 1978; issue of *Revue de littérature comparée,* no. 4 (1976). *Costumbrismo:* Montesinos, 1965. *Roman à thèse:* Suleiman, 1983. Personal diary: Boerner, 1969; Didier, 1976; Jurgensen, 1979; Picard, 1981. Detective novel: Porter, 1981. Fantastic story: Carilla, 1968; Todorov, 1970; Solmi, 1978; Finné, 1980; Alazraki, 1983. And the prose poem: Bernard, 1959; Johnson, 1979; and Caws and Riffaterre, 1983.

13. Forms

1. Cervantes, 1967, p. 11.
2. Marot, 1958, p. 17.
3. See Lausberg, 1960, I, pp. 175, 187–190.
4. Sacks, 1964, p. 228.
5. Hartman, 1970.
6. See Striedter, 1969, pp. 33, 35. For bibliography see Chapter 12, note 5, above.
7. Tynyanov in ibid., p. 405.
8. See Tynyanov in ibid., p. 439; and Striedter, 1989, p. 59.
9. Jameson, 1972, p. 52.

10. See Hansen-Löve, 1978.
11. Fokkema and Kunne-Ibsch, 1977, p. 20.
12. D. Alonso, 1950, p. 32.
13. See Riffaterre, 1971, chap. 7.
14. Ibid., pp. 37–40.
15. Genette, 1980, p. 32.
16. See Willis, 1953.
17. Martín de Riquer, in his edition of *Quijote* (Barcelona, 1969), is to be com-mended for restoring the original division of the first edition (1605). The 1615 edition abandons the subdivision (and the intercalation of stories), like most later edititions of the complete *Quixote*. The division is very significant: the second section of the first part, which begins with chapter IX ("In the first part of this history we left . . ."), introduces the distancing device of Cide Hamete Bengeli, and so on. See Riquer's note p. 91.
18. See Francisco García Lorca, 1984, pp. 41–56.
19. On syllepsis, for example, see O'Brien, 1954; Todorov, 1971, p. 37; and Rif-faterre, 1980; or in Quevedo, C. Guillén, 1982. More generally, see "Antike Rhetorik und vergleichende Literaturwissenschaft," in Curtius, 1950 (or earlier in *CL* 1, [1949], 24–43). And on the resurgence of rhetoric, see Yllera, 1974, p. 15.
20. On the idea of form, see D. W. Gotshalk, "Form," in Vivas and Krieger, 1953; "Sentimiento e intuición en la lírica" and "El ideal clásico de la forma poética," in A. Alonso, 1954; E. Wilkinson, "'Form' and 'Content' in the Aesthetics of German Classicism," in Boeckmann, 1959; LaDrière, 1959b; Rousset, preface, 1962b; "Concepts of Form and Structure in Twentieth-Century Criticism," in Wellek, 1963; and C. Guillén, 1978b.
21. Rousset, 1962b, p. x: "L'épanouissement simultané d'une structure et d'une pensée, l'amalgame d'une forme et d'une expérience dont la genèse et la croiss-ance sont solidaire." For a dynamic conception of poetic form, see also Bou-soño, 1956b.
22. C. Blanco Aguinaga, *Ultimos poemas,* preface by Prados, Malaga, (1965), p. 10.
23. Bakhtin, 1981, p. 254.
24. See Zubiría, 1955, chap. 1; Riffaterre, 1971, chap. 2; Jakobson, 1987c, p. 127: "one may state that in poetry similarity is superimposed on contiguity, and hence equivalence is promoted to the constitutive device of the sequence."
25. See C. Guillén, 1977b, where Jakobson's idea is considered in some detail.
26. Rousset, 1962b, pp. 13, 16.
27. See "Spatial Form in Modern Literature," in Frank, 1963, pp. 3–62.
28. See C. Guillén, 1978b.
29. See Wellek and Warren, 1956, p. 152. Claus Uhlig writes about a *Schichten-theorie* (theory of levels) of antiquity; see Uhlig, 1982, pp. 89–99; and Martí-nez Bonati, 1983.

30. See Catalán, 1979 and 1984a, pp. 19–25.

31. LaDrière, 1959b, p. 35.

32. See LaDrière, 1959a, p. 171.

33. Ibid., p. 170. On prosody, see also Hrushovski, 1960, 1972; Lotz, 1960; Chatman, 1965; LaDrière, 1965; Wimsatt, 1972; Jakobson, 1979. Zhirmunsky's *Rifma* (St. Petersburg, 1923), was reissued in 1970 in Munich with a new prologue-summary in German.

34. Hrushovski, 1972, p. 1.197b.

35. See Pfister, 1977, pp. 18–19. For tradition—not only in regard to dramatic genres—that continues in our century, see Staiger, 1956; or Hamburger, 1957. A more analytic discussion is found in Fergusson, 1949.

36. See Ingarden, 1960; and Bogatyrev, 1971.

37. Barthes, 1972, p. 42.

38. Díez Borque in Díez Borque and García Lorenzo, 1975, p. 57. Concerning practices of contemporary theater, see Szondi, 1956. See also, from a theoretical and bibliographical point of view, Vowles, 1956; Diederichsen, 1966; Bentley, 1968.

39. Cited by García Lorenzo, in Díez Borque and García Lorenzo, 1975, p. 105. See Kowzan, 1968.

40. Eco, 1975, p. 101 (French version in Helbo, 1975, pp. 33–45). See also Bouissac, 1973.

41. Barthes, 1967, p. 41: "As soon as there is a society, every usage is converted into a sign of itself."

42. See Segre, 1982a.

43. See Pérez Gállego, 1975.

44. See Díez Borque in Díez Borque and García Lorenzo, 1975, p. 86.

45. See García Lorenzo, "Elementos paraverbales," in ibid.

46. Díez Borque in ibid., p. 56. For the semiological approach to the theater, see notes 39–43 above and Helbo, 1975; Ubersfeld, 1978; Elam, 1980 (has a good bibliography); Pavis, 1980; *Poetics Today* 2, no. 3 (1981); De Marinis, 1982.

47. See Metz, 1971 and 1971–72; and Jeanne-Marie Clerc, "Littérature et cinéma," in Pageaux, 1983, pp. 157–171.

48. Eco, 1975, p. 96.

49. See "Significante y significado," in D. Alonso, 1950.

50. See L. Prieto, *Messages et signaux* (Paris, 1966); Mounin, 1971; and, more generally, Sebeok, 1975; Eco, 1979; and Greimas and Courtès, 1979.

51. Mounin, 1971, p. 14.

52. Ibid., p. 92.

53. Ibid., p. 94.

54. Quoted in ibid., p. 88.

55. See Segre, 1984, p. 11.

56. See Propp, 1970, pp. 30–31.

57. See Bremond, 1964, 1966; Barthes, 1966; Greimas, 1966; Todorov, 1969. In

1950 E. Souriau had published *Les deux cent mille situations dramatiques*. See Beristáin, 1982. There are historical summaries in Meijer, 1981; and in the valuable manual of S. Rimmon-Kenan, *Narrative Fiction* (London, 1983).

58. Todorov, 1969, p. 125.

59. Ibid., p. 15.

60. Ibid., p. 12.

61. Genette, 1972; Lotman, 1973, 1974; Segre, 1974; Chatman, 1978; Cohn, 1978; and Stanzel, 1984.

62. Genette, 1980, p. 94. See also Genette's additions, 1983.

63. Genette, 1980, pp. 94, 102–106. Regarding descriptions in the story, see Pérez Gállego, 1973, pp. 115–135: there is tension between dialogue and description; dialogue proceeds from description and is opposed to it. For the art of description, in addition to Chapter 12, note 85, above, see Ricardou, 1972; Gelley, 1979; and Hamon, 1981.

64. Genette, 1980, p. 72.

65. See ibid., pp. 106–109.

66. Cervantes, 1961, p. 202.

67. Carmen Martín Gaite, *Ritmo lento* (Barcelona, 1981), p. 20. On tempo in the novel, see Villanueva, 1977.

68. See Genette, 1980, pp. 35–40.

69. Ibid., p. 67. See Rico, 1983, p. 14, and also his edition of *Caballero de Olmedo* (Salamanca, 1967).

70. Lazarillo de Tormes, 1973, p. 21.

71. Stendhal, 1977, pp. 171, 166.

72. Mario Vargas Llosa, "*Los Miserables:* El último clásico," in *Cielo abierto* (Lima) 8 (1983), 38.

73. See Stanzel, 1984, p. 5: "the distinguishing characteristic of the figural narrative situation is that the illusion of immediacy is superimposed over mediacy." See B. H. Smith, 1978, chap. 2; Pagnini, 1980, pp. 27–34; and Elliott, 1982. In 1971 Francisco Ayala wrote in "Reflexiones sobre la estructura narrativa" (p. 420): "at bottom, all poetry turns out to be narration."

74. Stanzel, 1978, p. 247. On the concept of *Ideal type,* see Stanzel's interesting explications, 1984, pp. 7–9 and 60–62.

75. See Stanzel, 1984, p. 16.

76. See ibid., pp. 63–66. On Stanzel's theory see the review by D. Cohn, "The Encirclement of Narrative," in *Poetics Today* 2, no. 2 (1981), 157–182, and, in the same issue, dedicated to narratology, especially the bibliographies; Mieke Bal, "Notes on Narrative Embedding," pp. 49–59; and, by Stanzel himself, "Teller-Characters and Reflector-Characters in Narrative Theory," pp. 5–15.

77. See Genette, 1980, pp. 194–198.

78. I am grateful to Stephen Gilman for pointing out (years ago) the Goethe-Valera parallel.

79. Cohn, 1978, p. 7.

80. See C. Guillén, 1971, p. 124.
81. See Prieto, 1975, pp. 30–39.
82. See Cohn, 1978, chaps. 4, 5, and 6.
83. See ibid., pp. 112–115.
84. Ibid., p. 34.
85. Ibid., p. 103.
86. See Jenny, 1976.
87. Milosz, 1983, p. 66.
88. Ibid., p. 71.
89. Catalán, 1984a, p. 20.
90. Catalán, 1978, p. 248.
91. Ibid., p. 250.
92. Ibid., p. 261.
93. Catalán, 1984a, pp. 173–174 (I have modernized the orthography).
94. See ibid., p. 92.
95. Quoted in Lord, 1960, p. 3.
96. Lord, 1960, p. 30, repeats Parry's definition.
97. See Zumthor, 1990.
98. See Lord, 1960, pp. 54, 131, and the bibliography of p. 284, n. 17; and Catalán, 1984a, p. 169: the hemistich is often a semantic unity; but "narration advances, ordinarily, line by line."
99. Nagy, 1982, p. 45. See Lord, 1960, pp. 50–54.
100. See Edwards, 1971.
101. Catalán, 1984a, p. 81.
102. See Lord, 1960, pp. 143, 291.
103. Catalán, 1984a, p. 177.
104. Lord, 1960, p. 5.
105. Menéndez Pidal, 1953, II, p. 44.
106. Catalán, 1984b, p. 6.
107. Ibid.
108. Nagy, 1982, p. 46.
109. See Díaz Viana, Díaz, and Delfín Val, 1979, pp. 116–117—here is the shortest version:

> La Virgen se está peinando a la sombra de una higuera,
> los peines eran de plata, las cintas de primavera.
> Pasó por allí José, diciendo de esta manera:
> ¿Por qué no canta la linda? ¿Por qué no canta la bella?
> —-¿Cómo quieres que yo cante si soy de tierras ajenas
> y aquel hijo que tenía, más blanco que la azucena,
> me le están crucificando en una cruz de madera?

> The Virgin was combing her hair in the shade of a fig tree
> the combs were of silver, the ribbons of springtime.

Joseph passed by there, speaking in this way:
Why does the lovely one not sing? Why does the beautiful one not
sing?
—How do you think I can sing if I am from far-off lands
and that son I had, whiter than a lily
they are crucifying upon a wooden cross.

110. Lord, 1960, p. 184.

111. For the bibliography on oral literature, which is vast, see Bynum, 1969; Stolz and Shannon, 1976; Finnegan, 1977; Zumthor, 1990, pp. 233–247; and Chapter 12, note 41, above. On the "formulaic" technique in the *Chanson de Roland,*, see Duggan, 1973; on *El Cid,* Duggan, 1975; on African literature, Görog-Karady, 1982. See the bibliography of Catalán, Armistead, and Sánchez Romeralo, 1979; and *Proceedings V,* pt. 2.

112. See Derrida, 1978.

113. See Zumthor, 1990, pp. 5–8. Logocentric illusion, this mutation of the voice in writing, according to Derrida, 1967.

114. See Menéndez Pidal, 1953, I, pp. 45–47.

115. See Zumthor, 1990, pp. 22–23.

116. Ibid., p. 27. See Alfonso Reyes, "Lo oral y lo escrito," in *Obras completas,* XXI (Mexico City, 1963), pp. 265–269.

117. On repetition, see Hock, 1915; Deleuze, 1968; Said, 1976; Szegedy-Maszák, 1979; Rimmon-Kenan, 1980. Kierkegaard's *Repetition* is from 1843 (English translation, 1941). Also repeated by J. Cohen, 1976.

118. Todorov, 1984, p. 45.

119. See Genette, 1980, pp. 228–229; Bal, 1981; and, on *The Arabian Nights,* Todorov, 1973, pp. 107–110 and 164–165. There are certainly other important formal approaches, such as the *Wendepunkt* (turning point) that the theory of the novella brings to light; see Wiese, 1963; Hell, 1976. On ends or conclusions, see Kermode, 1967; and on beginnings, Said, 1975; and Pere Gimferrer, *Dietari 1979–1980* (Barcelona, 1981), p. 187.

120. See Morrissette, 1971; and Dällenbach, 1977, which has a bibliography, pp. 235–242.

121. Mishima, 1975. The level of intertextuality of the *Tale of Genji* and other Japanese classics is considerable.

122. Foulquié, 1958, p. 12.

123. Regarding dialogue many monologues have been published. See Bakhtin (all his works, without exception); Fries, 1975; Aubailly, 1976; the special issue of the *Canadian Review of Comparative Literature* 3 (1976); Bauer, 1977; Gray, 1977; Mukařovský, 1977; and Kushner, 1982, 1983.

124. See C. Guillén, 1979a.

125. Bakhtin, 1984b, p. 279.

126. C. Guillén, 1979a, p. 644.

127. Bakhtin, 1981, p. 349.

128. On the textual history of Bakhtin's work, see M. Holquist in Bakhtin, 1981, pp. xxvi–xxxiv; and Todorov, 1984, pp. 5–13.
129. See Todorov, 1981, pp. 151–152.
130. Gilman, 1956, pp. 20, 23.
131. See Chapter 15 and Kristeva, 1986.
132. Bakhtin, 1984b, p. 293.
133. Bakhtin, 1984a, p. 366.
134. See Todorov, 1984; and Holquist in Bakhtin, 1981, p. 428.
135. Bakhtin, 1981, p. 293.
136. Todorov, 1984, p. 87.
137. Bakhtin, 1981, p. 276.
138. Todorov, 1984, pp. 56–57.
139. Bakhtin, 1981, p. 32.
140. Bakhtin, 1984b, p. 291.
141. Ibid., p. 279.
142. I am quoting from the unpublished talk given by Donald Fanger, which will one day surely be amplified by the author, but whose interest is such that it admits of no delay, "Dostoyevsky and Cervantes in the Theory of Bakhtin: The Theory of Bakhtin in Cervantes and Dostoyevsky." I am grateful to him for this opportunity, with his permission, to practice the dialogism that Bakhtin professed.
143. Díaz Viana, Díaz, and Delfín Val, 1979, p. 66; translation by Cola Franzen and Alicia Borinsky. On the theory of metaphors, see "La mythologie blanche," in Derrida, 1972; Ricoeur, 1975; de Man, 1978; Ortony, 1979, which has a good bibliography; Sacks, 1979; the issue of *Poetics Today* 2 (1980–81), 1 *b*.
144. See de Man, 1971 and 1979. The methodology of the approximation to the singular text is not a basic preoccupation of comparativism; it goes beyond the bounds of this book. That explains the absence of allusions to deconstructionism, whose neo-avant-gardism, moreover, seems to me invalid. Not so the proposals of Paul de Man, who, without messianic or global pataphysical pretensions, illuminates with singular delicacy the rhetorical character of the language of literature. According to him the rhetorical figures are not tools of a persuasive language but constituents of the paradigmatic structure of all literary communication (see de Man, 1979, p. 106). The sign is a space where a referential sense and another figurative sense, whose context is extralinguistic, are interlaced in a problematic way. In addition, the grammatical form carries the words along with it, distancing them from all reference to actual experience: "the logic of grammar generates texts only in the absence of referential meaning" (de Man, 1979, p. 269). Independently of Derrida, de Man's orientation is already found in the essays of *Blindness and Insight*, 1971: a rhetorical conception of the text, the examination of philosophical texts as if they were literary ones, the assimilation of criticism to literature.

Note that de Man does not reduce *everything* to rhetoric, which would have the effect of suppressing the peculiarities of rhetoric as well as its historical trajectory. This is not the case with Miller, 1971. See Culler, 1982.

145. See C. Guillén, foreword to Francisco García Lorca, 1984.

146. Barthes, 1967, pp. 12, 20; 1974 p. 15; see Kristeva, 1968, pp. 299, 301; and Hirsch, 1976, p. 21. A few words more, mine this time, regarding a certain recent fondness in literary studies: a fondness for disintegration. It is to be supposed that Barthes denounced the "ideology of the whole" for two reasons: because of the dogma of totality, and because of its transparent origin or ideological intention. Isn't the ideology of disintegration just as transparent, programmatic, extraliterary, and pretentious? I am referring, obviously, to the most ingenuous "deconstructionists." The text dismantles itself, according to Miller, 1976, p. 341, and the critic has only to observe and continue the dismantling. To begin with, the faith in the will of form and its perfect efficacy seems to me just as unilateral as faith in chaos. How much they resemble each other! The deconstructionists search for an illogical, aberrant element, "differencing device," and so on. But the only one who would go looking for such elements and devices is the one who does not recognize from the beginning that the dialectic of the one and the many is the constituent impulse of literary work. Everyone who reads poetry with sensibility knows that the poem encloses discordances, evasions, self-contradictions. Without them the will of form would find neither resistance nor materials. I have already emphasized (Chapter 10) that not all is parallelism in poetry, that its tensions and interactions are basic. Well then, as a practical matter, critics are perfectly free to dedicate themselves exclusively to the destructive and desintegrative desires and elements—so typical, as is very well known, of the retarded or belated movements of the neo-avant-garde.

147. Bakhtin, 1981, p. 362.

148. See Flaker, 1973; and Zmegač, 1970, pp. 387–397 (complete version in *Stilovi i razdoblja* [Zagreb, 1964], pp. 158–170).

149. Spitzer, 1955a, p. 23.

150. See Sempoux, 1960. For useful introductions to stylistics see Aguiar e Silva, 1968, chap. 15; and Yllera, 1974.

151. The detail does not coincide totally with the whole of the work or exemplify it absolutely, either—according to what Lázaro Carreter points out in his reservations about stylistics, which I share; see Lázaro Carreter, 1979, pp. 51–52; there is a "circular movement," which alone justifies the "impression of the critic."

152. See A. Alonso, 1955, pp. 257–300; C. Guillén, 1971.

153. Figueiredo, 1962, p. 257.

154. Wellek, 1970, p. 342.

155. See, for example, Corti, 1976; in a singular text there are crisscrosses and superpositions of different "registers"; this density of registers may allow the

poem to be a "hypersign," capable of communicating a complex or elevated level of information.

156. See Riffaterre, 1971, chap. 2; also 1978, 1979. Lázaro Carreter also rejects the theory of the deviation or deflection, 1980, pp. 193–206; literary language is not reduced to a unified standard; each particular poetics determines in particular the use of the different recourses of a writer, a plurality whose conjugation and equilibrium condition the writer's stance toward the "common language."

157. Paz, 1974, p. 5. On the earlier attitude—my fifth point—of veneration of the work of art, see Caramaschi, 1984, p. 34.

14. Themes

1. See Van Tieghem, 1951, p. 87; Block, 1970, p. 22. For the old thematic, see A. Graf, *La leggenda del paradiso terrestre* (Rome, 1878); Max Koch, "Zur Einführung," *Zeitschrift für vergleichende Literaturwissenschaft*, 1 (1887); Gaston Paris, *Légendes du Moyen Age,* 3d ed. (Paris, 1912); or A. Farinelli, *La vita è un sogno* (Turin, 1916).

2. "The Revolt against Positivism in Recent European Scholarship," in Wellek, 1963, pp. 256–281.

3. On this issue debated in the manuals and histories of comparativism, see Weisstein, 1968, chap. 7; and Jost, 1974, chap. 5 (see his bibliography). On the recent flowering of thematology, Beller, 1970, is very useful; and for present-day France, J. Dugast and P. Chardin in Pageaux, 1983, pp. 19–26.

4. Quoted in Derrida, 1978, p. 29.

5. See Beller, 1970, p. 2. Also very useful is Beller's summary, with a bibliography on thematology, in Schmeling, 1981.

6. Schiller to Goethe, March 27, 1801; see *Briefe,* ed. F. Jonas (Leipzig, 1892–1896), VI, p. 262.

7. See H. Levin, 1972, p. 95.

8. In Federico García Lorca, 1983, p. 19.

9. Alberti, 1976, I, p. 4.

10. Federico García Lorca, 1931, 1929, and 1981 (the version quoted here). "Ballad . . . ," translated by David K. Loughran, and the following "Serenade," translated by Alan S. Trueblood, both from Frederico García Lorca, 1991.

11. Sena, 1982, p. 202; translation by Fritz Hensey.

12. See J. L. Borges, "El arte narrativo y la magia," in *Discusión* (Buenos Aires, 1961), pp. 86–88.

13. On the rhetorical concept of topos, see Veit, 1963; and Beller, 1970; Beller, 1979, recommends the study of brief entities, "kleinere formale Einheiten."

14. See Fanger, 1965, chap. 5; and Festa-McCormick, 1979. For the historical thematization of space, the studies of delimitation and interpretation of space in

literature are important, such as Weisgerber, 1978. In this respect Bakhtin was a thematologist of historical orientation, interested in what he calls "chronotopes"—spatial-temporal complexes—as well as the encounter, the road, the test required of the hero or the fool; see Bakhtin, 1981, pp. 99, 244, 388, 404. On space and metonomy, see Gelley, 1980. The study of space in Gogol by Lotman, 1973, is excellent, as is Ingarden, 1960.

15. See H. Levin, 1968, p. 93.
16. See Greimas, 1970, pp. 249–270.
17. See Trousson, 1965.
18. See Blume, 1966.
19. See Prawer, 1973, pp. 99–100.
20. Juan Marichal, preface to Pedro Salinas, *Poesías completas,* ed. S. Salinas de Marichal (Barcelona, 1981), p. 24.
21. See Salinas, 1946, pp. 44, 37, 47, 72; variation 13, pp. 68–69; and 1950, pp. 53, 43, 55, 86, and 83.
22. See J. M. Blecua, 1945; also Navarro González, 1963.
23. A. Romero Márquez, preface to J. Guillén, 1981, p. 11. On the sea in Romantic English poetry, see W. H. Auden, *The Enchafed Flood* (New York, 1950).
24. Garibay, 1953–1954, I, p. 100.
25. Soseki, 1977, p. 9.
26. Pla, 1950, p. 229; translation by Fritz Hensey.
27. See Michaëlsson, 1959.
28. See Mathieu-Castellani, 1980.
29. Translation by Jeffrey Mehlman. See Rousset, 1961.
30. See Charles S. Houston, *Going High: The Story of Man and Altitude* (Burlington, Vt., 1980); Nicolson, 1959; and Konrad Gesner, *Libellus de lacte . . . cum epistola ad Iacobum Aiuenum de montium admiratione* (Zurich, 1541).
31. See Castro, 1977b.
32. Hugo, 1977; translation by Jeffrey Mehlman.
33. See Motekat, 1961.
34. Palmier, 1972, p. 207.
35. Trakl, 1987 and 1989.
36. See Balakian, 1967.
37. Translation by Jeffrey Mehlman.
38. See Schulman, 1960.
39. Quoted in Silva Castro, 1959, p. 94.
40. Stevens, 1971, p. 133.
41. Jay Rubin, "Sanchiro and Soseki," in Soseki, 1977, p. 218.
42. See Palmier, 1972, p. 226.
43. See Sonnenfeld, 1960, p. 48.
44. Mix, 1960, p. 2.
45. Jiménez, 1987, p. 14. A later version of the poem by Juan Ramón, that of *Leyenda,* A. Sánchez Romeralo (Madrid, 1978), no. 308, is very different—

"Abril de dios venía, lleno todo de gracias amarillas . . ."—but it keeps the monochromaticism. And what about the monochromaticism of the first line of "Romance sonámbulo": "Verde que te quiero verde"?

46. "Bell," in Frederico García Lorca, 1991; See also idem, 1983, pp. 68, 90–95, 134, 254.
47. Translation by Cola Franzen and Alicia Borinsky.
48. W. Kaiser, 1963, p. 5.
49. Ibid., p. 7.
50. Such as Fra Mariano and Domenico Brandino, nicknamed "il Cordiale"; see A. Graf, "Un bufone de Leone X," in *Attraverso el Cinquecento* (Turin, 1926), p. 300; cited by Márquez Villanueva, 1983, p. 208.
51. See Deleite y Piñuela, 1935, pp. 121–129; J. Moreno Villa, *Locos, enanos, negros y niños palaciegos* (Mexico City, 1939); Bigeard, 1972; and Zuñiga, 1981, pp. 23–35.
52. See W. Kaiser, 1963, pp. 285, 9–10.
53. Cited by ibid., p. 11.
54. See Giamatti, 1966.
55. Lida de Malkiel, 1975, p. 37.
56. On Vives' *Fabula* see Rico, 1970, pp. 121–128.
57. Montaigne, 1958.
58. Giamatti, 1968, pp. 444, 472–475.
59. See Georg Brandes, *Main Currents in Nineteenth-Century Literature* (London and New York, 1906), IV, pp. 1–2. On Braudel's terms, mentioned various times here, see Braudel, 1958 and 1966.
60. See Frye, 1968, pp. 85–105.
61. Quental, 1989; translation by Fritz Hensey.
62. See Gilman, 1981, p. 148.
63. Manrique in J. M. Cohen, 1988, pp. 72, 73.
64. Bécquer, 1977, pp. 96–100. See Ariès, 1975; and Pagliano, 1983. Like the poetry of Jorge Manrique, a peerless example of conscious death, meaningful, and, so to speak, shared, is the actual death of Etienne La Boétie, as described in detail by Montaigne in August 1563 in a letter to his father a short while after the event (see 1965, pp. 1.352–354). Pale and exhausted earlier, La Boétie recovers strength ("il semblait . . . comme par miracle, reprendre quelque nouvelle vigueur"), speaks, expresses himself clearly and at length, calling—thematically, we would say—on the stoic topics of *consolatio:* it is better to die young than old, and so on. La Boétie dies consciously, philosophically, and actively. He dies surrounded by loved ones, principally three people—his uncle M. de Builhonnas, his wife, and Montaigne—who do not grieve but admire and understand his *ars moriendi,* meaningful and exemplary for them. Finally, La Boétie remains alone with Montaigne, his best friend, who would never forget the event, as is well known.
65. "Fuera del mundo," in Guillén, 1987, V, p. 345; translation by Alicia Borinsky.

66. See Gorer, 1965, pp. 169–175.
67. Lapesa, 1976, p. 7.
68. See Castro, 1977a.
69. For the study of themes, Frenzel, 1970a, 1970b, and 1980 are indispensable, along with Baldensperger and Friederich, 1950.
70. See Borges, 1979, p. 71.
71. See Veit, 1963 and 1983; Beller, 1970.
72. See Lida de Malkiel, 1975, pp. 36–38, 121.
73. From "Falleció César, fortunado y fuerte," in Quevedo, 1969–1971, I, p. 155.
74. Translation from Cruz, 1988.
75. The stag appears for the third time in stanza 29 of the "Cántico": "A las aves ligeras, / leones, ciervos, gamos saltadores . . ." ("Swift birds, lions, deer, leaping harts . . ."; translation from Rivers, 1988, p. 136). But it is no longer the wounded stag, but an enumeration close to the Song of Songs; see Lida de Malkiel, 1975, p. 78. For the theme of the stag, see also Asensio, 1957.
76. San Juan de la Cruz, 1973, stanza 1, p. 15; translation, Rivers, 1988, pp. 130–131.
77. D. Ynduráin, preface to San Juan de la Cruz, *Poesía* (Madrid, 1983), p. 90.
78. San Juan de la Cruz, 1973, pp. 134–136.
79. Lida de Malkiel, 1975, p. 69.
80. Translation from Rivers, 1988, p. 133.
81. Lida de Malkiel, 1975, p. 76.
82. See Giamatti, 1966; Beller, 1970, pp. 24–25. Steiner, 1975, p. 217, writes: "Language is the main instrument of man's refusal to accept the world as it is."
83. In Cristóbal Colón, *Textos y documentos completos,* ed. Consuelo Varela (Madrid, 1982), pp. 145, 119. See Veit, 1983.
84. See H. Levin, 1969, p. 93.
85. Quoted in ibid., p. 74.
86. From *Aminta,* II.2, quoted in ibid., p. 46; translation modified.
87. Quevedo, 1969–1971, III, p. 97.
88. See H. Levin, 1969, pp. 8–11.
89. See S. Sontag, "The Imagination of Disaster," in Rose, 1976, pp. 116–131; Stanislaw Lem, "The Time-Travel Story and Related Matters of SF Structuring," ibid., pp. 71–88; Lukács, 1971, p. 29.
90. Rico, 1970, p. 12.
91. Ibid., p. 267.
92. Ibid., p. 153.
93. See ibid., pp. 242–259; translation from Calderón de la Barca, 1970, p. 53.
94. Rico, 1970, p. 43.
95. Quoted in ibid., p. 271.
96. Quoted in Gilman, 1981, p. 78 and n. 47.
97. Paz, 1973a, p. 240.

98. A theme that could perhaps be analyzed as a diachronic structure; see Chapter 16.

99. See J.-J. Rousseau, 1979; and Rousset, 1981, p. 8.

100. See Rousset, 1981, pp. 24–27, 137–141; translation from Flaubert, 1904, p. 8.

101. See Rousset, 1981, p. 48.

102. Heliodorus, 1957, p. 73.

103. Martorell and Martí, 1984.

104. Rousset, 1981, p. 63.

105. On Stendhal, see ibid., pp. 108–113.

106. Cervantes, 1961, p. 192.

107. Ibid., pp. 248–249.

108. Salinas, 1949, pp. 22–23; translation, 1974, pp. 31–33.

109. Dutu, 1973, p. 317. See also Gilman, 1967.

110. See Wölfflin, 1915.

111. Dufour, 1977, p. 160.

112. Ibid., p. 161.

113. See Frenzel, 1970a, 1970b, and 1980.

114. Trousson, 1965, pp. 12–13. For a recapitulation, see Trousson, 1980.

115. See C. Guillén, 1955.

116. Castro, 1954, communication with author.

117. Curtius, 1950, p. 165.

118. Salinas, 1948, p. 48.

119. Darío, 1968, from "Eco y yo," p. 755.

120. Salinas, 1948, p. 50.

121. See Giraud, 1968; and Beller, 1970, pp. 9–10.

122. H. Levin, 1968, p. 101, n. 7.

123. See Lord, 1960, chap. 4.

124. See Poulet, 1949, 1952, 1961, 1968; Richard, 1954, 1955; Brombert, 1966, 1975; see Bachelard, 1943, 1948, 1958, 1974; Kushner, 1963.

125. See Durand, 1963, 1979; and Mauron, 1963. The "in-depth" perspective of which I speak in these pages can perhaps be joined with or related to the important study by Gerald Holton of the themes—*themata*—that guide the investigations of the natural sciences, *Thematic Origins of Scientific Thought: Kepler to Einstein* (Cambridge, Mass., 1973). Holton's "themes" are the preconceptions and earlier inclinations that guided investigations, independent of the empirical or analytic content of the findings: in Einstein, for instance, the search for continuity (in face of the division into discrete elements in quantum physics); or in general the love for simplicity and necessity. Holton's themes compose wholes, and various scientists of the same historical moment can share the same points of view (whereas the inclinations of Salinas or Curtius are individual in nature). It is curious that Holton also talks of an in-depth

thematic perspective: "In addition to the empirical or phenomenic *(x)* dimension and the heuristic-analytic *(y)* dimension, we can define a third, a *z* axis. This third dimension is the dimension of fundamental presuppositions, notions, terms, methodological judgments and decisions" (p. 41). What Holton calls content and theme can obviously coincide; thus, the continuity or *continuum* as an aspect of the solution of a problem and the empirical experiment itself that exemplifies the problem. To return to Salinas, in Rubén Darío the theme would be eroticism; and the empirical content or laboratory experiment, Leda or the garden of the peacocks. It is true that "the dichotomy between scientific and humanistic scholarship . . . becomes far less impressive if one looks carefully at the construction of scientific theories"; Holton, p. 35.

126. Interview by Natália Correia with A. Mega Ferreira, *Jornal de letras, artes e ideais* (Lisbon), 20 July–2 August 1982, p. 7.
127. See Pearce, 1969, pp. 20–25.
128. H. Levin, 1968, p. 101.
129. See Bodkin, 1934; Hyman, 1949; Wheelwright, 1954; Seboek, 1955; Weisinger, 1964; Ferdinandy, 1961; Schajowicz, 1962; the very complete anthology of Vickery, 1966; Jesi, 1968. A good example: the myths and actual narrative, M. Eliade and Juan Rulfo; see Durán, 1981.
130. See Frye, 1968, p. 69.
131. Ibid., p. 48.
132. H. Levin, 1969, p. xiii.
133. Frye, 1968, p. 110. See also W. K. Wimsatt, in Krieger, 1966, p. 76; Jameson, 1981, pp. 69–74; and Uhlig, 1982, p. 53.
134. See Wimsatt in Krieger, 1966, p. 106.
135. See Frye, 1957, chap. 1.
136. Frye, 1968, p. 56.
137. Northrop Frye in Vickery, 1966, p. 91.
138. Frye, 1968, p. 55.
139. Ibid., p. 71.
140. See Geoffrey Hartman in Krieger, 1966, p. 128.
141. Frye, 1957, p. 14. On the study of myths in France, see P. Brunel and A. Dabezies in Pageaux, 1983, pp. 51–65.

15. Literary Relations

1. Praz, 1952, p. 11.
2. Robert Shackleton in Aldridge, 1969, p. 293.
3. Mario Praz in Viscardi et al., 1948, p. 146. Translations of all quotations of Praz by Ruth Feldman.
4. Ibid., p. 148.
5. See ibid., p. 151.
6. Ibid., p. 159.

7. Ibid., p. 157.

8. Ibid., p. 169.

9. According to ibid., p. 171, until Luigi Baretti, *An Account of the Manners and Customs of Italy* (1768), which responds to the slanderous remarks of Samuel Sharp, *Letters from Italy*. On Italian comparativism see Vernon Lee, *Euphorion* (Boston, 1884); Pellegrini, 1947; Porta, 1951; Meregalli, 1976.

10. Vajda, 1964, p. 566.

11. See C. Guillén, 1971, pp. 46–52.

12. A. Croce in Viscardi, 1948, p. 110; translations of Croce by Ruth Feldman.

13. Ibid., p. 113.

14. On the problem of influences, see Chapter 7, notes 25 and 26, above; Hassan, 1955; Block, 1958; Hemerén, 1975; and Weisstein, 1981, chap. 5, including a bibliography, p. 207.

15. Goethe, 1984, p. 229.

16. Croce, 1923, p. 501.

17. Kristeva, 1986, p. 37.

18. Ibid., p. 36.

19. Ibid., p. 40, 36.

20. Ibid., pp. 35–36.

21. See Kristeva, 1969, pp. 278–350.

22. Kristeva, 1986, p. 41.

23. Roland Barthes, "Texte (théorie du)," in *Encyclopaedia universalis* (Paris, 1968), XV, p. 1.015c. I gladly take advantage of the occasion to confirm how sparingly this book admits the totalizing pretensions of certain literary theories. "Every text is an intertext" brings to mind statements like "All words are metaphors," formulated by an excellent North American critic in the throes of deconstructionism. Is the generalizing, absolutist inclination of theoretical thinking unavoidable? Perhaps it is. But let those who enter into a dialogue with such a theory from the point of view of experience of literature itself be on guard, cut away the excess, and question it. José Ferrater Mora includes in *De la materia a la razón* an article by C. Ulises Moulines ("Por qué no soy materialista," *Crítica*, 11, no. 26, 1977) that points out that every monist conception of the world, to be true, is so in a vacuum. "If we maintain that everything, or any x is P, we should provide a non-empty characteristic of P. Otherwise, to say that all x is P is to say nothing, since P can be understood in any way at all." In effect, to affirm that every word is a metaphor makes it difficult for a metaphor not to be emptied of all informative precision. When one affirms that every text is an intertext, the possibility becomes remote that the intertext may admit omissions or shadings, absences or presences, possess qualities not intermixed with every other text. The theory, avoiding intellectual terrorism, can indeed be opened to the diversity of the real. In sum, it is necessary to distinguish between *teoría* and *terroría* (theorizing and terrorizing)—permit me the pun.

24. Frye, 1959, p. 53. In this respect also see Brandt Corstius, 1968, pp. 71 and 139.
25. Du Bellay, 1910, p. 34; translation by Jeffrey Mehlman.
26. Riffaterre, 1979, p. 121.
27. Culler, 1981, p. 102.
28. Pascoli already preferred the expression *presupposti a fonti,* according to Croce, 1923, p. 501. On intertextuality, see the earlier quotations of Kristeva, Barthes, Riffaterre; also Riffaterre, 1978, pp. 116–124; idem, "La trace de l'intertexte," *La pensée,* October 1980; Bloom, 1975; Jenny, 1976; the special issue of *Poétique,* 1976, p. 27; Compagnon, 1979; Genette, 1982; and Segre, 1982b.
29. Alarcos Llorach, 1976, p. 249. Literary communication "is not in situation," says Pagnini also, 1980, p. 62; cited in Caramaschi, 1984, p. 14, n. 10.
30. Cernuda, 1977. For this suggestion, I am indebted to an unpublished work by Daniel Fernández, "El rincón del olvido."
31. Gilman, 1981, p. 521, n. 43.
32. Ibid., pp. 222, 162.
33. See ibid., pp. 75, 134.
34. See ibid., pp. 97–102.
35. See ibid., pp. 114–123, 176–184. Amado Alonso wrote (1954, p. 383): "the poet does not repeat, he replies. And it is clear that we can grasp the whole sense of the reply only if what incited it is known to us."
36. Eça de Queiróz, 1965, p. 630.
37. Flaubert, 1904, p. 326.
38. See Forster, 1970, p. 83. (The resulting poem is "Balsam cartouche"). The members of the avant-garde of the 1920s were often bilingual: Juan Larrea, Vicente Huidobro, among others. Earlier we recalled the surrealistic game of *cadavre exquis,* and Octavio Paz's *Renga.* On multilingual—or neological—Dadaism, see Steiner, 1975, pp. 192–196.
39. Quoted in Kushner, 1966, p. 582.
40. Forster, 1970, p. 66.
41. Quoted in ibid., p. 56.
42. Quoted in ibid., p. 65; translation by Jeffrey Mehlman.
43. Quoted in ibid., pp. 66–67; translation by Jeffrey Mehlman.
44. Steiner, 1971, p. 10.
45. Quoted in Forster, 1970, p. 29: "Weil ein Vers dir gelingt in einer gebildeten Sprache. Die für dich dichtet und denkt, glaubst du schon Dichter zu sein"; translation by Wolfgang Franzen.
46. See Alekseiev, 1975, p. 39.
47. See ibid., p. 40.
48. Ibid., p. 37.
49. See Berndt and Berndt, 1982, p. 41.
50. See Bakhtin, 1981, p. 64.

51. F. Jost in *Proceedings III*, p. 301.

52. See Dan Pagis, preface to Solomon ibn-Gabirol, *Poesía secular,* tr. E. Romero (Madrid, 1978), pp. xxiv, xxvi. And keep in mind the highly regarded bilingual poetry of some present-day Chicano poets (Tino Villanueva).

53. And perhaps to a lesser degree in other European capitals; see the letters sent from Vienna in 1808 by J. C. L. Simonde de Sismondi, *Un viaggio d'altri tempi* (Pescia, 1983), p. 72: "French is the universal language of society, but absolutely not that of the People." In Finland the official or dominant language until the eighteenth century was Swedish; see Laitinen, 1983.

54. See O. Rádl in L. I. Strakhovsky, *A Handbook of Slavic Studies* (Cambridge, Mass., 1949), p. 491.

55. See Friar, 1973.

56. Although earlier Rosalía de Castro used many Castilian expressions and Manuel Curros Enríquez essentially used the spoken language, Pondal enriched and ennobled Galician, even though the Galician-Portuguese songs of the Middle Ages were not revived until the 1920s; see R. Carballo Calero, *Historia da literatura galega contemporánea,* 2d ed. (Vigo, 1975). Almost all writers of Galician—like almost all writers of Catalan—had to write in Castilian also, and were in fact bilingual: "in a bilingual country, it is almost impossible not to write in the official language"; ibid., p. 749.

57. See Vildomec, 1963; and Weinreich, 1963.

58. See Birnbaum, 1974, p. 341; and V. Vratović, "Croatian Latinity in the Context of Croatian and European Literature," in Beker, 1981.

59. Waldapfel, 1968, p. 19.

60. See L. Sziklay in Sötér and Süpek, 1964, p. 330. Since 1895 Vienna and Prague have been intermediary cities for Croatia; see Flaker, 1976.

61. Klaniczay, 1967, p. 265; translation by Ruth Feldman.

62. See ibid. and Klaniczay, "Un machiavellista ungherese: Miklós Zrinyi," in Horányi and Klaniczay, 1967, pp. 185–199.

63. Nadal and Prats, 1982, p. 196; translation by Fritz Hensey.

64. Ibid., p. 315.

65. Seville was reconquered in 1248; Menorca was not finally taken until 1287. From 1200 to 1260 Gerona was an extremely active center of Jewish thought: Juda ben Yaqar, Ezra ben Salomon, Azriel, Jacob ben Shehet, and other cabalists.

66. According to J. Rubió i Balaguer, cited by Nadal and Prats, 1982, p. 312.

67. See Riquer, 1964, I, pp. 219, 235, 329.

68. See L. Sziklay in Sötér and Süpek, 1964, p. 342. A national culture can also serve as intermediary, as in the case of Italy between Germany and Spain; see Meregalli, 1978.

69. See Lara, 1947, p. 137.

70. Jean-Pierre Callach'h, *A genoux* (Paris, 1921,) pp. 20–21 (French translation by P. Mocaër): "il approche avec hâte, le dernier jour de notre chair périssable,

le jour du Grand Jugement, / Le jour de la mort des nations . . . / Nos bardes chantent 'l'autre Bretagne,' mais ils savent bien qu'il n'y a / Aucun paradis pour les nations . . ."

71. Cited in Pupo-Walker, 1982, p. 166; translated by Harold Livermore, *Royal Commentaries of the Incas* (Austin, 1966), p. 46.

72. See Forster, 1970, pp. 30–31.

73. See ibid., p. 51. M. Praz in Viscardi et al., 1948, stresses the influence of a *bembista* model and also that of Giovanni della Casa.

74. See Grabowicz, 1983, chap. 1.

75. See F. J. Nichols, 1975.

76. See Weintraub, 1969, pp. 663, 664, 670.

77. See Hartman, 1970, p. 372; and Bakhtin, 1968, pp. 465–476.

78. See D. Alonso, 1931, p. 51.

79. See van Dam, 1927; Elwert, 1960.

80. See Wytrzens, 1969. The use of Guaraní, also an official language of Paraguay, is perfectly functional in A. Roa Bastos' admirable *Hijo de hombre* (1960) (translated as *Son of Man*, 1965).

81. Cioran, 1973, p. 49.

82. Quoted in Riegel, 1934, p. 694.

83. See Everth, 1924, p. 15.

84. Quoted in Brunet, 1967, p. 469.

85. See Prado Coelho, 1966; and Lourenço, 1981.

86. See Bakhtin, 1981, pp. 61–68.

87. On multilingualism, in addition to those mentioned in notes 36–79, above, see Béziers, 1968; N. Anderson, 1969; Steiner, 1975, especially the bibliography p. 120, n. 1; Tassoni, 1981; the February 1982 issue of *Revista de Occidente*, on bilingualism; *Cuenta y razón*, 12 (1983); and Augusto Ponzio, "Oltre il monolinguismo," in Mariani, 1983, pp. 95–99.

88. Steiner, 1975, p. 24.

89. See ibid., chap. 1, "Understanding as Translation."

90. See ibid., chap. 4, "The Claims of Theory." The bibliography is fundamental, pp. 475–484.

91. Ibid., p. 90. The quotation is from E. S. Bates, *Intertraffic: Studies in Translation* (London, 1943), p. 15.

92. See R. Jakobson, "On Linguistic Aspects of Translation," in Brower, 1959, pp. 232–239. See also Diller and Kornelius, 1978.

93. See W. V. Quine, "Meaning and Translation," in Brower, 1959, pp. 148–172; Quine, 1960; Guenthner and Guenthner-Reutter, 1978.

94. Steiner, 1975, p. 107.

95. Lefevere, 1982, p. 145.

96. Arrowsmith and Shattuck, 1964, p. vi.

97. E. Nida in Brower, 1959, p. 14.

98. Jakobson in Brower, 1959, p. 234: "all cognitive experience and its classification is conveyable in any existing language."

99. See Escarpit, 1961 and 1966c; also Achilles Fang in Brower, 1959, p. 128. It is even appropriate to think of the translator, because of the freedom he exercises and his capacity for creative mistakes, as akin to the good reader—especially the reader/writer. Paul de Man says: "the specificity of literary language resides in the possibility of misreading and misinterpretation"; "Literature and Language: A Commentary," *NLH*, 1972, p. 184. It is unnecessary to recall Bloom, 1975, who extols theoretically fallacious readings and of course practices them.

100. See Gerchkovitch, 1975, pp. 56–57.

101. See Balakian, 1962, p. 28.

102. Arrowsmith and Shattuck, 1964, p. xiii.

103. See the issue of *CRCL*, 8 (1981), devoted to the translations of the Renaissance, especially the contributions of Paul Chavy ("Les traductions humanistes au début de la Renaissance française: Traductions médiévales, traductions modernes") and of Glyn P. Norton ("Humanist Foundation of Translation Theory, 1400–1450: A Study in the Dynamic of the Word").

104. See D. S. Carne-Ross, "Translation and Transposition," in Arrowsmith and Shattuck, 1964, pp. 5–28.

105. See Friar, 1973, p. 654.

106. See "Miseria y esplendor de la traducción," in J. Ortega y Gasset, *Obras completas* (Madrid, 1947), V, pp. 429–458.

107. See "Translation Types and Conventions" in Gaddis Rose, 1981, pp. 31–40; also E. Balcerzan, "Die Poetik der künstlerichen Uebersetung," in G. R. Kaiser, 1980b, pp. 155–168.

108. See Lefevere, 1982, p. 150.

109. See Vladimir Nabokov in Brower, 1959, pp. 98–99. It deals with the *Oeuvres de Lord Byron* (Paris, 1819), put into prose by Amédée Pichot.

110. See Lefevere, 1982, p. 150.

111. See Cotnam, 1970.

112. See Fang in Brower, 1959, p. 121; and the preface, "Translating Chinese Poetry," in Yip, 1976.

113. Translation by Fritz Hensey.

114. R. Poggioli in Brower, 1959, p. 141. Curtius thought the same thing about critics, drawn to certain authors and works by affinities and organized inclinations; see Curtius, 1950, p. 300: "The metaphysical background [of criticism] is the conviction that the intellectual world tends toward systems of affinity." The confessions of translators are very valuable, such as the extremely sincere one of J. M. Valverde, "Mi experiencia como traductor," in *Cuadernos de traducción e interpretación* (Barcelona, 1983), II, pp. 9–19.

115. Quoted by Haskell Block in Gaddis Rose, 1981, p. 120.

116. See Forster, 1970, p. 41.

117. J. J. Montesinos, preface to L. P. Arias Pérez, *Primavera y flor de los mejores romances* (1621), (Valencia, 1954), p. xv.
118. Arias Pérez, *Primavera y flor,* no. 3, pp. 15–16; C. Huygens, *De Gedichten* (Groningen, 1892–1898), II, p. 178.
119. Berman, 1984, p. 24.
120. See C. Guillén, 1971, pp. 498–499.
121. Lefevere, 1982, p. 140.
122. On translation, see, in addition to notes 87–118 above, the bibliograpies of B. Q. Morgan in Brower, 1959; Mounin, 1963; Paz, 1973a; Steiner, 1975, pp. 475–484; Lambert, 1976, 1981; Wilss, 1977; Toury, 1980; Even-Zohar, 1981; García Yebra, 1981; *Poetics Today,* 2, no. 4 (1981); Ayala, 1984, pp. 62–86; and Rodríguez Monroy, 1984.
123. See the reading of Marina Mayoral, "'Se equivocó la paloma . . .' de Rafael Alberti," in Amorós, 1973, pp. 343–350.
124. *Matthias Claudius Werke,* from *Sämtliche Werke,* . . . (1774), p. 520.
125. Quoted in Miner, 1979, p. 148.
126. Ha-Levi, 1983, pp. 75, 27.
127. Translation from Rivers, 1988, p. 528.

16. Historical Configurations

1. Although some historians such as Casalduero (1943, 1972, 1973), have tried to widen the European space of *Sturm und Drang,* and Nemoianu (1984) that of *Biedermeier,* making it coincide in general with the debilitation and ebbing of Romanticism around the middle of the nineteenth century.
2. See the attempt of Henri Peyre, *Les générations littéraires* (Paris, 1948).
3. See Wellek, 1963 and 1970. For a literary historiography, see the analysis and masterly summary of Jauss, 1967 and 1982, secs. 2–4. On its resurgence today see Szabolcsi, 1980.
4. Among his many works, see Casalduero, 1943, 1972, 1973, where such terms as *Naturalism, Impressionism, Expressionism,* and *Cubism* appear.
5. Barthes, 1963, p. 149.
6. See "The Tradition of Tradition" in H. Levin, 1958, pp. 17–26. See criticisms of the idea of tradition in Jauss, 1967 and 1982, sec. 4; C. Guillén, 1971, p. 453; and Uhlig, 1982, pp. 35–43.
7. See Paz, 1974.
8. Poggioli, 1968, p. 20.
9. Flaker, 1973, p. 187.
10. My article, "Second Thoughts on Currents and Periods," did not appear in the *Proceedings* of the Belgrade conference, but in the homage to Wellek, *The Disciplines of Criticism,* ed. Peter Demetz, Thomas Greene, and Lowry Nelson (New Haven, 1968), pp. 477–509. See an expanded version in C. Guillén, 1971, pp. 420–469.

11. See the bibliography in C. Guillén, 1971, p. 423, nn. 5 and 6.

12. On periodization see Wellek, 1941 and 1947; Teesing, 1949; Wellek and Warren, 1956, chap. 19; Barthes, 1963, p. 149; Binni, 1963; Fowler, 1972; Françoise Gaillard and Jacques Leenhardt in Bouazis, 1972; articles by A. Balakian, A. Dima, A. Flaker, C. Guillén, I. Sötér, A. O. Aldridge in the special issue of *Neohelicon* 1, no. 1, (1972); White, 1973; Margolin, 1975; Weisstein, 1973. There is a bibliography in Weisstein, 1981, p. 208; and another at the end of the chapter on periodization, useful in itself, by Martin Brunkhorst in Schmeling, 1981.

13. The *Histoire comparée,* sponsored by the ICLA, under the direction of Jacques Voisine, then Henry Remak, and later Jean Weisgerber, consists of volumes in French or English, written in collaboration by numerous specialists of western and eastern Europe and America. The following volumes have appeared: *Expressionism as an International Literary Phenomenon,* ed. U. Weisstein (Paris and Budapest, 1978); *Le tournant du Siècle des Lumières, 1760–1820: Les genres en vers des Lumières au Romantisme,* ed. G. M. Vajda (Budapest: Akadémiai Kiadó [which also published the following volumes], 1982); *The Symbolist Movement in the Literature of European Languages,* ed. A. Balakian (1982); *Les avant-gardes littéraires au XXe siècle,* vol. I: *Histoire;* vol. II: *Théorie,* ed. J. Weisgerber (1984).

14. See Chapter 14, note 59. Paul Cornea has commented on and emphasized this experience of diversity on the part of present-day historians; see Cornea, 1983, p. 46.

15. See F. De Sanctis, *Storia della letteratura italiana,* ed. B. Croce, 2 vols. (Bari, 1939). For a critical attitude that might have influenced Croce's reservations about periodization, see "Epoche cronologiche e epoche storiche," in *La storia come pensiero e come azione* 6th ed. (Bari, 1954), p. 308.

16. See J. Huizinga, *Wege der Kulturgeschichte,* tr. W. Kaegi (Munich, 1930), p. 119; or "Het probleem der Renaissance," in *Verzamelde Werken* (Haarlem, 1949), IV, p. 257.

17. See G. Brandes, *Main Currents in Nineteenth Century Literature,* 6 vols. (London, 1906). The Danish edition is from 1872–1890.

18. See C. Guillén, 1971, pp. 420–469.

19. See the historical summary of Julián Marías, with bibliography, in *El método histórico de las generaciones,* 3d ed. (Madrid, 1961). See also note 2 above.

20. See Sötér, 1974, p. 25. On international currents, see *Proceedings V,* pp. 1–428.

21. A. Blecua, 1981, p. 111.

22. See P. Vilar in *Première Conférence Internationale d'Histoire Economique. Contributions* (The Hague, 1960), p. 37.

23. See Kubler, 1962, p. 13. On the union of communities and ruptures, see Gsteiger, 1983b.

24. See Wellek, 1973, p. 439; and Uhlig, 1982.

25. To summarize quickly C. Guillén, 1977a, 1978a: Jean-Paul Sartre thought that

man, in directing himself toward a future, personalizes time, see *Critique de la raison dialectique* (Paris, 1960), p. 64: "it should be understood, indeed, that neither men nor their activities are *in time* but that time, like a concrete character of history, is made by men, on the basis of their original temporalization." Aristotle wrote, *Physics* VI.4.234b10: "everything that changes must be divisible."

26. On Mannerism as well as the baroque, see Hocke, 1961; Boase, 1962; Rousset, 1962a; Borgerhoff, 1963; "The Concept of Baroque in Literary Scholarship," in Wellek, 1963, pp. 69–127; Orozco Díaz, 1970; Nichols and Robinson, 1972; Warnke, 1972; Gérard, 1983.

27. Wellek, 1963, p. 129.

28. See Béguin, 1937; Gérard, 1957; Remak, 1961; "The Concept of Romanticism in Literary History" in Wellek, 1963, pp. 128–221; Hartman, 1954, 1962.

29. "Brauche ich . . . zusagen, dass ich in Fragen der *décadence* erfahren bin?"

30. Bauer, 1978b, p. 198; and on decadence, Bauer, 1978a.

31. See Fanger, 1965, chaps. 1 and 5.

32. Lévi-Strauss, 1979.

33. For example, see "The Story of Asdiwal," in Claude Lévi-Strauss, *Structural Anthropology*, vol. II, tr. Monique Layton (New York: Basic Books, 1976), pp. 146–197.

34. See Szabolcsi, 1969; Marino, 1977a, 1979a, 1980; Flaker, 1980, 1983; also Bergel, 1964; Goriely, 1967; Calinescu, 1969; Weightman, 1973; Paz, 1974; Vitiello, 1984. Beyond question the pioneer was Guillermo de Torre, *Literaturas europeas de vanguardia* (Madrid, 1925), expanded and reissued several times. I have already mentioned (note 13) the two monumental volumes of *Les avant-gardes littéraires au XXe siècle* (Budapest, 1984), edited by Jean Weisgerber.

35. Bloom, 1973, p. 30. See the criticisms by Culler, 1981, pp. 108–111; and by Uhlig, 1982, pp. 44–59, "Literarhistorische Pathologie."

36. What is new under the sun about awareness of error? Forty years ago Alexander Gillies emphasized the pertinence of past misreadings for comparativism; see Gillies, 1952, p. 23.

37. See Chapter 15, note 23.

38. See Danto, 1965, p. 152.

39. Collingwood, 1946, p. 240.

40. Dray, 1964, p. 19; Danto, 1965, p. 8.

41. See White, 1973. According to him, each class of history follows a generic inclination—romance, tragedy, comedy, satire—and also an interpretative inclination on the ethical, cognitive, or aesthetic level; that is, it is at one and the same time history and metahistory. The fundamental tropes are metaphor, metonymy, synecdoche, and irony.

42. See Laemmert, 1955, pp. 100–194.

43. A narrative phrase, according to Danto, 1965, p. 164, ought "to refer to two time-separated events and describe the earlier with reference to the later. In addition it logically requires, if it is to be true, the occurrence of *both* events."

See Jauss's critique, 1982, pp. 60–62. In my opinion, reception theory is perfectly compatible with the necessity of predicting from the past—or rather, of anticipating the future reading or reception of a work such as *Madame Bovary* (not of Georges Feydeau's *Fanny*).

44. Translation, Rivers, 1988, p. 42. See ibid., p. 342, for editions of Garcilaso's works.

45. Ortega y Gasset, 1947, VI, p. 39.

46. A. Machado, 1957b, p. 144; translation, 1963, p. 54. It is possible that the first sentence refers to an aphorism of Friedrich Schlegel (no. 80 of the *Athenäum*): "der Historiker ist ein rückwärts gekehrter Prophet" (the historian is a backward-turned prophet).

47. Karl Rahner in K. Schlecta, ed., *Der Mensch und seine Zukunft* (Darmstadt, 1967), p. 150: "Zukunft ist das Nichtevolutive, das Nichtgeplante, das Unverfügbare, und zwar in seiner Unbegreiflichkeit und Unendlichkeit." See also "Das Problem der Perspektive," in Lukács, 1961, pp. 254–260; and Franchini, 1972.

48. See E. Bloch, 1967, especially "Zur Ontologie des Noch-Nicht-Seins," pp. 41–66.

49. See Wimsatt, 1954.

50. See Hirsch, 1976, p. 90; and Newton de Molina, 1976.

51. See Binni, 1963, pp. 23–27; and Anceschi, 1990, pp. 21–42, who offers a historical summary of this critical current. Benedetto Croce also opposed what he considered a fallacy, "cattivo prodotto d poco pensanti pensatori" (poor product of thinkers who hardly think), in *Terze pagine sparse* (Bari, 1955), II, pp. 143–144.

52. See Binni, 1963, pp. 30, 48.

53. Del Río, 1963, p. 79.

54. Ibid.

55. Ibid., p. 82.

56. Ibid.

57. Ibid., p. 83.

58. Ibid., p. 85.

59. Ibid. Compare with Nemoianu, 1984.

60. See the suggestive distinctions between epic and novel in Bakhtin, 1981, pp. 32–40.

61. History is scientific knowledge inasmuch as its results are objectively debatable, with documents in hand; that is, the results can be falsified, as Popper would say. But in answer to a prediction one can only make another prediction.

62. See Even-Zohar, 1978.

63. In an article on systems in states of crisis, Yahalom, 1981, uses abbreviations based on French nomenclature, such as SC: cultural system; SL: literary system; SLN: system of national literature; PS: polysystem; STVNL: system of non-literary verbal texts; LT: translated literature; S-can: canonical system.

64. See Even-Zohar, 1978, p. 69.

65. Ibid., p 46.
66. Ibid., p. 54; and Even-Zohar, 1979.
67. Lambert, 1983, p. 362. On the concept of national literature and its history, see the fundamental articles of Tibor Klaniczay, Robert Escarpit, and Jean Weisgerber in *Proceedings IV;* Gsteiger, 1967; and Rama, 1979. From these works one can draw several useful inferences. One: the relations among nation (or nationality), state, and "national literature" are fluid, changing, debatable—see Escarpit, 1966b, p. 198: "Today it is absolutely impossible to find a constant and invariable rapport between the language and the nationality of a literature." Two: the itinerary of the idea of national literature is historical and perfectly definable chronologically; see Klaniczay, 1966, p. 188: national literatures are "special and complex historical formations, like the very developed phases in the evolution of various literatures." Spanish literature, as such a formation, for example (see C. Guillén, 1971, p. 501), will have endured some two hundred years, from the middle of the eighteenth century to the middle of the twentieth. Three: this idea, in many cases and moments, is a profession of faith, or a belief—see Weisgerber, 1966, p. 221: "the idea of nation is therefore the object of belief." Four: broader formations, such as European or Latin American or Hispanic literature, whose roots are not nationalistic but the awareness in different countries of a common culture, a common civilization, some common social and political conditions—as in Latin America; see Rama, 1979—open paths to an identical creative and imaginative line, providing access to myth, to folklore, to indigenous languages, and the stratification of cultural manifestations. The new formations, then, are multiple, plurilingual, complex; and the "intermediate" zones, of which Lambert speaks, are perhaps characteristic of the future; like Switzerland—see Gsteiger, 1967, p. 14: arena of literary mediation, "useful model, it seems, for a Europe and a future world where political frontiers will have fallen." European literature is and without doubt will be multiple, multilingual. The Latin American is and will be at least bilingual. A decentralized Spain—will it be, like Switzerland, at least triliterary? That would not signify uniformity or homogenization—a suppression of the fundamental structural difference that, for linguistic motives, distinguishes poetry written in one language from that written in others (see V. M. Zhirmunsky, *Rifma,* Munich, 1970, p. vii: the fact that dactylic rhyme is possible in Russian but not in French at first inhibited the possibilities of Russian verse)—but the complete contrary. For the new integrating approach to Latin American literature, see also Pizarro, 1980; and Rodríguez-Monegal, 1980. And going back to the example of Switzerland, *modèle valable,* read the beautiful *lettera semiseria* of Gsteiger, 1983b, which tells of the avatars of the future comparatist in a country where "the idea of a national tongue led *ad absurdum*" (p. 28).
68. See Lambert, 1983, p. 362. The term *self-organizing* is from Yuri Lotman.
69. Ibid., p. 367.
70. See Barthes, 1974; Lotman, 1977; Eco, 1976.

71. At a certain point one returns to the texts themselves, to their thematic and formal elements, and to such well-known conventions as genres. I am not ignoring the fact that a new model need not have only new consequences in order to demonstrate its efficacy; it suffices that *today* it be functional and suggestive (after the exhaustion of certain earlier models). (At this writing I do not have access to the most recent publications of D. W. Fokkema on Modernism. For now, I cite "Literary History from an International Point of View," text of the first of the Erasmus Lectures, given at Harvard University in March 1983.)

72. For example, the acceptance of the model as hypothetical construction, of a not objective but utilitarian character (Fokkema, 1982, pp. 9–10); the inseparable nature of comparativism and the theory of literature (Fokkema, 1982, pp. 2–4; see Chapter 9 above); the rejection of critical atomism, or rather, of the concept of the insularity or autonomy of the individual text (Fokkema, 1982, pp. 6–7). I should add, however, that Fokkema's objections to the New Criticism—the insularity of the text, the lack of historicity, the absence of a critical metalanguage—apply only to stylistics or *Stilistik* (German, Spanish, Italian, Belgian) as far as the first of these objections is concerned. Leo Spitzer takes into consideration the historicity of the texts and makes use of a metalanguage: that of rhetoric (enriched by modern linguistics).

73. See Segers, 1978.

74. See Fokkema, 1982, p. 3.

75. Ibid., p. 6.

76. Someone will tell me that ornithologists have little or nothing to do with birds (although some ornithologists manage to understand birds and are even influenced by them). What Fokkema advocates is the separation of literary science from literary criticism, which he relegates to the realm of teaching (1982, p. 15): "within the new paradigm the scientific study of literature on the one hand, and literary criticism and the teaching of literature on the other, are strictly differentiated. In my view this will benefit the scientific study as well as the criticism and teaching of literature. If one accepts the distinction between pure and applied science, literary criticism and the didactics of literature which utilize the results of literary scholarship can be considered forms of applied science." The models proposed by literary science, in my opinion, must be applicable to the literariness, to the forms and qualities of the style, to the values that characterize the works being considered (which certain receivers lived as an aesthetic experience). This adaptation presupposes a minimum of relation with what is perceived by the scientist-historian in his readings, in his activity as reader and critic. Otherwise, it seems unlikely to me that the results of literary science could be usable in classrooms, or rather, could be converted into applied science. It is true that criticism itself can refuse to consider itself a science (as a "science still"); but I do not believe that this kind of criticism—if it reserves for itself exclusively evaluation and artistic emotion—can be put into effect *after* science has abandoned all aesthetic considerations. Ordinarily that

would occur earlier. Or rather, a to-and-fro should exist, a going and coming, between criticism and science. The communicability of the two is what forms the basis of a complete study of literature, and what constitutes its difficulty. Theory makes constant use of the experiences of the reader (at least that is the intention here). The educated reader makes constant use of theory. The divorce proposed by Fokkema, like so many others, especially in France, where weariness of the classics and the *grand siècle* are evident, reveals an obvious historicity: that of the rejection in our time of the *institution* of literature. That is a circumstance very typical of our time and very worthy of study; but not as mere or total acceptance by those of us who are both scholars and lovers of literature; just as good ornithologists are both scholars and lovers of birds. (Hans Robert Jauss has demonstrated that the literary phenomenon conceived as a process of communication and the aesthetic experience are compatible and are necessary for each other; see Jauss, 1972, 1977.)

77. Lotman, 1973; p. 54. See ibid., p. 56.
78. Ibid., p. 48.
79. What I called earlier the pragmatic aspect of our approach to genres (Chapter 12).
80. In the widest sense of the word. On this current or period, see "What Was Modernism?" in H. Levin, 1966, pp. 271–295; the colloquium on modernism of the group Poetik und Hermeneutik, Iser, 1966; Howe, 1967; "Literarische Tradition und gegenwärtiges Beweusstein," in Jauss, 1970a; Bradbury and McFarlane, 1976; Lodge, 1977; and Fokkema, 1980, 1984. On the concept of postmodernism, begun by the theory of architecture (see Charles Jencks, *The Language of Post-Modern Architecture,* New York, 1977), see Howe, 1970; Merquior, 1972; and X. Rupert de Ventós, *Filosofía y política* (Barcelona, 1984), p. 57.
81. Fokkema, "Literary History from an International Point of View," p. 9.
82. Ibid., pp. 12–13.
83. Historicity, from the point of view of history on the move; historiability, from the point of view of historiography *a posteriori.*
84. See Iser, 1972. Carlos Bousoño (1956b; 1st ed. 1952) already emphasized that the poetic text encompasses a project of the reader, whose "consent" he asks for.
85. Very debatable opposition, as we said earlier (see Chapter 13, note 156), as a method of apprehending a style.
86. An extensive bibliography exists on typology and the various functions of reading. Here I will mention only Riffaterre, 1971; Warning, 1975; Eco, 1976; Naumann, 1976; Fokkema and Kunne-Ibsch, 1977, chap. 5; Gsteiger, 1980; F. Meregalli, 1980, 1983a; the chapter by Maria Moog-Grünewald in Schmeling, 1981; the foreword by Paul de Man in Jauss, 1982; Caramaschi, 1984, p. 35. The Congress of the ICLA in Innsbruck made known the encounter of comparativism with reception theory, see *Proceedings IX,* vol. II, ed. Manfred Nau-

mann and H. R. Jauss, with the introductory essays by Naumann and Jauss themselves. On the reception of surrealism in Spain, see García Gallego, 1984.

87. Multiplicity of durations that Fernand Braudel and E. Labrousse helped me to see (for my essay 1977a), the economic model of Labrousse being decisive above all else, with its diverse superimposed curves, which together lead to the revolutionary consciousness of the crisis (see his *La crise de l'économie française à la fin de l'Ancien Régime et au début de la Révolution*, Paris, 1943). At that time I did not know the writings of Siegfried Kracauer in which he supported Jauss.

88. Peter Szondi suggested that the object of history might be humanity in general: anonymous processes, "Folge von Zuständen und Veränderung von Systemen," which will have to lead to a descriptive history; see Szondi in Kosselleck and Stempel, 1973, p. 541.

89. Roger Bastide, "Evénement (sociologie)," in *Encyclopaedia Universalis* (Paris, 1968), Vp., 822c. Wolf-Dieter Stempel calls *Fakten* those elements that are not incorporated as events in the significant process of history; see Kosselleck and Stempel, 1973, p. 338.

90. Jauss, 1967 and 1982, thesis 4.

91. Jauss in Kosselleck and Stempel, 1973, p. 554.

92. Jauss, 1974, pp. 22–27.

93. Köpeczi, 1979, p. 8.

94. Beverley, 1980, p. 34.

95. Quoted in ibid., p. 28. In my opinion Beverley shows the function of a socioeconomic *moyenne durée* of a literary idea that is a *longue durée:* the usefulness of "exercise of wit" is a venerable topos. For St. Augustine (*De doctrina christiana,* II.6.8), the obscurity of the scriptures is an act of providence, and for St. Thomas also (*Summa,* I.1.9).

96. See C. Guillén, 1977a; and Jauss, 1967 and 1982, sec. 3. As for the *praxis* of thought and of criticism as antagonism, battle, or aversion, its best justification is in Sartre, *Questions de méthode;* see Caramaschi, 1984, p. 25: "interpretation . . . is based on divining the behavior of the enemy."

97. See Oleza, 1981.

98. Jameson, 1981, p. 19.

99. Ibid., p. 55.

100. Savater, 1982, p. 18.

101. Jameson, in speaking of Althusser's *causa ausente,* quotes a brilliant page from a novel by Sartre, *Le sursis* (Jameson, 1981, p. 55), in which the fragmentation of a thousand consciousnesses contrasts with the existence of the war: "but there is nobody to add the total. It exists only for God. But God doesn't exist. And yet war exists." Those of us who have participated in a war know that there is nothing more characteristic of the atmosphere produced by it— any detail whatsoever of daily life, time, friendships, sexuality—than its elusive and also unusual character, that it absorbs and transforms *everything,*

turning everything into wartime, atmosphere of war. Sartre was very well acquainted with it, as were Stendhal and Tolstoy before him. One must look for other models, such as the pragmatically diverse ones Victoria Camps seeks for our time. See her *La imaginación ética* (Barcelona, 1983), p. 34: "if the judgment of Max Scheler is true that the cognitive value of metaphysics is measured by the solidarity of the theoretical with the world, the thinker today cannot help but feel solidarity with a plural fragmentary and vulnerable existence."

102. See note 89 above.

103. See Jauss, 1982, p. 29.

104. López-Baralt, 1980, p. 40.

105. See Klaniczay, 1966.

106. See Schroeder, 1967, pp. 78, 93–95.

107. Krĕjeć, 1968, p. 136.

108. López-Baralt, 1980, p. 22.

109. See George, 1983, pp. 3–5.

110. See Hosillos, 1966.

111. See Paolucci, 1982; and the issue of the *Review of National Literatures,* 11 (1982), devoted to Australia.

112. See Dutu, 1976. Moreoever, it is clear that the translations of the Bible into vernacular languages continued to be a decisive factor for the literatures of the first phase (Germany, Sweden, Hungary, and others), and also for some of the second phase, and even today (Africa). On Africa, see Gérard, 1981.

113. See *The Poems of Ancient Tamil,* ed. George L. Hart (Berkeley, 1975), p. 7.

114. See Gobbi, 1708–09.

115. See Ibn Sa'id, *El libro de las banderas de los campeones,* ed. Emilio García Gómez (Madrid, 1942); or *Moorish Poetry,* ed. A. J. Arberry (Cambridge, 1953). More recent translations into English include *The Banners of the Champions,* tr. James A. Bellamy and Patricia Owen Steiner (Madison, Wis., 1989); and *Poems of Arab Andalusia,* tr. Cola Franzen (San Francisco, 1989).

116. See Hightower, 1966, p. 46.

117. See Hutton, 1946, pp. 13–33.

118. Palgrave, 1863, p. xii: the poems chosen are "as episodes to that great Poem which all poets, like the cooperating thoughts of one great mind, have built up since the beginning of the world."

119. Ibn Sa'id, *El libro de las banderas de los campeones,* cuts and fragments larger pieces. A. T. Quiller-Couch's edition of *The Oxford Book of English Verse* (1900) noticeably favored the song, the epigram, the lyric. Note that Callimachus, who made possible the Virgilian model (the *Georgiics,* which without doubt compose a scrupulously structured book), and Meleager, author of the first *Greek Anthology* (first century B.C.), belong to the same Hellenistic era, as does also the beginnings of the Museum, *Mouseion,* an institution compa-

rable to the anthology, and one to which the questions posed above could be applied. See Paul Valéry's reservations on the subject ("Le problème des musées," in *Oeuvres*, J. Hytier, Paris, 1960, II, pp. 1.290–293) regarding that strange organized order, "étrange désordre organisé," that impoverishes and makes the head swim: "vertige du mélange, dont nous infligeons le supplice à l'art du passé" (p. 1.293).

120. Georges Bonneau, translation of Ki No Tsurayuki's, *Préface au Kokinshu* (Paris, 1933), p. 27: "la Poésie c'est de laisser exprimer son coeur à travers les choses qu'on voit et qu'on entend. C'est dan les fleurs le chant du rossignol; c'est sur les eaux la voix de la grenouille."

121. See Hightower, 1966, p. 42. There is a metaphor of indisputable universality that manifests the volition of unity of the anthology, that of a bouquet or garland of flowers, or a grove or arbor, or wreath *(stephanos): florilegio* is the Latin version of anthology. Thus we have the *Arbor of Amorous Devices* (London, 1597) and so many more. The title of a lost Japanese collection, *Ruiju-karin,* means "grove of arranged trees." As for the very important *Man'yōshū,* its title means "collection [*shu*] of a thousand leaves [*yo*]," the sense of "leaves" being ambiguous, but not the botanical element of the image. (The bibliography on this theme is sparse. See Alfonso Reyes, "Teoría de la antología," in *Obras completas,* Mexico City, 1963, XIV, pp. 137–141. And vol. I, *The Literary Canon,* of *Comparative Criticism: A Yearbook,* ed. Elinor Shaffer, 1979.) I believe that in this manner the investigation of the diachronic structures—existing and available for study—permits us, in agreement with René Etiemble, with Adrian Marino, with the scholars of East/West studies, and in spite of some comparatists (see Gifford, 1969, p. 30), to overcome the literary Eurocentrism in a visible way, an attitude that expresses so inadequately the capacity of creation and the European imagination.

122. Marino, 1979b, p. 157.

123. See ibid., p. 162.

124. See Marino, 1977b, p. 308.

125. See Lotman and Uspenski, 1975, p. 67: "il principio stesso dell'alternatività."

126. Ibid., p. 65; translated by Ruth Feldman.

127. See C. Guillén, 1978b.

128. Delacampagne, 1977, p. 187.

129. See Dray, 1964, p. 19.

130. See Fernando Savater, "Violencia y comunicación," in *Contra las patrias* (Madrid, 1984), p. 173: "the discourse of violence is based on a principle of universal *indifference:* it makes no difference, if it is not what I want. Any gradation, distinction, or relative preference is a form of complicity with absolute evil . . . This annihilation out of contempt for nuances is completely contrary to the differentiating task of love, which consists in finding the unrepeatable there where objectivity sees nothing more than routine: parents listening to

the first word spoken by the child, dawn shared by lovers . . ." See also the protest of Hazard Adams against critical violence, 1969, chap. 7, "System and Violence."

131. See the recent formulation by Douwe Fokkema, 1982, p. 9: "such mental constructions are designed to guide the observation, to aid the analysis, and to provide a model for describing the object in terms which make comparison with other, similarly examined objects, possible and testable."

132. Roland Mortier in *Les Lumières en Hongrie, en Europe Centrale et en Europe Orientale,* (Budapest, 1975), p. 174; quoted in Cornea, 1983, p. 45.

133. Caramaschi, 1984, p. 18.

134. Auerbach, 1952, pp. 39, 41, 49.

135. See Debray, 1984, p. 157.

136. See Francisco Ayala, "La identidad nacional," *El país,* March 19, 1984, p. 9.

137. Benedetto Croce, *Nuovi saggi de estetica,* 4th ed. (Bari, 1958), p. 271; translation by Ruth Feldman.

138. Interview with Eduardo Chillida by José Luis Barbería, *El país,* November 26, 1983, p. 5.

139. See Guy Scarpetta, *Eloge du cosmopolitisme* (Paris, 1981).

140. Quoted by Auerbach, 1952, p. 49: "magnum virtutis principium est, ut discat paulatim exercitatus animus visibilia haec et transitoria primum commutare, ut postmodum possit etiam derelilnquere. Delicatus ille est adhuc cui patria dulcis est, fortis autem cui omne solum patria est, perfectus vero cui mundus totus exilium est . . ."; translation by Stephen Scully.

141. J. Ferrater Mora, *De la materia a la razón* (Madrid, 1979), p. 28.

142. See Frye, 1957, p. 15.

143. See Iser, 1966.

144. Caramaschi, 1984, p. 7. For an example of hermeneutic analysis, see Valdés, 1982, chap. 8.

145. See Marino, 1982b and 1979b, p. 161.

146. C. Castilla del Pino, "Razón y modernidad," *El país,* May 2, 1984, p. 26.

147. Quoted by Patricia Hampl, "Czeslaw Milosz and Memory," *Ironwood,* 18 (1981), 57.

148. H. Levin, 1966, p. 286. See note 80 above.

Bibliography

Abrams, M. H., 1953. *The Mirror and the Lamp: Romantic Theory and the Critical Tradition.* New York, Oxford University Press. (Reissued 1958, New York, W. W. Norton.)

Adam, Antoine, Georges Lerminier, and Edouard Morot-Sir, 1972. *Littérature française.* 2 vols. Paris, Larousse.

Adams, Hazard, 1969. *The Interests of Criticism.* New York, Harcourt, Brace and World.

Aguiar e Silva, Vítor Manuel de, 1968. *Teoria da literatura.* 2nd ed. Coimbra, Libr. Almendina.

Alarcos Llorach, Emilio, 1976. *Ensayos y estudios literarios.* Madrid, Júcar.

Alas, Leopoldo ("Clarín"), 1984. *La regenta.* Tr. John Rutherford. London, Penguin.

Alazraki, Jaime, 1983. *En busca del unicornio: Los cuentos de Julio Cortázar.* Madrid, Gredos.

Alberti, R., 1976. *Baladas y canciones del Paraná.* Buenos Aires, Losada.

Aldana, Francisco de. 1978. *Epistolario poético completo.* Madrid, Turner, D. L.

Aldridge, A. Owen, 1963. "The Brazilian Maxim." *CL,* 15, 45–69.

——, ed. 1969. *Comparative Literature: Matter and Method.* Urbana, University of Illinois Press.

Aleixandre, Vicente, 1977. *Sombra del paraíso.* In *Antología total,* 171–217. Barcelona, Seix Barral.

——1987. *Shadow of Paradise/Sombra del paraíso.* Bilingual ed. Tr. Hugh A. Harter. Berkeley, University of California Press.

Alekseiev, M. P., 1975. "Le plurilinguisme et la création littéraire." *Proceedings VI,* 37–40.

Alonso, Amado, 1940. *Poesía y estilo de Pablo Neruda.* Buenos Aires, Losada. (Reissued 1960, Buenos Aires, Sudamericana.)

——1942. *Ensayo sobre la novela histórica.* Buenos Aires, Coni.

——1952. "Lope de Vega y sus fuentes." *Thesaurus* (Bogotá), 8, 1–24.

——1954. *Materia y forma en poesía.* Madrid, Gredos.

——1955. "Estructura de las *Sonatas* de Valle-Inclan." In *Materia y forma en poesía.* 2nd ed. Madrid, Gredos. (Originally published in *Verbum,* no. 71 [1928], 6–42.)

Alonso, Dámaso, 1931. Review of D. Alemany, *Vocabulario de D. Luis de Góngora. Revista de filología española,* 18, 40–55.

———1950. *Poesía española.* Madrid, Gredos.

Amorós, Andrés, ed., 1973. *El comentario de textos.* 2nd ed. Madrid, Castalia.

———1979. *Introducción a la literatura.* Madrid, Castalia.

Ampère, J.-J., 1867. "De l'histoire de la poésie." In *Mélanges d'histoire littéraire et de littérature.* Vol. I. Paris.

Anceschi, Luciano, 1968. *Le istituzioni della poesia.* Milan, Bompiani.

———1990. *Le poetiche del Novecento in Italia.* 2nd ed. Venice, Marsilio.

Anderson, Margaret, ed., 1953. *The Little Review Anthology.* New York, Hermitage House.

Anderson, Nels, ed., 1969. *Studies in Multilingualism.* Leiden, Brill.

Anderson Imbert, Enrique, 1967. *La originalidad de Rubén Darío.* Buenos Aires, Centro Editor de América Latina.

Arce, Joaquín, 1973. *Tasso y la poesía española.* Barcelona, Planeta.

Ariès, Philippe, 1975. *Essais sur l'histoire de la mort en occident du Moyen-Age à nos jours.* Paris, Seuil.

Arrowsmith, William, and Roger Shattuck, eds., 1964. *The Craft and Context of Translation.* 2nd ed. Garden City, N.Y., Anchor Books.

Asensio, Eugenio, 1957. *Poética y realidad del Cancionero penisular de la Edad Media.* Madrid, Gredos.

Aubailly, J.-C., 1976. *Le monologue, le dialogue et la sottie.* Paris, Champion.

Auerbach, Erich, 1952. "Philologie der Weltliteratur." In *Weltliteratur: Festgabe für Fritz Strich zum 70. Geburtstag,* 39–50 Bern, Francke.

Avalle-Arce, Juan Bautista, and E. C. Riley, eds., 1973. *Suma cervantina.* London, Thames.

Ayala, Francisco, 1972. *Los ensayos: Teoría y crítica literaria.* Madrid, Aguilar.

———1984. *La estructura narrativa.* Barcelona, Crítica.

Bachelard, Gaston, 1943. *L'air et les songes.* Paris, Corti.

———1948. *La terre et les rêveries du repos.* Paris, Corti.

———1958. *La psychanalyse du feu.* Paris, Gallimard.

———1974. *L'eau et les rêves.* Paris, Corti.

Backvis, Claude, 1968. "Quelques remarques sur l'élément bucolique dans la 'Dafnis' de Samuel Twardoski." In *Kultura i literatura dawnej Polski: Studia* (Homage to J. Nowak-Dluzewski), 319–353. Warsaw, PWN.

Bakhtin, M. M., 1968. *Rabelais and His World.* Tr. I. Iswolsky. Cambridge, Mass., MIT Press.

———1981. *The Dialogic Imagination.* Ed. M. Holquist and C. Emerson. Austin, University of Texas Press.

———1984a. *L'esthétique de la création verbale.* Tr. Alfreda Aucouturier. Paris, Gallimard.

————1984b. *Problems of Dostoevsky's Poetics*. Tr. Caryl Emerson, Minneapolis, University of Minnesota Press.

Bal, Mieke, 1981. "Narrative Embedding." *PT*, 2, no. 2, 41–59.

Balakian, Anna, 1962. "Influence and Literary Fortune." *YCGL*, 11, 24–31.

————1967. *The Symbolist Movement*. New York, Random House.

Baldensperger, Fernand, 1921. "Littérature comparée: Le mot et la chose." *RLC*, 1, 5–29.

Baldensperger, Fernand, and Werner P. Friederich, 1950. *Bibliography of Comparative Literature*. Chapel Hill, University of North Carolina Press.

Barricelli, Jean-Pierre, 1978. "Critical Limitations in Musico-Literary Study." *Science/Technology and the Humanities*, 1, 127–132.

Barricelli, Jean-Pierre, and Joseph Gibaldi, eds., 1982. *Interrelations of Literature*. New York, Modern Language Association.

Barthes, Roland, 1963. *Sur Racine*. Paris, Seuil.

————1966. "Introduction à l'analyse structurelle des récits." *Communications*, 8, 1–27.

————1967. *Writing Degree Zero*. Tr. Annette Lavers and Colin Smith. New York, Farrar, Straus and Giroux.

————1972. *Critical Essays and Elements of Semiology*. Tr. Richard Howard, Evanston, Ill., Northwestern University Press.

————1974. *S/Z*. Tr. Richard Miller. New York, Farrar, Straus and Giroux.

Bassy, Alain-Marie, 1973. "Iconographie et littérature: Essai de réflection critique et méthodologique." *Revue française d'histoire du livre*, 5, 3–33.

Bataillon, Marcel, 1952. *Etudes sur le Portugal au temps de l'humanisme*. Coimbra, Universidade.

Bate, W. Jackson, 1946. *From Classic to Romantic*. Cambridge, Mass., Harvard University Press.

Bauer, Roger, 1977. "'Ein Sohn der Philosophie': Über den Dialog als literarische Gattung." In *Deutsche Akademie für Sprache und Dichtung: Darmstadt, Jahrbuch 1976*, 29–44. Heidelberg, Lambert Schneider.

————1978a. "'Décadence': Histoire d'un mot et d'une idée." *CREL*, 1, 55–71.

————1978b. "Dernier voyage à Cythère: La redécouverte du rococo dans la littérature européenne du 19e siècle." In B. Fabian, ed., *Festschrift für Rainer Gruenter*, 187–200. Heidelberg.

Beall, Chandler B., 1942. *La fortune du Tasse en France*. Eugene, Oreg., University of Oregon and Modern Language Association.

Beaujour, Michel, 1980. *Miroirs d'encre: Rhétorique de l'autoportrait*. Paris, Seuil.

Bécquer, Gustavo A., 1977. *Rimas y leyendas*. Salamanca, Edicionas Almar.

Béguin, Albert, 1937. *L'âme romantique et le rêve*. 2 vols. Marseilles, Editions des cahiers du sud.

Beker, Miroslav, ed., 1981. *Comparative Studies in Croatian Literature*. Zagreb, Univerzitet.

Beller, Manfred, 1970. "Von der Stoffgeschichte zur Thematologie." *Arcadia* (Berlin), 5, 1–38.

———1979. *Jupiter Tonans: Studien zur Darstellung der Macht in der Poesie.* Heidelberg, Winter.

Bender, Helmut, and Ulrich Melzer, 1958. "Zur Geschichte des Begriffes 'Weltliteratur.'" *Saeculum,* 9, 113–123.

Benedetto, Luigi Foscolo, 1953. "La letteratura mondiale." In *Uomini e tempi,* 3–20. Milan, Ricciardi.

Bentley, Eric, ed., 1968. *The Theory of the Modern Stage.* Harmondsworth, Penguin.

Bergel, Lienhard, 1964. "The Avant-Garde Mind and Its Expression." *CLS,* 1, 115–125.

Berger, Bruno, 1964. *Der Essay.* Bern, Francke.

Bergmann, Emilie L., 1979. *Art Inscribed: Essays on Ekphrasis in Spanish Golden Age Poetry.* Cambridge, Mass., Harvard University Press.

Beristáin, Helena, 1982. *Análysis estructural del relato literario.* Mexico City, UNAM.

Berman, Antoine, 1984. *L'épreuve de l'étranger: Culture et traduction dans l'Allemagne romantique.* Paris, Gallimard.

Bernard, Suzanne, 1959. *Le poème en prose de Baudelaire jusqu'à nos jours.* Paris, Nizet.

Berndt, Catherine, and Ronald Berndt, 1982. "Aboriginal Australia: Literature in an Oral Tradition." *Review of National Literatures,* 11, 39–63.

Beverley, John, 1980. "The Production of Solitude: Góngora and the State." *Ideologies and Literature,* 13, 23–41.

Béziers, Monique, 1968. *Le bilinguisme.* Louvain, Libr. universitaire.

Biesterfeld, Wolfgang, 1974. *Die literarische Utopie.* Stuttgart, Metzler.

Bigeard, Martiné, 1972. *La folie et les fous littéraires en Espagne, 1500–1650.* Paris, Institut d'études hispaniques.

Binni, Walter, 1963. *Poetica, critica e storia letteraria.* Bari, Laterza.

Birnbaum, Henrik, 1974. *On Medieval and Renaissance Slavic Writing.* The Hague, Mouton.

Blecua, Alberto, 1981. "La literatura, signo histórico-literario." In J. Romera Castillo, ed., *La literatura como signo.* 110–144. Madrid, Playor.

Blecua, José Manuel, 1945. *El mar en la poesía española.* Madrid, Editorial hispánica.

Bloch, Ernst, 1967. *Auswahl aus seinem Schriften.* Ed. H. H. Holz. Frankfurt am Main, Fischer Bücherei.

Bloch, Marc, 1953. *The Historian's Craft.* Tr. Peter Putnam. New York, Alfred A. Knopf.

Block, Haskell M., 1958. "The Concept of Influence in Comparative Literature." *YCGL,* 7, 30–37.

———1970. *Nouvelles tendances en littérature comparée.* Paris, Nizet.

Bloom, Harold, 1973. *The Anxiety of Influence*. New York, Oxford University Press.

———1975. *A Map of Misreading*. New York, Oxford University Press.

Bloomfield, Morton W., ed., 1981. *Allegory, Myth, and Symbol*. Cambridge, Mass., Harvard University Press.

Bluestone, George, 1957. *Novels into Film*. Baltimore, Johns Hopkins University Press.

Blume, Bernard, 1966. "Lebendiger Quell und Flut des Todes—ein Beitrag zu einer Literaturgeschichte des Wassers." *Arcadia* (Berlin), 1, 18–30.

Boase, A. M., 1962. "The Definition of Mannerism." *Proceedings III*, 143–155.

Bodkin, Maud, 1934. *Archetypal Patterns in Poetry*. Oxford. Reissued 1978, New York, AMS Press.

Boeckmann, Paul, ed., 1959. *Stil- und Formprobleme in der Literatur*. Heidelberg, Winter.

Boerner, Peter, 1969. *Tagebuch*. Stuttgart, Metzler.

Bogatyrev, P., 1971. "Les signes du théâtre." *Poétique*, 2, 517–530.

Booth, Wayne C., 1961. *The Rhetoric of Fiction*. Chicago, University of Chicago Press.

———1974. *A Rhetoric of Irony*. Chicago, University of Chicago Press.

Borgerhoff, E. B. O., 1963. "Mannerism and Baroque: A Simple Plea." *CL*, 5, 323–331.

Borges, J. L., 1964a. "The Analytical Language of John Wilkins." In *Other Inquisitions*. Tr. Ruth L. C. Sims. Austin, University of Texas Press.

———1964b. *Obra poética*. Buenos Aires, Emecé editores.

———1979. "La metáfora." In *Historia de la eternidad*. 4th ed. Madrid, Alianza; and Buenos Aires, Emecé.

———1989. *Obras completas*. Buenos Aires, Emecé editores.

Bouazis, Charles, ed., 1972. *Analyse de la périodisation littéraire*. Paris, Editions universitaires.

Bouissac, Paul, 1973. *La mesure des gestes*. The Hague, Mouton.

Bousoño, Carlos, 1956a. *La poesía de Vicente Aleixandre*. 2nd ed. Madrid, Gredos.

———1956b. *Teoría de la expresión poética*. 2nd ed. Madrid, Gredos.

Bradbury, Malcolm, and James McFarlane, eds., 1976. *Modernism 1890–1930*. Harmondsworth, Penguin.

Brandt Corstius, Jan C., 1963. "Writing Histories of World Literature." *YCGL*, 12, 5–14.

———1968. *Introduction to the Comparative Study of Literature*. New York, Random House.

Braudel, Fernand, 1958. "Histoire et sciences sociales." *Annales E. S. C.*, October–December, 725–753.

———1966. *La Méditerranée et le monde méditerranéen à l'époque de Philippe II*. 2nd ed. Paris, Colin.

Bremond, Claude, 1964. "Le message narratif." *Communications*, 4, 4–32.

———1966. "La logique des possibles narratifs." *Communications*, 8, 60–76.

———1973. *Logique du récit*. Paris, Seuil.

Brody, Jules, and Leo Spitzer, 1980. *Approches textuelles des Mémoires de Saint-Simon*. Paris, Place; and Tübingen, Narr.

Brombert, Victor, 1966. *The Novels of Flaubert*. Princeton, Princeton University Press.

———1975. *La prison romantique*. Paris, Corti.

Bronson, B. B., 1967. "Literature and Music." In Thorpe, 1967, 127–148.

Brooks, Peter, 1976. *The Melodramatic Imagination*. New Haven, Yale University Press.

———1978. "Freud's Masterplot." *Yale French Studies*, 280–300.

———1982. "Narrative Transaction and Transference (Unburying *Le Colonel Chabert*)." *Novel. A Forum on Fiction*, 15, no. 2, 101–110.

———1984. *Reading for the Plot*. Oxford, Clarendon Press.

Brower, Ruben, ed., 1959. *On Translation*. Cambridge, Mass., Harvard University Press.

Brown, Calvin, 1948. *Music and Literature*. Athens, University of Georgia Press.

———1970a. "Musico-Literary Research in the Last Two Decades." *YCGL*, 19, 5–27.

———1970b. "The Relations between Music and Literature as a Field of Study." *CL*, 22, 97–107.

———1978. "Theme and Variations as a Literary Form." *YCGL*, 27, 35–43.

Brunel, Pierre, Claude Pichois, and André-Marie Rousseau, 1983. *Qu'est-ce que la littérature comparée?* Paris, Colin.

Brunet, Georges, 1967. *C. F. Meyer et la nouvelle*. Paris, Didier.

Brunetière, F., 1900. "La littérature européenne." *Varietés littéraires* (Paris), September.

Buxó, José Pascual, 1978. *Introducción à la poética de Roman Jakobson*. Mexico City, UNAM.

Bynum, David, 1969. "The Generic Nature of Oral Epic Poetry." *Genres*, 2, 236–258.

Cabanis, P., 1824. *Oeuvres complètes*. Paris, Bossange frères.

Calderón de la Barca, P., 1969. *Obras completas*. Vol. I, *Dramas*. Madrid, Aguilar.

———1970. *Life Is a Dream*. Tr. Edwin Honig. New York, Hill and Wang.

Calinescu, Matei, 1969. "L'avant-garde littéraire en Roumanie et ses rapports avec l'avant-garde internationale dans l'entre-deux-guerres." *Proceedings V*, 343–354.

Calvino, Italo, 1986. "Levels of Reality in Literature." In *The Uses of Literature*, 101–121. Tr. Patrick Creagh. New York, Harcourt Brace Jovanovich.

Cambon, Glauco, 1979. "The Future of That Unlikely Thing, Comparative Literature." *Michigan Germanic Studies*, 5, 159–169.

Campbell, Jackson J., 1978. "Adaptation of Classical Rhetoric in Old English Literature." In J. J. Murphy, ed., *Medieval Eloquence*, 173–197. Berkeley, University of California Press.

Caramaschi, Enzo, 1974. *Essai sur la critique française de la fin-de-siècle*. Paris, Nizet.

——1984. *"Pietik und Hermeneutik" (A propos d'Apollinaire)*. Lecce, Adriatica.

Carilla, Emilio, 1968. *El cuento fantástico*. Buenos Aires, Ediciones Nova.

Carpeaux, Otto Maria, 1959–1966. *História da literatura ocidental*. 8 vols. Rio de Janeiro, Edicões O Cruzeiro.

Casalduero, Joaquín, 1943. *Vida y obra de Galdós*. Buenos Aires, Losada. (2nd ed., Madrid, Gredos, 1961.)

——1972. *Estudios sobre el teatro español*. 3rd ed. Madrid, Gredos.

——1973. *Estudios de literatura española*. 3rd ed. Madrid, Gredos.

Castex, P.-G., 1969. *Baudelaire critique d'art*. Paris, Société d'édition d'enseignement supérieur.

Castro, Américo, 1977a. "The Presence of the Sultan Saladin in the Romance Languages." In S. Gilman and E. L. King, eds., *An Idea of History*, 241–269. Columbus, Ohio University Press. (Previously published in *Diogenes* 8 [1954].)

——1977b. "In the Alps." In ibid., pp. 271–276. (Previously published in *El national* [Caracas], August 3, 1956.)

Catalán, Diego, 1978. "Los modos de producción y 'reproducción' del texto literario y la noción de apertura." In A. Carreira, ed., *Homenaje a Julio Caro Baroja*, 245–270. Madrid, Centro de investigaciones sociólogicas.

——1979. "Análisis semiótico de estructuras abiertas: El modelo 'Romancero.'" In D. Catalán, S. G. Armistead, and A. Sánchez Romeralo, eds., *El romancero hoy: Poética*, 231–249. Madrid, Gredos.

——1984a. *Catálogo general del romancero (pan-hispánico)*. Vol. I, *Teoría general y metodología*. Madrid, Gredos.

——1984b. "El romancero, hoy." *Boletín informativo. Fundación Juan March*, 133, 3–14.

Caws, Mary Ann, and Hermine Riffaterre, 1983. *The Prose Poem in France*. New York, Columbia University Press.

Célis, Raphael, ed., 1982. *Littérature et musique*. Brussels, Publs. Faculté universitaires Saint Louis.

Cernuda, Luis, 1977. *Donde habite el olvido*. Vol. V of *Poesía completa*. Barcelona, Barral.

Cervantes Saavedra, Miguel de, 1961. *Six Exemplary Novels*. Tr. Harriet de Onís. Barrons Educational Series. Woodbury, N.Y., Barrons.

——1967. *The Ingenious Gentleman Don Quixote de La Mancha*. Tr. Samuel Putnam. New York, Viking Press.

Chasles, P., 1847. *Etudes sur l'antiquité*. Paris, Amyot.

——1867. *Questions du temps*. Paris, G. Baillière.

Chatman, Seymour, 1965. *A Theory of Meter*. The Hague, Mouton.

————1978. *Story and Discourse*. Ithaca, N.Y., Cornell University Press.

Cioran, E. M., 1973. *De l'inconvenient d'être né*. Paris, Gallimard. (Translated by Richard Howard as *The Trouble with Being Born.* New York, Viking Press, 1976.)

Cioranescu, Alejandro (Alejandru), 1964. *Principios de literatura comparada*. La Laguna, Universidad.

Clebsch, William A., 1964. *England's Earliest Protestants: 1520–1535*. New Haven, Yale University Press.

Clover, Carol J., 1980. "The Germanic Context of the Unfer *þ* Episode." *Speculum*, 55, 444–468.

Clüver, Claus, 1978. "Painting into Poetry." *YCGL*, 27, 19–34.

Cohen, Jean, 1976. "Poésie et redondance." *Poétique*, 28, 413–422.

Cohen, J. M., ed. and tr., 1988. *The Penguin Book of Spanish Verse*. London, Penguin.

Cohen, Ralph, ed., 1974. *New Directions in Literary History*. Baltimore, Johns Hopkins University Press.

Cohn, Dorrit, 1978. *Transparent Minds*. Princeton, Princeton University Press.

————1981. "The Encirclement of Narrative." *PT*, 2, no. 2, 157–182.

Colie, Rosalie, 1973. *The Resources of Kind: Genre Theory in the Renaissance*. Berkeley, University of California Press.

Collingwood, R. G., 1946. *The Idea of History*. Oxford, Oxford University Press. (Reissued 1956, Oxford, Oxford University Press.)

Compagnon, Antoine, 1979. *La seconde main, ou le travail de la citation*. Paris, Seuil.

Compte, A., 1974. *The Essential Comte*. Stanislav Andreski. Tr. and ann. Margaret Clarke. London, Croom Helm; New York, Harper & Row.

Cornea, Paul, 1976. "Tendances et orientations actuelles dans la sociologie de la littérature." *Synthesis* (Bucharest), 3, 205–214.

————1983. "Trois lectures actuelles au sujet des Lumières." In Z. Kostaninovic et al., ed., *Sur l'actualité des lumières: Aufklärung heute*, 43–49. Innsbrucker Beiträge zur Kulturwissenschaft no. 54. Innsbruck.

Corsini, Gianfranco, 1974. *L'istituzione letteraria*. Naples, Liguori.

Corti, Maria, 1976. *Principi della communicazione letteraria*. Milan, Bompiani.

Cotnam, J., 1970. "André Gide et le cosmopolitisme littéraire." *Revue d'histoire littéraire de la France*, 70, 267–285.

Cox, L., 1899. *The Arte or Crafte of Rhetoryke*. Ed. F. I. Carpenter. Chicago, University of Chicago Press.

Cremona, Isida, 1977. *L'influence de l'Aminta sur la pastorale dramatique française*. Paris, Vrin.

Croce, Benedetto, 1923. *Problemi de estetica*. 2nd ed., Bari, Laterza.

Cros, Edmond, 1976. "Propositions pour une sociocritique." *Les langues modernes*, 6, 458–479.

————1983. *Théorie et pratique sociocritiques*. Paris, Editions sociales.

Cruz, Sor Juana Inés de la, 1988. *A Sor Juana Anthology.* Tr. Alan S. Trueblood. Cambridge, Mass., Harvard University Press.

Culler, Jonathan, 1975. *Structuralist Poetics.* London, Routledge and Kegan Paul.

———1979. "Comparative Literature and Literary Theory." *Michigan Germanic Studies,* 5, 170–184.

———1981. *The Pursuit of Signs.* Ithaca, N.Y., Cornell University Press.

———1982. *On Deconstruction.* Ithaca, N.Y., Cornell University Press.

Curtius, Ernst Robert, 1950. *Kritische Essays zur europäischen Literatur.* Bern, Francke.

———1962. *Gesammelte Aufsätze zur romanischen Philologie.* Bern, Francke.

———1973. *Essays on European Literature.* Tr. Michael Kowal. Princeton, Princeton University Press.

Dalla Valle, Daniela, 1973. *Pastorale barocca.* Ravenna, Longo.

———1980. "Le thème et la structure de l'écho dans la pastorale dramatique française au XVIIe siècle." In Longeon, 1980, 193–197.

Dällenbach, Lucien, 1977. *Le récit spéculaire.* Paris, Seuil.

Dante Alighieri, 1973a. *Dante's Vita Nuova.* Tr. Mark Musa. Bloomington, Indiana University Press.

———1973b. *The Divine Comedy.* Bilingual. Tr. Charles S. Singleton. Princeton, Princeton University Press.

Danto, Arthur C., 1965. *Analytical Philosophy of History.* Cambridge, Cambridge University Press.

Darío, Rubén, 1968. *Poesías completas.* Madrid, Aguilar.

Darnton, R. 1982. "What Is the History of Books?" *Daedalus,* Summer, 65–83.

Debray, Régis, 1984. *La puissance et les rêves.* Paris, Gallimard.

Dédéyan, Charles, 1944. *Montaigne chez ses amis anglo-saxons.* 2 vols. Paris, Boivin.

Deeney, J. J., 1970. "Comparative Literature Studies in Taiwan." *TR,* 1, 119–145.

———1978. "Comparative Literature and China: A Bibliographical Review of Materials in English." *New Asia Academic Bulletin,* 1, 278–301.

———, ed., 1980. *Chinese-Western Comparative Literature.* Hong Kong, Chinese University Press.

Delacampagne, C., 1977. *Figures de l'oppression.* Paris, Presses universitaires de France.

Deleite y Piñuela, José, 1935. *El rey se divierte.* Madrid, Espesa-Calpe.

Deleuze, Gilles, 1968. *Différence et répétition.* Paris, Presses universitaires de France.

Del Río, A., 1963. *Historia de la literatura española.* 2nd ed. New York, Holt, Rinehart and Winston.

de Man, Paul, 1969. "The Rhetoric of Temporality." In C. S. Singleton, ed., *Interpretation,* 173–209. Baltimore, Johns Hopkins University Press.

———1971. *Blindness and Insight.* New York, Oxford University Press.

———1978. "The Epistemology of Metaphor." *Critical Inquiry,* 5, 11–19.

———1979. *Allegories of Reading.* New Haven, Yale University Press.

De Marinis, Marco, 1982. *Semiótica del teatro.* Milan, Bompiani.

Démoris, René, 1975. *Le roman à la première personne.* Paris, Colin.

Derrida, Jacques, 1967. *De la grammatologie.* Paris, Minuit.

———1972. *Marges de la philosophie.* Paris, Minuit.

———1978. *Writing and Difference.* Tr. Alan Bass. Chicago, University of Chicago Press.

De Sanctis, Francesco, 1952. *Saggi critici.* Ed. L. Russo. 3 vols. Bari, Laterza.

Díaz Viana, Luis, Joaquín Díaz, and José Delfín Val, 1979. *Catálogo folklórico de la Provincia de Valladolid.* Vol. II, *Romances tradicionales.* Valladolid, Institutión cultura simancas.

Dickens, Charles, 1981. *David Copperfield.* New York, Oxford University Press.

Didier, Béatrice, 1976. *Le journal intime.* Paris, Presses universitaires de France.

Diederichsen, Diedrich, 1966. "Theaterwissenschaft und Literaturwissenschaft." *Euphorion,* 60, 402–424.

Díez Borque, José María, and Luciano García Lorenzo, eds., 1975. *Semiología del teatro.* Barcelona, Planeta.

Dijkstra, Bram, 1969. *Cubism, Stieglitz, and the Early Poetry of William Carlos Williams.* Princeton, Princeton University Press.

Diller, Hans-Jürgen, and Joachim Kornelius, 1978. *Linguistische Probleme der Uebersetzung.* Tübingen, Niemeyer.

Donadoni, Sergio, 1957. *Storia della letteratura egiziana antica.* Milan, Accademia.

Dray, W., 1964. *Philosophy of History.* Englewood Cliffs, N.J., Prentice-Hall.

du Bellay, Joachim, 1910. *Oeuvres poétiques,* Vol. II. Paris, Edouard Cornély.

Dubois, Page, 1982. *History, Rhetorical Description and the Epic.* Cambridge, D. S. Brewer.

Dubrow, Heather, 1982. *Genre.* London, Methuen.

Duchet, Claude, ed., 1979. *Sociocritique* (Colloquium at Vincennes, 1977). Paris, Nathan.

Dufour, Pierre, 1977. "La relation peinture/littérature: Notes pour un comparatisme interdisciplinaire." *Neohelicon* (Budapest), 5, no. 1, 141–190.

Duggan, Joseph J., 1973. *The Song of Roland: Formulaic Craft, Poetic Craft.* Berkeley, University of California Press.

———1975. "Formulaic Diction in the Cantar de mío Cid." In J. J. Duggan, ed., *Oral Literature.* Edinburgh, Scottish Academy Press.

Durán, Manuel, 1981. "La obra de Juan Rulfo vista a través de Mircea Eliade." *INTI revista de literatura hispánica,* 13–14, 25–33.

Durand, Gilbert, 1963. *Les structures anthropologiques de l'imaginaire.* 2nd ed. Paris, Presses universitaires de France.

———1979. *Figures mythiques et visages de l'oeuvre: De la mythocritique à la mythanalyse.* Paris, Berg International.

Ďurišin, Dionýz, 1967. *Problémy literárnej Komparatistiky.* Bratislava, Slovenská Akad. vied.

————1972. *Vergleichende Literaturforschung.* Berlin, Akademie-Verlag.

————1977. "Comparative Investigation in Literature and Art." *Neohelicon* (Budapest), 5, 125–140.

Dutu, Alexandru, 1973. "Les livres de délectation dans la culture roumaine." *Revue des études sud-est européennes,* 11, 307–325.

————1976. "Modèles, images, comparaisons." *Synthesis* (Bucharest), 3, 5–10.

————1979. "Travellers and National Images: Romanian Perceptions of British Culture." *CREL,* 1, 13–21.

Dyserinck, Hugo, 1966. "Zum Problem der 'images' und 'mirages' und ihrer Untersuchung im Rahmen der Vergleichenden Literaturwissenshaft." *Arcadia* (Berlin), 1, 107–120.

————1977. *Komparatistik: Eine Einführung.* Bonn, Bouvier.

Eça de Queiróz, José Maria, 1965. *The Maias.* Tr. Patricia McGowan Pinheiro and Ann Stevens. London, The Bodley Head.

Eco, Umberto, 1975. "Elementos preteatrales de una semiótica del teatro." In Díez Borque and García Lorenzo, 1975, 95–102.

————1976. *A Theory of Semiotics.* Bloomington, Indiana University Press.

————1979. *Lector in fabula.* Milan, Bompiani.

Edwards, G. P., 1971. *The Language of Hesiod in Its Traditional Context.* Oxford, Blackwell.

Eimermacher, Karl, and Serge Shishkoff, 1977. *Bibliography of Soviet Semiotics: The Moscow-Tartú School.* Ann Arbor, University of Michigan Press.

Elam, Keir, 1980. *The Semiotics of Theatre and Drama.* London, Methuen.

Elliott, Robert C., 1960. *The Power of Satire.* Princeton, Princeton University Press.

————1962. "The Definition of Satire." *YCGL,* 11, 19–23.

————1970. *The Shape of Utopia.* Chicago, University of Chicago Press.

————1982. *Literary Persona.* Chicago, University of Chicago Press.

Elwert, Wilhelm Theodor, 1960. "L'emploi des langues étrangères comme procédé stylistique." *RLC,* 35, 409–437.

Empson, William, 1960. *Some Versions of Pastoral.* Norfolk, Conn., New Directions. (Reissued 1986, London, Hogarth Press; 1st ed. London, 1935.)

Erlich, Victor, 1959. "Alexander Veselovsky." *YCGL,* 8, 33–36.

————1969. *Russian Formalism.* 3rd ed. New Haven, Yale University Press. (1st ed. 1955).

Erman, Adolf, 1896. "Gespräch eines Lebensmüden mit seiner Seele." *Abhandlungen der Königl. Akademie der Wissenschaften zu Berlin,* 2, 67–68.

————1925a. *Die ägyptischen Schulerhandschriften.* Berlin, Verlag der Akademie der Wissenschaften.

————1925b. *Papyrus Lansing.* Copenhagen, A. F. Host and Sons.

Escarpit, Robert, 1961. "'Creative Treason' as a Key to Literature." *YCGL,* 10, 16–21.

————1966a. *The Book Revolution.* London, Harrap; and Paris, UNESCO.

————1966b. "Les cadres de l'histoire littéraire." *Proceedings IV,* I, 195–202.

————1966c. *Sociologie de la littérature.* Paris, Presses universitaires de France. (1st ed., 1958.)

Esteban, Claude, 1979. *Un lieu hors de tout lieu.* Paris, Galilée.

Ethé, Hermann, 1882. "Über perische Tenzonen." *Verhandlungen des 5. Internationalen Orientalisten-Congresses,* 48–135. Berlin.

Etiemble, René, 1963. *Comparaison n'est pas raison.* Paris, Gallimard.

————1966. "Faut-it réviser la notion de Weltliteratur?" *Proceedings IV,* 5–16.

Even-Zohar, Itamar, 1978. *Papers in Historical Poetics.* Tel Aviv, Porter Institute.

————1979. "Polysystem Theory." *PT,* 1, no. 1–2, 287–310.

————1981. "Translation Theory Today." *PT,* 2, no. 4, 1–7.

Everth, Erich, 1924. *Conrad Ferdinand Meyer.* Dresden, Sibyllen-Verlag.

Falkenstein, A., 1959. "Ein Sumerischer Brief an den Mondgott." *Analecta Biblica,* 12, 69–77.

Fanger, Donald, 1962. "Romanticism and Comparative Literature." *CL,* 14, 153–166.

————1965. *Dostoevsky and Romantic Realism: A Study of Dostoevsky in Relation to Balzac, Dickens, and Gogol.* Chicago, University of Chicago Press.

————1979. *The Creation of Nicolai Gogol.* Cambridge, Mass., Harvard University Press.

Farinelli, Arturo, 1925. *Petrarca, Manzoni, Leopardi: Il sogno di una letteratura "mondiale."* Turin, Fratelli Bocca.

Felman, Shoshona, ed., 1982. *Literature and Psychoanalysis.* Baltimore, Johns Hopkins University Press.

Ferdinandy, Miguel de (Mihály), 1961. *En torno al pensar mítico.* Berlin, Colloquium Verlag.

Fergusson, Francis, 1949. *The Idea of a Theatre.* Princeton, Princeton University Press.

Fernandez, Ramon, 1926. *Messages.* Paris, Editiones de la nouvelle revue française. (Translated by Montgomery Belgion. Port Washington, N.Y., Kennikat Press, 1964.)

Fernández Montesinos, José, 1965. *Costumbrismo y novela.* 2nd ed. Madrid, Castalia.

Festa-McCormick, Diana, 1979. *The City as Catalyst.* Rutherford, N.J., Fairleigh Dickinson University Press.

Figueiredo, Fidelino de, 1935. *Pyrene.* Lisbon, Emprêsa nacional de publicidade.

————1962. *Ideario crítico de . . . ,* ed. C. de Assis Pereira. São Paulo, Universidade.

Fink, A. H., 1934. *Maxime und Fragment.* Munich, Max Hueber Verlag.

Finné, Jacques, 1980. *La littérature fantastique.* Brussels, Université.

Finnegan, Ruth H., 1977. *Oral Poetry.* Cambridge, Cambridge University Press.

Fiore, Silvestro, 1966. "La tenson en Espagne et en Babylonie: Evolution ou polygenèse?" *Proceedings IV,* II, 983–992.

Flaker, Aleksandar, 1970. "Motivation und Stil." In Zmegač, 1970, 287–397.

————1973. "Stylistic Formation." *Neohelicon* (Budapest), 1, 183–207.

————1976. *Die slavischen Literaturen 1870–1900.* Neues Handbuch der Literaturwissenschaft, 18. Wiesbaden, Athenaion.

————1980. "Discriminations of the Concept of *Avant-Garde.*" *Proceedings VIII,* I, 925–928.

————1983. "The Croatian Avant-Garde." *Russian Literature,* 14, 1–16.

Flaubert, Gustave, 1904. *Sentimental Education.* Tr. M. Walter Dunne. Akron, Ohio, St. Dunstan Society.

Fletcher, Angus, 1964. *Allegory.* Ithaca, N.Y., Cornell University Press.

Foa, Raffaele V., 1956. *L'arte e la vita in Guiseppe Mazzini.* Genoa, Associazione mazziniana italiana.

Focke, Friedrich, 1923. "Synkrisis." *Hermes,* 58, 327–368.

Fokkema, Douwe W., 1980. "The Code of Modernism." *Proceedings VIII,* I, 679–684.

————1982. "Comparative Literature and the New Paradigm." *CRCL,* 9, no. 1, 1–18.

————1984. *Het Modernisme in de Europese Letterkunde.* Amsterdam, Arbeiderspers.

Fokkema, Douwe W., and Elrud Kunne-Ibsch, 1977. *Theories of Literature in the Twentieth Century.* London, C. Hurst.

Folkierski, Wladyslaw, 1925. *Entre le classicisme et le romantisme: Etude sur l'esthétique et les esthéticiens du XVIIIe siècle.* Cracow, Académie polonaise des sciences et les lettres.

Forster, Leonard, 1970. *The Poet's Tongues: Multilingualism in Literature.* Cambridge, Cambridge University Press.

Fosca, François, 1960. *De Diderot à Valéry: Les écrivains et les arts visuels.* Paris, Michel.

Foster, Lawrence, and J. W. Swanson, eds., 1970. *Experience and Theory.* Amherst, University of Massachusetts Press.

Foulquié, Paul, 1958. *La dialectique.* Paris, Presses universitaires de France.

Fowler, Alastair, 1972. "Periodization and Interart Analogies." *NLH,* 3, 487–510.

————1982. *Kinds of Literature.* Cambridge, Mass., Harvard University Press.

Franchini, Raffaello, 1972. *Teoria della previsione.* 2nd ed. Naples, Giannini.

Frank, Joseph, 1963. *The Widening Gyre.* New Brunswick, N.J., Rutgers University Press.

Freedman, Ralph, 1963. *The Lyrical Novel.* Princeton, Princeton University Press.

Frenk, Margit, 1979. "La lírica pretrovadoresca." In E. Köhler, ed., *Les genres lyriques* Grundriss der romanischen Literaturen des Mittelalters. Heidelberg, Winter.

Frenz, Horst, ed., 1959. *Asia and the Humanities: Second Conference on Oriental-Western Relations.* Bloomington, Indiana University Press.

Frenz, Horst, and G. L. Anderson, eds., 1955. *Indiana University Conference on Oriental-Western Literary Relations.* Chapel Hill, University of North Carolina Press.

Frenzel, Elisabeth, 1970a. *Stoffe der Weltliteratur.* 3rd ed. Stuttgart, Kröner. (6th ed. 1983.)

———1970b. *Stoff-, Motiv- und Symbolforschung.* 3rd ed. Stuttgart, Metzler.

———1980. *Motive der Weltliteratur.* 2nd ed. Stuttgart, Kröner.

Friar, Kimon, 1973. *Modern Greek Poetry.* New York, Simon and Schuster.

Fried, István, Zoltán Kanyó, and József Pál, eds., 1983. *Essays Presented to György Mihály Vajda.* Szeged, Attila Tudományegyetem.

Fries, Udo, 1975. "Topics and Problems in Dialogue Linguistics." *Studia Anglica Posaniensa,* 7, 7–15.

Fry, D. K., 1969. "Themes and Type-Scenes in *Elene* 1–113." *Speculum,* 44, 34–45.

Frye, Northrop, 1957. *The Anatomy of Criticism.* Princeton, Princeton University Press.

———1959. "Literature as Context: Milton's *Lycidas.*" *Proceedings II,* I, 44–53.

———1968. *The Educated Imagination.* Bloomington, Indiana University Press.

Fubini, Mario, 1973. "Genesi e storia dei generi letterari." *Critica e poesia.* 3rd ed., 121–212. Rome, Bonacci.

Fuentes, Carlos, 1976. *Cervantes o la crítica de la lectura.* Mexico City, J. Mortiz.

Gaddis Rose, Marilyn, ed., 1981. *Translation Spectrum.* Albany, State University of New York Press.

Galdós, B. Pérez, 1954. *El abuelo.* Buenos Aires, Espasa-Calpe Argentina.

———1986. *Fortunata and Jacinta.* Tr. Agnes Moncy Gullón. Athens, University of Georgia Press.

Gallego Morell, Antonio, Andrés Soria, and Nicholás Marín, eds., 1971. *Estudios sobre literatura y arte: Dedicados al profesor Emilio Orozco Díaz.* 3 vols. Granada, Universidad.

García Berrio, Antonio, 1973. *Significado actual del formalismo ruso.* Barcelona, Planeta.

———1978a. "Lingüística del texto y texto lírico." *Revista de la Sociedad española de lingüística,* 8, 19–75.

———1978b. "Tipología textual de los sonetos españoles sobre el 'carpe diem.'" *Dispositio,* 3, 243–293.

———1981. "Macrocomponente textual y sistematismo tipológico: el soneto amoroso español de los siglos XVI y XVII y las reglas del género." *Zeitschrift für romanische Philologie,* 97, 146–171.

García Gallego, Jesús, 1984. *La recepción del surrealismo en España (1924–1931).* Granada, Antonio Ubago.

García Lorca, Federico, 1929. *Canciones.* Málaga, Revista de occidente.

———1931. *Poema del cante jondo.* Madrid, Ulises.

———1955. *Obras completas.* 2nd ed. Prologue by J. Guillén. Madrid, Aguilar. (19th ed. 1974.)

———1981. *Amor de don Perlimplín.* Madrid, Taurus.

———1983. *Suites.* Ed. A. Balamich. Barcelona.

————1991. *Collected Poems*. Bilingual ed. Ed. Christopher Maurer. New York, Farrar, Straus and Giroux.

García Lorca, Francisco, 1984. *De Garciloso a Lorca*. Ed. C. Guillén. Madrid, Istmo.

García Márquez, Gabriel, 1982. *Chronicle of a Death Foretold*. Tr. Gregory Rabassa. New York, Alfred A. Knopf.

García Yebra, Valentín, 1981. "La traducción en el nacimiento y desarrollo de las literaturas." *1616*, 4, 7–24.

Garcilaso de la Vega ("El Inca"), 1966. *Royal Commentaries of the Incas*. 2 vols. Tr. Harold Livermore. Austin, University of Texas Press.

Garibay, Angel María, 1953–1954. *Historia de la literatura náhuatl*. 2 vols. Mexico City, Porrúa.

Gelley, Alexander, 1979. "The Represented World: Toward a Phenomenological Theory of Description in the Novel." *Journal of Aesthetics and Art Criticism*, 37, 415–422.

————1980. "Metonymy, Schematism, and the Space of Literature." *NLH*, 11, 469–487.

Gendarme de Bévotte, Georges, 1906–1929. *La légende de Don Juan*. 2 vols. Paris, Hachette.

Genette, Gérard, 1972. "Discours du récit." In *Figures III*, 62–282. Paris, Seuil.

————1977. "Genres, 'types,' modes." *Poétique*, 32, 389–421.

————1980. *Narrative Discourse*. Tr. Jane E. Lewin. Ithaca, N.Y., Cornell University Press.

————1982. *Palimpsestes*. Paris, Seuil.

————1983. *Nouveau discours du récit*. Paris, Seuil.

George, Emery, ed., 1983. *Contemporary East European Poetry*. Ann Arbor, Ardis.

Gérard, Albert, 1957. "On the Logic of Romanticism." *Essays in Criticism*, 7, 262–273.

————1981. *African Language Literatures*. Harlow, England, Longman.

————1983. "Baroque classique et classicisme post-baroque." *Romanistische Zeitschrift für Literaturgeschichte*, 3–4, 298–307.

Gerchkovitch, Aleksandr A., 1975. "Le théâtre est-européen à la charnière des lumières et du romantisme." *Neohelicon* (Budapest), 3, 51–67.

Gerhardt, Mia I., 1950. *La pastorale*. Assen, Van Gorcum.

Giamatti, A. Bartlett, 1966. *The Earthly Paradise and the Renaissance Epic*. Princeton, Princeton University Press.

————1968. "Proteus Unbound: Some Versions of the Sea God in the Renaissance." In P. Demertz et al., eds., *The Disciplines of Criticism*, 437–475. New Haven, Yale University Press.

Gicovate, Bernardo, 1962. *Conceptos fundamentales de literatura comparada: Iniciación de la poesía modernista*. San Juan, Puerto Rico, Asomante.

Gifford, Henry, 1969. *Comparative Literature*. London, Routledge and Kegan Paul.

Gillespie, Gerald, 1967. "Novela, Nouvelle, Novelle, Short Novel? A Review of Terms." *Neophilologus,* 51, 117–122, 225–230.

Gillies, Alexander, 1952. "Some Thoughts on Comparative Literature." *YCGL,* 1, 15–25.

Gilman, Stephen, 1956. *The Art of "La Celestina."* Madison, University of Wisconsin Press.

———1967. *The Tower as Emblem: Chapters VIII, IX, XIX and XX of the Chartreuse de Parme.* Frankfurt am Main, Klostermann.

———1981. *Galdós and the Art of the European Novel: 1867–1887.* Princeton, Princeton University Press.

Giraud, Yves F.-A., 1968. *La fable de Daphné.* Geneva, Droz.

Gobbi, Agostino, 1708–09. *Scelta de Sonetti e Canzoni d' più eccellenti Rimatori d'ogni secolo.* Vol. I, *Discorso.* Venice, Presso L. Bassegio.

Goethe, Wolfgang, 1902–1907. *Sämtliche Werke.* Ed. E. von der Hellen (Jubiläums Ausgabe). Stuttgart, J. G. Cotta'che Buchandlung Nachfolger.

———1984. *Conversations with Eckermann (1823–1832).* Tr. John Oxenford. San Francisco, North Point Press.

Goldknopf, David, 1972. *The Life of the Novel.* Chicago, University of Chicago Press.

Gorer, Geoffrey, 1965. *Death, Grief and Mourning in Contemporary Britain.* London, Cresset.

Goriely, Benjamin, 1967. *Le avanguardie letterarie in Europa.* Milan, Feltrinelli.

Görog-Karady, Veronika, ed., 1982. *Genres, Forms, Meanings: Essays in African Oral Literature.* JASO Occasional Papers. Oxford.

Grabowicz, George G., 1983. *The Poet as Mythmaker: A Study of Symbolic Meaning in Taras Sevcenko.* Cambridge, Mass., Harvard University Press.

Gracián, Baltazar, 1987 (first pub. 1642). *Agadeza y arte de ingenio.* Madrid, Castalia.

Grahor, Olga, 1977. *France in the Work and Ideas of Antun Gustav Matoš.* Munich, Sagner.

Gray, Bennison, 1977. "From Discourse to 'Dialog.'" *Journal of Pragmatics,* 3, 283–297.

Greimas, A.-J., 1966. *Sémantique structurale.* Paris, Flammarion.

———1970. *Du sens.* Paris, Seuil.

Greimas, A.-J., and Joseph Courtès, 1979. *Sémiotique: Dictionnaire raisonné de la théorie du langage.* Paris, Hachette.

Griffith, G. O., 1932. *Mazzini.* London, Hodder and Stoughton.

Gsteiger, Manfred, 1967. *Littérature nationale et comparatisme.* Neuchâtel, Université.

———1980. "Littérature comparée et esthétique de la réception." *Proceedings VIII,* II, 527–533.

———1983a. "Komparatistik als Vorwand und Rückhalt: Halbernster Brief über eine langwierige Auffindung." *Arcadia* (Berlin), 23–30.

————1983b. "Les modèles en histoire littéraire et le paradigme 'continuité' et 'rupture.' " *Etude de lettres*, 3, 55–63.

Guenther, Herbert, 1960. *Künstlerische Doppelbegabungen*. 2nd ed. Munich, Heimeran.

Guenthner, Franz, and M. Guenthner-Reutter, 1978. *Meaning and Translation*. London, Duckworth.

Guillén, Claudio, 1955. "Problemas de tematología: *Die verführte Unschuld* de H. Petriconi." *Romanische Forschungen*, 66, 397–406.

————1957. "Estilística del silencio." *Revista hispánica moderna*, 23, 260–291.

————1962. "Perspectivas de la literatura comparada." *Boletín informativo del seminario del derecho político* (Salamanca), 27, 57–70.

————1971. *Literature as System*. Princeton, Princeton University Press.

————1971–72. "Some Observations on Parallel Forms." *TR*, 2–3, 395–415.

————1972. "Sátira y poética en Garcilaso." In R. Pincus Siegele and G. Sobejano, eds., *Homenaje a Joaquín Casalduero*, 209–233. Madrid, Gredos.

————1977a. "Literary Change and Multiple Relations." *CLS*, 14, 100–118.

————1977b. "Proceso y orden inminente en *Campos de Castilla*." In J. Angeles, ed., *Estudios sobre Antonio Machado*, 195–216. Barcelona, Ariel.

————1978a. "Cambio literario y múltiple duración." In A. Carreira, ed., *Homenaje a Julio Caro Baroja*, 533–549. Madrid, Centro de investigaciones sociológicas.

————1978b. "De la forma a la estructura: Fusiones y confusiones." *1616*, 23–40.

————1979a. "Cervantes y la dialéctica, o el diálogo inacabado." In *Les cultures ibériques en devenir . . . Essais . . . à la mémoire de Marcel Bataillon*, 631–645. Paris, Fondation Singer-Polignac.

————1979b. "De influencias y convenciones." *1616*, 2, 87–97.

————1982. "Quevedo y los géneros literarios." In J. Iffland, ed., *Quevedo in Perspective*, 1–16. Newark, Del., Juan de la Cuesta.

————1988. *El primer siglo de oro. Estudios sobre géneros y modelos*. Barcelona, Editorial Crítica.

Guillén, Jorge, 1981. *Antología del mar*. Málaga, Libr. Agora.

————1987. *Aire nuestro*. 5 vols. (I, *Cántico;* II, *Clamor;* III, *Homenaje;* IV, *Y otras poemas;* V, *Final*). Valladolid, Centro de estudios de Jorge Guillén, Diputación de Valladolid.

Gurney, O. R., 1957. "The Sultantepe Tablets: VI: A Letter of Gilgamesh." *Anatolian Studies*, 7, 127–136.

Guthke, Karl S., 1966. *Modern Tragicomedy*. New York, Random House.

Guyard, Marius-François, 1951. *La littérature comparée*. Paris, Presses universitaires de France. (6th ed. rev. with R. Lauverjat, 1978.)

Haas, Gerhard, 1969. *Essay*. Stuttgart, Metzler.

Hagstrum, Jean H., 1953. *The Sister Arts*. Chicago, University of Chicago Press.

ha-Levi, Judah, 1983. *Antología poética*. Tr. Rosa Castillo. Madrid, Altalena editores.

Hamburger, Käte, 1957. *Die Logik der Dichtung.* Stuttgart, Klett.

Hamon, Philippe, 1981. *Introduction à l'analyse du descriptif.* Paris, Hachette.

Hankiss, János, 1938. "Littérature universelle?" *Helicon,* 1, 156–171.

Hansen-Löve, Aage A., 1978. *Der russische Formalismus: Methodologische Rekonstruction seiner Entwicklung aus dem Prinzip der Verfremdung.* Vienna, Oesterreichische. Akademie der Wissenschaften.

Harris, Joseph, 1979. "The *Senna:* From Description to Literary Theory." *Michigan Germanic Studies,* 5, 65–74.

Hartman, Geoffrey H., 1954. *The Unmediated Vision.* New Haven, Yale University Press.

———1962. "Romanticism and 'Antiself-consciousness'." *Centennial Review,* 6, 553–565.

———1970. *Beyond Formalism.* New Haven, Yale University Press.

Hassan, Ihab B., 1955. "The Problem of Influence in Literary History: Notes toward a Definition." *Journal of Aesthetics and Art Criticism,* 14, 66–76.

Hatto, Arthur T., 1965. *Eos: An Enquiry into the Theme of Lovers' Meetings and Partings at Dawn in Poetry.* London, Mouton.

Haufe, Heinz, 1935. *Jean-Jacques Ampère, 1800–1864.* Dresden, Risse-Verlag.

Hauser, Arnold, 1951. *The Social History of Art.* 2 vols. New York, Alfred A. Knopf.

Helbo, André, ed., 1975. *Sémiologie de la représentation.* Brussels, Eds. complexe.

Heliodorus, 1957. *An Ethiopian Romance.* Tr. Moses Hadas. Ann Arbor, University of Michigan Press.

Hell, Victor, 1976. "L'art de la brèveté: Genèse et formes du récit court: 'Short stories' et 'Kurzgeschichte'." *RLC,* 50, 389–401.

Hemerén, Göran, 1975. *Influence in Art and Literature.* Princeton, Princeton University Press.

Hempfer, Klaus W., 1973. *Gattungstheorie.* Munich, Fink.

Henkel, Arthur, and Albrecht Schoene, 1967. *Emblemata.* Stuttgart, Metzler. (2nd ed. 1976.)

Herder, J. G., 1877–1913. *Sämmtliche Werke.* Ed. Bernhard Suphan. 23 vols. Berlin, Weidmannsche Buchhandlung.

———1957. *Mensch und Geschichte.* Ed. Willi A. Koch. Stuttgart, Alfred Kröner Verlag.

Hermann, Fritz, 1959. *Die "Revue Blanche" und die "Nabis."* 2 vols. Munich, Mikrokopie.

Hernadi, Paul, 1972. *Beyond Genre.* Ithaca, N.Y., Cornell University Press.

———, ed. 1978. *What Is Literature?* Bloomington, Indiana University Press.

Herrick, M. T., 1955. *Tragicomedy.* Urbana, Illinois University Press.

Highet, Gilbert, 1962. *The Anatomy of Satire.* Princeton, Princeton University Press.

Hightower, James R., 1966. *Topics in Chinese Literature.* Cambridge, Mass., Harvard University Press.

Higman, Perry, tr., 1986. *Love Poems from Spain and Latin America.* San Francisco, City Lights.

Hirsch, E. D., Jr., 1976. *The Aims of Interpretation.* Chicago, University of Chicago Press.

Hock, S., 1915. "Ueber die Wiederholung in der Dichtung." In *Festschrift für Wilhelm Jersalem zu seinem 60. Geburtstag,* 100–122. Vienna.

Hocke, G. R., 1961. *Manierismus in der Literatur.* Hamburg, Rowohlt.

Hoffman, Frederick J., Charles Allen, and Carolyn F. Ulrich, 1946. *The Little Magazine.* Princeton, Princeton University Press.

Holmes, James, José Lambert, and Raymond Van den Broeck, 1978. *Literature and Translation.* Louvain, Acco.

Horányi, Mátyás, and Tibor Klaniczay, eds., 1967. *Italia ed Ungheria.* Budapest, Akademiái Kiadó.

Hosillos, Lucila V., 1966. "Filipino Literature: Its Emergence and Quest for National Identity." *Proceedings IV,* II, 1370–1377.

Howe, Irving, ed., 1967. *The Idea of the Modern in Literature and the Arts.* New York, Horizon Press.

Howe, Irving, 1970. "Mass Society and Postmodern Fiction." In I. Howe, ed., *Decline of the New.* New York, Harcourt, Brace and World.

Hrushovski, Benjamin, 1960. "On Free Rhythms in Modern Poetry." In Thomas A. Seboek, ed., *Style in Language,* 173–190. Cambridge, Mass., MIT Press.

———1972. "Prosody, Hebrew." *Encyclopaedica Judaica,* XIII, 1.195–1.240.

Hugo, Victor, 1977. *Les châtiments.* Paris, Gallimard.

Hunt, John Dickson, ed., 1971. *Encounters: Essays on Literature and the Visual Arts.* New York, W. W. Norton.

Hutton, James, 1946. *The Greek Anthology in France and in the Latin Writers of the Netherlands to the Year 1800.* Ithaca, N.Y., Cornell University Press.

Hyman, Stanley Edgar, 1949. "Myth, Ritual and Nonsense." *Kenyon Review,* 11, 463–466.

Iffland, James, 1972. *Quevedo and the Grotesque.* London, Thames.

Ingarden, Roman, 1960. *Das literarische Kunstwerk.* 2d ed. Tübingen, Niemeyer (1st ed. Halle, 1931).

Iser, Wolfgang, ed., 1966. *Immanente Aesthetik, aesthetische Reflexion: Lyrik als Paradigma der Moderne.* Munich, Fink.

———1972. *Der implizite Leser.* Munich, Fink.

Jabbour, A., 1969. "Memorial Transmission in Old English Poetry." *Chaucer Review,* 3, 174–190.

Jackson, A. B., 1960. *La revue blanche (1889–1903).* Paris, Minard.

Jakobson, Roman, 1979. *On Verse, Its Masters and Explorers.* Ed. S. Rudy and M. Taylor. The Hague, Mouton.

———1987a. "Grammatical Parallelism and Its Russian Aspects." In Krystyna Pomorska and Stephen Rudy, eds., *Language in Literature,* 145–179. Cambridge, Mass., Harvard University Press.

————1987b. "Linguistics and Poetics." In ibid., pp. 62–94.

————1987c. "Poetry of Grammar and Grammar of Poetry." In ibid., 121–144.

Jakobson, Roman, and Claude Lévi-Strauss, 1962. "'Les chats' de Charles Baudelaire." *L'homme*, 2, no. 1, 5–21.

Jameson, Fredric, 1971. *Marxism and Form*. Princeton, Princeton University Press.

————1972. *The Prison-House of Language*. Princeton, Princeton University Press.

————1975. "Magical Narrative: Romance as Genre." *NLH*, 7, 135–163.

————1981. *The Political Unconscious*. Ithaca, N.Y., Cornell University Press.

Jauss, Hans Robert, 1967. *Literaturgeschichte als Provokation der Literaturwissenschaft*. Konstanzer Universitätsreden 3. Constance, Universitätsverlag.

————1970a. *Literaturgeschichte als Provokation*. Frankfurt am Main, Suhrkamp.

————1970b. "Littérature médiévale et théorie des genres." *Poétique*, 1, 79–101.

————1972. *Kleine Apologie der ästhetischen Erfahrung*. Konstanzer Universitätsreden 59. Constance, Universitätsverlag.

————1974. "Literary History as a Challenge to Literary Theory." Tr. Elizabeth Benzinger. In Cohen, 1974, pp. 11–41.

————1977. *Aesthetische Erfahrung und Literarische Hemeneutik*. Munich, Fink.

————1982. *Toward an Aesthetic of Reception*. Tr. Timothy Bahti. Foreword by Paul de Man. Minneapolis, University of Minnesota Press.

Jechová, Hana, 1982. *L'image poétique dans le mouvement romantique slave*. Lille-Paris, Didier.

Jenny, Laurent, 1976. "La stratégie de la forme." *Poétique*, 27, 257–281.

Jesi, Furio, 1968. *Letteratura e mito*. Turin, Einaudi.

Jeune, Simon, 1968. *Littérature générale et littérature comparée*. Paris, Minard.

Jiménez, Juan Ramón, 1987. *Light and Shadows: Selected Poems and Prose*. Ed. and tr. Dennis Maloney. Fredonia, N.Y., White Pine Press.

Jiménez Millán, Antonio, 1983. *Los poemas de Picasso*. Málaga, Impr. Dardo.

Johnson, Barbara, 1979. *Défigurations du langage poétique*. Paris, Flammarion.

Jones, David J., 1934. *La tenson provençale*. Paris, Droz.

Jost, François, 1974. *Introduction to Comparative Literature*. Indianapolis, Bobbs-Merrill.

Jrapchenko, M. B., 1968. "Typologische Literaturforschung und ihre Principien." In Ziegengeist, 1968, 17–46.

Jurgensen, Manfred, 1979. *Das fiktionale Ich: Untersuchungen zum Tagebuch*. Bern, Francke.

Kadić, Ante, 1962. "The Croatian Renaissance." *Slavic Review*, 21, 65–88.

Kaiser, Gerhard R., 1980a. *Einführung in die vergleichende Literaturwissenschaft*. Darmstadt, Wissenschaftliche Buchgesellschaft.

————, ed., 1980b. *Vergleichende Literaturforschung in den sozialistischen Ländern: 1963–1979*. Stuttgart, Metzler.

Kaiser, Walter, 1963. *Praisers of Folly: Erasmus, Rabelais, Shakespeare*. Cambridge, Mass., Harvard University Press.

Kappler, Arno, 1976. *Der literaische Vergleich: Beiträge zu einer Vorgeschichte der Komparatistik*. Bern, Herbert Lang.

Kayser, Wolfgang, 1957. *Das Groteske*. Oldburg, Stalling.

Kerman, Joseph, 1956. *Opera as Drama*. New York, Alfred A. Knopf. (Reissued 1959, New York, Vintage Books.)

Kermode, Frank, 1967. *The Sense of an Ending*. New York, Oxford University Press.

Kernan, Alvin, 1959. *The Cankered Muse*. New Haven, Yale University Press.

Kierkegaard, S., 1944. *Either/Or*. Vol. I tr. David F. Swenson and Lillian Marvin Swenson; vol. 2 tr. Walter Lowrie. Princeton, Princeton University Press.

King, Edmund L., 1953. *Gustavo Adolfo Bécquer: From Painter to Poet*. Mexico City, Porrúa.

Kirschbaum, J. M., 1966. *Pan Slavism in Slovak Literature: Ján Kollár, Poet of Pan-Slavism (1793–1852)*. Cleveland, Ohio, Slovak Institute.

Klaniczay, Tibor, 1966. "Que faut-it entendre par littérature nationale?" *Proceedings IV*, I, 187–194.

———1967. "Niccolò Zrinyi, Venezia e la letteratura della ragion de stato." In *Mélanges de littérature comparée et philologie offerts à Mieczslaw Brahmer*, 265–273. Warsaw, PWN.

Klein, Jürgen, 1975. *Der gotische Roman und die Aesthetik des Bösen*. Darmstadt, Wissenschaftliche Buchgesellschaft.

Knox, Norman, 1961. *The Word Irony and Its Context, 1500–1755*. Durham, N.C., Duke University Press.

Kohut, Karl, 1973. "Ingeniosa comparación entre lo antiguo y lo presente: Aufnahme und Kritik der antiken Tradition im Spanischen Humanismus." In *Renatae Litterae . . . August Buck zum 60. Geburtstag*, 217–243. Frankfurt/Main, Heiman und Schroeder.

Köpeczi, Béla, 1979. *Idee, Geschichte, Literatur*. Berlin, Aufnahme-Verlag.

Koskennemie, Heikki, 1956. *Studien zur Idee und Phraseologie des griechischen Briefs bis 400 n. Chr.* Helsinki, Tiedeakatemian toimituksia.

Kosselleck, Reinhart, and Wolf-Dieter Stempel, eds., 1973. *Ereignis und Erzählung*. Munich, Fink.

Kowzan, Tadeusz, 1968. "Le signe au théâtre." *Diogène*, 61, 52–80.

———1975. *Littérature et spectacle*. The Hague, Mouton.

Kramer, Samuel Noah, 1979. *From the Poetry of Sumer*. Berkeley, University of California Press.

Kraus, F. R., 1980. "Der Brief des Gilgamesh." *Anatolian Studies*, 30, 109–121.

Krějeć, J., 1968. "Zur Entwicklung der Präromantik in europäischen Nationalliteraturen des 18. und 19. Jahrhunderts." In Ziegengeist, 1968, 230–239.

Krieger, Murray, ed., 1966. *Northrop Frye in Modern Criticism*. New York, Columbia University Press.

———1973. *The Tragic Vision: The Confrontation of Extremity*. Baltimore, Johns Hopkins Press.

Kristeva, Julia, 1968. "Problèmes de la structuration du texte." In P. Sollers, ed., *Théorie d'ensemble*. Paris, Seuil.

———1969. "L'engendrement de la formule." In *Semiotiké*. Paris, Seuil.

———1986. "Word, Dialogue and Novel." In *The Kristeva Reader,* 35–61. Oxford, Basil Blackwell.

Krueger, Manfred, 1973. *Wandlungen des tragischen.* Stuttgart, Freies Geistesleben.

Kubler, George, 1962. *The Shape of Time.* New Haven, Yale University Press.

Kugel, James L., 1981. *The Idea of Biblical Poetry: Parallelism and its History.* New Haven, Yale University Press.

Kushner, Eva, 1963. "The Critical Method of Gaston Bachelard." In B. Slote, ed., *Myth and Symbol,* 39–50. Lincoln, University of Nebraska Press.

———1966. "Yvan Goll: Deux langages, une âme." *Proceedings IV,* II, 576–582.

———1982. "Le dialogue de 1580 à 1630: Articulations et fonctions." In J. Lafond, and A. Stegmann, eds., *L'Automne de la Renaissance,* 149–162. Paris, Vrin.

———1983. "Vers une poétique du dialogue de la Renaissance." In Fried, Kanyó, and Pál, 1983, 131–136.

LaDrière, Craig, 1959a. "The Comparative Method in the Study of Prosody." *Proceedings II,* I, 160–175.

———, 1959b. "Literary Form and Form in the Other Arts." In Boeckmann, 1959, 28–37.

———1965. "Prosody." In A. Preminger, ed., *Encyclopedia of Poetry and Poetics,* 669–677. Princeton, Princeton University Press.

Laemmert, Eberhard, 1955. *Bauformen des Erzählens.* Stuttgart, Metzler. (Reissued 1970.)

Laitinen, Kai, 1983. "Finland and World Literatures." *World Literature Today,* 393–398.

Lambert, José, 1976. *Ludwig Tieck dans les lettres françaises: Aspects d'une résistance au Romantisme allemand.* Louvain, Presses universitaires.

———1981. "Théorie de la littérature et théorie de la traduction en France (1800–1850)." *PT,* 2, 4, 161–170.

———1983. "L'éternelle question des frontières: Littératures nationales et systèmes littéraires." In C. Angelet, et al., eds., *Langue, dialecte, littérature: Etudes romanes à la mémoire de Hugo Plomteux,* 355–370. Louvain, Université.

Lapesa, Rafael, 1976. "Garcilaso y Fray Luis de León: Coincidencias temáticas y contrastes de actitudes." *Archivum* (Oviedo), 2, 7–17.

Lara, Jesús, 1947. *La poesía quechua.* Cochabamba, Bolivia, Universidad Mayor de San Simón.

Lausberg, Heinrich, 1960. *Handbuch der literarischen Rhetorik.* 2 vols. Munich, Max Hueber.

Lazarillo of Tormes, 1973. *The Life of Lazarillo of Tormes: His Fortunes and Misfortunes, as Told by Himself.* Tr. Robert S. Rudder. New York, Frederick Ungar.

Lázaro Carreter, Fernando, 1979. *Estudios de poética.* Madrid, Taurus.

———1980. *Estudios de lingüística.* Barcelona, Crítica.

Lee, Rensselaer W., 1940. "Ut Pictura Poesis: The Humanistic Theory of Painting." *Art Bulletin,* 22, 197–269.

Leenhardt, Jacques, 1973. *Lecture politique du roman: La Jalousie d'Alain Robbe-Grillet*. Paris, Minuit.

Lefevere, André, 1973. *Translating Literature: The German Tradition from Luther to Rosenzweig*. Assen, Van Gorcum.

———1978. "Some Tactical Steps toward a Common Poetics." *New Asia Academic Bulletin*, 1, 9–16.

———1982. "Théorie littéraire et littérature traduite." *CRCL*, 9, 137–156.

Lejeune, Philippe, 1975. *Le pacte autobiographique*. Paris, Seuil.

———1980. *Je est un autre*. Paris, Seuil.

Lejeune, Rita, Jacques Stiennon, 1965. *La légende de Roland dans l'art du Moyen Age*. 2 vols. Brussels, Arcade.

Lemon, L. T., and M. J. Reis, 1965. *Russian Formalist Criticism: Four Essays*. Lincoln, University of Nebraska Press.

Lenson, David, 1975. *Achilles' Choice: Examples of Modern Tragedy*. Princeton, Princeton University Press.

Levin, A., 1957. *The Legacy of Philarète Chasles*. Chapel Hill, University of North Carolina Press.

Levin, Harry, 1953. "La littérature comparée: Point de vue d'outre-Atlantique." *RLC*, 27, 17–26.

———1958. *Contexts of Criticism*. Cambridge, Mass., Harvard University Press.

———1963. *The Gates of Horn*. New York, Oxford University Press.

———1966. *Refractions*. New York, Oxford University Press.

———1968. "Thematics of Criticism." In P. Demetz, T. Greene, and L. Nelson, Jr., eds., *The Discipline of Criticism*. New Haven, Yale University Press.

———1969. *The Myth of the Golden Age in the Renaissance*. New York, Oxford University Press.

———1972. *Grounds for Comparison*. Cambridge, Mass., Harvard University Press.

———1975–76. "Towards World Literature." *TR*, 6–7, 21–30.

Lévi-Strauss, Claude, 1979. *From Honey to Ashes: Introduction to a Science of Mythology*. Tr. John and Doreen Weightman. New York, Octagon Books, Farrar, Straus and Giroux.

Lida de Malkiel, María Rosa, 1975. *La tradición clásica en España*. Barcelona, Ariel.

Lima, Sergio, 1964. *Ensaio sôbre a essência de ensaio*. 2nd ed. Coimbra, Amado.

Liu, James J. Y., 1975a. *Chinese Theories of Literature*. Chicago, University of Chicago Press.

———, 1975b. "The Study of Chinese Literature in the West: Recent Developments, Current Trends, Future Prospects." *Journal of Asian Studies*, 35, 21–30.

Lodge, David, 1977. *The Modes of Modern Writing*. Ithaca, N.Y., Cornell University Press.

Longeon, Claude, ed., 1980. *Le genre pastoral en Europe du XVe au XVIIe siècle*. Saint-Étienne, Université.

López-Baralt, Luce, 1980. "Crónica de la destrucción de un mundo: La literatura Aljamiado-Morisca." *Bulletin hispanique,* 82, 16–58.

López-Baralt, Mercedes, 1979. "Millenarianism as Liminality: An Interpretation of the Andean Myth of *Inkarrí.*" *Punto de contacto,* 6, 65–82.

———1980. "The Quechuan Elegy of the All-Powerful Inka Atawallpa." *Latin American Indian Literatures,* 4, 79–86.

Lord, Albert B., 1960. *The Singer of Tales.* Cambridge, Mass., Harvard University Press.

Lotman, Yuri, 1969. "Il problema di una tipologia della cultura." In R. Faccani and U. Eco, eds., *I sistemi di segni e lo struttualismo sovietico.* Milan, Bompiani.

———1973. *La structure du texte artistique.* Tr. A. Fournier. Paris, Gallimard.

———1974. *Aufsätze zur Theorie und Methodologie der Literatur und Kultur.* Ed. K. Eimermacher. Kronberg, Scriptor.

———1977. *The Structure of the Artistic Text.* Tr. Ronald Vroon. Ann Arbor, University of Michigan Press.

Lotman, Yuri, and Boris A. Uspenski, 1975. *Tipololgia della cultura.* Ed. R. Faccani and M. Marzaduri. Milan, Bompiani.

Lotz, J., 1960. "Metric Typology." In Seboek, 1960, 135–148.

Lourenço, Eduardo, 1981. *Fernando Pessoa revisitado.* 2nd ed. Lisbon, Moraes.

Loveluck, Juan, 1982. "Esquividad y concreción del ensayo." *Literatura Chilena,* 22 (October–December), 2–7.

Lowenthal, Leo, 1948. "The Sociology of Literature." In W. Schramm, ed., *Communications in Modern Society,* 82–100. Urbana, University of Illinois Press.

Lukács, Georg, 1955. *Der historische Roman.* Berlin, Aufbau-Verlag.

———1961. *Schriften zur Literatursoziologie.* Ed. P. Ludz. Neuwied, Luchterhand.

———1971. *The Theory of the Novel.* Tr. Anna Bostock. Cambridge, Mass., MIT Press.

Lyotard, Jean-François, 1971. *Discours, figure.* Paris, Klincksieck.

Machado, Alvaro Manuel, and Daniel-Henri Pageaux, 1981. *Literatura portuguesa, literatura comparada, teoria da literatura.* Lisbon, Eds. 70.

Machado, Antonio, 1957a. "Los complementarios." In Antonio and Manuel Machado, *Obras completas.* 3rd ed. Madrid, Editorial Plenitud.

———1957b. *Juan de Mairena.* In ibid.

———1963. *Juan de Mairena.* Tr. Ben Belitt. Berkeley, University of California Press.

Malmede, Hans Hermann, 1966. *Wege zur Novelle.* Stuttgart, Kohlhammer.

Malone, David, 1954. "The 'Comparative' in Comparative Literature." *YCGL,* 3, 13–20.

Manrique, Jorge, 1981. *Coplas por la muerte de su padre.* Madrid, Turner. Translation in Cohen, 1988.

Manuel, Frank E., and Fritzie P. Manuel, 1979. *Utopian Thought in the Western World.* Cambridge, Mass., Harvard University Press.

Marasso, Arturo, 1941. *Rubén Darío y su creación poética*. 2nd ed. Buenos Aires, Imprenta López.

Maravall, J.-A., 1966. *Antiguos y modernos*. Madrid, Sociedad de estudios y publicacions.

Margolin, Uri, 1975. "On the Object of Study in Literary History." *Neohelicon* (Budapest), 3, 287–328.

Mariani, Franca, ed., 1983. *Letteratura: Percorsi possibili*. Ravenna, Longo.

Marichal, Juan, 1957. *La voluntad de estilo*. Barcelona, Seix Barral. (2nd ed. 1971, Madrid, Revista de occidente.)

Marin, Louis, 1972a. *Etudes sémiologiques*. Paris, Klincksieck.

———1972b. "La lecture du tableau d'après Poussin." *Cahiers de l'Association internationale des études françaises*, 24, 251–266.

Marino, Adrian, 1974. *Critica ideilor literare*. Cluj, Dacia.

———1975. "Où situer la littérature universelle." *CREL*, 3, 64–81.

———1977a. "L'avant-garde et l'histoire retrouvée." *Synthesis* (Bucharest), 4, 227–241.

———1977b. *La critique des idées littéraires*. Brussels, Complexe.

———1979a. "Analyse comparatiste du cycle de l'avant-garde." *CREL*, 84–93.

———1979b. "Etiemble, les 'invariants' et la littérature comparée." In *Le mythe d'Etiemble*, 157–167. Paris, Didier.

———1980. "Comment définir l'avant-garde?" *Proceedings VIII*, I, 889–895.

———1982a. *Etiemble ou le comparatisme militant*. Paris, Gallimard.

———1982b. "In Favour of a Hermeneutics of the Idea of Literature." *CREL*, 34–47.

———1982c. *Littérature roumaine; littératures occidentales*. Bucharest, Ed. sciintifica enciclopedica.

Markiewicz, Henryk, 1980. "Forschungsbereich und Systematik der vergleichenden Literaturwissenschaft." In G. R. Kaiser, 1980b, 113–122.

Marot, C., 1958. *L'adolescence clémentine*. Ed. V. L. Salnier. Paris, Colin.

———1964. *Les epîtres*. London, C. A. Mayer.

Márquez Villanueva, Francisco, 1973. *Fuentes literarias cervantinas*. Madrid, Gredos.

———1983. "Nueva visión de la leyenda de Don Juan." In K.-H. Körner, and D. Briesemeister, eds., *Aureum Saeculum Hispanum . . . Festschrift für Hans Flasche,*, 203–216. Wiesbaden, Steiner.

Martínez Bonati, Félix, 1983. *La estructura de la obra literaria*. 3rd. ed. Barcelona, Ariel.

Martínez Estrada, Ezequiel, 1946. *Panorama de las literaturas*. Buenos Aires, Editorial claridad.

Martini, Carlo, ed., 1956. *"La voce": Storia e bibliografia*. Pisa, Nistri-Lischi.

Martorell, Joannot, and Martí Joan de Galba, 1983. *Tirant lo blanc* (1490). Ed. Martí de Riquer. Barcelona, Ediciones 62.

————1984. *Triant lo Blanc.* Tr. David H. Rosenthal. New York, Schocken Books.

Matejka, Ladislav, and Krystyna Pomorska, 1971. *Readings in Russian Poetics.* Cambridge, Mass., MIT Press.

Mathieu-Castellani, Gisèle, 1980. "La poétique du fleuve dans les *Bergeries* de Racan." In Longeon, 1980, 223–232.

Mauron, Charles, 1963. *Des métaphors obsédantes au mythe personnel.* Paris, Corti.

Maury, Paul, 1934. *Arts et littératures comparées.* Paris, Les belles lettres.

Mautner, Franz H., 1966. "Maxim(e)s, sentences, fragmente, aphormismen." *Proceedings IV,* 812–819.

May, Georges, 1979. *L'autobiographie.* Paris, Presses universitaires de France.

Mayo, Robert S., 1969. *Herder and the Beginnings of Comparative Literature.* Chapel Hill, University of North Carolina Press.

McLeod, Russell, 1976. "The Baroque as a Period Concept in Chinese Literature." *TR,* 7, 2, 185–206.

Meijer, Pieter de, 1981. "L'analyse du récit." In A. Kibédy-Varga, ed., *Théorie de la littérature,* 177–189. Paris, Picard.

Menéndez Pidal, Ramón, 1953. *Romancero hispánico.* 2 vols. Madrid, Espasa Calpe.

————1969. *Flor nueva de romances viejos.* 18th ed. Buenos Aires, Espasa-Calpe Argentina.

Meregalli, Franco, 1976. "La littérature comparée en Italie." *Neohelicon* (Budapest), 4, 303–314.

————1978. "L'Italia mediatrice tra il teatro spagnolo a la Germania nel Settecento." *Arcadia* (Berlin), 13, 242–254.

————1980. "Sur la réception littéraire." *RLC,* 54, 133–149.

————1983a. "Lettori e letture." *Annali dell'Istituto universitario orientale (Sezione romanza),* 25, no. 1, 125–137.

————1983b. Summary of *Proceedings IX,* vol. II, *CRCL,* 86–91.

Merian-Genast, E., 1927. "Voltaire und die Entwicklung der Idee der Weltliteratur." *Romanische Forschungen,* 40, 1–226.

Merquior, José Guilherme, 1972. "O significado do pós-modernismo." *Colóquio: Letras,* 52, 5–15.

Metz, Christian, 1971. *Langage et cinéma.* Paris, Larousse.

————1971–72. *Essais sur la signification au cinéma.* 2 vols. Paris, Klincksieck.

Michaëlsson, Erik, 1959. "L'eau, centre de métaphores et de métamorphoses dans la littérature française de la première moitié du XVIIe siècle." *Orbis Litterarum,* 14, 121–173.

————1980. "Remarques sur la réception en tant qu'événement historique et social." *Proceedings IX,* II, 27–33.

Miller, J. Hillis, 1971. "The Fiction of Realism." In J. Hillis Miller and D. Borowitz, *Charles Dickens and George Cruikshank,* 1–69. Los Angeles, W. A. Clark Memorial Library.

———1976. "Stevens' Rock and Criticism as Cure, II." *Georgia Review,* 30, no. 2, 330–348.

Milosz, Czeslaw, 1983. *The Witness of Poetry.* Cambridge, Mass., Harvard University Press.

Miner, Earl, 1979. *Japanese Linked Poetry,* Princeton, Princeton University Press.

Mishima, Y., 1975. *Runaway Horses.* Tr. Michael Gallagher. New York, Alfred A. Knopf. (Reinssued 1990.)

Mitxelena, Koldo, 1960. *Historia de la literatura vasca.* Madrid, Minotauro.

Mix, Katherine Lyon, 1960. *A Study in Yellow: The "Yellow Book" and Its Contributions.* Lawrence, University of Kansas Press.

Moisés, Massaud, 1968. *A criação literária.* 2nd ed. São Paulo, Eds. Melhoramentos.

Molière, 1981. *Oeuvres complètes.* 2 vols. Paris, Gallimard.

Mönch, Walter, 1954. *Das Sonett.* Heidelberg, Kerle.

Montaigne, Michel Eyquem de, 1958. *The Complete Essays of Montaigne.* Tr. Donald M. Frame. Stanford, Stanford University Press.

———1965. *Oeuvres complètes.* Ed. A. Thibaudet and M. Rat. Paris, Gallimard.

Montale, Eugenio, 1975. *L'opera in versi.* Turin, Giulio Einaudi.

Montesinos, José Fernández, 1965. *Costumbrismo y novela: Ensayo sobre el redescubrimineto de la realidad española.* Valencia, Editorial Castalia.

Mooji, J. J. A., 1979. "The Nature and Function of Literary Theories." *PT,* 1, nos. 1–2, 111–135.

Morris, E. P., 1931. "The Form of the Epistle in Horace." *Yale Classical Studies,* 2, 81–114.

Morrissette, Bruce, 1971. "Un héritage d'André Gide: La duplication intérieure." *CLS,* 8, 125–142.

Morson, Gary S., 1981. *The Boundaries of Genre: Dostoyevsky's "Diary of a Writer" and the Traditions of Literary Utopia.* Austin, University of Texas Press.

Motekat, Helmut, 1961. "Variations in Blue." *YCGL,* 10, 39–48.

Mounin, Georges, 1963. *Les problèmes théoriques de la traduction.* Paris, Gallimard.

———1971. *Introduction à la sémiologie.* Paris, Minuit.

Mukařovský, Jan, 1970. *Kapitel aus der Aesthetik.* Frankfurt am Main, Suhrkamp.

———1977. *The Word and Verbal Art.* Tr. J. Burbank and P. Steiner. New Haven, Yale University Press.

Müller, Adam. 1807. *Vorlesungen über die deutsche Wissenschaft und Literatur.* Munich and Dresden, Arnold.

Nadal, Josep M., and Modest Prats, 1982. *Història de la llengua catalana.* Vol. I. Barcelona, Edicions 62.

Nagy, Gregory, 1982. "Hesiod (Eighth Century B.C.)." In T. J. Luce, ed., *Ancient Writers: Greece and Rome,* 43–73. New York, Scribner.

Naumann, Manfred, 1976. "Das Dilemma der Rezeptionsästhetik." *Poetica*, 451–466.

———1980. "Remarques sur la reception en tant qu'événement historique et social." *Proceedings IX*, II, 27–33.

Navarro González, Alberto, 1963. *El mar en la literatura medieval castellana*. La Laguna, Universidad.

Nelson, Lowry, Jr., 1963. "Night Thoughts on the Gothic Novel." *Yale Review*, 52, 237–257.

———1980. "Earliest Provençal Lyric: Some Historical Conditions of 'Rezeptionsgeschichte'." *Proceedings IX*, II, 217–221.

Nemoianu, Virgil, 1977. *Micro-Harmony: The Growth and Uses of the Idyllic Model in Literature*. Bern, Peter Lang.

———1984. *The Taming of Romanticism: European Literature and the Age of Biedermeier*. Cambridge, Mass., Harvard University Press.

Newton de Molina, David, ed., 1976. *On Literary Intention*. Edinburgh, University of Edinburgh Press.

Nichols, Fred J., 1975. "The Renewal of Latin Poetry in the Renaissance: Rhetoric and Experience." *Proceedings VI*, 89–98.

Nichols, Stephen G., Jr., and Franklin W. Robinson, eds., 1972. *The Meaning of Mannerism*. Hanover, N.H., University Press of New England.

Nicolson, Marjorie Hope, 1959. *Mountain Gloom and Mountain Glory: The Development of the Aesthetics of the Infinite*. Ithaca, N.Y., Cornell University Press.

Nolting-Hauff, Ilse, 1974. *Visión, sátira y agudeza en los "Sueños" de Quevedo*. Madrid, Gredos.

O'Brien, Justin, 1954. "Proust's Use of Syllepsis." *PMLA*, 69, 741–752.

O'Connor, W. Van, 1962. *The Grotesque*. Carbondale, Southern Illinois Press.

Oleza, Juan, 1981. "La literatura, signo ideológico." In J. Romera Castillo, ed., *La literatura como signo*, 176–226. Madrid, Playo.

Omesco, Ion, 1978. *La métamorphose de la tragédie*. Paris, Presses universitaires de France.

Onís, José de, 1962. "Literatura comparada como disciplina literaria." *Cuadernos* (Paris), 63–69.

Orecchioni, Pierre, 1970. "Pour une histoire sociologique de la littérature." In R. Escarpit, ed., *Le littéraire et le social*, 45–53. Paris, Flammarion.

Orozco Díaz, Emilio, 1947. *Temas del barroco, de poesía y pintura*. Granada, Universidad.

———1970. *Manierismo y barroco*. Salamanca, Anaya.

Ortega y Gasset, J., 1947. *Obras completas*. Madrid, Revista de Occidente.

———1957a. "Teoría del clasicismo." In *Obras completas*, 2d ed. Madrid, Revista de Occidente. (First published in *El imparcial*, 1907.)

———1957b. *Historia como sistema*. In ibid.

Ortony, Andrew, ed., 1979. *Metaphor and Thought.* Cambridge, Cambridge University Press.

Owen, Stephen, 1975. *The Great Age of Chinese Poetry: The High T'ang.* New Haven, Yale University Press.

———1977. *The Poetry of Early T'ang.* New Haven, Yale University Press.

Pageaux, Daniel-Henri, 1971. *Images du Portugal dans les lettres françaises (1700–1755).* Paris, Fund. Gulbenkian.

———1981. "Une perspective d'études en littérature comparée: L'imagerie culturelle." *Synthesis* (Bucharest), 8, 169–185.

———, ed., 1983. *La recherche en littérature générale et comparée en France.* Paris, SFLGC.

Pagliano, Jean-Paul, 1983. "La mort au Moyen Age (quelques aspects)." In Fried, Kanyó, and Pál, 1983, 221–231.

Pagnini, Marcello, 1980. *Pragmatica della lettertura.* Palermo, Sellerio.

Palgrave, Francis Turner, 1863. *The Golden Treasury of the Best Songs and Lyrical Poems in the English Language.* Cambridge, Mass., Sever and Francis.

Palmier, Jean-Michel, 1972. *Situation de Georg Trakl.* Paris, Belfond.

Paolucci, Anne, 1982. "The 'Coming of Age' of Australian Literature." *Review of National Literatures,* 11, 11–15.

Paris, Gaston, 1892. *Les origines de la poésie en France au Moyen Age.* Paris, Imprimerie Nationale.

Park, Roy, 1969. "Ut Pictura Poesis: The Nineteenth-Century Aftermath." *Journal of Aesthetics and Art Criticism,* 28, 155–164.

Parry, Milman, 1971. *The Making of Homeric Verse: The Collected Papers of Milman Parry.* Ed. A. Parry. Oxford, Clarendon.

Paulson, Ronald, 1967. *The Fictions of Satire.* Baltimore, Johns Hopkins University Press.

Pavel, Thomas G., 1980. "Narrative Domains." *PT,* 4, no. 1, 105–114.

Pavis, Patrice, 1980. *Dictionnaire du théâtre.* Paris, Editions sociales.

Paz, Octavio, 1967. *Puertas al campo.* 2nd ed. Mexico City, UNAM.

———1973a. *The Bow and the Lyre.* Tr. Ruth L. C. Simms. Austin, University of Texas Press.

———1973b. *El signo y el garabato.* Mexico City, J. Mortiz.

———1974. *Children of the Mire: Modern Poetry from Romanticism to the Avant-Garde.* Tr. Rachel Phillips. Cambridge, Mass., Harvard University Press.

———1983. "Pintado en México." *El país* (Madrid), November 7, p. 21.

Pearce, Roy Harvey, 1969. *Historicism Once More.* Princeton, Princeton University Press.

Pellegrini, Carlo, 1947. *Tradizione italiana e cultura europea.* Messina.

Pérez Gállego, Cándido, 1973. *Morfonovelística.* Madrid, Fundamentos.

———1975. "Dentro-fuera y presente-ausente en teatro." In Diéz Borque and García Lorenzo, 1975, 167–191.

Pessoa, F., 1982. *Livro do desassossego*. Lisbon, Ed. de Prado Coelo.

———1991. *The Book of Disquiet*, Tr. Margaret Jull Costa. London and New York, Serpent's Tail.

Petsch, Robert, 1942. *Wesen und Formen der Erzählkunst*. 2nd ed. Halle, M. Niemeyer. (1st ed. 1934.)

Peyre, Henri, 1935. *Shelley et la France*. Cairo, Imprimerie Paul Barbey.

———1952. "A Glance at Comparative Literature in America." *YCGL*, 1, 1–8.

Pfister, Manfred, 1977. *Das Drama*. Munich, Fink.

Picard, Hans Rudolf, 1981. "El diario como género entre lo íntimo y lo público." *1616*, 4, 115–122.

Pichois, Claude, 1957. *L'image de la Belgique dans les lettres françaises de 1830 à 1870*. Paris, Nizet.

———1965. *Philarète Chasles et la vie littéraire au temps du romantisme*. Paris, Colin.

Pichois, Claude, and André-Marie Rousseau, 1967. *La littérature comparée*. Paris, A. Colin.

Pizarro, Ana, 1980. "La dépendence culturelle en Amérique hispanique." *Proceedings VIII*, I, 155–161.

Pla, Josep, 1950. *Bodegó amb peixos*. Barcelona, Editorial Selecta.

Poggioli, Renato, 1943. "Comparative Literature." In J. T. Shipley, ed., *Dictionary of World Literature*, 114–116. New York.

———1959. "Poetics and Metrics." *Proceedings II*, I, 192–204.

———1968. *The Theory of the Avant-Garde*. Cambridge, Mass., Harvard University Press.

———1975. *The Oaten Flute*. Cambridge, Mass., Harvard University Press.

Poli, Bernard J., 1967. *Ford Madox Ford and the Transatlantic Review*. Syracuse, N.Y., Syracuse University Press.

Porta, Antonio, 1951. *La letteratura comparata nella storia e nella critica*. Milan, C. Marzorati.

Porter, Dennis, 1981. *The Pursuit of Crime*. New Haven, Yale University Press.

Poulet, Georges, 1949. *Etudes sur le temps humain*. Edinburgh, Edinburgh University Press. (Reissued 1972, Paris, Union générale d'éditions.)

———1952. *La distance intérieure*. Paris, Plon.

———1961. *Les métamophoses du cercle*. Paris, Plon.

———1968. *Mesure de l'instant*. Paris, Plon.

Poyán Díaz, Daniel, 1966. "Burla y convite de Don Juan: Constitución y destitución de un mito." *Proceedings IV*, I, 488–494.

Prado Coelho, Jacinto do, 1966. "Nationalisme et cosmopolitisme chez Fernando Pessoa." *Proceedings IV*, I, 481–487.

Prampolini, Giacomo, 1959–1961. *Storia universale della letteratura*. 3rd ed. 7 vols. Turin, UTET.

Prawer, S. S., 1973. *Comparative Literature Studies: An Introduction*. London, Duckworth.

Praz, Mario, 1952. *La casa della fama*. Milan, Ricciardi.

——1970. *Mnemosyne: The Parallel between Literature and the Visual Arts*. Princeton, Princeton University Press.

Prieto, Antonio, 1975. *Morfología de la novela*. Barcelona, Planeta.

Propp, Vladimir, 1958. *Morphology of the Folk Tale*. Tr. L. Scott. Bloomington, Indiana University Press. (Rev. ed. Austin, University of Texas Press, 1968.)

——1970. *Morphologie du conte*. Ed. M. Derrida, T. Todorov, and C. Kahn. Paris, Seuil.

Puibusque, A. de, 1843. *Histoire comparée des littératures espagnole et française*. Paris, G.-A. Dentu.

Punter, David, 1980. *The Literature of Terror*. London, Longman.

Pupo-Walker, Enrique, 1982. *Historia, creation and profecía en los textos del Inca Garcilaso de la Vega*. Madrid, Porrúa Turanzas.

Queneau, Raymond, ed., 1955–1958. *Histoires des littératures*. 3 vols. Paris, Gallimard.

Quental, Antero de, 1989. *"Hino de manhã" e outras poesias do mesmo ciclo*. Lisbon, Horizonte.

Quevedo, F., 1969–1971. *Obras poéticas*. Vol. III. Madrid, Ed. Blecua.

Quilligan, Maureen, 1979. *The Language of Allegory*. Ithaca, N.Y., Cornell University Press.

Quine, W. Van, 1960. *Word and Object*. Cambridge, Mass., MIT Press.

Rajna, Pio, 1900. *Le fonti dell'Orlando furioso*. 2nd ed. Florence, G. C. Sansoni.

Rama, Angel, 1979. "Un proceso autonómico: De las literaturas nacionales a la literatura latinoamericana." *Proceedings VII*, I, 35–42.

Remak, H. H. H., 1960. "Comparative Literature at the Crossroads: Diagnosis, Therapy and Prognosis." *YCGL*, 9, 1–28.

——1961. "West-European Romanticism: Definition and Scope." In Stallknecht and Frenz, 1961, 223–259.

——1980. "The Future of Comparative Literature." *Proceedings VIII*, II, 429–439.

Reyes, Alfonso, 1963. "Apuntes para la teoría literaria." In *Obras completas*. Vol. XV, 424–455. Mexico City, Fondo de cultura económica.

Ricardou, Jean, 1972. "Qu'est-ce qu'une description?" *Poétique*, 3, 465–485.

Richard, Jean-Pierre, 1954. *Littérature et sensation*. Paris, Seuil.

——1955. *Poésie et profondeur*. Paris, Seuil.

Richter, G., 1938. "Zur Enstehungsgeschichte der altarabischen Qaside." *Zeitschrift der deutschen Morgenländischen Gesellschaft*, 92, 552–569.

Rico, Francisco, 1970. *El pequeño mundo del hombre*. Madrid, Castalia.

——1983. "Literatura e historia de la literatura." *Boletín informativo: Fundación Juan March*, 127, 3–16.

Ricoeur, Paul, 1975. *La métaphore vive*. Paris, Seuil.

Riegel, René, 1934. *Adalbert de Chamisso*. Paris, Les editions internationales.

Riffaterre, Michael, 1971. *Essais de stylistique structurale*. Paris, Flammarion.

———1972. "Système d'un genre descriptif." *Poétique,* 9, 15–30.

———1978. *Semiotics of Poetry.* Bloomington, Indiana University Press.

———1979. *La production du texte.* Paris, Seuil.

———1980. "Syllepsis." *Critical Inquiry,* 625–638.

Rimmon-Kenan, Shlomith, 1980. "The Paradoxical Status of Repetition." *PT,* 1, 4, 151–159.

Riquer, Martín de, 1964. *Història de la literatura catalana.* 3 vols. Barcelona, Ariel.

———1975. *Los trovadores: Historia literaria y textos.* 3 vols. Barcelona, Planeta.

Riquer, Martín de, and J. M. Valverde, 1957–1974. *Historia de la literatura universal.* 4 vols. Barcelona, Editorial Planeta.

Rivers, Elias L., 1954. "The Horatian Epistle and Its Introduction into Spanish Literature." *Hispanic Review,* 22, 175–194.

———, ed. and tr., 1988. *Renaissance and Baroque Poetry of Spain.* Prospect Heights, Ill., Waveland Press.

Rodríguez Adrados, Francisco, 1980. "Música y literatura en la Grecia antigua." *1616,* 3, 130–137.

Rodríguez-Monegal, Emir, 1980. "The Integration of Latin-American Cultures." *Proceedings VIII,* I, 111–116.

Rodríguez Monroy, Amalia, 1984. "An English 'Imitation' of Rimbaud: An Exercise in Comparative Translation." *Cuadernos de traducción e interpretación* (Barcelona), 3, 7–22.

Romero Márquez, A., 1981. Introduction to Jorge Guillén, *Antología del mar.* Málaga, Libr. Agora.

Ropars-Wuilleumier, Marie-Claire, 1981. *Le texte divisé: Essai sur l'écriture filmique.* Paris, Presses universitaires de France.

Rose, Mark, ed., 1976. *Science Fiction.* Englewood Cliffs, N.J., Prentice-Hall.

Rosengren, Karl Erik, 1968. *Sociological Aspects of the Literary System.* Stockholm, Natur och Kultur.

Rosenmeyer, Thomas G., 1969. *The Green Cabinet.* Berkeley, University of California Press.

Rosso, Corrado, 1968. *La "Maxime."* Naples, E. S. I.

Rousseau, André-Marie, 1977. "Arts et Littérature: Un état présent et quelques réflexions." *Synthesis* (Bucharest), 4, 35–51.

Rousseau, J.-J., 1979. *The Reveries of the Solitary Walker. Tenth Walk.* Tr. Charles E. Butterworth. New York, New York University Press.

Rousset, Jean, 1961. *Anthologie de la poésie baroque française.* 2 vols. Paris, Colin.

———1962a. "La définition du terme baroque." *Proceedings III,* 167–178.

———1962b. *Forme et signification.* Paris, Corti.

———1967. "L'île enchantée: Fête et théâtre au XVIIe siècle." In *Mélanges de littérature comparée et de philologie offerts à Mieczyslaw Brahmer,* 435–441. Warsaw, PWN.

———1973. *Narcisse romancier: Essai sur la première personne dans le roman.* Paris, Corti.

————1981. *Les yeux se rencontrèrent*. Paris, Corti.

Ruitenbeek, Hendrik M., ed., 1964. *Psychoanalysis and Literature*. New York, Dutton.

Russo, Luigi, 1946. *La critica letteraria contemporanea*. Bari. (Reissued 1967, Florence, Sansoni.)

Sacks, Sheldon, 1964. *Fiction and the Shape of Belief: A Study of Henry Fielding*. Berkeley, University of California Press.

————, ed., 1979. *On Metaphor*. Chicago, University of Chicago Press.

Said, Edward W., 1975. *Beginnings*. New York, Basic Books.

————1976. "On Repetition." In A. Fletcher, ed., *The Literature of Fact: Selected Papers from the English Institute*, 141–147. New York, Columbia University Press.

————1978. *Orientalism*. New York, Pantheon.

Said Armesto, Víctor, 1908. *La leyenda de Don Juan*. Madrid, Sucesores de Hernando.

Sainte-Beuve, Charles A., 1869. *Poésies complètes*. Paris, Charpentier.

Saint-John Perse, 1972. *Exil*. In *Selected Poems*, 46, 48. Bilingual ed. Ed. Mary Ann Caws. Tr. Denis Devlin, pp. 47, 49. New York, New Directions.

Salinas, Pedro, 1946. *El contemplado: Tema con variaciones*. Mexico City, Editorial stylo.

————1948. *La poesía de Rubén Darío*. Buenos Aires, Losada.

————1949. *La roz a ti debida*. Buenos Aires, Losada. (First published 1933.)

————1950. *Sea of San Juan: A Contemplation*. Tr. Eleanor L. Turnbull. Boston, Bruce Humphries.

————1955. *Confianza*. Madrid, Aguilar.

————1974. *To Live in Pronouns*. Tr. Edith Helman and Norma Farber. New York, W. W. Norton.

Sammons, Jeffrey L., 1977. *Literary Sociology and Practical Criticism*. Bloomington, Indiana University Press.

Samurović-Pavlović, Liliana, 1969. *Les lettres hispano-américaines au "Mercure de France" (1897–1915)*. Belgrade, Filoloski Fakultet.

San Juan de la Cruz, 1973. *Poesias completas y comentarios en prosa a los poemas mayores*. Madrid, Aguilar.

Saraiva, António José, and Oscar Lopes, n.d. *História da literatura portuguesa*. 2nd ed. Oporto, Empresa literária fluminense.

Savater, Fernando, 1982. *Panfleto contra del Todo*. Madrid, Alianza.

Schajowicz, Ludwig, 1962. *Mito y existencia*. San Juan, Puerto Rico, Eds. de la Torre.

Scher, Steven P., 1982. "Literature and Music." In Barricelli and Gibaldi, 1982, 225–250.

————, ed., 1984. *Literatur und Musik*. Berlin, Erich Schmidt.

Schlegel, F., 1967. *Kritische Ausgabe*. Munich, Paderborn, and Vienna, Ed. E. Behler.

Schlocker-Schmidt, Hildegard, 1961. *Jean-Jacques Ampère*. Munich, Mikrokopie.

Schmeling, Manfred, ed., 1981. *Vergleichende Literaturwissenschaft.* Wiesbaden, Athenaion.

Schober, Rita, 1970. *Von der wirklichen Welt in der Dichtung.* Berlin, Aufbau-Verlag.

Scholes, Robert E., and Robert Kellogg, 1963. *The Nature of Narrative.* New York, Oxford University Press.

Schon, P. M., 1954. *Vorformen des Essays in Antike und Humanismus.* Wiesbaden, Steiner.

Schrimpf, Hans Joachim, 1968. *Goethes Begriff der Weltliteratur.* Stuttgart, Metzler.

Schroeder, Klaus-Henning, 1967. *Einführung in das Studium des Rumänischen.* Berlin, Schmidt.

Schulman, Ivan A., 1960. "Génesis del Azul Modernista." *Revista iberoamericana,* 25, 251–271.

Schweizer, N. R., 1972. *The Ut Pictura Poesis Controversy in Eighteenth-Century England and Germany.* Frankfurt am Main, Lang.

Scott, Clive, 1976. "The Limit of the Sonnet: Towards a Proper Contemporary Approach." *RLC,* 50, 237–250.

Seboek, Thomas A., ed., 1955. *Myth.* Bloomington, Indiana University Press.

——, ed., 1960. *Style in Language.* Cambridge, Mass., MIT Press.

——1974. *Structure and Texture: Selected Essays in Cheremis Verbal Art.* The Hague, Mouton.

——, ed., 1975. *The Tell-Tale Sign: A Survey of Semiotics.* Lisse, Peter de Ridde.

Segers, Rien T., 1978. *The Evaluation of Literary Texts: An Experimental Investigation into the Rationalization of Value Judgments with Reference to Semiotics and Aesthetics of Reception.* Lisse, Peter de Ridde.

Segre, Cesare, 1974. *Le strutture e il tempo.* Turin, Einaudi.

——1982a. "Contribution to the Semiotics of the Theatre." *PT,* 1, 4, 39–48.

——1982b. "Intertestuale-interdiscorsivo: Appunti per una fenomenologia delle fonti." In C. Girolamo, and C. di I. Paccagnella, eds., *La parola ritrovata,* 15–28. Palermo, Sellerio.

——1984. *Teatro e romanzo.* Turin, Einaudi.

Seidler, Herbert, 1973. "Was ist vergleichende Literaturwissenschaft?" *Sitzungsberichte der Oesterr. Akad. der Wissenschaften. Philosophische-Historische Klasse* (Vienna), 284, no. 4, 3–18.

Selbach, L., 1886. *Das Streitgedicht in der altprovenzalischen Lyrik.* Marburg, C. L. Pfeil'sche univ.-buchdr.

Selig, Karl-Ludwig, 1963. "Emblem Literature: Directions in Recent Scholarship." *YCGL,* 12, 36–41.

Sempoux, André, 1960. "Trois principes fondamentaux de l'analyse du style." *Revue belge de philologie et d'histoire,* 38, 809–814.

Sena, Jorge de, 1982. *Visão perpetua.* Lisbon, Edições 70.

Serpieri, Alessandro, 1983. "Analisi e psiconalisi letteraria." In Franca Mariani, ed., *Letteratura: Percorsi possibili,* 53–68. Ravenna, Longo.

Serra, Edelweis, 1978. *Tipología del cuento literario: Textos hispanoamericanos.* Madrid, Cupsa.

Setschkareff, Wsevolod, 1952. *Die Dichtungen Gunduličs und ihr poetischer Stil.* Bonn, Athenäum.

Seznec, Jean, 1948. "Don Quixote and His French Illustrators." *Gazette des beaux-arts* (Paris), 173–229.

———1949. *Nouvelles études sur la Tentation de Saint Antoine.* London, Warburg Institute.

———1972. "Art and Literature: A Plea for Humility." *NLH,* 3, 563–574.

———1980. *La Survivance des dieux antiques.* 2nd ed. Paris, Flammarion.

Sieburth, Richard, 1978. *Instigations: Ezra Pound and Rémy de Gourmont.* Cambridge, Mass., Harvard University Press.

Silva Castro, Raúl, 1959. "El ciclo de lo 'azul' en Rubén Darío." *Revista hispánica moderna,* 25, 81–95.

Simpson, Joyce G., 1962. *Le Tasse et la littérature et l'art baroques en France.* Paris, Nizet.

Singer, A. E., 1965. *The Don Juan Theme, Versions and Criticism: A Bibliography.* Morgantown, West Virginia University Press.

Skura, Meredith Anne, 1981. *The Literary Use of the Psychoanalytic Process.* New Haven, Yale University Press.

Smith, Barbara Herrstein, 1978. *On the Margins of Discourse.* Chicago, University of Chicago Press.

Smith, Patrick J., 1970. *The Tenth Muse: A Historical Study of the Opera Libretto.* New York, Alfred A. Knopf.

Sobejano, Gonzalo, 1967. *Nietzsche en España.* Madrid, Gredos.

Solmi, Sergio, 1978. *Saggi sul fantastico.* Turin, Einaudi.

Solt, Mary Ellen, 1970. *Concrete Poetry.* Bloomington, Indiana University Press.

Sonnenfeld, Albert, 1960. *L'oeuvre poétique de Tristan Corbière.* Paris, Presses universitaires de France.

Sopeña Ibáñez, Federico, 1974. *Música y literatura.* Madrid, Rialp.

Soseki, Natsume, 1977. *Sanshiro.* Tr. J. Rubin. Seattle, University of Washington Press.

Sötér, István, ed., 1963. *La littérature comparée en Europe orientale.* Budapest, Akadémiai Kiadó.

Sötér, István, 1974. "On the Comparatist Method." *Neohelicon* (Budapest), 2, 9–30.

Sötér, István, and Otto Süpek, eds., 1964. *Littérature hongroise, littérature européenne.* Budapest, Akadémiai Kiadó.

Spitzer, Leo, 1955a. *Lingüística e historia literaria.* Madrid, Gredos.

———1955b. "The 'Ode on a Grecian Urn,' or Content vs. Metagrammar." *CL,* 7, 203–225.

Staiger, Emil, 1956. *Grundbegriffe der Poetik.* 2nd ed. Zurich, Atlantis (1st ed. 1946).

Stallknecht, N. P., and Horst Frenz, 1961. *Comparative Literature: Method and Perspective*. Carbondale, Southern Illinois University Press.

Stamnitz, Susanne, 1977. *Prettie Tales of Wolues and Sheepe. Tragikomik, Pastorale und Satire im Drama der englischen und italienischen Renaissance, 1550–1648*. Heidelberg, Winter.

Stanzel, Franz K., 1963. *Die typischen Erzählsituationen im Roman*. Vienna, Braumüller.

———1978. "Second Thoughts on Narrative Situations in the Novel: Towards a Grammar of Fiction." *Novel: A Forum on Fiction*, 11, 247–264.

———1981. "Teller-Character and Reflector-Character in Narrative Theory." *PT*, 2, no. 2, 5–15.

———1984. *A Theory of Narrative*. Tr. Charlotte Goedsche. Cambridge, Cambridge University Press.

Stégen, Guillaume, 1960. *Essai sur la composition de cinq Epîtres d'Horace*. Namur, Wesmael-Charlier.

Steiner, George, 1961. *The Death of Tragedy*. New York, Alfred A. Knopf. (Reissued 1981, New York, Oxford University Press.)

———1971. *Extra-territorial*. New York, Atheneum.

———1975. *After Babel*. New York, Oxford University Press.

Steinitz, Wolfgang, 1934. *Der Parallelismus in der finnisch-karelischen Volksdichtung*. Helsinki.

Stempel, Wolf-Dieter, 1969–1972. *Texte der russischen Formalisten*. 2 vols. Munich, Fink.

Stendhal, 1977. *The Charterhouse of Parma*. Tr. C. K. Scott-Moncrief. London, The Folio Society.

Stevens, Wallace, 1971. "The Man with the Blue Guitar." In *The Palm at the End of the Mind*. New York, Alfred A. Knopf.

Stiennon, Jacques, 1973. "Réflexions sur l'étude comparée des arts plastiques et littéraires." In *Approches de l'art: Mélanges d'esthétique et de sciences de l'art offerts à Arsène Soreil*, 115–124. Brussels, Renaissance du livre.

Stolz, Benjamin, A., and Richard S. Shannon, eds., 1976. *Oral Literature and the Formula*. Ann Arbor, University of Michigan Press.

Strelka, Joseph P., ed., 1973. *Literary Criticism and Sociology*. University Park, Pennsylvania State University Press.

———, ed., 1978. *Theories of Literary Genre*. University Park, Pennsylvania State University Press.

Strich, Fritz, 1946. *Goethe und die Weltliteratur*. Bern, Francke.

Striedter, Yuri, 1969. *Texte der russischen Formalisten*. Vol. I. Munich, Fink.

———1989. *Literary Structure, Evolution, and Value*. Cambridge, Mass., Harvard University Press.

Struve, Gleb, 1955. "Comparative Literature in the Soviet Union, Today and Yesterday." *YCGL*, 4, 1–20.

Styan, J. L., 1968. *The Dark Comedy*. 2nd ed. Cambridge, Cambridge University Press.

Suleiman, Susan R., 1983. *Le Roman à thèse ou l'autorité fictive*. Paris, Presses universitaires de France.

Suleiman, Susan R., and Inge Crossman, 1980. *The Reader in the Text*. Princeton, Princeton University Press.

Szabolcsi, Miklós, 1969. "L'avant-garde littéraire et artistique comme phénomène international." *Proceedings V*, 317–334.

———1980. "La renaissance des méthodes historiques et la littérature comparée." *Proceedings VIII*, 469–473.

Szegedy-Maszák, Mihály, 1979. "One of the Basic Concepts of Research in Historical Poetics in Hungary: Repetition." In J. Oldmark, ed., *Language, Literature and Meaning*, 361–417. Amsterdam, Benjamins.

Szondi, Peter, 1956. *Theorie des modernen Dramas*. Frankfurt am Main, Suhrkamp.

———1964. *Versuch über das Tragische*. 2nd ed. Frankfurt am Main, Insel.

Taine, H., 1866. *Histoire de la littérature anglaise*. Paris, Hachette.

Tassoni, Luigi, ed., 1981. *Studi sulla poesia dialettale del Novecento*. Catanzaro, Assessorato, P. I. e cultura.

Teesing, H. P. H., 1949. *Das Problem der Perioden in der Literaturgeschichte*. Gronigen, Academische Proefschrift.

———1963. "Literature and the Other Arts." *YCGL*, 12, 27–35.

Terrasse, Jean, 1977. *Rhétorique de l'essai littéraire*. Montreal, Université de Québec Press.

Texte, Joseph, 1895. *Jean-Jacques Rousseau et les origines du cosmopolitisme littéraire*. Paris, Hachette.

———1898. "L'histoire comparée des littératures." In *Etudes de littérature européenne*, 1–24. Paris, Colin.

Thibaudet, Albert, 1938. *Réflections sur le roman*. Paris, Gallimard.

Thomson, Patricia, 1964. *Sir Thomas Wyatt and His Background*. Stanford, Stanford University Press.

Thorpe, James, ed., 1967. *Relations of Literary Study: Essays on Interdisciplinary Contributions*. New York, Modern Language Association.

Todorov, Tzvetan, 1965. *Théorie de la littérature: Textes des formalists russes*. Paris, Seuil.

———1969. *Grammaire du Décaméron*. The Hague, Mouton.

———1970. *Introduction à la littérature fantastique*. Paris, Seuil.

———1971. *Poétique de la prose*. Paris, Seuil.

———1973. *The Fantastic*. Tr. Richard Howard. Cleveland, Press of Case Western Reserve.

———1976. "The Origin of Genres." *NLH*, 8, 159–170.

———1981. *Mikhail Bakhtine: le principe dialogique*. Paris, Seuil.

———1984. *Mikhail Bakhtin: The Dialogical Principle*. Tr. Wlad Godzich. Minneapolis, University of Minnesota Press.

Tókei, Ferenc, 1971. *Genre Theory in China from the IIId to the VIth Centuries*. Budapest, Adakémiai Kiadó.

Torbarina, Josip, 1967. "A Great Forerunner of Shakespeare." *Studia romanica et anglica zobrabiensa*, 24, 5–21.

Torre, Guillermo de, 1956. "Goethe y la literatura universal." In *Las metamorfosis de Proteo*, 278–289. Buenos Aires, Losada.

———1957. "Ortega, teórico de la literatura." *Papeles de Son Armadans*, 19, 22–49.

———1962. *La aventura estética de nuestra edad*. Barcelona, Seix Barral.

Toury, Gideon, 1980. *In Search of a Theory of Translation*. Tel Aviv, Porter Institute.

Trakl, Georg, 1987. *Dichtungen und Briefe*. Salzburg, O. Müller.

———1989. *Autumn Sonata*. Bilingual ed. Tr. Daniel Simko. Mt. Kisco, N.Y., Moyer-Bell.

Trimpi, Wesley, 1973. "The Meaning of Horace's *Ut Pictura Poesis*." *Journal of the Warburg and Courtauld Institute*, 36, 1–34.

Trogrančič, Franjo, 1953. *Storia della letteratura croata*. Rome, Studium.

Trousson, Raymond, 1964. *Le mythe de Prométhée dans la littérature européenne*. 2 vols. Geneva, Groz.

———1965. *Un problème de littérature comparée: Les études des thèmes*. Paris, Lettres Modernes.

———1980. "Les études des thèmes hier et aujourd'hui." *Proceedings VIII*, II, 499–503.

Ubersfeld, Anne, 1978. *Lire le théâtre*. Paris, Editions sociales.

Uhlig, Claus, 1982. *Theorie der Literarhistorie*. Heidelberg, Winter.

Unamuno, Miguel de, 1895. *Obras selectas*. Madrid. Editorial Plenitud. (Reissued in 1960.)

Urrutia, Jorge, 1983. *Réflexión de la literatura*. Sevilla, Universidad.

Vajda, György M., 1964. "Essai d'une histoire de la littérature comparée en Hongrie." In Sötér and Süpek, 1964, 525–588.

———1968. "Goethes Anregung zur vergleichenden Literaturbetrachtung." *Acta Litteraria Academiae Scientiarum Hungaricae*, 10, nos. 3–4, 211–238.

Valdés, Mario, 1982. *Shadows in the Cave: A Phenomenological Approach to Literary Criticism Based on Hispanic Texts*. Toronto, University of Toronto Press.

van Dam, C. F. A., 1927. "Lope de Vega y el neerlandés." *Revista de filología española*, 14, 282–286.

Van Tieghem, Paul, 1951. *La littérature comparée*. 4th ed. Paris, Colin. (1st ed. 1931.)

Vauthier, Gabriel, 1913. *Villemain (1790–1870)*. Paris, Perrin.

Veit, Walter, 1963. "Toposforschung- ein Forschungsbericht." *Deutsche Viert. f. Literaturw. und Geistesgeschichte*, 37, 120–163.

———1983. "The Topoi of the European Imagining of the Non-European World." *Arcadia* (Berlin), 18, 1–23.

Versini, Laurent, 1979. *Le roman épistolaire*. Paris, Presses universitaires de France.

Vickers, Brian, 1973. *Comparative Tragedy*. London, Longman.

Vickery, John B., ed., 1966. *Myth and Literature*. Lincoln, University of Nebraska Press.

Viëtor, Karl, 1931. "Probleme der literarischen Gattungsgeschichte." *Deutsche Viert. f. Literaturw. und Geistesgeschichte*, 9, 425–447. (Reprinted in *Geist und Form*, Bern, Francke, 1952; abr. in *Poétique*, 32 [1977], 490–506.)

Vildomec, Véroboj, 1963. *Multilingualism*. Leiden, Synthoff.

Villanueva, Darío, 1977. *Estructura y tiempo reducido en la novela*. Valencia, Bello.

Virgil, 1985. *The Aeneid*. Tr. Robert Fitzgerald. 2nd ed. New York, Random House.

Viscardi, Antonio, et al., eds., 1948. *Letteratura comparate*. Milan, Marzorati.

Vitiello, Ciro, 1984. *Teoria e tecnica dell-avanguardia*. Milan, Mursia.

Vivas, Eliseo, and Murray Krieger, eds., 1953. *The Problems of Aesthetics*. New York, Rinehart.

Voisine, Jacques, 1976. "Racine et Shakespeare, ou la naissance de l'opéra anglais *(Dido and Aeneas)*." *RLC*, 50, 49–68.

Vossler, Karl, 1928. "Nationalliteratur und Weltliteratur." *Zeitwende*, 4, no. 1, 193–204.

Vowles, Richard B., 1956. *Drama Theory: A Bibliography*. New York, New York Public Library. (From *Bulletin of the New York Public Library*, 59, 1955, 412–428.)

Wais, Kurt, 1936. *Symbiose der Künste*. Stuttgart, W. Kohlhammer.

Waldapfel, József, 1968. *A travers siècles et frontières: Etudes sur la littérature hongroise et la littérature comparée*. Budapest, Akadémiai Kiadó.

Walter, Hans, 1920. *Das Streitgedicht in der lateinischen Literatur des Mittelalters*. Munich, C. H. Beck.

Walzel, Oskar, 1912. *Deutsche Romantik*. Leipzig, B. G. Teubner.

——1917. *Wechselseitige Erhellung der Künste*. Berlin, Reuther and Reichard.

Wang, Ching-hsien, 1974. *The Bell and the Drum: Shih Ching as Formulaic Poetry in an Oral Tradition*. Berkeley, University of California Press.

——1975. "Toward Defining a Chinese Heroism." *Journal of the American Oriental Society*, 95, 25–35.

Warning, Rainer, ed., 1975. *Rezeptionsästhetik*. Munich, Fink.

Warnke, Frank J., 1972. *Versions of the Baroque*. New Haven, Yale University Press.

Watson, Burton, 1962. *Early Chinese Literature*. New York, Columbia University Press.

Watt, Ian, 1957. *The Rise of the Novel*. Berkeley, University of California Press.

Wehrli, Max, 1941. "Der historische Roman." *Helicon*, 3, 89–109.

Weightman, John, 1973. *The Concept of the Avant-Garde*. London, Alcove.

Weimann, Robert, 1971. *Literaturgeschichte und Mythologie*. Berlin, Aufbau-Verlag.

Weinberg, Bernard, 1961. *A History of Literary Criticism in the Italian Renaissance*. 2 vols. Chicago, University of Chicago Press.

Weinreich, Uriel, 1963. *Languages in Contact*. The Hague, Mouton.

Weinstein, Leo, 1967. *The Metamorphoses of Don Juan*. New York, AMS Press.

Weintraub, Wiktor, 1969. "The Latin and the Polish Kochanowski: The Two Faces of a Poet." *Proceedings V,* 663–670.

Weisgerber, Jean, 1966. "Examen critique de la notion de nationalisme et de quelques problèmes qu'elle soulève en histoire littéraire." *Proceedings IV,* I, 218–228.

————1968. *Faulkner et Dostoïevsky.* Brussels, Presses universitaires.

————1978. *L'espace romanesque.* Lausanne, L'age d'homme.

Weisinger, Herbert, 1953. *Tragedy and the Paradox of the Fortunate Fall.* East Lansing, Michigan State University Press.

————1964. *The Agony and the Triumph: Papers on the Use and Abuse of Myth.* East Lansing, Michigan State University Press.

Weisstein, Ulrich, 1968. *Einführung in die vergleichende Literaturwissenschaft.* Stuttgart, Kohlhammer.

————1973. *Comparative Literature and Literary Theory: Survey and Introduction.* Tr. William Riggan in collaboration with the author. Bloomington, Indiana University Press.

————1975. "Influences and Parallels: The Place and Function of Analogy Studies in Comparative Literature." In B. Allemann and E. Koppen, eds., *Teilnahme und Spiegelung: Festschrift für Horst Rüdiger,* 593–609. Berlin, De Gruyter.

————1977. "Die wechselseitige Erhellung von Literatur und Musik: ein Arbeitsgebiet der Komparastik?" *Neohelicon* (Budapest), 5, 93–123.

————1978. "Verbal Paintings, Fugal Poems, Literary Collages and the Metamorphic Comparatist." *YCGL,* 28, 7–16.

————1981. *Vergleichende Literaturwissenschaft: Erster Bericht: 1968–1977.* Jahrbuch für Internationale Germanistik, C, 2. Bern.

————1982. "Bibliography of Literature and the Visual Arts." *Comparative Criticism,* 4, 324–334.

Weitz, Morris, 1970. "Genre and Style." In H. E. Kiefer and M. K. Munitz, eds., *Perspectives in Education, Religion, and the Arts,* 183–218. Albany, State University of New York Press.

Wellek, René, 1941. "Periods and Movements in Literary History." *English Institute Annual: 1940,* 79–93. New York.

————1947. "Six Types of Literary History." *English Institute Essays: 1946,* 107–126. New York.

————1955–. *A History of Modern Criticism: 1750–1950.* 2 vols. to date. New Haven, Yale University Press.

————1963. *Concepts of Criticism.* Ed. S. G. Nichols, Jr. New Haven, Yale University Press.

————1966. "Literature, Fiction and Literariness." *Proceedings IV,* I, 19–25.

————1970. *Discriminations.* New Haven, Yale University Press.

————1973. "The Fall of Literary History." In Koselleck and Stempel, 1973, 427–440.

Wellek, René, and A. Warren, 1956. *Theory of Literature*. 3rd ed. New York, Harcourt, Brace. (1st ed. 1949.)

Wheelwright, Philip, 1954. *The Burning Fountain*. Bloomington, Indiana University Press.

White, Hayden, 1973. *Metahistory: The Historical Imagination in Nineteenth-Century Europe*. Baltimore, Johns Hopkins University Press.

Whitman, Walt, 1990. "Song of Myself." In *Leaves of Grass*. Oxford, Oxford University Press.

Wiese, Benno von, 1963. *Novelle*. Stuttgart, Metzler (6th ed. 1975).

Williams, Raymond, 1973. *The Country and the City*. London, Chatto and Windus.

———1977. *Marxism and Literature*. Oxford, Oxford University Press.

Willis, Raymond S., 1953. *The Phantom Chapters of the Quijote*. New York, Hispanic Institute.

Wilss, Wolfram, 1977. *Uebersetzungswissenschaft*. Stuttgart, Klett.

Wimsatt, W. K., 1954. *The Verbal Icon*. Lexington, Kentucky University Press.

———, ed., 1972. *Versification*. New York, Modern Language Association.

Witke, Charles, 1971–72. "Comparative Literature and the Classics: East and West." *TR*, 2–3, 11–16.

Wölfflin, H., 1915. *Kuntsgeschlichtliche Grundbegriffe*. Munich, H. Bruckmann.

Wong, Tak-wai, 1978. "Period Style and Periodization: A Survey of Theory and Practice in the Histories of Chinese and European Literatures." *New Asia Academic Bulletin*, 1, 45–69.

Wytrzens, Günther, 1969. "Das Deutsche als Kunstmittel bei Marina Cvetaeva." *Wiener Slavistisches Jahrbuch*, 15, 57–70.

Yahalom, Shelly, 1981. "Le système littéraire en état de crise: Contacts intersystémiques et comportement traductionnel." *PT*, 2, no. 4, 143–160.

Yip, Wai-lim, 1969. *Ezra Pound's Cathay*. Princeton, Princeton University Press.

———1975–76. "The Use of 'Models' in East-West Comparative Literature." *TR*, 6–7, 109–126.

———1976. *Chinese Poetry*. Berkeley, University of California Press.

Yllera, Alicia, 1974. *Estilística poética y semiótica literaria*. Madrid, Alianza.

———1981. "La autobiografía como género renovador de la novela: *Lazarillo, Guzmán, Robinson, Moll Flanders, Marianne y Manon*." *1616*, 4, 163–192.

Yu, Anthony C., 1974. "Problems and Prospects in Chinese-Western Literary Relations." *YCGL*, 23, 47–53.

———1983. "The Literary Examples of Religious Pilgrimage: The *Commedia* and *The Journey to the West*." *History of Religions*, 22, 202–230.

Yuan, Heh-hsiang, 1980. "East-West Comparative Literature: An Inquiry into Possibilities." In Deeney, 1980, 1–24.

Zavala, Antonio, 1964. *Bosquejo de historia del bersolarismo*. San Sebastián, Auñamendi.

Zhirmunsky, V. M., 1961. *Vergleichende Epenforschung.* Berlin, Akademie-Verlag.

————1965. "Syntakitischer Parallelismus und rhytmische Bindung im alttürkischen epischen Vers." In *Beiträge zur Sprachwissenschaft, Volkskunde und Literaturforschung, Wolfgang Steinitz zum 60. Geburtstag.* Berlin, Akademie-Verlag.

————1967. "On the Study of Comparative Literature." *Oxford Slavonic Papers,* 13, 1–13.

————1969. "Les courants littéraires en tant que phénomèmes internationeaux." *Proceedings V,* 3–21.

Zhirmunksy, V. M., and N. K. Chadwick, 1969. *Oral Epics of Central Asia.* Cambridge, Cambridge University Press.

Ziegengeist, Gerhard, ed., 1968. *Aktuelle Probleme der vergleichenden Literaturforschung.* Berlin, Akademie-Verlag.

Zmegać, Viktor, ed., 1970. *Marxistische Literaturkritik.* Bad Homburg, Athenäum.

Zubiría, Ramón de, 1955. *La poesía de Antonio Machado.* Madrid, Gredos.

Zumthor, Paul, 1990. *Oral Poetry: An Introduction.* Minneapolis, University of Minnesota Press.

Zúñiga, Francesillo de, 1981. *Crónica burlesca del Emperador Carlos V.* Ed. Diana Pamp de Avalle-Arce. Barcelona, Crítica.

Credits

Rafael Alberti. From *Baladas y canciones del Paraná*, Editorial Seix Barral, S.A., 1979.

Vicente Aleixandre. "Sierpe de amor," in *Sombra del paraíso*. Copyright © 1941 Editorial Castalia, S.A. English translation: *Shadow of Paradise*, trans. Hugh Harter. Copyright © 1987 The Regents of the University of California.

Matsuo Basho. Haiku. English translation in *Japanese Linked Poetry*, trans. Earl Miner. Copyright © 1979 Princeton University Press.

Jorge Luis Borges. From *Obras Completas*, Emecé Editores.

Pedro Calderón de la Barca. From *Life Is a Dream*. Trans. copyright © 1970 Edwin Honig.

San Juan de la Cruz. "Spiritual Canticle," "Moral Epistle to Fabio," in *Renaissance and Baroque Poetry of Spain*, trans. Elias L. Rivers. Copyright © 1966 reissued 1988 by Waveland Press, Inc., Prospect Heights, Ill.; reprinted with permission from the publisher.

Dante Alighieri. From *The Divine Comedy* LXXX, Vol. 2, *Purgatorio*, trans. C. S. Singleton. Copyright © 1973 Routledge.

Federico García Lorca. "Baladilla de los tres ríos," "Serenata," "Campana," in *Poema del cante jondo*. Copyright 1921 Fundación Federico García Lorca. English translation: "Ballad of the Three Rivers," "Serenade," "Bell," in *Collected Poems*, trans. Christopher Maurer, Copyright © 1990, 1991, by the Estate of Federico García Lorca. Reprinted by permission of Farrar, Straus & Giroux, Inc.

Garcilaso de la Vega. "Third Eclogue," in *Renaissance and Baroque Poetry of Spain*, trans. Elias L. Rivers. Copyright © 1966, reissued 1988 by Waveland Press, Inc., Prospect Heights, Ill.; reprinted with permission from the publisher.

Victor Hugo. From "Chatimento," trans. Jeffrey Mehlman. Reprinted with permission of The Athlone Press.

Juan Ramón Jiménez. "Yellow Spring," in *Light and Shadows*, trans. Dennis Maloney. Copyright © 1987 White Pine Press.

Jorge Manrique. From *The Penguin Book of Spanish Verse*, ed. J. M. Cohen, 3d ed., Penguin Books, 1988, copyright © J. M. Cohen, 1956, 1960, 1988.

Saint-John Perse. From *Exil.* Copyright 1942 Editions Gallimard. English translation: *Selected Poems,* trans. Denis Devlin. Copyright © 1982 New Directions; reprinted by permission of New Directions Pub. Corp.

Pedro Salinas. "El Contemplado," in *Poesías completas.* Copyright © 1981 Solita Salinas de Marichal and Jaime Salinas. English translation: *To Live in Pronouns,* Selected Love Poems, trans. Edith Helman and Norma Farber, by permission of W. W. Norton & Company, Inc. Copyright © 1974 by Edith Helman and Norma Farber.

Sappho. From Sappho and Alcaeus, *Greek Lyric I,* Loeb Classical Library 142, trans. D. A. Campbell, Cambridge, Mass: Harvard University Press, 1982; reprinted by permission of the publishers and the Loeb Classical Library.

Jorge de Sena. "Cantiga de roda," "Envoi," in *Visão perpetua.* Copyright © 1982 Mécia de Sena.

Wallace Stevens. "The Man with the Blue Guitar," in Wallace Stevens, *Collected Poems.* Copyright 1936 by Wallace Stevens and renewed 1964 by Holly Stevens. Reprinted by permission of Alfred A. Knopf, Inc., and by Faber & Faber Ltd.

Bernart de Ventadorn. From Paul Blackburn, *Proensa: An Anthology of Troubadour Poetry,* trans. George Economou. Copyright © 1978 Joan Blackburn.

Anonymous works:

Byliny, in Roman Jakobson, *Language in Literature,* trans. Stephen Rudy. Copyright © 1987 the Jakobson Foundation.

Ode, from *Shih Ching,* trans. Burton Watson, in *Early Chinese Literature.* Copyright © 1962 Columbia University Press.

Sumerian creation myth. From Samuel Kramer, *From the Poetry of Sumer: Creation, Glorification, Adoration.* Copyright © 1979 The Regents of the University of California.

Index

433

Harvard Studies in Comparative Literature